THIRD EDITION REVISED

Computer Organization and Design

THE HARDWARE/SOFTWARE INTERFACE

ACKNOWLEDGMENTS

Figures 1.9, 1.15 Courtesy of Intel.

Figure 1.11 Courtesy of Storage Technology Corp.

Figures 1.7.1, 1.7.2, 6.13.2 Courtesy of the Charles Babbage Institute, University of Minnesota Libraries, Minneapolis.

Figures 1.7.3, 6.13.1, 6.13.3, 7.9.3, 8.11.2 Courtesy of IBM.

Figure 1.7.4 Courtesy of Cray Inc.

Figure 1.7.5 Courtesy of Apple Computer, Inc.

Figure 1.7.6 Courtesy of the Computer History Museum.

Figure 7.33 Courtesy of AMD.

Figures 7.9.1, 7.9.2 Courtesy of Museum of Science, Boston.

Figure 7.9.4 Courtesy of MIPS Technologies, Inc.

Figure 8.3 © Peg Skorpinski.

Figure 8.11.1 Courtesy of the Computer Museum of America.

Figure 8.11.3 Courtesy of the Commercial Computing Museum.

Figures 9.11.2, 9.11.3 Courtesy of NASA Ames Research Center.

Figure 9.11.4 Courtesy of Lawrence Livermore National Laboratory.

Computers in the Real World:

Photo of "A Laotian villager," courtesy of David Sanger.

Photo of an "Indian villager," property of Encore Software, Ltd., India.

Photos of "Block and students" and "a pop-up archival satellite tag," courtesy of Professor Barbara Block. Photos by Scott Taylor.

Photos of "Professor Dawson and student" and "the Mica micromote," courtesy of AP/World Wide Photos.

Photos of "images of pottery fragments" and "a computer reconstruction," courtesy of Andrew Willis and David B. Cooper, Brown University, Division of Engineering.

Photo of "the Eurostar TGV train," by Jos van der Kolk.

Photo of "the interior of a Eurostar TGV cab," by Andy Veitch.

Photo of "firefighter Ken Whitten," courtesy of World Economic Forum.

Graphic of an "artificial retina," © The San Francisco Chronicle. Reprinted by permission.

Image of "A laser scan of Michelangelo's statue of David," courtesy of Marc Levoy and Dr. Franca Falletti, director of the Galleria dell'Accademia, Italy.

"An image from the Sistine Chapel," courtesy of Luca Pezzati. IR image recorded using the scanner for IR reflectography of the INOA (National Institute for Applied Optics, http://arte.ino.it) at the Opificio delle Pietre Dure in Florence.

THIRD EDITION REVISED

Computer Organization and Design

THE HARDWARE/SOFTWARE INTERFACE

David A. Patterson
University of California, Berkeley

John L. Hennessy
Stanford University

With contributions by

Peter J. Ashenden
Ashenden Designs Pty Ltd

James R. Larus
Microsoft Research

Daniel J. Sorin
Duke University

ELSEVIER

AMSTERDAM · BOSTON · HEIDELBERG · LONDON
NEW YORK · OXFORD · PARIS · SAN DIEGO
SAN FRANCISCO · SINGAPORE · SYDNEY · TOKYO

Morgan Kaufmann is an imprint of Elsevier

MORGAN KAUFMANN PUBLISHERS

Publishing Director	Joanne Tracy
Publisher	Denise E. M. Penrose
Publishing Services Manager	George Morrison
Senior Project Manager	Brandy Lilly
Senior Developmental Editor	Nathaniel McFadden
Assistant Editor	Kimberlee Honjo
Cover Design	Ross Caron Design
Cover and Chapter Illustration	Chris Asimoudis
Text Design	GCS Book Services
Composition	Nancy Logan
Technical Illustration	diacriTech
Proofreader	Jacqueline Brownstein, Jennifer McClain
Interior printer	Courier
Cover printer	Phoenix Color

Morgan Kaufmann Publishers is an imprint of Elsevier.
30 Corporate Drive, Suite 400, Burlington, MA 01803, USA

This book is printed on acid-free paper.

Library of Congress Cataloging-in-Publication Data
Application submitted

ISBN: 978-0-12-370606-5

For information on all Morgan Kaufmann publications,
visit our Web site at *www.mkp.com* or *www.books.elsevier.com*.

Printed in the United States of America
08 09 10 11   5 4 3 2

Contents

COMPUTERS IN THE REAL WORLD
Helping Save Our Environment with Data   156

3   Arithmetic for Computers   158

COMPUTERS IN THE REAL WORLD
Reconstructing the Ancient World   236

4   Assessing and Understanding Performance   238

COMPUTERS IN THE REAL WORLD
Moving People Faster and More Safely   280

5 **The Processor: Datapath and Control 282**

COMPUTERS IN THE REAL WORLD
Empowering the Disabled 366

6 **Enhancing Performance with Pipelining 368**

COMPUTERS IN THE REAL WORLD
Mass Communication without Gatekeepers 464

A P P E N D I C E S

Assemblers, Linkers, and the SPIM Simulator   A-2

The Basics of Logic Design   B-2

Preface

The most beautiful thing we can experience is the mysterious.
It is the source of all true art and science.

Albert Einstein, *What I Believe*, 1930

About This Book

We believe that learning in computer science and engineering should reflect the current state of the field, as well as introduce the principles that are shaping computing. We also feel that readers in every specialty of computing need to appreciate the organizational paradigms that determine the capabilities, performance, and, ultimately, the success of computer systems.

Modern computer technology requires professionals of every computing specialty to understand both hardware and software. The interaction between hardware and software at a variety of levels also offers a framework for understanding the fundamentals of computing. Whether your primary interest is hardware or software, computer science or electrical engineering, the central ideas in computer organization and design are the same. Thus, our emphasis in this book is to show the relationship between hardware and software and to focus on the concepts that are the basis for current computers.

The audience for this book includes those with little experience in assembly language or logic design who need to understand basic computer organization as well as readers with backgrounds in assembly language and/or logic design who want to learn how to design a computer or understand how a system works and why it performs as it does.

About the Other Book

Some readers may be familiar with *Computer Architecture: A Quantitative Approach*, popularly known as Hennessy and Patterson. (This book in turn is called Patterson and Hennessy.) Our motivation in writing that book was to describe the principles of computer architecture using solid engineering fundamentals and quantitative cost/performance trade-offs. We used an approach that combined examples and measurements, based on commercial systems, to create realistic design experiences. Our goal was to demonstrate that computer architecture could be learned using quantitative methodologies instead of a descriptive approach. It was intended for the serious computing professional who wanted a detailed understanding of computers.

A majority of the readers for this book do not plan to become computer architects. The performance of future software systems will be dramatically affected, however, by how well software designers understand the basic hardware techniques at work in a system. Thus, compiler writers, operating system designers, database programmers, and most other software engineers need a firm grounding in the principles presented in this book. Similarly, hardware designers must understand clearly the effects of their work on software applications.

Thus, we knew that this book had to be much more than a subset of the material in *Computer Architecture*, and the material was extensively revised to match the different audience. We were so happy with the result that the subsequent editions of *Computer Architecture* were revised to remove most of the introductory material; hence, there is much less overlap today than with the first editions of both books.

Changes for the Third Edition

We had six major goals for the third edition of *Computer Organization and Design:* make the book work equally well for readers with a software focus or with a hardware focus; improve pedagogy in general; enhance understanding of program performance; update the technical content to reflect changes in the industry since the publication of the second edition in 1998; tie the ideas from the book more closely to the real world *outside* the computing industry; and reduce the size of the book.

First, the table on the next page shows the hardware and software paths through the material. Chapters 1, 4, and 7 are found on both paths, no matter what the experience or the focus. Chapters 2 and 3 are likely to be review material for the hardware-oriented, but are essential reading for the software-oriented, especially for those readers interested in learning more about compilers and object-oriented programming languages. The first sections of Chapters 5 and 6 give overviews for those with a software focus. Those with a hardware focus, however, will find that these chapters present core material; they may also, depending on background, want to read Appendix B on logic design first and the sections on microprogramming and how to use hardware description languages to specify control. Chapter 8 on input/output is key to readers with a software focus and should be read by others if time permits. The last chapter on multiprocessors and clusters is again a question of time for the reader. Even the history sections show this balanced focus; they include short histories of programming languages, compilers, numerical software, operating systems, networking protocols, and databases.

Chapter or appendix	*Sections*	*Software focus*	*Hardware focus*
1. Computer Abstractions and Technology	1.1 to 1.6	Read carefully	Read carefully
	1.7 (History)	Read for culture	Read for culture
2. Instructions: Language of the Computer	2.1 to 2.11	Read carefully	Review or read
	2.12 (Compilers)	Read if have time	
	2.13 (C sort)	Read carefully	Review or read
	2.14 (Java)	Read if have time	
	2.15 to 2.18	Read carefully	Review or read
	2.19 (History)	Read for culture	Read for culture
3. Arithmetic for Computers	3.1 to 3.9	Read carefully	Review or read
	3.10 (History)	Read for culture	Read for culture
D. RISC instruction set architectures	D.1 to D.19	Read if have time	
4. Assessing and Understanding Performance	4.1 to 4.6	Read carefully	Read carefully
	4.7 (History)	Read for culture	Read for culture
B. The Basics of Logic Design	B.1 to B.13		Review or read
5. The Processor: Datapath and Control	5.1 (Overview)	Read carefully	Read carefully
	5.2 to 5.6		Read carefully
	5.7 (Microcode)		Read if have time
	5.8 (Verilog)		Read carefully
	5.9 to 5.12	Read carefully	Read carefully
	5.13 (History)	Read for culture	Read for culture
C. Mapping Control to Hardware	C.1 to C.6		Read if have time
6. Enhancing Performance with Pipelining	6.1 (Overview)	Read carefully	Read carefully
	6.2 to 6.6		Read carefully
	6.7 (Verilog)		Read carefully
	6.8 to 6.9		Read carefully
	6.10 to 6.12	Read carefully	Read carefully
	6.13 (History)	Read for culture	Read for culture
7. Large and Fast: Exploiting Memory Hierarchy	7.1 to 7.8	Read carefully	Read carefully
	7.9 (History)	Read for culture	Read for culture
8. Storage, Networks, and Other Peripherals	8.1 to 8.2	Read carefully	Read if have time
	8.3 (Networks)	Read if have time	Read if have time
	8.4 to 8.10	Read carefully	Read if have time
	8.11 (History)	Read for culture	Read for culture
9. Multiprocessors and Clusters	9.1 to 9.10	Read if have time	
	9.11 (History)	Read for culture	
A. Assemblers, Linkers, and the SPIM Simulator	A.1 to A.12	Reference	Reference
Computers in the Real World	Between chapters	Read for culture	Read for culture

Read carefully — Read if have time — Reference
Review or read — Read for culture

(2.16–2.18 for culture) — also read all of Waldron
* via own notes + Waldron reading
(culture)

The second goal was to improve the exposition of the ideas in the book, based on difficulties mentioned by readers of the second edition. We added five new book elements to help. To make the book work better as a reference, we placed definitions of new terms in the margins at their first occurrence. We hope this will help readers find the sections when they want to refer to material they have already read. Another change was the insertion of the "Check Yourself" sections, which we added to help readers to check their comprehension of the material on the first time through it. A third change is that we added extra exercises in the "For More Practice" section. Fourth, we added the answers to the "Check Yourself" sections and to the "For More Practice" exercises to help readers see for themselves if they understand the material by comparing their answers to the book. The final new book element was inspired by the "Green Card" of the IBM System/360. We believe that you will find that the MIPS Reference Data Card will be a handy reference when writing MIPS assembly language programs. Our idea is that you will remove the card from the front of the book, fold it in half, and keep it in your pocket, just as IBM S/360 programmers did in the 1960s.

Third, computers are so complex today that understanding the performance of a program involves understanding a good deal about the underlying principles and the organization of a given computer. Our goal is that readers of this book should be able to understand the performance of their programs and how to improve it. To aid in that goal, we added a new book element called "Understanding Program Performance" in several chapters. These sections often give concrete examples of how ideas in the chapter affect performance of real programs.

Fourth, in the interval since the second edition of this book, Moore's law has marched onward so that we now have processors with 200 million transistors, DRAM chips with a billion transistors, and clock rates of multiple gigahertz. The "Real Stuff" examples have been updated to describe such chips. This edition also includes AMD64/IA-32e, the 64-bit address version of the long-lived 8086 architecture, which appears to be the nemesis of the more recent IA-64. It also reflects the transition from parallel buses to serial networks and switches. Later chapters describe Google, which was born after the second edition, in terms of its cluster technology and in novel uses of search.

Fifth, although many computer science and engineering students enjoy information technology for technology's sake, some have more altruistic interests. This latter group tends to have more women and underrepresented minorities. Consequently, we have added a new book element, "Computers in the Real World," two-page layouts found between each chapter. Our perspective is that information technology is more valuable for humanity than most other topics you could study—whether it is preserving our art heritage, helping the Third World, saving our environment, or even changing political systems—and so we demonstrate our view with concrete examples of nontraditional applications. We think readers of these segments will have a greater appreciation of the computing culture beyond the inherently interesting technology, much like those who read the history sections at the end of each chapter.

Finally, books are like people: they usually get larger as they get older. By using technology, we have managed to do all the above and yet shrink the page count by hundreds of pages. As the table illustrates, the core portion of the book for hardware and software readers is on paper, but sections that some readers would value more than others are found on the companion CD. This technology also allows your authors to provide longer histories and more extensive exercises without concerns about lengthening the book. Once we added the CD to the book, we could then include a great deal of free software and tutorials that many instructors have told us they would like to use in their courses. This hybrid paper–CD publication weighs about 30% less than it did six years ago—an impressive goal for books as well as for people.

Instructor Support

We have collected a great deal of material to help instructors teach courses using this book. Solutions to exercises, figures from the book, lecture notes, lecture slides, and other materials are available to adopters from the publisher. Check the publisher's Web site for more information:

www.mkp.com/companions/1558606041

Concluding Remarks

If you read the following acknowledgments section, you will see that we went to great lengths to correct mistakes. Since a book goes through many printings, we have the opportunity to make even more corrections. If you uncover any remaining, resilient bugs, please contact the publisher by electronic mail at *cod3bugs@mkp.com* or by low-tech mail using the address found on the copyright page. The first person to report a technical error will be awarded a $1.00 bounty upon its implementation in future printings of the book!

This book is truly collaborative, despite one of us running a major university. Together we brainstormed about the ideas and method of presentation, then individually wrote about one-half of the chapters and acted as reviewer for every draft of the other half. The page count suggests we again wrote almost exactly the same number of pages. Thus, we equally share the blame for what you are about to read.

Acknowledgments for the Third Edition

We'd like to again express our appreciation to **Jim Larus** for his willingness in contributing his expertise on assembly language programming, as well as for welcoming readers of this book to use the simulator he developed and maintains. Our exercise editor **Dan Sorin** took on the Herculean task of adding new exercises and answers. **Peter Ashenden** worked similarly hard to collect and organize the companion CD.

We are grateful to the many instructors who answered the publisher's surveys, reviewed our proposals, and attended focus groups to analyze and respond to our plans for this edition. They include the following individuals: Michael Anderson (University of Hartford), David Bader (University of New Mexico), Rusty Baldwin (Air Force Institute of Technology), John Barr (Ithaca College), Jack Briner (Charleston Southern University), Mats Brorsson (KTH, Sweden), Colin Brown (Franklin University), Lori Carter (Point Loma Nazarene University), John Casey (Northeastern University), Gene Chase (Messiah College), George Cheney (University of Massachusetts, Lowell), Daniel Citron (Jerusalem College of Technology, Israel), Albert Cohen (INRIA, France), Lloyd Dickman (PathScale), Jose Duato (Universidad Politécnica de Valencia, Spain), Ben Dugan (University of Washington), Derek Eager (University of Saskatchewan, Canada), Magnus Ekman (Chalmers University of Technology, Sweden), Ata Elahi (Southern Connecticut State University), Soundararajan Ezekiel (Indiana University of Pennsylvania), Ernest Ferguson (Northwest Missouri State University), Michael Fry (Lebanon Valley College, Pennsylvania), R. Gaede (University of Arkansas at Little Rock), Jean-Luc Gaudiot (University of California, Irvine), Thomas Gendreau (University of Wisconsin, La Crosse), George Georgiou (California State University, San Bernardino), Paul Gillard (Memorial University of Newfoundland, Canada), Joe Grimes (California Polytechnic State University, SLO), Max Hailperin (Gustavus Adolphus College), Jayantha Herath (St. Cloud State University, Minnesota), Mark Hill (University of Wisconsin, Madison), Michael Hsaio (Virginia Tech), Richard Hughey (University of California, Santa Cruz), Tony Jebara (Columbia University), Elizabeth Johnson (Xavier University), Peter Kogge (University of Notre Dame), Morris Lancaster (BAH), Doug Lawrence (University of Montana), David Lilja (University of Minnesota), Nam Ling (Santa Clara University, California), Paul Lum (Agilent Technologies), Stephen Mann (University of Waterloo, Canada), Diana Marculescu (Carnegie Mellon University), Margaret McMahon (U.S. Naval Academy Computer Science), Uwe Meyer-Baese (Florida State University), Chris Milner (University of Virginia), Tom Pittman (Southwest Baptist University), Jalel Rejeb (San Jose State University, California), Bill Siever (University of Missouri, Rolla), Kevin Skadron (University of Virginia), Pam Smallwood (Regis University, Colorado), K. Stuart Smith (Rocky Mountain College), William J. Taffe (Plymouth State University), Michael E. Thomodakis (Texas A&M University), Ruppa K. Thulasiram (University of Manitoba, Canada), Ye Tung (University of South Alabama), Steve VanderLeest (Calvin College), Neal R. Wagner (University of Texas at San Antonio), and Kent Wilken (University of California, Davis).

We are grateful too to those who carefully read our draft manuscripts; some read successive drafts to help ensure new errors didn't creep in as we revised. They include Krste Asanovic (Massachusetts Institute of Technology), Jean-Loup Baer (University of Washington), David Brooks (Harvard University), Doug Clark (Princeton University), Dan Connors (University of Colorado at Boulder), Matt Farrens (University of California, Davis), Manoj Franklin (University of Maryland, College Park), John Greiner (Rice University), David Harris (Harvey Mudd College), Paul Hilfinger (University of California, Berkeley), Norm Jouppi (Hewlett-Packard), David Kaeli (Northeastern University), David Oppenheimer (University of California, Berkeley), Timothy Pinkston (University of Southern California), Mark Smotherman (Clemson University), and David Wood (University of Wisconsin, Madison).

To help us meet our goal of creating 70% new exercises and solutions for this edition, we recruited several graduate students recommended to us by their professors. We are grateful for their creativity and persistence: Michael Black (University of Maryland), Lei Chen (University of Rochester), Nirav Dave (Massachusetts Institute of Technology), Wael El Essawy (University of Rochester), Nikil Mehta (Brown University), Nicholas Nelson (University of Rochester), Aaron Smith (University of Texas, Austin), and Charlie Wang (Duke University).

We would like to especially thank **Mark Smotherman** for making a careful final pass to find technical and writing glitches that significantly improved the quality of this edition.

We wish to thank the extended Morgan Kaufmann family for agreeing to publish this book again under the able leadership of **Denise Penrose**. She developed the vision of the hybrid paper–CD book and recruited the many people above who played important roles in developing the book.

Brandy Lilly managed the book production process, and **Nathaniel McFadden** and **Kimberlee Honjo** coordinated the surveying of users and their responses. We thank also the many freelance vendors who contributed to this volume, especially **Nancy Logan**, our compositor.

The contributions of the nearly 100 people we mentioned here have made this third edition our best book yet. Enjoy!

David A. Patterson   **John L. Hennessy**

1

Computer Abstractions and Technology

*Civilization advances by extending
the number of important operations
which we can perform without
thinking about them.*

Alfred North Whitehead
An Introduction to Mathematics, 1911

1.1   Introduction

Welcome to this book! We're delighted to have this opportunity to convey the excitement of the world of computer systems. This is not a dry and dreary field, where progress is glacial and where new ideas atrophy from neglect. No! Computers are the product of the incredibly vibrant information technology industry, all aspects of which are responsible for almost 10% of the gross national product of the United States. This unusual industry embraces innovation at a breathtaking rate. Since 1985 there have been a number of new computers whose introduction appeared to revolutionize the computing industry; these revolutions were cut short only because someone else built an even better computer.

This race to innovate has led to unprecedented progress since the inception of electronic computing in the late 1940s. Had the transportation industry kept pace with the computer industry, for example, today we could travel coast to coast in about a second for roughly a few cents. Take just a moment to contemplate how such an improvement would change society—living in Tahiti while working in San Francisco, going to Moscow for an evening at the Bolshoi Ballet—and you can appreciate the implications of such a change.

Computers have led to a third revolution for civilization, with the information revolution taking its place alongside the agricultural and the industrial revolutions. The resulting multiplication of humankind's intellectual strength and reach naturally has affected our everyday lives profoundly and also changed the ways in which the search for new knowledge is carried out. There is now a new vein of scientific investigation, with computational scientists joining theoretical and experimental scientists in the exploration of new frontiers in astronomy, biology, chemistry, physics, ...

The computer revolution continues. Each time the cost of computing improves by another factor of 10, the opportunities for computers multiply. Applications that were economically infeasible suddenly become practical. In the recent past, the following applications were "computer science fiction."

- *Automatic teller machines:* A computer placed in the wall of banks to distribute and collect cash would have been a ridiculous concept in the 1950s, when the cheapest computer cost at least $500,000 and was the size of a car.

- *Computers in automobiles:* Until microprocessors improved dramatically in price and performance in the early 1980s, computer control of cars was ludicrous. Today, computers reduce pollution and improve fuel efficiency via engine controls and increase safety through the prevention of dangerous skids and through the inflation of air bags to protect occupants in a crash.

- *Laptop computers:* Who would have dreamed that advances in computer systems would lead to laptop computers, allowing students to bring computers to coffeehouses and on airplanes?

- *Human genome project:* The cost of computer equipment to map and analyze human DNA sequences is hundreds of millions of dollars. It's unlikely that anyone would have considered this project had the computer costs been 10 to 100 times higher, as they would have been 10 to 20 years ago.

- *World Wide Web:* Not in existence at the time of the first edition of this book, the World Wide Web has transformed our society. Among its uses are distributing news, sending flowers, buying from online catalogues, taking electronic tours to help pick vacation spots, finding others who share your esoteric interests, and even more mundane topics like finding the lecture notes of the authors of your textbooks.

Clearly, advances in this technology now affect almost every aspect of our society. Hardware advances have allowed programmers to create wonderfully useful software, and explain why computers are omnipresent. Tomorrow's science fiction computer applications are the cashless society, automated intelligent highways, and genuinely ubiquitous computing: no one carries computers because they are available everywhere.

Classes of Computing Applications and Their Characteristics

Although a common set of hardware technologies (discussed in Sections 1.3 and 1.4) is used in computers ranging from smart home appliances to cell phones to the largest supercomputers, these different applications have different design requirements and employ the core hardware technologies in different ways. Broadly speaking, computers are used in three different classes of applications.

Desktop computers are possibly the best-known form of computing and are characterized by the personal computer, which most readers of this book have probably used extensively. Desktop computers emphasize delivering good performance to a single user at low cost and usually are used to execute third-party software, also called shrink-wrap software. Desktop computing is one of the largest markets for computers, and the evolution of many computing technologies is driven by this class of computing, which is only about 30 years old!

Servers are the modern form of what was once mainframes, minicomputers, and supercomputers, and are usually accessed only via a network. Servers are oriented to carrying large workloads, which may consist of either single complex applications, usually a scientific or engineering application, or handling many small jobs, such as would occur in building a large Web server. These applications are often based on software from another source (such as a database or simulation system), but are often modified or customized for a particular function. Servers are built from the same basic technology as desktop computers, but provide for greater expandability of both computing and input/output capacity. As we will see in Chapter 4, the performance of a server can be measured in several different ways, depending on the application of interest. In general, servers also place a greater emphasis on dependability, since a crash is usually more costly than it would be on a single-user desktop computer.

Servers span the widest range in cost and capability. At the low end, a server may be little more than a desktop machine without a screen or keyboard and with a cost of a thousand dollars. These low-end servers are typically used for file storage, small business applications, or simple Web serving. At the other extreme are **supercomputers,** which at the present consist of hundreds to thousands of processors, and usually gigabytes to **terabytes** of memory and terabytes to petabytes of storage, and cost millions to hundreds of millions of dollars. Supercomputers are usually used for high-end scientific and engineering calculations, such as weather forecasting, oil exploration, protein structure determination, and other large-scale problems. Although such supercomputers represent the peak of computing capability, they are a relatively small fraction of the servers and a relatively small fraction of the overall computer market in terms of total revenue.

Embedded computers are the largest class of computers and span the widest range of applications and performance. Embedded computers include the microprocessors found in your washing machine and car, the computers in a cell phone

desktop computer A computer designed for use by an individual, usually incorporating a graphics display, keyboard, and mouse.

Server A computer used for running larger programs for multiple users often simultaneously and typically accessed only via a network.

supercomputer A class of computers with the highest performance and cost; they are configured as servers and typically cost millions of dollars.

terabyte Originally 1,099,511,627,776 (2^{40}) bytes, although some communications and secondary storage systems have redefined it to mean 1,000,000,000,000 (10^{12}) bytes.

embedded computer A computer inside another device used for running one predetermined application or collection of software.

or personal digital assistant, the computers in a video game or digital television, and the networks of processors that control a modern airplane or cargo ship. Embedded computing systems are designed to run one application or one set of related applications, which is normally integrated with the hardware and delivered as a single system; thus, despite the large number of embedded computers, most users never really see that they are using a computer!

Embedded applications often have unique application requirements that combine a minimum performance with stringent limitations on cost or power. For example, consider a cell phone: the processor need only be as fast as necessary to handle its limited function, and beyond that, minimizing cost and power are the most important objectives. Despite their low cost, embedded computers often have the least tolerance for failure, since the results can vary from upsetting (when your new television crashes) to devastating (such as might occur when the computer in a plane or car crashes). In consumer-oriented embedded applications, such as a digital home appliance, dependability is achieved primarily through simplicity—the emphasis is on doing one function, as perfectly as possible. In large embedded systems, techniques of redundancy, which are used in servers, are often employed. Although this book focuses on general-purpose computers, most of the concepts apply directly, or with slight modifications, to embedded computers. In several places, we will touch on some of the unique aspects of embedded computers.

Figure 1.1 shows that during the last several years, the growth in the number of embedded computers has been much faster (40% compounded annual growth rate) than the growth rate among desktop computers and servers (9% annually). Note that the embedded computers include cell phones, video games, digital TVs and set-top boxes, personal digital assistants, and a variety of such consumer devices. Note that this data does not include low-end embedded control devices that use 8-bit and 16-bit processors.

Elaboration: Elaborations are short sections used throughout the text to provide more detail on a particular subject, which may be of interest. Disinterested readers may skip over an elaboration, since the subsequent material will never depend on the contents of the elaboration.

Many embedded processors are designed using *processor cores*, a version of a processor written in a hardware description language, such as Verilog or VHDL. The core allows a designer to integrate other application-specific hardware with the processor core for fabrication on a single chip. The availability of synthesis tools that can generate a chip from a Verilog specification, together with the capacity of modern silicon chips, has made such special-purpose processors highly attractive. Since the core can be synthesized for different semiconductor manufacturing lines, using a core provides flexibility in choosing a manufacturer as well. In the last few years, the use of cores has

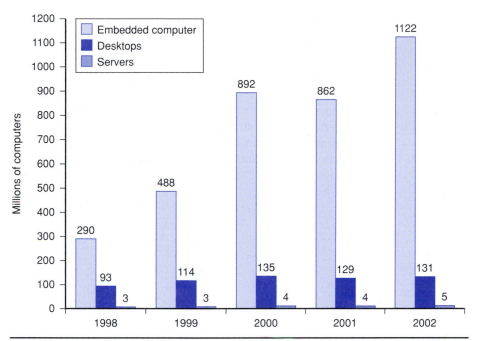

FIGURE 1.1 The number of distinct processors sold between 1998 and 2002. These counts are obtained somewhat differently, so some caution is required in interpreting the results. For example, the totals for desktops and servers count complete computer systems; because some fraction of these include multiple processors, the number of processors sold is somewhat higher, but probably by only 10–20% in total (since the servers, which may average more than one processor per system, are only about 3% of the desktop sales, which are predominantly single-processor systems). The totals for embedded computers actually count processors, many of which are not even visible, and in some cases there may be multiple processors per device.

been growing very fast. For example, in 1998 only 31% of the embedded processors were cores. By 2002, 56% of the embedded processors were cores. Furthermore, while the overall growth rate in the embedded market has been 40% per year, this growth has been primarily driven by cores, where the compounded annual growth rate has been 63%!

Figure 1.2 shows the major architectures sold in these markets with counts for each architecture, across all three types of products (embedded, desktop, and server). Only 32-bit and 64-bit processors are included, although 32-bit processors are the vast majority for most of the architectures.

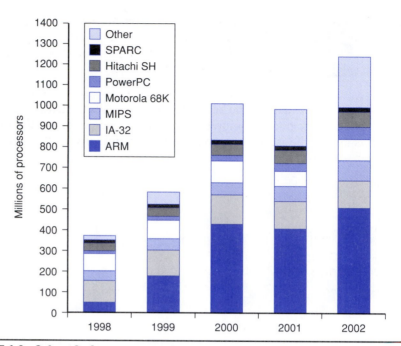

FIGURE 1.2   Sales of microprocessors between 1998 and 2002 by instruction set architecture combining all uses. The "other" category refers to processors that are either application-specific or customized architectures. In the case of ARM, roughly 80% of the sales are for cell phones, where an ARM core is used in conjunction with application-specific logic on a chip.

What You Can Learn in This Book

Successful programmers have always been concerned about the performance of their programs because getting results to the user quickly is critical in creating successful software. In the 1960s and 1970s, a primary constraint on computer performance was the size of the computer's memory. Thus programmers often followed a simple credo: Minimize memory space to make programs fast. In the last decade, advances in computer design and memory technology have greatly reduced the importance of small memory size in most applications other than those in embedded computing systems.

Programmers interested in performance now need to understand the issues that have replaced the simple memory model of the 1960s: the hierarchical nature of memories and the parallel nature of processors. Programmers who seek to build competitive versions of compilers, operating systems, databases, and even applications will therefore need to increase their knowledge of computer organization.

We are honored to have the opportunity to explain what's inside this revolutionary machine, unraveling the software below your program and the hardware under the covers of your computer. By the time you complete this book, we believe you will be able to answer the following questions:

- How are programs written in a high-level language, such as C or Java, translated into the language of the hardware, and how does the hardware execute the resulting program? Comprehending these concepts forms the basis of understanding the aspects of both the hardware and software that affect program performance.

- What is the interface between the software and the hardware, and how does software instruct the hardware to perform needed functions? These concepts are vital to understanding how to write many kinds of software.

- What determines the performance of a program, and how can a programmer improve the performance? As we will see, this depends on the original program, the software translation of that program into the computer's language, and the effectiveness of the hardware in executing the program.

- What techniques can be used by hardware designers to improve performance? This book will introduce the basic concepts of modern computer design. The interested reader will find much more material on this topic in our advanced book, *Computer Architecture: A Quantitative Approach*.

Without understanding the answers to these questions, improving the performance of your program on a modern computer, or evaluating what features might make one computer better than another for a particular application, will be a complex process of trial and error, rather than a scientific procedure driven by insight and analysis.

This first chapter lays the foundation for the rest of the book. It introduces the basic ideas and definitions, places the major components of software and hardware in perspective, and introduces integrated circuits, the technology that fuels the computer revolution. In this chapter, and later ones, you will likely see a lot of new words, or words that you may have heard, but are not sure what they mean. Don't panic! Yes, there is a lot of special terminology used in describing modern computers, but the terminology actually helps since it enables us to describe precisely a function or capability. In addition, computer designers (including your authors) *love* using **acronyms**, which are *easy* to understand once you know what the letters stand for! To help you remember and locate terms, we have included a highlighted definition of every term, the first time it appears in the text. After a short time of working with the terminology, you will be fluent, and your friends

acronym A word constructed by taking the initial letters of a string of words. For example: RAM is an acronym for Random Access Memory, and CPU is an acronym for Central Processing Unit.

will be impressed as you correctly use words such as BIOS, DIMM, CPU, cache, DRAM, ATA, PCI, and many others.

To reinforce how the software and hardware systems used to run a program will affect performance, we use a special section, "Understanding Program Performance," throughout the book, with the first one appearing below. These elements summarize important insights into program performance.

Understanding Program Performance

The performance of a program depends on a combination of the effectiveness of the algorithms used in the program, the software systems used to create and translate the program into machine instructions, and the effectiveness of the computer in executing those instructions, which may include input/output (I/O) operations. The following table summarizes how the hardware and software affect performance.

Hardware or software component	How this component affects performance	Where is this topic covered?
Algorithm	Determines both the number of source-level statements and the number of I/O operations executed	Other books!
Programming language, compiler, and architecture	Determines the number of machine instructions for each source-level statement	Chapters 2 and 3
Processor and memory system	Determines how fast instructions can be executed	Chapters 5, 6, and 7
I/O system (hardware and operating system)	Determines how fast I/O operations may be executed	Chapter 8

Check Yourself

"Check Yourself" sections are designed to help readers assess whether they have comprehended the major concepts introduced in a chapter and understand the implications of those concepts. Some "Check Yourself" questions have simple answers; others are for discussion among a group. Answers to the specific questions can be found at the end of the chapter. "Check Yourself" questions appear only at the end of a section, making it easy to skip them if you are sure you understand the material.

1. Section 1.1 showed that the number of embedded processors sold every year greatly outnumbers the number of desktop processors. Can you confirm or deny this insight based on your own experience? Try to count the number of embedded processors in your home. How does it compare with the number of desktop computers in your home?

2. As mentioned earlier, both the software and hardware affect the performance of a program. Can you think of examples where each of the following is the right place to look for a performance bottleneck?

   ■ The algorithm chosen

   ■ The programming language or compiler

   ■ The operating system

   ■ The processor

   ■ The I/O system and devices

1.2 Below Your Program

A typical application, such as a word processor or a large database system, may consist of hundreds of thousands to millions of lines of code and rely on sophisticated software libraries that implement complex functions in support of the application. As we will see, the hardware in a computer can only execute extremely simple low-level instructions. To go from a complex application to the simple instructions involves several layers of software that interpret or translate high-level operations into simple computer instructions.

These layers of software are organized primarily in a hierarchical fashion, with applications being the outermost ring and a variety of **systems software** sitting between the hardware and applications software, as shown in Figure 1.3.

There are many types of systems software, but two types of systems software are central to every computer system today: an operating system and a compiler. An **operating system** interfaces between a user's program and the hardware and provides a variety of services and supervisory functions. Among the most important functions are

   ■ handling basic input and output operations

   ■ allocating storage and memory

   ■ providing for sharing the computer among multiple applications using it simultaneously

Examples of operating systems in use today are Windows, Linux, and MacOS.

Compilers perform another vital function: the translation of a program written in a high-level language, such as C or Java, into instructions that the hardware

In Paris they simply stared when I spoke to them in French; I never did succeed in making those idiots understand their own language.

Mark Twain, *The Innocents Abroad*, 1869

systems software Software that provides services that are commonly useful, including operating systems, compilers, and assemblers.

operating system Supervising program that manages the resources of a computer for the benefit of the programs that run on that machine.

compiler A program that translates high-level language statements into assembly language statements.

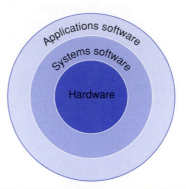

FIGURE 1.3   A simplified view of hardware and software as hierarchical layers, shown as concentric circles with hardware in the center and applications software outermost. In complex applications there are often multiple layers of application software as well. For example, a database system may run on top of the systems software hosting an application, which in turn runs on top of the database.

can execute. Given the sophistication of modern programming languages and the simple instructions executed by the hardware, the translation from a high-level language program to hardware instructions is complex. We will give a brief overview of the process and return to the subject in Chapter 2.

From a High-Level Language to the Language of Hardware

To actually speak to an electronic machine, you need to send electrical signals. The easiest signals for machines to understand are *on* and *off*, and so the machine alphabet is just two letters. Just as the 26 letters of the English alphabet do not limit how much can be written, the two letters of the computer alphabet do not limit what computers can do. The two symbols for these two letters are the numbers 0 and 1, and we commonly think of the machine language as numbers in base 2, or *binary numbers*. We refer to each "letter" as a **binary digit** or **bit**. Computers are slaves to our commands, which are called instructions. Instructions, which are just collections of bits that the computer understands, can be thought of as numbers. For example, the bits

    1000110010100000

tell one computer to add two numbers. Chapter 3 explains why we use numbers for instructions *and* data; we don't want to steal that chapter's thunder, but using numbers for both instructions and data is a foundation of computing.

binary digit Also called a **bit**. One of the two numbers in base 2 (0 or 1) that are the components of information.

The first programmers communicated to computers in binary numbers, but this was so tedious that they quickly invented new notations that were closer to the way humans think. At first these notations were translated to binary by hand, but this process was still tiresome. Using the machine to help program the machine, the pioneers invented programs to translate from symbolic notation to binary. The first of these programs was named an **assembler**. This program translates a symbolic version of an instruction into the binary version. For example, the programmer would write

```
add A,B
```

and the assembler would translate this notation into

```
1000110010100000
```

This instruction tells the computer to add the two numbers A and B. The name coined for this symbolic language, still used today, is **assembly language**.

Although a tremendous improvement, assembly language is still far from the notation a scientist might like to use to simulate fluid flow or that an accountant might use to balance the books. Assembly language requires the programmer to write one line for every instruction that the machine will follow, forcing the programmer to think like the machine.

The recognition that a program could be written to translate a more powerful language into computer instructions was one of the great breakthroughs in the early days of computing. Programmers today owe their productivity—and their sanity—to the creation of **high-level programming languages** and compilers that translate programs in such languages into instructions.

A compiler enables a programmer to write this high-level language expression:

```
A + B
```

The compiler would compile it into this assembly language statement:

```
add A,B
```

The assembler would translate this statement into the binary instruction that tells the computer to add the two numbers A and B:

```
1000110010100000
```

Figure 1.4 shows the relationships among these programs and languages.

High-level programming languages offer several important benefits. First, they allow the programmer to think in a more natural language, using English words and algebraic notation, resulting in programs that look much more like text than like tables of cryptic symbols (see Figure 1.4). Moreover, they allow languages to

assembler A program that translates a symbolic version of instructions into the binary version.

assembly language A symbolic representation of machine instructions.

high-level programming language A portable language such as C, Fortran, or Java composed of words and algebraic notation that can be translated by a compiler into assembly language.

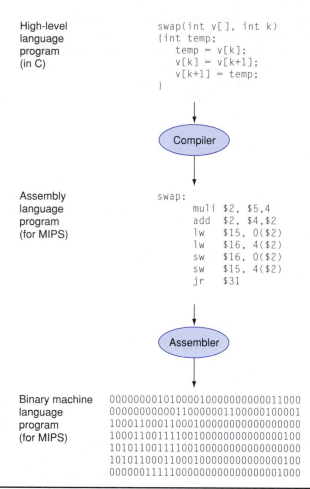

FIGURE 1.4   C program compiled into assembly language and then assembled into binary machine language. Although the translation from high-level language to binary machine language is shown in two steps, some compilers cut out the middleman and produce binary machine language directly. These languages and this program are examined in more detail in Chapter 2.

be designed according to their intended use. Hence, Fortran was designed for scientific computation, Cobol for business data processing, Lisp for symbol manipulation, and so on.

The second advantage of programming languages is improved programmer productivity. One of the few areas of widespread agreement in software development is that it takes less time to develop programs when they are written in languages that require fewer lines to express an idea. Conciseness is a clear advantage of high-level languages over assembly language.

The final advantage is that programming languages allow programs to be independent of the computer on which they were developed, since compilers and assemblers can translate high-level language programs to the binary instructions of any machine. These three advantages are so strong that today little programming is done in assembly language.

1.3   Under the Covers

Now that we have looked below your program to uncover the underlying software, let's open the covers of the computer to learn about the underlying hardware. The underlying hardware in any computer performs the same basic functions: inputting data, outputting data, processing data, and storing data. How these functions are performed is the primary topic of this book, and subsequent chapters deal with different parts of these four tasks. When we come to an important point in this book, a point so important that we hope you will remember it forever, we emphasize it by identifying it as a "Big Picture" item. We have about a dozen Big Pictures in this book, with the first being the five components of a computer that perform the tasks of inputting, outputting, processing, and storing data.

The five classic components of a computer are input, output, memory, datapath, and control, with the last two sometimes combined and called the processor. Figure 1.5 shows the standard organization of a computer. This organization is independent of hardware technology: you can place every piece of every computer, past and present, into one of these five categories. To help you keep all this in perspective, the five components of a computer are shown on the front page of the following chapters, with the portion of interest to that chapter highlighted.

The BIG Picture

Figure 1.6 shows a typical desktop computer with keyboard, mouse, screen, and a box containing even more hardware. What is not visible in the photograph is a network that connects the computer to other computers. This photograph reveals two of the key components of computers: **input devices**, such as the keyboard and mouse, and **output devices**, such as the screen. As the names suggest, input feeds the computer, and output is the result of computation sent to the user. Some devices, such as networks and disks, provide both input and output to the computer.

input device A mechanism through which the computer is fed information, such as the keyboard or mouse.

output device A mechanism that conveys the result of a computation to a user or another computer.

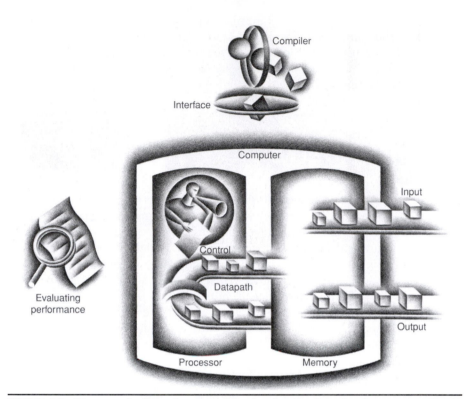

FIGURE 1.5   The organization of a computer, showing the five classic components. The processor gets instructions and data from memory. Input writes data to memory, and output reads data from memory. Control sends the signals that determine the operations of the datapath, memory, input, and output.

Chapter 8 describes input/output (I/O) devices in more detail, but let's take an introductory tour through the computer hardware, starting with the external I/O devices.

Anatomy of a Mouse

I got the idea for the mouse while attending a talk at a computer conference. The speaker was so boring that I started daydreaming and hit upon the idea.

Doug Engelbart

Although many users now take mice for granted, the idea of a pointing device such as a mouse was first shown by Engelbart using a research prototype in 1967. The Alto, which was the inspiration for all workstations as well as for the Macintosh, included a mouse as its pointing device in 1973. By the 1990s, all desktop computers included this device, and new user interfaces based on graphics displays and mice became the norm.

FIGURE 1.6   A desktop computer. The liquid crystal display (LCD) screen is the primary output device, and the keyboard and mouse are the primary input devices. The box contains the processor as well as additional I/O devices. This system is a Dell Optiplex GX260.

The original mouse was electromechanical and used a large ball that when rolled across a surface would cause an x and y counter to be incremented. The amount of increase in each counter told how far the mouse had been moved.

The electromechanical mouse has largely been replaced by the newer all-optical mouse. The optical mouse is actually a miniature optical processor including an LED to provide lighting, a tiny black-and-white camera, and a simple optical processor. The LED illuminates the surface underneath the mouse; the camera takes 1500 sample pictures a second under the illumination. Successive pictures are sent to a simple optical processor that compares the images and determines whether the mouse has moved and how far. The replacement of the electromechanical mouse by the electro-optical mouse is an illustration of a common phenomenon where the decreasing costs and higher reliability of electronics cause an electronic solution to replace the older electromechanical technology.

cathode ray tube (CRT) display A display, such as a television set, that displays an image using an electron beam scanned across a screen.

pixel The smallest individual picture element. Screens are composed of hundreds of thousands to millions of pixels, organized in a matrix.

flat panel display, liquid crystal display A display technology using a thin layer of liquid polymers that can be used to transmit or block light according to whether a charge is applied.

active matrix display A liquid crystal display using a transistor to control the transmission of light at each individual pixel.

Through the Looking Glass

The most fascinating I/O device is probably the graphics display. Based on television technology, a **cathode ray tube (CRT) display** scans an image one line at a time, 30 to 75 times per second. At this *refresh rate*, people don't notice a flicker on the screen.

The image is composed of a matrix of picture elements, or **pixels**, which can be represented as a matrix of bits, called a *bit map*. Depending on the size of the screen and the resolution, the display matrix ranges in size from 640×480 to 2560×1600 pixels in 2007. The simplest display has 1 bit per pixel, allowing it to be black or white. For displays that support 256 different shades of black and white, sometimes called *gray-scale* displays, 8 bits per pixel are required. A color display might use 8 bits for each of the three colors (red, blue, and green), for 24 bits per pixel, permitting millions of different colors to be displayed.

All laptop and handheld computers, calculators, cellular phones, and most desktop computers use **flat-panel** or **liquid crystal displays (LCDs)** instead of CRTs to get a thin, low-power display. The main difference is that the LCD pixel is not the source of light; instead it controls the transmission of light. A typical LCD includes rod-shaped molecules in a liquid that form a twisting helix that bends light entering the display, from either a light source behind the display or less often from reflected light. The rods straighten out when a current is applied and no longer bend the light; since the liquid crystal material is between two screens polarized at 90 degrees, the light cannot pass through unless it is bent. Today, most LCD displays use an **active matrix** that has a tiny transistor switch at each pixel to precisely control current and make sharper images. As in a CRT, a red-green-blue mask associated with each pixel determines the intensity of the three color components in the final image; in a color active matrix LCD, there are three transistor switches at each pixel.

No matter what the display, the computer hardware support for graphics consists mainly of a *raster refresh buffer*, or *frame buffer*, to store the bit map. The image to be represented on-screen is stored in the frame buffer, and the bit pattern per pixel is read out to the graphics display at the refresh rate. Figure 1.7 shows a frame buffer with 4 bits per pixel.

The goal of the bit map is to faithfully represent what is on the screen. The challenges in graphics systems arise because the human eye is very good at detecting even subtle changes on the screen. For example, when the screen is being updated, the eye can detect the inconsistency between the portion of the screen that has changed and that which hasn't.

Opening the Box

If we open the box containing the computer, we see a fascinating board of thin green plastic, covered with dozens of small gray or black rectangles. Figure 1.8

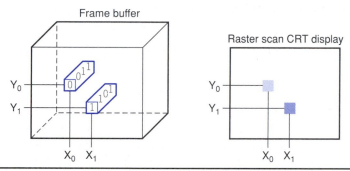

FIGURE 1.7 Each coordinate in the frame buffer on the left determines the shade of the corresponding coordinate for the raster scan CRT display on the right. Pixel (X_0, Y_0) contains the bit pattern 0011, which is a lighter shade of gray on the screen than the bit pattern 1101 in pixel (X_1, Y_1).

FIGURE 1.8 Inside the personal computer of Figure 1.6 on page 17. This packaging is sometimes called a clamshell because of the way it opens with hinges on one side. To see what's inside, let's start on the top left-hand side. The shiny metal box on the top far left side is the power supply. Just below that on the far left is the fan, with its cover pulled back. To the right and below the fan is a printed circuit board (PC board), called the *motherboard* in a PC, that contains most of the electronics of the computer; Figure 1.10 is a close-up of that board. The processor is the large raised rectangle just to the right of the fan. On the right side we see the bays designed to hold types of disk drives. The top bay contains a DVD drive, the middle bay a Zip drive, and the bottom bay contains a hard disk.

motherboard A plastic board containing packages of integrated circuits or chips, including processor, cache, memory, and connectors for I/O devices such as networks and disks.

integrated circuit Also called **chip**. A device combining dozens to millions of transistors.

memory The storage area in which programs are kept when they are running and that contains the data needed by the running programs.

central processor unit (CPU) Also called processor. The active part of the computer, which contains the datapath and control and which adds numbers, tests numbers, signals I/O devices to activate, and so on.

datapath The component of the processor that performs arithmetic operations.

control The component of the processor that commands the datapath, memory, and I/O devices according to the instructions of the program.

dynamic random access memory (DRAM) Memory built as an integrated circuit, it provides random access to any location.

cache memory A small, fast memory that acts as a buffer for a slower, larger memory.

shows the contents of the desktop computer in Figure 1.6. This **motherboard** is shown vertically on the left with the power supply. Three disk drives—a DVD drive, Zip drive, and hard drive—appear on the right.

The small rectangles on the motherboard contain the devices that drive our advancing technology, **integrated circuits** or **chips**. The board is composed of three pieces: the piece connecting to the I/O devices mentioned earlier, the memory, and the processor. The I/O devices are connected via the two large boards attached perpendicularly to the motherboard toward the middle on the right-hand side.

The **memory** is where the programs are kept when they are running; it also contains the data needed by the running programs. In Figure 1.8, memory is found on the two small boards that are attached perpendicularly toward the middle of the motherboard. Each small memory board contains eight integrated circuits.

The *processor* is the active part of the board, following the instructions of a program to the letter. It adds numbers, tests numbers, signals I/O devices to activate, and so on. The processor is under the fan and covered by a heat sink on the left side of Figure 1.8. Occasionally, people call the processor the *CPU*, for the more bureaucratic-sounding **central processor unit**.

Descending even lower into the hardware, Figure 1.9 reveals details of the processor in Figure 1.8. The processor comprises two main components: datapath and control, the respective brawn and brain of the processor. The **datapath** performs the arithmetic operations, and **control** tells the datapath, memory, and I/O devices what to do according to the wishes of the instructions of the program. Chapter 5 explains the datapath and control for a straightforward implementation, and Chapter 6 describes the changes needed for a higher-performance design.

Descending into the depths of any component of the hardware reveals insights into the machine. The memory in Figure 1.10 is built from DRAM chips. *DRAM* stands for **dynamic random access memory**. Several DRAMs are used together to contain the instructions and data of a program. In contrast to sequential access memories, such as magnetic tapes, the *RAM* portion of the term DRAM means that memory accesses take the same amount of time no matter what portion of the memory is read. Inside the processor is another type of memory—cache memory. **Cache memory** consists of a small, fast memory that acts as a buffer for the DRAM memory. (The nontechnical definition of *cache* is a safe place for hiding things.) Cache is built using a different memory technology, static random access memory (SRAM). SRAM is faster but less dense, and hence more expensive, than DRAM.

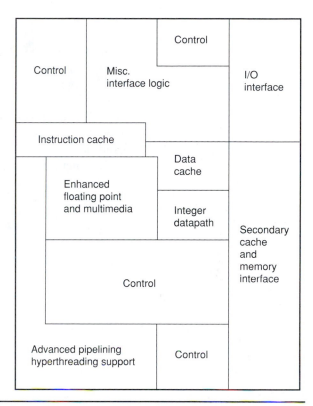

FIGURE 1.9 **Inside the processor chip used on the board shown in Figure 1.8.** The left-hand side is a microphotograph of the Pentium 4 processor chip, and the right-hand side shows the major blocks in the processor.

You may have noticed a common theme in both the software and the hardware descriptions: delving into the depths of hardware or software reveals more information or, conversely, lower-level details are hidden to offer a simpler model at higher levels. The use of such layers, or **abstractions**, is a principal technique for designing very sophisticated computer systems.

One of the most important abstractions is the interface between the hardware and the lowest-level software. Because of its importance, it is given a special

abstraction A model that renders lower-level details of computer systems temporarily invisible in order to facilitate design of sophisticated systems.

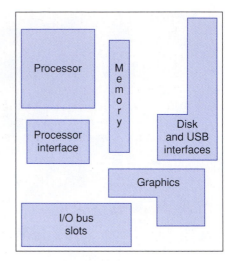

DIMM (dual inline memory module) A small board that contains DRAM chips on both sides. SIMMs have DRAMs on only one side. Both DIMMs and SIMMs are meant to be plugged into memory slots, usually on a motherboard.

FIGURE 1.10   Close-up of PC motherboard. This board uses the Intel Pentium 4 processor, which is located on the upper-left quadrant of the board. It is covered by a set of metal fins, which look like a radiator. This structure is the *heat sink,* used to help cool the chip. The main memory is contained on one or more small boards that are perpendicular to the motherboard near the middle. The DRAM chips are mounted on these boards (called DIMMs, for dual inline memory modules) and then plugged into the connectors. Much of the rest of the board comprises connectors for external I/O devices: audio/MIDI and parallel/serial at the right edge, two PCI card slots near the bottom, and an ATA connector used for attaching hard disks.

instruction set architecture Also called **architecture**. An abstract interface between the hardware and the lowest-level software of a machine that encompasses all the information necessary to write a machine language program that will run correctly, including instructions, registers, memory access, I/O, and so on.

application binary interface (ABI) The user portion of the instruction set plus the operating system interfaces used by application programmers. Defines a standard for binary portability across computers.

implementation Hardware that obeys the architecture abstraction.

name: the **instruction set architecture**, or simply **architecture**, of a machine. The instruction set architecture includes anything programmers need to know to make a binary machine language program work correctly, including instructions, I/O devices, and so on. Typically, the operating system will encapsulate the details of doing I/O, allocating memory, and other low-level system functions, so that application programmers do not need to worry about such details. The combination of the basic instruction set and the operating system interface provided for application programmers is called the **application binary interface** (ABI).

An instruction set architecture allows computer designers to talk about functions independently from the hardware that performs them. For example, we can talk about the functions of a digital clock (keeping time, displaying the time, setting the alarm) independently from the clock hardware (quartz crystal, LED displays, plastic buttons). Computer designers distinguish architecture from an **implementation** of an architecture along the same lines: an implementation is hardware that obeys the architecture abstraction. These ideas bring us to another Big Picture.

Both hardware and software consist of hierarchical layers, with each lower layer hiding details from the level above. This principle of *abstraction* is the way both hardware designers and software designers cope with the complexity of computer systems. One key interface between the levels of abstraction is the *instruction set architecture*—the interface between the hardware and low-level software. This abstract interface enables many *implementations* of varying cost and performance to run identical software.

The BIG Picture

A Safe Place for Data

Thus far we have seen how to input data, compute using the data, and display data. If we were to lose power to the computer, however, everything would be lost because the **memory** inside the computer is **volatile**—that is, when it loses power, it forgets. In contrast, a cassette tape for a stereo doesn't forget the recorded music when you turn off the power because the tape is magnetic and is thus a **nonvolatile memory** technology.

To distinguish between the memory used to hold programs while they are running and this nonvolatile memory used to store programs between runs, the term **primary memory** or **main memory** is used for the former, and **secondary memory** for the latter. DRAMs have dominated main memory since 1975, but **magnetic disks** have dominated secondary memory since 1965. In embedded applications, FLASH, a nonvolatile semiconductor memory, is also used.

Today the primary nonvolatile storage used on all desktop and server computers is the magnetic hard disk. As Figure 1.11 shows, a magnetic hard disk consists of a collection of platters, which rotate on a spindle at 5400 to 15,000 revolutions per minute. The metal platters are covered with magnetic recording material on both sides, similar to the material found on a cassette or videotape. To read and write information on a hard disk, a movable *arm* containing a small electromagnetic coil called a *read/write head* is located just above each surface. The entire drive is permanently sealed to control the environment inside the drive, which, in turn, allows the disk heads to be much closer to the drive surface.

Diameters of hard disks vary by more than a factor of 3 today, from less than 1 inch to 3.5 inches, and have been shrunk over the years to fit into new products; workstation servers, personal computers, laptops, palmtops, and digital cameras have all inspired new disk form factors. Traditionally, the widest disks have the highest performance, the smallest disks have the lowest unit cost, and the best cost per **megabyte** is usually a disk in between. Although most hard drives appear inside computers (as in Figure 1.8), hard drives can also be attached using external interfaces such as Firewire or USB.

memory The storage area in which programs are kept when they are running and that contains the data needed by the running programs.

volatile memory Storage, such as DRAM, that retains data only if it is receiving power.

nonvolatile memory A form of memory that retains data even in the absence of a power source and that is used to store programs between runs. Magnetic disk is nonvolatile and DRAM is not.

primary memory Also called **main memory**. Volatile memory used to hold programs while they are running; typically consists of DRAM in today's computers.

secondary memory Nonvolatile memory used to store programs and data between runs; typically consists of magnetic disks in today's computers.

magnetic disk Also called **hard disk**. A form of nonvolatile secondary memory composed of rotating platters coated with a magnetic recording material.

megabyte Traditionally 1,048,576 (2^{20}) bytes, although some communications and secondary storage systems have redefined it to mean 1,000,000 (10^{6}) bytes.

FIGURE 1.11   A disk showing 10 disk platters and the read/write heads.

The use of mechanical components means that access times for magnetic disks are much slower than for DRAMs: disks typically take 5–15 milliseconds, while DRAMs take 40–80 nanoseconds—making DRAMs about 100,000 times faster. Yet disks have much lower costs than DRAM for the same storage capacity because the production costs for a given amount of disk storage are lower than for the same amount of integrated circuit. In 2007, the cost per megabyte of disk is more than 100 times less expensive than DRAM.

Thus there are three primary differences between magnetic disks and main memory: disks are nonvolatile because they are magnetic; they have a slower access time because they are mechanical devices; and they are cheaper per megabyte because they have very high storage capacity at a modest cost.

Although hard drives are not removable, there are several storage technologies in use that include the following:

- Optical disks, including both compact disks (CDs) and digital video disks (DVDs), constitute the most common form of removable storage.

- Magnetic tape provides only slow serial access and has been used to back up disks, in a role now often replaced by duplicate hard drives.

- FLASH-based removable memory cards typically attach by a USB (Universal Serial Bus) connection and are often used to transfer files.

- Floppy drives and Zip drives are a version of magnetic disk technology with removable flexible disks. **Floppy disks** were the original primary storage for personal computers, but have now largely vanished.

Optical disk technology works in a completely different way than magnetic disk technology. In a CD, data is recorded in a spiral fashion, with individual bits being recorded by burning small pits—approximately 1 micron (10^{-6} meters) in diameter—into the disk surface. The disk is read by shining a laser at the CD surface and determining by examining the reflected light whether there is a pit or flat (reflective) surface. DVDs use the same approach of bouncing a laser beam off a series of pits and flat surfaces. In addition, there are multiple layers that the laser beam can be focused on, and the size of each bit is much smaller, which together yield a significant increase in capacity.

CD and DVD writers in personal computers use a laser to make the pits in the recording layer on the CD or DVD surface. This writing process is relatively slow, taking from tens of minutes (for a full CD) to close to an hour (for a full DVD). Thus, for large quantities a different technique called *pressing* is used, which costs only pennies per CD or DVD.

Rewritable CDs and DVDs use a different recording surface that has a crystalline, reflective material; pits are formed that are not reflective in a manner similar to that for a write-once CD or DVD. To erase the CD or DVD, the surface is heated and cooled slowly, allowing an annealing process to restore the surface recording layer to its crystalline structure. These rewritable disks are the most expensive, with write-once being cheaper; for read-only disks—used to distribute software, music, or movies—both the disk cost and recording cost are much lower.

floppy disk A portable form of secondary memory composed of a rotating Mylar platter coated with a magnetic recording material.

Communicating with Other Computers

We've explained how we can input, compute, display, and save data, but there is still one missing item found in today's computers: computer networks. Just as the processor shown in Figure 1.5 on page 16 is connected to memory and I/O devices, networks connect whole computers, allowing computer users to extend the power of computing by including communication. Networks have become so popular that they are the backbone of current computer systems; a new machine without an optional network interface would be ridiculed. Networked computers have several major advantages:

- *Communication:* Information is exchanged between computers at high speeds.

- *Resource sharing:* Rather than each machine having its own I/O devices, devices can be shared by computers on the network.

- *Nonlocal access:* By connecting computers over long distances, users need not be near the computer they are using.

Networks vary in length and performance, with the cost of communication increasing according to both the speed of communication and the distance that information travels. Perhaps the most popular type of network is the *Ethernet.* Its length is limited to about a kilometer, and the most popular version in 2007 takes about a tenth of a second to send 1 million bytes of data; gigabit Ethernet technology, which is ten times faster, is also widely available. Its length and speed make Ethernet useful to connect computers on the same floor of a building; hence, it is an example of what is generically called a **local area network**. Local area networks are interconnected with switches that can also provide routing services and security. **Wide area networks** cross continents and are the backbone of the Internet, which supports the World Wide Web. They are typically based on optical fibers and are leased from telecommunication companies.

local area network (LAN) A network designed to carry data within a geographically confined area, typically within a single building.

wide area network (WAN) A network extended over hundreds of kilometers that can span a continent.

Networks have changed the face of computing in the last 25 years both by becoming much more ubiquitous and by dramatic increases in performance. In the 1970s, very few individuals had access to electronic mail, the Internet and Web did not exist, and physically mailing magnetic tapes was the primary way to transfer large amounts of data between two locations. In the 1970s, local area networks were almost nonexistent, and the few existing wide area networks had limited capacity and restricted access.

As networking technology improved, it became much cheaper and had a much higher capacity. For example, the first standardized local area network technology developed about 25 years ago was a version of Ethernet that had a maximum capacity (also called bandwidth) of 10 million bits per second, typically shared by tens of, if not a hundred, computers. Today, local area network technology offers a capacity of from 100 million bits per second to a gigabit per second, usually shared by at most a few computers. Furthermore, 10-gigabit technology is in development! Optical communications technology has allowed similar growth in the capacity of wide area networks from hundreds of kilobits to gigabits, and from hundreds of computers connected to a worldwide network to millions of computers connected. This combination of dramatic rise in deployment of networking combined with the increases in capacity have made network technology central to the information revolution of the last 25 years.

Recently, another innovation in networking is reshaping the way computers communicate. Wireless technology has become widely deployed, and most laptops now incorporate this technology. The ability to make a radio in the same low-cost semiconductor technology (CMOS) used for memory and microprocessors enabled a significant improvement in price, leading to an explosion in deployment. Currently available wireless technologies, called by the IEEE standard name 802.11, allow for transmission rates from 1 to less than 100 million bits per second. Wireless technology is quite a bit different from wire-based networks, since all users in an immediate area share the airwaves.

1. Semiconductor DRAM and disk storage differ significantly. Describe the fundamental difference for each of the following: volatility, access time, and cost.

Check Yourself

Technologies for Building Processors and Memory

Processors and memory have improved at an incredible rate because computer designers have long embraced the latest in electronic technology to try to win the race to design a better computer. Figure 1.12 shows the technologies that have been used over time, with an estimate of the relative performance per unit cost for each technology. This section explores the technology that has fueled the computer industry since 1975 and will continue to do so for the foreseeable future. Since this technology shapes what computers will be able to do and how quickly they will evolve, we believe all computer professionals should be familiar with the basics of integrated circuits.

A **transistor** is simply an on/off switch controlled by electricity. The *integrated circuit* (IC) combined dozens to hundreds of transistors into a single chip. To describe the tremendous increase in the number of transistors from hundreds to

transistor An on/off switch controlled by an electric signal.

Year	Technology used in computers	Relative performance/unit cost
1951	Vacuum tube	1
1965	Transistor	35
1975	Integrated circuit	900
1995	Very large scale integrated circuit	2,400,000
2005	Ultra large scale integrated circuit	6,200,000,000

FIGURE 1.12 Relative performance per unit cost of technologies used in computers over time. Source: Computer Museum, Boston, with 2005 extrapolated by the authors.

vacuum tube An electronic component, predecessor of the transistor, that consists of a hollow glass tube about 5 to 10 cm long from which as much air has been removed as possible and that uses an electron beam to transfer data.

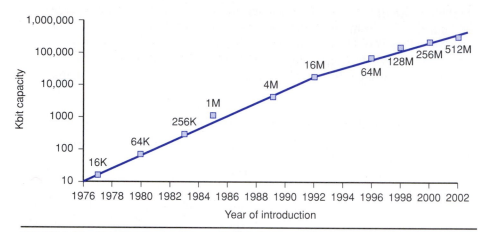

FIGURE 1.13   Growth of capacity per DRAM chip over time. The *y*-axis is measured in Kbits, where K = 1024 (2^{10}). The DRAM industry quadrupled capacity almost every 3 years, a 60% increase per year, for 20 years. This "four times every three years" estimate was called the *DRAM growth rule*. In recent years, the rate has slowed down somewhat and is somewhat closer to doubling every two years, or four times every four years.

very large scale integrated (VLSI) circuit A device containing hundreds of thousands to millions of transistors.

millions, the adjective *very large scale* is added to the term, creating the abbreviation *VLSI*, for **very large scale integrated circuit**.

This rate of increasing integration has been remarkably stable. Figure 1.13 shows the growth in DRAM capacity since 1977. For 20 years, the industry has consistently quadrupled capacity every 3 years, resulting in an increase in excess of 16,000 times! This increase in transistor count for an integrated circuit is popularly known as Moore's law, which states that transistor capacity doubles every 18–24 months. Moore's law resulted from a prediction of such growth in IC capacity made by Gordon Moore, one of the founders of Intel during the 1960s.

Sustaining this rate of progress for almost 40 years has required incredible innovation in manufacturing techniques. In Section 1.4, we discuss how integrated circuits are manufactured.

I thought [computers] would be a universally applicable idea, like a book is. But I didn't think it would develop as fast as it did, because I didn't envision we'd be able to get as many parts on a chip as we finally got. The transistor came along unexpectedly. It all happened much faster than we expected.

J. Presper Eckert, coinventor of ENIAC, speaking in 1991

1.4   Real Stuff: Manufacturing Pentium 4 Chips

Each chapter has a section entitled "Real Stuff" that ties the concepts in the book with a computer you may use every day. These sections cover the technology underlying the IBM-compatible PC, the Apple Macintosh, a common server, or an embedded computer. For this first "Real Stuff" section, we look at how integrated circuits are manufactured, with the Pentium 4 as an example.

Let's start at the beginning. The manufacture of a chip begins with **silicon**, a substance found in sand. Because silicon does not conduct electricity well, it is called a **semiconductor**. With a special chemical process, it is possible to add materials to silicon that allow tiny areas to transform into one of three devices:

- Excellent conductors of electricity (using either microscopic copper or aluminum wire)

- Excellent insulators from electricity (like plastic sheathing or glass)

- Areas that can conduct *or* insulate under special conditions (as a switch)

Transistors fall in the last category. A VLSI circuit, then, is just billions of combinations of conductors, insulators, and switches manufactured in a single, small package.

The manufacturing process for integrated circuits is critical to the cost of the chips and hence important to computer designers. Figure 1.14 shows that process. The process starts with a **silicon crystal ingot**, which looks like a giant sausage. Today, ingots are 8–12 inches in diameter and about 12–24 inches long. An ingot is finely sliced into **wafers** no more than 0.1 inch thick. These wafers then go through a series of processing steps, during which patterns of chemicals are placed

silicon A natural element that is a semiconductor.

semiconductor A substance that does not conduct electricity well.

silicon crystal ingot A rod composed of a silicon crystal that is between 8 and 12 inches in diameter and about 12 to 24 inches long.

wafer A slice from a silicon ingot no more than 0.1 inch thick, used to create chips.

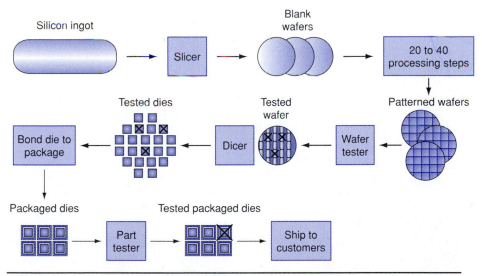

FIGURE 1.14   The chip manufacturing process. After being sliced from the silicon ingot, blank wafers are put through 20 to 40 steps to create patterned wafers (see Figure 1.15 on page 31). These patterned wafers are then tested with a wafer tester and a map of the good parts is made. Then, the wafers are diced into dies (see Figure 1.9 on page 21). In this figure, one wafer produced 20 dies, of which 17 passed testing. (*X* means the die is bad.) The yield of good dies in this case was 17/20, or 85%. These good dies are then bonded into packages and tested one more time before shipping the packaged parts to customers. One bad packaged part was found in this final test.

defect A microscopic flaw in a wafer or in patterning steps that can result in the failure of the die containing that defect.

die The individual rectangular sections that are cut from a wafer, more informally known as **chips**.

yield The percentage of good dies from the total number of dies on the wafer.

on each wafer, creating the transistors, conductors, and insulators discussed earlier. Today's integrated circuits contain only one layer of transistors but may have from two to eight levels of metal conductor, separated by layers of insulators.

A single microscopic flaw in the wafer itself or in one of the dozens of patterning steps can result in that area of the wafer failing. These **defects**, as they are called, make it virtually impossible to manufacture a perfect wafer. To cope with imperfection, several strategies have been used, but the simplest is to place many independent components on a single wafer. The patterned wafer is then chopped up, or *diced,* into these components, called **dies** and more informally known as **chips**. Figure 1.15 is a photograph of a wafer containing Pentium 4 microprocessors before they have been diced; earlier, Figure 1.9 on page 21 showed an individual die of the Pentium 4 and its major components.

Dicing enables you to discard only those dies that were unlucky enough to contain the flaws, rather than the whole wafer. This concept is quantified by the **yield** of a process, which is defined as the percentage of good dies from the total number of dies on the wafer.

The cost of an integrated circuit rises quickly as the die size increases, due both to the lower yield and the smaller number of large dies that fit on a wafer. To reduce the cost, a large die is often "shrunk" by using the next generation process, which incorporates smaller sizes for both transistors and wires. This improves the yield and the die count per wafer. (An ◉ **Integrated Circuit Cost** section on the CD probes these issues further.)

Once you've found good dies, they are connected to the input/output pins of a package, using a process called *bonding*. These packaged parts are tested a final time, since mistakes can occur in packaging, and then they are shipped to customers.

Another increasingly important design constraint is power. Power is a challenge for two reasons. First, power must be brought in and distributed around the chip; modern microprocessors use hundreds of pins just for power and ground! Similarly, multiple levels of interconnect are used solely for power and ground distribution to portions of the chip. Second, power is dissipated as heat and must be removed. An Intel Pentium 4 at 3.06 GHz burns 82 watts, which must be removed from a chip whose surface area is just over 1 cm^2! Figure 1.16 shows a 3.06 GHz Pentium 4 mounted on top of its heat sink, which in turn sits right next to the fan in the box shown in Figure 1.8 (on page 19)!

What determines the power consumed by an integrated circuit? Ignoring technology and circuit specifics, the power is proportional to the product of the number of transistors switched times the frequency they are switched. Thus, in general, higher clock rates or higher transistor counts lead to higher power. For example, the Intel Itanium 2 has four times the transistors of the Intel Pentium 4; although its clock rate is only one-half that of the Pentium 4, the Itanium burns 130 watts

FIGURE 1.15   An 8-inch (200-mm) diameter wafer containing Intel Pentium 4 processors.
The number of Pentium dies per wafer at 100% yield is 165. Figure 1.9 on page 21 is a photomicrograph of one of these Pentium 4 dies. The die area is 250 mm^2, and it contains about 55 million transistors. This die uses a 0.18 micron technology, which means that the smallest transistors are approximately 0.18 microns in size, although they are typically somewhat smaller than the actual feature size, which refers to the size of the transistors as "drawn" versus the final manufactured size. The Pentium 4 is also made using a more advanced 0.13 micron technology. The several dozen partially rounded chips at the boundaries of the wafer are useless; they are included because it's easier to create the masks used to pattern the silicon.

compared to the 82 watts consumed by the Pentium 4. As we will see in later chapters, both performance and power consumption vary widely.

Elaboration: In CMOS (complementary metal oxide semiconductor), which is the dominant technology for integrated circuits, the primary source of power dissipation is so-called dynamic power—that is, power that is consumed during switching. CMOS technology, unlike earlier technologies, does not directly consume power when it is idle—hence the use of low clock rates to allow a processor to "sleep" and conserve power. The dynamic power dissipation depends on the capacitive loading of each transistor, the voltage applied, and the frequency that the transistor is switched:

$$\text{Power} = \text{Capacitive load} \times \text{Voltage}^2 \times \text{Frequency switched}$$

FIGURE 1.16   An Intel Pentium 4 (3.06 GHz) mounted on top of its heat sink, which is designed to remove the 82 watts generated within the die.

Power can be reduced by lowering the voltage, which typically occurs with a new generation of technology; in 20 years, voltages have gone from 5V to 1.5V, significantly reducing power. The capacitive load per transistor is a function of both the number of transistors connected to an output (called the *fanout*) and the technology, which determines the capacitance of both wires and transistors.

Although dynamic power is the primary source of power dissipation in CMOS, static power dissipation occurs because of leakage current that flows even when a transistor is off. In 2007, leakage is typically responsible for more than one-third of the power consumption. Thus, increasing the number of transistors increases power dissipation, even if the transistors are always off. A variety of design techniques and technology innovations have been deployed to control leakage.

A key factor in determining the cost of an integrated circuit is volume. Which of the following are reasons why a chip made in high volume should cost less?

Check Yourself

1. With high volumes, the manufacturing process can be tuned to a particular design, increasing the yield.

2. It is less work to design a high-volume part than a low-volume part.

3. The masks used to make the chip are expensive, so the cost per chip is lower for higher volumes.

4. Engineering development costs are high and largely independent of volume; thus, the development cost per die is lower with high-volume parts.

5. High-volume parts usually have smaller die sizes than low-volume parts and therefore have higher yield per wafer.

1.5 Fallacies and Pitfalls

Science must begin with myths, and the criticism of myths.

Sir Karl Popper, *The Philosophy of Science,* 1957

The purpose of a section on fallacies and pitfalls, which will be found in every chapter, is to explain some commonly held misconceptions that you might encounter. We call such misbeliefs *fallacies*. When discussing a fallacy, we try to give a counterexample. We also discuss *pitfalls*, or easily made mistakes. Often pitfalls are generalizations of principles that are true in a limited context. The purpose of these sections is to help you avoid making these mistakes in the machines you may design or use.

Fallacy: Computers have been built in the same, old-fashioned way for far too long, and this antiquated model of computation is running out of steam.

For an antiquated model of computation, it surely is improving quickly. Figure 1.17 plots the top performance per year of workstations between 1987 and 2003. (Chapter 4 explains the proper way to measure performance.) The graph shows a line indicating an improvement of 1.54 per year, or doubling performance approximately every 18 months. In contrast to the statement above, computers are improving in performance faster today than at any time in their history, with over a thousandfold improvement between 1987 and 2003!

Pitfall: Ignoring the inexorable progress of hardware when planning a new machine.

Suppose you plan to introduce a machine in three years, and you claim the machine will be a terrific seller because it's three times as fast as anything available today. Unfortunately, the machine will probably sell poorly because the average

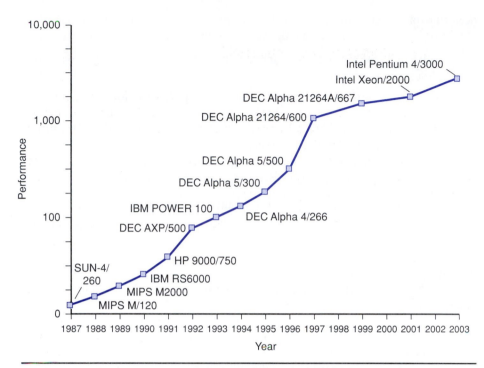

FIGURE 1.17 Performance increase of workstations, 1987–2003. Here performance is given as approximately the number of times faster than the VAX-11/780, which was a commonly used yardstick. The rate of performance improvement is between 1.5 and 1.6 times per year. These performance numbers are based on SPECint performance (see Chapter 2) and scaled over time to deal with changing benchmark sets. For processors listed with *x/y* after their name, *x* is the model number and *y* is the speed in megahertz.

performance growth rate for the industry will yield machines with the same performance. For example, assuming a 50% yearly growth rate in performance, a machine with performance *x* today can be expected to have performance $1.5^3x = 3.4x$ in three years. Your machine would have no performance advantage! Many projects within computer companies are canceled, either because they ignore this rule or because the project is completed late and the performance of the delayed machine is below the industry average. This phenomenon may occur in any industry, but rapid improvements in cost/performance make it a major concern in the computer industry.

1.6 Concluding Remarks

Where . . . the ENIAC is equipped with 18,000 vacuum tubes and weighs 30 tons, computers in the future may have 1,000 vacuum tubes and perhaps weigh just $1^{1}/_{2}$ tons.

Popular Mechanics, March 1949

Although it is difficult to predict exactly what level of cost/performance computers will have in the future, it's a safe bet that they will be much better than they are today. To participate in these advances, computer designers and programmers must understand a wider variety of issues.

Both hardware and software designers construct computer systems in hierarchical layers, with each lower layer hiding details from the level above. This principle of abstraction is fundamental to understanding today's computer systems, but it does not mean that designers can limit themselves to knowing a single technology. Perhaps the most important example of abstraction is the interface between hardware and low-level software, called the *instruction set architecture.* Maintaining the instruction set architecture as a constant enables many implementations of that architecture—presumably varying in cost and performance—to run identical software. On the downside, the architecture may preclude introducing innovations that require the interface to change.

Key technologies for modern processors are compilers and silicon. Clearly, to participate you must understand some of the characteristics of both. Equal in importance to an understanding of integrated circuit technology is an understanding of the expected rates of technological change. While silicon fuels the rapid advance of hardware, new ideas in the organization of computers have improved price/performance. Two of the key ideas are exploiting parallelism in the processor, typically via pipelining, and exploiting locality of accesses to a memory hierarchy, typically via caches.

Road Map for This Book

At the bottom of these abstractions are the five classic components of a computer: datapath, control, memory, input, and output (refer to Figure 1.5). These five components also serve as the framework for the rest of the chapters in this book:

- *Datapath:* Chapters 3, 5, and 6
- *Control:* Chapters 5 and 6
- *Memory:* Chapter 7
- *Input:* Chapter 8
- *Output:* Chapter 8

Chapter 6 describes how processor pipelining exploits parallelism, and Chapter 7 describes how the memory hierarchy exploits locality. The remaining chapters provide the introduction and the conclusion to this material. Chapter 2 describes instruction sets—the interface between compilers and the machine—and emphasizes the role of compilers and programming languages in using the features of the instruction set. Chapter 3 describes how computers perform arithmetic operations and handle arithmetic data. Chapter 4 covers performance and thus describes how to evaluate the whole computer. Chapter 9 describes multiprocessors and is included on the CD. Appendix B, also on the CD, discusses logic design.

> *An active field of science is like an immense anthill; the individual almost vanishes into the mass of minds tumbling over each other, carrying information from place to place, passing it around at the speed of light.*
>
> Lewis Thomas, "Natural Science," in *The Lives of a Cell*, 1974

1.7 Historical Perspective and Further Reading

For each chapter in the text, a section devoted to a historical perspective can be found on the CD that accompanies this book. We may trace the development of an idea through a series of machines or describe some important projects, and we provide references in case you are interested in probing further.

The historical perspective for this chapter provides a background for some of the key ideas presented in this opening chapter. Its purpose is to give you the human story behind the technological advances and to place achievements in their historical context. By understanding the past, you may be better able to understand the forces that will shape computing in the future. Each historical perspectives section on the CD ends with suggestions for further reading, which are also collected separately on the CD under the section "**Further Reading**." The rest of this ⊙ **Section 1.7** is on the CD.

1.8 Exercises

The relative time ratings of exercises are shown in square brackets after each exercise number. On average, an exercise rated [10] will take you twice as long as one rated [5]. Sections of the text that should be read before attempting an exercise will be given in angled brackets; for example, <§1.3> means you should have read Section 1.3, "Under the Covers," to help you solve this exercise. If the solution to an exercise depends on others, they will be listed in curly brackets; for example, {Ex.1.1} means that you should answer Exercise 1.1 before trying this exercise.

⊙ **In More Depth** exercises introduce a new topic or explore a topic in more detail. Such exercises include sufficient background to understand the concepts, as well as to explore their implication or use. The "In More Depth" sections appear on the CD associated with the specific chapter.

Starting in Chapter 2, you will also find "For More Practice" exercises. "For More Practice" exercises include additional problems intended to give the interested reader more practice in dealing with a subject. These exercises have been collected primarily from earlier editions of this book as well as in some cases developed by other instructors. The "For More Practice" sections appear on the CD associated with the specific chapter.

Exercises 1.1 through 1.28 Find the word or phrase from the list below that best matches the description in the following questions. Use the numbers to the left of words in the answer. Each answer should be used only once.

1	abstraction	15	embedded system
2	assembler	16	instruction
3	bit	17	instruction set architecture
4	cache	18	local area network (LAN)
5	central processor unit (CPU)	19	memory
6	chip	20	operating system
7	compiler	21	semiconductor
8	computer family	22	server
9	control	23	supercomputer
10	datapath	24	transistor
11	desktop or personal computer	25	VLSI (very large scale integrated circuit)
12	digital video disk (DVD)	26	wafer
13	defect	27	wide area network (WAN)
14	DRAM (dynamic random access memory)	28	yield

1.1 [2] Active part of the computer, following the instructions of the programs to the letter. It adds numbers, tests numbers, controls other components, and so on.

1.2 [2] Approach to the design of hardware or software. The system consists of hierarchical layers, with each lower layer hiding details from the level above.

1.3 [2] Binary digit.

1.4 [2] Collection of implementations of the same instruction set architecture. They are usually made by the same company and vary in price and performance.

19   **1.5** [2] Component of the computer where all running programs and associated data reside.

10   **1.6** [2] Component of the processor that performs arithmetic operations.

9   **1.7** [2] Component of the processor that tells the datapath, memory, and I/O devices what to do according to the instructions of the program.

11   **1.8** [2] Computer designed for use by an individual, usually incorporating a graphics display, keyboard, and mouse.

15   **1.9** [2] Computer inside another device used for running one predetermined application or collection of software.

22   **1.10** [2] Computer used for running larger programs for multiple users often simultaneously and typically accessed only by a network.

18   **1.11** [2] Computer network that connects a group of computers by a common transmission cable or wireless link within a small geographic area (for example, within the same floor of a building).

27   **1.12** [2] Computer networks that connect computers spanning great distances, the backbone of the Internet.

23   **1.13** [2] High-performance machine, costing more than $1 million.

14   **1.14** [2] Integrated circuit commonly used to construct main memory.

13   **1.15** [2] Microscopic flaw in a wafer.

6   **1.16** [2] Nickname for a die or integrated circuit.

24   **1.17** [2] On/off switch controlled by electricity.

12   **1.18** [2] Optical storage medium with a storage capacity of more than 4.7 GB. It was initially marketed for entertainment and later for computer users.

28   **1.19** [2] Percentage of good dies from the total number of dies on the wafer.

2   **1.20** [2] Program that converts a symbolic version of an instruction into the binary version.

20   **1.21** [2] Program that manages the resources of a computer for the benefit of the programs that run on that machine.

7   **1.22** [2] Program that translates from a higher-level notation to assembly language.

25   **1.23** [2] Technology in which single chip contains hundreds of thousands to millions of transistors.

16 **1.24** [2] Single software command to a processor.

9 **1.25** [2] Small, fast memory that acts as a buffer for the main memory.

17 **1.26** [2] Specific interface that the hardware provides the low-level software.

21 **1.27** [2] Substance that does not conduct electricity well but is the foundation of integrated circuits.

26 **1.28** [2] Thin disk sliced from a silicon crystal ingot, which will be later divided into dies.

Exercises 1.29 through 1.45 Using the categories in the list below, classify the following examples. Use the letters to the left of the words in the answer. Unlike the previous exercises, answers in this group may be used more than once.

a	applications software	f	personal computer
b	high-level programming language	g	semiconductor
c	input device	h	supercomputer
d	integrated circuit	i	systems software
e	output device		

1.29 [1] Assembler *i*

1.30 [1] C++ *b*

1.31 [1] Liquid crystal display (LCD) *e*

1.32 [1] Compiler *i*

1.33 [1] Cray-1 *h*

1.34 [1] DRAM *d*

1.35 [1] IBM PC *f*

1.36 [1] Java *b*

1.37 [1] Scanner *c*

1.38 [1] Macintosh *f*

1.39 [1] Microprocessor *d*

1.40 [1] Microsoft Word *a*

1.41 [1] Mouse *c*

1.42 [1] Operating system *i*

1.43 [1] Printer

1.44 [1] Silicon

1.45 [1] Spreadsheet

1.46 [15] <§1.3> In a magnetic disk, the disks containing the data are constantly rotating. On average it should take half a revolution for the desired data on the disk to spin under the read/write head. Assuming that the disk is rotating at 7200 revolutions per minute (RPM), what is the average time for the data to rotate under the disk head? What is the average time if the disk is spinning at 10,000 revolutions per minute?

1.47 [5] <§1.3> A DVD drive, however, works in the constant linear velocity (CLV) mode. The read head must interact with the concentric circles at a constant rate, whether it is accessing data from the inner or outermost portions of the disk. This is affected by varying the rotation speed of the disk, from 1600 RPM at the center, to 570 RPM at the outside. Assuming that the DVD drive reads 1.35 MB of user data per second, how many bytes can the center circle store? How many bytes can the outside circle store?

1.48 [5] <§1.3> If a computer issues 30 network requests per second and each request is on average 64 KB, will a 100 Mbit Ethernet link be sufficient?

1.49 [5] <§1.3> What kinds of networks do you use on a regular basis? What kinds of media do they use? How much bandwidth do they provide?

1.50 [15] <§1.3> End-to-end delay is an important performance metric for networks. It is the time between the point when the source starts to send data and the point when the data is completely delivered to the destination. Consider two hosts A and B, connected by a single link of rate R bps. Suppose the two hosts are separated by m meters, and suppose the propagation speed along the link is s m/sec. Host A is sending a file of size L bits to host B.

   a. Obtain an expression for the end-to-end delay in terms of R, L, m, and s.

   b. Suppose there is a router between A and B, and the data from A must be forwarded to B by the router. If the forwarding process takes t sec, then what is the end-to-end delay?

   c. Suppose the router is configured to provide QoS (quality of service) control for different kinds of data. If the data is a multimedia stream, such as video-conference data, it will forward it at a shorter delay of $t/2$ sec. For other kinds of data, the delay is t sec. If host A is sending a multimedia stream of size $2L$, what is the end-to-end delay?

1.51 [15] <§§1.4, 1.5> Assume you are in a company that will market a certain IC chip. The fixed costs, including R&D, fabrication and equipment, and so on, add up to $500,000. The cost per wafer is $6000, and each wafer can be diced into 1500 dies. The die yield is 50%. Finally, the dies are packaged and tested, with a cost of $10 per chip. The test yield is 90%; only those that pass the test will be sold to customers. If the retail price is 40% more than the cost, at least how many chips have to be sold to break even?

1.52 [8] <§1.6> In this exercise, you will evaluate the performance difference between two CPU architectures, CISC (complex instruction set computing) and RISC (reduced instruction set computing). Generally speaking, CISC CPUs have more complex instructions than RISC CPUs and therefore need fewer instructions to perform the same tasks. However, typically one CISC instruction, since it is more complex, takes more time to complete than a RISC instruction. Assume that a certain task needs P CISC instructions and $2P$ RISC instructions, and that one CISC instruction takes $8T$ ns to complete, and one RISC instruction takes $2T$ ns. Under this assumption, which one has the better performance?

1.53 [15] <§§1.3, 1.6> Suppose there are five computers connected together to form a local area network. The maximum data transport rate (bandwidth) that the network cable can provide is 10 Mbps. If we use a low-end device (Hub) to connect them, all the computers in the network share the 10 Mbps bandwidth. If we use a high-end device (Switch), then any two of the computers can communicate with each other without disturbing the other computers. If you want to download a 10 MB file from a remote server, which is located outside your local network, how long will it take if using a Hub? How long will it take if using a Switch? Assume the other four computers only communicate with each other, and each has a constant data rate of 2 Mbps.

1.54 [8] <§1.6> Sometimes software optimization can dramatically improve the performance of a computer system. Assume that a CPU can perform a multiplication operation in 10 ns, and a subtraction operation in 1 ns. How long will it take for the CPU to calculate the result of $d = a \times b - a \times c$? Could you optimize the equation so that it will take less time?

1.55 [8] <§§1.1–1.5> This book covers abstractions for computer systems at many different levels of detail. Pick another system with which you are familiar and write one or two paragraphs describing some of the many different levels of abstraction inherent in that system. Some possibilities include automobiles, homes, airplanes, geometry, the economy, a city, and the government. Be sure to identify both high-level and low-level abstractions.

1.56 [15] <§§1.1–1.5> A less technically inclined friend has asked you to explain how computers work. Write a detailed, one-page description for your friend.

1.57 [10] <§§1.1–1.5> In what ways do you lack a clear understanding of how computers work? Are there levels of abstraction with which you are particularly unfamiliar? Are there levels of abstraction with which you are familiar but still have specific questions about? Write at least one paragraph addressing each of these questions.

1.58 [15] <§1.3> In this exercise, you will learn more about interfaces or abstractions. For example, we can provide an abstraction for a disk like this:

Performance characteristics:

- Capacity (how much data can it store?)
- Bandwidth (how fast can data be transferred between the computer and disk?)
- Latency (how long does it take to find a specific position for access?)

Functions the interface provides:

- Read/write data
- Seek to a specific position
- Status report (is the disk ready to read/write, etc.?)

Following this pattern, please provide an abstraction for a network card.

1.59 [5] <§§1.4, 1.5> ⊙ **In More Depth:** Integrated Circuit Cost

1.60 [15] <§§1.4, 1.5> ⊙ **In More Depth:** Integrated Circuit Cost

1.61 [10] <§§1.4, 1.5> ⊙ **In More Depth:** Integrated Circuit Cost

1.62 [5] <§§1.4, 1.5> ⊙ **In More Depth:** Integrated Circuit Cost

1.63 [10] <§§1.4, 1.5> ⊙ **In More Depth:** Integrated Circuit Cost

1.64 [10] <§§1.4, 1.5> ⊙ **In More Depth:** Integrated Circuit Cost

Answers to Check Yourself

§1.1, page 10: Discussion questions: lots of answers are acceptable.

§1.3, page 27: Disk memory: nonvolatile, long access time (milliseconds), and cost $2–4/GB. Semiconductor memory: volatile, short access time (nanoseconds), and cost $200–400/GB.

§1.4, page 33: 1, 3, and 4 are valid reasons.

Computers in the Real World

Throughout this book you will see sections entitled "Computers in the Real World." These sections describe compelling uses for computers outside of their typical functions in office automation and data processing. The goal of these sections is to illustrate the diversity of uses for information technology.

Problem to solve: Make information technology available to the rest of humanity, such as farmers in rural villages, beyond a multilingual character set like Unicode.

Solution: Develop a computer, software, and a communication system for a rural farming village. However, there is no electricity, no telephone, and no technical support, and the villagers do not read English.

The Jhai Foundation took on this challenge for five villages in the Hin Heup district of Laos. This American-Lao foundation was founded to raise the standard of living for rural Laos by developing an export economy. It also built schools, installed wells, and started a weaving cooperative. When asked what they wanted next, villagers said they wanted access to the Internet! First, they wanted to learn the prices before taking their crops to the nearest market, which is 35 kilometers away. They could also learn about the market abroad to make better decisions on what crops to grow and to increase their bargaining power when it was time to sell them. Second, they wanted to use Internet telephony to talk to relatives in Laos and beyond.

The goal was "a rugged computer and printer assembled from off-the-shelf components that draws less than 20 watts in normal use—less than 70 watts when the printer is printing—and that can survive dirt, heat, and immersion in water."

The resulting Jhai PC design uses flash memory instead of a disk drive, thereby eliminating moving parts from the PC to make it more rugged and easier to maintain. Rather than use a power-hungry cathode ray tube, it has a liquid crystal display. To lower costs and power, it uses an 80486 microprocessor. The power is supplied by a car battery, which can be charged by a turning bicycle crank. An old

A Laotian villager who wanted access to the Internet.

designed this personal digital assistant, which is similar to the Palm Pilot, to meet the needs of villagers in third world countries. Input is through a touch screen and speech recognition so that people need not be able to write to use it. It uses three AAA batteries, which last 3 to 4 hours. The cost is $250, and there is no special solution for communication. It's unclear whether villagers in the developing world would spend $250 on a PDA, where even batteries are a luxury.

dot matrix printer completes the hardware, bringing the cost to about $400. The operating system is Linux, and the applications are accounting, email, and letter writing, which expatriates are tailoring to the Lao language.

The communication solution is to adapt the WiFi (IEEE 802.11b) wireless network (see Chapter 8). The plan is to boost the signal using larger antennas and then place repeater stations on the hilltops between the village and the market city. These repeaters get their power from solar cells. The local phone system ties to it at the far end, which completes the connection to the Internet. Twenty-five volunteers in Silicon Valley are developing this Jhai PC network.

An alternative attempt is the *simputer*, which stands for "simple, inexpensive, multilingual computer." Indian computer scientists

To learn more, see these references on the ◉ library:

"Making the Web world-wide," *The Economist*, September 26, 2002, *www.jhai.org/economist*

The Jhai Foundation, *www.jhai.org/*

"Computers for the third world," *Scientific American*, October 2002

Indian villager using the simputer.

Instructions:
Language of
the Computer

I speak Spanish to God,
Italian to women,
French to men,
and German to my horse.

Charles V, King of France
1337–1380

The Five Classic Components of a Computer

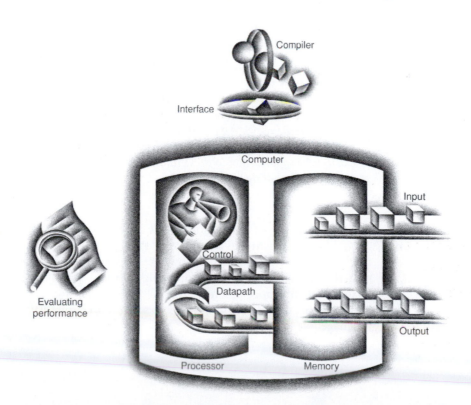

2.1   Introduction

instruction set The vocabulary of commands understood by a given architecture.

To command a computer's hardware, you must speak its language. The words of a computer's language are called *instructions*, and its vocabulary is called an **instruction set**. In this chapter, you will see the instruction set of a real computer, both in the form written by humans and in the form read by the computer. We introduce instructions in a top-down fashion. Starting from a notation that looks like a restricted programming language, we refine it step-by-step until you see the real language of a real computer. Chapter 3 continues our downward descent, unveiling the representation of integer and floating-point numbers and the hardware that operates on them.

You might think that the languages of computers would be as diverse as those of humans, but in reality computer languages are quite similar, more like regional dialects than like independent languages. Hence, once you learn one, it is easy to pick up others. This similarity occurs because all computers are constructed from hardware technologies based on similar underlying principles and because there are a few basic operations that all computers must provide. Moreover, computer designers have a common goal: to find a language that makes it easy to build the hardware and the compiler while maximizing performance and minimizing cost. This goal is time honored; the following quote was written before you could buy a computer, and it is as true today as it was in 1947:

> *It is easy to see by formal-logical methods that there exist certain [instruction sets] that are in abstract adequate to control and cause the execution of any sequence of operations. . . . The really decisive considerations from the present point of view, in selecting an [instruction set], are more of a practical nature: simplicity of the equipment demanded by the [instruction set], and the clarity of its application to the actually important problems together with the speed of its handling of those problems.*

> Burks, Goldstine, and von Neumann, 1947

The "simplicity of the equipment" is as valuable a consideration for computers of the 2000s as it was for those of the 1950s. The goal of this chapter is to teach an instruction set that follows this advice, showing both how it is represented in hardware and the relationship between high-level programming languages and this more primitive one. Our examples are in the C programming language; Section 2.14 shows how these would change for an object-oriented language like Java.

By learning how to represent instructions, you will also discover the secret of computing: the **stored-program concept**. Moreover, you will exercise your "foreign language" skills by writing programs in the language of the computer and running them on the simulator that comes with this book. You will also see the impact of programming languages and compiler optimization on performance. We conclude with a look at the historical evolution of instruction sets and an overview of other computer dialects.

stored-program concept The idea that instructions and data of many types can be stored in memory as numbers, leading to the stored-program computer.

The chosen instruction set comes from MIPS, which is typical of instruction sets designed since the 1980s. Almost 100 million of these popular microprocessors were manufactured in 2002, and they are found in products from ATI Technologies, Broadcom, Cisco, NEC, Nintendo, Silicon Graphics, Sony, Texas Instruments, and Toshiba, among others.

We reveal the MIPS instruction set a piece at a time, giving the rationale along with the computer structures. This top-down, step-by-step tutorial weaves the components with their explanations, making assembly language more palatable. To keep the overall picture in mind, each section ends with a figure summarizing the MIPS instruction set revealed thus far, highlighting the portions presented in that section.

2.2 Operations of the Computer Hardware

There must certainly be instructions for performing the fundamental arithmetic operations.

Burks, Goldstine, and von Neumann, 1947

Every computer must be able to perform arithmetic. The MIPS assembly language notation

```
add a, b, c
```

instructs a computer to add the two variables b and c and to put their sum in a.

This notation is rigid in that each MIPS arithmetic instruction performs only one operation and must always have exactly three variables. For example, suppose we want to place the sum of variables b, c, d, and e into variable a. (In this section we are being deliberately vague about what a "variable" is; in the next section we'll explain in detail.)

The following sequence of instructions adds the four variables:

```
add a, b, c    # The sum of b and c is placed in a.
add a, a, d    # The sum of b, c, and d is now in a.
add a, a, e    # The sum of b, c, d, and e is now in a.
```

Thus, it takes three instructions to take the sum of four variables.

The words to the right of the sharp symbol (#) on each line above are *comments* for the human reader, and the computer ignores them. Note that unlike other programming languages, each line of this language can contain at most one instruction. Another difference from C is that comments always terminate at the end of a line.

The natural number of operands for an operation like addition is three: the two numbers being added together and a place to put the sum. Requiring every instruction to have exactly three operands, no more and no less, conforms to the philosophy of keeping the hardware simple: hardware for a variable number of operands is more complicated than hardware for a fixed number. This situation illustrates the first of four underlying principles of hardware design:

Design Principle 1: Simplicity favors regularity.

We can now show, in the two examples that follow, the relationship of programs written in higher-level programming languages to programs in this more primitive notation.

Compiling Two C Assignment Statements into MIPS

EXAMPLE

This segment of a C program contains the five variables a, b, c, d, and e. Since Java evolved from C, this example and the next few work for either high-level programming language:

```
a = b + c;
d = a - e;
```

The translation from C to MIPS assembly language instructions is performed by the *compiler*. Show the MIPS code produced by a compiler.

ANSWER

A MIPS instruction operates on two source operands and places the result in one destination operand. Hence, the two simple statements above compile directly into these two MIPS assembly language instructions:

```
add a, b, c
sub d, a, e
```

Compiling a Complex C Assignment into MIPS

A somewhat complex statement contains the five variables f, g, h, i, and j:

```
f = (g + h) - (i + j);
```

What might a C compiler produce?

EXAMPLE

EXAMPLE

ANSWER

The compiler must break this statement into several assembly instructions since only one operation is performed per MIPS instruction. The first MIPS instruction calculates the sum of g and h. We must place the result somewhere, so the compiler creates a temporary variable, called t0:

```
add t0,g,h # temporary variable t0 contains g + h
```

Although the next operation is subtract, we need to calculate the sum of i and j before we can subtract. Thus, the second instruction places the sum i and j in another temporary variable created by the compiler, called t1:

```
add t1,i,j  # temporary variable t1 contains i + j
```

Finally, the subtract instruction subtracts the second sum from the first and places the difference in the variable f, completing the compiled code:

```
sub f,t0,t1 # f gets t0 - t1, which is (g + h)-(i + j)
```

Figure 2.1 summarizes the portions of MIPS assembly language described in this section. These instructions are symbolic representations of what the MIPS processor actually understands. In the next few sections, we will evolve this symbolic representation into the real language of MIPS, with each step making the symbolic representation more concrete.

MIPS assembly language

Category	Instruction	Example	Meaning	Comments
Arithmetic	add	add a,b,c	a = b + c	Always three operands
	subtract	sub a,b,c	a = b - c	Always three operands

FIGURE 2.1 MIPS architecture revealed in Section 2.2. The real computer operands will be unveiled in the next section. Highlighted portions in such summaries show MIPS assembly language structures introduced in this section; for this first figure, all is new.

**Check
Yourself**
For a given function, which programming language likely takes the most lines of code? Put the three representations below in order.

1. Java
2. C
3. MIPS assembly language

Elaboration: To increase portability, Java was originally envisioned as relying on a software interpreter. The instruction set of this interpreter is called *Java bytecodes,* which is quite different from the MIPS instruction set. To get performance close to the equivalent C program, Java systems today typically compile Java bytecodes into the native instruction sets like MIPS. Because this compilation is normally done much later than for C programs, such Java compilers are often called *Just In Time* (JIT) compilers. Section 2.10 shows how JITs are used later than C compilers in the start-up process, and Section 2.13 shows the performance consequences of compiling versus interpreting Java programs. The Java examples in this chapter skip the Java bytecode step and just show the MIPS code that is produced by a compiler.

2.3   Operands of the Computer Hardware

Unlike programs in high-level languages, the operands of arithmetic instructions are restricted; they must be from a limited number of special locations built directly in hardware called *registers*. Registers are the bricks of computer construction: registers are primitives used in hardware design that are also visible to the programmer when the computer is completed. The size of a register in the MIPS architecture is 32 bits; groups of 32 bits occur so frequently that they are given the name **word** in the MIPS architecture.

word The natural unit of access in a computer, usually a group of 32 bits; corresponds to the size of a register in the MIPS architecture.

One major difference between the variables of a programming language and registers is the limited number of registers, typically 32 on current computers. MIPS has 32 registers. (See Section 2.19 for the history of the number of registers.) Thus, continuing in our top-down, stepwise evolution of the symbolic representation of the MIPS language, in this section we have added the restriction that the three operands of MIPS arithmetic instructions must each be chosen from one of the 32 32-bit registers.

The reason for the limit of 32 registers may be found in the second of our four underlying design principles of hardware technology:

Design Principle 2: Smaller is faster.

A very large number of registers may increase the clock cycle time simply because it takes electronic signals longer when they must travel farther.

Guidelines such as "smaller is faster" are not absolutes; 31 registers may not be faster than 32. Yet, the truth behind such observations causes computer designers to take them seriously. In this case, the designer must balance the craving of programs for more registers with the designer's desire to keep the clock cycle fast. Another reason for not using more than 32 is the number of bits it would take in the instruction format, as Section 2.4 demonstrates.

Chapters 5 and 6 show the central role that registers play in hardware construction; as we shall see in this chapter, effective use of registers is key to program performance.

Although we could simply write instructions using numbers for registers, from 0 to 31, the MIPS convention is to use two-character names following a dollar sign to represent a register. Section 2.7 will explain the reasons behind these names. For now, we will use $s0, $s1, ... for registers that correspond to variables in C and Java programs and $t0, $t1, ... for temporary registers needed to compile the program into MIPS instructions.

Compiling a C Assignment Using Registers

It is the compiler's job to associate program variables with registers. Take, for instance, the assignment statement from our earlier example:

```
f = (g + h) - (i + j);
```

The variables f, g, h, i, and j are assigned to the registers $s0, $s1, $s2, $s3, and $s4, respectively. What is the compiled MIPS code?

EXAMPLE

The compiled program is very similar to the prior example, except we replace the variables with the register names mentioned above plus two temporary registers, $t0 and $t1, which correspond to the temporary variables above:

```
add $t0,$s1,$s2 # register $t0 contains g + h
add $t1,$s3,$s4 # register $t1 contains i + j
sub $s0,$t0,$t1 # f gets $t0 - $t1, which is (g + h)-(i + j)
```

ANSWER

Memory Operands

Programming languages have simple variables that contain single data elements as in these examples, but they also have more complex data structures—arrays and structures. These complex data structures can contain many more data elements than there are registers in a computer. How can a computer represent and access such large structures?

Recall the five components of a computer introduced in Chapter 1 and depicted on page 47. The processor can keep only a small amount of data in registers, but computer memory contains millions of data elements. Hence, data structures (arrays and structures) are kept in memory.

As explained above, arithmetic operations occur only on registers in MIPS instructions; thus, MIPS must include instructions that transfer data between memory and registers. Such instructions are called **data transfer instructions**. To access a word in memory, the instruction must supply the memory **address**. Memory is just a large, single-dimensional array, with the address acting as the index to that array, starting at 0. For example, in Figure 2.2, the address of the third data element is 2, and the value of Memory[2] is 10.

The data transfer instruction that copies data from memory to a register is traditionally called *load*. The format of the load instruction is the name of the operation followed by the register to be loaded, then a constant and register used to access memory. The sum of the constant portion of the instruction and the contents of the second register forms the memory address. The actual MIPS name for this instruction is `lw`, standing for *load word*.

> **data transfer instruction** A command that moves data between memory and registers.
>
> **address** A value used to delineate the location of a specific data element within a memory array.

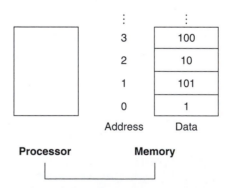

FIGURE 2.2   Memory addresses and contents of memory at those locations. This is a simplification of the MIPS addressing; Figure 2.3 shows the actual MIPS addressing for sequential word addresses in memory.

Compiling an Assignment When an Operand Is in Memory

Let's assume that A is an array of 100 words and that the compiler has associated the variables g and h with the registers $s1 and $s2 as before. Let's also assume that the starting address, or *base address,* of the array is in $s3. Compile this C assignment statement:

```
g = h + A[8];
```

Although there is a single operation in this assignment statement, one of the operands is in memory, so we must first transfer A[8] to a register. The address of this array element is the sum of the base of the array A, found in register $s3, plus the number to select element 8. The data should be placed in a temporary register for use in the next instruction. Based on Figure 2.2, the first compiled instruction is

```
lw    $t0,8($s3) # Temporary reg $t0 gets A[8]
```

(On the next page we'll make a slight adjustment to this instruction, but we'll use this simplified version for now.) The following instruction can operate on the value in $t0 (which equals A[8]) since it is in a register. The instruction must add h (contained in $s2) to A[8] ($t0) and put the sum in the register corresponding to g (associated with $s1):

```
add   $s1,$s2,$t0 # g = h + A[8]
```

The constant in a data transfer instruction is called the *offset,* and the register added to form the address is called the *base register.*

Hardware/ Software Interface

alignment restriction
A requirement that data be aligned in memory on natural boundaries

In addition to associating variables with registers, the compiler allocates data structures like arrays and structures to locations in memory. The compiler can then place the proper starting address into the data transfer instructions.

Since 8-bit *bytes* are useful in many programs, most architectures address individual bytes. Therefore, the address of a word matches the address of one of the 4 bytes within the word. Hence, addresses of sequential words differ by 4. For example, Figure 2.3 shows the actual MIPS addresses for Figure 2.2; the byte address of the third word is 8.

In MIPS, words must start at addresses that are multiples of 4. This requirement is called an **alignment restriction**, and many architectures have it. (Chapter 5 suggests why alignment leads to faster data transfers.)

Computers divide into those that use the address of the leftmost or "big end" byte as the word address versus those that use the rightmost or "little end" byte. MIPS is in the *big-endian* camp. (Appendix A, page A-42, shows the two options to number bytes in a word.)

Byte addressing also affects the array index. To get the proper byte address in the code above, *the offset to be added to the base register $s3 must be 4 × 8, or 32,* so that the load address will select A[8] and not A[8/4]. (See the related pitfall on page 144 of Section 2.17.)

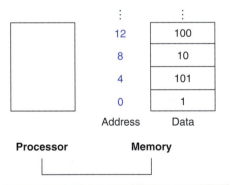

Address	Data
12	100
8	10
4	101
0	1

Processor   Memory

FIGURE 2.3   Actual MIPS memory addresses and contents of memory for those words.
The changed addresses are highlighted to contrast with Figure 2.2. Since MIPS addresses each byte, word addresses are multiples of 4: there are 4 bytes in a word.

The instruction complementary to load is traditionally called *store;* it copies data from a register to memory. The format of a store is similar to that of a load: the name of the operation, followed by the register to be stored, then offset to select the array element, and finally the base register. Once again, the MIPS address is specified in part by a constant and in part by the contents of a register. The actual MIPS name is sw, standing for *store word*.

Compiling Using Load and Store

EXAMPLE

Assume variable h is associated with register $s2 and the base address of the array A is in $s3. What is the MIPS assembly code for the C assignment statement below?

```
A[12] = h + A[8];
```

ANSWER

Although there is a single operation in the C statement, now two of the operands are in memory, so we need even more MIPS instructions. The first two instructions are the same as the prior example, except this time we use the proper offset for byte addressing in the load word instruction to select A[8], and the add instruction places the sum in $t0:

```
lw    $t0,32($s3)   # Temporary reg $t0 gets A[8]

add   $t0,$s2,$t0   # Temporary reg $t0 gets h + A[8]
```

The final instruction stores the sum into A[12], using 48 as the offset and register $s3 as the base register.

```
sw    $t0,48($s3)   # Stores h + A[8] back into A[12]
```

Constant or Immediate Operands

Many times a program will use a constant in an operation—for example, incrementing an index to point to the next element of an array. In fact, more than half of the MIPS arithmetic instructions have a constant as an operand when running the SPEC2000 benchmarks.

Hardware/ Software Interface

Many programs have more variables than computers have registers. Consequently, the compiler tries to keep the most frequently used variables in registers and places the rest in memory, using loads and stores to move variables between registers and memory. The process of putting less commonly used variables (or those needed later) into memory is called *spilling* registers.

The hardware principle relating size and speed suggests that memory must be slower than registers since registers are smaller. This is indeed the case; data accesses are faster if data is in registers instead of memory.

Moreover, data is more useful when in a register. A MIPS arithmetic instruction can read two registers, operate on them, and write the result. A MIPS data transfer instruction only reads one operand or writes one operand, without operating on it.

Thus, MIPS registers take less time to access *and* have higher throughput than memory—a rare combination—making data in registers both faster to access and simpler to use. To achieve highest performance, compilers must use registers efficiently.

Using only the instructions we have seen so far, we would have to load a constant from memory to use one. (The constants would have been placed in memory when the program was loaded.) For example, to add the constant 4 to register $s3, we could use the code

```
lw   $t0, AddrConstant4($s1) # $t0 = constant 4
add  $s3,$s3,$t0             # $s3 = $s3 + $t0 ($t0 == 4)
```

assuming that AddrConstant4 is the memory address of the constant 4.

An alternative that avoids the load instruction is to offer versions of the arithmetic instructions in which one operand is a constant. This quick add instruction with one constant operand is called *add immediate* or addi. To add 4 to register $s3, we just write

```
addi    $s3,$s3,4          # $s3 = $s3 + 4
```

Immediate instructions illustrate the third hardware design principle, first mentioned in the Fallacies and Pitfalls of Chapter 1:

Design Principle 3: Make the common case fast.

Constant operands occur frequently, and by including constants inside arithmetic instructions, they are much faster than if constants were loaded from memory.

MIPS operands

Name	Example	Comments
32 registers	$s0, $s1, . . . , $t0, $t1, . . .	Fast locations for data. In MIPS, data must be in registers to perform arithmetic.
2^{30} memory words	Memory[0], Memory[4], . . . , Memory[4294967292]	Accessed only by data transfer instructions in MIPS. MIPS uses byte addresses, so sequential word addresses differ by 4. Memory holds data structures, arrays, and spilled registers.

MIPS assembly language

Category	Instruction	Example	Meaning	Comments
Arithmetic	add	add $s1,$s2,$s3	$s1 = $s2 + $s3	Three operands; data in registers
	subtract	sub $s1,$s2,$s3	$s1 = $s2 − $s3	Three operands; data in registers
	add immediate	addi $s1,$s2,100	$s1 = $s2 + 100	Used to add constants
Data transfer	load word	lw $s1,100($s2)	$s1 = Memory[$s2 + 100]	Data from memory to register
	store word	sw $s1,100($s2)	Memory[$s2 + 100] = $s1	Data from register to memory

FIGURE 2.4   MIPS architecture revealed through Section 2.3. Highlighted portions show MIPS assembly language structures introduced in Section 2.3.

Figure 2.4 summarizes the portions of the symbolic representation of the MIPS instruction set described in this section. Load word and store word are the instructions that copy words between memory and registers in the MIPS architecture. Other brands of computers use instructions along with load and store to transfer data. An architecture with such alternatives is the Intel IA-32, described in Section 2.16.

Given the importance of registers, what is the rate of increase in the number of registers in a chip over time?

Check Yourself

1. Very fast: They increase as fast as Moore's law, which predicts doubling the number of transistors on a chip every 18 months.

2. Very slow: Since programs are usually distributed in the language of the computer, there is inertia in instruction set architecture, and so the number of registers increases only as fast as new instruction sets become viable.

Elaboration: Although the MIPS registers in this book are 32 bits wide, there is a 64-bit version of the MIPS instruction set with 32 64-bit registers. To keep them straight, they are officially called MIPS-32 and MIPS-64. In this chapter, we use a subset of MIPS-32. Appendix D shows the differences between MIPS-32 and MIPS-64.

The MIPS offset plus base register addressing is an excellent match to structures as well as arrays, since the register can point to the beginning of the structure and the offset can select the desired element. We'll see such an example in Section 2.13.

The register in the data transfer instructions was originally invented to hold an index of an array with the offset used for the starting address of an array. Thus, the base register is also called the *index register*. Today's memories are much larger and the software model of data allocation is more sophisticated, so the base address of the array is normally passed in a register since it won't fit in the offset, as we shall see.

Section 2.4 explains that since MIPS supports negative constants, there is no need for subtract immediate in MIPS.

2.4 Representing Instructions in the Computer

We are now ready to explain the difference between the way humans instruct computers and the way computers see instructions. First, let's quickly review how a computer represents numbers.

Humans are taught to think in base 10, but numbers may be represented in any base. For example, 123 base 10 = 1111011 base 2.

Numbers are kept in computer hardware as a series of high and low electronic signals, and so they are considered base 2 numbers. (Just as base 10 numbers are called *decimal* numbers, base 2 numbers are called *binary* numbers.) A single digit of a binary number is thus the "atom" of computing, since all information is composed of **binary digits** or *bits*. This fundamental building block can be one of two values, which can be thought of as several alternatives: high or low, on or off, true or false, or 1 or 0.

Instructions are also kept in the computer as a series of high and low electronic signals and may be represented as numbers. In fact, each piece of an instruction can be considered as an individual number, and placing these numbers side by side forms the instruction.

Since registers are part of almost all instructions, there must be a convention to map register names into numbers. In MIPS assembly language, registers $s0 to $s7 map onto registers 16 to 23, and registers $t0 to $t7 map onto registers 8 to 15. Hence, $s0 means register 16, $s1 means register 17, $s2 means register 18, . . . , $t0 means register 8, $t1 means register 9, and so on. We'll describe the convention for the rest of the 32 registers in the following sections.

binary digit Also called **binary bit**. One of the two numbers in base 2, 0 or 1, that are the components of information.

Translating a MIPS Assembly Instruction into a Machine Instruction

Let's do the next step in the refinement of the MIPS language as an example. We'll show the real MIPS language version of the instruction represented symbolically as

```
add $t0,$s1,$s2
```

first as a combination of decimal numbers and then of binary numbers.

EXAMPLE

The decimal representation is

ANSWER

0	17	18	8	0	32

Each of these segments of an instruction is called a *field*. The first and last fields (containing 0 and 32 in this case) in combination tell the MIPS computer that this instruction performs addition. The second field gives the number of the register that is the first source operand of the addition operation (17 = $s1), and the third field gives the other source operand for the addition (18 = $s2). The fourth field contains the number of the register that is to receive the sum (8 = $t0). The fifth field is unused in this instruction, so it is set to 0. Thus, this instruction adds register $s1 to register $s2 and places the sum in register $t0.

This instruction can also be represented as fields of binary numbers as opposed to decimal:

000000	10001	10010	01000	00000	100000
6 bits	5 bits	5 bits	5 bits	5 bits	6 bits

To distinguish it from assembly language, we call the numeric version of instructions **machine language** and a sequence of such instructions *machine code*.

This layout of the instruction is called the **instruction format**. As you can see from counting the number of bits, this MIPS instruction takes exactly 32 bits—the same size as a data word. In keeping with our design principle that simplicity favors regularity, all MIPS instructions are 32 bits long.

It would appear that you would now be reading and writing long, tedious strings of binary numbers. We avoid that tedium by using a higher base than binary that

machine language Binary representation used for communication within a computer system.

instruction format A form of representation of an instruction composed of fields of binary numbers.

Hexadecimal	Binary	Hexadecimal	Binary	Hexadecimal	Binary	Hexadecimal	Binary
0_{hex}	0000_{two}	4_{hex}	0100_{two}	8_{hex}	1000_{two}	c_{hex}	1100_{two}
1_{hex}	0001_{two}	5_{hex}	0101_{two}	9_{hex}	1001_{two}	d_{hex}	1101_{two}
2_{hex}	0010_{two}	6_{hex}	0110_{two}	a_{hex}	1010_{two}	e_{hex}	1110_{two}
3_{hex}	0011_{two}	7_{hex}	0111_{two}	b_{hex}	1011_{two}	f_{hex}	1111_{two}

FIGURE 2.5   The hexadecimal-binary conversion table. Just replace one hexadecimal digit by the corresponding four binary digits, and vice versa. If the length of the binary number is not a multiple of 4, go from right to left.

hexadecimal Numbers in base 16.

converts easily into binary. Since almost all computer data sizes are multiples of 4, **hexadecimal** (base 16) numbers are popular. Since base 16 is a power of 2, we can trivially convert by replacing each group of four binary digits by a single hexadecimal digit, and vice versa. Figure 2.5 converts hexadecimal to binary, and vice versa.

Because we frequently deal with different number bases, to avoid confusion we will subscript decimal numbers with *ten*, binary numbers with *two*, and hexadecimal numbers with *hex*. (If there is no subscript, the default is base 10.) By the way, C and Java use the notation 0x*nnnn* for hexadecimal numbers.

Binary to Hexadecimal and Back

EXAMPLE

Convert the following hexadecimal and binary numbers into the other base:
eca8 6420_{hex}

0001 0011 0101 0111 1001 1011 1101 1111_{two}

ANSWER

Just a table lookup one way:

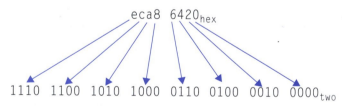

eca8 6420_{hex}

1110 1100 1010 1000 0110 0100 0010 0000_{two}

And then the other direction too:

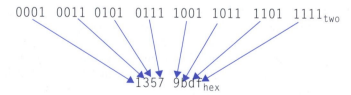

0001 0011 0101 0111 1001 1011 1101 1111_{two}

1357 $9bdf_{hex}$

MIPS Fields

MIPS fields are given names to make them easier to discuss:

op	rs	rt	rd	shamt	funct
6 bits	5 bits	5 bits	5 bits	5 bits	6 bits

Here is the meaning of each name of the fields in MIPS instructions:

- *op:* Basic operation of the instruction, traditionally called the **opcode**.

- *rs:* The first register source operand.

- *rt:* The second register source operand.

- *rd:* The register destination operand. It gets the result of the operation.

- *shamt:* Shift amount. (Section 2.5 explains shift instructions and this term; it will not be used until then, and hence the field contains zero.)

- *funct:* Function. This field selects the specific variant of the operation in the op field and is sometimes called the *function code.*

opcode The field that denotes the operation and format of an instruction.

A problem occurs when an instruction needs longer fields than those shown above. For example, the load word instruction must specify two registers and a constant. If the address were to use one of the 5-bit fields in the format above, the constant within the load word instruction would be limited to only 2^5 or 32. This constant is used to select elements from arrays or data structures, and it often needs to be much larger than 32. This 5-bit field is too small to be useful.

Hence, we have a conflict between the desire to keep all instructions the same length and the desire to have a single instruction format. This leads us to the final hardware design principle:

Design Principle 4: Good design demands good compromises.

The compromise chosen by the MIPS designers is to keep all instructions the same length, thereby requiring different kinds of instruction formats for different kinds of instructions. For example, the format above is called *R-type* (for register) or *R-format*. A second type of instruction format is called *I-type* (for immediate) or *I-format* and is used by the immediate and data transfer instructions. The fields of I-format are

op	rs	rt	constant or address
6 bits	5 bits	5 bits	16 bits

The 16-bit address means a load word instruction can load any word within a region of $\pm 2^{15}$ or 32,768 bytes ($\pm 2^{13}$ or 8192 words) of the address in the base register rs. Similarly, add immediate is limited to constants no larger than $\pm 2^{15}$. (Chapter 3 explains how to represent negative numbers.) We see that more than 32 registers would be difficult in this format, as the rs and rt fields would each need another bit, making it harder to fit everything in one word.

Let's look at the load word instruction from page 57:

```
lw   $t0,32($s3)    # Temporary reg $t0 gets A[8]
```

Here, 19 (for $s3) is placed in the rs field, 8 (for $t0) is placed in the rt field, and 32 is placed in the address field. Note that the meaning of the rt field has changed for this instruction: in a load word instruction, the rt field specifies the *destination* register, which receives the result of the load.

Although multiple formats complicate the hardware, we can reduce the complexity by keeping the formats similar. For example, the first three fields of the R-type and I-type formats are the same size and have the same names; the fourth field in I-type is equal to the length of the last three fields of R-type.

In case you were wondering, the formats are distinguished by the values in the first field: each format is assigned a distinct set of values in the first field (op) so that the hardware knows whether to treat the last half of the instruction as three fields (R-type) or as a single field (I-type). Figure 2.6 shows the numbers used in each field for the MIPS instructions covered through Section 2.3.

Instruction	Format	op	rs	rt	rd	shamt	funct	address
add	R	0	reg	reg	reg	0	32_{ten}	n.a.
sub (subtract)	R	0	reg	reg	reg	0	34_{ten}	n.a.
add immediate	I	8_{ten}	reg	reg	n.a.	n.a.	n.a.	constant
lw (load word)	I	35_{ten}	reg	reg	n.a.	n.a.	n.a.	address
sw (store word)	I	43_{ten}	reg	reg	n.a.	n.a.	n.a.	address

FIGURE 2.6   MIPS instruction encoding. In the table above, "reg" means a register number between 0 and 31, "address" means a 16-bit address, and "n.a." (not applicable) means this field does not appear in this format. Note that add and sub instructions have the same value in the op field; the hardware uses the funct field to decide the variant of the operation: add (32) or subtract (34).

Translating MIPS Assembly Language into Machine Language

EXAMPLE

We can now take an example all the way from what the programmer writes to what the computer executes. If $t1 has the base of the array A and $s2 corresponds to h, the assignment statement

    A[300] = h + A[300];

is compiled into

    lw $t0,1200($t1) # Temporary reg $t0 gets A[300]

    add $t0,$s2,$t0   # Temporary reg $t0 gets h + A[300]

    sw $t0,1200($t1) # Stores h + A[300] back into A[300]

What is the MIPS machine language code for these three instructions?

ANSWER

For convenience, let's first represent the machine language instructions using decimal numbers. From Figure 2.6, we can determine the three machine language instructions:

op	rs	rt	rd	address/ shamt	funct
35	9	8		1200	
0	18	8	8	0	32
43	9	8		1200	

The lw instruction is identified by 35 (see Figure 2.6) in the first field (op). The base register 9 ($t1) is specified in the second field (rs), and the destination register 8 ($t0) is specified in the third field (rt). The offset to select A[300] (1200 = 300 × 4) is found in the final field (address).

The add instruction that follows is specified with 0 in the first field (op) and 32 in the last field (funct). The three register operands (18, 8, and 8) are found in the second, third, and fourth fields and correspond to $s2, $t0, and $t0.

The sw instruction is identified with 43 in the first field. The rest of this final instruction is identical to the lw instruction.

The binary equivalent to the decimal form is the following (1200 in base 10 is 0000 0100 1011 0000 base 2):

100011	01001	01000	0000 0100 1011 0000		
000000	10010	01000	01000	00000	100000
101011	01001	01000	0000 0100 1011 0000		

Note the similarity of the binary representations of the first and last instructions. The only difference is in the third bit from the left.

Figure 2.7 summarizes the portions of MIPS assembly language described in this section. As we shall see in Chapters 5 and 6, the similarity of the binary representations of related instructions simplifies hardware design. These instructions are another example of regularity in the MIPS architecture.

Check Yourself

Why doesn't MIPS have a subtract immediate instruction?

1. Negative constants appear much less frequently in C and Java, so they are not the common case and do not merit special support.

2. Since the immediate field holds both negative and positive constants, add immediate with a negative number is equivalent to subtract immediate with a positive number, so subtract immediate is superfluous.

The BIG Picture

Today's computers are built on two key principles:

1. Instructions are represented as numbers.

2. Programs are stored in memory to be read or written, just like numbers.

These principles lead to the *stored-program* concept; its invention let the computing genie out of its bottle. Figure 2.8 shows the power of the concept; specifically, memory can contain the source code for an editor program, the corresponding compiled machine code, the text that the compiled program is using, and even the compiler that generated the machine code.

One consequence of instructions as numbers is that programs are often shipped as files of binary numbers. The commercial implication is that computers can inherit ready-made software provided they are compatible with an existing instruction set. Such "binary compatibility" often leads industry to align around a small number of instruction set architectures.

MIPS operands

Name	Example	Comments
32 registers	$s0, $s1, ..., $s7 $t0, $t1, ..., $t7	Fast locations for data. In MIPS, data must be in registers to perform arithmetic. Registers $s0-$s7 map to 16–23 and $t0-$t7 map to 8–15.
2^{30} memory words	Memory[0], Memory[4], ..., Memory[4294967292]	Accessed only by data transfer instructions in MIPS. MIPS uses byte addresses, so sequential word addresses differ by 4. Memory holds data structures, arrays, and spilled registers.

MIPS assembly language

Category	Instruction	Example	Meaning	Comments
Arithmetic	add	add $s1,$s2,$s3	$s1 = $s2 + $s3	Three operands; data in registers
	subtract	sub $s1,$s2,$s3	$s1 = $s2 - $s3	Three operands; data in registers
Data transfer	load word	lw $s1,100($s2)	$s1 = Memory[$s2 + 100]	Data from memory to register
	store word	sw $s1,100($s2)	Memory[$s2 + 100] = $s1	Data from register to memory

MIPS machine language

Name	Format	Example						Comments
add	R	0	18	19	17	0	32	add $s1,$s2,$s3
sub	R	0	18	19	17	0	34	sub $s1,$s2,$s3
addi	I	8	18	17	100			addi $s1,$s2,100
lw	I	35	18	17	100			lw $s1,100($s2)
sw	I	43	18	17	100			sw $s1,100($s2)
Field size		6 bits	5 bits	5 bits	5 bits	5 bits	6 bits	All MIPS instructions 32 bits
R-format	R	op	rs	rt	rd	shamt	funct	Arithmetic instruction format
I-format	I	op	rs	rt	address			Data transfer format

FIGURE 2.7   MIPS architecture revealed through Section 2.4. Highlighted portions show MIPS machine language structures introduced in Section 2.4. The two MIPS instruction formats so far are R and I. The first 16 bits are the same: both contain an *op* field, giving the base operation; an *rs* field, giving one of the sources; and the *rt* field, which specifies the other source operand, except for load word, where it specifies the destination register. R-format divides the last 16 bits into an *rd* field, specifying the destination register; *shamt* field, which Section 2.5 explains; and the *funct* field, which specifies the specific operation of R-format instructions. I-format keeps the last 16 bits as a single *address* field.

Elaboration: Representing decimal numbers in base 2 gives an easy way to represent positive integers in computer words. Chapter 3 explains how to represent negative numbers, but for now take it on faith that a 32-bit word can represent integers between -2^{31} and $+2^{31} - 1$ or –2,147,483,648 to +2,147,483,647, and the 16-bit constant field really holds -2^{15} to $+2^{15} - 1$ or –32,768 to 32,767. Such integers are called *two's complement* numbers. Chapter 3 shows how we would encode addi $t0,$t0,-1 or lw $t0, -4 ($s0), which require negative numbers in the constant field of the immediate format.

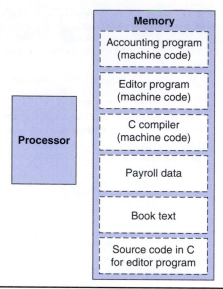

FIGURE 2.8   The stored-program concept. Stored programs allow a computer that performs accounting to become, in the blink of an eye, a computer that helps an author write a book. The switch happens simply by loading memory with programs and data and then telling the computer to begin executing at a given location in memory. Treating instructions in the same way as data greatly simplifies both the memory hardware and the software of computer systems. Specifically, the memory technology needed for data can also be used for programs, and programs like compilers, for instance, can translate code written in a notation far more convenient for humans into code that the computer can understand.

"Contrariwise," continued Tweedledee, "if it was so, it might be; and if it were so, it would be; but as it isn't, it ain't. That's logic."

Lewis Carroll, *Alice's Adventures in Wonderland*, 1865

2.5   Logical Operations

Although the first computers concentrated on full words, it soon became clear that it was useful to operate on fields of bits within a word or even on individual bits. Examining characters within a word, each of which is stored as 8 bits, is one example of such an operation. It follows that instructions were added to simplify, among other things, the packing and unpacking of bits into words. These instructions are called logical operations. Figure 2.9 shows logical operations in C and Java.

Logical operations	C operators	Java operators	MIPS instructions
Shift left	<<	<<	sll
Shift right	>>	>>>	srl
Bit-by-bit AND	&	&	and, andi
Bit-by-bit OR	|	|	or, ori
Bit-by-bit NOT	~	~	nor

FIGURE 2.9   C and Java logical operators and their corresponding MIPS instructions. MIPS implements NOT using a NOR with one operand being zero.

The first class of such operations is called *shifts*. They move all the bits in a word to the left or right, filling the emptied bits with 0s. For example, if register $s0 contained

$$0000\ 0000\ 0000\ 0000\ 0000\ 0000\ 0000\ 1001_{two} = 9_{ten}$$

and the instruction to shift left by 4 was executed, the new value would look like this:

$$0000\ 0000\ 0000\ 0000\ 0000\ 0000\ 1001\ 0000_{two} = 144_{ten}$$

The dual of a shift left is a shift right. The actual name of the two MIPS shift instructions are called *shift left logical* (sll) and *shift right logical* (srl). The following instruction performs the operation above, assuming that the result should go in register $t2:

```
sll   $t2,$s0,4   # reg $t2 = reg $s0 << 4 bits
```

We delayed explaining the *shamt* field in the R-format. It stands for *shift amount* and is used in shift instructions. Hence, the machine language version of the instruction above is

op	rs	rt	rd	shamt	funct
0	0	16	10	4	0

The encoding of sll is 0 in both the op and funct fields, rd contains $t2, rt contains $s0, and shamt contains 4. The rs field is unused, and thus is set to 0.

Shift left logical provides a bonus benefit. Shifting left by i bits gives the same result as multiplying by 2^i (Chapter 3 explains why). For example, the above sll shifts by 4, which gives the same result as multiplying by 2^4 or 16.

The first bit pattern above represents 9, and 9 × 16 = 144, the value of the second bit pattern.

Another useful operation that isolates fields is *AND*. (We capitalize the word to avoid confusion between the operation and the English conjunction.) AND is a bit-by-bit operation that leaves a 1 in the result only if both bits of the operands are 1. For example, if register $t2 still contains

$$0000\ 0000\ 0000\ 0000\ 0000\ 1101\ 0000\ 0000_{two}$$

and register $t1 contains

$$0000\ 0000\ 0000\ 0000\ 0011\ 1100\ 0000\ 0000_{two}$$

then, after executing the MIPS instruction

```
and $t0,$t1,$t2     # reg $t0 = reg $t1 & reg $t2
```

the value of register $t0 would be

$$0000\ 0000\ 0000\ 0000\ 0000\ 1100\ 0000\ 0000_{two}$$

As you can see, AND can apply a bit pattern to a set of bits to force 0s where there is a 0 in the bit pattern. Such a bit pattern in conjunction with AND is traditionally called a *mask*, since the mask "conceals" some bits.

To place a value into one of these seas of 0s, there is the dual to AND, called *OR*. It is a bit-by-bit operation that places a 1 in the result if *either* operand bit is a 1. To elaborate, if the registers $t1 and $t2 are unchanged from the preceding example, the result of the MIPS instruction

```
or $t0,$t1,$t2 # reg $t0 = reg $t1 | reg $t2
```

is this value in register $t0:

$$0000\ 0000\ 0000\ 0000\ 0011\ 1101\ 0000\ 0000_{two}$$

NOT A logical bit-by-bit operation with one operand that inverts the bits; that is, it replaces every 1 with a 0, and every 0 with a 1.

NOR A logical bit-by-bit operation with two operands that calculates the NOT of the OR of the two operands.

The final logical operation is a contrarian. **NOT** takes one operand and places a 1 in the result if one operand bit is a 0, and vice versa. In keeping with the two-operand format, the designers of MIPS decided to include the instruction **NOR** (NOT OR) instead of NOT. If one operand is zero, then it is equivalent to NOT. For example, A NOR 0 = NOT (A OR 0) = NOT (A).

If the register $t1 is unchanged from the preceding example and register $t3 has the value 0, the result of the MIPS instruction

```
nor $t0,$t1,$t3 # reg $t0 = ~ (reg $t1 | reg $t3)
```

is this value in register $t0:

$$1111\ 1111\ 1111\ 1111\ 1100\ 0011\ 1111\ 1111_{two}$$

Figure 2.9 above shows the relationship between the C and Java operators and the MIPS instructions. Constants are useful in AND and OR logical operations as well as in arithmetic operations, so MIPS also provides the instructions *and immediate* (andi) and *or immediate* (ori). Constants are rare for NOR, since its main use is to invert the bits of a single operand; thus, the hardware has no immediate version. Figure 2.10, which summarizes the MIPS instructions seen thus far, highlights the logical instructions.

MIPS operands

Name	Example	Comments
32 registers	$s0, $s1, ..., $s7 $t0, $t1, ..., $t7	Fast locations for data. In MIPS, data must be in registers to perform arithmetic. Registers $s0-$s7 map to 16–23 and $t0-$t7 map to 8–15.
2^{30} memory words	Memory[0], Memory[4], ..., Memory[4294967292]	Accessed only by data transfer instructions. MIPS uses byte addresses, so sequential word addresses differ by 4. Memory holds data structures, arrays, and spilled registers.

MIPS assembly language

Category	Instruction	Example		Meaning	Comments
Arithmetic	add	add	$s1,$s2,$s3	$s1 = $s2 + $s3	Three operands; overflow detected
	subtract	sub	$s1,$s2,$s3	$s1 = $s2 − $s3	Three operands; overflow detected
	add immediate	addi	$s1,$s2,100	$s1 = $s2 + 100	+ constant; overflow detected
Logical	and	and	$s1,$s2,$s3	$s1 = $s2 & $s3	Three reg. operands; bit-by-bit AND
	or	or	$s1,$s2,$s3	$s1 = $s2 | $s3	Three reg. operands; bit-by-bit OR
	nor	nor	$s1,$s2,$s3	$s1 = ~ ($s2 | $s3)	Three reg. operands; bit-by-bit NOR
	and immediate	andi	$s1,$s2,100	$s1 = $s2 & 100	Bit-by-bit AND reg with constant
	or immediate	ori	$s1,$s2,100	$s1 = $s2 | 100	Bit-by-bit OR reg with constant
	shift left logical	sll	$s1,$s2,10	$s1 = $s2 << 10	Shift left by constant
	shift right logical	srl	$s1,$s2,10	$s1 = $s2 >> 10	Shift right by constant
Data transfer	load word	lw	$s1,100($s2)	$s1 = Memory[$s2 + 100]	Word from memory to register
	store word	sw	$s1,100($s2)	Memory[$s2 + 100] = $s1	Word from register to memory

FIGURE 2.10 MIPS architecture revealed thus far. Color indicates the portions introduced since Figure 2.7 on page 67. The back endpapers of this book also list the MIPS machine language.

The utility of an automatic computer lies in the possibility of using a given sequence of instructions repeatedly, the number of times it is iterated being dependent upon the results of the computation. When the iteration is completed a different sequence of [instructions] is to be followed, so we must, in most cases, give two parallel trains of [instructions] preceded by an instruction as to which routine is to be followed. This choice can be made to depend upon the sign of a number (zero being reckoned as plus for machine purposes). Consequently, we introduce an [instruction] (the conditional transfer [instruction]) which will, depending on the sign of a given number, cause the proper one of two routines to be executed.

Burks, Goldstine, and von Neumann, 1947

2.6   Instructions for Making Decisions

What distinguishes a computer from a simple calculator is its ability to make decisions. Based on the input data and the values created during computation, different instructions execute. Decision making is commonly represented in programming languages using the *if* statement, sometimes combined with *go to* statements and labels. MIPS assembly language includes two decision-making instructions, similar to an *if* statement with a *go to*. The first instruction is

```
beq register1, register2, L1
```

This instruction means go to the statement labeled L1 if the value in register1 equals the value in register2. The mnemonic beq stands for *branch if equal*. The second instruction is

```
bne register1, register2, L1
```

It means go to the statement labeled L1 if the value in register1 does *not* equal the value in register2. The mnemonic bne stands for *branch if not equal*. These two instructions are traditionally called **conditional branches**.

EXAMPLE

Compiling *if-then-else* into Conditional Branches

In the following code segment, f, g, h, i, and j are variables. If the five variables f through j correspond to the five registers $s0 through $s4, what is the compiled MIPS code for this C *if* statement?

```
if (i == j) f = g + h; else f = g - h;
```

ANSWER

Figure 2.11 is a flowchart of what the MIPS code should do. The first expression compares for equality, so it would seem that we would want beq. In general, the code will be more efficient if we test for the opposite condition to branch over the code that performs the subsequent *then* part of the *if* (the label Else is defined below):

```
bne $s3,$s4,Else    # go to Else if i ≠ j
```

The next assignment statement performs a single operation, and if all the operands are allocated to registers, it is just one instruction:

```
add $s0,$s1,$s2    # f = g + h (skipped if i ≠ j)
```

conditional branch An instruction that requires the comparison of two values and that allows for a subsequent transfer of control to a new address in the program based on the outcome of the comparison.

We now need to go to the end of the *if* statement. This example introduces another kind of branch, often called an *unconditional branch*. This instruction says that the processor always follows the branch. To distinguish between conditional and unconditional branches, the MIPS name for this type of instruction is *jump*, abbreviated as j (the label Exit is defined below).

```
j Exit     # go to Exit
```

The assignment statement in the *else* portion of the *if* statement can again be compiled into a single instruction. We just need to append the label Else to this instruction. We also show the label Exit that is after this instruction, showing the end of the *if-then-else* compiled code:

```
Else:sub $s0,$s1,$s2    # f = g - h (skipped if i = j)
Exit:
```

Notice that the assembler relieves the compiler and the assembly language programmer from the tedium of calculating addresses for branches, just as it does for calculating data addresses for loads and stores (see Section 2.10).

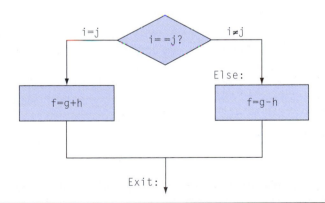

FIGURE 2.11 Illustration of the options in the *if* statement above. The left box corresponds to the *then* part of the *if* statement, and the right box corresponds to the *else* part.

**Hardware/
Software
Interface**

Compilers frequently create branches and labels where they do not appear in the programming language. Avoiding the burden of writing explicit labels and branches is one benefit of writing in high-level programming languages and is a reason coding is faster at that level.

Loops

Decisions are important both for choosing between two alternatives—found in *if* statements—and for iterating a computation—found in loops. The same assembly instructions are the building blocks for both cases.

Compiling a *while* Loop in C

EXAMPLE

Here is a traditional loop in C:

```
while (save[i] == k)
      i += 1;
```

Assume that i and k correspond to registers $s3 and $s5 and the base of the array save is in $s6. What is the MIPS assembly code corresponding to this C segment?

ANSWER

The first step is to load save[i] into a temporary register. Before we can load save[i] into a temporary register, we need to have its address. Before we can add i to the base of array save to form the address, we must multiply the index i by 4 due to the byte addressing problem. Fortunately, we can use shift left logical since shifting left by 2 bits multiplies by 4 (see page 69 in Section 2.5). We need to add the label Loop to it so that we can branch back to that instruction at the end of the loop:

```
Loop: sll  $t1,$s3,2    # Temp reg $t1 = 4 * i
```

To get the address of save[i], we need to add $t1 and the base of save in $s6:

```
      add $t1,$t1,$s6    # $t1 = address of save[i]
```

Now we can use that address to load save[i] into a temporary register:

```
      lw  $t0,0($t1)    # Temp reg $t0 = save[i]
```

The next instruction performs the loop test, exiting if save[i] ≠ k:

```
    bne   $t0,$s5, Exit   # go to Exit if save[i] ≠ k
```

The next instruction adds 1 to i:

```
    addi  $s3,$s3,1     # i = i + 1
```

The end of the loop branches back to the *while* test at the top of the loop. We just add the Exit label after it, and we're done:

```
    j     Loop          # go to Loop
Exit:
```

(See Exercise 2.33 for an optimization of this sequence.)

<table>
<tr><td>

Such sequences of instructions that end in a branch are so fundamental to compiling that they are given their own buzzword: a **basic block** is a sequence of instructions without branches, except possibly at the end, and without branch targets or branch labels, except possibly at the beginning. One of the first early phases of compilation is breaking the program into basic blocks.

</td><td>

Hardware/ Software Interface

</td></tr>
</table>

The test for equality or inequality is probably the most popular test, but sometimes it is useful to see if a variable is less than another variable. For example, a *for* loop may want to test to see if the index variable is less than 0. Such comparisons are accomplished in MIPS assembly language with an instruction that compares two registers and sets a third register to 1 if the first is less than the second; otherwise, it is set to 0. The MIPS instruction is called *set on less than*, or slt. For example,

basic block A sequence of instructions without branches (except possibly at the end) and without branch targets or branch labels (except possibly at the beginning).

```
    slt    $t0, $s3, $s4
```

means that register $t0 is set to 1 if the value in register $s3 is less than the value in register $s4; otherwise, register $t0 is set to 0.

Constant operands are popular in comparisons. Since register $zero always has 0, we can already compare to 0. To compare to other values, there is an immediate version of the set on less than instruction. To test if register $s2 is less than the constant 10, we can just write

```
    slti    $t0,$s2,10     # $t0 = 1 if $s2 < 10
```

Heeding von Neumann's warning about the simplicity of the "equipment," the MIPS architecture doesn't include branch on less than because it is too complicated; either it would stretch the clock cycle time or it would take extra clock cycles per instruction. Two faster instructions are more useful.

**Hardware/
Software
Interface**

MIPS compilers use the slt, slti, beq, bne, and the fixed value of 0 (always available by reading register $zero) to create all relative conditions: equal, not equal, less than, less than or equal, greater than, greater than or equal. (As you might expect, register $zero maps to register 0.)

Case/Switch Statement

Most programming languages have a *case* or *switch* statement that allows the programmer to select one of many alternatives depending on a single value. The simplest way to implement *switch* is via a sequence of conditional tests, turning the *switch* statement into a chain of *if-then-else* statements.

jump address table Also called **jump table**. A table of addresses of alternative instruction sequences.

Sometimes the alternatives may be more efficiently encoded as a table of addresses of alternative instruction sequences, called a **jump address table**, and the program needs only to index into the table and then jump to the appropriate sequence. The **jump table** is then just an array of words containing addresses that correspond to labels in the code. See the "In More Depth" exercises in Section 2.20 for more details on jump address tables.

To support such situations, computers like MIPS include a *jump register* instruction (jr), meaning an unconditional jump to the address specified in a register. The program loads the appropriate entry from the jump table into a register, and then it jumps to the proper address using a jump register. This instruction is described in Section 2.7.

**Hardware/
Software
Interface**

Although there are many statements for decisions and loops in programming languages like C and Java, the bedrock statement that implements them at the next lower level is the conditional branch.

Figure 2.12 summarizes the portions of MIPS assembly language described in this section, and Figure 2.13 summarizes the corresponding MIPS machine language. This step along the evolution of the MIPS language has added branches and jumps to our symbolic representation, and fixes the useful value 0 permanently in a register.

Elaboration: If you have heard about *delayed branches*, covered in Chapter 6, don't worry: the MIPS assembler makes them invisible to the assembly language programmer.

MIPS operands

Name	Example	Comments
32 registers	$s0, $s1, ..., $s7 $t0, $t1, ..., $t7, $zero	Fast locations for data. In MIPS, data must be in registers to perform arithmetic. Registers $s0–$s7 map to 16–23 and $t0–$t7 map to 8–15. MIPS register $zero always equals 0.
2^{30} memory words	Memory[0], Memory[4], ..., Memory[4294967292]	Accessed only by data transfer instructions in MIPS. MIPS uses byte addresses, so sequential word addresses differ by 4. Memory holds data structures, arrays, and spilled registers.

MIPS assembly language

Category	Instruction	Example	Meaning	Comments
Arithmetic	add	add $s1,$s2,$s3	$s1 = $s2 + $s3	Three operands; data in registers
	subtract	sub $s1,$s2,$s3	$s1 = $s2 − $s3	Three operands; data in registers
Data transfer	load word	lw $s1,100($s2)	$s1 = Memory[$s2 + 100]	Data from memory to register
	store word	sw $s1,100($s2)	Memory[$s2 + 100] = $s1	Data from register to memory
Logical	and	and $s1,$s2,$s3	$s1 = $s2 & $s3	Three reg. operands; bit-by-bit AND
	or	or $s1,$s2,$s3	$s1 = $s2	$s3	Three reg. operands; bit-by-bit OR
	nor	nor $s1,$s2,$s3	$s1 = ~ ($s2 | $s3)	Three reg. operands; bit-by-bit NOR
	and immediate	andi $s1,$s2,100	$s1 = $s2 & 100	Bit-by-bit AND reg with constant
	or immediate	ori $s1,$s2,100	$s1 = $s2	100	Bit-by-bit OR reg with constant
	shift left logical	sll $s1,$s2,10	$s1 = $s2 << 10	Shift left by constant
	shift right logical	srl $s1,$s2,10	$s1 = $s2 >> 10	Shift right by constant
Conditional branch	branch on equal	beq $s1,$s2,L	if ($s1 == $s2) go to L	Equal test and branch
	branch on not equal	bne $s1,$s2,L	if ($s1 != $s2) go to L	Not equal test and branch
	set on less than	slt $s1,$s2,$s3	if ($s2 < $s3) $s1 = 1; else $s1 = 0	Compare less than; used with beq, bne
	set on less than immediate	slti $s1,$s2,100	if ($s2 < 100) $s1 = 1; else $s1 = 0	Compare less than immediate; used with beq, bne
Unconditional jump	jump	j L	go to L	Jump to target address

FIGURE 2.12   MIPS architecture revealed through Section 2.6. Highlighted portions show MIPS structures introduced in Section 2.6.

C has many statements for decisions and loops while MIPS has few. Which of the following do or do not explain this imbalance? Why?

Check Yourself

1. More decision statements make code easier to read and understand.

2. Fewer decision statements simplify the task of the underlying layer that is responsible for execution.

MIPS machine language

Name	Format	Example						Comments
add	R	0	18	19	17	0	32	add $s1,$s2,$s3
sub	R	0	18	19	17	0	34	sub $s1,$s2,$s3
lw	I	35	18	17	100			lw $s1,100($s2)
sw	I	43	18	17	100			sw $s1,100($s2)
and	R	0	18	19	17	0	36	and $s1,$s2,$s3
or	R	0	18	19	17	0	37	or $s1,$s2,$s3
nor	R	0	18	19	17	0	39	nor $s1,$s2,$s3
andi	I	12	18	17	100			andi $s1,$s2,100
ori	I	13	18	17	100			ori $s1,$s2,100
sll	R	0	0	18	17	10	0	sll $s1,$s2,10
srl	R	0	0	18	17	10	2	srl $s1,$s2,10
beq	I	4	17	18	25			beq $s1,$s2,100
bne	I	5	17	18	25			bne $s1,$s2,100
slt	R	0	18	19	17	0	42	slt $s1,$s2,$s3
j	J	2	2500					j 10000 (see Section 2.9)
Field size		6 bits	5 bits	5 bits	5 bits	5 bits	6 bits	All MIPS instructions 32 bits
R-format	R	op	rs	rt	rd	shamt	funct	Arithmetic instruction format
I-format	I	op	rs	rt	address			Data transfer, branch format

FIGURE 2.13 MIPS machine language revealed through Section 2.6. Highlighted portions show MIPS structures introduced in Section 2.6. The J-format, used for jump instructions, is explained in Section 2.9. Section 2.9 also explains the proper values in address fields of branch instructions.

3. More decision statements mean fewer lines of code, which generally reduces coding time.

4. More decision statements mean fewer lines of code, which generally results in the execution of fewer operations.

Why does C provide two sets of operators for AND (& and &&) and two sets of operators for OR (| and ||) while MIPS doesn't?

1. Logical operations AND and OR implement & and | while conditional branches implement && and ||.

2. The previous statement has it backwards: && and || correspond to logical operations while & and | map to conditional branches.

3. They are redundant and mean the same thing: && and || are simply inherited from the programming language B, the predecessor of C.

<table>
<tr><td>**2.7**</td><td></td></tr>
</table>

2.7 Supporting Procedures in Computer Hardware

A **procedure** or function is one tool C or Java programmers use to structure programs, both to make them easier to understand and to allow code to be reused. Procedures allow the programmer to concentrate on just one portion of the task at a time, with parameters acting as a barrier between the procedure and the rest of the program and data, allowing it to be passed values and return results. We describe the equivalent in Java at the end of this section, but Java needs everything from a computer that C needs.

You can think of a procedure like a spy who leaves with a secret plan, acquires resources, performs the task, covers his tracks, and then returns to the point of origin with the desired result. Nothing else should be perturbed once the mission is complete. Moreover, a spy operates on only a "need to know" basis, so the spy can't make assumptions about his employer.

Similarly, in the execution of a procedure, the program must follow these six steps:

1. Place parameters in a place where the procedure can access them.

2. Transfer control to the procedure.

3. Acquire the storage resources needed for the procedure.

4. Perform the desired task.

5. Place the result value in a place where the calling program can access it.

6. Return control to the point of origin, since a procedure can be called from several points in a program.

As mentioned above, registers are the fastest place to hold data in a computer, so we want to use them as much as possible. MIPS software follows the following convention in allocating its 32 registers for procedure calling:

■ $a0–$a3: four argument registers in which to pass parameters

■ $v0–$v1: two value registers in which to return values

■ $ra: one return address register to return to the point of origin

In addition to allocating these registers, MIPS assembly language includes an instruction just for the procedures: it jumps to an address and simultaneously saves the address of the following instruction in register $ra. The **jump-and-link instruction** (jal) is simply written

procedure A stored subroutine that performs a specific task based on the parameters with which it is provided.

jump-and-link instruction An instruction that jumps to an address and simultaneously saves the address of the following instruction in a register ($ra in MIPS).

```
jal ProcedureAddress
```

The *link* portion of the name means that an address or link is formed that points to the calling site to allow the procedure to return to the proper address. This "link," stored in register $ra, is called the **return address**. The return address is needed because the same procedure could be called from several parts of the program.

return address A link to the calling site that allows a procedure to return to the proper address; in MIPS it is stored in register $ra.

program counter (PC) The register containing the address of the instruction in the program being executed.

Implicit in the stored-program idea is the need to have a register to hold the address of the current instruction being executed. For historical reasons, this register is almost always called the **program counter**, abbreviated *PC* in the MIPS architecture, although a more sensible name would have been *instruction address register*. The jal instruction saves PC + 4 in register $ra to link to the following instruction to set up the procedure return.

To support such situations, computers like MIPS use a *jump register* instruction (jr), meaning an unconditional jump to the address specified in a register:

```
jr   $ra
```

caller The program that instigates a procedure and provides the necessary parameter values.

callee A procedure that executes a series of stored instructions based on parameters provided by the caller and then returns control to the caller.

The jump register instruction jumps to the address stored in register $ra—which is just what we want. Thus, the calling program, or **caller**, puts the parameter values in $a0–$a3 and uses jal X to jump to procedure X (sometimes named the **callee**). The callee then performs the calculations, places the results in $v0–$v1, and returns control to the caller using jr $ra.

Using More Registers

Suppose a compiler needs more registers for a procedure than the four argument and two return value registers. Since we must cover our tracks after our mission is complete, any registers needed by the caller must be restored to the values that they contained *before* the procedure was invoked. This situation is an example in which we need to spill registers to memory, as mentioned in the "Hardware/Software Interface" section on page 58.

stack A data structure for spilling registers organized as a last-in-first-out queue.

stack pointer A value denoting the most recently allocated address in a stack that shows where registers should be spilled or where old register values can be found.

The ideal data structure for spilling registers is a **stack**—a last-in-first-out queue. A stack needs a pointer to the most recently allocated address in the stack to show where the next procedure should place the registers to be spilled or where old register values are found. The **stack pointer** is adjusted by one word for each register that is saved or restored. Stacks are so popular that they have their own buzzwords for transferring data to and from the stack: placing data onto the stack is called a *push*, and removing data from the stack is called a *pop*.

MIPS software allocates another register just for the stack: the stack pointer ($sp), used to save the registers needed by the callee. By historical precedent, stacks "grow" from higher addresses to lower addresses. This convention means that you push values onto the stack by subtracting from the stack pointer. Adding to the stack pointer shrinks the stack, thereby popping values off the stack.

Compiling a C Procedure That Doesn't Call Another Procedure

Let's turn the example on page 51 into a C procedure:

```
int leaf_example (int g, int h, int i, int j)
{
    int f;

    f = (g + h) - (i + j);
    return f;
}
```

What is the compiled MIPS assembly code?

EXAMPLE

The parameter variables g, h, i, and j correspond to the argument registers $a0, $a1, $a2, and $a3, and f corresponds to $s0. The compiled program starts with the label of the procedure:

ANSWER

```
leaf_example:
```

The next step is to save the registers used by the procedure. The C assignment statement in the procedure body is identical to the example on page 51, which uses two temporary registers. Thus, we need to save three registers: $s0, $t0, and $t1. We "push" the old values onto the stack by creating space for three words on the stack and then store them:

```
addi $sp,$sp,-12 # adjust stack to make room for 3 items
sw   $t1, 8($sp)  # save register $t1 for use afterwards
sw   $t0, 4($sp)  # save register $t0 for use afterwards
sw   $s0, 0($sp)  # save register $s0 for use afterwards
```

Figure 2.14 shows the stack before, during, and after the procedure call. The next three statements correspond to the body of the procedure, which follows the example on page 51:

```
add $t0,$a0,$a1 # register $t0 contains g + h
add $t1,$a2,$a3 # register $t1 contains i + j
sub $s0,$t0,$t1 # f = $t0 - $t1, which is (g + h)-(i + j)
```

To return the value of f, we copy it into a return value register:

```
add $v0,$s0,$zero # returns f ($v0 = $s0 + 0)
```

Before returning, we restore the three old values of the registers we saved by "popping" them from the stack:

```
lw   $s0, 0($sp)  # restore register $s0 for caller
lw   $t0, 4($sp)  # restore register $t0 for caller
lw   $t1, 8($sp)  # restore register $t1 for caller
addi $sp,$sp,12   # adjust stack to delete 3 items
```

The procedure ends with a jump register using the return address:

```
jr   $ra     # jump back to calling routine
```

In the example above we used temporary registers and assumed their old values must be saved and restored. To avoid saving and restoring a register whose value is never used, which might happen with a temporary register, MIPS software separates 18 of the registers into two groups:

- $t0–$t9 : 10 temporary registers that are *not* preserved by the callee (called procedure) on a procedure call

- $s0–$s7 : 8 saved registers that must be preserved on a procedure call (if used, the callee saves and restores them)

This simple convention reduces register spilling. In the example above, since the caller (procedure doing the calling) does not expect registers $t0 and $t1 to be preserved across a procedure call, we can drop two stores and two loads from the code. We still must save and restore $s0, since the callee must assume that the caller needs its value.

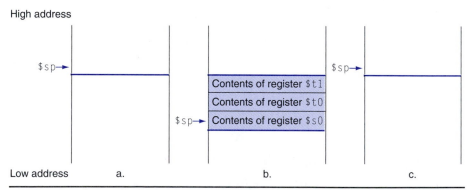

FIGURE 2.14   The values of the stack pointer and the stack (a) before, (b) during, and (c) after the procedure call. The stack pointer always points to the "top" of the stack, or the last word in the stack in this drawing.

Nested Procedures

Procedures that do not call others are called *leaf* procedures. Life would be simple if all procedures were leaf procedures, but they aren't. Just as a spy might employ other spies as part of a mission, who in turn might use even more spies, so do procedures invoke other procedures. Moreover, recursive procedures even invoke "clones" of themselves. Just as we need to be careful when using registers in procedures, more care must also be taken when invoking nonleaf procedures.

For example, suppose that the main program calls procedure A with an argument of 3, by placing the value 3 into register $a0 and then using jal A. Then suppose that procedure A calls procedure B via jal B with an argument of 7, also placed in $a0. Since A hasn't finished its task yet, there is a conflict over the use of register $a0. Similarly, there is a conflict over the return address in register $ra, since it now has the return address for B. Unless we take steps to prevent the problem, this conflict will eliminate procedure A's ability to return to its caller.

One solution is to push all the other registers that must be preserved onto the stack, just as we did with the saved registers. The caller pushes any argument registers ($a0–$a3) or temporary registers ($t0–$t9) that are needed after the call. The callee pushes the return address register $ra and any saved registers ($s0–$s7) used by the callee. The stack pointer $sp is adjusted to account for the number of registers placed on the stack. Upon the return, the registers are restored from memory and the stack pointer is readjusted.

Compiling a Recursive C Procedure, Showing Nested Procedure Linking

Let's tackle a recursive procedure that calculates factorial:

```
int fact (int n)
{
    if (n < 1) return (1);
        else return (n * fact(n-1));
}
```

What is the MIPS assembly code?

EXAMPLE

ANSWER

The parameter variable n corresponds to the argument register $a0. The compiled program starts with the label of the procedure and then saves two registers on the stack, the return address and $a0:

```
fact:
    addi   $sp,$sp,-8  # adjust stack for 2 items
    sw     $ra, 4($sp) # save the return address
    sw     $a0, 0($sp) # save the argument n
```

The first time fact is called, sw saves an address in the program that called fact. The next two instructions test if n is less than 1, going to L1 if n ≥ 1.

```
    slti   $t0,$a0,1      # test for n < 1
    beq    $t0,$zero,L1   # if n >= 1, go to L1
```

If n is less than 1, fact returns 1 by putting 1 into a value register: it adds 1 to 0 and places that sum in $v0. It then pops the two saved values off the stack and jumps to the return address:

```
    addi   $v0,$zero,1  # return 1
    addi   $sp,$sp,8    # pop 2 items off stack
    jr     $ra          # return to after jal
```

Before popping two items off the stack, we could have loaded $a0 and $ra. Since $a0 and $ra don't change when n is less than 1, we skip those instructions.

If n is not less than 1, the argument n is decremented and then fact is called again with the decremented value:

```
L1: addi $a0,$a0,-1   # n >= 1: argument gets (n - 1)
    jal  fact         # call fact with (n - 1)
```

The next instruction is where fact returns. Now the old return address and old argument are restored, along with the stack pointer:

```
    lw   $a0, 0($sp)  # return from jal:restore argument n
    lw   $ra, 4($sp)  # restore the return address
    addi $sp, $sp,8   # adjust stack pointer to pop 2 items
```

Next, the value register $v0 gets the product of old argument $a0 and the current value of the value register. We assume a multiply instruction is available, even though it is not covered until Chapter 3:

```
mul  $v0,$a0,$v0  # return n * fact (n - 1)
```

Finally, fact jumps again to the return address:

```
jr   $ra            # return to the caller
```

A C variable is a location in storage, and its interpretation depends both on its *type* and *storage class*. Types are discussed in detail in Chapter 3, but examples include integers and characters. C has two storage classes: *automatic* and *static*. Automatic variables are local to a procedure and are discarded when the procedure exits. Static variables exist across exits from and entries to procedures. C variables declared outside all procedures are considered static, as are any variables declared using the keyword static. The rest are automatic. To simplify access to static data, MIPS software reserves another register, called the **global pointer**, or $gp.

Hardware/ Software Interface

global pointer The register that is reserved to point to static data.

Figure 2.15 summarizes what is preserved across a procedure call. Note that several schemes preserve the stack. The stack above $sp is preserved simply by making sure the callee does not write above $sp; $sp is itself preserved by the callee adding exactly the same amount that was subtracted from it, and the other registers are preserved by saving them on the stack (if they are used) and restoring them from there. These actions also guarantee that the caller will get the same data back on a load from the stack as it put into the stack on a store because the callee promises to preserve $sp and because the callee also promises not to modify the caller's portion of the stack, that is, the area above the $sp at the time of the call.

Preserved	Not preserved
Saved registers: $s0–$s7	Temporary registers: $t0–$t9
Stack pointer register: $sp	Argument registers: $a0–$a3
Return address register: $ra	Return value registers: $v0–$v1
Stack above the stack pointer	Stack below the stack pointer

FIGURE 2.15   What is and what is not preserved across a procedure call. If the software relies on the frame pointer register or on the global pointer register, discussed in the following sections, they are also preserved.

Allocating Space for New Data on the Stack

procedure frame Also called **activation record**. The segment of the stack containing a procedure's saved registers and local variables.

frame pointer A value denoting the location of the saved registers and local variables for a given procedure.

The final complexity is that the stack is also used to store variables that are local to the procedure that do not fit in registers, such as local arrays or structures. The segment of the stack containing a procedure's saved registers and local variables is called a **procedure frame** or **activation record**. Figure 2.16 shows the state of the stack before, during, and after the procedure call.

Some MIPS software uses a **frame pointer** ($fp) to point to the first word of the frame of a procedure. A stack pointer might change during the procedure, and so references to a local variable in memory might have different offsets depending on where they are in the procedure, making the procedure harder to understand. Alternatively, a frame pointer offers a stable base register within a procedure for local memory references. Note that an activation record appears on the stack whether or not an explicit frame pointer is used. We've been avoiding $fp by avoiding changes to $sp within a procedure: in our examples, the stack is adjusted only on entry and exit of the procedure.

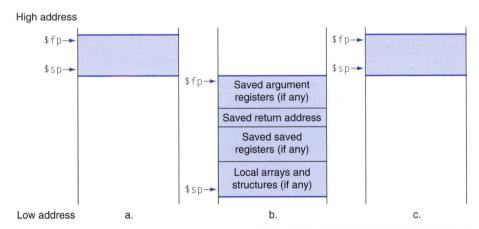

FIGURE 2.16 Illustration of the stack allocation (a) before, (b) during, and (c) after the procedure call. The frame pointer ($fp) points to the first word of the frame, often a saved argument register, and the stack pointer ($sp) points to the top of the stack. The stack is adjusted to make room for all the saved registers and any memory-resident local variables. Since the stack pointer may change during program execution, it's easier for programmers to reference variables via the stable frame pointer, although it could be done just with the stack pointer and a little address arithmetic. If there are no local variables on the stack within a procedure, the compiler will save time by *not* setting and restoring the frame pointer. When a frame pointer is used, it is initialized using the address in $sp on a call, and $sp is restored using $fp. This information is also found in column 4 of the MIPS Reference Data Card at the front of this book.

Allocating Space for New Data on the Heap

In addition to automatic variables that are local to procedures, C programmers need space in memory for static variables and for dynamic data structures. Figure 2.17 shows the MIPS convention for allocation of memory. The stack starts in the high end of memory and grows down. The first part of the low end of memory is reserved, followed by the home of the MIPS machine code, traditionally called the **text segment**. Above the code is the *static data segment*, which is the place for constants and other static variables. Although arrays tend to be to a fixed length and thus are a good match to the static data segment, data structures like linked lists tend to grow and shrink during their lifetimes. The segment for such data structures is traditionally called the *heap*, and it is placed next in memory. Note that this allocation allows the stack and heap to grow toward each other, thereby allowing the efficient use of memory as the two segments wax and wane.

C allocates and frees space on the heap with explicit functions. `malloc()` allocates space on the heap and returns a pointer to it, and `free()` releases space on the stack to which the pointer points. Memory allocation is controlled by programs in C, and it is the source of many common and difficult bugs. Forgetting to free space

text segment The segment of a Unix object file that contains the machine language code for routines in the source file.

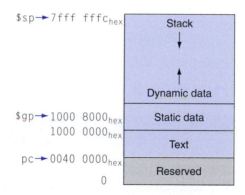

FIGURE 2.17 The MIPS memory allocation for program and data. These addresses are only a software convention, and not part of the MIPS architecture. Starting top down, the stack pointer is initialized to $7fff\ fffc_{hex}$ and grows down toward the data segment. At the other end, the program code ("text") starts at $0040\ 0000_{hex}$. The static data starts at $1000\ 0000_{hex}$. Dynamic data, allocated by malloc in C and via new in Java, is next and grows up toward the stack in an area called the heap. The global pointer, $gp, is set to an address to make it easy to access data. It is initialized to $1000\ 8000_{hex}$ so that it can access from $1000\ 0000_{hex}$ to $1000\ ffff_{hex}$ using the positive and negative 16-bit offsets from $gp (see two's complement addressing in Chapter 3). This information is also found in column 4 of the MIPS Reference Data Card at the front of this book.

leads to a "memory leak," which eventually uses up so much memory that the operating system may crash. Freeing space too early leads to "dangling pointers," which can cause pointers to point to things that the program never intended.

Figure 2.18 summarizes the register conventions for the MIPS assembly language. Figures 2.19 and 2.20 summarize the parts of the MIPS assembly instructions described so far and the corresponding MIPS machine instructions.

Elaboration: What if there are more than four parameters? The MIPS convention is to place the extra parameters on the stack just above the frame pointer. The procedure then expects the first four parameters to be in registers $a0 through $a3 and the rest in memory, addressable via the frame pointer.

As mentioned in the caption of Figure 2.16, the frame pointer is convenient because all references to variables in the stack within a procedure will have the same offset. The frame pointer is not necessary, however. The GNU MIPS C compiler uses a frame pointer, but the C compiler from MIPS/Silicon Graphics does not; it uses register 30 as another save register ($s8).

jal actually saves the address of the instruction that *follows* jal into register $ra, thereby allowing a procedure return to be simply jr $ra.

Check Yourself

Which of the following statements about C and Java are generally true?

1. Procedure calls in C are faster than method invocation in Java.

2. C programmers manage data explicitly while it's automatic in Java.

3. C leads to more pointer bugs and memory leak bugs than does Java.

4. C passes parameters in registers while Java passes them on the stack.

Name	Register number	Usage	Preserved on call?
$zero	0	The constant value 0	n.a.
$v0–$v1	2–3	Values for results and expression evaluation	no
$a0–$a3	4–7	Arguments	no
$t0–$t7	8–15	Temporaries	no
$s0–$s7	16–23	Saved	yes
$t8–$t9	24–25	More temporaries	no
$gp	28	Global pointer	yes
$sp	29	Stack pointer	yes
$fp	30	Frame pointer	yes
$ra	31	Return address	yes

FIGURE 2.18   MIPS register conventions. Register 1, called $at, is reserved for the assembler (see Section 2.10), and registers 26–27, called $k0–$k1, are reserved for the operating system. This information is also found in column 2 of the MIPS Reference Data Card at the front of this book.

MIPS operands

Name	Example	Comments
32 registers	$s0–$s7, $t0–$t9, $zero, $a0–$a3, $v0–$v1, $gp, $fp, $sp, $ra	Fast locations for data. In MIPS, data must be in registers to perform arithmetic. MIPS register $zero always equals 0. $gp (28) is the global pointer, $sp (29) is the stack pointer, $fp (30) is the frame pointer, and $ra (31) is the return address.
2^{30} memory words	Memory[0], Memory[4], . . . , Memory[4294967292]	Accessed only by data transfer instructions. MIPS uses byte addresses, so sequential word addresses differ by 4. Memory holds data structures, arrays, and spilled registers, such as those saved on procedure calls.

MIPS assembly language

Category	Instruction	Example	Meaning	Comments
Arithmetic	add	add $s1,$s2,$s3	$s1 = $s2 + $s3	Three register operands
	subtract	sub $s1,$s2,$s3	$s1 = $s2 - $s3	Three register operands
Data transfer	load word	lw $s1,100($s2)	$s1 = Memory[$s2 + 100]	Data from memory to register
	store word	sw $s1,100($s2)	Memory[$s2 + 100] = $s1	Data from register to memory
Logical	and	and $s1,$s2,$s3	$s1 = $s2 & $s3	Three reg. operands; bit-by-bit AND
	or	or $s1,$s2,$s3	$s1 = $s2	$s3	Three reg. operands; bit-by-bit OR
	nor	nor $s1,$s2,$s3	$s1 = ~ ($s2 |$s3)	Three reg. operands; bit-by-bit NOR
	and immediate	andi $s1,$s2,100	$s1 = $s2 & 100	Bit-by-bit AND reg with constant
	or immediate	ori $s1,$s2,100	$s1 = $s2	100	Bit-by-bit OR reg with constant
	shift left logical	sll $s1,$s2,10	$s1 = $s2 << 10	Shift left by constant
	shift right logical	srl $s1,$s2,10	$s1 = $s2 >> 10	Shift right by constant
Conditional branch	branch on equal	beq $s1,$s2,L	if ($s1 == $s2) go to L	Equal test and branch
	branch on not equal	bne $s1,$s2,L	if ($s1 != $s2) go to L	Not equal test and branch
	set on less than	slt $s1,$s2,$s3	if ($s2 < $s3) $s1 = 1; else $s1 = 0	Compare less than; used with beq, bne
	set on less than immediate	slti $s1,$s2,100	if ($s2 < 100) $s1 = 1; else $s1 = 0	Compare less than immediate; used with beq, bne
Unconditional jump	jump	j L	go to L	Jump to target address
	jump register	jr $ra	go to $ra	For procedure return
	jump and link	jal L	$ra = PC + 4; go to L	For procedure call

FIGURE 2.19 MIPS architecture revealed through Section 2.7. Highlighted portions show MIPS assembly language structures introduced in Section 2.7. The J-format, used for jump and jump-and-link instructions, is explained in Section 2.9.

MIPS machine language

Name	Format	Example						Comments
add	R	0	18	19	17	0	32	add $s1,$s2,$s3
sub	R	0	18	19	17	0	34	sub $s1,$s2,$s3
lw	I	35	18	17	100			lw $s1,100($s2)
sw	I	43	18	17	100			sw $s1,100($s2)
and	R	0	18	19	17	0	36	and $s1,$s2,$s3
or	R	0	18	19	17	0	37	or $s1,$s2,$s3
nor	R	0	18	19	17	0	39	nor $s1,$s2,$s3
andi	I	12	18	17	100			andi $s1,$s2,100
ori	I	13	18	17	100			ori $s1,$s2,100
sll	R	0	0	18	17	10	0	sll $s1,$s2,10
srl	R	0	0	18	17	10	2	srl $s1,$s2,10
beq	I	4	17	18	25			beq $s1,$s2,100
bne	I	5	17	18	25			bne $s1,$s2,100
slt	R	0	18	19	17	0	42	slt $s1,$s2,$s3
j	J	2	2500					j 10000 (see Section 2.9)
jr	R	0	31	0	0	0	8	jr $ra
jal	J	3	2500					jal 10000 (see Section 2.9)
Field size		6 bits	5 bits	5 bits	5 bits	5 bits	6 bits	All MIPS instructions 32 bits
R-format	R	op	rs	rt	rd	shamt	funct	Arithmetic instruction format
I-format	I	op	rs	rt	address			Data transfer, branch format

FIGURE 2.20   MIPS machine language revealed through Section 2.7. Highlighted portions show MIPS assembly language structures introduced in Section 2.7. The J-format, used for jump and jump-and-link instructions, is explained in Section 2.9. This section also explains why putting 25 in the address field of beq and bne machine language instructions is equivalent to 100 in assembly language.

!(@ | = >
(wow open tab at bar is great)

Fourth line of the keyboard poem "Hatless Atlas," 1991 (some give names to ASCII characters: "!" is "wow," "(" is open, "|" is bar, and so on).

2.8   Communicating with People

Computers were invented to crunch numbers, but as soon as they became commercially viable they were used to process text. Most computers today use 8-bit bytes to represent characters, with the American Standard Code for Information Interchange (ASCII) being the representation that nearly everyone follows. Figure 2.21 summarizes ASCII.

A series of instructions can extract a byte from a word, so load word and store word are sufficient for transferring bytes as well as words. Because of the popularity

ASCII value	Char- acter	ASCII value	Char- acter	ASCII value	Char- acter	ASCII value	Char- acter	ASCII value	Char- acter	ASCII value	Char- acter
32	space	48	0	64	@	80	P	96	`	112	p
33	!	49	1	65	A	81	Q	97	a	113	q
34	"	50	2	66	B	82	R	98	b	114	r
35	#	51	3	67	C	83	S	99	c	115	s
36	$	52	4	68	D	84	T	100	d	116	t
37	%	53	5	69	E	85	U	101	e	117	u
38	&	54	6	70	F	86	V	102	f	118	v
39	'	55	7	71	G	87	W	103	g	119	w
40	(	56	8	72	H	88	X	104	h	120	x
41	)	57	9	73	I	89	Y	105	i	121	y
42	*	58	:	74	J	90	Z	106	j	122	z
43	+	59	;	75	K	91	[	107	k	123	{
44	,	60	<	76	L	92	\	108	l	124		
45	-	61	=	77	M	93	]	109	m	125	}
46	.	62	>	78	N	94	^	110	n	126	~
47	/	63	?	79	O	95	_	111	o	127	DEL

FIGURE 2.21 ASCII representation of characters. Note that upper- and lowercase letters differ by exactly 32; this observation can lead to short-cuts in checking or changing upper- and lowercase. Values not shown include formatting characters. For example, 8 represents backspace, 9 represents a tab character, and 13 a carriage return. Another useful value is 0 for null, the value the programming language C uses to mark the end of a string. This information is also found in column 3 of the MIPS Reference Data Card at the front of this book.

of text in some programs, however, MIPS provides instructions to move bytes. Load byte (lb) loads a byte from memory, placing it in the rightmost 8 bits of a register. Store byte (sb) takes a byte from the rightmost 8 bits of a register and writes it to memory. Thus, we copy a byte with the sequence

```
lb $t0,0($sp)      # Read byte from source
sb $t0,0($gp)      # Write byte to destination
```

Characters are normally combined into strings, which have a variable number of characters. There are three choices for representing a string: (1) the first position of the string is reserved to give the length of a string, (2) an accompanying variable has the length of the string (as in a structure), or (3) the last position of a string is indicated by a character used to mark the end of a string. C uses the third choice, terminating a string with a byte whose value is 0 (named null in ASCII). Thus, the string "Cal" is represented in C by the following 4 bytes, shown as decimal numbers: 67, 97, 108, 0.

EXAMPLE

Compiling a String Copy Procedure, Showing How to Use C Strings

The procedure `strcpy` copies string `y` to string `x` using the null byte termination convention of C:

```
void strcpy (char x[], char y[])
{
    int i;

    i = 0;
    while ((x[i] = y[i]) != '\0') /* copy & test byte */
     i += 1;
}
```

What is the MIPS assembly code?

ANSWER

Below is the basic MIPS assembly code segment. Assume that base addresses for arrays x and y are found in $a0 and $a1, while i is in $s0. `strcpy` adjusts the stack pointer and then saves the saved register $s0 on the stack:

```
strcpy:
    addi  $sp,$sp,-4  # adjust stack for 1 more item
    sw    $s0, 0($sp) # save $s0
```

To initialize i to 0, the next instruction sets $s0 to 0 by adding 0 to 0 and placing that sum in $s0:

```
    add   $s0,$zero,$zero  # i = 0 + 0
```

This is the beginning of the loop. The address of y[i] is first formed by adding i to y[]:

```
L1: add   $t1,$s0,$a1  # address of y[i] in $t1
```

Note that we don't have to multiply i by 4 since y is an array of *bytes* and not of words, as in prior examples.

To load the character in y[i], we use load byte, which puts the character into $t2:

```
    lb    $t2, 0($t1)  # $t2 = y[i]
```

A similar address calculation puts the address of x[i] in $t3, and then the character in $t2 is stored at that address.

```
add    $t3,$s0,$a0  # address of x[i] in $t3
sb     $t2, 0($t3)  # x[i] = y[i]
```

Next we exit the loop if the character was 0; that is, if it is the last character of the string:

```
beq    $t2,$zero,L2 # if y[i] == 0, go to L2
```

If not, we increment i and loop back:

```
addi   $s0, $s0,1   # i = i + 1
j      L1           # go to L1
```

If we don't loop back, it was the last character of the string; we restore $s0 and the stack pointer, and then return.

```
L2: lw    $s0, 0($sp)  # y[i] == 0: end of string;
                       # restore old $s0
    addi  $sp,$sp,4    # pop 1 word off stack
    jr    $ra          # return
```

String copies usually use pointers instead of arrays in C to avoid the operations on i in the code above. See Section 2.15 for an explanation of arrays versus pointers.

Since the procedure strcpy above is a leaf procedure, the compiler could allocate i to a temporary register and avoid saving and restoring $s0. Hence, instead of thinking of the $t registers as being just for temporaries, we can think of them as registers that the callee should use whenever convenient. When a compiler finds a leaf procedure, it exhausts all temporary registers before using registers it must save.

Characters and Strings in Java

Unicode is a universal encoding of the alphabets of most human languages. Figure 2.22 is a list of Unicode alphabets; there are about as many *alphabets* in Unicode as there are useful *symbols* in ASCII. To be more inclusive, Java uses Unicode for characters. By default, it uses 16 bits to represent a character.

Latin	Malayalam	Tagbanwa	General Punctuation
Greek	Sinhala	Khmer	Spacing Modifier Letters
Cyrillic	Thai	Mongolian	Currency Symbols
Armenian	Lao	Limbu	Combining Diacritical Marks
Hebrew	Tibetan	Tai Le	Combining Marks for Symbols
Arabic	Myanmar	Kangxi Radicals	Superscripts and Subscripts
Syriac	Georgian	Hiragana	Number Forms
Thaana	Hangul Jamo	Katakana	Mathematical Operators
Devanagari	Ethiopic	Bopomofo	Mathematical Alphanumeric Symbols
Bengali	Cherokee	Kanbun	Braille Patterns
Gurmukhi	Unified Canadian Aboriginal Syllabic	Shavian	Optical Character Recognition
Gujarati	Ogham	Osmanya	Byzantine Musical Symbols
Oriya	Runic	Cypriot Syllabary	Musical Symbols
Tamil	Tagalog	Tai Xuan Jing Symbols	Arrows
Telugu	Hanunoo	Yijing Hexagram Symbols	Box Drawing
Kannada	Buhid	Aegean Numbers	Geometric Shapes

FIGURE 2.22   Example alphabets in Unicode. Unicode version 4.0 has more than 160 "blocks," which is their name for a collection of symbols. Each block is a multiple of 16. For example, Greek starts at 0370_{hex}, and Cyrillic at 0400_{hex}. The first three columns show 48 blocks that correspond to human languages in roughly Unicode numerical order. The last column has 16 blocks that are multilingual and are not in order. A 16-bit encoding, called UTF-16, is the default. A variable-length encoding, called UTF-8, keeps the ASCII subset as 8 bits and uses 16–32 bits for the other characters. UTF-32 uses 32 bits per character. To learn more, see *www.unicode.org*.

The MIPS instruction set has explicit instructions to load and store such 16-bit quantities, called *halfwords*. Load half (lh) loads a halfword from memory, placing it in the rightmost 16 bits of a register. Store half (sh) takes a halfword from the rightmost 16 bits of a register and writes it to memory. We copy a halfword with the sequence

```
lh $t0,0($sp)   # Read halfword (16 bits) from source
sh $t0,0($gp)   # Write halfword (16 bits) to destination
```

Strings are a standard Java class with special built-in support and predefined methods for concatenation, comparison, and conversion. Unlike C, Java includes a word that gives the length of the string, similar to Java arrays.

Elaboration: MIPS software tries to keep the stack aligned to word addresses, allowing the program to always use lw and sw (which must be aligned) to access the stack. This convention means that a char variable allocated on the stack occupies 4 bytes, even though it needs less. However, a C string variable or an array of bytes *will* pack 4 bytes per word, and a Java string variable or array of shorts packs 2 halfwords per word.

Which of the following statements about characters and strings in C and Java are true?

1. A string in C takes about half the memory as the same string in Java.

2. Strings are just an informal name for single-dimension arrays of characters in C and Java.

3. Strings in C and Java use null (0) to mark the end of a string.

4. Operations on strings, like length, are faster in C than in Java.

2.9   MIPS Addressing for 32-Bit Immediates and Addresses

Although keeping all MIPS instructions 32 bits long simplifies the hardware, there are times where it would be convenient to have a 32-bit constant or 32-bit address. This section starts with the general solution for large constants, and then shows the optimizations for instruction addresses used in branches and jumps.

32-Bit Immediate Operands

Although constants are frequently short and fit into the 16-bit field, sometimes they are bigger. The MIPS instruction set includes the instruction *load upper immediate* (lui) specifically to set the upper 16 bits of a constant in a register, allowing a subsequent instruction to specify the lower 16 bits of the constant. Figure 2.23 shows the operation of lui.

The machine language version of lui $t0, 255   # $t0 is register 8:

001111	00000	01000	0000 0000 1111 1111

Contents of register $t0 after executing lui $t0, 255:

0000 0000 1111 1111	0000 0000 0000 0000

FIGURE 2.23   The effect of the lui **instruction.** The instruction lui transfers the 16-bit immediate constant field value into the leftmost 16 bits of the register, filling the lower 16 bits with 0s.

Hardware/ Software Interface

Either the compiler or the assembler must break large constants into pieces and then reassemble them into a register. As you might expect, the immediate field's size restriction may be a problem for memory addresses in loads and stores as well as for constants in immediate instructions. If this job falls to the assembler, as it does for MIPS software, then the assembler must have a temporary register available in which to create the long values. This is a reason for the register $at, which is reserved for the assembler.

Hence, the symbolic representation of the MIPS machine language is no longer limited by the hardware, but to whatever the creator of an assembler chooses to include (see Section 2.10). We stick close to the hardware to explain the architecture of the computer, noting when we use the enhanced language of the assembler that is not found in the processor.

Loading a 32-Bit Constant

EXAMPLE

What is the MIPS assembly code to load this 32-bit constant into register $s0?

```
0000 0000 0011 1101 0000 1001 0000 0000
```

ANSWER

First, we would load the upper 16 bits, which is 61 in decimal, using lui:

```
lui $s0, 61    # 61 decimal = 0000 0000 0011 1101 binary
```

The value of register $s0 afterward is

```
0000 0000 0011 1101 0000 0000 0000 0000
```

The next step is to add the lower 16 bits, whose decimal value is 2304:

```
ori $s0, $s0, 2304 # 2304 decimal = 0000 1001 0000 0000
```

The final value in register $s0 is the desired value:

```
0000 0000 0011 1101 0000 1001 0000 0000
```

Elaboration: Creating 32-bit constants needs care. The instruction addi copies the leftmost bit of the 16-bit immediate field of the instruction into the upper 16 bits of a word. *Logical or immediate* from Section 2.5 loads 0s into the upper 16 bits and hence is used by the assembler in conjunction with lui to create 32-bit constants.

Addressing in Branches and Jumps

The MIPS jump instructions have the simplest addressing. They use the final MIPS instruction format, called the *J-type*, which consists of 6 bits for the operation field and the rest of the bits for the address field. Thus,

```
j    10000    # go to location 10000
```

could be assembled into this format (it's actually a bit more complicated, as we will see on the next page):

2	10000
6 bits	26 bits

where the value of the jump opcode is 2 and the jump address is `10000`.

Unlike the jump instruction, the conditional branch instruction must specify two operands in addition to the branch address. Thus,

```
bne  $s0,$s1,Exit    # go to Exit if $s0 ≠ $s1
```

is assembled into this instruction, leaving only 16 bits for the branch address:

5	16	17	Exit
6 bits	5 bits	5 bits	16 bits

If addresses of the program had to fit in this 16-bit field, it would mean that no program could be bigger than 2^{16}, which is far too small to be a realistic option today. An alternative would be to specify a register that would always be added to the branch address, so that a branch instruction would calculate the following:

$$\text{Program counter} = \text{Register} + \text{Branch address}$$

This sum allows the program to be as large as 2^{32} and still be able to use conditional branches, solving the branch address size problem. The question is then, which register?

The answer comes from seeing how conditional branches are used. Conditional branches are found in loops and in *if* statements, so they tend to branch to a nearby instruction. For example, about half of all conditional branches in SPEC2000 benchmarks go to locations less than 16 instructions away. Since the program counter (PC) contains the address of the current instruction, we can

PC-relative addressing An addressing regime in which the address is the sum of the program counter (PC) and a constant in the instruction.

branch within $\pm 2^{15}$ words of the current instruction if we use the PC as the register to be added to the address. Almost all loops and *if* statements are much smaller than 2^{16} words, so the PC is the ideal choice.

This form of branch addressing is called **PC-relative addressing**. As we shall see in Chapter 5, it is convenient for the hardware to increment the PC early to point to the next instruction. Hence, the MIPS address is actually relative to the address of the following instruction (PC + 4) as opposed to the current instruction (PC).

Like most recent computers, MIPS uses PC-relative addressing for all conditional branches because the destination of these instructions is likely to be close to the branch. On the other hand, jump-and-link instructions invoke procedures that have no reason to be near the call, and so they normally use other forms of addressing. Hence, the MIPS architecture offers long addresses for procedure calls by using the J-type format for both jump and jump-and-link instructions.

Since all MIPS instructions are 4 bytes long, MIPS stretches the distance of the branch by having PC-relative addressing refer to the number of *words* to the next instruction instead of the number of bytes. Thus, the 16-bit field can branch four times as far by interpreting the field as a relative word address rather than as a relative byte address. Similarly, the 26-bit field in jump instructions is also a word address, meaning that it represents a 28-bit byte address.

Elaboration: Since the PC is 32 bits, 4 bits must come from somewhere else. The MIPS jump instruction replaces only the lower 28 bits of the PC, leaving the upper 4 bits of the PC unchanged. The loader and linker (Section 2.9) must be careful to avoid placing a program across an address boundary of 256 MB (64 million instructions); otherwise a jump must be replaced by a jump register instruction preceded by other instructions to load the full 32-bit address into a register.

Showing Branch Offset in Machine Language

EXAMPLE

The *while* loop on page 74 was compiled into this MIPS assembler code:

```
Loop:sll    $t1,$s3,2    # Temp reg $t1 = 4 * i
     add $t1,$t1,$s6     # $t1 = address of save[i]
     lw  $t0,0($t1)      # Temp reg $t0 = save[i]
     bne $t0,$s5, Exit   # go to Exit if save[i] ≠ k
     addi $s3,$s3,1      # i = i + 1
     j   Loop            # go to Loop
Exit:
```

If we assume we place the loop starting at location 80000 in memory, what is the MIPS machine code for this loop?

The assembled instructions and their addresses would look like this:

80000	0	0	19	9	2	0
80004	0	9	22	9	0	32
80008	35	9	8		0	
80012	5	8	21		2	
80016	8	19	19		1	
80020	2			20000		
80024	. . .					

Remember that MIPS instructions have byte addresses, so addresses of sequential words differ by 4, the number of bytes in a word. The bne instruction on the fourth line adds 2 words or 8 bytes to the address of the *following* instruction (80016), specifying the branch destination relative to that following instruction (8 + 80016) instead of relative to the branch instruction (12 + 80012) or using the full destination address (80024). The jump instruction on the last line does use the full address (20000 × 4 = 80000), corresponding to the label Loop.

Nearly every conditional branch is to a nearby location, but occasionally it branches far away, farther than can be represented in the 16 bits of the conditional branch instruction. The assembler comes to the rescue just as it did with large addresses or constants: it inserts an unconditional jump to the branch target, and inverts the condition so that the branch decides whether to skip the jump.

Hardware/ Software Interface

Branching Far Away

Given a branch on register $s0 being equal to register $s1,

        beq $s0,$s1, L1

replace it by a pair of instructions that offers a much greater branching distance.

ANSWER

These instructions replace the short-address conditional branch:

```
        bne     $s0,$s1, L2
        j       L1
  L2:
```

MIPS Addressing Mode Summary

addressing mode One of several addressing regimes delimited by their varied use of operands and/or addresses.

Multiple forms of addressing are generically called **addressing modes**. The MIPS addressing modes are the following:

1. *Register addressing,* where the operand is a register

2. *Base* or *displacement addressing,* where the operand is at the memory location whose address is the sum of a register and a constant in the instruction

3. *Immediate addressing,* where the operand is a constant within the instruction itself

4. *PC-relative addressing,* where the address is the sum of the PC and a constant in the instruction

5. *Pseudodirect addressing,* where the jump address is the 26 bits of the instruction concatenated with the upper bits of the PC

Hardware/ Software Interface

Although we show the MIPS architecture as having 32-bit addresses, nearly all microprocessors (including MIPS) have 64-bit address extensions (see ◉ **Appendix D**). These extensions were in response to the needs of software for larger programs. The process of instruction set extension allows architectures to expand in a way that lets software move compatibly upward to the next generation of architecture.

Note that a single operation can use more than one addressing mode. Add, for example, uses both immediate (addi) and register (add) addressing. Figure 2.24 shows how operands are identified for each addressing mode. ◉ **In More Depth** shows other addressing modes found in the IBM PowerPC.

Decoding Machine Language

Sometimes you are forced to reverse-engineer machine language to create the original assembly language. One example is when looking at a core dump. Figure 2.25 shows the MIPS encoding of the fields for the MIPS machine language. This figure helps when translating by hand between assembly language and machine language.

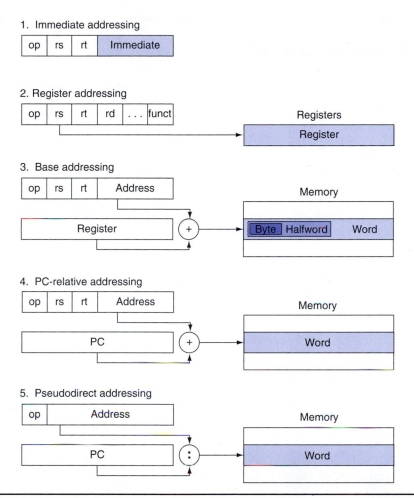

FIGURE 2.24 Illustration of the five MIPS addressing modes. The operands are shaded in color. The operand of mode 3 is in memory, whereas the operand for mode 2 is a register. Note that versions of load and store access bytes, halfwords, or words. For mode 1, the operand is 16 bits of the instruction itself. Modes 4 and 5 address instructions in memory, with mode 4 adding a 16-bit address shifted left 2 bits to the PC and mode 5 concatenating a 26-bit address shifted left 2 bits with the 4 upper bits of the PC.

EXAMPLE

Decoding Machine Code

What is the assembly language statement corresponding to this machine instruction?

    00af8020hex

ANSWER

The first step in converting hexadecimal to binary is to find the op fields:

(Bits: 31   28   26   5   2   0)
      0000 0000 1010 1111 1000 0000 0010 0000

We look at the op field to determine the operation. Referring to Figure 2.25, when bits 31–29 are 000 and bits 28–26 are 000, it is an R-format instruction. Let's reformat the binary instruction into R-format fields, listed in Figure 2.26:

op	rs	rt	rd	shamt	funct
000000	00101	01111	10000	00000	100000

The bottom portion of Figure 2.25 determines the operation of an R-format instruction. In this case, bits 5–3 are 100 and bits 2–0 are 000, which means this binary pattern represents an add instruction.

We decode the rest of the instruction by looking at the field values. The decimal values are 5 for the rs field, 15 for rt, and 16 for rd (shamt is unused). Figure 2.18 says these numbers represent registers $a1, $t7, and $s0. Now we can show the assembly instruction:

    add $s0,$a1,$t7

Figure 2.26 shows all the MIPS instruction formats. Figure 2.27 shows the MIPS assembly language revealed in this chapter; the remaining hidden portion of MIPS instructions deals mainly with arithmetic covered in the next chapter.

op(31:26)								
28–26 31–29	0(000)	1(001)	2(010)	3(011)	4(100)	5(101)	6(110)	7(111)
0(000)	R-format	Bltz/gez	jump	jump & link	branch eq	branch ne	blez	bgtz
1(001)	add immediate	addiu	set less than imm.	sltiu	andi	ori	xori	load upper imm
2(010)	TLB	FlPt						
3(011)								
4(100)	load byte	load half	lwl	load word	lbu	lhu	lwr	
5(101)	store byte	store half	swl	store word			swr	
6(110)	lwc0	lwc1						
7(111)	swc0	swc1						

op(31:26)=010000 (TLB), rs(25:21)								
23–21 25–24	0(000)	1(001)	2(010)	3(011)	4(100)	5(101)	6(110)	7(111)
0(00)	mfc0		cfc0		mtc0		ctc0	
1(01)								
2(10)								
3(11)								

op(31:26)=000000 (R-format), funct(5:0)								
2–0 5–3	0(000)	1(001)	2(010)	3(011)	4(100)	5(101)	6(110)	7(111)
0(000)	shift left logical		shift right logical	sra	sllv		srlv	srav
1(001)	jump reg.	jalr			syscall	break		
2(010)	mfhi	mthi	mflo	mtlo				
3(011)	mult	multu	div	divu				
4(100)	add	addu	subtract	subu	and	or	xor	not or (nor)
5(101)			set l.t.	sltu				
6(110)								
7(111)								

FIGURE 2.25 MIPS instruction encoding. This notation gives the value of a field by row and by column. For example, the top portion of the figure shows load word in row number 4 (100_{two} for bits 31–29 of the instruction) and column number 3 (011_{two} for bits 28–26 of the instruction), so the corresponding value of the op field (bits 31–26) is 100011_{two}. Underscore means the field is used elsewhere. For example, R-format in row 0 and column 0 (op = 000000_{two}) is defined in the bottom part of the figure. Hence, subtract in row 4 and column 2 of the bottom section means that the funct field (bits 5–0) of the instruction is 100010_{two} and the op field (bits 31–26) is 000000_{two}. The FlPt value in row 2, column 1 is defined in Figure 3.20 in Chapter 3. Bltz/gez is the opcode for four instructions found in Appendix A: bltz, bgez, bltzal, and bgezal. This chapter describes instructions given in full name using color, while Chapter 3 describes instructions given in mnemonics using color. Appendix A covers all instructions.

Name	Fields						Comments
Field size	6 bits	5 bits	5 bits	5 bits	5 bits	6 bits	All MIPS instructions 32 bits
R-format	op	rs	rt	rd	shamt	funct	Arithmetic instruction format
I-format	op	rs	rt	address/immediate			Transfer, branch, imm. format
J-format	op	target address					Jump instruction format

FIGURE 2.26   MIPS instruction formats in this chapter. Highlighted portions show instruction formats introduced in this section.

Check Yourself

What is the range of addresses for conditional branches in MIPS (K = 1024)?

1. Addresses between 0 and 64K − 1
2. Addresses between 0 and 256K − 1
3. Addresses up to about 32K before the branch to about 32K after
4. Addresses up to about 128K before the branch to about 128K after

What is the range of addresses for jump and jump and link in MIPS (M = 1024K)?

1. Addresses between 0 and 64M − 1
2. Addresses between 0 and 256M − 1
3. Addresses up to about 32M before the branch to about 32M after
4. Addresses up to about 128M before the branch to about 128M after
5. Anywhere within a block of 64M addresses where the PC supplies the upper 6 bits
6. Anywhere within a block of 256M addresses where the PC supplies the upper 4 bits

What is the MIPS assembly language instruction corresponding to the machine instruction with the value 0000 0000$_{hex}$?

1. j
2. R-format
3. addi
4. sll
5. mfc0
6. Undefined opcode: there is no legal instruction that corresponds to 0.

MIPS operands

Name	Example	Comments
32 registers	$s0–$s7, $t0–$t9, $zero, $a0–$a3, $v0–$v1, $gp, $fp, $sp, $ra, $at	Fast locations for data. In MIPS, data must be in registers to perform arithmetic. MIPS register $zero always equals 0. Register $at is reserved for the assembler to handle large constants.
2^{30} memory words	Memory[0], Memory[4], . . . , Memory[4294967292]	Accessed only by data transfer instructions. MIPS uses byte addresses, so sequential word addresses differ by 4. Memory holds data structures, arrays, and spilled registers, such as those saved on procedure calls.

MIPS assembly language

Category	Instruction	Example	Meaning	Comments
Arithmetic	add	add $s1,$s2,$s3	$s1 = $s2 + $s3	Three register operands
	subtract	sub $s1,$s2,$s3	$s1 = $s2 – $s3	Three register operands
	add immediate	addi $s1,$s2,100	$s1 = $s2 + 100	Used to add constants
Data transfer	load word	lw $s1,100($s2)	$s1 = Memory[$s2 + 100]	Word from memory to register
	store word	sw $s1,100($s2)	Memory[$s2 + 100] = $s1	Word from register to memory
	load half	lh $s1,100($s2)	$s1 = Memory[$s2 + 100]	Halfword memory to register
	store half	sh $s1,100($s2)	Memory[$s2 + 100] = $s1	Halfword register to memory
	load byte	lb $s1,100($s2)	$s1 = Memory[$s2 + 100]	Byte from memory to register
	store byte	sb $s1,100($s2)	Memory[$s2 + 100] = $s1	Byte from register to memory
	load upper immed.	lui $s1,100	$s1 = 100 * 2^{16}	Loads constant in upper 16 bits
Logical	and	and $s1,$s2,$s3	$s1 = $s2 & $s3	Three reg. operands; bit-by-bit AND
	or	or $s1,$s2,$s3	$s1 = $s2	$s3	Three reg. operands; bit-by-bit OR
	nor	nor $s1,$s2,$s3	$s1 = ~ ($s2 |$s3)	Three reg. operands; bit-by-bit NOR
	and immediate	andi $s1,$s2,100	$s1 = $s2 & 100	Bit-by-bit AND reg with constant
	or immediate	ori $s1,$s2,100	$s1 = $s2	100	Bit-by-bit OR reg with constant
	shift left logical	sll $s1,$s2,10	$s1 = $s2 << 10	Shift left by constant
	shift right logical	srl $s1,$s2,10	$s1 = $s2 >> 10	Shift right by constant
Conditional branch	branch on equal	beq $s1,$s2,25	if ($s1 == $s2) go to PC + 4 + 100	Equal test; PC-relative branch
	branch on not equal	bne $s1,$s2,25	if ($s1 != $s2) go to PC + 4 + 100	Not equal test; PC-relative
	set on less than	slt $s1,$s2,$s3	if ($s2 < $s3) $s1 = 1; else $s1 = 0	Compare less than; for beq, bne
	set less than immediate	slti $s1,$s2,100	if ($s2 < 100) $s1 = 1; else $s1 = 0	Compare less than constant
Unconditional jump	jump	j 2500	go to 10000	Jump to target address
	jump register	jr $ra	go to $ra	For switch, procedure return
	jump and link	jal 2500	$ra = PC + 4; go to 10000	For procedure call

FIGURE 2.27 MIPS assembly language revealed in this chapter. Highlighted portions show instructions from Sections 2.8 and 2.9. This information is also found in column 1 of the MIPS Reference Data Card at the front of this book.

2.10   Translating and Starting a Program

This section describes the four steps in transforming a C program in a file on disk into a program running on a computer. Figure 2.28 shows the translation hierarchy. Some systems combine these steps to reduce translation time, but these are the logical four phases that programs go through. This section follows this translation hierarchy.

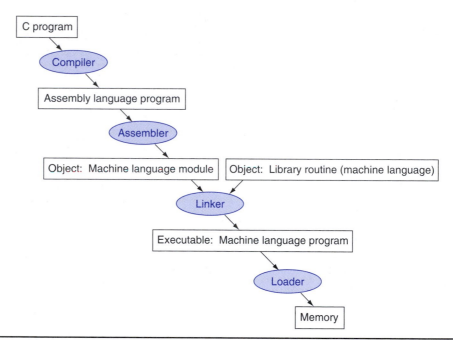

FIGURE 2.28   A translation hierarchy for C. A high-level language program is first compiled into an assembly language program and then assembled into an object module in machine language. The linker combines multiple modules with library routines to resolve all references. The loader then places the machine code into the proper memory locations for execution by the processor. To speed up the translation process, some steps are skipped or combined. Some compilers produce object modules directly, and some systems use linking loaders that perform the last two steps. To identify the type of file, Unix follows a suffix convention for files: C source files are named `x.c`, assembly files are `x.s`, object files are named `x.o`, statically linked library routines are `x.a`, dynamically linked library routes are `x.so`, and executable files by default are called `a.out`. MS-DOS uses the suffixes `.C`, `.ASM`, `.OBJ`, `.LIB`, `.DLL`, and `.EXE` to the same effect.

Compiler

The compiler transforms the C program into an *assembly language program*, a symbolic form of what the machine understands. High-level language programs take many fewer lines of code than assembly language, so programmer productivity is much higher.

In 1975, many operating systems and assemblers were written in **assembly language** because memories were small and compilers were inefficient. The 128,000-fold increase in memory capacity per single DRAM chip has reduced program size concerns, and optimizing compilers today can produce assembly language programs nearly as good as an assembly language expert, and sometimes even better for large programs.

assembly language A symbolic language that can be translated into binary.

Assembler

As mentioned on page 96, since assembly language is the interface to higher-level software, the assembler can also treat common variations of machine language instructions as if they were instructions in their own right. The hardware need not implement these instructions; however, their appearance in assembly language simplifies translation and programming. Such instructions are called **pseudoinstructions.**

As mentioned above, the MIPS hardware makes sure that register $zero always has the value 0. That is, whenever register $zero is used, it supplies a 0, and the programmer cannot change the value of register $zero. Register $zero is used to create the assembly language instruction move that copies the contents of one register to another. Thus the MIPS assembler accepts this instruction even though it is not found in the MIPS architecture:

pseudoinstruction A common variation of assembly language instructions often treated as if it were an instruction in its own right.

```
move $t0,$t1       # register $t0 gets register $t1
```

The assembler converts this assembly language instruction into the machine language equivalent of the following instruction:

```
add  $t0,$zero,$t1 # register $t0 gets 0 + register $t1
```

The MIPS assembler also converts blt (branch on less than) into the two instructions slt and bne mentioned in the example on page 96. Other examples include bgt, bge, and ble. It also converts branches to faraway locations into a branch and jump. As mentioned above, the MIPS assembler allows 32-bit constants to be loaded into a register despite the 16-bit limit of the immediate instructions.

In summary, pseudoinstructions give MIPS a richer set of assembly language instructions than those implemented by the hardware. The only cost is reserving one register, $at, for use by the assembler. If you are going to write assembly programs, use pseudoinstructions to simplify your task. To understand the MIPS

machine language Binary representation used for communication within a computer system.

symbol table A table that matches names of labels to the addresses of the memory words that instructions occupy.

architecture and to be sure to get best performance, however, study the real MIPS instructions found in Figures 2.25 and 2.27.

Assemblers will also accept numbers in a variety of bases. In addition to binary and decimal, they usually accept a base that is more succinct than binary yet converts easily to a bit pattern. MIPS assemblers use hexadecimal.

Such features are convenient, but the primary task of an assembler is assembly into machine code. The assembler turns the assembly language program into an *object file*, which is a combination of **machine language** instructions, data, and information needed to place instructions properly in memory.

To produce the binary version of each instruction in the assembly language program, the assembler must determine the addresses corresponding to all labels. Assemblers keep track of labels used in branches and data transfer instructions in a **symbol table**. As you might expect, the table contains pairs of symbols and addresses.

The object file for Unix systems typically contains six distinct pieces:

- The *object file header* describes the size and position of the other pieces of the object file.

- The *text segment* contains the machine language code.

- The *static data segment* contains data allocated for the life of the program. (Unix allows programs to use either *static data,* which is allocated throughout the program, or *dynamic data,* which can grow or shrink as needed by the program.)

- The *relocation information* identifies instructions and data words that depend on absolute addresses when the program is loaded into memory.

- The *symbol table* contains the remaining labels that are not defined, such as external references.

- The *debugging information* contains a concise description of how the modules were compiled so that a debugger can associate machine instructions with C source files and make data structures readable.

The next subsection shows how to attach such routines that have already been assembled, such as library routines.

Linker

What we have presented so far suggests that a single change to one line of one procedure requires compiling and assembling the whole program. Complete retranslation is a terrible waste of computing resources. This repetition is particularly wasteful for standard library routines because programmers would be compiling and assembling routines that by definition almost never change. An alternative is to compile and assemble each procedure independently, so that a change to one line would require compiling and assembling only one procedure. This alternative requires a new systems program, called a **link editor** or **linker**, which takes all the independently assembled machine language programs and "stitches" them together.

There are three steps for the linker:

1. Place code and data modules symbolically in memory.

2. Determine the addresses of data and instruction labels.

3. Patch both the internal and external references.

The linker uses the relocation information and symbol table in each object module to resolve all undefined labels. Such references occur in branch instructions, jump instructions, and data addresses, so the job of this program is much like that of an editor: it finds the old addresses and replaces them with the new addresses. Editing is the origin of the name "link editor," or linker for short. The reason a linker makes sense is that it is much faster to patch code than it is to recompile and reassemble.

If all external references are resolved, the linker next determines the memory locations each module will occupy. Recall that Figure 2.17 on page 87 shows the MIPS convention for allocation of program and data to memory. Since the files were assembled in isolation, the assembler could not know where a module's instructions and data would be placed relative to other modules. When the linker places a module in memory, all *absolute* references, that is, memory addresses that are not relative to a register, must be *relocated* to reflect its true location.

The linker produces an **executable file** that can be run on a computer. Typically, this file has the same format as an object file, except that it contains no unresolved references. It is possible to have partially linked files, such as library routines, which still have unresolved addresses and hence result in object files.

linker Also called **link editor**. A systems program that combines independently assembled machine language programs and resolves all undefined labels into an executable file.

executable file A functional program in the format of an object file that contains no unresolved references, relocation information, symbol tables, or debugging information.

Linking Object Files

Link the two object files below. Show updated addresses of the first few instructions of the completed executable file. We show the instructions in assembly language just to make the example understandable; in reality, the instructions would be numbers.

Note that in the object files we have highlighted the addresses and symbols that must be updated in the link process: the instructions that refer to the addresses of procedures A and B and the instructions that refer to the addresses of data words X and Y.

EXAMPLE

Object file header			
	Name	Procedure A	
	Text size	100_{hex}	
	Data size	20_{hex}	
Text segment	Address	Instruction	
	0	`lw $a0, 0($gp)`	
	4	`jal 0`	
	…	…	
Data segment	0	(X)	
	…	…	
Relocation information	Address	Instruction type	Dependency
	0	`lw`	X
	4	`jal`	B
Symbol table	Label	Address	
	X	—	
	B	—	
Object file header			
	Name	Procedure B	
	Text size	200_{hex}	
	Data size	30_{hex}	
Text segment	Address	Instruction	
	0	`sw $a1, 0($gp)`	
	4	`jal 0`	
	…	…	
Data segment	0	(Y)	
	…	…	
Relocation information	Address	Instruction type	Dependency
	0	`sw`	Y
	4	`jal`	A
Symbol table	Label	Address	
	Y	—	
	A	—	

ANSWER

Procedure A needs to find the address for the variable labeled X to put in the load instruction and to find the address of procedure B to place in the `jal` instruction. Procedure B needs the address of the variable labeled Y for the store instruction and the address of procedure A for its `jal` instruction.

From Figure 2.17 on page 87, we know that the text segment starts at address $40\ 0000_{hex}$ and the data segment at $1000\ 0000_{hex}$. The text of procedure A is placed at the first address and its data at the second. The object file header for procedure A says that its text is 100_{hex} bytes and its data is 20_{hex} bytes, so the starting address for procedure B text is $40\ 0100_{hex}$, and its data starts at $1000\ 0020_{hex}$.

Executable file header		
	Text size	300_{hex}
	Data size	50_{hex}
Text segment	Address	Instruction
	$0040\ 0000_{hex}$	lw $a0, 8000_{hex}($gp)
	$0040\ 0004_{hex}$	jal 40 0100_{hex}
	...	...
	$0040\ 0100_{hex}$	sw $a1, 8020_{hex}($gp)
	$0040\ 0104_{hex}$	jal 40 0000_{hex}
	...	...
Data segment	Address	
	$1000\ 0000_{hex}$	(X)
	...	...
	$1000\ 0020_{hex}$	(Y)
	...	...

From Figure 2.17 on page 87, we know that the text segment starts at address $40\ 0000_{hex}$ and the data segment at $1000\ 0000_{hex}$. The text of procedure A is placed at the first address and its data at the second. The object file header for procedure A says that its text is 100_{hex} bytes and its data is 20_{hex} bytes, so the starting address for procedure B text is $40\ 0100_{hex}$, and its data starts at $1000\ 0020_{hex}$.

Now the linker updates the address fields of the instructions. It uses the instruction type field to know the format of the address to be edited. We have two types here:

1. The jals are easy because they use pseudodirect addressing. The jal at address $40\ 0004_{hex}$ gets $40\ 0100_{hex}$ (the address of procedure B) in its address field, and the jal at $40\ 0104_{hex}$ gets $40\ 0000_{hex}$ (the address of procedure A) in its address field.

2. The load and store addresses are harder because they are relative to a base register. This example uses the global pointer as the base register. Figure 2.17 shows that $gp is initialized to $1000\ 8000_{hex}$. To get the address $1000\ 0000_{hex}$ (the address of word X), we place 8000_{hex} in the address field of lw at address $40\ 0000_{hex}$. Chapter 3 explains 16-bit two's complement computer arithmetic, which is why 8000_{hex} in the address field yields $1000\ 0000_{hex}$ as the address. Similarly, we place 8020_{hex} in the address field of sw at address $40\ 0100_{hex}$ to get the address $1000\ 0020_{hex}$ (the address of word Y).

Loader

Now that the executable file is on disk, the operating system reads it to memory and starts it. It follows these steps in Unix systems:

1. Reads the executable file header to determine size of the text and data segments.

2. Creates an address space large enough for the text and data.

3. Copies the instructions and data from the executable file into memory.

4. Copies the parameters (if any) to the main program onto the stack.

5. Initializes the machine registers and sets the stack pointer to the first free location.

6. Jumps to a start-up routine that copies the parameters into the argument registers and calls the main routine of the program. When the main routine returns, the start-up routine terminates the program with an `exit` system call.

loader A systems program that places an object program in main memory so that it is ready to execute.

Sections A.3 and A.4 in Appendix A describe linkers and **loaders** in more detail.

Dynamically Linked Libraries

The first part of this section describes the traditional approach to linking libraries before the program is run. Although this static approach is the fastest way to call library routines, it has a few disadvantages:

- The library routines become part of the executable code. If a new version of the library is released that fixes bugs or supports new hardware devices, the statically linked program keeps using the old version.

- It loads all routines in the library that are called anywhere in the executable, even if those calls are not executed. The library can be large relative to the program; for example, the standard C library is 2.5 MB.

These disadvantages lead to dynamically linked libraries (DLLs), where the library routines are not linked and loaded until the program is run. Both the program and library routines keep extra information on the location of nonlocal procedures and their names. In the initial version of DLLs, the loader ran a dynamic linker, using the extra information in the file to find the appropriate libraries and to update all external references.

The downside of the initial version of DLLs was that it still linked all routines of the library that might be called versus those that are called during the running of the program. This observation led to the lazy procedure linkage version of DLLs, where each routine is linked only *after* it is called.

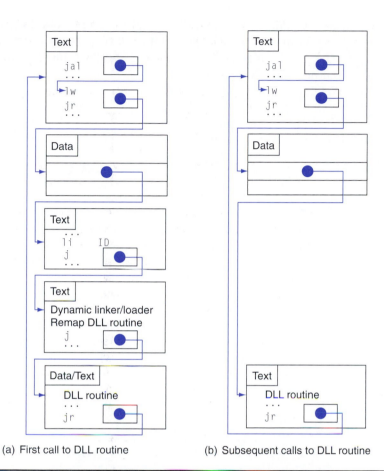

(a) First call to DLL routine   (b) Subsequent calls to DLL routine

FIGURE 2.29 Dynamically linked library via lazy procedure linkage. (a) Steps for the first time a call is made to the DLL routine. (b) The steps to find the routine, remap it, and link it are skipped on subsequent calls. As we will see in Chapter 7, the operating system may avoid copying the desired routine by remapping it using virtual memory management.

Like many instances in our field, this trick relies on a level of indirection. Figure 2.29 shows the technique. It starts with the nonlocal routines calling a set of dummy routines at the end of the program, with one entry per nonlocal routine. These dummy entries each contain an indirect jump.

The first time the library routine is called, the program calls the dummy entry and follows the indirect jump. It points to code that puts a number in a register to identify the desired library routine and then jumps to the dynamic linker/loader.

The linker/loader finds the desired routine, remaps it, and changes the address in the indirect jump location to point to that routine. It then jumps to it. When the routine completes, it returns to the original calling site. Thereafter, it jumps indirectly to the routine without the extra hops.

In summary, DLLs require extra space for the information needed for dynamic linking, but do not require that whole libraries be copied or linked. They pay a good deal of overhead the first time a routine is called, but only a single indirect jump thereafter. Note that the return from the library pays no extra overhead. Microsoft's Windows relies extensively on lazy dynamically linked libraries, and it is also the normal way of executing programs on Unix systems today.

Starting a Java Program

The discussion above captures the traditional model of executing a program, where the emphasis is on fast execution time for a program targeted to a specific instruction set architecture, or even a specific implementation of that architecture. Indeed, it is possible to execute Java programs just like C. Java was invented with a different set of goals, however. One was to quickly run safely on any computer, even if it might slow execution time.

Figure 2.30 shows the typical translation and execution steps for Java. Rather than compile to the assembly language of a target computer, Java is compiled first to instructions that are easy to interpret: the **Java bytecode** instruction set. This instruction set is designed to be close to the Java language so that this com-

Java bytecode Instruction from an instruction set designed to interpret Java programs.

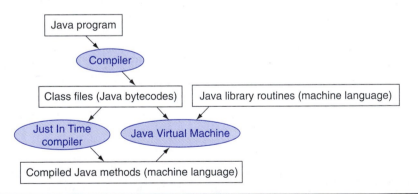

FIGURE 2.30   A translation hierarchy for Java. A Java program is first compiled into a binary version of Java bytecodes, with all addresses defined by the compiler. The Java program is now ready to run on the interpreter, called the Java Virtual Machine (JVM). The JVM links to desired methods in the Java library while the program is running. To achieve greater performance, the JVM can invoke the Just In Time (JIT) compiler, which selectively compiles methods into the native machine language of the machine on which it is running.

pilation step is trivial. Virtually no optimizations are performed. Like the C compiler, the Java compiler checks the types of data and produces the proper operation for each type. Java programs are distributed in the binary version of these bytecodes.

A software interpreter, called a **Java Virtual Machine** (JVM), can execute Java bytecodes. An interpreter is a program that simulates an instruction set architecture. For example, the MIPS simulator used with this book is an interpreter. There is no need for a separate assembly step since either the translation is so simple that the compiler fills in the addresses or JVM finds them at runtime.

Java Virtual Machine (JVM) The program that interprets Java bytecodes.

The upside of interpretation is portability. The availability of software Java virtual machines meant that most could write and run Java programs shortly after Java was announced. Today Java virtual machines are found in millions of devices, in everything from cell phones to Internet browsers.

The downside of interpretation is low performance. The incredible advances in performance of the 1980s and 1990s made interpretation viable for many important applications, but the factor of 10 slowdown when compared to traditionally compiled C programs made Java unattractive for some applications.

To preserve portability and improve execution speed, the next phase of Java development was compilers that translated *while* the program was running. Such **Just In Time compilers (JIT)** typically profile the running program to find where the "hot" methods are, and then compile them into the native instruction set on which the virtual machine is running. The compiled portion is saved for the next time the program is run, so that it can run faster each time it is run. This balance of interpretation and compilation evolves over time, so that frequently run Java programs suffer little of the overhead of interpretation.

Just In Time compiler (JIT) The name commonly given to a compiler that operates at runtime, translating the interpreted code segments into the native code of the computer.

As computers get faster so that compilers can do more, and as researchers invent betters ways to compile Java on the fly, the performance gap between Java and C or C++ is closing. Section 2.14 goes into much greater depth on the implementation of Java, Java bytecodes, JVM, and JIT compilers.

Which of the advantages of an interpreter over a translator do you think was most important for the designers of Java?

Check Yourself

1. Ease of writing an interpreter

2. Better error messages

3. Smaller object code

4. Machine independence

2.11   How Compilers Optimize

Because the compiler will significantly affect the performance of a computer, under-standing compiler technology today is critical to understanding performance. The purpose of this section is to give a brief overview of optimizations a compiler uses to achieve performance. The following section introduces the internal anatomy of a compiler. To start, Figure 2.31 shows the structure of recent compilers, and we describe the optimizations in the order of the passes of that structure.

High-Level Optimizations

High-level optimizations are transformations that are done at something close to the source level.

The most common high-level transformation is probably *procedure inlining*, which replaces a call to a function by the body of the function, substituting the caller's arguments for the procedure's parameters. Other high-level optimizations

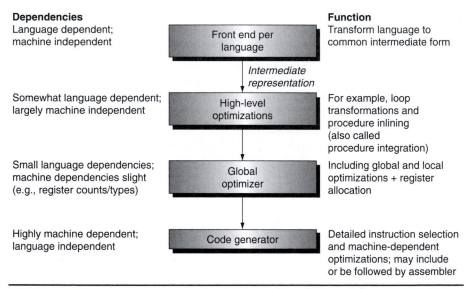

FIGURE 2.31 The structure of a modern optimizing compiler consists of a number of passes or phases. Logically, each pass can be thought of as running to completion before the next occurs. In practice, some passes may handle a procedure at a time, essentially interleaving with another pass.

involve loop transformations that can reduce loop overhead, improve memory access, and exploit the hardware more effectively. For example, in loops that execute many iterations, such as those traditionally controlled by a *for* statement, the optimization of **loop unrolling** is often useful. Loop unrolling involves taking a loop and replicating the body multiple times and executing the transformed loop fewer times. Loop unrolling reduces the loop overhead and provides opportunities for many other optimizations. Other types of high-level transformations include sophisticated loop transformations such as interchanging nested loops and blocking loops to obtain better memory behavior; see Chapter 7 for examples.

loop unrolling A technique to get more performance from loops that access arrays, in which multiple copies of the loop body are made and instructions from different iterations are scheduled together.

Local and Global Optimizations

Within the pass dedicated to local and global optimization, three classes of optimizations are performed:

1. *Local optimization* works within a single basic block. A local optimization pass is often run as a precursor and successor to global optimization to "clean up" the code before and after global optimization.

2. *Global optimization* works across multiple basic blocks; we will see an example of this shortly.

3. Global *register allocation* allocates variables to registers for regions of the code. Register allocation is crucial to getting good performance in modern processors.

Several optimizations are performed both locally and globally, including common subexpression elimination, constant propagation, copy propagation, dead store elimination, and strength reduction. Let's look at some simple examples of these optimizations.

Common subexpression elimination finds multiple instances of the same expression and replaces the second one by a reference to the first. Consider, for example, a code segment to add 4 to an array element:

```
x[i] = x[i] + 4
```

The address calculation for x[i] occurs twice and is identical since neither the starting address of x nor the value of i changes. Thus, the calculation can be reused. Let's look at the intermediate code for this fragment, since it allows several other optimizations to be performed. Here is the unoptimized intermediate code on the left, and on the right is the code with common subexpression elimination replacing the second address calculation with the first. Note that the register allocation has not yet occurred, so the compiler is using virtual register numbers like R100 here.

```
# x[i] + 4                      # x[i] + 4
li R100,x                       li R100,x
lw R101,i                       lw R101,i
mult R102,R101,4                mult R102,R101,4
add R103,R100,R102              add R103,R100,R102
lw R104,0(R103)                 lw R104,0(R103)
# value of x[i] is in R104      # value of x[i] is in R104
add R105,R104,4                 add R105,R104,4
# x[i] =                        # x[i] =
li R106,x                       sw R105,0(R103)
lw R107,i
mult R108,R107,4
add R109,R106,R107
sw R105,0(R109)
```

If the same optimization was possible across two basic blocks, it would then be an instance of *global common subexpression elimination.*

Let's consider some of the other optimizations:

- *Strength reduction* replaces complex operations by simpler ones and can be applied to this code segment, replacing the `mult` by a shift left.

- *Constant propagation* and its sibling *constant folding* find constants in code and propagate them, collapsing constant values whenever possible.

- *Copy propagation* propagates values that are simple copies, eliminating the need to reload values and possibly enabling other optimizations such as common subexpression elimination.

- *Dead store elimination* finds stores to values that are not used again and eliminates the store; its "cousin" is *dead code elimination*, which finds unused code—code that cannot affect the final result of the program—and eliminates it. With the heavy use of macros, templates, and the similar techniques designed to reuse code in high-level languages, dead code occurs surprisingly often.

Programmers concerned about performance of critical loops, especially in real-time or embedded applications, often find themselves staring at the assembly language produced by a compiler and wondering why the compiler failed to perform some global optimization or to allocate a variable to a register throughout a loop. The answer often lies in the dictate that the compiler be conservative. The opportunity for improving the code may seem obvious to the programmer, but then the programmer often has knowledge that the compiler does not have, such as the absence of aliasing between two pointers or the absence of side effects by a function call. The compiler may indeed be able to perform the transformation with a little help, which could eliminate the worst-case behavior that it must assume. This insight also illustrates an important observation: programmers who use pointers to try to improve performance in accessing variables, especially pointers to values on the stack that also have names as variables or as elements of arrays, are likely to disable many compiler optimizations. The end result is that the lower-level pointer code may run no better, or perhaps even worse, than the higher-level code optimized by the compiler.

Understanding Program Performance

Compilers must be *conservative*. The first task of a compiler is to produce correct code; its second task is usually to produce fast code although other factors such as code size may sometimes be important as well. Code that is fast but incorrect—for any possible combination of inputs—is simply wrong. Thus, when we say a compiler is "conservative," we mean that it performs an optimization only if it knows with 100% certainty that, no matter what the inputs, the code will perform as the user wrote it. Since most compilers translate and optimize one function or procedure at a time, most compilers, especially at lower optimization levels, assume the worst about function calls and about their own parameters.

Global Code Optimizations

Many global code optimizations have the same aims as those used in the local case, including common subexpression elimination, constant propagation, copy propagation, and dead store and dead code elimination.

There are two other important global optimizations: code motion and induction variable elimination. Both are loop optimizations; that is, they are aimed at code in loops. *Code motion* finds code that is loop invariant: a particular piece of code computes the same value on every loop iteration and, hence, may be computed once outside the loop. *Induction variable elimination* is a combination of transformations that reduce overhead on indexing arrays, essentially replacing array indexing with pointer accesses. Rather than examine induction variable elimination in depth, we point the reader to Section 2.15, which compares the use of array indexing and pointers; for most loops, the transformation from the more obvious array code to the pointer code can be performed by a modern optimizing compiler.

Optimization Summary

Figure 2.32 gives examples of typical optimizations, and the last column indicates where the optimization is performed in the gcc compiler. It is sometimes difficult to separate some of the simpler optimizations—local and processor-dependent optimizations—from transformations done in the code generator, and some optimizations are done multiple times, especially local optimizations, which may be performed before and after global optimization as well as during code generation.

Optimization name	Explanation	gcc level
High level	*At or near the source level; processor independent*	
Procedure integration	Replace procedure call by procedure body	O3
Local	*Within straight-line code*	
Common subexpression elimination	Replace two instances of the same computation by single copy	O1
Constant propagation	Replace all instances of a variable that is assigned a constant with the constant	O1
Stack height reduction	Rearrange expression tree to minimize resources needed for expression evaluation	O1
Global	*Across a branch*	
Global common subexpression elimination	Same as local, but this version crosses branches	O2
Copy propagation	Replace all instances of a variable A that has been assigned X (i.e., $A = X$) with X	O2
Code motion	Remove code from a loop that computes same value each iteration of the loop	O2
Induction variable elimination	Simplify/eliminate array addressing calculations within loops	O2
Processor dependent	*Depends on processor knowledge*	
Strength reduction	Many examples; replace multiply by a constant with shifts	O1
Pipeline scheduling	Reorder instructions to improve pipeline performance	O1
Branch offset optimization	Choose the shortest branch displacement that reaches target	O1

FIGURE 2.32   Major types of optimizations and explanation of each class. The third column shows when these occur at different levels of optimization in gcc. The Gnu organization calls the three optimization levels medium (O1), full (O2), and full with integration of small procedures (O3).

Today, essentially all programming for desktop and server applications is done in high-level languages, as is most programming for embedded applications. This development means that since most instructions executed are the output of a compiler, an instruction set architecture is essentially a compiler target. With Moore's law comes the temptation of adding sophisticated operations in an instruction set. The challenge is that they may not exactly match what the compiler needs to produce or be so general that they aren't fast. For example, consider special loop instructions found in some computers. Suppose that instead of decrementing by one, the compiler wanted to increment by four, or instead of branching on not equal zero, the compiler wanted to branch if the index was less than or equal to the limit. The loop instruction may be a mismatch. When faced with such objections, the instruction set designer might then generalize the operation, adding another operand to specify the increment and perhaps an option on which branch condition to use. Then the danger is that a common case, say, incrementing by one, will be slower than a sequence of simple operations.

How Compilers Work: An Introduction

The purpose of this section is to give a brief overview of the compiler function, which will help the reader understand how the compiler translates a high-level language program into machine instructions. Keep in mind that the subject of compiler construction is usually taught in a one- or two-semester course; our introduction will necessarily only touch on the basics. The rest of this section is on the CD.

2.13 A C Sort Example to Put It All Together

One danger of showing assembly language code in snippets is that you will have no idea what a full assembly language program looks like. In this section, we derive the MIPS code from two procedures written in C: one to swap array elements and one to sort them.

The Procedure `swap`

Let's start with the code for the procedure `swap` in Figure 2.33. This procedure simply swaps two locations in memory. When translating from C to assembly language by hand, we follow these general steps:

1. Allocate registers to program variables.

2. Produce code for the body of the procedure.

3. Preserve registers across the procedure invocation.

This section describes the `swap` procedure in these three pieces, concluding by putting all the pieces together.

Register Allocation for `swap`

As mentioned on page 79, the MIPS convention on parameter passing is to use registers $a0, $a1, $a2, and $a3. Since swap has just two parameters, v and k, they will be found in registers $a0 and $a1. The only other variable is temp, which we associate with register $t0 since `swap` is a leaf procedure (see page 83). This register allocation corresponds to the variable declarations in the first part of the `swap` procedure in Figure 2.33.

Code for the Body of the Procedure `swap`

The remaining lines of C code in `swap` are

```
temp = v[k];
v[k] = v[k+1];
v[k+1] = temp;
```

Recall that the memory address for MIPS refers to the *byte* address, and so words are really 4 bytes apart. Hence we need to multiply the index k by 4 before

```
void swap(int v[], int k)
{
 int temp;
 temp = v[k];
 v[k] = v[k+1];
 v[k+1] = temp;
}
```

FIGURE 2.33   A C procedure that swaps two locations in memory. This subsection uses this procedure in a sorting example.

adding it to the address. *Forgetting that sequential word addresses differ by 4 instead of by 1 is a common mistake in assembly language programming.* Hence the first step is to get the address of v[k] by multiplying k by 4:

```
sll    $t1, $a1,2      # reg $t1 = k * 4
add    $t1, $a0,$t1    # reg $t1 = v + (k * 4)
                       # reg $t1 has the address of v[k]
```

Now we load v[k] using $t1, and then v[k+1] by adding 4 to $t1:

```
lw     $t0, 0($t1)     # reg $t0 (temp) = v[k]
lw     $t2, 4($t1)     # reg $t2 = v[k + 1]
                       # refers to next element of v
```

Next we store $t0 and $t2 to the swapped addresses:

```
sw     $t2, 0($t1)     # v[k] = reg $t2
sw     $t0, 4($t1)     # v[k+1] = reg $t0 (temp)
```

Now we have allocated registers and written the code to perform the operations of the procedure. What is missing is the code for preserving the saved registers used within swap. Since we are not using saved registers in this leaf procedure, there is nothing to preserve.

The Full swap Procedure

We are now ready for the whole routine, which includes the procedure label and the return jump. To make it easier to follow, we identify in Figure 2.34 each block of code with its purpose in the procedure.

The Procedure sort

To ensure that you appreciate the rigor of programming in assembly language, we'll try a second, longer example. In this case, we'll build a routine that calls the swap procedure. This program sorts an array of integers, using bubble or exchange sort, which is one of the simplest if not the fastest sorts. Figure 2.35 shows the C version of the program. Once again, we present this procedure in several steps, concluding with the full procedure.

Register Allocation for sort

The two parameters of the procedure sort, v and n, are in the parameter registers $a0 and $a1, and we assign register $s0 to i and register $s1 to j.

Procedure body			
swap:	sll	$t1, $a1, 2	# reg $t1 = k * 4
	add	$t1, $a0, $t1	# reg $t1 = v + (k * 4)
			# reg $t1 has the address of v[k]
	lw	$t0, 0($t1)	# reg $t0 (temp) = v[k]
	lw	$t2, 4($t1)	# reg $t2 = v[k + 1]
			# refers to next element of v
	sw	$t2, 0($t1)	# v[k] = reg $t2
	sw	$t0, 4($t1)	# v[k+1] = reg $t0 (temp)

Procedure return		
jr	$ra	# return to calling routine

FIGURE 2.34   MIPS assembly code of the procedure swap **in Figure 2.33.**

```
void sort (int v[], int n)
{
    int i, j;
    for (i = 0; i < n; i += 1) {
        for (j = i - 1; j >= 0 && v[j] > v[j + 1]; j -= 1) {
            swap(v,j);
        }
    }
}
```

FIGURE 2.35   A C procedure that performs a sort on the array v.

Code for the Body of the Procedure sort

The procedure body consists of two nested *for* loops and a call to swap that includes parameters. Let's unwrap the code from the outside to the middle.

The first translation step is the first *for* loop:

```
for (i = 0; i < n; i += 1) {
```

Recall that the C *for* statement has three parts: initialization, loop test, and iteration increment. It takes just one instruction to initialize i to 0, the first part of the *for* statement:

```
move    $s0, $zero      # i = 0
```

(Remember that move is a pseudoinstruction provided by the assembler for the convenience of the assembly language programmer; see page 107.) It also takes just one instruction to increment i, the last part of the *for* statement:

```
addi    $s0, $s0, 1     # i += 1
```

The loop should be exited if i < n is *not* true or, said another way, should be exited if i ≥ n. The set on less than instruction sets register $t0 to 1 if $s0 < $a1 and 0 otherwise. Since we want to test if $s0 ≥ $a1, we branch if register $t0 is 0. This test takes two instructions:

```
for1tst:slt $t0, $s0, $a1    # reg $t0 = 0 if $s0 ≥ $a1 (i≥n)
         beq $t0, $zero,exit1 # go to exit1 if $s0≥$a1 (i≥n)
```

The bottom of the loop just jumps back to the loop test:

```
        j   for1tst          # jump to test of outer loop
  exit1:
```

The skeleton code of the first *for* loop is then

```
        move  $s0, $zero       # i = 0
for1tst:slt $t0, $s0, $a1    # reg $t0 = 0 if $s0 ≥ $a1 (i≥n)
        beq   $t0, $zero,exit1 # go to exit1 if $s0≥$a1 (i≥n)
        . . .
        (body of first for loop)
        . . .
        addi  $s0, $s0, 1      # i += 1
        j     for1tst          # jump to test of outer loop
  exit1:
```

Voila! Exercise 2.14 explores writing faster code for similar loops.

The second *for* loop looks like this in C:

```
for (j = i - 1; j >= 0 && v[j] > v[j + 1]; j -= 1) {
```

The initialization portion of this loop is again one instruction:

```
addi    $s1, $s0, -1 # j = i - 1
```

The decrement of j at the end of the loop is also one instruction:

```
addi    $s1, $s1, -1 # j -= 1
```

The loop test has two parts. We exit the loop if either condition fails, so the first test must exit the loop if it fails (j < 0):

```
for2tst:slti$t0, $s1, 0      # reg $t0 = 1 if $s1 < 0 (j < 0)
        bne $t0, $zero, exit2 # go to exit2 if $s1<0 (j < 0)
```

This branch will skip over the second condition test. If it doesn't skip, j ≥ 0.

The second test exits if v[j] > v[j + 1] is *not* true, or exits if v[j] ≤ v[j + 1]. First we create the address by multiplying j by 4 (since we need a byte address) and add it to the base address of v:

```
sll     $t1, $s1,2     # reg $t1 = j * 4
add     $t2, $a0,$t1   # reg $t2 = v + (j * 4)
```

Now we load v[j]:

```
lw      $t3, 0($t2)    # reg $t3    = v[j]
```

Since we know that the second element is just the following word, we add 4 to the address in register $t2 to get v[j + 1]:

```
lw      $t4, 4($t2)    # reg $t4    = v[j + 1]
```

The test of v[j] ≤ v[j + 1] is the same as v[j + 1] ≥ v[j], so the two instructions of the exit test are

```
slt     $t0, $t4, $t3      # reg $t0 = 0 if $t4 ≥ $t3
beq     $t0, $zero,exit2   # go to exit2 if $t4 ≥ $t3
```

The bottom of the loop jumps back to the inner loop test:

```
j       for2tst    # jump to test of inner loop
```

Combining the pieces, the skeleton of the second *for* loop looks like this:

```
        addi $s1, $s0, -1     # j = i - 1
for2tst:slti $t0, $s1, 0      # reg $t0 = 1 if $s1 < 0 (j<0)
        bne  $t0, $zero,exit2 # go to exit2 if $s1<0 (j<0)
        sll  $t1, $s1,2       # reg $t1 = j * 4
        add  $t2, $a0,$t1     # reg $t2 = v + (j * 4)
        lw   $t3, 0($t2)      # reg $t3    = v[j]
        lw   $t4, 4($t2)      # reg $t4    = v[j + 1]
        slt  $t0, $t4, $t3    # reg $t0 = 0 if $t4 ≥ $t3
        beq  $t0, $zero,exit2 # go to exit2 if $t4 ≥ $t3
        ...
        (body of second for loop)
        ...
        addi $s1, $s1, -1     # j -= 1
        j    for2tst          # jump to test of inner loop
exit2:
```

The Procedure Call in sort

The next step is the body of the second *for* loop:

```
swap(v,j);
```

Calling `swap` is easy enough:

```
jal     swap
```

Passing Parameters in `sort`

The problem comes when we want to pass parameters because the `sort` procedure needs the values in registers $a0 and $a1, yet the `swap` procedure needs to have its parameters placed in those same registers. One solution is to copy the parameters for `sort` into other registers earlier in the procedure, making registers $a0 and $a1 available for the call of `swap`. (This copy is faster than saving and restoring on the stack.) We first copy $a0 and $a1 into $s2 and $s3 during the procedure:

```
move    $s2, $a0     # copy parameter $a0 into $s2
move    $s3, $a1     # copy parameter $a1 into $s3
```

Then we pass the parameters to `swap` with these two instructions:

```
move    $a0, $s2     # first swap parameter is v
move    $a1, $s1     # second swap parameter is j
```

Preserving Registers in `sort`

The only remaining code is the saving and restoring of registers. Clearly, we must save the return address in register $ra, since `sort` is a procedure and is called itself. The `sort` procedure also uses the saved registers $s0, $s1, $s2, and $s3, so they must be saved. The prologue of the `sort` procedure is then

```
addi    $sp,$sp,-20    # make room on stack for 5 regs
sw      $ra,16($sp)    # save $ra on stack
sw      $s3,12($sp)    # save $s3 on stack
sw      $s2, 8($sp)    # save $s2 on stack
sw      $s1, 4($sp)    # save $s1 on stack
sw      $s0, 0($sp)    # save $s0 on stack
```

The tail of the procedure simply reverses all these instructions, then adds a `jr` to return.

The Full Procedure `sort`

Now we put all the pieces together in Figure 2.36, being careful to replace references to registers $a0 and $a1 in the *for* loops with references to registers $s2 and $s3. Once again to make the code easier to follow, we identify each block of code with its purpose in the procedure. In this example, 9 lines of the `sort` procedure in C became 35 lines in the MIPS assembly language.

Saving registers			
sort:	addi	$sp,$sp, -20	# make room on stack for 5 registers
	sw	$ra, 16($sp)	# save $ra on stack
	sw	$s3,12($sp)	# save $s3 on stack
	sw	$s2, 8($sp)	# save $s2 on stack
	sw	$s1, 4($sp)	# save $s1 on stack
	sw	$s0, 0($sp)	# save $s0 on stack

Procedure body			
Move parameters	move	$s2, $a0	# copy parameter $a0 into $s2 (save $a0)
	move	$s3, $a1	# copy parameter $a1 into $s3 (save $a1)
	move	$s0, $zero	# i = 0
Outer loop	for1tst:slt	$t0, $s0, $s3	# reg $t0 = 0 if $s0 ≥ $s3 (i ≥ n)
	beq	$t0, $zero, exit1	# go to exit1 if $s0 ≥ $s3 (i ≥ n)
	addi	$s1, $s0, -1	# j = i - 1
	for2tst:slti	$t0, $s1, 0	# reg $t0 = 1 if $s1 < 0 (j < 0)
	bne	$t0, $zero, exit2	# go to exit2 if $s1 < 0 (j < 0)
	sll	$t1, $s1, 2	# reg $t1 = j * 4
Inner loop	add	$t2, $s2, $t1	# reg $t2 = v + (j * 4)
	lw	$t3, 0($t2)	# reg $t3 = v[j]
	lw	$t4, 4($t2)	# reg $t4 = v[j + 1]
	slt	$t0, $t4, $t3	# reg $t0 = 0 if $t4 ≥ $t3
	beq	$t0, $zero, exit2	# go to exit2 if $t4 ≥ $t3
Pass parameters and call	move	$a0, $s2	# 1st parameter of swap is v (old $a0)
	move	$a1, $s1	# 2nd parameter of swap is j
	jal	swap	# swap code shown in Figure 2.34
Inner loop	addi	$s1, $s1, -1	# j -= 1
	j	for2tst	# jump to test of inner loop
Outer loop	exit2: addi	$s0, $s0, 1	# i += 1
	j	for1tst	# jump to test of outer loop

Restoring registers			
exit1:	lw	$s0, 0($sp)	# restore $s0 from stack
	lw	$s1, 4($sp)	# restore $s1 from stack
	lw	$s2, 8($sp)	# restore $s2 from stack
	lw	$s3,12($sp)	# restore $s3 from stack
	lw	$ra,16($sp)	# restore $ra from stack
	addi	$sp,$sp, 20	# restore stack pointer

Procedure return			
	jr	$ra	# return to calling routine

FIGURE 2.36   MIPS assembly version of procedure sort **in Figure 2.35 on page 124.**

Elaboration: One optimization that works with this example is *procedure inlining*, mentioned in Section 2.11. Instead of passing arguments in parameters and invoking the code with a jal instruction, the compiler would copy the code from the body of the swap procedure where the call to swap appears in the code. Inlining would avoid four instructions in this example. The downside of the inlining optimization is that the compiled code would be bigger if the inlined procedure is called from several locations. Such a code expansion might turn into *lower* performance if it increased the cache miss rate; see Chapter 7.

The MIPS compilers always save room on the stack for the arguments in case they need to be stored, so in reality they always decrement $sp by 16 to make room for all four argument registers (16 bytes). One reason is that C provides a `vararg` option that allows a pointer to pick, say, the third argument to a procedure. When the compiler encounters the rare `vararg`, it copies the four argument registers onto the stack into the four reserved locations.

Understanding Program Performance

Figure 2.37 shows the impact of compiler optimization on sort program performance, compile time, clock cycles, instruction count, and CPI. Note that unoptimized code has the best CPI and O1 optimization has the lowest instruction count, but O3 is the fastest, reminding us that time is the only accurate measure of program performance.

Figure 2.38 compares the impact of programming languages, compilation versus interpretation, and algorithms on performance of sorts. The fourth column shows that the unoptimized C program is 8.3 times faster than the interpreted Java code for Bubble Sort. Using the Just In Time Java compiler makes Java 2.1 times *faster* than the unoptimized C and within a factor of 1.13 of the highest optimized C code. (The next section gives more details on interpretation versus compilation of Java and the Java and MIPS code for Bubble Sort.) The ratios aren't as close for Quicksort in column 5, presumably because it is harder to amortize the cost of runtime compilation over the shorter execution time. The last column demonstrates the impact of a better algorithm, offering three orders of magnitude performance increase when sorting 100,000 items. Even comparing interpreted Java in column 5 to the C compiler at highest optimization in column 4, Quicksort beats Bubble Sort by a factor of 50 (0.05 × 2468 or 123 versus 2.41).

gcc optimization	Relative performance	Clock cycles (millions)	Instruction count (millions)	CPI
None	1.00	158,615	114,938	1.38
O1 (medium)	2.37	66,990	37,470	1.79
O2 (full)	2.38	66,521	39,993	1.66
O3 (procedure integration)	2.41	65,747	44,993	1.46

FIGURE 2.37 Comparing performance, instruction count, and CPI using compiler optimization for Bubble Sort. The programs sorted 100,000 words with the array initialized to random values. These programs were run on a Pentium 4 with a clock rate of 3.06 GHz and a 533 MHz system bus with 2 GB of PC2100 DDR SDRAM. It used Linux version 2.4.20.

Language	Execution method	Optimization	Bubble Sort relative performance	Quicksort relative performance	Speedup Quicksort vs. Bubble Sort
C	Compiler	None	1.00	1.00	2468
	Compiler	01	2.37	1.50	1562
	Compiler	02	2.38	1.50	1555
	Compiler	03	2.41	1.91	1955
Java	Interpreter	—	0.12	0.05	1050
	Just In Time compiler	—	2.13	0.29	338

FIGURE 2.38   Performance of two sort algorithms in C and Java using interpretation and optimizing compilers relative to unoptimized C version. The last column shows the advantage in performance of Quicksort over Bubble Sort for each language and execution option. These programs were run on the same system as Figure 2.37. The JVM is Sun version 1.3.1, and the JIT is Sun Hotspot version 1.3.1.

2.14   Implementing an Object-Oriented Language

object-oriented language A programming language that is oriented around objects rather than actions, or data versus logic.

This section is for readers interested in seeing how an **objected-oriented language** like Java executes on a MIPS architecture. It shows the Java bytecodes used for interpretation and the MIPS code for the Java version of some of the C segments in prior sections, including Bubble Sort. The rest of this section is on the CD.

2.15   Arrays versus Pointers

A challenging topic for any new programmer is understanding pointers. Comparing assembly code that uses arrays and array indices to the assembly code that uses pointers offers insights about pointers. This section shows C and MIPS assembly versions of two procedures to clear a sequence of words in memory: one using array indices and one using pointers. Figure 2.39 shows the two C procedures.

The purpose of this section is to show how pointers map into MIPS instructions, and not to endorse a dated programming style. We'll see the impact of modern compiler optimization on these two procedures at the end of the section.

Array Version of Clear

Let's start with the array version, clear1, focusing on the body of the loop and ignoring the procedure linkage code. We assume that the two parameters array and size are found in the registers $a0 and $a1, and that i is allocated to register $t0.

```
clear1(int array[], int size)
{
  int i;
  for (i = 0; i < size; i += 1)
      array[i] = 0;
}


clear2(int *array, int size)
{
  int *p;
  for (p = &array[0]; p < &array[size]; p = p + 1)
      *p = 0;
}
```

FIGURE 2.39   Two C procedures for setting an array to all zeros. Clear1 uses indices, while clear2 uses pointers. The second procedure needs some explanation for those unfamiliar with C. The address of a variable is indicated by &, and referring to the object pointed to by a pointer is indicated by *. The declarations declare that array and p are pointers to integers. The first part of the *for* loop in clear2 assigns the address of the first element of array to the pointer p. The second part of the *for* loop tests to see if the pointer is pointing beyond the last element of array. Incrementing a pointer by one, in the last part of the *for* loop, means moving the pointer to the next sequential object of its declared size. Since p is a pointer to integers, the compiler will generate MIPS instructions to increment p by four, the number of bytes in a MIPS integer. The assignment in the loop places 0 in the object pointed to by p.

The initialization of i, the first part of the *for* loop, is straightforward:

```
        move    $t0,$zero       # i = 0 (register $t0 = 0)
```

To set array[i] to 0 we must first get its address. Start by multiplying i by 4 to get the byte address:

```
loop1:  sll     $t1,$t0,2       # $t1 = i * 4
```

Since the starting address of the array is in a register, we must add it to the index to get the address of array[i] using an add instruction:

```
        add     $t2,$a0,$t1     # $t2 = address of array[i]
```

(This example is an ideal situation for indexed addressing; see ⊙ **In More Depth** in Section 2.20.) Finally, we can store 0 in that address:

```
        sw      $zero, 0($t2)   # array[i] = 0
```

This instruction is the end of the body of the loop, so the next step is to increment i:

```
        addi    $t0,$t0,1       # i = i + 1
```

The loop test checks if i is less than size:

```
slt    $t3,$t0,$a1      # $t3 = (i < size)
bne    $t3,$zero,loop1  # if (i < size) go to loop1
```

We have now seen all the pieces of the procedure. Here is the MIPS code for clearing an array using indices:

```
        move   $t0,$zero        # i = 0
loop1:  sll    $t1,$t0,2        # $t1 = i * 4
        add    $t2,$a0,$t1      # $t2 = address of array[i]
        sw     $zero, 0($t2)    # array[i] = 0
        addi   $t0,$t0,1        # i = i + 1
        slt    $t3,$t0,$a1      # $t3 = (i < size)
        bne    $t3,$zero,loop1  # if (i < size) go to loop1
```

(This code works as long as size is greater than 0; ANSI C requires a test of size before the loop, but we'll skip that legality here.)

Pointer Version of Clear

The second procedure that uses pointers allocates the two parameters array and size to the registers $a0 and $a1 and allocates p to register $t0. The code for the second procedure starts with assigning the pointer p to the address of the first element of the array:

```
        move   $t0,$a0          # p = address of array[0]
```

The next code is the body of the *for* loop, which simply stores 0 into p:

```
loop2:  sw     $zero,0($t0)     # Memory[p] = 0
```

This instruction implements the body of the loop, so the next code is the iteration increment, which changes p to point to the next word:

```
        addi   $t0,$t0,4        # p = p + 4
```

Incrementing a pointer by 1 means moving the pointer to the next sequential object in C. Since p is a pointer to integers, each of which use 4 bytes, the compiler increments p by 4.

The loop test is next. The first step is calculating the address of the last element of array. Start with multiplying size by 4 to get its byte address:

```
        sll    $t1,$a1,2        # $t1 = size * 4
```

and then we add the product to the starting address of the array to get the address of the first word *after* the array:

```
    add   $t2,$a0,$t1      # $t2 = address of array[size]
```

The loop test is simply to see if p is less than the last element of array:

```
    slt   $t3,$t0,$t2      # $t3 = (p<&array[size])
    bne   $t3,$zero,loop2  # if (p<&array[size]) go to loop2
```

With all the pieces completed, we can show a pointer version of the code to zero an array:

```
      move  $t0,$a0          # p = address of array[0]
loop2:sw$zero,0($t0)         # Memory[p] = 0
      addi  $t0,$t0,4        # p = p + 4
      sll   $t1,$a1,2        # $t1 = size * 4
      add   $t2,$a0,$t1      # $t2 = address of array[size]
      slt   $t3,$t0,$t2      # $t3 = (p<&array[size])
      bne   $t3,$zero,loop2  # if (p<&array[size]) go to loop2
```

As in the first example, this code assumes size is greater than 0.

Note that this program calculates the address of the end of the array in every iteration of the loop, even though it does not change. A faster version of the code moves this calculation outside the loop:

```
      move  $t0,$a0          # p = address of array[0]
      sll   $t1,$a1,2        # $t1 = size * 4
      add   $t2,$a0,$t1      # $t2 = address of array[size]
loop2:sw    $zero,0($t0)     # Memory[p] = 0
      addi  $t0,$t0,4        # p = p + 4
      slt   $t3,$t0,$t2      # $t3 = (p<&array[size])
      bne   $t3,$zero,loop2  # if (p<&array[size]) go to loop2
```

Comparing the Two Versions of Clear

Comparing the two code sequences side by side illustrates the difference between array indices and pointers (the changes introduced by the pointer version are highlighted):

```
      move $t0,$zero    # i = 0               move $t0,$a0          # p = & array[0]
loop1:sll  $t1,$t0,2    # $t1 = i * 4         sll  $t1,$a1,2        # $t1 = size * 4
      add  $t2,$a0,$t1  # $t2 = &array[i]     add  $t2,$a0,$t1      # $t2 = &array[size]
      sw   $zero, 0($t2)# array[i] = 0  loop2:sw    $zero,0($t0)    # Memory[p] = 0
      addi $t0,$t0,1    # i = i + 1           addi $t0,$t0,4        # p = p + 4
      slt  $t3,$t0,$a1  # $t3 = (i < size)    slt  $t3,$t0,$t2      # $t3=(p<&array[size])
      bne  $t3,$zero,loop1# if () go to loop1 bne  $t3,$zero,loop2# if () go to loop2
```

The version on the left must have the "multiply" and add inside the loop because i is incremented and each address must be recalculated from the new index; the memory pointer version on the right increments the pointer p directly. The pointer version reduces the instructions executed per iteration from 6 to 4. This manual optimization corresponds to the compiler optimization of strength reduction (shift instead of multiply) and induction variable elimination (eliminating array address calculations within loops).

Elaboration: The C compiler would add a test to be sure that size is greater than 0. One way would be to add a jump just before the first instruction of the loop to the slt instruction.

Understanding Program Performance

People used to be taught to use pointers in C to get greater efficiency than that available with arrays: "Use pointers, even if you can't understand the code." Modern optimizing compilers can produce code for the array version that is just as good. Most programmers today prefer that the compiler do the heavy lifting.

Beauty is altogether in the eye of the beholder.

Margaret Wolfe Hungerford, *Molly Bawn*, 1877

2.16 Real Stuff: IA-32 Instructions

Designers of instruction sets sometimes provide more powerful operations than those found in MIPS. The goal is generally to reduce the number of instructions executed by a program. The danger is that this reduction can occur at the cost of simplicity, increasing the time a program takes to execute because the instructions are slower. This slowness may be the result of a slower clock cycle time or of requiring more clock cycles than a simpler sequence (see Section 4.8).

The path toward operation complexity is thus fraught with peril. To avoid these problems, designers have moved toward simpler instructions. Section 2.17 demonstrates the pitfalls of complexity.

The Intel IA-32

MIPS was the vision of a single small group in 1985; the pieces of this architecture fit nicely together, and the whole architecture can be described succinctly. Such is not the case for the IA-32; it is the product of several independent groups who evolved the architecture over almost 20 years, adding new features to the original instruction set as someone might add clothing to a packed bag. Here are important IA-32 milestones.

- **1978**: The Intel 8086 architecture was announced as an assembly-language-compatible extension of the then-successful Intel 8080, an 8-bit microprocessor. The 8086 is a 16-bit architecture, with all internal registers 16 bits wide. Unlike MIPS, the registers have dedicated uses, and hence the 8086 is not considered a **general-purpose register** architecture.

- **1980**: The Intel 8087 floating-point coprocessor is announced. This architecture extends the 8086 with about 60 floating-point instructions. Instead of using registers, it relies on a stack (see Sections 2.19 and 3.9).

- **1982**: The 80286 extended the 8086 architecture by increasing the address space to 24 bits, by creating an elaborate memory-mapping and protection model (see Chapter 7), and by adding a few instructions to round out the instruction set and to manipulate the protection model.

- **1985**: The 80386 extended the 80286 architecture to 32 bits. In addition to a 32-bit architecture with 32-bit registers and a 32-bit address space, the 80386 added new addressing modes and additional operations. The added instructions make the 80386 nearly a general-purpose register machine. The 80386 also added paging support in addition to segmented addressing (see Chapter 7). Like the 80286, the 80386 has a mode to execute 8086 programs without change.

- **1989–95**: The subsequent 80486 in 1989, Pentium in 1992, and Pentium Pro in 1995 were aimed at higher performance, with only four instructions added to the user-visible instruction set: three to help with multiprocessing (Chapter 9) and a conditional move instruction.

- **1997**: After the Pentium and Pentium Pro were shipping, Intel announced that it would expand the Pentium and the Pentium Pro architectures with MMX (Multi Media Extensions). This new set of 57 instructions uses the floating-point stack to accelerate multimedia and communication applications. MMX instructions typically operate on multiple short data elements at a time, in the tradition of single instruction, multiple data (SIMD) architectures (see Chapter 9). Pentium II did not introduce any new instructions.

- **1999**: Intel added another 70 instructions, labeled SSE (Streaming SIMD Extensions) as part of Pentium III. The primary changes were to add eight separate registers, double their width to 128 bits, and add a single precision floating-point data type. Hence four 32-bit floating-point operations can be performed in parallel. To improve memory performance, SSE includes cache prefetch instructions plus streaming store instructions that bypass the caches and write directly to memory.

general-purpose register (GPR) A register that can be used for addresses or for data with virtually any instruction.

■ **2001**: Intel added yet another 144 instructions, this time labeled SSE2. The new data type is double precision arithmetic, which allows pairs of 64-bit floating-point operations in parallel. Almost all of these 144 instructions are versions of existing MMX and SSE instructions that operate on 64 bits of data in parallel. Not only does this change enable more multimedia operations, it gives the compiler a different target for floating-point operations than the unique stack architecture. Compilers can choose to use the eight SSE registers as floating-point registers like those found in other computers. This change has boosted floating-point performance on the Pentium 4, the first microprocessor to include SSE2 instructions.

■ **2003**: A company other than Intel enhanced the IA-32 architecture this time. AMD announced a set of architectural extensions to increase the address space from 32 to 64 bits. Similar to the transition from a 16- to 32-bit address space in 1985 with the 80386, AMD64 widens all registers to 64 bits. It also increases the number of registers to 16 and increases the number of 128-bit SSE registers to 16. The primary ISA change comes from adding a new mode called *long mode* that redefines the execution of all IA-32 instructions with 64-bit addresses and data. To address the larger number of registers, it adds a new prefix to instructions. Depending how you count, long mode also adds 4 to 10 new instructions and drops 27 old ones. PC-relative data addressing is another extension. AMD64 still has a mode that is identical to IA-32 (*legacy mode*) plus a mode that restricts user programs to IA-32 but allows operating systems to use AMD64 (*compatability mode*). These modes allow a more graceful transition to 64-bit addressing than the HP/Intel IA-64 architecture.

■ **2004**: Intel capitulates and embraces AMD64, relabeling it Extended Memory 64 Technology (EM64T). The major difference is that Intel added a 128-bit atomic compare and swap instruction, which probably should have been included in AMD64. At the same time, Intel announced another generation of media extensions. SSE3 adds 13 instructions to support complex arithmetic, graphics operations on arrays of structures, video encoding, floating-point conversion, and thread synchronization (see Chapter 9). AMD will offer SSE3 in subsequent chips and it will almost certainly add the missing atomic swap instruction to AMD64 to maintain binary compatibility with Intel.

This history illustrates the impact of the "golden handcuffs" of compatibility on the IA-32, as the existing software base at each step was too important to jeopardize with significant architectural changes.

Whatever the artistic failures of the IA-32, keep in mind that there are more instances of this architectural family on desktops than of any other architecture, increasing by 100 million per year. Nevertheless, this checkered ancestry has led to an architecture that is difficult to explain and impossible to love.

Brace yourself for what you are about to see! Do *not* try to read this section with the care you would need to write IA-32 programs; the goal instead is to give you familiarity with the strengths and weaknesses of the world's most popular desktop architecture.

Rather than show the entire 16-bit and 32-bit instruction set, in this section we concentrate on the 32-bit subset that originated with the 80386, as this portion of the architecture is what is used. We start our explanation with the registers and addressing modes, move on to the integer operations, and conclude with an examination of instruction encoding.

IA-32 Registers and Data Addressing Modes

The registers of the 80386 show the evolution of the instruction set (Figure 2.40). The 80386 extended all 16-bit registers (except the segment registers) to 32 bits,

FIGURE 2.40 The 80386 register set. Starting with the 80386, the top eight registers were extended to 32 bits and could also be used as general-purpose registers.

Source/destination operand type	Second source operand
Register	Register
Register	Immediate
Register	Memory
Memory	Register
Memory	Immediate

FIGURE 2.41   Instruction types for the arithmetic, logical, and data transfer instructions. The IA-32 allows the combinations shown. The only restriction is the absence of a memory-memory mode. Immediates may be 8, 16, or 32 bits in length; a register is any one of the 14 major registers in Figure 2.40 (not EIP or EFLAGS).

prefixing an *E* to their name to indicate the 32-bit version. We'll refer to them generically as GPRs (general-purpose registers). The 80386 contains only eight GPRs. This means MIPS programs can use four times as many.

The arithmetic, logical, and data transfer instructions are two-operand instructions that allow the combinations shown in Figure 2.41. There are two important differences here. The IA-32 arithmetic and logical instructions must have one operand act as both a source and a destination; MIPS allows separate registers for source and destination. This restriction puts more pressure on the limited registers, since one source register must be modified. The second important difference is that one of the operands can be in memory. Thus virtually any instruction may have one operand in memory, unlike MIPS and PowerPC.

The seven data memory-addressing modes, described in detail below, offer two sizes of addresses within the instruction. These so-called *displacements* can be 8 bits or 32 bits.

Although a memory operand can use any addressing mode, there are restrictions on which *registers* can be used in a mode. Figure 2.42 shows the IA-32 addressing modes and which GPRs cannot be used with that mode, plus how you would get the same effect using MIPS instructions.

IA-32 Integer Operations

The 8086 provides support for both 8-bit (*byte*) and 16-bit (*word*) data types. The 80386 adds 32-bit addresses and data (*double words)* in the IA-32. The data type distinctions apply to register operations as well as memory accesses. Almost every operation works on both 8-bit data and on one longer data size. That size is determined by the mode and is either 16 bits or 32 bits.

Clearly, some programs want to operate on data of all three sizes, so the 80386 architects provide a convenient way to specify each version without expanding code size significantly. They decided that either 16-bit or 32-bit data dominates

Mode	Description	Register restrictions	MIPS equivalent
Register indirect	Address is in a register.	Not ESP or EBP	`lw $s0,0($s1)`
Based mode with 8- or 32-bit displacement	Address is contents of base register plus displacement.	Not ESP	`lw $s0,100($s1) # ≤16-bit` `# displacement`

Base plus scaled index	The address is
	Base + (2^Scale x Index)
	where Scale has the value 0, 1, 2, or 3.
		Base: any GPR
		Index: not ESP
			`mul $t0,$s2,4`
			`add $t0,$t0,$s1`
			`lw $s0,0($t0)`

Base plus scaled index with 8- or 32-bit displacement	The address is
	Base + (2^Scale x Index) + displacement
	where Scale has the value 0, 1, 2, or 3.
		Base: any GPR
		Index: not ESP
			`mul $t0,$s2,4`
			`add $t0,$t0,$s1`
			`lw $s0,100($t0) # ≤16-bit`
			`# displacement`

FIGURE 2.42 IA-32 32-bit addressing modes with register restrictions and the equivalent MIPS code. The Base plus Scaled Index addressing mode, not found in MIPS or the PowerPC, is included to avoid the multiplies by 4 (scale factor of 2) to turn an index in a register into a byte address (see Figures 2.34 and 2.36). A scale factor of 1 is used for 16-bit data, and a scale factor of 3 for 64-bit data. A scale factor of 0 means the address is not scaled. If the displacement is longer than 16 bits in the second or fourth modes, then the MIPS equivalent mode would need two more instructions: a `lui` to load the upper 16 bits of the displacement and an `add` to sum the upper address with the base register $s1. (Intel gives two different names to what is called Based addressing mode—Based and Indexed—but they are essentially identical and we combine them here.)

most programs, and so it made sense to be able to set a default large size. This default data size is set by a bit in the code segment register. To override the default data size, an 8-bit *prefix* is attached to the instruction to tell the machine to use the other large size for this instruction.

The prefix solution was borrowed from the 8086, which allows multiple prefixes to modify instruction behavior. The three original prefixes override the default segment register, lock the bus to support a semaphore (see Chapter 9), or repeat the following instruction until the register ECX counts down to 0. This last prefix was intended to be paired with a byte move instruction to move a variable number of bytes. The 80386 also added a prefix to override the default address size.

The IA-32 integer operations can be divided into four major classes:

1. Data movement instructions, including move, push, and pop

2. Arithmetic and logic instructions, including test, integer, and decimal arithmetic operations

3. Control flow, including conditional branches, unconditional jumps, calls, and returns

4. String instructions, including string move and string compare

The first two categories are unremarkable, except that the arithmetic and logic instruction operations allow the destination to be either a register or a memory location. Figure 2.43 shows some typical IA-32 instructions and their functions.

Instruction	Function
`JE name`	`if equal(condition code) {EIP=name};` `EIP-128 ≤ name < EIP+128`
`JMP name`	`EIP=name`
`CALL name`	`SP=SP-4; M[SP]=EIP+5; EIP=name;`
`MOVW EBX,[EDI+45]`	`EBX=M[EDI+45]`
`PUSH ESI`	`SP=SP-4; M[SP]=ESI`
`POP EDI`	`EDI=M[SP]; SP=SP+4`
`ADD EAX,#6765`	`EAX= EAX+6765`
`TEST EDX,#42`	Set condition code (flags) with EDX and 42
`MOVSL`	`M[EDI]=M[ESI];` `EDI=EDI+4; ESI=ESI+4`

FIGURE 2.43   Some typical IA-32 instructions and their functions. A list of frequent operations appears in Figure 2.44. The `CALL` saves the EIP of the next instruction on the stack. (EIP is the Intel PC.)

Conditional branches on the IA-32 are based on *condition codes* or *flags*. Condition codes are set as a side effect of an operation; most are used to compare the value of a result to 0. Branches then test the condition codes. The argument for condition codes is that they occur as part of normal operations and are faster to test than the time it takes to compare registers, as MIPS does for `beq` and `bne`. The argument against condition codes is that the compare to 0 extends the time of the operation, since it uses extra hardware after the operation, and that often the programmer must use compare instructions to test a value that is not the result of an operation. Moreover, PC-relative branch addresses must be specified in the number of bytes, since unlike MIPS, 80386 instructions are not all 4 bytes in length.

String instructions are part of the 8080 ancestry of the IA-32 and are not commonly executed in most programs. They are often slower than equivalent software routines (see the fallacy on page 143).

Figure 2.44 lists some of the integer IA-32 instructions. Many of the instructions are available in both byte and word formats.

IA-32 Instruction Encoding

Saving the worst for last, the encoding of instructions in the 80386 is complex, with many different instruction formats. Instructions for the 80386 may vary from 1 byte, when there are no operands, up to 15 bytes.

Figure 2.45 shows the instruction format for several of the example instructions in Figure 2.43. The opcode byte usually contains a bit saying whether the operand is

Instruction	Meaning
Control	**Conditional and unconditional branches**
JNZ, JZ	Jump if condition to EIP + 8-bit offset; JNE (for JNZ), JE (for JZ) are alternative names
JMP	Unconditional jump—8-bit or 16-bit offset
CALL	Subroutine call—16-bit offset; return address pushed onto stack
RET	Pops return address from stack and jumps to it
LOOP	Loop branch—decrement ECX; jump to EIP + 8-bit displacement if ECX $\neq$ 0
Data transfer	**Move data between registers or between register and memory**
MOV	Move between two registers or between register and memory
PUSH, POP	Push source operand on stack; pop operand from stack top to a register
LES	Load ES and one of the GPRs from memory
Arithmetic, logical	**Arithmetic and logical operations using the data registers and memory**
ADD, SUB	Add source to destination; subtract source from destination; register-memory format
CMP	Compare source and destination; register-memory format
SHL, SHR, RCR	Shift left; shift logical right; rotate right with carry condition code as fill
CBW	Convert byte in 8 rightmost bits of EAX to 16-bit word in right of EAX
TEST	Logical AND of source and destination sets condition codes
INC, DEC	Increment destination, decrement destination
OR, XOR	Logical OR; exclusive OR; register-memory format
String	**Move between string operands; length given by a repeat prefix**
MOVS	Copies from string source to destination by incrementing ESI and EDI; may be repeated
LODS	Loads a byte, word, or doubleword of a string into the EAX register

FIGURE 2.44   Some typical operations on the IA-32. Many operations use register-memory format, where either the source or the destination may be memory and the other may be a register or immediate operand.

8 bits or 32 bits. For some instructions, the opcode may include the addressing mode and the register; this is true in many instructions that have the form "register = register op immediate." Other instructions use a "postbyte" or extra opcode byte, labeled "mod, reg, r/m," which contains the addressing mode information. This postbyte is used for many of the instructions that address memory. The base plus scaled index mode uses a second postbyte, labeled "sc, index, base."

Figure 2.46 shows the encoding of the two postbyte address specifiers for both 16-bit and 32-bit mode. Unfortunately, to fully understand which registers and which addressing modes are available, you need to see the encoding of all addressing modes and sometimes even the encoding of the instructions.

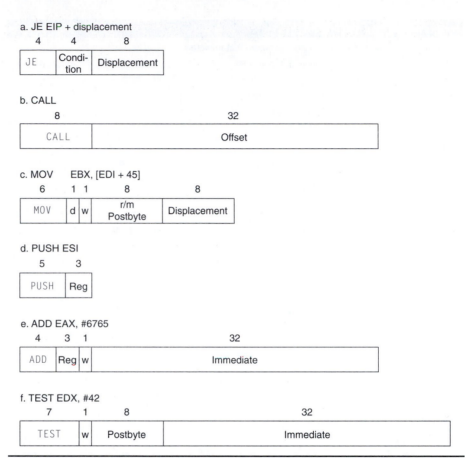

FIGURE 2.45 Typical IA-32 instruction formats. Figure 2.46 shows the encoding of the postbyte. Many instructions contain the 1-bit field w, which says whether the operation is a byte or a doubleword. The d field in MOV is used in instructions that may move to or from memory and shows the direction of the move. The ADD instruction requires 32 bits for the immediate field because in 32-bit mode the immediates are either 8 bits or 32 bits. The immediate field in the TEST is 32 bits long because there is no 8-bit immediate for test in 32-bit mode. Overall, instructions may vary from 1 to 17 bytes in length. The long length comes from extra 1-byte prefixes, having both a 4-byte immediate and a 4-byte displacement address, using an opcode of 2 bytes, and using the scaled index mode specifier, which adds another byte.

IA-32 Conclusion

Intel had a 16-bit microprocessor two years before its competitors' more elegant architectures, such as the Motorola 68000, and this head start led to the selection of the 8086 as the CPU for the IBM PC. Intel engineers generally acknowledge that the IA-32 is more difficult to build than machines like MIPS, but the much larger

reg	w = 0	w = 1		r/m	mod = 0		mod = 1		mod = 2		mod = 3
		16b	32b		16b	32b	16b	32b	16b	32b	
0	AL	AX	EAX	0	addr=BX+SI	=EAX	same	same	same	same	same
1	CL	CX	ECX	1	addr=BX+DI	=ECX	addr as	addr as	addr as	addr as	as
2	DL	DX	EDX	2	addr=BP+SI	=EDX	mod=0	mod=0	mod=0	mod=0	reg
3	BL	BX	EBX	3	addr=BP+SI	=EBX	+ disp8	+ disp8	+ disp16	+ disp32	field
4	AH	SP	ESP	4	addr=SI	=(sib)	SI+disp8	(sib)+disp8	SI+disp8	(sib)+disp32	"
5	CH	BP	EBP	5	addr=DI	=disp32	DI+disp8	EBP+disp8	DI+disp16	EBP+disp32	"
6	DH	SI	ESI	6	addr=disp16	=ESI	BP+disp8	ESI+disp8	BP+disp16	ESI+disp32	"
7	BH	DI	EDI	7	addr=BX	=EDI	BX+disp8	EDI+disp8	BX+disp16	EDI+disp32	"

FIGURE 2.46 The encoding of the first address specifier of the IA-32: mod, reg, r/m. The first four columns show the encoding of the 3-bit reg field, which depends on the w bit from the opcode and whether the machine is in 16-bit mode (8086) or 32-bit mode (80386). The remaining columns explain the mod and r/m fields. The meaning of the 3-bit r/m field depends on the value in the 2-bit mod field and the address size. Basically, the registers used in the address calculation are listed in the sixth and seventh columns, under mod = 0, with mod = 1 adding an 8-bit displacement and mod = 2 adding a 16-bit or 32-bit displacement, depending on the address mode. The exceptions are r/m = 6 when mod = 1 or mod = 2 in 16-bit mode selects BP plus the displacement; r/m = 5 when mod = 1 or mod = 2 in 32-bit mode selects EBP plus displacement; and r/m = 4 in 32-bit mode when mod ≠ 3, where (sib) means use the scaled index mode shown in Figure 2.42. When mod = 3, the r/m field indicates a register, using the same encoding as the reg field combined with the w bit.

market means Intel can afford more resources to help overcome the added complexity. What the IA-32 lacks in style is made up in quantity, making it beautiful from the right perspective.

The saving grace is that the most frequently used IA-32 architectural components are not too difficult to implement, as Intel has demonstrated by rapidly improving performance of integer programs since 1978. To get that performance, compilers must avoid the portions of the architecture that are hard to implement fast.

2.17 Fallacies and Pitfalls

Fallacy: More powerful instructions mean higher performance.

Part of the power of the Intel IA-32 is the prefixes that can modify the execution of the following instruction. One prefix can repeat the following instruction until a counter counts down to 0. Thus, to move data in memory, it would seem that the natural instruction sequence is to use move with the repeat prefix to perform 32-bit memory-to-memory moves.

An alternative method, which uses the standard instructions found in all computers, is to load the data into the registers and then store the registers back to memory. This second version of this program, with the code replicated to reduce loop overhead, copies at about 1.5 times faster. A third version, which uses the larger floating-point registers instead of the integer registers of the IA-32, copies at about 2.0 times faster than the complex instruction.

Fallacy: Write in assembly language to obtain the highest performance.

At one time compilers for programming languages produced naive instruction sequences; the increasing sophistication of compilers means the gap between compiled code and code produced by hand is closing fast. In fact, to compete with current compilers, the assembly language programmer needs to thoroughly understand the concepts in Chapters 6 and 7 (processor pipelining and memory hierarchy).

This battle between compilers and assembly language coders is one situation in which humans are losing ground. For example, C offers the programmer a chance to give a hint to the compiler about which variables to keep in registers versus spilled to memory. When compilers were poor at register allocation, such hints were vital to performance. In fact, some C textbooks spent a fair amount of time giving examples that effectively use register hints. Today's C compilers generally ignore such hints because the compiler does a better job at allocation than the programmer.

Even *if* writing by hand resulted in faster code, the dangers of writing in assembly language are longer time spent coding and debugging, the loss in portability, and the difficulty of maintaining such code. One of the few widely accepted axioms of software engineering is that coding takes longer if you write more lines, and it clearly takes many more lines to write a program in assembly language than in C. Moreover, once it is coded, the next danger is that it will become a popular program. Such programs always live longer than expected, meaning that someone will have to update the code over several years and make it work with new releases of operating systems and new models of machines. Writing in higher-level language instead of assembly language not only allows future compilers to tailor the code to future machines, it also makes the software easier to maintain and allows the program to run on more brands of computers.

Pitfall: Forgetting that sequential word addresses in machines with byte addressing do not differ by one.

Many an assembly language programmer has toiled over errors made by assuming that the address of the next word can be found by incrementing the address in a register by one instead of by the word size in bytes. Forewarned is forearmed!

Pitfall: Using a pointer to an automatic variable outside its defining procedure.

A common mistake in dealing with pointers is to pass a result from a procedure that includes a pointer to an array that is local to that procedure. Following the stack discipline in Figure 2.16, the memory that contains the local array will be reused as soon as the procedure returns. Pointers to automatic variables can lead to chaos.

Less is more.

Robert Browning, *Andrea del Sarto*, 1855

2.18 Concluding Remarks

The two principles of the *stored-program* computer are the use of instructions that are indistinguishable from numbers and the use of alterable memory for programs. These principles allow a single machine to aid environmental scientists, financial advisers, and novelists in their specialties. The selection of a set of instructions that the machine can understand demands a delicate balance among the number of instructions needed to execute a program, the number of clock cycles needed by an instruction, and the speed of the clock. Four design principles guide the authors of instruction sets in making that delicate balance:

1. *Simplicity favors regularity.* Regularity motivates many features of the MIPS instruction set: keeping all instructions a single size, always requiring three register operands in arithmetic instructions, and keeping the register fields in the same place in each instruction format.

2. *Smaller is faster.* The desire for speed is the reason that MIPS has 32 registers rather than many more.

3. *Make the common case fast.* Examples of making the common MIPS case fast include PC-relative addressing for conditional branches and immediate addressing for constant operands.

4. *Good design demands good compromises.* One MIPS example was the compromise between providing for larger addresses and constants in instructions and keeping all instructions the same length.

Above this machine level is assembly language, a language that humans can read. The assembler translates it into the binary numbers that machines can understand, and it even "extends" the instruction set by creating symbolic instructions that aren't in the hardware. For instance, constants or addresses that are too big are broken into properly sized pieces, common variations of instructions are given their own name, and so on. Figure 2.47 lists the MIPS instructions we have covered so far, both real and pseudoinstructions.

These instructions are not born equal; the popularity of the few dominates the many. For example, Figure 2.48 shows the popularity of each class of instructions for SPEC2000. The varying popularity of instructions plays an important role in the chapters on performance, datapath, control, and pipelining.

Each category of MIPS instructions is associated with constructs that appear in programming languages:

MIPS instructions	Name	Format	Pseudo MIPS	Name	Format
add	add	R	move	move	R
subtract	sub	R	multiply	mult	R
add immediate	addi	I	multiply immediate	multi	I
load word	lw	I	load immediate	li	I
store word	sw	I	branch less than	blt	I
load half	lh	I	branch less than or equal	ble	I
store half	sh	I	branch greater than	bgt	I
load byte	lb	I	branch greater than or equal	bge	I
store byte	sb	I			
load upper immediate	lui	I			
and	and	R			
or	or	R			
nor	nor	R			
and immediate	andi	I			
or immediate	ori	I			
shift left logical	sll	R			
shift right logical	srl	R			
branch on equal	beq	I			
branch on not equal	bne	I			
set less than	slt	R			
set less than immediate	slti	I			
jump	j	J			
jump register	jr	R			
jump and link	jal	J			

FIGURE 2.47   The MIPS instruction set covered so far, with the real MIPS instructions on the left and the pseudoinstructions on the right. Appendix A (Section A.10, page A-44) describes the full MIPS architecture. Figure 2.27 shows more details of the MIPS architecture revealed in this chapter. The information given here is also found in columns 1 and 2 of the MIPS Reference Data Card at the front of the book.

Instruction class	MIPS examples	HLL correspondence	Frequency	
			Integer	Ft. pt.
Arithmetic	add, sub, addi	Operations in assignment statements	24%	48%
Data transfer	lw, sw, lb, sb, lui	References to data structures, such as arrays	36%	39%
Logical	and, or, nor, andi, ori, sll, srl	Operations in assignment statements	18%	4%
Conditional branch	beq, bne, slt, slti	*If* statements and loops	18%	6%
Jump	j, jr, jal	Procedure calls, returns, and *case/switch* statements	3%	0%

FIGURE 2.48   MIPS instruction classes, examples, correspondence to high-level program language constructs, and percentage of MIPS instructions executed by category for average of five SPEC2000 integer programs and five SPEC2000 floating-point programs. Figure 3.26 shows the percentage of the individual MIPS instructions executed.

- The arithmetic instructions correspond to the operations found in assignment statements.

- Data transfer instructions are most likely to occur when dealing with data structures like arrays or structures.

- The conditional branches are used in *if* statements and in loops.

- The unconditional jumps are used in procedure calls and returns and for *case/switch* statements.

After we explain computer arithmetic in Chapter 3, we reveal more of the MIPS instruction set architecture.

2.19 Historical Perspective and Further Reading

This section surveys the history of instruction set architraves over time, and we give a short history of programming languages and compilers. ISAs include accumulator architectures, general-purpose register architectures, stack architectures, and a brief history of the IA-32. We also review the controversial subjects of high-level-language computer architectures and reduced instruction set computer architectures. The history of programming languages includes Fortran, Lisp, Algol, C, Cobol, Pascal, Simula, Smalltalk, C++, and Java, and the history of compilers includes the key milestones and the pioneers who achieved them. The rest of this section is on the CD.

2.20 Exercises

Appendix A describes the MIPS simulator, which is helpful for these exercises. Although the simulator accepts pseudoinstructions, try not to use pseudoinstructions for any exercises that ask you to produce MIPS code. Your goal should be to learn the real MIPS instruction set, and if you are asked to count instructions, your count should reflect the actual instructions that will be executed and not the pseudoinstructions.

There are some cases where pseudoinstructions must be used (for example, the la instruction when an actual value is not known at assembly time). In many cases, they are quite convenient and result in more readable code (for example, the li and move instructions). If you choose to use pseudoinstructions for these reasons, please add a sentence or two to your solution stating which pseudoinstructions you have used and why.

2.1 [15] <§2.4> ⊚ **For More Practice:** Instruction Formats

2.2 [5] <§2.4> What binary number does this hexadecimal number represent: 7fff fffa$_{hex}$? What decimal number does it represent?

2.3 [5] <§2.4> What hexadecimal number does this binary number represent: 1100 1010 1111 1110 1111 1010 1100 1110$_{two}$?

2.4 [5] <§2.4> Why doesn't MIPS have a subtract immediate instruction?

2.5 [15] <§2.5> ⊚ **For More Practice:** MIPS Code and Logical Operations

2.6 [15] <§2.5> Some computers have explicit instructions to extract an arbitrary field from a 32-bit register and to place it in the least significant bits of a register. The figure below shows the desired operation:

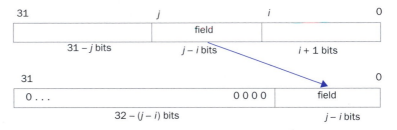

Find the shortest sequence of MIPS instructions that extracts a field for the constant values $i = 5$ and $j = 22$ from register $t3 and places it in register $t0. (Hint: It can be done in two instructions.)

2.7 [10] <§2.5> ⊚ **For More Practice:** Logical Operations in MIPS

2.8 [20] <§2.5> ⊚ **In More Depth:** Bit Fields in C

2.9 [12] <§2.5> ⊚ **In More Depth:** Bit Fields in C

2.10 [20] <§2.5> ⊚ **In More Depth:** Jump Tables

2.11 [20] <§2.5> ⊚ **In More Depth:** Jump Tables

2.12 [20] <§2.5> ⊚ **In More Depth:** Jump Tables

2.13 [10] <§2.6> Construct a control flow graph (like the one shown in Fig. 2.11) for the following section of C or Java code:

```
for (i=0; i<x; i=i+1)
    y = y + i;
```

2.14 [10] <§2.6> 🔘 **For More Practice:** Writing Assembly Code

2.15 [25] <§2.7> Implement the following C code in MIPS, assuming that set_array is the first function called:

```
int i;
void set_array(int num) {
    int array[10];
    for (i=0; i<10; i++) {
        array[i] = compare(num, i);
    }
}
int compare(int a, int b) {
    if (sub(a, b) >= 0)
        return 1;
    else
        return 0;
}
int sub (int a, int b) {
    return a-b;
}
```

Be sure to handle the stack and frame pointers appropriately. The variable code font is allocated on the stack, and i corresponds to $s0. Draw the status of the stack before calling set_array and during each function call. Indicate the names of registers and variables stored on the stack and mark the location of $sp and $fp.

2.16 [30] <§2.7> 🔘 **In More Depth:** Tail Recursion

2.17 [30] <§2.7> 🔘 **In More Depth:** Tail Recursion

2.18 [20] <§2.7> 🔘 **In More Depth:** Tail Recursion

2.19 [5] <§2.8> Iris and Julie are students in computer engineering who are learning about ASCII and Unicode character sets. Help them by spelling their names and your first name in both ASCII (using decimal notation) and Unicode (using hex notation and the Basic Latin character set).

2.20 [10] <§2.8> Compute the decimal byte values that form the null-terminated ASCII representation of the following string:

```
A byte is 8 bits
```

2.21 [30] <§§2.7, 2.8> 🔵 **For More Practice:** MIPS Coding and ASCII Strings

2.22 [20] <§§2.7, 2.8> 🔵 **For More Practice:** MIPS Coding and ASCII Strings

2.23 [20] <§§2.7, 2.8> 🔵 **For More Practice:** MIPS Coding and ASCII Strings

2.24 [30] <§§2.7, 2.8> 🔵 **For More Practice:** MIPS Coding and ASCII Strings

2.25 <§2.8> 🔵 **For More Practice:** Comparing C/Java to MIPS

2.26 <§2.8> 🔵 **For More Practice:** Translating MIPS to C

2.27 <§2.8> 🔵 **For More Practice:** Understanding MIPS Code

2.28 <§2.8> 🔵 **For More Practice:** Understanding MIPS Code

2.29 [5] <§§2.3, 2.6, 2.9> Add comments to the following MIPS code and describe in one sentence what it computes. Assume that $a0 and $a1 are used for the input and both initially contain the integers a and b, respectively. Assume that $v0 is used for the output.

```
               add    $t0, $zero, $zero
loop:          beq    $a1, $zero, finish
               add    $t0, $t0, $a0
               sub    $a1, $a1, 1
               j      loop
finish:        addi   $t0, $t0, 100
               add    $v0, $t0, $zero
```

2.30 [12] <§§2.3, 2.6, 2.9> The following code fragment processes two arrays and produces an important value in register $v0. Assume that each array consists of 2500 words indexed 0 through 2499, that the base addresses of the arrays are stored in $a0 and $a1, respectively, and their sizes (2500) are stored in $a2 and $a3, respectively. Add comments to the code and describe in one sentence what this code does. Specifically, what will be returned in $v0?

```
          sll    $a2, $a2, 2
          sll    $a3, $a3, 2
          add    $v0, $zero, $zero
          add    $t0, $zero, $zero
outer:    add    $t4, $a0, $t0
```

```
            lw      $t4, 0($t4)
            add     $t1, $zero, $zero
   inner:   add     $t3, $a1, $t1
            lw      $t3, 0($t3)
            bne     $t3, $t4, skip
            addi    $v0, $v0, 1
   skip:    addi    $t1, $t1, 4
            bne     $t1, $a3, inner
            addi    $t0, $t0, 4
            bne     $t0, $a2, outer
```

2.31 [10] <§§2.3, 2.6, 2.9> Assume that the code from Exercise 2.30 is run on a machine with a 2 GHz clock that requires the following number of cycles for each instruction:

Instruction	Cycles
add,addi,sll	1
lw, bne	2

In the worst case, how many seconds will it take to execute this code?

2.32 [5] <§2.9> Show the single MIPS instruction or minimal sequence of instructions for this C statement:

```
    b = 25 | a;
```

Assume that a corresponds to register $t0 and b corresponds to register $t1.

2.33 [10] <§2.9> ◉ **For More Practice:** Translating from C to MIPS

2.34 [10] <§§ 2.3, 2.6, 2.9> The following program tries to copy words from the address in register $a0 to the address in register $a1, counting the number of words copied in register $v0. The program stops copying when it finds a word equal to 0. You do not have to preserve the contents of registers $v1, $a0, and $a1. This terminating word should be copied but not counted.

```
      addi $v0, $zero, 0 # Initialize count
loop: lw   $v1, 0($a0)   # Read next word from source
      sw   $v1, 0($a1)   # Write to destination
      addi $a0, $a0, 4   # Advance pointer to next source
      addi $a1, $a1, 4   # Advance pointer to next destination
```

```
beq $v1, $zero, loop  # Loop if word copied != zero
```

There are multiple bugs in this MIPS program; fix them and turn in a bug-free version. Like many of the exercises in this chapter, the easiest way to write MIPS programs is to use the simulator described in Appendix A.

2.35 [10] <§§2.2, 2.3, 2.6, 2.9> ⊙ **For More Practice:** Reverse Translation from MIPS to C

2.36 <§2.9> ⊙ **For More Practice:** Reverse Translation from MIPS to C

2.37 [25] <§2.10> As discussed on page 107 (Section 2.10, "Assembler"), pseudoinstructions are not part of the MIPS instruction set but often appear in MIPS programs. For each pseudoinstruction in the following table, produce a minimal sequence of actual MIPS instructions to accomplish the same thing. You may need to use $at for some of the sequences. In the following table, big refers to a specific number that requires 32 bits to represent and small to a number that can fit in 16 bits.

Pseudoinstruction	What it accomplishes
move $t1, $t2	$t1 = $t2
clear $t0	$t0 = 0
beq $t1, small, L	if ($t1 == small) go to L
beq $t2, big, L	if ($t2 == big) go to L
li $t1, small	$t1 = small
li $t2, big	$t2 = big
ble $t3, $t5, L	if ($t3 <= $t5) go to L
bgt $t4, $t5, L	if ($t4 > $t5) go to L
bge $t5, $t3, L	if ($t5 >= $t3) go to L
addi $t0, $t2, big	$t0 = $t2 + big
lw $t5, big($t2)	$t5 = Memory[$t2 + big]

2.38 [5] <§§2.9, 2.10> Given your understanding of PC-relative addressing, explain why an assembler might have problems directly implementing the branch instruction in the following code sequence:

```
here:           beq    $s0, $s2, there
...
there           add    $s0, $s0, $s0
```

Show how the assembler might rewrite this code sequence to solve these problems.

2.39 <§2.10> ⊙ **For More Practice:** MIPS Pseudoinstructions

2.40 <§2.10> ⊙ **For More Practice:** Linking MIPS Code

2.41 <§2.10> ⊚ **For More Practice:** Linking MIPS Code

2.42 [20] <§2.11>Find a large program written in C (for example, gcc, which can be obtained from *http://gcc.gnu.org*) and compile the program twice, once with optimizations (use -03) and once without. Compare the compilation time and runtime of the program. Are the results what you expect?

2.43 [20] <§2.12> ⊚ **For More Practice:** Enhancing MIPS Addressing Modes

2.44 [10] <§2.12> ⊚ **For More Practice:** Enhancing MIPS Addressing Modes

2.45 [10] <§2.12> ⊚ **In More Depth:** The IBM/Motorola PowerPC

2.46 [15] <§§2.6, 2.14> The MIPS translation of the C (or Java) segment

```
while (save[i] == k)
    i += 1;
```

on page 74 ("Compiling a *while* Loop in C") uses both a conditional branch and an unconditional jump each time through the loop. Only poor compilers would produce code with this loop overhead. Assuming that this code is in Java (not C), rewrite the assembly code so that it uses at most one branch or jump each time through the loop. Additionally, add code to perform the Java checking for index out of bounds and ensure that this code uses at most one branch or jump each time through the loop. How many instructions are executed before and after the optimization if the number of iterations of the loop is 10 and the value of i is never out of bounds?

2.47 [30] <§§2.6, 2.14> Consider the following fragment of Java code:

```
for (i=0; i<=100; i=i+1)
    a[i] = b[i] + c;
```

Assume that a and b are arrays of words and that the base address of a is in $a0 and the base address of b is in $a1. Register $t0 is associated with variable i and register $s0 with the value of c. You may also assume that any address constants you need are available to be loaded from memory. Write the code for MIPS. How many instructions are executed during the running of this code if there are no array out-of-bounds exceptions thrown? How many memory data references will be made during execution?

2.48 [5] <§2.14> Write the MIPS code for the Java method compareTo (found in Figure 2.14.3 in ⊚ **Section 2.14** (page 2.14-8).

2.49 [15] <§2.17> When designing memory systems, it becomes useful to know the frequency of memory reads versus writes as well as the frequency of accesses for instructions versus data. Using the average instruction mix information for MIPS for the program SPEC2000int in Figure 2.48 (on page 146), find the following:

a. The percentage of all memory accesses (both data and instruction) that are for data.

b. The percentage of all memory accesses (both data and instruction) that are for reads. Assume that two-thirds of data transfers are loads.

2.50 [10] <§2.17> Perform the same calculations as for Exercise 2.49, but replace the program SPEC2000int with SPEC2000fp.

2.51 [15] <§2.17> Suppose we have made the following measurements of average CPI for instructions:

Instruction	Average CPI
Arithmetic, Logical	1.0 clock cycles
Data transfer	1.4 clock cycles
Conditional branch	1.7 clock cycles
Jump	1.2 clock cycles

Compute the effective CPI for MIPS. Average the instruction frequencies for SPEC2000int and SPEC2000fp in Figure 2.48 on page 146 to obtain the instruction mix.

2.52 [20] <§2.18> ◉ **In More Depth:** Instruction Set Styles

2.53 [20] <§2.18> ◉ **In More Depth:** Instruction Set Styles

2.54 [10] <§2.18> ◉ **In More Depth:** The Single Instruction Computer

2.55 [20] <§2.18> ◉ **In More Depth:** The Single Instruction Computer

2.56 [5] <§2.19>The stored-program concept, introduced in the late 1940s, brought about a significant change in how computers were designed and operated. What is a possible example of a nonstored-program machine, and what are the problems with such a machine? How can these problems be overcome by a stored-program machine?

2.57 [5] <§2.19> ◉ **In More Depth:** The IBM/Motorola PowerPC

2.58 [15] <§2.19> ◉ **In More Depth:** The IBM/Motorola PowerPC

2.59 [15] <§2.5> ◉ **In More Depth:** Logical Instructions

Computers in the Real World

Helping Save Our Environment with Data

Problem to solve: Monitor plants and animals of our environment to collect information that may influence environmental policies.

Solution: Develop rugged, battery-operated, embedded computers with sensors, wireless communication, and appropriate software.

Stanford biologist Barbara Block studies bluefin tuna. One policy question was whether the tuna on one side of the Atlantic are different from those on the other side. If so, then each region could set its own quotas. If not, then we need oceanwide quotas.

To answer this question, she started implanting tuna with devices that could monitor their journeys. Every two minutes a pop-up satellite archival tag (PSAT) records water pressure, ambient light, temperature, time of day, and other measurements. The data is saved in 1 MB of flash memory. The onboard 8-bit microprocessor estimates depth from the water pressure. It finds longitude using light intensity data and time of day. It determines sunrise, sunset, and therefore high noon, and calculates the time shift between local noon and Greenwich Mean Time noon, like a navigator using a sextant and chronometer. The water temperature is later matched to satellite records to determine latitude. Block does not rely on fishermen to catch the tuna and return PSATs. A PSAT is attached to a fish with a pin that dissolves via electrolysis after the computer turns on a battery. The tag then floats to the surface and begins transmitting data to satellites. The floating tag can transmit for up to two weeks, sending the data directly to Block's lab.

Block and students tag a bluefin tuna, which can grow to 2000 pounds and 10 feet in length.

A pop-up archival satellite tag and internal electronics.

Block discovered that bluefin tuna travel more than 10,000 miles per year; tuna tagged near the East Coast of the United States will cross the Atlantic and spawn in both the Gulf of Mexico and the Eastern Mediterranean. Her discovery changed regulations so that tuna are no longer managed separately in the Eastern and Western Atlantic. She is now developing a census of Pacific marine life using smaller tags for smaller animals and tags that transmit each time a fish surfaces. She speculates that tagged tuna could be ideal "vehicles" to monitor ocean change.

Berkeley biologist Todd Dawson studies the ecology of the coastal redwood, *Sequoia sempervirens,* particularly the interaction of sea fog with trees. For years his research involved installing 50 kilograms of gear and kilometers of wire strung to sensors. This work is often done more than 80 meters above the ground. Data could only be retrieved by climbing up to a printer-sized data logger.

Berkeley computer scientist David Culler proposed a new approach. Dawson is now placing miniature wireless sensors the size of film canisters in these trees. Each micromote is less than 3 cubic inches, can transmit up to 40 KB/sec, and can run for months on a C battery. Since micromotes are small and cheap, many can be placed in a tree. Data is collected with a compatible laptop by simply walking to the base of the tree.

Dawson found that summertime fog accounts for 25% to 40% of the water that the redwoods receive for the whole year. The trees may even be drinking water directly from fog via a symbiotic relationship with fungi living on their leaves.

Dawson predicts wireless sensor networks will change the way people do ecological research.

To learn more, see these references on the 🔘 library:

Block et al., "Migratory movements, depth preferences, and thermal biology of Atlantic bluefin tuna," *Science* 293: 1310–1314, 2001

"Redwoods," Prof. Dawson's laboratory site

"Redwoods drinking water from fog," *The Forestry Source*, November 2002

"Tagging of the Pacific Pelagics," *www.toppcensus.org*

Professor Dawson and student climbing a redwood to install fog monitors.

The Mica micromote with C battery. It is about the size of a film canister.

3

Arithmetic for Computers

*Numerical precision
is the very soul
of science.*

Sir D'arcy Wentworth Thompson
On Growth and Form, 1917

The Five Classic Components of a Computer

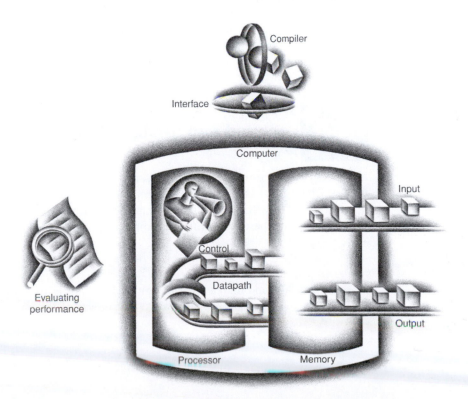

3.1 Introduction

Computer words are composed of bits; thus words can be represented as binary numbers. Although the natural numbers 0, 1, 2, and so on can be represented either in decimal or binary form, what about the other numbers that commonly occur? For example:

- How are negative numbers represented?

- What is the largest number that can be represented in a computer word?

- What happens if an operation creates a number bigger than can be represented?

- What about fractions and other real numbers?

And underlying all these questions is a mystery: How does hardware really multiply or divide numbers?

The goal of this chapter is to unravel this mystery, including representation of numbers, arithmetic algorithms, hardware that follows these algorithms, and the implications of all this for instruction sets. These insights may even explain quirks that you have already encountered with computers. (If you are familiar with signed binary numbers, you may wish to skip the next section and go to Section 3.3 on page 170.)

3.2 Signed and Unsigned Numbers

Numbers can be represented in any base; humans prefer base 10 and, as we examined in Chapter 2, base 2 is best for computers. To avoid confusion we subscript decimal numbers with *ten* and binary numbers with *two*.

In any number base, the value of ith digit d is

$$d \times \text{Base}^i$$

where i starts at 0 and increases from right to left. This leads to an obvious way to number the bits in the word: simply use the power of the base for that bit. For example,

1011_{two}

represents

$$
\begin{aligned}
&(1 \times 2^3) & + (0 \times 2^2) & + (1 \times 2^1) & + (1 \times 2^0)_{ten} \\
&= (1 \times 8) & + (0 \times 4) & + (1 \times 2) & + (1 \times 1)_{ten} \\
&= \quad 8 & + \quad 0 & + \quad 2 & + \quad 1_{ten} \\
&= 11_{ten}
\end{aligned}
$$

Hence the bits are numbered 0, 1, 2, 3, . . . from *right to left* in a word. The drawing below shows the numbering of bits within a MIPS word and the placement of the number 1011_{two}:

31 30 29 28	27 26 25 24	23 22 21 20	19 18 17 16	15 14 13 12	11 10 9 8	7 6 5 4	3 2 1 0
0 0 0 0	0 0 0 0	0 0 0 0	0 0 0 0	0 0 0 0	0 0 0 0	0 0 0 0	1 0 1 1

(32 bits wide)

Since words are drawn vertically as well as horizontally, leftmost and rightmost may be unclear. Hence, the phrase **least significant bit** is used to refer to the rightmost bit (bit 0 above) and **most significant bit** to the leftmost bit (bit 31).

The MIPS word is 32 bits long, so we can represent 2^{32} different 32-bit patterns. It is natural to let these combinations represent the numbers from 0 to $2^{32} - 1$ ($4{,}294{,}967{,}295_{ten}$):

```
0000 0000 0000 0000 0000 0000 0000 0000 two = 0 ten
0000 0000 0000 0000 0000 0000 0000 0001 two = 1 ten
0000 0000 0000 0000 0000 0000 0000 0010 two = 2 ten
. . .                       . . .
1111 1111 1111 1111 1111 1111 1111 1101 two = 4,294,967,293 ten
1111 1111 1111 1111 1111 1111 1111 1110 two = 4,294,967,294 ten
1111 1111 1111 1111 1111 1111 1111 1111 two = 4,294,967,295 ten
```

That is, 32-bit binary numbers can be represented in terms of the bit value times a power of 2 (here *xi* means the *i*th bit of *x*):

$$(x31 \times 2^{31}) + (x30 \times 2^{30}) + (x29 \times 2^{29}) + \ldots + (x1 \times 2^1) + (x0 \times 2^0)$$

least significant bit The rightmost bit in a MIPS word.

most significant bit The leftmost bit in a MIPS word.

Base 2 is not natural to human beings; we have 10 fingers and so find base 10 natural. Why didn't computers use decimal? In fact, the first commercial computer *did* offer decimal arithmetic. The problem was that the computer still used on and off signals, so a decimal digit was simply represented by several binary digits. Decimal proved so inefficient that subsequent computers reverted to all binary, converting to base 10 only for the relatively infrequent input/output events.

Hardware/ Software Interface

EXAMPLE

ASCII versus Binary Numbers

We could represent numbers as strings of ASCII digits instead of as integers (see Figure 2.21 on page 91). How much does storage increase if the number 1 billion is represented in ASCII versus a 32-bit integer?

ANSWER

One billion is 1 000 000 000, so it would take 10 ASCII digits, each 8 bits long. Thus the storage expansion would be $(10 \times 8)/32$ or 2.5. In addition to the expansion in storage, the hardware to add, subtract, multiply, and divide such numbers is difficult. Such difficulties explain why computing professionals are raised to believe that binary is natural and that the occasional decimal computer is bizarre.

Keep in mind that the binary bit patterns above are simply *representatives* of numbers. Numbers really have an infinite number of digits, with almost all being 0 except for a few of the rightmost digits. We just don't normally show leading 0s.

Hardware can be designed to add, subtract, multiply, and divide these binary bit patterns. If the number that is the proper result of such operations cannot be represented by these rightmost hardware bits, *overflow* is said to have occurred. It's up to the operating system and program to determine what to do if overflow occurs.

Computer programs calculate both positive and negative numbers, so we need a representation that distinguishes the positive from the negative. The most obvious solution is to add a separate sign, which conveniently can be represented in a single bit; the name for this representation is *sign and magnitude*.

Alas, sign and magnitude representation has several shortcomings. First, it's not obvious where to put the sign bit. To the right? To the left? Early computers tried both. Second, adders for sign and magnitude may need an extra step to set the sign because we can't know in advance what the proper sign will be. Finally, a separate sign bit means that sign and magnitude has both a positive and a negative zero, which can lead to problems for inattentive programmers. As a result of these shortcomings, sign and magnitude was soon abandoned.

In the search for a more attractive alternative, the question arose as to what would be the result for unsigned numbers if we tried to subtract a large number from a small one. The answer is that it would try to borrow from a string of leading 0s, so the result would have a string of leading 1s.

Given that there was no obvious better alternative, the final solution was to pick the representation that made the hardware simple: leading 0s mean positive, and leading 1s mean negative. This convention for representing signed binary numbers is called *two's complement* representation:

$$
\begin{aligned}
0000\ 0000\ 0000\ 0000\ 0000\ 0000\ 0000\ 0000_{two} &= 0_{ten} \\
0000\ 0000\ 0000\ 0000\ 0000\ 0000\ 0000\ 0001_{two} &= 1_{ten} \\
0000\ 0000\ 0000\ 0000\ 0000\ 0000\ 0000\ 0010_{two} &= 2_{ten}
\end{aligned}
$$

. . .   . . .

$$
\begin{aligned}
0111\ 1111\ 1111\ 1111\ 1111\ 1111\ 1111\ 1101_{two} &= 2,147,483,645_{ten} \\
0111\ 1111\ 1111\ 1111\ 1111\ 1111\ 1111\ 1110_{two} &= 2,147,483,646_{ten} \\
0111\ 1111\ 1111\ 1111\ 1111\ 1111\ 1111\ 1111_{two} &= 2,147,483,647_{ten} \\
1000\ 0000\ 0000\ 0000\ 0000\ 0000\ 0000\ 0000_{two} &= -2,147,483,648_{ten} \\
1000\ 0000\ 0000\ 0000\ 0000\ 0000\ 0000\ 0001_{two} &= -2,147,483,647_{ten} \\
1000\ 0000\ 0000\ 0000\ 0000\ 0000\ 0000\ 0010_{two} &= -2,147,483,646_{ten}
\end{aligned}
$$

. . .   . . .

$$
\begin{aligned}
1111\ 1111\ 1111\ 1111\ 1111\ 1111\ 1111\ 1101_{two} &= -3_{ten} \\
1111\ 1111\ 1111\ 1111\ 1111\ 1111\ 1111\ 1110_{two} &= -2_{ten} \\
1111\ 1111\ 1111\ 1111\ 1111\ 1111\ 1111\ 1111_{two} &= -1_{ten}
\end{aligned}
$$

The positive half of the numbers, from 0 to $2,147,483,647_{ten}$ ($2^{31} - 1$), use the same representation as before. The following bit pattern ($1000 \ldots 0000_{two}$) represents the most negative number $-2,147,483,648_{ten}$ (-2^{31}). It is followed by a declining set of negative numbers: $-2,147,483,647_{ten}$ ($1000 \ldots 0001_{two}$) down to -1_{ten} ($1111 \ldots 1111_{two}$).

Two's complement does have one negative number, $-2,147,483,648_{ten}$, that has no corresponding positive number. Such imbalance was a worry to the inattentive programmer, but sign and magnitude had problems for both the programmer *and* the hardware designer. Consequently, every computer today uses two's complement binary representations for signed numbers.

Two's complement representation has the advantage that all negative numbers have a 1 in the most significant bit. Consequently, hardware needs to test only this bit to see if a number is positive or negative (with 0 considered positive). This bit is often called the *sign bit*. By recognizing the role of the sign bit, we can represent positive and negative 32-bit numbers in terms of the bit value times a power of 2:

$$
(x31 \times -2^{31}) + (x30 \times 2^{30}) + (x29 \times 2^{29}) + \ldots + (x1 \times 2^{1}) + (x0 \times 2^{0})
$$

The sign bit is multiplied by -2^{31}, and the rest of the bits are then multiplied by positive versions of their respective base values.

EXAMPLE

Binary to Decimal Conversion

What is the decimal value of this 32-bit two's complement number?

$$1111\ 1111\ 1111\ 1111\ 1111\ 1111\ 1111\ 1100_{two}$$

ANSWER

Substituting the number's bit values into the formula above:

$$(1 \times -2^{31}) + (1 \times 2^{30}) + (1 \times 2^{29}) + \ldots + (1 \times 2^2) + (0 \times 2^1) + (0 \times 2^0)$$
$$= -2^{31}\ \ +\ \ 2^{30}\ \ +\ \ 2^{29}\ \ +\ldots+\ \ 2^2\ \ +\ \ 0\ \ +\ \ 0$$
$$= -2{,}147{,}483{,}648_{ten} + 2{,}147{,}483{,}644_{ten}$$
$$= -4_{ten}$$

We'll see a shortcut to simplify conversion soon.

Just as an operation on unsigned numbers can overflow the capacity of hardware to represent the result, so can an operation on two's complement numbers. Overflow occurs when the leftmost retained bit of the binary bit pattern is not the same as the infinite number of digits to the left (the sign bit is incorrect): a 0 on the left of the bit pattern when the number is negative or a 1 when the number is positive.

Hardware/ Software Interface

Signed versus unsigned applies to loads as well as to arithmetic. The *function* of a signed load is to copy the sign repeatedly to fill the rest of the register—called *sign extension*—but its *purpose* is to place a correct representation of the number within that register. Unsigned loads simply fill with 0s to the left of the data, since the number represented by the bit pattern is unsigned.

When loading a 32-bit word into a 32-bit register, the point is moot; signed and unsigned loads are identical. MIPS does offer two flavors of byte loads: *load byte* (lb) treats the byte as a signed number and thus sign-extends to fill the 24 leftmost bits of the register, while *load byte unsigned* (lbu) works with unsigned integers. Since C programs almost always use bytes to represent characters rather than consider bytes as very short signed integers, lbu is used practically exclusively for byte loads. For similar reasons, *load half* (lh) treats the halfword as a signed number and thus sign-extends to fill the 16 leftmost bits of the register, while *load halfword unsigned* (lhu) works with unsigned integers.

Unlike the numbers discussed above, memory addresses naturally start at 0 and continue to the largest address. Put another way, negative addresses make no sense. Thus, programs want to deal sometimes with numbers that can be positive or negative and sometimes with numbers that can be only positive. Some programming languages reflect this distinction. C, for example, names the former *integers* (declared as `int` in the program) and the latter *unsigned integers* (`unsigned int`). Some C style guides even recommend declaring the former as `signed int` to keep the distinction clear.

Comparison instructions must deal with this dichotomy. Sometimes a bit pattern with a 1 in the most significant bit represents a negative number and, of course, is less than any positive number, which must have a 0 in the most significant bit. With unsigned integers, on the other hand, a 1 in the most significant bit represents a number that is *larger* than any that begins with a 0. (We'll take advantage of this dual meaning of the most significant bit to reduce the cost of the array bounds checking in a few pages.)

MIPS offers two versions of the set on less than comparison to handle these alternatives. *Set on less than* (`slt`) and *set on less than immediate* (`slti`) work with signed integers. Unsigned integers are compared using *set on less than unsigned* (`sltu`) and *set on less than immediate unsigned* (`sltiu`).

Hardware/ Software Interface

Signed versus Unsigned Comparison

Suppose register $s0 has the binary number

1111 1111 1111 1111 1111 1111 1111 1111$_{two}$

and that register $s1 has the binary number

0000 0000 0000 0000 0000 0000 0000 0001$_{two}$

What are the values of registers $t0 and $t1 after these two instructions?

```
slt    $t0, $s0, $s1 # signed comparison
sltu   $t1, $s0, $s1 # unsigned comparison
```

EXAMPLE

ANSWER

The value in register $\$s0$ represents –1 if it is an integer and $4{,}294{,}967{,}295_{ten}$ if it is an unsigned integer. The value in register $\$s1$ represents 1 in either case. Then register $\$t0$ has the value 1, since $-1_{ten} < 1_{ten}$, and register $\$t1$ has the value 0, since $4{,}294{,}967{,}295_{ten} > 1_{ten}$.

Before going on to addition and subtraction, let's examine a few useful shortcuts when working with two's complement numbers.

The first shortcut is a quick way to negate a two's complement binary number. Simply invert every 0 to 1 and every 1 to 0, then add one to the result. This shortcut is based on the observation that the sum of a number and its inverted representation must be $111 \ldots 111_{two}$, which represents –1. Since $x + \bar{x} \equiv -1$, therefore $x + \bar{x} + 1 = 0$ or $\bar{x} + 1 = -x$.

Negation Shortcut

Negate 2_{ten}, and then check the result by negating -2_{ten}.

EXAMPLE

ANSWER

$2_{ten} = 0000\ 0000\ 0000\ 0000\ 0000\ 0000\ 0000\ 0010_{two}$

Negating this number by inverting the bits and adding one,

$$
\begin{array}{rl}
 & 1111\ 1111\ 1111\ 1111\ 1111\ 1111\ 1111\ 1101_{two} \\
+ & \underline{\hspace{6cm} 1_{two}} \\
= & 1111\ 1111\ 1111\ 1111\ 1111\ 1111\ 1111\ 1110_{two} \\
= & -2_{ten}
\end{array}
$$

Going the other direction,

$$1111\ 1111\ 1111\ 1111\ 1111\ 1111\ 1111\ 1110_{two}$$

is first inverted and then incremented:

$$
\begin{array}{rl}
 & 0000\ 0000\ 0000\ 0000\ 0000\ 0000\ 0000\ 0001_{two} \\
+ & \underline{\hspace{6cm} 1_{two}} \\
= & 0000\ 0000\ 0000\ 0000\ 0000\ 0000\ 0000\ 0010_{two} \\
= & 2_{ten}
\end{array}
$$

The second shortcut tells us how to convert a binary number represented in n bits to a number represented with more than n bits. For example, the immediate field in the load, store, branch, add, and set on less than instructions contains a two's complement 16-bit number, representing $-32,768_{ten}$ (-2^{15}) to $32,767_{ten}$ ($2^{15} - 1$). To add the immediate field to a 32-bit register, the computer must convert that 16-bit number to its 32-bit equivalent. The shortcut is to take the most significant bit from the smaller quantity—the sign bit—and replicate it to fill the new bits of the larger quantity. The old bits are simply copied into the right portion of the new word. This shortcut is commonly called *sign extension*.

Sign Extension Shortcut

Convert 16-bit binary versions of 2_{ten} and -2_{ten} to 32-bit binary numbers.

EXAMPLE

ANSWER

The 16-bit binary version of the number 2 is

$$0000\ 0000\ 0000\ 0010_{two} = 2_{ten}$$

It is converted to a 32-bit number by making 16 copies of the value in the most significant bit (0) and placing that in the left-hand half of the word. The right half gets the old value:

$$0000\ 0000\ 0000\ 0000\ 0000\ 0000\ 0000\ 0010_{two} = 2_{ten}$$

Let's negate the 16-bit version of 2 using the earlier shortcut. Thus,

$$0000\ 0000\ 0000\ 0010_{two}$$

becomes

$$
\begin{array}{r}
1111\ 1111\ 1111\ 1101_{two} \\
+ \qquad\qquad\qquad\quad 1_{two} \\
\hline
\end{array}
$$

$$= 1111\ 1111\ 1111\ 1110_{two}$$

Creating a 32-bit version of the negative number means copying the sign bit 16 times and placing it on the left:

$$1111\ 1111\ 1111\ 1111\ 1111\ 1111\ 1111\ 1110_{two} = -2_{ten}$$

This trick works because positive two's complement numbers really have an infinite number of 0s on the left and negative two's complement numbers have an infinite number of 1s. The binary bit pattern representing a number hides leading bits to fit the width of the hardware; sign extension simply restores some of them.

The third shortcut reduces the cost of checking if $0 \leq x < y$, which matches the index out-of-bounds check for arrays. The key is that negative integers in two's complement notation look like large numbers in unsigned notation; that is, the most significant bit is a sign bit in the former notation but a large part of the number in the latter. Thus, an unsigned comparison of $x < y$ also checks if x is negative.

EXAMPLE

ANSWER

Bounds Check Shortcut

Use this shortcut to reduce an index-out-of-bounds check: jump to Index-OutOfBounds if $a1 ≥ $t2 or if $a1 is negative.

The checking code just uses sltu to do both checks:

```
sltu $t0,$a1,$t2 # Temp reg $t0=0 if k>=length or k<0
beq  $t0,$zero,IndexOutOfBounds #if bad, goto Error
```

Summary

The main point of this section is that we need to represent both positive and negative integers within a computer word, and although there are pros and cons to any option, the overwhelming choice since 1965 has been two's complement. Figure 3.1 shows the additions to the MIPS assembly language revealed in this section. (The MIPS machine language is also illustrated on the MIPS Reference Data Card at the front of the book.)

Check Yourself

Which type of variable that can contain $1{,}000{,}000{,}000_{ten}$ takes the most memory space?

1. int in C

2. string in C

3. string in Java (which uses Unicode)

MIPS operands

Name	Example	Comments
32 registers	`$s0–$s7, $t0–$t9, $gp, $fp, $zero, $sp, $ra, $at`	Fast locations for data. In MIPS, data must be in registers to perform arithmetic. MIPS register `$zero` always equals 0. Register `$at` is reserved for the assembler to handle large constants.
2^{30} memory words	Memory[0], Memory[4], . . . , Memory[4294967292]	Accessed only by data transfer instructions. MIPS uses byte addresses, so sequential word addresses differ by 4. Memory holds data structures, such as arrays, and spilled registers, such as those saved on procedure calls.

MIPS assembly language

Category	Instruction	Example	Meaning	Comments
Arithmetic	add	`add $s1,$s2,$s3`	`$s1 = $s2 + $s3`	Three operands
	subtract	`sub $s1,$s2,$s3`	`$s1 = $s2 – $s3`	Three operands
	add immediate	`addi $s1,$s2,100`	`$s1 = $s2 + 100`	+ constant
Data transfer	load word	`lw $s1,100($s2)`	`$s1 = Memory[$s2 + 100]`	Word from memory to register
	store word	`sw $s1,100($s2)`	`Memory[$s2 + 100] = $s1`	Word from register to memory
	load half unsigned	`lhu $s1,100($s2)`	`$s1 = Memory[$s2 + 100]`	Halfword memory to register
	store half	`sh $s1,100($s2)`	`Memory[$s2 + 100] = $s1`	Halfword register to memory
	load byte unsigned	`lbu $s1,100($s2)`	`$s1 = Memory[$s2 + 100]`	Byte from memory to register
	store byte	`sb $s1,100($s2)`	`Memory[$s2 + 100] = $s1`	Byte from register to memory
	load upper immediate	`lui $s1,100`	`$s1 = 100 * 2^{16}`	Loads constant in upper 16 bits
Logical	and	`and $s1,$s2,$s3`	`$s1 = $s2 & $s3`	Three reg. operands; bit-by-bit AND
	or	`or $s1,$s2,$s3`	`$s1 = $s2	$s3`	Three reg. operands; bit-by-bit OR
	nor	`nor $s1,$s2,$s3`	`$s1 = ~ ($s2 |$s3)`	Three reg. operands; bit-by-bit NOR
	and immediate	`andi $s1,$s2,100`	`$s1 = $s2 & 100`	Bit-by-bit AND with constant
	or immediate	`ori $s1,$s2,100`	`$s1 = $s2	100`	Bit-by-bit OR with constant
	shift left logical	`sll $s1,$s2,10`	`$s1 = $s2 << 10`	Shift left by constant
	shift right logical	`srl $s1,$s2,10`	`$s1 = $s2 >> 10`	Shift right by constant
Conditional branch	branch on equal	`beq $s1,$s2,25`	if (`$s1 == $s2`) go to PC + 4 + 100	Equal test; PC-relative branch
	branch on not equal	`bne $s1,$s2,25`	if (`$s1 != $s2`) go to PC + 4 + 100	Not equal test; PC-relative
	set on less than	`slt $s1,$s2,$s3`	if (`$s2 < $s3`) `$s1 = 1`; else `$s1 = 0`	Compare less than; two's complement
	set less than immediate	`slti $s1,$s2,100`	if (`$s2 < 100`) `$s1 = 1`; else `$s1 = 0`	Compare < constant; two's complement
	set less than unsigned	`sltu $s1,$s2,$s3`	if (`$s2 < $s3`) `$s1 = 1`; else `$s1 = 0`	Compare less than; unsigned numbers
	set less than immediate unsigned	`sltiu $s1,$s2,100`	if (`$s2 < 100`) `$s1 = 1`; else `$s1 = 0`	Compare < constant; unsigned numbers
Uncondi-tional jump	jump	`j 2500`	go to 10000	Jump to target address
	jump register	`jr $ra`	go to `$ra`	For switch, procedure return
	jump and link	`jal 2500`	`$ra = PC + 4`; go to 10000	For procedure call

FIGURE 3.1 MIPS architecture revealed thus far. Color indicates portions from this section added to the MIPS architecture revealed in Chapter 2 (Figure 3.26 on page 228). MIPS machine language is listed in the MIPS Reference Data Card in the front of this book.

Elaboration: Two's complement gets its name from the rule that the unsigned sum of an n-bit number and its negative is 2^n; hence, the complement or negation of a two's complement number x is $2^n - x$.

A third alternative representation is called *one's complement*. The negative of a one's complement is found by inverting each bit, from 0 to 1 and from 1 to 0, which helps explain its name since the complement of x is $2^n - x - 1$. It was also an attempt to be a better solution than sign and magnitude, and several scientific computers did use the notation. This representation is similar to two's complement except that it also has two 0s: $00 \ldots 00_{two}$ is positive 0 and $11 \ldots 11_{two}$ is negative 0. The most negative number $10 \ldots 000_{two}$ represents $-2,147,483,647_{ten}$, and so the positives and negatives are balanced. One's complement adders did need an extra step to subtract a number, and hence two's complement dominates today.

A final notation, which we will look at when we discuss floating point, is to represent the most negative value by $00 \ldots 000_{two}$ and the most positive value by $11 \ldots 11_{two}$, with 0 typically having the value $10 \ldots 00_{two}$. This is called a biased notation, since it biases the number such that the number plus the bias has a nonnegative representation.

Elaboration: For signed decimal numbers we used "−" to represent negative because there are no limits to the size of a decimal number. Given a fixed word size, binary and hexadecimal bit strings can encode the sign, and hence we do not normally use "+" or "−" with binary or hexadecimal notation.

biased notation A notation that represents the most negative value by $00 \ldots 000_{two}$ and the most positive value by $11 \ldots 11_{two}$, with 0 typically having the value $10 \ldots 00_{two}$, thereby biasing the number such that the number plus the bias has a nonnegative representation.

Subtraction: Addition's Tricky Pal

No. 10, Top Ten Courses for Athletes at a Football Factory, David Letterman et al., *Book of Top Ten Lists*, 1990

3.3   Addition and Subtraction

Addition is just what you would expect in computers. Digits are added bit by bit from right to left, with carries passed to the next digit to the left, just as you would do by hand. Subtraction uses addition: the appropriate operand is simply negated before being added.

Binary Addition and Subtraction

Let's try adding 6_{ten} to 7_{ten} in binary and then subtracting 6_{ten} from 7_{ten} in binary.

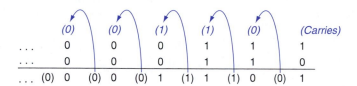

FIGURE 3.2 Binary addition, showing carries from right to left. The rightmost bit adds 1 to 0, resulting in the sum of this bit being 1 and the carry out from this bit being 0. Hence, the operation for the second digit to the right is 0 + 1 + 1. This generates a 0 for this sum bit and a carry out of 1. The third digit is the sum of 1 + 1 + 1, resulting in a carry out of 1 and a sum bit of 1. The fourth bit is 1 + 0 + 0, yielding a 1 sum and no carry.

$$
\begin{array}{rll}
 & 0000\ 0000\ 0000\ 0000\ 0000\ 0000\ 0000\ 0111_{two} & =\ 7_{ten} \\
+ & 0000\ 0000\ 0000\ 0000\ 0000\ 0000\ 0000\ 0110_{two} & =\ 6_{ten} \\
\hline
= & 0000\ 0000\ 0000\ 0000\ 0000\ 0000\ 0000\ 1101_{two} & =\ 13_{ten}
\end{array}
$$

The 4 bits to the right have all the action; Figure 3.2 shows the sums and carries. The carries are shown in parentheses, with the arrows showing how they are passed.

Subtracting 6_{ten} from 7_{ten} can be done directly:

$$
\begin{array}{rll}
 & 0000\ 0000\ 0000\ 0000\ 0000\ 0000\ 0000\ 0111_{two} & =\ 7_{ten} \\
- & 0000\ 0000\ 0000\ 0000\ 0000\ 0000\ 0000\ 0110_{two} & =\ 6_{ten} \\
\hline
= & 0000\ 0000\ 0000\ 0000\ 0000\ 0000\ 0000\ 0001_{two} & =\ 1_{ten}
\end{array}
$$

or via addition using the two's complement representation of −6:

$$
\begin{array}{rll}
 & 0000\ 0000\ 0000\ 0000\ 0000\ 0000\ 0000\ 0111_{two} & =\ 7_{ten} \\
+ & 1111\ 1111\ 1111\ 1111\ 1111\ 1111\ 1111\ 1010_{two} & =\ -6_{ten} \\
\hline
= & 0000\ 0000\ 0000\ 0000\ 0000\ 0000\ 0000\ 0001_{two} & =\ 1_{ten}
\end{array}
$$

We said earlier that overflow occurs when the result from an operation cannot be represented with the available hardware, in this case a 32-bit word. When can overflow occur in addition? When adding operands with different signs, overflow cannot occur. The reason is the sum must be no larger than one of the operands. For example, −10 + 4 = −6. Since the operands fit in 32 bits and the sum is no larger than an operand, the sum must fit in 32 bits as well. Therefore, no overflow can occur when adding positive and negative operands.

There are similar restrictions to the occurrence of overflow during subtract, but it's just the opposite principle: when the signs of the operands are the *same*, overflow cannot occur. To see this, remember that $x - y = x + (-y)$ because we subtract by negating the second operand and then add. So, when we subtract operands of the same sign we end up by *adding* operands of *different* signs. From the prior paragraph, we know that overflow cannot occur in this case either.

Having examined when overflow cannot occur in addition and subtraction, we still haven't answered how to detect when it *does* occur. Overflow occurs when adding two positive numbers and the sum is negative, or vice versa. Clearly, adding or subtracting two 32-bit numbers can yield a result that needs 33 bits to be fully expressed. The lack of a 33rd bit means that when overflow occurs the sign bit is being set with the *value* of the result instead of the proper sign of the result. Since we need just one extra bit, only the sign bit can be wrong. This means a carry out occurred into the sign bit.

Overflow occurs in subtraction when we subtract a negative number from a positive number and get a negative result, or when we subtract a positive number from a negative number and get a positive result. This means a borrow occurred from the sign bit. Figure 3.3 shows the combination of operations, operands, and results that indicate an overflow.

We have just seen how to detect overflow for two's complement numbers in a computer. What about unsigned integers? Unsigned integers are commonly used for memory addresses where overflows are ignored.

The computer designer must therefore provide a way to ignore overflow in some cases and to recognize it in others. The MIPS solution is to have two kinds of arithmetic instructions to recognize the two choices:

- Add (`add`), add immediate (`addi`), and subtract (`sub`) cause exceptions on overflow.

- Add unsigned (`addu`), add immediate unsigned (`addiu`), and subtract unsigned (`subu`) do *not* cause exceptions on overflow.

Because C ignores overflows, the MIPS C compilers will always generate the unsigned versions of the arithmetic instructions `addu`, `addiu`, and `subu` no matter what the type of the variables. The MIPS Fortran compilers, however, pick the appropriate arithmetic instructions, depending on the type of the operands.

Operation	Operand A	Operand B	Result indicating overflow
A + B	≥ 0	≥ 0	< 0
A + B	< 0	< 0	≥ 0
A − B	≥ 0	< 0	< 0
A − B	< 0	≥ 0	≥ 0

FIGURE 3.3 Overflow conditions for addition and subtraction.

The computer designer must decide how to handle arithmetic overflows. Although some languages like C ignore integer overflow, languages like Ada and Fortran require that the program be notified. The programmer or the programming environment must then decide what to do when overflow occurs.

MIPS detects overflow with an **exception**, also called an **interrupt** on many computers. An exception or interrupt is essentially an unscheduled procedure call. The address of the instruction that overflowed is saved in a register, and the computer jumps to a predefined address to invoke the appropriate routine for that exception. The interrupted address is saved so that in some situations the program can continue after corrective code is executed. (Section 5.6 covers exceptions in more detail; Chapters 7 and 8 describe other situations where exceptions and interrupts occur.)

MIPS includes a register called the *exception program counter* (EPC) to contain the address of the instruction that caused the exception. The instruction *move from system control* (mfc0) is used to copy EPC into a general-purpose register so that MIPS software has the option of returning to the offending instruction via a jump register instruction.

Hardware/ Software Interface

exception Also called **interrupt**. An unscheduled event that disrupts program execution; used to detect overflow.

interrupt An exception that comes from outside of the processor. (Some architectures use the term *interrupt* for all exceptions.)

Elaboration: MIPS can trap on overflow, but unlike many other computers there is no conditional branch to test overflow. A sequence of MIPS instructions can discover overflow. For signed addition, the sequence is the following (see the "In More Depth" segment on logical instruction in Chapter 2 for the definition of the xor instructions):

```
addu $t0, $t1, $t2 # $t0 = sum, but don't trap
xor  $t3, $t1, $t2 # Check if signs differ
slt  $t3, $t3, $zero # $t3 = 1 if signs differ
bne  $t3, $zero, No_overflow # $t1, $t2 signs ≠,
so no overflow
xor  $t3, $t0, $t1 # signs =; sign of sum match too?
                   # $t3 negative if sum sign different
slt  $t3, $t3, $zero # $t3 = 1 if sum sign different
bne  $t3, $zero, Overflow # All three signs ≠; go to
overflow
```

For unsigned addition ($t0 = $t1 + $t2), the test is

```
addu $t0, $t1, $t2 # $t0 = sum
nor  $t3, $t1, $zero # $t3 = NOT $t1
         # (2's comp - 1: 2^32 - $t1 - 1)
sltu $t3, $t3, $t2 # (2^32 - $t1 - 1) < $t2
         # ⟹ 2^32 - 1 < $t1 + $t2
bne $t3,$zero,Overflow # if(2^32-1 < $t1 + $t2) go to
overflow
```

Summary

The main point of this section is that, independent of the representation, the finite word size of computers means that arithmetic operations can create results that are too large to fit in this fixed word size. It's easy to detect overflow in unsigned numbers, although these are almost always ignored because programs don't want to detect overflow for address arithmetic, the most common use of natural numbers. Two's complement presents a greater challenge, yet some software systems require detection of overflow, so today all computers have a way to detect it. Figure 3.4 shows the additions to the MIPS architecture from this section.

Check Yourself

Some programming languages allow two's complement integer arithmetic on variables declared byte and half. What MIPS instructions would be used?

1. Load with lbu, lhu; arithmetic with add, sub, mult, div; then store using sb, sh.

2. Load with lb, lh; arithmetic with add, sub, mult, div; then store using sb, sh.

3. Loads with lb, lh; arithmetic with add, sub, mult, div, using and to mask result to 8 or 16 bits after each operation; then store using sb, sh.

Elaboration: In the preceding text, we said that you copy EPC into a register via mfc0 and then return to the interrupted code via jump register. This leads to an interesting question: Since you must first transfer EPC to a register to use with jump register, how can jump register return to the interrupted code *and* restore the original values of *all* registers? Either you restore the old registers first, thereby destroying your return address from EPC that you placed in a register for use in jump register, or you restore all registers but the one with the return address so that you can jump—meaning an exception would result in changing that one register at any time during program execution! Neither option is satisfactory.

To rescue the hardware from this dilemma, MIPS programmers agreed to reserve registers $k0 and $k1 for the operating system; these registers are *not* restored on exceptions. Just as the MIPS compilers avoid using register $at so that the assembler

MIPS assembly language

Category	Instruction	Example	Meaning	Comments
Arithmetic	add	`add  $s1,$s2,$s3`	$s1 = $s2 + $s3	Three operands; overflow detected
	subtract	`sub  $s1,$s2,$s3`	$s1 = $s2 - $s3	Three operands; overflow detected
	add immediate	`addi $s1,$s2,100`	$s1 = $s2 + 100	+ constant; overflow detected
	add unsigned	`addu $s1,$s2,$s3`	$s1 = $s2 + $s3	Three operands; overflow undetected
	subtract unsigned	`subu $s1,$s2,$s3`	$s1 = $s2 - $s3	Three operands; overflow undetected
	add immediate unsigned	`addiu $s1,$s2,100`	$s1 = $s2 + 100	+ constant; overflow undetected
	move from coprocessor register	`mfc0 $s1,$epc`	$s1 = $epc	Used to copy Exception PC plus other special registers
Data transfer	load word	`lw   $s1,100($s2)`	$s1 = Memory[$s2 + 100]	Word from memory to register
	store word	`sw   $s1,100($s2)`	Memory[$s2 + 100] = $s1	Word from register to memory
	load half unsigned	`lhu  $s1,100($s2)`	$s1 = Memory[$s2 + 100]	Halfword memory to register
	store half	`sh   $s1,100($s2)`	Memory[$s2 + 100] = $s1	Halfword register to memory
	load byte unsigned	`lbu  $s1,100($s2)`	$s1 = Memory[$s2 + 100]	Byte from memory to register
	store byte	`sb   $s1,100($s2)`	Memory[$s2 + 100] = $s1	Byte from register to memory
	load upper immediate	`lui  $s1,100`	$s1 = 100 * 2^{16}	Loads constant in upper 16 bits
Logical	and	`and  $s1,$s2,$s3`	$s1 = $s2 & $s3	Three reg. operands; bit-by-bit AND
	or	`or   $s1,$s2,$s3`	$s1 = $s2 | $s3	Three reg. operands; bit-by-bit OR
	nor	`nor  $s1,$s2,$s3`	$s1 = ~ ($s2 |$s3)	Three reg. operands; bit-by-bit NOR
	and immediate	`andi $s1,$s2,100`	$s1 = $s2 & 100	Bit-by-bit AND with constant
	or immediate	`ori  $s1,$s2,100`	$s1 = $s2 | 100	Bit-by-bit OR with constant
	shift left logical	`sll  $s1,$s2,10`	$s1 = $s2 << 10	Shift left by constant
	shift right logical	`srl  $s1,$s2,10`	$s1 = $s2 >> 10	Shift right by constant
Conditional branch	branch on equal	`beq  $s1,$s2,25`	if ($s1 == $s2) go to PC + 4 + 100	Equal test; PC-relative branch
	branch on not equal	`bne  $s1,$s2,25`	if ($s1 != $s2) go to PC + 4 + 100	Not equal test; PC-relative
	set on less than	`slt  $s1,$s2,$s3`	if ($s2 < $s3) $s1 = 1; else $s1 = 0	Compare less than; two's complement
	set less than immediate	`slti $s1,$s2,100`	if ($s2 < 100) $s1 = 1; else $s1 = 0	Compare < constant; two's complement
	set less than unsigned	`sltu $s1,$s2,$s3`	if ($s2 < $s3) $s1 = 1; else $s1 = 0	Compare less than; unsigned
	set less than immediate unsigned	`sltiu $s1,$s2,100`	if ($s2 < 100) $s1 = 1; else $s1 = 0	Compare < constant; unsigned
Unconditional jump	jump	`j    2500`	go to 10000	Jump to target address
	jump register	`jr   $ra`	go to $ra	For switch, procedure return
	jump and link	`jal  2500`	$ra = PC + 4; go to 10000	For procedure call

FIGURE 3.4 MIPS architecture revealed thus far. To save space in the table, it does not include the registers and memory found in Figure 3.1 on page 169. Color indicates the portions revealed since Figure 3.1. MIPS machine language is also on the MIPS Reference Data Card.

can use it as a temporary register (see the "Hardware/Software Interface" section on page 96 in Chapter 2), compilers also abstain from using registers $k0 and $k1 to make them available for the operating system. Exception routines place the return address in one of these registers and then use jump register to restore the instruction address.

Multiplication is vexation,
Division is as bad;
The rule of three doth puzzle me,
And practice drives me mad.

Anonymous, Elizabethan manuscript, 1570

3.4   Multiplication

Now that we have completed the explanation of addition and subtraction, we are ready to build the more vexing operation of multiply.

But first let's review the multiplication of decimal numbers in longhand to remind ourselves of the steps and the names of the operands. For reasons that will become clear shortly, we limit this decimal example to using only the digits 0 and 1. Multiplying 1000_{ten} by 1001_{ten}:

Multiplicand		1000_{ten}
Multiplier	x	1001_{ten}
		1000
		0000
		0000
		1000
Product		1001000_{ten}

The first operand is called the *multiplicand* and the second the *multiplier*. The final result is called the *product*. As you may recall, the algorithm learned in grammar school is to take the digits of the multiplier one at a time from right to left, multiplying the multiplicand by the single digit of the multiplier and shifting the intermediate product one digit to the left of the earlier intermediate products.

The first observation is that the number of digits in the product is considerably larger than the number in either the multiplicand or the multiplier. In fact, if we ignore the sign bits, the length of the multiplication of an n-bit multiplicand and an m-bit multiplier is a product that is $n + m$ bits long. That is, $n + m$ bits are required to represent all possible products. Hence, like add, multiply must cope with overflow because we frequently want a 32-bit product as the result of multiplying two 32-bit numbers.

In this example we restricted the decimal digits to 0 and 1. With only two choices, each step of the multiplication is simple:

1. Just place a copy of the multiplicand (1 × multiplicand) in the proper place if the multiplier digit is a 1, or

2. Place 0 (0 × multiplicand) in the proper place if the digit is 0.

Although the decimal example above happened to use only 0 and 1, multiplication of binary numbers must always use 0 and 1, and thus always offers only these two choices.

Now that we have reviewed the basics of multiplication, the traditional next step is to provide the highly optimized multiply hardware. We break with tradition in the belief that you will gain a better understanding by seeing the evolution of the multiply hardware and algorithm through multiple generations. For now, let's assume that we are multiplying only positive numbers.

Sequential Version of the Multiplication Algorithm and Hardware

This design mimics the algorithm we learned in grammar school; the hardware is shown in Figure 3.5. We have drawn the hardware so that data flows from top to bottom to more closely resemble the paper-and-pencil method.

Let's assume that the multiplier is in the 32-bit Multiplier register and that the 64-bit Product register is initialized to 0. From the paper-and-pencil example above, it's clear that we will need to move the multiplicand left one digit each step as it may be added to the intermediate products. Over 32 steps a 32-bit multiplicand would move 32 bits to the left. Hence we need a 64-bit Multiplicand register, initialized with the 32-bit multiplicand in the right half and 0 in the left half. This register is then shifted left 1 bit each step to align the multiplicand with the sum being accumulated in the 64-bit Product register.

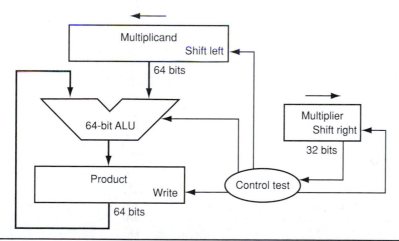

FIGURE 3.5   First version of the multiplication hardware. The Multiplicand register, ALU, and Product register are all 64 bits wide, with only the Multiplier register containing 32 bits. The 32-bit multiplicand starts in the right half of the Multiplicand register and is shifted left 1 bit on each step. The multiplier is shifted in the opposite direction at each step. The algorithm starts with the product initialized to 0. Control decides when to shift the Multiplicand and Multiplier registers and when to write new values into the Product register.

Figure 3.6 shows the three basic steps needed for each bit. The least significant bit of the multiplier (Multiplier0) determines whether the multiplicand is added to the Product register. The left shift in step 2 has the effect of moving the intermediate operands to the left, just as when multiplying by hand. The shift right in step 3 gives us the next bit of the multiplier to examine in the following iteration. These three steps are repeated 32 times to obtain the product. If each step took a

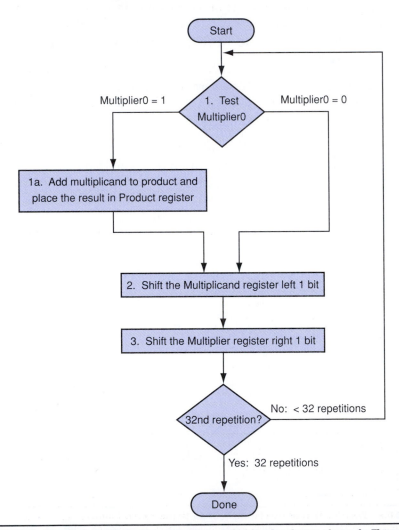

FIGURE 3.6 The first multiplication algorithm, using the hardware shown in Figure 3.5. If the least significant bit of the multiplier is 1, add the multiplicand to the product. If not, go to the next step. Shift the multiplicand left and the multiplier right in the next two steps. These three steps are repeated 32 times.

clock cycle, this algorithm would require almost 100 clock cycles to multiply two 32-bit numbers. The relative importance of arithmetic operations like multiply varies with the program, but addition and subtraction may be anywhere from 5 to 100 times more popular than multiply. Accordingly, in many applications, multiply can take multiple clock cycles without significantly affecting performance. Yet Amdahl's law (see Chapter 4, page 267) reminds us that even a moderate frequency for a slow operation can limit performance.

This algorithm and hardware are easily refined to take 1 clock cycle per step. The speedup comes from performing the operations in parallel: the multiplier and multiplicand are shifted while the multiplicand is added to the product if the multiplier bit is a 1. The hardware just has to ensure that it tests the right bit of the multiplier and gets the preshifted version of the multiplicand. The hardware is usually further optimized to halve the width of the adder and registers by noticing where there are unused portions of registers and adders. Figure 3.7 shows the revised hardware.

Replacing arithmetic by shifts can also occur when multiplying by constants. Some compilers replace multiplies by short constants with a series of shifts and adds. Because one bit to the left represents a number twice as large in base 2, shifting the bits left has the same effect as multiplying by a power of 2. As mentioned in Chapter 2, almost every compiler will perform the strength reduction optimization of substituting a left shift for a multiply by a power of 2.

Hardware/ Software Interface

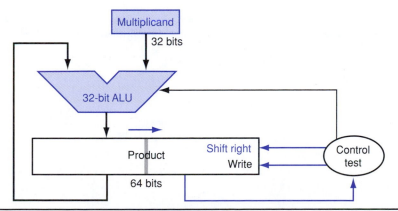

FIGURE 3.7 Refined version of the multiplication hardware. Compare with the first version in Figure 3.5. The Multiplicand register, ALU, and Multiplier register are all 32 bits wide, with only the Product register left at 64 bits. Now the product is shifted right. The separate Multiplier register also disappeared. The multiplier is placed instead in the right half of the Product register. These changes are highlighted in color. (The Product register should really be 65 bits to hold the carryout of the adder, but it's shown here as 64 bits to highlight the evolution from Figure 3.5.)

EXAMPLE

ANSWER

A Multiply Algorithm

Using 4-bit numbers to save space, multiply $2_{ten} \times 3_{ten}$, or $0010_{two} \times 0011_{two}$.

Figure 3.8 shows the value of each register for each of the steps labeled according to Figure 3.6, with the final value of $0000\ 0110_{two}$ or 6_{ten}. Color is used to indicate the register values that change on that step, and the bit circled is the one examined to determine the operation of the next step.

Signed Multiplication

So far we have dealt with positive numbers. The easiest way to understand how to deal with signed numbers is to first convert the multiplier and multiplicand to positive numbers and then remember the original signs. The algorithms should then be run for 31 iterations, leaving the signs out of the calculation. As we learned in grammar school, we need negate the product only if the original signs disagree.

It turns out that the last algorithm will work for signed numbers provided that we remember that the numbers we are dealing with have infinite digits, and that we are only representing them with 32 bits. Hence, the shifting steps would need to extend the sign of the product for signed numbers. When the algorithm completes, the lower word would have the 32-bit product.

Iteration	Step	Multiplier	Multiplicand	Product
0	Initial values	0011	0000 0010	0000 0000
1	1a: 1 ⟹ Prod = Prod + Mcand	0011	0000 0010	0000 0010
	2: Shift left Multiplicand	0011	0000 0100	0000 0010
	3: Shift right Multiplier	0001	0000 0100	0000 0010
2	1a: 1 ⟹ Prod = Prod + Mcand	0001	0000 0100	0000 0110
	2: Shift left Multiplicand	0001	0000 1000	0000 0110
	3: Shift right Multiplier	0000	0000 1000	0000 0110
3	1: 0 ⟹ No operation	0000	0000 1000	0000 0110
	2: Shift left Multiplicand	0000	0001 0000	0000 0110
	3: Shift right Multiplier	0000	0001 0000	0000 0110
4	1: 0 ⟹ No operation	0000	0001 0000	0000 0110
	2: Shift left Multiplicand	0000	0010 0000	0000 0110
	3: Shift right Multiplier	0000	0010 0000	0000 0110

FIGURE 3.8 Multiply example using algorithm in Figure 3.6. The bit examined to determine the next step is circled in color.

Faster Multiplication

Moore's law has provided so much more in resources that hardware designers can now build a much faster multiplication hardware. Whether the multiplicand is to be added or not is known at the beginning of the multiplication by looking at each of the 32 multiplier bits. Faster multiplications are possible by essentially providing one 32-bit adder for each bit of the multiplier: one input is the multiplicand ANDed with a multiplier bit and the other is the output of a prior adder. Figure 3.9 shows how they would be connected.

Why is this much hardware faster? The sequential multiplier pays the overhead of a clock for each bit of the product. This multiplier array of adders does not. A second reason is this large collection of adders lends itself to many optimizations to gain further improvements. One example is using *carry save adders* to add such a large column of numbers; see Exercises 3.24 and 3.49. A third reason is that it is easy to pipeline such a design to be able to support many multiplies simultaneously (see Chapter 6).

Multiply in MIPS

MIPS provides a separate pair of 32-bit registers to contain the 64-bit product, called *Hi* and *Lo*. To produce a properly signed or unsigned product, MIPS has two instructions: multiply (`mult`) and multiply unsigned (`multu`). To fetch the integer 32-bit product, the programmer uses *move from lo* (`mflo`). The MIPS assembler generates a pseudoinstruction for multiply that specifies three general-purpose registers, generating `mflo` and `mfhi` instructions to place the product into registers.

Summary

Multiplication is accomplished by simple shift and add hardware, derived from the paper-and-pencil method learned in grammar school. Compilers even use shift instructions for multiplications by powers of 2.

Both MIPS multiply instructions ignore overflow, so it is up to the software to check to see if the product is too big to fit in 32 bits. There is no overflow if Hi is 0 for `multu` or the replicated sign of Lo for `mult`. The instruction *move from hi* (`mfhi`) can be used to transfer Hi to a general-purpose register to test for overflow.

Hardware/ Software Interface

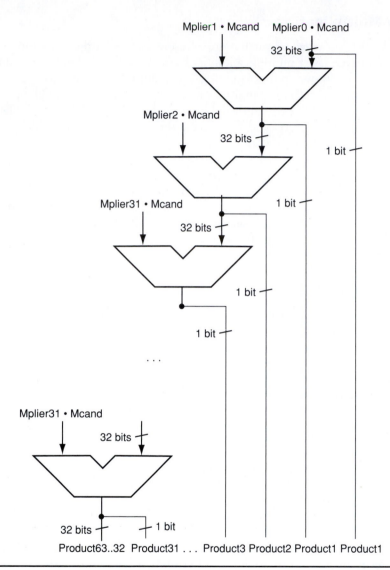

FIGURE 3.9 Fast multiplication hardware. Rather than use a single 32-bit adder 31 times, this hardware "unrolls the loop" to use 31 adders. Each adder produces a 32-bit sum and a carry out. The least significant bit is a bit of the product, and the carry out and the upper 31 bits of the sum are passed along to the next adder.

3.5   **Division**

Divide et impera.

Latin for "Divide and rule,"
ancient political maxim cited
by Machiavelli, 1532

The reciprocal operation of multiply is divide, an operation that is even less frequent and even more quirky. It even offers the opportunity to perform a mathematically invalid operation: dividing by 0.

Let's start with an example of long division using decimal numbers to recall the names of the operands and the grammar school division algorithm. For reasons similar to those in the previous section, we limit the decimal digits to just 0 or 1. The example is dividing $1,001,010_{ten}$ by 1000_{ten}:

$$
\begin{array}{r}
1001_{ten} \quad \text{Quotient} \\
\text{Divisor } 1000_{ten} \overline{\smash)1001010_{ten}} \quad \text{Dividend} \\
-1000 \\
\hline
10 \\
101 \\
1010 \\
-1000 \\
\hline
10_{ten} \quad \text{Remainder}
\end{array}
$$

The two operands (**dividend** and **divisor**) and the result (**quotient**) of divide are accompanied by a second result called the **remainder**. Here is another way to express the relationship between the components:

$$\text{Dividend} = \text{Quotient} \times \text{Divisor} + \text{Remainder}$$

where the remainder is smaller than the divisor. Infrequently, programs use the divide instruction just to get the remainder, ignoring the quotient.

The basic grammar school division algorithm tries to see how big a number can be subtracted, creating a digit of the quotient on each attempt. Our carefully selected decimal example uses only the numbers 0 and 1, so it's easy to figure out how many times the divisor goes into the portion of the dividend: it's either 0 times or 1 time. Binary numbers contain only 0 or 1, so binary division is restricted to these two choices, thereby simplifying binary division.

Let's assume that both the dividend and the divisor are positive and hence the quotient and the remainder are nonnegative. The division operands and both results are 32-bit values, and we will ignore the sign for now.

dividend A number being divided.

divisor A number that the dividend is divided by.

quotient The primary result of a division; a number that when multiplied by the divisor and added to the remainder produces the dividend.

remainder The secondary result of a division; a number that when added to the product of the quotient and the divisor produces the dividend.

A Division Algorithm and Hardware

Figure 3.10 shows hardware to mimic our grammar school algorithm. We start with the 32-bit Quotient register set to 0. Each iteration of the algorithm needs to move the divisor to the right one digit, so we start with the divisor placed in the left half of the 64-bit Divisor register and shift it right 1 bit each step to align it with the dividend. The Remainder register is initialized with the dividend.

Figure 3.11 shows three steps of the first division algorithm. Unlike a human, the computer isn't smart enough to know in advance whether the divisor is smaller than the dividend. It must first subtract the divisor in step 1; remember that this is how we performed the comparison in the set on less than instruction. If the result is positive, the divisor was smaller or equal to the dividend, so we generate a 1 in the quotient (step 2a). If the result is negative, the next step is to restore the original value by adding the divisor back to the remainder and generate a 0 in the quotient (step 2b). The divisor is shifted right and then we iterate again. The remainder and quotient will be found in their namesake registers after the iterations are complete.

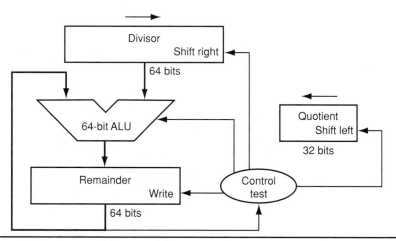

FIGURE 3.10   First version of the division hardware. The Divisor register, ALU, and Remainder register are all 64 bits wide, with only the Quotient register being 32 bits. The 32-bit divisor starts in the left half of the Divisor register and is shifted right 1 bit on each iteration. The remainder is initialized with the dividend. Control decides when to shift the Divisor and Quotient registers and when to write the new value into the Remainder register.

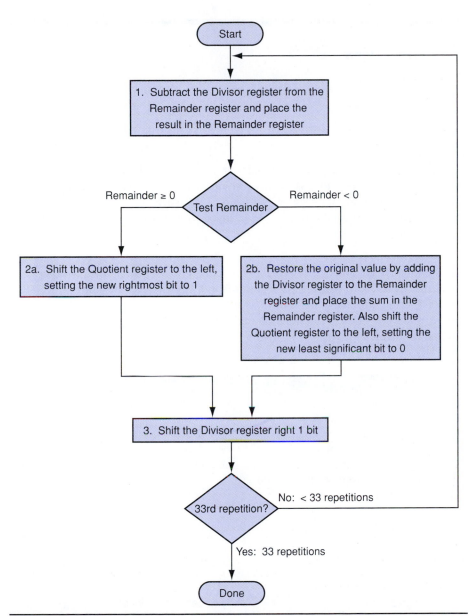

FIGURE 3.11 A division algorithm, using the hardware in Figure 3.10. If the Remainder is positive, the divisor did go into the dividend, so step 2a generates a 1 in the quotient. A negative Remainder after step 1 means that the divisor did not go into the dividend, so step 2b generates a 0 in the quotient and adds the divisor to the remainder, thereby reversing the subtraction of step 1. The final shift, in step 3, aligns the divisor properly, relative to the dividend for the next iteration. These steps are repeated 33 times.

A Divide Algorithm

Using a 4-bit version of the algorithm to save pages, let's try dividing 7_{ten} by 2_{ten}, or $0000\ 0111_{two}$ by 0010_{two}.

Figure 3.12 shows the value of each register for each of the steps, with the quotient being 3_{ten} and the remainder 1_{ten}. Notice that the test in step 2 of whether the remainder is positive or negative simply tests whether the sign bit of the Remainder register is a 0 or 1. The surprising requirement of this algorithm is that it takes $n + 1$ steps to get the proper quotient and remainder.

This algorithm and hardware can be refined to be faster and cheaper. The speedup comes from shifting the operands and quotient at the same time as the subtract. This refinement halves the width of the adder and registers by noticing where there are unused portions of registers and adders. Figure 3.13 shows the revised hardware.

Iteration	Step	Quotient	Divisor	Remainder
0	Initial values	0000	0010 0000	0000 0111
1	1: Rem = Rem – Div	0000	0010 0000	①110 0111
	2b: Rem < 0 ⟹ +Div, sll Q, Q0 = 0	0000	0010 0000	0000 0111
	3: Shift Div right	0000	0001 0000	0000 0111
2	1: Rem = Rem – Div	0000	0001 0000	①111 0111
	2b: Rem < 0 ⟹ +Div, sll Q, Q0 = 0	0000	0001 0000	0000 0111
	3: Shift Div right	0000	0000 1000	0000 0111
3	1: Rem = Rem – Div	0000	0000 1000	①111 1111
	2b: Rem < 0 ⟹ +Div, sll Q, Q0 = 0	0000	0000 1000	0000 0111
	3: Shift Div right	0000	0000 0100	0000 0111
4	1: Rem = Rem – Div	0000	0000 0100	⓪000 0011
	2a: Rem ≥ 0 ⟹ sll Q, Q0 = 1	0001	0000 0100	0000 0011
	3: Shift Div right	0001	0000 0010	0000 0011
5	1: Rem = Rem – Div	0001	0000 0010	⓪000 0001
	2a: Rem ≥ 0 ⟹ sll Q, Q0 = 1	0011	0000 0010	0000 0001
	3: Shift Div right	0011	0000 0001	0000 0001

FIGURE 3.12   Division example using the algorithm in Figure 3.11. The bit examined to determine the next step is circled in color.

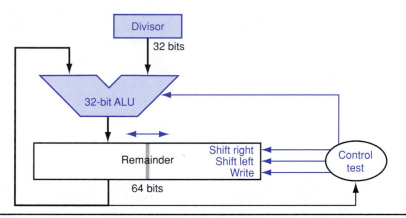

FIGURE 3.13 An improved version of the division hardware. The Divisor register, ALU, and Quotient register are all 32 bits wide, with only the Remainder register left at 64 bits. Compared to Figure 3.10, the ALU and Divisor registers are halved and the remainder is shifted left. This version also combines the Quotient register with the right half of the Remainder register. (As in Figure 3.7, the Remainder register should really be 65 bits to make sure the carryout of the adder is not lost.)

Signed Division

So far we have ignored signed numbers in division. The simplest solution is to remember the signs of the divisor and dividend and then negate the quotient if the signs disagree.

Elaboration: The one complication of signed division is that we must also set the sign of the remainder. Remember that the following equation must always hold:

Dividend = Quotient × Divisor + Remainder

To understand how to set the sign of the remainder, let's look at the example of dividing all the combinations of $\pm7_{ten}$ by $\pm2_{ten}$. The first case is easy:

+7 ÷ +2: Quotient = +3, Remainder = +1

Checking the results:

7 = 3 × 2 + (+1) = 6 + 1

If we change the sign of the dividend, the quotient must change as well:

−7 ÷ +2: Quotient = −3

Rewriting our basic formula to calculate the remainder:

Remainder = (Dividend − Quotient × Divisor) = −7 − (−3 × +2) = −7−(−6) = −1

So,

−7 ÷ +2: Quotient = −3, Remainder = −1

Checking the results again:

−7 = −3 × 2 + (−1) = −6 − 1

The reason the answer isn't a quotient of −4 and a remainder of +1, which would also fit this formula, is that the absolute value of the quotient would then change depending on the sign of the dividend and the divisor! Clearly, if

$$-(x \div y) \neq (-x) \div y$$

programming would be an even greater challenge. This anomalous behavior is avoided by following the rule that the dividend and remainder must have the same signs, no matter what the signs of the divisor and quotient.

We calculate the other combinations by following the same rule:

+7 ÷ −2: Quotient = −3, Remainder = +1
−7 ÷ −2: Quotient = +3, Remainder = −1

Thus the correctly signed division algorithm negates the quotient if the signs of the operands are opposite and makes the sign of the nonzero remainder match the dividend.

Faster Division

We used 32 adders to speed up multiply, but we cannot do the same trick for divide. The reason is that we need to know the sign of the difference before we can perform the next step of the algorithm, whereas with multiply we could calculate the 32 partial products immediately.

There are techniques to produce more than one bit of the quotient per bit. The *SRT division* technique tries to guess several quotient bits per step, using a table lookup based on the upper bits of the dividend and remainder. It relies on subsequent steps to correct wrong guesses. A typical value today is 4 bits. The key is guessing the value to subtract. With binary division there is only a single choice. These algorithms use 6 bits from the remainder and 4 bits from the divisor to index a table that determines the guess for each step.

The accuracy of this fast method depends on having proper values in the lookup table. The fallacy on page 222 in Section 3.8 shows what can happen if the table is incorrect.

Divide in MIPS

You may have already observed that the same sequential hardware can be used for both multiply and divide in Figures 3.7 and 3.13. The only requirement is a 64-bit register that can shift left or right and a 32-bit ALU that adds or subtracts. Hence, MIPS uses the 32-bit Hi and 32-bit Lo registers for both multiply and divide. As we might expect from the algorithm above, Hi contains the remainder, and Lo contains the quotient after the divide instruction completes.

To handle both signed integers and unsigned integers, MIPS has two instructions: *divide* (div) and *divide unsigned* (divu). The MIPS assembler allows divide instructions to specify three registers, generating the mflo or mfhi instructions to place the desired result into a general-purpose register.

Summary

The common hardware support for multiply and divide allows MIPS to provide a single pair of 32-bit registers that are used both for multiply and divide. Figure 3.14 summarizes the additions to the MIPS architecture for the last two sections.

MIPS divide instructions ignore overflow, so software must determine if the quotient is too large. In addition to overflow, division can also result in an improper calculation: division by 0. Some computers distinguish these two anomalous events. MIPS software must check the divisor to discover division by 0 as well as overflow.

Hardware/ Software Interface

Elaboration: An even faster algorithm does not immediately add the divisor back if the remainder is negative. It simply *adds* the dividend to the shifted remainder in the following step since $(r + d) \times 2 - d = r \times 2 + d \times 2 - d = r \times 2 + d$. This *nonrestoring* division algorithm, which takes 1 clock cycle per step, is explored further in Exercise 3.29; the algorithm here is called *restoring* division.

3.6 Floating Point

Speed gets you nowhere if you're headed the wrong way.

American proverb

Going beyond signed and unsigned integers, programming languages support numbers with fractions, which are called *reals* in mathematics. Here are some examples of reals:

$3.14159265\ldots_{ten}$ (π)

$2.71828\ldots_{ten}$ (e)

0.000000001_{ten} or $1.0_{ten} \times 10^{-9}$ (seconds in a nanosecond)

$3{,}155{,}760{,}000_{ten}$ or $3.15576_{ten} \times 10^{9}$ (seconds in a typical century)

Notice that in the last case, the number didn't represent a small fraction, but it was bigger than we could represent with a 32-bit signed integer. The alternative notation for the last two numbers is called **scientific notation**, which has a single digit to the left of the decimal point. A number in scientific notation that has no leading 0s is called a **normalized** number, which is the usual way to write it. For example, $1.0_{ten} \times 10^{-9}$ is in normalized scientific notation, but $0.1_{ten} \times 10^{-8}$ and $10.0_{ten} \times 10^{-10}$ are not.

scientific notation A notation that renders numbers with a single digit to the left of the decimal point.

normalized A number in floating-point notation that has no leading 0s.

MIPS assembly language

Category	Instruction	Example	Meaning	Comments
Arithmetic	add	add $s1,$s2,$s3	$s1 = $s2 + $s3	Three operands; overflow detected
	subtract	sub $s1,$s2,$s3	$s1 = $s2 − $s3	Three operands; overflow detected
	add immediate	addi $s1,$s2,100	$s1 = $s2 + 100	+ constant; overflow detected
	add unsigned	addu $s1,$s2,$s3	$s1 = $s2 + $s3	Three operands; overflow undetected
	subtract unsigned	subu $s1,$s2,$s3	$s1 = $s2 − $s3	Three operands; overflow undetected
	add immediate unsigned	addiu $s1,$s2,100	$s1 = $s2 + 100	+ constant; overflow undetected
	move from coprocessor register	mfc0 $s1,$epc	$s1 = $epc	Copy Exception PC + special regs
	multiply	mult $s2,$s3	Hi, Lo = $s2 × $s3	64-bit signed product in Hi, Lo
	multiply unsigned	multu $s2,$s3	Hi, Lo = $s2 × $s3	64-bit unsigned product in Hi, Lo
	divide	div $s2,$s3	Lo = $s2 / $s3, Hi = $s2 mod $s3	Lo = quotient, Hi = remainder
	divide unsigned	divu $s2,$s3	Lo = $s2 / $s3, Hi = $s2 mod $s3	Unsigned quotient and remainder
	move from Hi	mfhi $s1	$s1 = Hi	Used to get copy of Hi
	move from Lo	mflo $s1	$s1 = Lo	Used to get copy of Lo
Data transfer	load word	lw $s1,100($s2)	$s1 = Memory[$s2 + 100]	Word from memory to register
	store word	sw $s1,100($s2)	Memory[$s2 + 100] = $s1	Word from register to memory
	load half unsigned	lhu $s1,100($s2)	$s1 = Memory[$s2 + 100]	Halfword memory to register
	store half	sh $s1,100($s2)	Memory[$s2 + 100] = $s1	Halfword register to memory
	load byte unsigned	lbu $s1,100($s2)	$s1 = Memory[$s2 + 100]	Byte from memory to register
	store byte	sb $s1,100($s2)	Memory[$s2 + 100] = $s1	Byte from register to memory
	load upper immediate	lui $s1,100	$s1 = $100 * 2^{16}$	Loads constant in upper 16 bits
Logical	and	and $s1,$s2,$s3	$s1 = $s2 & $s3	Three reg. operands; bit-by-bit AND
	or	or $s1,$s2,$s3	$s1 = $s2 | $s3	Three reg. operands; bit-by-bit OR
	nor	nor $s1,$s2,$s3	$s1 = ~ ($s2 |$s3)	Three reg. operands; bit-by-bit NOR
	and immediate	andi $s1,$s2,100	$s1 = $s2 & 100	Bit-by-bit AND with constant
	or immediate	ori $s1,$s2,100	$s1 = $s2 | 100	Bit-by-bit OR with constant
	shift left logical	sll $s1,$s2,10	$s1 = $s2 << 10	Shift left by constant
	shift right logical	srl $s1,$s2,10	$s1 = $s2 >> 10	Shift right by constant
Conditional branch	branch on equal	beq $s1,$s2,25	if ($s1 == $s2) go to PC + 4 + 100	Equal test; PC-relative branch
	branch on not equal	bne $s1,$s2,25	if ($s1 != $s2) go to PC + 4 + 100	Not equal test; PC-relative
	set on less than	slt $s1,$s2,$s3	if ($s2 < $s3) $s1 = 1; else $s1 = 0	Compare less than; two's complement
	set less than immediate	slti $s1,$s2,100	if ($s2 < 100) $s1 = 1; else $s1=0	Compare < constant; two's complement
	set less than unsigned	sltu $s1,$s2,$s3	if ($s2 < $s3) $s1 = 1; else $s1=0	Compare less than; natural numbers
	set less than immediate unsigned	sltiu $s1,$s2,100	if ($s2 < 100) $s1 = 1; else $s1 = 0	Compare < constant; natural numbers
Unconditional jump	jump	j 2500	go to 10000	Jump to target address
	jump register	jr $ra	go to $ra	For switch, procedure return
	jump and link	jal 2500	$ra = PC + 4; go to 10000	For procedure call

FIGURE 3.14 MIPS architecture revealed thus far. The memory and registers of the MIPS architecture are not included for space reasons, but this section added the Hi and Lo registers to support multiply and divide. Color indicates the portions revealed since Figure 3.4 on page 175. MIPS machine language is listed in the MIPS Reference Data Card at the front of this book.

Just as we can show decimal numbers in scientific notation, we can also show binary numbers in scientific notation:

$$1.0_{\text{two}} \times 2^{-1}$$

To keep a binary number in normalized form, we need a base that we can increase or decrease by exactly the number of bits the number must be shifted to have one nonzero digit to the left of the decimal point. Only a base of 2 fulfills our need. Since the base is not 10, we also need a new name for decimal point; *binary point* will do fine.

Computer arithmetic that supports such numbers is called **floating point** because it represents numbers in which the binary point is not fixed, as it is for integers. The programming language C uses the name *float* for such numbers. Just as in scientific notation, numbers are represented as a single nonzero digit to the left of the binary point. In binary, the form is

$$1.xxxxxxxxx_{\text{two}} \times 2^{yyyy}$$

(Although the computer represents the exponent in base 2 as well as the rest of the number, to simplify the notation we show the exponent in decimal.)

A standard scientific notation for reals in normalized form offers three advantages. It simplifies exchange of data that includes floating-point numbers; it simplifies the floating-point arithmetic algorithms to know that numbers will always be in this form; and it increases the accuracy of the numbers that can be stored in a word, since the unnecessary leading 0s are replaced by real digits to the right of the binary point.

> **floating point** Computer arithmetic that represents numbers in which the binary point is not fixed.

Floating-Point Representation

A designer of a floating-point representation must find a compromise between the size of the **fraction** and the size of the **exponent** because a fixed word size means you must take a bit from one to add a bit to the other. This trade-off is between precision and range: increasing the size of the fraction enhances the precision of the fraction, while increasing the size of the exponent increases the range of numbers that can be represented. As our design guideline from Chapter 2 reminds us, good design demands good compromise.

Floating-point numbers are usually a multiple of the size of a word. The representation of a MIPS floating-point number is shown below, where *s* is the sign of the floating-point number (1 meaning negative), *exponent* is the value of the 8-bit exponent field (including the sign of the exponent), and *fraction* is the 23-bit number. This representation is called *sign and magnitude*, since the sign has a separate bit from the rest of the number.

> **fraction** The value, generally between 0 and 1, placed in the fraction field.

> **exponent** In the numerical representation system of floating-point arithmetic, the value that is placed in the exponent field.

31	30	29	28	27	26	25	24	23	22	21	20	19	18	17	16	15	14	13	12	11	10	9	8	7	6	5	4	3	2	1	0
s	exponent								fraction																						

  1 bit   8 bits   23 bits

In general, floating-point numbers are of the form

$$(-1)^S \times F \times 2^E$$

F involves the value in the fraction field and E involves the value in the exponent field; the exact relationship to these fields will be spelled out soon. (We will shortly see that MIPS does something slightly more sophisticated.)

These chosen sizes of exponent and fraction give MIPS computer arithmetic an extraordinary range. Fractions almost as small as $2.0_{ten} \times 10^{-38}$ and numbers almost as large as $2.0_{ten} \times 10^{38}$ can be represented in a computer. Alas, extraordinary differs from infinite, so it is still possible for numbers to be too large. Thus, overflow interrupts can occur in floating-point arithmetic as well as in integer arithmetic. Notice that **overflow** here means that the exponent is too large to be represented in the exponent field.

overflow (floating-point) A situation in which a positive exponent becomes too large to fit in the exponent field.

Floating point offers a new kind of exceptional event as well. Just as programmers will want to know when they have calculated a number that is too large to be represented, they will want to know if the nonzero fraction they are calculating has become so small that it cannot be represented; either event could result in a program giving incorrect answers. To distinguish it from overflow, people call this event **underflow**. This situation occurs when the negative exponent is too large to fit in the exponent field.

underflow (floating-point) A situation in which a negative exponent becomes too large to fit in the exponent field.

One way to reduce chances of underflow or overflow is to offer another format that has a larger exponent. In C this number is called *double*, and operations on doubles are called **double precision** floating-point arithmetic; **single precision** floating point is the name of the earlier format.

double precision A floating-point value represented in two 32-bit words.

The representation of a double precision floating-point number takes two MIPS words, as shown below, where s is still the sign of the number, *exponent* is the value of the 11-bit exponent field, and *fraction* is the 52-bit number in the fraction field.

single precision A floating-point value represented in a single 32-bit word.

31	30	29	28	27	26	25	24	23	22	21	20	19	18	17	16	15	14	13	12	11	10	9	8	7	6	5	4	3	2	1	0
s	exponent											fraction																			

  1 bit   11 bits   20 bits

fraction (continued)

                                      32 bits

MIPS double precision allows numbers almost as small as $2.0_{ten} \times 10^{-308}$ and almost as large as $2.0_{ten} \times 10^{308}$. Although double precision does increase the exponent range, its primary advantage is its greater precision because of the larger significand.

These formats go beyond MIPS. They are part of the *IEEE 754 floating-point standard*, found in virtually every computer invented since 1980. This standard has greatly improved both the ease of porting floating-point programs and the quality of computer arithmetic.

To pack even more bits into the significand, IEEE 754 makes the leading 1 bit of normalized binary numbers implicit. Hence, the number is actually 24 bits long in single precision (implied 1 and a 23-bit fraction), and 53 bits long in double precision (1 + 52). To be precise, we use the term *significand* to represent the 24- or 53-bit number that is 1 plus the fraction, and *fraction* when we mean the 23- or 52-bit number. Since 0 has no leading 1, it is given the reserved exponent value 0 so that the hardware won't attach a leading 1 to it.

Thus $00 \ldots 00_{two}$ represents 0; the representation of the rest of the numbers uses the form from before with the hidden 1 added:

$$(-1)^S \times (1 + \text{Fraction}) \times 2^E$$

where the bits of the fraction represent a number between 0 and 1 and E specifies the value in the exponent field, to be given in detail shortly. If we number the bits of the fraction from *left to right* s1, s2, s3, $\ldots$, then the value is

$$(-1)^S \times (1 + (s1 \times 2^{-1}) + (s2 \times 2^{-2}) + (s3 \times 2^{-3}) + (s4 \times 2^{-4}) + \ldots) \times 2^E$$

Figure 3.15 shows the encodings of IEEE 754 floating-point numbers. Other features of IEEE 754 are special symbols to represent unusual events. For example, instead of interrupting on a divide by 0, software can set the result to a bit pattern representing $+\infty$ or $-\infty$; the largest exponent is reserved for these special symbols. When the programmer prints the results, the program will print an infinity symbol. (For the mathematically trained, the purpose of infinity is to form topological closure of the reals.)

IEEE 754 even has a symbol for the result of invalid operations, such as 0/0 or subtracting infinity from infinity. This symbol is *NaN*, for *Not a Number*. The purpose of NaNs is to allow programmers to postpone some tests and decisions to a later time in the program when it is convenient.

The designers of IEEE 754 also wanted a floating-point representation that could be easily processed by integer comparisons, especially for sorting. This desire is why the sign is in the most significant bit, allowing a quick test of less than, greater than, or equal to 0. (It's a little more complicated than a simple integer sort, since this notation is essentially sign and magnitude rather than two's complement.)

Single precision		Double precision		Object represented
Exponent	Fraction	Exponent	Fraction	
0	0	0	0	0
0	Nonzero	0	Nonzero	± denormalized number
1–254	Anything	1–2046	Anything	± floating-point number
255	0	2047	0	± infinity
255	Nonzero	2047	Nonzero	NaN (Not a Number)

FIGURE 3.15   IEEE 754 encoding of floating-point numbers. A separate sign bit determines the sign. Denormalized numbers are described in the elaboration on page 217. This information is also found in column 4 of the MIPS Reference Data Card at the front of this book.

Placing the exponent before the significand also simplifies sorting of floating-point numbers using integer comparison instructions, since numbers with bigger exponents look larger than numbers with smaller exponents, as long as both exponents have the same sign.

Negative exponents pose a challenge to simplified sorting. If we use two's complement or any other notation in which negative exponents have a 1 in the most significant bit of the exponent field, a negative exponent will look like a big number. For example, $1.0_{two} \times 2^{-1}$ would be represented as

31	30	29	28	27	26	25	24	23	22	21	20	19	18	17	16	15	14	13	12	11	10	9	8	7	6	5	4	3	2	1	0
0	1	1	1	1	1	1	1	1	0	0	0	0	0	0	0	0	0	0	0	0	0	0	0	0	0	0	0	0	0	.	. .

(Remember that the leading 1 is implicit in the significand.) The value $1.0_{two} \times 2^{+1}$ would look like the smaller binary number

31	30	29	28	27	26	25	24	23	22	21	20	19	18	17	16	15	14	13	12	11	10	9	8	7	6	5	4	3	2	1	0
0	0	0	0	0	0	0	0	1	0	0	0	0	0	0	0	0	0	0	0	0	0	0	0	0	0	0	0	0	0	.	. .

The desirable notation must therefore represent the most negative exponent as $00 \ldots 00_{two}$ and the most positive as $11 \ldots 11_{two}$. This convention is called *biased notation*, with the bias being the number subtracted from the normal, unsigned representation to determine the real value.

IEEE 754 uses a bias of 127 for single precision, so −1 is represented by the bit pattern of the value $-1 + 127_{ten}$, or $126_{ten} = 0111\ 1110_{two}$, and +1 is represented by $1 + 127$, or $128_{ten} = 1000\ 0000_{two}$. Biased exponent means that the value represented by a floating-point number is really

$$(-1)^S \times (1 + \text{Fraction}) \times 2^{(\text{Exponent} - \text{Bias})}$$

The exponent bias for double precision is 1023.

Thus IEEE 754 notation can be processed by integer compares to accelerate sorting of floating-point numbers. Let's show the representation.

Floating-Point Representation

Show the IEEE 754 binary representation of the number -0.75_{ten} in single and double precision.

EXAMPLE

ANSWER

The number -0.75_{ten} is also

$$-3/4_{ten} \text{ or } -3/2^2{}_{ten}$$

It is also represented by the binary fraction

$$-11_{two}/2^2{}_{ten} \text{ or } -0.11_{two}$$

In scientific notation, the value is

$$-0.11_{two} \times 2^0$$

and in normalized scientific notation, it is

$$-1.1_{two} \times 2^{-1}$$

The general representation for a single precision number is

$$(-1)^S \times (1 + \text{Fraction}) \times 2^{(\text{Exponent} - 127)}$$

When we subtract the bias 127 from the exponent of $-1.1_{two} \times 2^{-1}$, the result is

$$(-1)^1 \times (1 + .1000\ 0000\ 0000\ 0000\ 0000\ 000_{two}) \times 2^{(126 - 127)}$$

The single precision binary representation of -0.75_{ten} is then

31	30	29	28	27	26	25	24	23	22	21	20	19	18	17	16	15	14	13	12	11	10	9	8	7	6	5	4	3	2	1	0
1	0	1	1	1	1	1	1	0	1	0	0	0	0	0	0	0	0	0	0	0	0	0	0	0	0	0	0	0	0	0	0

1 bit   8 bits   23 bits

The double precision representation is

$(-1)^1 \times (1 + .1000\ 0000\ 0000\ 0000\ 0000\ 0000\ 0000\ 0000\ 0000\ 0000\ 0000\ 0000\ 0000_{two}) \times 2^{(1022-1023)}$

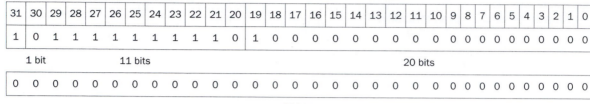

31	30	29	28	27	26	25	24	23	22	21	20	19	18	17	16	15	14	13	12	11	10	9	8	7	6	5	4	3	2	1	0
1	0	1	1	1	1	1	1	1	1	1	0	1	0	0	0	0	0	0	0	0	0	0	0	0	0	0	0	0	0	0	0

1 bit   11 bits   20 bits

0	0	0	0	0	0	0	0	0	0	0	0	0	0	0	0	0	0	0	0	0	0	0	0	0	0	0	0	0	0	0	0

32 bits

Now let's try going the other direction.

Converting Binary to Decimal Floating Point

EXAMPLE

What decimal number is represented by this single precision float?

31	30	29	28	27	26	25	24	23	22	21	20	19	18	17	16	15	14	13	12	11	10	9	8	7	6	5	4	3	2	1	0
1	1	0	0	0	0	0	0	1	0	1	0	0	0	0	0	0	0	0	0	0	0	0	0	0	0	0	0	0	.	.	.

ANSWER

The sign bit is 1, the exponent field contains 129, and the fraction field contains $1 \times 2^{-2} = 1/4$, or 0.25. Using the basic equation,

$$
\begin{aligned}
(-1)^S \times (1 + \text{Fraction}) \times 2^{(\text{Exponent} - \text{Bias})} &= (-1)^1 \times (1 + 0.25) \times 2^{(129-127)} \\
&= -1 \times 1.25 \times 2^2 \\
&= -1.25 \times 4 \\
&= -5.0
\end{aligned}
$$

In the next sections we will give the algorithms for floating-point addition and multiplication. At their core, they use the corresponding integer operations on the significands, but extra bookkeeping is necessary to handle the exponents and normalize the result. We first give an intuitive derivation of the algorithms in decimal, and then give a more detailed, binary version in the figures.

Elaboration: In an attempt to increase range without removing bits from the significand, some computers before the IEEE 754 standard used a base other than 2. For example, the IBM 360 and 370 mainframe computers use base 16. Since changing the IBM exponent by one means shifting the significand by 4 bits, "normalized" base 16 numbers can have up to 3 leading bits of 0s! Hence, hexadecimal digits mean that up to 3 bits must be dropped from the significand, which leads to surprising problems in the accuracy of floating-point arithmetic, as noted in Section 3.6. Recent IBM mainframes support IEEE 755 as well as the hex format.

Floating-Point Addition

Let's add numbers in scientific notation by hand to illustrate the problems in floating-point addition: $9.999_{ten} \times 10^1 + 1.610_{ten} \times 10^{-1}$. Assume that we can store only four decimal digits of the significand and two decimal digits of the exponent.

Step 1. To be able to add these numbers properly, we must align the decimal point of the number that has the smaller exponent. Hence, we need a form of the smaller number, $1.610_{ten} \times 10^{-1}$, that matches the larger exponent. We obtain this by observing that there are multiple representations of an unnormalized floating-point number in scientific notation:

$$1.610_{ten} \times 10^{-1} = 0.1610_{ten} \times 10^0 = 0.01610_{ten} \times 10^1$$

The number on the right is the version we desire, since its exponent matches the exponent of the larger number, $9.999_{ten} \times 10^1$. Thus the first step shifts the significand of the smaller number to the right until its corrected exponent matches that of the larger number. But we can represent only four decimal digits so, after shifting, the number is really

$$0.016_{ten} \times 10^1$$

Step 2. Next comes the addition of the significands:

$$\begin{array}{r} 9.999_{ten} \\ +\quad 0.016_{ten} \\ \hline 10.015_{ten} \end{array}$$

The sum is $10.015_{ten} \times 10^1$.

Step 3. This sum is not in normalized scientific notation, so we need to adjust it:

$$10.015_{ten} \times 10^1 = 1.0015_{ten} \times 10^2$$

Thus, after the addition we may have to shift the sum to put it into normalized form, adjusting the exponent appropriately. This example shows shifting to the right, but if one number were positive and the other were negative, it would be possible for the sum to have many leading 0s, requiring left shifts. Whenever the exponent is increased or decreased, we must check for overflow or underflow—that is, we must make sure that the exponent still fits in its field.

Step 4.   Since we assumed that the significand can be only four digits long (excluding the sign), we must round the number. In our grammar school algorithm, the rules truncate the number if the digit to the right of the desired point is between 0 and 4 and add 1 to the digit if the number to the right is between 5 and 9. The number

$$1.0015_{ten} \times 10^2$$

is rounded to four digits in the significand to

$$1.002_{ten} \times 10^2$$

since the fourth digit to the right of the decimal point was between 5 and 9. Notice that if we have bad luck on rounding, such as adding 1 to a string of 9s, the sum may no longer be normalized and we would need to perform step 3 again.

Figure 3.16 shows the algorithm for binary floating-point addition that follows this decimal example. Steps 1 and 2 are similar to the example just discussed: adjust the significand of the number with the smaller exponent and then add the two significands. Step 3 normalizes the results, forcing a check for overflow or underflow. The test for overflow and underflow in step 3 depends on the precision of the operands. Recall that the pattern of all 0 bits in the exponent is reserved and used for the floating-point representation of zero. Also, the pattern of all 1 bits in the exponent is reserved for indicating values and situations outside the scope of normal floating-point numbers (see the elaboration on page 217). Thus, for single precision, the maximum exponent is 127, and the minimum exponent is −126. The limits for double precision are 1023 and −1022.

EXAMPLE

Decimal Floating-Point Addition

Try adding the numbers 0.5_{ten} and -0.4375_{ten} in binary using the algorithm in Figure 3.16.

Let's first look at the binary version of the two numbers in normalized scientific notation, assuming that we keep 4 bits of precision:

$$0.5_{ten} = 1/2_{ten} = 1/2^1_{ten}$$
$$= 0.1_{two} = 0.1_{two} \times 2^0 = 1.000_{two} \times 2^{-1}$$
$$-0.4375_{ten} = -7/16_{ten} = -7/2^4_{ten}$$
$$= -0.0111_{two} = -0.0111_{two} \times 2^0 = -1.110_{two} \times 2^{-2}$$

Now we follow the algorithm:

Step 1. The significand of the number with the lesser exponent ($-1.11_{two} \times 2^{-2}$) is shifted right until its exponent matches the larger number:

$$-1.110_{two} \times 2^{-2} = -0.111_{two} \times 2^{-1}$$

Step 2. Add the significands:

$$1.000_{two} \times 2^{-1} + (-0.111_{two} \times 2^{-1}) = 0.001_{two} \times 2^{-1}$$

Step 3. Normalize the sum, checking for overflow or underflow:

$$0.001_{two} \times 2^{-1} = 0.010_{two} \times 2^{-2} = 0.100_{two} \times 2^{-3}$$
$$= 1.000_{two} \times 2^{-4}$$

Since $127 \geq -4 \geq -126$, there is no overflow or underflow. (The biased exponent would be $-4 + 127$, or 123, which is between 1 and 254, the smallest and largest unreserved biased exponents.)

Step 4. Round the sum:

$$1.000_{two} \times 2^{-4}$$

The sum already fits exactly in 4 bits, so there is no change to the bits due to rounding.
This sum is then

$$1.000_{two} \times 2^{-4} = 0.0001000_{two} = 0.0001_{two}$$
$$= 1/2^4_{ten} = 1/16_{ten} = 0.0625_{ten}$$

This sum is what we would expect from adding 0.5_{ten} to -0.4375_{ten}.

Many computers dedicate hardware to run floating-point operations as fast as possible. Figure 3.17 sketches the basic organization of hardware for floating-point addition.

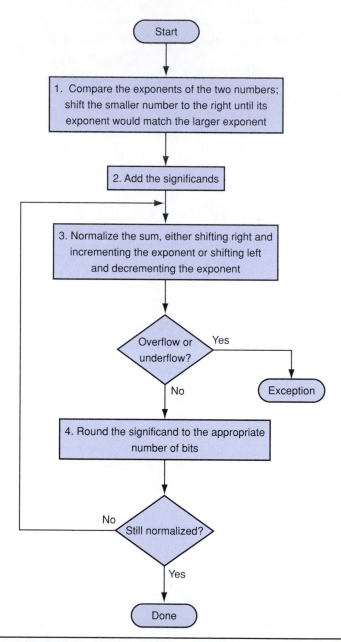

FIGURE 3.16   Floating-point addition. The normal path is to execute steps 3 and 4 once, but if rounding causes the sum to be unnormalized, we must repeat step 3.

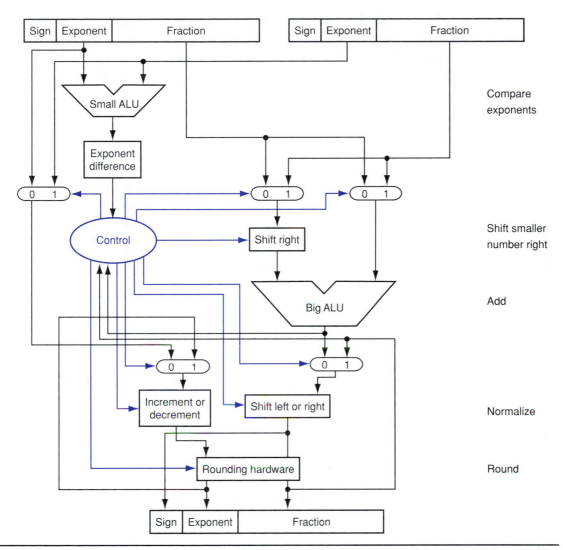

FIGURE 3.17 Block diagram of an arithmetic unit dedicated to floating-point addition. The steps of Figure 3.16 correspond to each block, from top to bottom. First, the exponent of one operand is subtracted from the other using the small ALU to determine which is larger and by how much. This difference controls the three multiplexors; from left to right, they select the larger exponent, the significand of the smaller number, and the significand of the larger number. The smaller significand is shifted right, and then the significands are added together using the big ALU. The normalization step then shifts the sum left or right and increments or decrements the exponent. Rounding then creates the final result, which may require normalizing again to produce the final result.

Floating-Point Multiplication

Now that we have explained floating-point addition, let's try floating-point multiplication. We start by multiplying decimal numbers in scientific notation by hand: $1.110_{ten} \times 10^{10} \times 9.200_{ten} \times 10^{-5}$. Assume that we can store only four digits of the significand and two digits of the exponent.

Step 1. Unlike addition, we calculate the exponent of the product by simply adding the exponents of the operands together:

$$\text{New exponent} = 10 + (-5) = 5$$

Let's do this with the biased exponents as well to make sure we obtain the same result: $10 + 127 = 137$, and $-5 + 127 = 122$, so

$$\text{New exponent} = 137 + 122 = 259$$

This result is too large for the 8-bit exponent field, so something is amiss! The problem is with the bias because we are adding the biases as well as the exponents:

$$\text{New exponent} = (10 + 127) + (-5 + 127) = (5 + 2 \times 127) = 259$$

Accordingly, to get the correct biased sum when we add biased numbers, we must subtract the bias from the sum:

$$\text{New exponent} = 137 + 122 - 127 = 259 - 127 = 132 = (5 + 127)$$

and 5 is indeed the exponent we calculated initially.

Step 2. Next comes the multiplication of the significands:

$$
\begin{array}{r}
1.110_{ten} \\
\times\ 9.200_{ten} \\
\hline
0000 \\
0000 \\
2220 \\
9990 \\
\hline
10212000_{ten} \\
\end{array}
$$

There are three digits to the right of the decimal for each operand, so the decimal point is placed six digits from the right in the product significand:

$$10.212000_{ten}$$

Assuming that we can keep only three digits to the right of the decimal point, the product is 10.212×10^5.

Step 3. This product is unnormalized, so we need to normalize it:

$$10.212_{ten} \times 10^5 = 1.0212_{ten} \times 10^6$$

Thus, after the multiplication, the product can be shifted right one digit to put it in normalized form, adding 1 to the exponent. At this point, we can check for overflow and underflow. Underflow may occur if both operands are small—that is, if both have large negative exponents.

Step 4. We assumed that the significand is only four digits long (excluding the sign), so we must round the number. The number

$$1.0212_{ten} \times 10^6$$

is rounded to four digits in the significand to

$$1.021_{ten} \times 10^6$$

Step 5. The sign of the product depends on the signs of the original operands. If they are both the same, the sign is positive; otherwise it's negative. Hence the product is

$$+1.021_{ten} \times 10^6$$

The sign of the sum in the addition algorithm was determined by addition of the significands, but in multiplication the sign of the product is determined by the signs of the operands.

Once again, as Figure 3.18 shows, multiplication of binary floating-point numbers is quite similar to the steps we have just completed. We start with calculating the new exponent of the product by adding the biased exponents, being sure to subtract one bias to get the proper result. Next is multiplication of significands, followed by an optional normalization step. The size of the exponent is checked for overflow or underflow, and then the product is rounded. If rounding leads to further normalization, we once again check for exponent size. Finally, set the sign bit to 1 if the signs of the operands were different (negative product) or to 0 if they were the same (positive product).

Decimal Floating-Point Multiplication

Let's try multiplying the numbers 0.5_{ten} and -0.4375_{ten}, using the steps in Figure 3.18.

EXAMPLE

ANSWER

In binary, the task is multiplying $1.000_{two} \times 2^{-1}$ by $-1.110_{two} \times 2^{-2}$.

Step 1. Adding the exponents without bias:

$$-1 + (-2) = -3$$

or, using the biased representation:

$$(-1 + 127) + (-2 + 127) - 127 = (-1 - 2) + (127 + 127 - 127)$$
$$= -3 + 127 = 124$$

Step 2. Multiplying the significands:

$$
\begin{array}{r}
1.000_{two} \\
\times \quad 1.110_{two} \\
\hline
0000 \\
1000 \\
1000 \\
1000 \\
\hline
1110000_{two}
\end{array}
$$

The product is $1.110000_{two} \times 2^{-3}$, but we need to keep it to 4 bits, so it is $1.110_{two} \times 2^{-3}$.

Step 3. Now we check the product to make sure it is normalized, and then check the exponent for overflow or underflow. The product is already normalized and, since $127 \geq -3 \geq -126$, there is no overflow or underflow. (Using the biased representation, $254 \geq 124 \geq 1$, so the exponent fits.)

Step 4. Rounding the product makes no change:

$$1.110_{two} \times 2^{-3}$$

Step 5. Since the signs of the original operands differ, make the sign of the product negative. Hence the product is

$$-1.110_{two} \times 2^{-3}$$

Converting to decimal to check our results:

$$-1.110_{two} \times 2^{-3} = -0.001110_{two} = -0.00111_{two}$$
$$= -7/2^5{}_{ten} = -7/32_{ten} = -0.21875_{ten}$$

The product of 0.5_{ten} and -0.4375_{ten} is indeed -0.21875_{ten}.

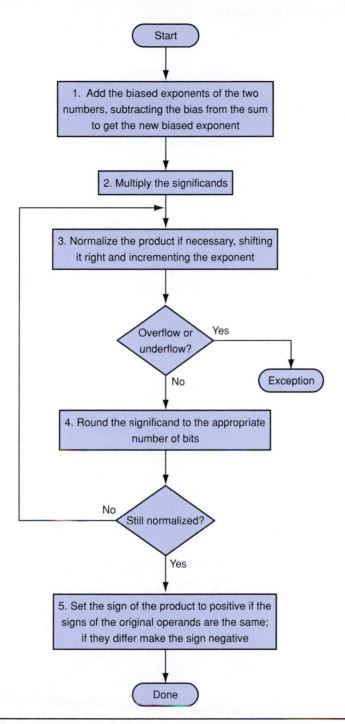

FIGURE 3.18 Floating-point multiplication. The normal path is to execute steps 3 and 4 once, but if rounding causes the sum to be unnormalized, we must repeat step 3.

Floating-Point Instructions in MIPS

MIPS supports the IEEE 754 single precision and double precision formats with these instructions:

- Floating-point *addition, single* (add.s) and *addition, double* (add.d)

- Floating-point *subtraction, single* (sub.s) and *subtraction, double* (sub.d)

- Floating-point *multiplication, single* (mul.s) and *multiplication, double* (mul.d)

- Floating-point *division, single* (div.s) and *division, double* (div.d)

- Floating-point *comparison, single* (c.x.s) and *comparison, double* (c.x.d), where x may be *equal* (eq), *not equal* (neq), *less than* (lt), *less than or equal* (le), *greater than* (gt), or *greater than or equal* (ge)

- Floating-point *branch, true* (bc1t) and *branch, false* (bc1f)

Floating-point comparison sets a bit to true or false, depending on the comparison condition, and a floating-point branch then decides whether or not to branch, depending on the condition.

The MIPS designers decided to add separate floating-point registers—called $f0, $f1, $f2, ...—used either for single precision or double precision. Hence, they included separate loads and stores for floating-point registers: lwc1 and swc1. The base registers for floating-point data transfers remain integer registers. The MIPS code to load two single precision numbers from memory, add them, and then store the sum might look like this:

```
lwc1    $f4,x($sp)  # Load 32-bit F.P. number into F4
lwc1    $f6,y($sp)  # Load 32-bit F.P. number into F6
add.s   $f2,$f4,$f6 # F2 = F4 + F6 single precision
swc1    $f2,z($sp)  # Store 32-bit F.P. number from F2
```

A double precision register is really an even-odd pair of single precision registers, using the even register number as its name.

Figure 3.19 summarizes the floating-point portion of the MIPS architecture revealed in this chapter, with the additions to support floating point shown in color. Similar to Figure 2.25 on page 103 in Chapter 2, we show the encoding of these instructions in Figure 3.20.

MIPS floating-point operands

Name	Example	Comments
32 floating-point registers	$f0, $f1, $f2, . . . , $f31	MIPS floating-point registers are used in pairs for double precision numbers.
2^{30} memory words	Memory[0], Memory[4], . . . , Memory[4294967292]	Accessed only by data transfer instructions. MIPS uses byte addresses, so sequential word addresses differ by 4. Memory holds data structures, such as arrays, and spilled registers, such as those saved on procedure calls.

MIPS floating-point assembly language

Category	Instruction	Example	Meaning	Comments
Arithmetic	FP add single	add.s $f2,$f4,$f6	$f2 = $f4 + $f6	FP add (single precision)
	FP subtract single	sub.s $f2,$f4,$f6	$f2 = $f4 - $f6	FP sub (single precision)
	FP multiply single	mul.s $f2,$f4,$f6	$f2 = $f4 × $f6	FP multiply (single precision)
	FP divide single	div.s $f2,$f4,$f6	$f2 = $f4 / $f6	FP divide (single precision)
	FP add double	add.d $f2,$f4,$f6	$f2 = $f4 + $f6	FP add (double precision)
	FP subtract double	sub.d $f2,$f4,$f6	$f2 = $f4 - $f6	FP sub (double precision)
	FP multiply double	mul.d $f2,$f4,$f6	$f2 = $f4 × $f6	FP multiply (double precision)
	FP divide double	div.d $f2,$f4,$f6	$f2 = $f4 / $f6	FP divide (double precision)
Data transfer	load word copr. 1	lwc1 $f1,100($s2)	$f1 = Memory[$s2 + 100]	32-bit data to FP register
	store word copr. 1	swc1 $f1,100($s2)	Memory[$s2 + 100] = $f1	32-bit data to memory
Conditional branch	branch on FP true	bc1t 25	if (cond == 1) go to PC + 4 + 100	PC-relative branch if FP cond.
	branch on FP false	bc1f 25	if (cond == 0) go to PC + 4 + 100	PC-relative branch if not cond.
	FP compare single (eq,ne,lt,le,gt,ge)	c.lt.s $f2,$f4	if ($f2 < $f4) cond = 1; else cond = 0	FP compare less than single precision
	FP compare double (eq,ne,lt,le,gt,ge)	c.lt.d $f2,$f4	if ($f2 < $f4) cond = 1; else cond = 0	FP compare less than double precision

MIPS floating-point machine language

Name	Format			Example				Comments
add.s	R	17	16	6	4	2	0	add.s $f2,$f4,$f6
sub.s	R	17	16	6	4	2	1	sub.s $f2,$f4,$f6
mul.s	R	17	16	6	4	2	2	mul.s $f2,$f4,$f6
div.s	R	17	16	6	4	2	3	div.s $f2,$f4,$f6
add.d	R	17	17	6	4	2	0	add.d $f2,$f4,$f6
sub.d	R	17	17	6	4	2	1	sub.d $f2,$f4,$f6
mul.d	R	17	17	6	4	2	2	mul.d $f2,$f4,$f6
div.d	R	17	17	6	4	2	3	div.d $f2,$f4,$f6
lwc1	I	49	20	2	100			lwc1 $f2,100($s4)
swc1	I	57	20	2	100			swc1 $f2,100($s4)
bc1t	I	17	8	1	25			bc1t 25
bc1f	I	17	8	0	25			bc1f 25
c.lt.s	R	17	16	4	2	0	60	c.lt.s $f2,$f4
c.lt.d	R	17	17	4	2	0	60	c.lt.d $f2,$f4
Field size		6 bits	5 bits	5 bits	5 bits	5 bits	6 bits	All MIPS instructions 32 bits

FIGURE 3.19   MIPS floating-point architecture revealed thus far. See Appendix A, Section A.10, page A-48, for more detail. This information is also found in column 2 of the MIPS Reference Data Card at the front of this book.

op(31:26):								
28–26 31–29	0(000)	1(001)	2(010)	3(011)	4(100)	5(101)	6(110)	7(111)
0(000)	Rfmt	Bltz/gez	j	jal	beq	bne	blez	bgtz
1(001)	addi	addiu	slti	sltiu	andi	ori	xori	lui
2(010)	TLB	FlPt						
3(011)								
4(100)	lb	lh	lwl	lw	lbu	lhu	lwr	
5(101)	sb	sh	swl	sw			swr	
6(110)	lwc0	lwc1						
7(111)	swc0	swc1						

op(31:26) = 010001 (FlPt), (rt(16:16) = 0 => c = f, rt(16:16) = 1 => c = t), rs(25:21):								
23–21 25–24	0(000)	1(001)	2(010)	3(011)	4(100)	5(101)	6(110)	7(111)
0(00)	mfc1		cfc1		mtc1		ctc1	
1(01)	bc1.c							
2(10)	f = single	f = double						
3(11)								

op(31:26) = 010001 (FlPt), (f above: 10000 => f = s, 10001 => f = d), funct(5:0):								
2–0 5–3	0(000)	1(001)	2(010)	3(011)	4(100)	5(101)	6(110)	7(111)
0(000)	add.f	sub.f	mul.f	div.f		abs.f	mov.f	neg.f
1(001)								
2(010)								
3(011)								
4(100)	cvt.s.f	cvt.d.f			cvt.w.f			
5(101)								
6(110)	c.f.f	c.un.f	c.eq.f	c.ueq.f	c.olt.f	c.ult.f	c.ole.f	c.ule.f
7(111)	c.sf.f	c.ngle.f	c.seq.f	c.ngl.f	c.lt.f	c.nge.f	c.le.f	c.ngt.f

FIGURE 3.20　MIPS floating-point instruction encoding. This notation gives the value of a field by row and by column. For example, in the top portion of the figure lw is found in row number 4 (100_{two} for bits 31–29 of the instruction) and column number 3 (011_{two} for bits 28–26 of the instruction), so the corresponding value of the op field (bits 31–26) is 100011_{two}. Underscore means the field is used elsewhere. For example, FlPt in row 2 and column 1 (op = 010001_{two}) is defined in the bottom part of the figure. Hence sub.f in row 0 and column 1 of the bottom section means that the funct field (bits 5–0) of the instruction is 000001_{two} and the op field (bits 31–26) is 010001_{two}. Note that the 5-bit rs field, specified in the middle portion of the figure, determines whether the operation is single precision (f = s so rs = 10000) or double precision (f = d so rs = 10001). Similarly, bit 16 of the instruction determines if the bc1.c instruction tests for true (bit 16 = 1 =>bc1.t) or false (bit 16 = 0 =>bc1.f). Instructions in color are described in Chapter 2 or this chapter, with Appendix A covering all instructions. This information is also found in column 2 of the MIPS Reference Data Card at the front of this book.

One issue that computer designers face in supporting floating-point arithmetic is whether to use the same registers used by the integer instructions or to add a special set for floating point. Because programs normally perform integer operations and floating-point operations on different data, separating the registers will only slightly increase the number of instructions needed to execute a program. The major impact is to create a separate set of data transfer instructions to move data between floating-point registers and memory.

The benefits of separate floating-point registers are having twice as many registers without using up more bits in the instruction format, having twice the register bandwidth by having separate integer and floating-point register sets, and being able to customize registers to floating point; for example, some computers convert all sized operands in registers into a single internal format.

Compiling a Floating-Point C Program into MIPS Assembly Code

Let's convert a temperature in Fahrenheit to Celsius:

```
float f2c (float fahr)
        {
                return ((5.0/9.0) * (fahr - 32.0));
        }
```

Assume that the floating-point argument `fahr` is passed in `$f12` and the result should go in `$f0`. (Unlike integer registers, floating-point register 0 can contain a number.) What is the MIPS assembly code?

EXAMPLE

We assume that the compiler places the three floating-point constants in memory within easy reach of the global pointer `$gp`. The first two instructions load the constants 5.0 and 9.0 into floating-point registers:

```
f2c:
        lwc1 $f16,const5($gp) # $f16 = 5.0 (5.0 in memory)
        lwc1 $f18,const9($gp) # $f18 = 9.0 (9.0 in memory)
```

ANSWER

They are then divided to get the fraction 5.0/9.0:

```
div.s $f16, $f16, $f18 # $f16 = 5.0 / 9.0
```

(Many compilers would divide 5.0 by 9.0 at compile time and save the single constant 5.0/9.0 in memory, thereby avoiding the divide at runtime.) Next we load the constant 32.0 and then subtract it from fahr ($f12):

```
lwc1 $f18, const32($gp) # $f18 = 32.0
sub.s $f18, $f12, $f18 # $f18 = fahr - 32.0
```

Finally, we multiply the two intermediate results, placing the product in $f0 as the return result, and then return

```
mul.s$f0,  $f16, $f18 # $f0 = (5/9)*(fahr - 32.0)
jr   $ra # return
```

Now let's perform floating-point operations on matrices, code commonly found in scientific programs.

EXAMPLE

Compiling Floating-Point C Procedure with Two-Dimensional Matrices into MIPS

Most floating-point calculations are performed in double precision. Let's perform matrix multiply of X = X + Y * Z. Let's assume X, Y, and Z are all square matrices with 32 elements in each dimension.

```
void mm (double x[][], double y[][], double z[][])
{
        int i, j, k;

        for (i = 0; i! = 32; i = i + 1)
        for (j = 0; j! = 32; j = j + 1)
        for (k = 0; k! = 32; k = k + 1)
          x[i][j] = x[i][j] + y[i][k] * z[k][j];
}
```

The array starting addresses are parameters, so they are in $a0, $a1, and $a2. Assume that the integer variables are in $s0, $s1, and $s2, respectively. What is the MIPS assembly code for the body of the procedure?

Note that x[i][j] is used in the innermost loop above. Since the loop index is k, the index does not affect x[i][j], so we can avoid loading and storing x[i][j] each iteration. Instead, the compiler loads x[i][j] into a register outside the loop, accumulates the sum of the products of y[i][k] and z[k][j] in that same register, and then stores the sum into x[i][j] upon termination of the innermost loop.

We keep the code simpler by using the assembly language pseudoinstructions li (which loads a constant into a register), and l.d and s.d (which the assembler turns into a pair of data transfer instructions, lwc1 or swc1, to a pair of floating-point registers).

The body of the procedure starts with saving the loop termination value of 32 in a temporary register and then initializing the three *for* loop variables:

```
mm:...
        li      $t1, 32  # $t1 = 32 (row size/loop end)
        li      $s0, 0   # i = 0; initialize 1st for loop
L1:     li      $s1, 0   # j = 0; restart 2nd for loop
L2:     li      $s2, 0   # k = 0; restart 3rd for loop
```

To calculate the address of x[i][j], we need to know how a 32 × 32, two-dimensional array is stored in memory. As you might expect, its layout is the same as if there were 32 single-dimension arrays, each with 32 elements. So the first step is to skip over the i "single-dimensional arrays," or rows, to get the one we want. Thus we multiply the index in the first dimension by the size of the row, 32. Since 32 is a power of 2, we can use a shift instead:

```
sll  $t2, $s0, 5 # $t2 = i * 2^5 (size of row of x)
```

Now we add the second index to select the jth element of the desired row:

```
addu  $t2, $t2, $s1 # $t2 = i * size(row) + j
```

To turn this sum into a byte index, we multiply it by the size of a matrix element in bytes. Since each element is 8 bytes for double precision, we can instead shift left by 3:

```
sll  $t2, $t2, 3 # $t2 = byte offset of [i][j]
```

Next we add this sum to the base address of x, giving the address of x[i][j], and then load the double precision number x[i][j] into $f4:

```
addu  $t2, $a0, $t2 # $t2 = byte address of x[i][j]
l.d   $f4, 0($t2) # $f4 = 8 bytes of x[i][j]
```

The following five instructions are virtually identical to the last five: calculate the address and then load the double precision number z[k][j].

```
L3:     sll $t0, $s2, 5 # $t0 = k * 2⁵ (size of row of z)
        addu $t0, $t0, $s1 # $t0 = k * size(row) + j
        sll $t0, $t0, 3 # $t0 = byte offset of [k][j]
        addu $t0, $a2, $t0 # $t0 = byte address of z[k][j]
        l.d $f16, 0($t0) # $f16 = 8 bytes of z[k][j]
```

Similarly, the next five instructions are like the last five: calculate the address and then load the double precision number y[i][k].

```
sll       $t0, $s0, 5 # $t0 = i * 2⁵ (size of row of y)
addu      $t0, $t0, $s2 # $t0 = i * size(row) + k
sll       $t0, $t0, 3 # $t0 = byte offset of [i][k]
addu      $t0, $a1, $t0 # $t0 = byte address of y[i][k]
l.d       $f18, 0($t0) # $f18 = 8 bytes of y[i][k]
```

Now that we have loaded all the data, we are finally ready to do some floating-point operations! We multiply elements of y and z located in registers $f18 and $f16, and then accumulate the sum in $f4.

```
mul.d $f16, $f18, $f16 # $f16 = y[i][k] * z[k][j]
add.d $f4, $f4, $f16 # f4 = x[i][j]+ y[i][k] * z[k][j]
```

The final block increments the index k and loops back if the index is not 32. If it is 32, and thus the end of the innermost loop, we need to store the sum accumulated in $f4 into x[i][j].

```
addiu  $s2, $s2, 1 # $k k + 1
bne    $s2, $t1, L3 # if (k != 32) go to L3
s.d    $f4, 0($t2) # x[i][j] = $f4
```

Similarly, these final four instructions increment the index variable of the middle and outermost loops, looping back if the index is not 32 and exiting if the index is 32.

```
addiu  $s1, $s1, 1 # $j = j + 1
bne    $s1, $t1, L2 # if (j != 32) go to L2
addiu  $s0, $s0, 1 # $i = i + 1
bne    $s0, $t1, L1 # if (i != 32) go to L1
. . .
```

Elaboration: The array layout discussed in the example, called *row-major order,* is used by C and many other programming languages. Fortran instead uses *column-major order,* whereby the array is stored column by column.

Only 16 of the 32 MIPS floating-point registers could originally be used for single precision operations: $f0, $f2, $f4,..., $f30. Double precision is computed using pairs of these registers. The odd-numbered floating-point registers were used only to load and store the right half of 64-bit floating-point numbers. MIPS-32 added `l.d` and `s.d` to the instruction set. MIPS-32 also added "paired single" versions of all floating-point instructions, where a single instruction results in two parallel floating-point operations on two 32-bit operands inside 64-bit registers. For example, `add.ps F0, F2, F4` is equivalent to `add.s F0, F2, F4` followed by `add.s F1, F3, F5`.

Another reason for separate integers and floating-point registers is that microprocessors in the 1980s didn't have enough transistors to put the floating-point unit on the same chip as the integer unit. Hence the floating-point unit, including the floating-point registers, was optionally available as a second chip. Such optional accelerator chips are called *coprocessors,* and explain the acronym for floating-point loads in MIPS: `lwc1` means load word to coprocessor 1, the floating-point unit. (Coprocessor 0 deals with virtual memory, described in Chapter 7.) Since the early 1990s, microprocessors have integrated floating point (and just about everything else) on chip, and hence the term "coprocessor" joins "accumulator" and "core memory" as quaint terms that date the speaker.

Elaboration: Although there are many ways to throw hardware at floating-point multiply to make it go fast, floating-point division is considerably more challenging to make fast and accurate. Slow divides in early computers led to removal of divides from many algorithms, but parallel computers have inspired rediscovery of divide-intensive algorithms that work better on these computers. Hence, we may need faster divides.

One technique to leverage a fast multiplier is *Newton's iteration*, where division is recast as finding the zero of a function to find the reciprocal $1/x$, which is then multiplied by the other operand. Iteration techniques *cannot* be rounded properly without calculating many extra bits. A TI chip solves this problem by calculating an extra-precise reciprocal.

Elaboration: Java embraces IEEE 754 by name in its definition of Java floating-point data types and operations. Thus, the code in the first example could have well been generated for a class method that converted Fahrenheit to Celsius.

The second example uses multiple dimensional arrays, which are not explicitly supported in Java. Java allows arrays of arrays, but each array may have its own length, unlike multiple dimensional arrays in C. Like the examples in Chapter 2, a Java version of this second example would require a good deal of checking code for array bounds, including a new length calculation at the end of row access. It would also need to check that the object reference is not null.

Accurate Arithmetic

Unlike integers, which can represent exactly every number between the smallest and largest number, floating-point numbers are normally approximations for a number they can't really represent. The reason is that an infinite variety of real numbers exists between, say, 0 and 1, but no more than 2^{53} can be represented

guard The first of two extra bits kept on the right during intermediate calculations of floating-point numbers; used to improve rounding accuracy.

round Method to make the intermediate floating-point result fit the floating-point format; the goal is typically to find the nearest number that can be represented in the format.

exactly in double precision floating point. The best we can do is get the floating-point representation close to the actual number. Thus, IEEE 754 offers several modes of rounding to let the programmer pick the desired approximation.

Rounding sounds simple enough, but to round accurately requires the hardware to include extra bits in the calculation. In the preceding examples, we were vague on the number of bits that an intermediate representation can occupy, but clearly if every intermediate result had to be truncated to the exact number of digits, there would be no opportunity to round. IEEE 754, therefore, always keeps 2 extra bits on the right during intermediate additions, called **guard** and **round**, respectively. Let's do a decimal example to illustrate the value of these extra digits.

EXAMPLE

ANSWER

Rounding with Guard Digits

Add $2.56_{ten} \times 10^0$ to $2.34_{ten} \times 10^2$, assuming that we have three significant decimal digits. Round to the nearest decimal number with three significant decimal digits, first with guard and round digits, and then without them.

First we must shift the smaller number to the right to align the exponents, so $2.56_{ten} \times 10^0$ becomes $0.0256_{ten} \times 10^2$. Since we have guard and round digits, we are able to represent the two least significant digits when we align exponents. The guard digit holds 5 and the round digit holds 6. The sum is

$$
\begin{array}{r}
2.3400_{ten} \\
+\ \ 0.0256_{ten} \\
\hline
2.3656_{ten}
\end{array}
$$

Thus the sum is $2.3656_{ten} \times 10^2$. Since we have two digits to round, we want values 0 to 49 to round down and 51 to 99 to round up, with 50 being the tie-breaker. Rounding the sum up with three significant digits yields $2.37_{ten} \times 10^2$.

Doing this *without* guard and round digits drops two digits from the calculation. The new sum is then

$$
\begin{array}{r}
2.34_{ten} \\
+\ \ 0.02_{ten} \\
\hline
2.36_{ten}
\end{array}
$$

The answer is $2.36_{ten} \times 10^2$, off by 1 in the last digit from the sum above.

Since the worst case for rounding would be when the actual number is halfway between two floating-point representations, accuracy in floating point is normally measured in terms of the number of bits in error in the least significant bits of the significand; the measure is called the number of **units in the last place**, or **ulp**. If a number was off by 2 in the least significant bits, it would be called off by 2 ulps. Provided there is no overflow, underflow, or invalid operation exceptions, IEEE 754 guarantees that the computer uses the number that is within one-half ulp.

units in the last place (ulp) The number of bits in error in the least significant bits of the significand between the actual number and the number that can be represented.

Elaboration: Although the example above really needed just one extra digit, multiply can need two. A binary product may have one leading 0 bit; hence, the normalizing step must shift the product 1 bit left. This shifts the guard digit into the least significant bit of the product, leaving the round bit to help accurately round the product.

There are four rounding modes: always round up (toward $+\infty$), always round down (toward $-\infty$), truncate, and round to nearest even. The final mode determines what to do if the number is exactly halfway in between. The Internal Revenue Service always rounds 0.50 dollars up, possibly to the benefit of the IRS. A more equitable way would be to round up this case half the time and round down the other half. IEEE 754 says that if the least significant bit retained in a halfway case would be odd, add one; if it's even, truncate. This method always creates a 0 in the least significant bit in the tie-breaking case, giving the rounding mode its name. This mode is the most commonly used, and the only one that Java supports.

The goal of the extra rounding bits is to allow the computer to get the same results as if the intermediate results were calculated to infinite precision and then rounded.

To support this goal and rounding to the nearest even, the standard has a third bit in addition to guard and round; it is set whenever there are nonzero bits to the right of the round bit. This sticky bit allows the computer to see the difference between $0.50 \ldots 00_{ten}$ and $0.50 \ldots 01_{ten}$ when rounding.

sticky bit A bit used in rounding in addition to guard and round that is set whenever there are nonzero bits to the right of the round bit.

The sticky bit may be set, for example, during addition, when the smaller number is shifted to the right. Suppose we added $5.01_{ten} \times 10^{-1}$ to $2.34_{ten} \times 10^{2}$ in the example above. Even with guard and round, we would be adding 0.0050 to 2.34, with a sum of 2.3450. The sticky bit would be set since there are nonzero bits to the right. Without the sticky bit to remember whether any 1s were shifted off, we would assume the number is equal to $2.345000 \ldots 00$ and round to the nearest even of 2.34. With the sticky bit to remember that the number is larger than $2.345000 \ldots 00$, we round instead to 2.35.

Summary

The Big Picture that follows reinforces the stored-program concept from Chapter 2; the meaning of the information cannot be determined just by looking at the bits, for the same bits can represent a variety of objects. This section shows that computer arithmetic is finite and thus can disagree with natural arithmetic. For example, the IEEE 754 standard floating-point representation

$$(-1)^{S} \times (1 + Fraction) \times 2^{(Exponent - Bias)}$$

is almost always an approximation of the real number. Computer systems must take care to minimize this gap between computer arithmetic and arithmetic in the real world, and programmers at times need to be aware of the implications of this approximation.

C type	Java type	Data transfers	Operations
int	int	lw, sw, lui	addu, addiu, subu, mult, div, and, andi, or, ori, nor, slt, slti
unsigned int	—	lw, sw, lui	addu, addiu, subu, multu, divu, and, andi, or, ori, nor, sltu, sltiu
char	—	lb, sb, lui	addu, addiu, subu, multu, divu, and, andi, or, ori, nor, sltu, sltiu
—	char	lh, sh, lui	addu, addiu, subu, multu, divu, and, andi, or, ori, nor, sltu, sltiu
float	float	lwc1, swc1	add.s, sub.s, mult.s, div.s, c.eq.s, c.lt.s, c.le.s
double	double	l.d, s.d	add.d, sub.d, mult.d, div.d, c.eq.d, c.lt.d, c.le.d

The BIG Picture

Bit patterns have no inherent meaning. They may represent signed integers, unsigned integers, floating-point numbers, instructions, and so on. What is represented depends on the instruction that operates on the bits in the word.

The major difference between computer numbers and numbers in the real world is that computer numbers have limited size, hence limited precision; it's possible to calculate a number too big or too small to be represented in a word. Programmers must remember these limits and write programs accordingly.

Hardware/ Software Interface

In the last chapter we presented the storage classes of the programming language C (see the "Hardware/Software Interface" section on page 85). The table above shows some of the C and Java data types, the MIPS data transfer instructions, and instructions that operate on those types that appear in Chapter 2 and this chapter. Note that Java omits unsigned integers.

Suppose there was a 16-bit IEEE 754 floating-point format with 5 exponent bits. What would be the likely range of numbers it could represent?

Check Yourself

1. $1.0000\ 0000\ 00 \times 2^0$ to $1.1111\ 1111\ 11 \times 2^{31}$, 0

2. $\pm 1.0000\ 0000\ 0 \times 2^{-14}$ to $\pm 1.1111\ 1111\ 1 \times 2^{15}$, $\pm 0, \pm\infty$, NaN

3. $\pm 1.0000\ 0000\ 00 \times 2^{-14}$ to $\pm 1.1111\ 1111\ 11 \times 2^{15}$, $\pm 0, \pm\infty$, NaN

4. $\pm 1.0000\ 0000\ 00 \times 2^{-15}$ to $\pm 1.1111\ 1111\ 11 \times 2^{14}$, $\pm 0, \pm\infty$, NaN

Elaboration: To accommodate comparisons that may include NaNs, the standard includes *ordered* and *unordered* as options for compares. Hence the full MIPS instruction set has many flavors of compares to support NaNs. (Java does not support unordered compares.)

In an attempt to squeeze every last bit of precision from a floating-point operation, the standard allows some numbers to be represented in unnormalized form. Rather than having a gap between 0 and the smallest normalized number, IEEE allows *denormalized numbers* (also known as *denorms* or *subnormals*). They have the same exponent as zero but a nonzero significand. They allow a number to degrade in significance until it becomes 0, called *gradual underflow*. For example, the smallest positive single precision normalized number is

$1.0000\ 0000\ 0000\ 0000\ 0000\ 000_{\text{two}} \times 2^{-126}$

but the smallest single precision denormalized number is

$0.0000\ 0000\ 0000\ 0000\ 0000\ 001_{\text{two}} \times 2^{-126}$, or $1.0_{\text{two}} \times 2^{-149}$

For double precision, the denorm gap goes from 1.0×2^{-1022} to 1.0×2^{-1074}.

The possibility of an occasional unnormalized operand has given headaches to floating-point designers who are trying to build fast floating-point units. Hence, many computers cause an exception if an operand is denormalized, letting software complete the operation. Although software implementations are perfectly valid, their lower performance has lessened the popularity of denorms in portable floating-point software. Also, if programmers do not expect denorms, their programs may be surprised.

3.7 Real Stuff: Floating Point in the IA-32

The IA-32 has regular multiply and divide instructions that operate entirely on registers, unlike the reliance on Hi and Lo in MIPS. (In fact, later versions of the MIPS instruction set have added similar instructions.)

The main differences are found in floating-point instructions. The IA-32 floating-point architecture is different from all other computers in the world.

The IA-32 Floating-Point Architecture

The Intel 8087 floating-point coprocessor was announced in 1980. This architecture extended the 8086 with about 60 floating-point instructions.

Intel provided a stack architecture with its floating-point instructions: loads push numbers onto the stack, operations find operands in the two top elements of the stacks, and stores can pop elements off the stack. Intel supplemented this stack architecture with instructions and addressing modes that allow the architecture to have some of the benefits of a register-memory model. In addition to finding operands in the top two elements of the stack, one operand can be in memory or in one of the seven registers on-chip below the top of the stack. Thus, a complete stack instruction set is supplemented by a limited set of register-memory instructions.

This hybrid is still a restricted register-memory model, however, since loads always move data to the top of the stack while incrementing the top-of-stack pointer and stores can only move the top of stack to memory. Intel uses the notation ST to indicate the top of stack, and ST(i) to represent the *i*th register below the top of stack.

Another novel feature of this architecture is that the operands are wider in the register stack than they are stored in memory, and all operations are performed at this wide internal precision. Unlike the maximum of 64 bits on MIPS, the IA-32 floating-point operands on the stack are 80 bits wide. Numbers are automatically converted to the internal 80-bit format on a load and converted back to the appropriate size on a store. This *double extended precision* is not supported by programming languages, although it has been useful to programmers of mathematical software.

Memory data can be 32-bit (single precision) or 64-bit (double precision) floating-point numbers. The register-memory version of these instructions will then convert the memory operand to this Intel 80-bit format before performing the operation. The data transfer instructions also will automatically convert 16- and 32-bit integers to floating point, and vice versa, for integer loads and stores.

The IA-32 floating-point operations can be divided into four major classes:

1. Data movement instructions, including load, load constant, and store

2. Arithmetic instructions, including add, subtract, multiply, divide, square root, and absolute value

3. Comparison, including instructions to send the result to the integer processor so that it can branch

4. Transcendental instructions, including sine, cosine, log, and exponentiation

Figure 3.21 shows some of the 60 floating-point operations. Note that we get even more combinations when including the operand modes for these operations. Figure 3.22 shows the many options for floating-point add.

Data transfer	Arithmetic	Compare	Transcendental
F{I}LD mem/ST(i)	F{I}ADD{P} mem/ST(i)	F{I}COM{P}	FPATAN
F{I}ST{P} mem/ST(i)	F{I}SUB{R}{P} mem/ST(i)	F{I}UCOM{P}{P}	F2XM1
FLDPI	F{I}MUL{P} mem/ST(i)	FSTSW AX/mem	FCOS
FLD1	F{I}DIV{R}{P} mem/ST(i)		FPTAN
FLDZ	FSQRT		FPREM
	FABS		FSIN
	FRNDINT		FYL2X

FIGURE 3.21 The floating-point instructions of the IA-32. We use the curly brackets {} to show optional variations of the basic operations: {I} means there is an integer version of the instruction, {P} means this variation will pop one operand off the stack after the operation, and {R} means reverse the order of the operands in this operation. The first column shows the data transfer instructions, which move data to memory or to one of the registers below the top of the stack. The last three operations in the first column push constants on the stack: pi, 1.0, and 0.0. The second column contains the arithmetic operations described above. Note that the last three operate only on the top of stack. The third column is the compare instructions. Since there are no special floating-point branch instructions, the result of the compare must be transferred to the integer CPU via the FSTSW instruction, either into the AX register or into memory, followed by an SAHF instruction to set the condition codes. The floating-point comparison can then be tested using integer branch instructions. The final column gives the higher-level floating-point operations. Not all combinations suggested by the notation are provided. Hence, F{I}SUB{R}{P} operations represent these instructions found in the IA-32: FSUB, FISUB, FSUBR, FISUBR, FSUBP, FSUBRP. For the integer subtract instructions, there is no pop (FISUBP) or reverse pop (FISUBRP).

Instruction	Operands	Comment
FADD		Both operands in stack; result replaces top of stack.
FADD	ST(i)	One source operand is *i*th register below the top of stack; result replaces the top of stack.
FADD	ST(i), S1	One source operand is the top of stack; result replaces *i*th register below the top of stack.
FADD	mem32	One source operand is a 32-bit location in memory; result replaces the top of stack.
FADD	mem64	One source operand is a 64-bit location in memory; result replaces the top of stack.

FIGURE 3.22 The variations of operands for floating-point add in the IA-32.

The floating-point instructions are encoded using the ESC opcode of the 8086 and the postbyte address specifier (see Figure 2.46 on page 143). The memory operations reserve 2 bits to decide whether the operand is a 32- or 64-bit floating point or a 16- or 32-bit integer. Those same 2 bits are used in versions that do not access memory to decide whether the stack should be popped after the operation and whether the top of stack or a lower register should get the result.

Floating-point performance of the IA-32 family has traditionally lagged far behind other computers. Whether it is simply a lack of attention by Intel engineers or a flaw with its architecture is hard to know. We can say that many new architectures have been announced since 1980, and none have followed in Intel's footsteps. In addition, Intel created a more traditional floating-point architecture as part of SSE2.

The Intel Streaming SIMD Extension 2 (SSE2) Floating-Point Architecture

Chapter 2 notes that in 2001 Intel added 144 instructions to its architecture, including double precision floating-point registers and operations. It includes eight registers that can be used for floating-point operands, giving the compiler a different target for floating-point operations than the unique stack architecture. Compilers can choose to use the eight SSE2 registers as floating-point registers like those found in other computers. AMD expanded the number to 16 as part of AMD64, which Intel relabled EM64T for its use.

In addition to holding a single precision or double precision number in a register, Intel allows multiple floating-point operands to be packed into a single 128-bit SSE2 register: four single precision or two double precision. If the operands can be arranged in memory as 128-bit aligned data, then 128-bit data transfers can load and store multiple operands per instruction. This packed floating-point format is supported by arithmetic operations that can operate simultaneously on four singles or two doubles. This new architecture can more than double performance over the stack architecture.

Thus mathematics may be defined as the subject in which we never know what we are talking about, nor whether what we are saying is true.

Bertrand Russell, *Recent Words on the Principles of Mathematics*, 1901

3.8   Fallacies and Pitfalls

Arithmetic fallacies and pitfalls generally stem from the difference between the limited precision of computer arithmetic and the unlimited precision of natural arithmetic.

Fallacy: Floating-point addition is associative; that is, $x + (y + z) = (x + y) + z$.

Given the great range of numbers that can be represented in floating point, problems occur when adding two large numbers of opposite signs plus a small number.

For example, suppose $x = -1.5_{ten} \times 10^{38}$, $y = 1.5_{ten} \times 10^{38}$, and $z = 1.0$, and that these are all single precision numbers. Then

$$
\begin{aligned}
x + (y + z) &= -1.5_{ten} \times 10^{38} + (1.5_{ten} \times 10^{38} + 1.0) \\
&= -1.5_{ten} \times 10^{38} + (1.5_{ten} \times 10^{38}) = 0.0 \\
(x + y) + z &= (-1.5_{ten} \times 10^{38} + 1.5_{ten} \times 10^{38}) + 1.0 \\
&= (0.0_{ten}) + 1.0 \\
&= 1.0
\end{aligned}
$$

Therefore, $x + (y + z) \neq (x + y) + z$.

Since floating-point numbers have limited precision and result in approximations of real results, $1.5_{ten} \times 10^{38}$ is so much larger than 1.0_{ten} that $1.5_{ten} \times 10^{38} + 1.0$ is still $1.5_{ten} \times 10^{38}$. That is why the sum of x, y, and z is 0.0 or 1.0, depending on the order of the floating-point additions, and hence floating-point add is *not* associative.

Fallacy: Just as a left shift instruction can replace an integer multiply by a power of 2, a right shift is the same as an integer division by a power of 2.

Recall that a binary number x, where xi means the ith bit, represents the number

$$
\ldots + (x3 \times 2^3) + (x2 \times 2^2) + (x1 \times 2^1) + (x0 \times 2^0)
$$

Shifting the bits of x right by n bits would seem to be the same as dividing by 2^n. And this *is* true for unsigned integers. The problem is with signed integers. For example, suppose we want to divide -5_{ten} by 4_{ten}; the quotient should be -1_{ten}. The two's complement representation of -5_{ten} is

$$1111\ 1111\ 1111\ 1111\ 1111\ 1111\ 1111\ 1011_{two}$$

According to this fallacy, shifting right by two should divide by 4_{ten} (2^2):

$$0011\ 1111\ 1111\ 1111\ 1111\ 1111\ 1111\ 1110_{two}$$

With a 0 in the sign bit, this result is clearly wrong. The value created by the shift right is actually $1,073,741,822_{ten}$ instead of -1_{ten}.

A solution would be to have an arithmetic right shift (see ⊙ **In More Depth: Booth's Algorithm**) that extends the sign bit instead of shifting in 0s. A 2-bit arithmetic shift right of -5_{ten} produces

$$1111\ 1111\ 1111\ 1111\ 1111\ 1111\ 1111\ 1110_{two}$$

The result is -2_{ten} instead of -1_{ten}; close, but no cigar.

The PowerPC, however, does have a fast shift instruction (*shift right algebraic*) that in conjunction with a special add (add with carry) gives the same answer as dividing by a power of 2.

Pitfall: The MIPS instruction add immediate unsigned `addiu` *sign-extends its 16-bit immediate field.*

Despite its name, add immediate unsigned (`addiu`) is used to add constants to signed integers when we don't care about overflow. MIPS has no subtract immediate instruction and negative numbers need sign extension, so the MIPS architects decided to sign-extend the immediate field.

Fallacy: Only theoretical mathematicians care about floating-point accuracy.

Newspaper headlines of November 1994 prove this statement is a fallacy (see Figure 3.23). The following is the inside story behind the headlines.

The Pentium uses a standard floating-point divide algorithm that generates multiple quotient bits per step, using the most significant bits of divisor and dividend to guess the next 2 bits of the quotient. The guess is taken from a lookup table containing −2, −1, 0, +1, or +2. The guess is multiplied by the divisor and

FIGURE 3.23   A sampling of newspaper and magazine articles from November 1994, including the *New York Times*, *San Jose Mercury News*, *San Francisco Chronicle*, and *Infoworld*. The Pentium floating-point divide bug even made the "Top 10 List" of the *David Letterman Late Show* on television. Intel eventually took a $300 million write-off to replace the buggy chips.

subtracted from the remainder to generate a new remainder. Like nonrestoring division (see Exercise 3.29), if a previous guess gets too large a remainder, the partial remainder is adjusted in a subsequent pass.

Evidently, there were five elements of the table from the 80486 that Intel thought could never be accessed, and they optimized the PLA to return 0 instead of 2 in these situations on the Pentium. Intel was wrong: while the first 11 bits were always correct, errors would show up occasionally in bits 12 to 52, or the 4th to 15th decimal digits.

The following is a time line of the Pentium bug morality play.

- *July 1994:* Intel discovers the bug in the Pentium. The actual cost to fix the bug was several hundred thousand dollars. Following normal bug fix procedures, it will take months to make the change, reverify, and put the corrected chip into production. Intel planned to put good chips into production in January 1995, estimating that 3 to 5 million Pentiums would be produced with the bug.

- *September 1994:* A math professor at Lynchburg College in Virginia, Thomas Nicely, discovers the bug. After calling Intel technical support and getting no official reaction, he posts his discovery on the Internet. It quickly gained a following, and some pointed out that even small errors become big when multiplying by big numbers: the fraction of people with a rare disease times the population of Europe, for example, might lead to the wrong estimate of the number of sick people.

- *November 7, 1994: Electronic Engineering Times* puts the story on its front page, which is soon picked up by other newspapers.

- *November 22, 1994:* Intel issues a press release, calling it a "glitch." The Pentium "can make errors in the ninth digit. . . . Even most engineers and financial analysts require accuracy only to the fourth or fifth decimal point. Spreadsheet and word processor users need not worry. . . . There are maybe several dozen people that this would affect. So far, we've only heard from one. . . . [Only] theoretical mathematicians (with Pentium computers purchased before the summer) should be concerned." What irked many was that customers were told to describe their application to Intel, and then *Intel* would decide whether or not their application merited a new Pentium without the divide bug.

- *December 5, 1994:* Intel claims the flaw happens once in 27,000 years for the typical spreadsheet user. Intel assumes a user does 1000 divides per day and multiplies the error rate assuming floating-point numbers are random, which is one in 9 billion, and then gets 9 million days, or 27,000 years.

Things begin to calm down, despite Intel neglecting to explain why a typical customer would access floating-point numbers randomly.

■ *December 12, 1994:* IBM Research Division disputes Intel's calculation of the rate of errors (you can access this article by visiting *www.mkp.com/books_catalog/cod/links.htm*). IBM claims that common spreadsheet programs, recalculating for 15 minutes a day, could produce Pentium-related errors as often as once every 24 days. IBM assumes 5000 divides per second, for 15 minutes, yielding 4.2 million divides per day, and does not assume random distribution of numbers, instead calculating the chances as one in 100 million. As a result, IBM immediately stops shipment of all IBM personal computers based on the Pentium. Things heat up again for Intel.

■ *December 21, 1994:* Intel releases the following, signed by Intel's president, chief executive officer, chief operating officer, and chairman of the board: "We at Intel wish to sincerely apologize for our handling of the recently publicized Pentium processor flaw. The Intel Inside symbol means that your computer has a microprocessor second to none in quality and performance. Thousands of Intel employees work very hard to ensure that this is true. But no microprocessor is ever perfect. What Intel continues to believe is technically an extremely minor problem has taken on a life of its own. Although Intel firmly stands behind the quality of the current version of the Pentium processor, we recognize that many users have concerns. We want to resolve these concerns. Intel will exchange the current version of the Pentium processor for an updated version, in which this floating-point divide flaw is corrected, for any owner who requests it, free of charge anytime during the life of their computer."Analysts estimate that this recall cost Intel $500 million, and Intel employees did not get a Christmas bonus that year.

This story brings up a few points for everyone to ponder. How much cheaper would it have been to fix the bug in July 1994? What was the cost to repair the damage to Intel's reputation? And what is the corporate responsibility in disclosing bugs in a product so widely used and relied upon as a microprocessor?

In April 1997 another floating-point bug was revealed in the Pentium Pro and Pentium II microprocessors. When the floating-point-to-integer store instructions (fist, fistp) encounter a negative floating-point number that is too large to fit in a 16- or 32-bit word after being converted to integer, they set the wrong bit in the FPO status word (precision exception instead of invalid operation exception). To Intel's credit, this time they publicly acknowledged the bug and offered a software patch to get around it—quite a different reaction from what they did in 1994.

3.9 Concluding Remarks

Computer arithmetic is distinguished from paper-and-pencil arithmetic by the constraints of limited precision. This limit may result in invalid operations through calculating numbers larger or smaller than the predefined limits. Such anomalies, called "overflow" or "underflow," may result in exceptions or interrupts, emergency events similar to unplanned subroutine calls. Chapter 5 discusses exceptions in more detail.

Floating-point arithmetic has the added challenge of being an approximation of real numbers, and care needs to be taken to ensure that the computer number selected is the representation closest to the actual number. The challenges of imprecision and limited representation are part of the inspiration for the field of numerical analysis.

Over the years, computer arithmetic has become largely standardized, greatly enhancing the portability of programs. Two's complement binary integer arithmetic and IEEE 754 binary floating-point arithmetic are found in the vast majority of computers sold today. For example, every desktop computer sold since this book was first printed follows these conventions.

A side effect of the stored-program computer is that bit patterns have no inherent meaning. The same bit pattern may represent a signed integer, unsigned integer, floating-point number, instruction, and so on. It is the instruction that operates on the word that determines its meaning.

With the explanation of computer arithmetic in this chapter comes a description of much more of the MIPS instruction set. One point of confusion is the instructions covered in these chapters versus instructions executed by MIPS chips versus the instructions accepted by MIPS assemblers. The next two figures try to make this clear.

Figure 3.24 lists the MIPS instructions covered in this chapter and Chapter 2. We call the set of instructions on the left-hand side of the figure the *MIPS core*. The instructions on the right we call the *MIPS arithmetic core*. On the left of Figure 3.25 are the instructions the MIPS processor executes that are not found in Figure 3.24. We call the full set of hardware instructions *MIPS-32*. On the right of Figure 3.25 are the instructions accepted by the assembler that are not part of MIPS-32. We call this set of instructions *Pseudo MIPS*.

Instruction subset	Integer	Fl. pt.
MIPS core	95%	57%
MIPS arithmetic core	0%	41%
Remaining MIPS-32	5%	2%

MIPS core instructions	Name	Format	MIPS arithmetic core	Name	Format
add	add	R	multiply	mult	R
add immediate	addi	I	multiply unsigned	multu	R
add unsigned	addu	R	divide	div	R
add immediate unsigned	addiu	I	divide unsigned	divu	R
subtract	sub	R	move from Hi	mfhi	R
subtract unsigned	subu	R	move from Lo	mflo	R
and	and	R	move from system control (EPC)	mfc0	R
and immediate	andi	I	floating-point add single	add.s	R
or	or	R	floating-point add double	add.d	R
or immediate	ori	I	floating-point subtract single	sub.s	R
nor	nor	R	floating-point subtract double	sub.d	R
shift left logical	sll	R	floating-point multiply single	mul.s	R
shift right logical	srl	R	floating-point multiply double	mul.d	R
load upper immediate	lui	I	floating-point divide single	div.s	R
load word	lw	I	floating-point divide double	div.d	R
store word	sw	I	load word to floating-point single	lwc1	I
load halfword unsigned	lhu	I	store word to floating-point single	swc1	I
store halfword	sh	I	load word to floating-point double	ldc1	I
load byte unsigned	lbu	I	store word to floating-point double	sdc1	I
store byte	sb	I	branch on floating-point true	bc1t	I
branch on equal	beq	I	branch on floating-point false	bc1f	I
branch on not equal	bne	I	floating-point compare single	c.x.s	R
jump	j	J	(x = eq, neq, lt, le, gt, ge)		
jump and link	jal	J	floating-point compare double	c.x.d	R
jump register	jr	R	(x = eq, neq, lt, le, gt, ge)		
set less than	slt	R			
set less than immediate	slti	I			
set less than unsigned	sltu	R			
set less than immediate unsigned	sltiu	I			

FIGURE 3.24   The MIPS instruction set covered so far. This book concentrates on the instructions in the left column. This information is also found in columns 1 and 2 of the MIPS Reference Data Card at the front of this book.

Remaining MIPS-32	Name	Format	Pseudo MIPS	Name	Format
exclusive or ($rs \oplus rt$)	xor	R	move	move	rd,rs
exclusive or immediate	xori	I	absolute value	abs	rd,rs
shift right arithmetic	sra	R	not ($\neg rs$)	not	rd,rs
shift left logical variable	sllv	R	negate (signed or unsigned)	neg*s*	rd,rs
shift right logical variable	srlv	R	rotate left	rol	rd,rs,rt
shift right arithmetic variable	srav	R	rotate right	ror	rd,rs,rt
move to Hi	mthi	R	multiply and don't check oflw (signed or uns.)	mul*s*	rd,rs,rt
move to Lo	mtlo	R	multiply and check oflw (signed or uns.)	mulo*s*	rd,rs,rt
load halfword	lh	I	divide and check overflow	div	rd,rs,rt
load byte	lb	I	divide and don't check overflow	divu	rd,rs,rt
load word left (unaligned)	lwl	I	remainder (signed or unsigned)	rem*s*	rd,rs,rt
load word right (unaligned)	lwr	I	load immediate	li	rd,imm
store word left (unaligned)	swl	I	load address	la	rd,addr
store word right (unaligned)	swr	I	load double	ld	rd,addr
load linked (atomic update)	ll	I	store double	sd	rd,addr
store cond. (atomic update)	sc	I	unaligned load word	ulw	rd,addr
move if zero	movz	R			
move if not zero	movn	R	unaligned store word	usw	rd,addr
multiply and add (S or uns.)	madd*s*	R			
multiply and subtract (S or uns.)	msub*s*	I	unaligned load halfword (signed or uns.)	ulh*s*	rd,addr
branch on ≥ zero and link	bgezal	I	unaligned store halfword	ush	rd,addr
branch on < zero and link	bltzal	I	branch	b	Label
jump and link register	jalr	R	branch on equal zero	beqz	rs,L
branch compare to zero	bxz	I	branch on compare (signed or unsigned)	bx*s*	rs,rt,L
branch compare to zero likely	bxzl	I	(x = lt, le, gt, ge)		
(x = lt, le, gt, ge)			set equal	seq	rd,rs,rt
branch compare reg likely	bxl	I	set not equal	sne	rd,rs,rt
trap if compare reg	tx	R	set on compare (signed or unsigned)	sx*s*	rd,rs,rt
trap if compare immediate	txi	I	(x = lt, le, gt, ge)		
(x = eq, neq, lt, le, gt, ge)			load to floating point (s or d)	l.*f*	rd,addr
return from exception	rfe	R	store from floating point (s or d)	s.*f*	rd,addr
system call	syscall	I			
break (cause exception)	break	I			
move from FP to integer	mfc1	R			
move to FP from integer	mtc1	R			
FP move (s or d)	mov.*f*	R			
FP move if zero (s or d)	movz.*f*	R			
FP move if not zero (s or d)	movn.*f*	R			
FP square root (s or d)	sqrt.*f*	R			
FP absolute value (s or d)	abs.*f*	R			
FP negate (s or d)	neg.*f*	R			
FP convert (w, s, or d)	cvt.*f.f*	R			
FP compare un (s or d)	c.x*n*.*f*	R			

FIGURE 3.25   Remaining MIPS-32 and "Pseudo MIPS" instruction sets. *f* means single (s) or double (d) precision floating-point instructions, and *s* means signed and unsigned (u) versions. MIPS-32 also has FP instructions for multiply and add/sub (madd.*f*/msub.*f*), ceiling (ceil.*f*), truncate (trunc.*f*), round (round.*f*), and reciprocal (recip.*f*). The underscore represents the letter to include to represent that datatype.

Figure 3.26 gives the popularity of the MIPS instructions for SPEC2000 integer and floating-point benchmarks. All instructions are listed that were responsible for at least 1% of the instructions executed.

Note that although programmers and compiler writers may use MIPS-32 to have a richer menu of options, MIPS core instructions dominate integer SPEC2000 execution, and the integer core plus arithmetic core dominate SPEC2000 floating point.

For the rest of the book, we concentrate on the MIPS core instructions—the integer instruction set excluding multiply and divide—to make the explanation of computer design easier. As you can see, the MIPS core includes the most popular MIPS instructions; be assured that understanding a computer that runs the MIPS core will give you sufficient background to understand even more ambitious computers.

Core MIPS	Name	Integer	Fl. pt.	Arithmetic core + MIPS-32	Name	Integer	Fl. pt.
add	add	0%	0%	FP add double	add.d	0%	8%
add immediate	addi	0%	0%	FP subtract double	sub.d	0%	3%
add unsigned	addu	7%	21%	FP multiply double	mul.d	0%	8%
add immediate unsigned	addiu	12%	2%	FP divide double	div.d	0%	0%
subtract unsigned	subu	3%	2%	load word to FP double	l.d	0%	15%
and	and	1%	0%	store word to FP double	s.d	0%	7%
and immediate	andi	3%	0%	shift right arithmetic	sra	1%	0%
or	or	7%	2%	load half	lhu	1%	0%
or immediate	ori	2%	0%	branch less than zero	bltz	1%	0%
nor	nor	3%	1%	branch greater or equal zero	bgez	1%	0%
shift left logical	sll	1%	1%	branch less or equal zero	blez	0%	1%
shift right logical	srl	0%	0%	multiply	mul	0%	1%
load upper immediate	lui	2%	5%				
load word	lw	24%	15%				
store word	sw	9%	2%				
load byte	lbu	1%	0%				
store byte	sb	1%	0%				
branch on equal (zero)	beq	6%	2%				
branch on not equal (zero)	bne	5%	1%				
jump and link	jal	1%	0%				
jump register	jr	1%	0%				
set less than	slt	2%	0%				
set less than immediate	slti	1%	0%				
set less than unsigned	sltu	1%	0%				
set less than imm. uns.	sltiu	1%	0%				

FIGURE 3.26   The frequency of the MIPS instructions for SPEC2000 integer and floating point. All instructions that accounted for at least 1% of the instructions are included in the table. Pseudoinstructions are converted into MIPS-32 before execution, and hence do not appear here. This data is from Chapter 2 of *Computer Architecture: A Quantitative Approach,* third edition.

Historical Perspective and Further Reading

This section surveys the history of the floating point going back to von Neumann, including the surprisingly controversial IEEE standards effort, plus the rationale for the 80-bit stack architecture for floating point in the IA-32. See ⊙ **Section 3.10**.

Gresham's Law ("Bad money drives out Good") for computers would say, "The Fast drives out the Slow even if the Fast is wrong."

W. Kahan, 1992

3.11 Exercises

Never give in, never give in, never, never, never—in nothing, great or small, large or petty—never give in.

Winston Churchill, address at Harrow School, 1941

3.1 [3] <§3.2> Convert 4096_{ten} into a 32-bit two's complement binary number.

3.2 [3] <§3.2> Convert -2047_{ten} into a 32-bit two's complement binary number.

3.3 [5] <§3.2> Convert $-2,000,000_{ten}$ into a 32-bit two's complement binary number.

3.4 [5] <§3.2> What decimal number does this two's complement binary number represent: $1111\ 1111\ 1111\ 1111\ 1111\ 1111\ 0000\ 0110_{two}$?

3.5 [5] <§3.2> What decimal number does this two's complement binary number represent: $1111\ 1111\ 1111\ 1111\ 1111\ 1111\ 1110\ 1111_{two}$?

3.6 [5] <§3.2> What decimal number does this two's complement binary number represent: $0111\ 1111\ 1111\ 1111\ 1111\ 1111\ 1110\ 1111_{two}$?

3.7 [10] <§3.2> Find the shortest sequence of MIPS instructions to determine the absolute value of a two's complement integer. Convert this instruction (accepted by the MIPS assembler):

```
abs    $t2,$t3
```

This instruction means that register $t2 has a copy of register $t3 if register $t3 is positive, and the two's complement of register $t3 if $t3 is negative. (Hint: It can be done with three instructions.)

3.8 [10] <§3.2> ⊙ **For More Practice:** Number Representations

3.9 [10] <§3.2> If A is a 32-bit address, typically an instruction sequence such as

```
lui $t0, A_upper
ori $t0, $t0, A_lower
lw $s0, 0($t0)
```

can be used to load the word at A into a register (in this case, $s0). Consider the following alternative, which is more efficient:

```
lui $t0, A_upper_adjusted
lw $s0, A_lower($t0)
```

Describe how A_upper is adjusted to allow this simpler code to work. (Hint: A_upper needs to be adjusted because A_lower will be sign-extended.)

3.10 [10] <§3.3> Find the shortest sequence of MIPS instructions to determine if there is a carry out from the addition of two registers, say, registers $t3 and $t4. Place a 0 or 1 in register $t2 if the carry out is 0 or 1, respectively. (Hint: It can be done in two instructions.)

3.11 [15] <§3.3> 💿 **For More Practice:** Writing MIPS Code to Perform Arithmetic

3.12 [15] <§3.3> Suppose that all of the conditional branch instructions except beq and bne were removed from the MIPS instruction set along with slt and all of its variants (slti, sltu, sltui). Show how to perform

```
slt $t0, $s0, $s1
```

using the modified instruction set in which slt is not available. (Hint: It requires more than two instructions.)

3.13 [10] <§3.3> Draw the gates for the Sum bit of an adder, given the equation on 💿 page B-28.

3.14 [5] <§3.6> 💿 **For More Practice:** Writing MIPS Code to Perform Arithmetic

3.15 [20] <§3.6> 💿 **For More Practice:** Writing MIPS Code to Perform Arithmetic

3.16 [2 weeks] <§3.4> 💿 **For More Practice:** Simulating MIPS Machines

3.17 [1 week] <§3.4> 💿 **For More Practice:** Simulating MIPS Machines

3.18 [5] <§3.4> 💿 **For More Practice:** Carry-Lookahead Adders

3.19 [15] <§3.4> 💿 **For More Practice:** Carry-Lookahead Adders

3.20 [10] <§3.4> 💿 **For More Practice:** Relative Performance of Adders

3.21 [15] <§3.4> ⊙ **For More Practice:** Relative Performance of Adders

3.22 [15] <§3.4> ⊙ **For More Practice:** Relative Performance of Adders

3.23 [30] <§3.4> ⊙ **In More Depth:** Booth's Algorithm

3.24 [30] <§3.4> ⊙ **For More Practice:** Relative Performance of Adders

3.25 [10] <§§3.5, 3.4> ⊙ **In More Depth:** The PowerPC's Multiply-Add Instruction

3.26 [20] <§3.5> ⊙ **In More Depth:** The PowerPC's Multiply-Add Instruction

3.27 <§§3.3, 3.4, 3.5> With $x = 0000\ 0000\ 0000\ 0000\ 0000\ 0000\ 0101\ 1011_{two}$ and $y = 0000\ 0000\ 0000\ 0000\ 0000\ 0000\ 0000\ 1101_{two}$ representing two's complement signed integers, perform, showing all work:

a. $x + y$

b. $x - y$

c. $x * y$

d. x/y

3.28 [20] <§§3.3, 3.4, 3.5> Perform the same operations as Exercise 3.27, but with $x = 1111\ 1111\ 1111\ 1111\ 1011\ 0011\ 0101\ 0011$ and $y = 0000\ 0000\ 0000\ 0000\ 0000\ 0010\ 1101\ 0111_{two}$.

3.29 [30] <§3.5> The division algorithm in Figure 3.11 on page 185 is called *restoring division*, since each time the result of subtracting the divisor from the dividend is negative you must add the divisor back into the dividend to restore the original value. Recall that shift left is the same as multiplying by 2. Let's look at the value of the left half of the Remainder again, starting with step 3b of the divide algorithm and then going to step 2:

$$(\text{Remainder} + \text{Divisor}) \times 2 - \text{Divisor}$$

This value is created from restoring the Remainder by adding the Divisor, shifting the sum left, and then subtracting the Divisor. Simplifying the result we get

$$\text{Remainder} \times 2 + \text{Divisor} \times 2 - \text{Divisor} = \text{Remainder} \times 2 + \text{Divisor}$$

Based on this observation, write a *nonrestoring division* algorithm using the notation of Figure 3.11 that does not add the Divisor to the Remainder in step 3b. Show that your algorithm works by dividing $0000\ 1011_{two}$ by 0011_{two}.

3.30 [15] <§§3.2, 3.6> "The Big Picture" on page 216 mentions that bits have no inherent meaning. Given the bit pattern

    1010 1101 0001 0000 0000 0000 0000 0010

what does it represent, assuming that it is

- a. a two's complement integer?
- b. an unsigned integer?
- c. a single precision floating-point number?
- d. a MIPS instruction?

You may find Figures 3.20 (page 208) and A.10.2 (page A-49) useful.

3.31 <§§3.2, 3.6> This exercise is similar to Exercise 3.30, but this time use the bit pattern

    0010 0100 1001 0010 0100 1001 0010 0100

3.32 [10] <§3.6> ◉ **For More Practice:** Floating-Point Number Representations

3.33 [10] <§3.6> ◉ **For More Practice:** Floating-Point Number Representations

3.34 [10] <§3.6> ◉ **For More Practice:** Writing MIPS Code to Perform FP Arithmetic

3.35 [5] <§3.6> Add $2.85_{ten} \times 10^3$ to $9.84_{ten} \times 10^4$, assuming that you have only three significant digits, first with guard and round digits and then without them.

3.36 [5] <§3.6> This exercise is similar to Exercise 3.35, but this time use the numbers $3.63_{ten} \times 10^4$ and $6.87_{ten} \times 10^3$.

3.37 [5] <§3.6> Show the IEEE 754 binary representation for the floating-point number 20_{ten} in single and double precision.

3.38 [5] <§3.6> This exercise is similar to Exercise 3.37, but this time replace the number 20_{ten} with 20.5_{ten}.

3.39 [10] <§3.6> This exercise is similar to Exercise 3.37, but this time replace the number 20_{ten} with 0.1_{ten}.

3.40 [10] <§3.6> This exercise is similar to Exercise 3.37, but this time replace the number 20_{ten} with the decimal fraction $-5/6$.

3.41 [10] <§3.6> Suppose we introduce a new instruction that adds three floating-point numbers. Assuming we add them together with a triple adder, with guard, round, and sticky bits, are we guaranteed results within 1 ulp of the results using two distinct add instructions?

3.42 [15] <§3.6> With $x = 0100\ 0110\ 1101\ 1000\ 0000\ 0000\ 0000\ 0000_{two}$ and $y = 1011\ 1110\ 1110\ 0000\ 0000\ 0000\ 0000\ 0000_{two}$ representing single precision IEEE 754 floating-point numbers, perform, showing all work:

a. $x + y$

b. $x * y$

3.43 [15] <§3.6> With $x = 0101\ 1111\ 1011\ 1110\ 0100\ 0000\ 0000\ 0000_{two}$, $y = 0011\ 1111\ 1111\ 1000\ 0000\ 0000\ 0000\ 0000_{two}$, and $z = 1101\ 1111\ 1011\ 1110\ 0100\ 0000\ 0000\ 0000_{two}$ representing single precision IEEE 754 floating-point numbers, perform, showing all work:

a. $x + y$

b. (result of a) $+ z$

c. Why is this result counterintuitive?

3.44 [20] <§§3.6, 3.7> The IEEE 754 floating-point standard specifies 64-bit double precision with a 53-bit significand (including the implied 1) and an 11-bit exponent. IA-32 offers an extended precision option with a 64-bit significand and a 16-bit exponent.

a. Assuming extended precision is similar to single and double precision, what is the bias in the exponent?

b. What is the range of numbers that can be represented by the extended precision option?

c. How much greater is this accuracy compared to double precision?

3.45 [5] <§§3.6, 3.7> The internal representation of floating-point numbers in IA-32 is 80 bits wide. This contains a 16-bit exponent. However, it also advertises a 64-bit significand. How is this possible?

3.46 [10] <§3.7> While the IA-32 allows 80-bit floating-point numbers internally, only 64-bit floating-point numbers can be loaded or stored. Starting with only 64-bit numbers, how many operations are required before the full range of the 80-bit exponents are used? Give an example.

3.47 [25] <§3.8> ⊙ **For More Practice:** Floating Point on Algorithms

3.48 [30] <§3.8> ⊙ **For More Practice:** Floating Point on Algorithms

3.49 [30] <§3.8> ⊙ **For More Practice:** Denormalized Numbers

3.50 [10] <§3.9> ⊙ **For More Practice:** Evaluating Instruction Frequencies

3.51 [10] <§3.9> ⊙ **For More Practice:** Evaluating Instruction Frequencies

3.52 [25] <§3.9> ⊙ **For More Practice:** Evaluating Instruction Frequencies

3.53 [10] <§3.9> ⊙ **For More Practice:** Evaluating Instruction Frequencies

3.54 [15] <§3.9> ⊙ **For More Practice:** Evaluating Performance

3.55 [15] <§3.9> ⊙ **For More Practice:** Evaluating Performance

**Answers to
Check Yourself**

§3.2. page 168: 3, since each character in a Java string takes 16 bits plus one word for length.
§3.3, page 174: 2.
§3.6, page 217: 3.

Computers in the Real World

Problem: Analyzing and understanding archeological sites is challenging. Can we find ways to use computers to help researchers to explore archeological sites and artifacts discovered at those sites?

Solution: Archeology is undergoing a revolution with the use of digital tools for mapping out ancient sites, reconstructing damaged artifacts, and re-creating ancient sites in three dimensions. Among the important new techniques being used to analyze and re-create sites are the following:

A digital photograph taken from a virtual reality model of the new temple at Chavín de Huántar.

■ The use of geographical information systems (GIS) to help accurately measure sites. GIS uses global positioning systems (GPS) to accurately pinpoint locations, allowing fast and precise measurements of a site.

■ Laser range finding to obtain accurate measurements of the two- and three-dimensional structure of objects. Laser range finding is even being used with low-flying aircraft to obtain height measurements.

■ Digital photography to obtain accurate images of sites as well as individual objects.

■ Virtual reality and three-dimensional visualization systems that use digital photographic data and accurate geospatial information to create realistic versions of archeological sites, allowing archeologists to gain new insights, as well as to share their work with other researchers and the general public.

These techniques have been used to explore and create an interactive virtual reality model of an archeological site called Chavín de Huántar, which is in the Peruvian highlands. The image on the previous page is a digital still photograph taken from the virtual reality model. Chavín de Huántar was occupied from about 1000 BCE and predates the classical Incan civilization by more than 1000 years. Highly detailed photos together with measurements of over 25,000 points allows a reconstruction of an accurate virtual model. The image on the previous page is from the new temple at Chavín, which played a key role in the establishment of formalized religious authority in the New World.

Three-dimensional modeling and reconstruction have also been used in the reconstruction of artifacts from fragments. The images on the left below are fragments of pottery found at Petra, the famous archeological site in Jordan. On the right is a computer reconstruction of the original vessel, highlighting the position of one of the fragments.

To learn more, see these references on the ⊚ library:

- Reconstructing objects from fragments at the SHAPE Laboratory at Brown University
- The Chavín de Huántar exploration (includes virtual reality tour of the site)

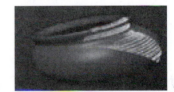

A computer reconstruction from the fragments in the adjacent photo.

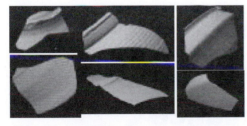

Images of pottery fragments found at Petra, Jordan.

4

Assessing and Understanding Performance

Time discovers truth.

Seneca

The Five Classic Components of a Computer

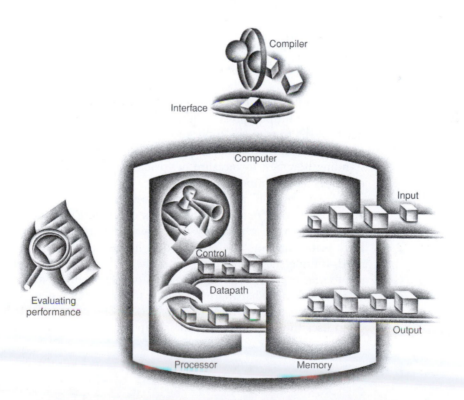

Compiler

Interface

Computer

Input

Evaluating performance

Control

Datapath

Processor

Memory

Output

4.1 Introduction

This chapter discusses how to measure, report, and summarize performance and describes the major factors that determine the performance of a computer. A primary reason for examining performance is that hardware performance is often key to the effectiveness of an entire system of hardware and software. Much of the material in this chapter, especially this section and the next, will be critical to understanding the next three chapters. The rest of the chapter provides important insights and principles that anyone seeking to evaluate the performance of a computer system should know. The material in Sections 4.3–4.5, however, is not necessary for the immediately following chapters and can be returned to later.

Assessing the performance of such a system can be quite challenging. The scale and intricacy of modern software systems, together with the wide range of performance improvement techniques employed by hardware designers, have made performance assessment much more difficult. It is simply impossible to sit down with an instruction set manual and a significant software system and determine, simply by analysis, how fast the software will run on the computer. In fact, for different types of applications, different performance metrics may be appropriate, and different aspects of a computer system may be the most significant in determining overall performance.

Of course, in trying to choose among different computers, performance is almost always an important attribute. Accurately measuring and comparing different computers is critical to purchasers, and therefore to designers. The people selling computers know this as well. Often, salespeople would like you to see their computer in the best possible light, whether or not this light accurately reflects the needs of the purchaser's application. In some cases, claims are made about computers that don't provide useful insight for any real applications. Hence, understanding how best to measure performance and the limitations of performance measurements is important in selecting a computer.

Our interest in performance, however, goes beyond issues of assessing performance only from the outside of a computer. To understand why a piece of software performs as it does, why one instruction set can be implemented to perform better than another, or how some hardware feature affects performance, we need to understand what determines the performance of a computer. For example, to improve the performance of a software system, we may need to understand what factors in the hardware contribute to the overall system performance and the relative importance of these factors. These factors may include how well the program uses the instructions of the computer, how well the underlying hardware implements the instructions, and how well the memory and I/O systems perform. Understanding how to determine the performance impact of these factors is crucial to understanding the motivation behind the design of particular aspects of the computer, as we will see in the chapters that follow.

The rest of this section describes different ways in which performance can be determined. In Section 4.2, we describe the metrics for measuring performance from the viewpoint of both a computer user and a designer. We also look at how these metrics are related and present the classical processor performance equation, which we will use throughout the text. Sections 4.3 and 4.4 describe how best to choose benchmarks to evaluate computers and how to accurately summarize the performance of a group of programs. Section 4.4 also describes one set of commonly used CPU benchmarks and examines measurements for a variety of Intel processors using those benchmarks. Finally, in Section 4.5, we'll examine some of the many pitfalls that have trapped designers and those who analyze and report performance.

Defining Performance

When we say one computer has better performance than another, what do we mean? Although this question might seem simple, an analogy with passenger airplanes shows how subtle the question of performance can be. Figure 4.1 shows some typical passenger airplanes, together with their cruising speed, range, and capacity. If we wanted to know which of the planes in this table had the best performance, we would first need to define performance. For example, considering different measures of performance, we see that the plane with the highest cruising speed is the Concorde, the plane with the longest range is the DC-8, and the plane with the largest capacity is the 747.

Let's suppose we define performance in terms of speed. This still leaves two possible definitions. You could define the fastest plane as the one with the highest cruising speed, taking a single passenger from one point to another in the least time. If you were interested in transporting 450 passengers from one point to another,

Airplane	Passenger capacity	Cruising range (miles)	Cruising speed (m.p.h.)	Passenger throughput (passengers x m.p.h.)
Boeing 777	375	4630	610	228,750
Boeing 747	470	4150	610	286,700
BAC/Sud Concorde	132	4000	1350	178,200
Douglas DC-8-50	146	8720	544	79,424

FIGURE 4.1 The capacity, range, and speed for a number of commercial airplanes. The last column shows the rate at which the airplane transports passengers, which is the capacity times the cruising speed (ignoring range and takeoff and landing times).

however, the 747 would clearly be the fastest, as the last column of the figure shows. Similarly, we can define computer performance in several different ways.

If you were running a program on two different desktop computers, you'd say that the faster one is the desktop computer that gets the job done first. If you were running a data center that had several servers running jobs submitted by many users, you'd say that the faster computer was the one that completed the most jobs during a day. As an individual computer user, you are interested in reducing **response time**—the time between the start and completion of a task—also referred to as **execution time**. Data center managers are often interested in increasing *throughput*—the total amount of work done in a given time. Hence, in most cases, we will need different performance metrics as well as different sets of applications to benchmark desktop computers versus servers, and embedded computers require yet other metrics and applications. We will see examples of this in Section 4.4 when we look at different SPEC benchmarks: one meant to measure CPU performance (SPEC CPU) and one meant to measure Web server performance (SPECweb99).

response time Also called **execution time**. The total time required for the computer to complete a task, including disk accesses, memory accesses, I/O activities, operating system overhead, CPU execution time, and so on.

EXAMPLE

Throughput and Response Time

Do the following changes to a computer system increase throughput, decrease response time, or both?

1. Replacing the processor in a computer with a faster version
2. Adding additional processors to a system that uses multiple processors for separate tasks—for example, searching the World Wide Web

ANSWER

Decreasing response time almost always improves throughput. Hence, in case 1, both response time and throughput are improved. In case 2, no one task gets work done faster, so only throughput increases. If, however, the demand for processing in the second case was almost as large as the throughput, the system might force requests to queue up. In this case, increasing the throughput could also improve response time, since it would reduce the waiting time in the queue. Thus, in many real computer systems, changing either execution time or throughput often affects the other.

In discussing the performance of computers, we will be primarily concerned with response time for the first few chapters. (In Chapter 8, on input/output systems, we will discuss throughput-related measures.) To maximize performance, we want to minimize response time or execution time for some task. Thus we can relate performance and execution time for a computer X:

$$\text{Performance}_X = \frac{1}{\text{Execution time}_X}$$

This means that for two computers X and Y, if the performance of X is greater than the performance of Y, we have

$$\text{Performance}_X > \text{Performance}_Y$$

$$\frac{1}{\text{Execution time}_X} > \frac{1}{\text{Execution time}_Y}$$

$$\text{Execution time}_Y > \text{Execution time}_X$$

That is, the execution time on Y is longer than that on X, if X is faster than Y.

In discussing a computer design, we often want to relate the performance of two different computers quantitatively. We will use the phrase "X is n times faster than Y"—or equivalently "X is n times as fast as Y"—to mean

$$\frac{\text{Performance}_X}{\text{Performance}_Y} = n$$

If X is n times faster than Y, then the execution time on Y is n times longer than it is on X:

$$\frac{\text{Performance}_X}{\text{Performance}_Y} = \frac{\text{Execution time}_Y}{\text{Execution time}_X} = n$$

Relative Performance

If computer A runs a program in 10 seconds and computer B runs the same program in 15 seconds, how much faster is A than B?

EXAMPLE

We know that A is n times faster than B if

$$\frac{\text{Performance}_A}{\text{Performance}_B} = \frac{\text{Execution time}_B}{\text{Execution time}_A} = n$$

ANSWER

Thus the performance ratio is

$$\frac{15}{10} = 1.5$$

and A is therefore 1.5 times faster than B.

In the above example, we could also say that computer B is 1.5 times *slower than* computer A, since

$$\frac{\text{Performance}_A}{\text{Performance}_B} = 1.5$$

means that

$$\frac{\text{Performance}_A}{1.5} = \text{Performance}_B$$

For simplicity, we will normally use the terminology *faster than* when we try to compare computers quantitatively. Because performance and execution time are reciprocals, increasing performance requires decreasing execution time. To avoid the potential confusion between the terms *increasing* and *decreasing*, we usually say "improve performance" or "improve execution time" when we mean "increase performance" and "decrease execution time."

Elaboration: Performance in embedded systems is often characterized by real-time constraints: that is, certain application-specific events must occur within a limited amount of time. There are two common types of real-time constraints: hard real time and soft real time. Hard real time defines a fixed bound on the time to respond to or process some event. For example, the embedded processor that controls an antilock brake system must respond within a hard limit from the time it receives a signal that the wheels are locked. In soft real-time systems, an average response or a response within a limited time to a large fraction of the events suffices. For example, handling video frames in a DVD playback system would be an example of a soft real-time constraint, since dropping a frame is permissible, if it happens very rarely. In embedded real-time applications, once the response-time performance constraint is met, designers often optimize throughput or try to reduce cost.

Measuring Performance

Time is the measure of computer performance: the computer that performs the same amount of work in the least time is the fastest. Program *execution time* is measured in seconds per program. But time can be defined in different ways, depending on what we count. The most straightforward definition of time is called *wall clock time*, *response time*, or *elapsed time*. These terms mean the total time to complete a task, including disk accesses, memory accesses, input/output (I/O) activities, operating system overhead—everything.

Computers are often shared, however, and a processor may work on several programs simultaneously. In such cases, the system may try to optimize throughput rather than attempt to minimize the elapsed time for one program. Hence, we often want to distinguish between the elapsed time and the time that the processor is working on our behalf. **CPU execution time** or simply **CPU time**, which recog-

CPU execution time Also called **CPU time**. The actual time the CPU spends computing for a specific task.

nizes this distinction, is the time the CPU spends computing for this task and does not include time spent waiting for I/O or running other programs. (Remember, though, that the response time experienced by the user will be the elapsed time of the program, not the CPU time.) CPU time can be further divided into the CPU time spent in the program, called **user CPU time**, and the CPU time spent in the operating system performing tasks on behalf of the program, called **system CPU time**. Differentiating between system and user CPU time is difficult to do accurately because it is often hard to assign responsibility for operating system activities to one user program rather than another and because of the functionality differences among operating systems.

For consistency, we maintain a distinction between performance based on elapsed time and that based on CPU execution time. We will use the term *system performance* to refer to elapsed time on an unloaded system and *CPU performance* to refer to user CPU time. We will focus on CPU performance in this chapter, although our discussions of how to summarize performance can be applied to either elapsed time or CPU time measurements.

Although as computer users we care about time, when we examine the details of a computer it's convenient to think about performance in other metrics. In particular, computer designers may want to think about a computer by using a measure that relates to how fast the hardware can perform basic functions. Almost all computers are constructed using a clock that runs at a constant rate and determines when events take place in the hardware. These discrete time intervals are called **clock cycles** (or ticks, clock ticks, clock periods, clocks, cycles). Designers refer to the length of a **clock period** both as the time for a complete *clock cycle* (e.g., 0.25 nanoseconds, 0.25 ns, 250 picoseconds, or 250 ps) and as the *clock rate* (e.g., 4 gigahertz, or 4 GHz), which is the inverse of the clock period. In the next section, we will formalize the relationship between the clock cycles of the hardware designer and the seconds of the computer user.

user CPU time The CPU time spent in a program itself.

system CPU time The CPU time spent in the operating system performing tasks on behalf of the program.

clock cycle Also called tick, clock tick, clock period, clock, cycle. The time for one clock period, usually of the processor clock, which runs at a constant rate.

clock period The length of each clock cycle.

Understanding Program Performance

Different applications are sensitive to different aspects of the performance of a computer system. Many applications, especially those running on servers, depend as much on I/O performance, which, in turn, relies on both hardware and software, and total elapsed time measured by a wall clock is the measurement of interest. In some application environments, the user may care about throughput, response time, or a complex combination of the two (e.g., maximum throughput with a worst-case response time). To improve the performance of a program, one must have a clear definition of what performance metric matters and then proceed to look for the performance bottlenecks by measuring program execution and looking for the likely bottlenecks. In the following chapters, we will describe how to search for bottlenecks and improve performance in various parts of the system.

Check
Yourself

1. Suppose we know that an application that uses both a desktop client and a remote server is limited by network performance. For the following changes state whether only the throughput improves, both response time and throughput improve, or neither improves.

   a. An extra network channel is added between the client and the server, increasing the total network throughput and reducing the delay to obtain network access (since there are now two channels).

   b. The networking software is improved, thereby reducing the network communication delay, but not increasing throughput.

   c. More memory is added to the computer.

2. Computer C's performance is 4 times better than the performance of computer B, which runs a given application in 28 seconds. How long will computer C take to run that application?

4.2   CPU Performance and Its Factors

Users and designers often examine performance using different metrics. If we could relate these different metrics, we could determine the effect of a design change on the performance as seen by the user. Since we are confining ourselves to CPU performance at this point, the bottom-line performance measure is CPU execution time. A simple formula relates the most basic metrics (clock cycles and clock cycle time) to CPU time:

$$\text{CPU execution time} \atop \text{for a program} = {\text{CPU clock cycles} \atop \text{for a program}} \times \text{Clock cycle time}$$

Alternatively, because clock rate and clock cycle time are inverses,

$$\text{CPU execution time} \atop \text{for a program} = \frac{\text{CPU clock cycles for a program}}{\text{Clock rate}}$$

This formula makes it clear that the hardware designer can improve performance by reducing either the length of the clock cycle or the number of clock cycles required for a program. As we will see in this chapter and later in Chapters 5, 6, and 7, the designer often faces a trade-off between the number of clock cycles needed for a program and the length of each cycle. Many techniques that decrease the number of clock cycles also increase the clock cycle time.

Improving Performance

Our favorite program runs in 10 seconds on computer A, which has a 4 GHz clock. We are trying to help a computer designer build a computer, B, that will run this program in 6 seconds. The designer has determined that a substantial increase in the clock rate is possible, but this increase will affect the rest of the CPU design, causing computer B to require 1.2 times as many clock cycles as computer A for this program. What clock rate should we tell the designer to target?

EXAMPLE

Let's first find the number of clock cycles required for the program on A:

$$\text{CPU time}_A = \frac{\text{CPU clock cycles}_A}{\text{Clock rate}_A}$$

$$10 \text{ seconds} = \frac{\text{CPU clock cycles}_A}{4 \times 10^9 \frac{\text{cycles}}{\text{second}}}$$

$$\text{CPU clock cycles}_A = 10 \text{ seconds} \times 4 \times 10^9 \frac{\text{cycles}}{\text{second}} = 40 \times 10^9 \text{cycles}$$

ANSWER

CPU time for B can be found using this equation:

$$\text{CPU time}_B = \frac{1.2 \times \text{CPU clock cycles}_A}{\text{Clock rate}_B}$$

$$6 \text{ seconds} = \frac{1.2 \times 40 \times 10^9 \text{cycles}}{\text{Clock rate}_B}$$

$$\text{Clock rate}_B = \frac{1.2 \times 40 \times 10^9 \text{cycles}}{6 \text{ seconds}} = \frac{8 \times 10^9 \text{cycles}}{\text{second}} = 8 \text{ GHz}$$

Computer B must therefore have twice the clock rate of A to run the program in 6 seconds.

Hardware/ Software Interface

The equations in our previous examples do not include any reference to the number of instructions needed for the program. However, since the compiler clearly generated instructions to execute, and the computer had to execute the instructions to run the program, the execution time must depend on the number of instructions in a program. One way to think about execution time is that it equals the number of instructions executed multiplied by the average time per instruction. Therefore, the number of clock cycles required for a program can be written as

$$\text{CPU clock cycles} = \text{Instructions for a program} \times \frac{\text{Average clock cycles}}{\text{per instruction}}$$

clock cycles per instruction (CPI) Average number of clock cycles per instruction for a program or program fragment.

The term **clock cycles per instruction**, which is the average number of clock cycles each instruction takes to execute, is often abbreviated as CPI. Since different instructions may take different amounts of time depending on what they do, CPI is an average of all the instructions executed in the program. CPI provides one way of comparing two different implementations of the same instruction set architecture, since the instruction count required for a program will, of course, be the same.

Using the Performance Equation

EXAMPLE

Suppose we have two implementations of the same instruction set architecture. Computer A has a clock cycle time of 250 ps and a CPI of 2.0 for some program, and computer B has a clock cycle time of 500 ps and a CPI of 1.2 for the same program. Which computer is faster for this program, and by how much?

ANSWER

We know that each computer executes the same number of instructions for the program; let's call this number I. First, find the number of processor clock cycles for each computer:

$$\text{CPU clock cycles}_A = I \times 2.0$$

$$\text{CPU clock cycles}_B = I \times 1.2$$

Now we can compute the CPU time for each computer:

$$\text{CPU time}_A = \text{CPU clock cycles}_A \times \text{Clock cycle time}_A$$

$$= I \times 2.0 \times 250 \text{ ps} = 500 \times I \text{ ps}$$

Likewise, for B:

$$\text{CPU time}_B = I \times 1.2 \times 500 \text{ ps} = 600 \times I \text{ ps}$$

Clearly, computer A is faster. The amount faster is given by the ratio of the execution times:

$$\frac{\text{CPU performance}_A}{\text{CPU performance}_B} = \frac{\text{Execution time}_B}{\text{Execution time}_A} = \frac{600 \times I \text{ ps}}{500 \times I \text{ ps}} = 1.2$$

We can conclude that computer A is 1.2 times as fast as computer B for this program.

We can now write this basic performance equation in terms of instruction count (the number of instructions executed by the program), CPI, and clock cycle time:

$$\text{CPU time} = \text{Instruction count} \times \text{CPI} \times \text{Clock cycle time}$$

or

$$\text{CPU time} = \frac{\text{Instruction count} \times \text{CPI}}{\text{Clock rate}}$$

These formulas are particularly useful because they separate the three key factors that affect performance. We can use these formulas to compare two different implementations or to evaluate a design alternative if we know its impact on these three parameters.

How can we determine the value of these factors in the performance equation? We can measure the CPU execution time by running the program, and the clock cycle time is usually published as part of the documentation for a computer. The instruction count and CPI can be more difficult to obtain. Of course, if we know the clock rate and CPU execution time, we need only one of the instruction count or the CPI to determine the other.

We can measure the instruction count by using software tools that profile the execution or by using a simulator of the architecture. Alternatively, we can use hardware counters, which are included on many processors, to record a variety of measurements, including the number of instructions executed, the average CPI, and often, the sources of performance loss. Since the instruction count depends

The BIG Picture

Figure 4.2 shows the basic measurements at different levels in the computer and what is being measured in each case. We can see how these factors are combined to yield execution time measured in seconds per program:

$$\text{Time} = \frac{\text{Seconds}}{\text{Program}} = \frac{\text{Instructions}}{\text{Program}} \times \frac{\text{Clock cycles}}{\text{Instruction}} \times \frac{\text{Seconds}}{\text{Clock cycle}}$$

Always bear in mind that the only complete and reliable measure of computer performance is time. For example, changing the instruction set to lower the instruction count may lead to an organization with a slower clock cycle time that offsets the improvement in instruction count. Similarly, because CPI depends on type of instructions executed, the code that executes the fewest number of instructions may not be the fastest.

Components of performance	Units of measure
CPU execution time for a program	Seconds for the program
Instruction count	Instructions executed for the program
Clock cycles per instruction (CPI)	Average number of clock cycles per instruction
Clock cycle time	Seconds per clock cycle

FIGURE 4.2   The basic components of performance and how each is measured.

on the architecture, but not on the exact implementation, we can measure the instruction count without knowing all the details of the implementation. The CPI, however, depends on a wide variety of design details in the computer, including both the memory system and the processor structure (as we will see in Chapters 5, 6, and 7), as well as on the mix of instruction types executed in an application. Thus, CPI varies by application, as well as among implementations with the same instruction set.

Designers often obtain CPI by a detailed simulation of an implementation or by using hardware counters, when a CPU is operational. Sometimes it is possible to compute the CPU clock cycles by looking at the different types of instructions and using their individual clock cycle counts. In such cases, the following formula is useful:

$$\text{CPU clock cycles} = \sum_{i=1}^{n} (\text{CPI}_i \times \text{C}_i)$$

where C_i is the count of the number of instructions of class i executed, CPI_i is the average number of cycles per instruction for that instruction class, and n is the number of instruction classes. Remember that overall CPI for a program will depend on both the number of cycles for each instruction type and the frequency of each instruction type in the program execution.

As we described in Chapter 1, the performance of a program depends on the algorithm, the language, the compiler, the architecture, and the actual hardware. The following table summarizes how these components affect the factors in the CPU performance equation.

Understanding Program Performance

Hardware or software component	Affects what?	How?
Algorithm	Instruction count, possibly CPI	The algorithm determines the number of source program instructions executed and hence the number of processor instructions executed. The algorithm may also affect the CPI, by favoring slower or faster instructions. For example, if the algorithm uses more floating-point operations, it will tend to have a higher CPI.
Programming language	Instruction count, CPI	The programming language certainly affects the instruction count, since statements in the language are translated to processor instructions, which determine instruction count. The language may also affect the CPI because of its features; for example, a language with heavy support for data abstraction (e.g., Java) will require indirect calls, which will use higher CPI instructions.
Compiler	Instruction count, CPI	The efficiency of the compiler affects both the instruction count and average cycles per instruction, since the compiler determines the translation of the source language instructions into computer instructions. The compiler's role can be very complex and affect the CPI in complex ways.
Instruction set architecture	Instruction count, clock rate, CPI	The instruction set architecture affects all three aspects of CPU performance, since it affects the instructions needed for a function, the cost in cycles of each instruction, and the overall clock rate of the processor.

EXAMPLE

Comparing Code Segments

A compiler designer is trying to decide between two code sequences for a particular computer. The hardware designers have supplied the following facts:

	CPI for this instruction class		
	A	B	C
CPI	1	2	3

For a particular high-level language statement, the compiler writer is considering two code sequences that require the following instruction counts:

	Instruction counts for instruction class		
Code sequence	A	B	C
1	2	1	2
2	4	1	1

Which code sequence executes the most instructions? Which will be faster? What is the CPI for each sequence?

ANSWER

Sequence 1 executes $2 + 1 + 2 = 5$ instructions. Sequence 2 executes $4 + 1 + 1 = 6$ instructions. So sequence 1 executes fewer instructions.

We can use the equation for CPU clock cycles based on instruction count and CPI to find the total number of clock cycles for each sequence:

$$\text{CPU clock cycles} = \sum_{i=1}^{n} (\text{CPI}_i \times C_i)$$

This yields

$\text{CPU clock cycles}_1 = (2 \times 1) + (1 \times 2) + (2 \times 3) = 2 + 2 + 6 = 10 \text{ cycles}$

$\text{CPU clock cycles}_2 = (4 \times 1) + (1 \times 2) + (1 \times 3) = 4 + 2 + 3 = 9 \text{ cycles}$

So code sequence 2 is faster, even though it actually executes one extra instruction. Since code sequence 2 takes fewer overall clock cycles but has more instructions, it must have a lower CPI. The CPI values can be computed by

$$CPI = \frac{CPU \text{ clock cycles}}{Instruction \text{ count}}$$

$$CPI_1 = \frac{CPU \text{ clock cycles}_1}{Instruction \text{ count}_1} = \frac{10}{5} = 2$$

$$CPI_2 = \frac{CPU \text{ clock cycles}_2}{Instruction \text{ count}_2} = \frac{9}{6} = 1.5$$

The above example shows the danger of using only one factor (instruction count) to assess performance. When comparing two computers, you must look at all three components, which combine to form execution time. If some of the factors are identical, like the clock rate in the above example, performance can be determined by comparing all the nonidentical factors. Since CPI varies by **instruction mix**, both instruction count and CPI must be compared, even if clock rates are identical. Several of the exercises ask you to evaluate a series of computer and compiler enhancements that affect clock rate, CPI, and instruction count. In the next section, we'll examine a common performance measurement that does not incorporate all the terms and can thus be misleading.

instruction mix A measure of the dynamic frequency of instructions across one or many programs.

Two of the major factors that affect CPI are the performance of the pipeline, which is the technique used by all modern processors to execute instructions, and the performance of the memory system. In Chapter 6, we will see how pipeline performance adds to the CPI through stalls, and in Chapter 7 we will see how the performance of the caches can increase the CPI due to stalls in the memory system.

A given application written in Java runs 15 seconds on a desktop processor. A new Java compiler is released that requires only 0.6 as many instructions as the old compiler. Unfortunately, it increases the CPI by 1.1. How fast can we expect the application to run using this new compiler?

Check Yourself

a. $\dfrac{15 \times 0.6}{1.1} = 8.2 \text{ sec}$

b. $15 \times 0.6 \times 1.1 = 9.9 \text{ sec}$

c. $\dfrac{15 \times 1.1}{0.6} = 27.5 \text{ sec}$

4.3   Evaluating Performance

A computer user who runs the same programs day in and day out would be the perfect candidate to evaluate a new computer. The set of programs run would form a **workload**. To evaluate two computer systems, a user would simply compare the execution time of the workload on the two computers. Most users, however, are not in this situation. Instead, they must rely on other methods that measure the performance of a candidate computer, hoping that the methods will reflect how well the computer will perform with the user's workload. This alternative is usually followed by evaluating the computer using a set of *benchmarks*—programs specifically chosen to measure performance. The benchmarks form a workload that the user hopes will predict the performance of the actual workload.

Today, it is widely understood that the best type of programs to use for benchmarks are real applications. These may be applications that the user employs regularly or simply applications that are typical. For example, in an environment where the users are primarily engineers, you might use a set of benchmarks containing several typical engineering or scientific applications. If the user community were primarily software development engineers, the best benchmarks would probably include such applications as a compiler or document processing system. Using real applications as benchmarks makes it much more difficult to find trivial ways to speed up the execution of the benchmark. Furthermore, when techniques are found to improve performance, such techniques are much more likely to help other programs in addition to the benchmark.

The use of benchmarks whose performance depends on very small code segments encourages optimizations in either the architecture or compiler that target these segments. The compiler optimizations might recognize special code fragments and generate an instruction sequence that is particularly efficient for this code fragment. Likewise, a designer might try to make some sequence of instructions run especially fast because the sequence occurs in a benchmark. In fact, several companies have introduced compilers with special-purpose optimizations targeted at specific benchmarks. Often these optimizations must be explicitly enabled with a specific compiler option, which would not be used when compiling other programs. Whether the compiler would produce good code, or even *correct* code, if a real application program used these switches, is unclear.

Sometimes in the quest to produce highly optimized code for benchmarks, engineers introduce erroneous optimizations. For example, in late 1995, Intel published a new performance rating for the integer SPEC benchmarks running on a Pentium processor and using an internal compiler, not used outside of Intel.

workload A set of programs run on a computer that is either the actual collection of applications run by a user or constructed from real programs to approximate such a mix. A typical workload specifies both the programs and the relative frequencies.

Unfortunately, the code produced for one of the benchmarks was wrong, a fact that was discovered when a competitor read through the binary to understand how Intel had sped up one of the programs in the benchmark suite so dramatically. In January 1996, Intel admitted the error and restated the performance. Small programs or programs that spend almost all their execution time in a very small code fragment are especially vulnerable to such efforts.

So why doesn't everyone run real programs to measure performance? One reason is that small benchmarks are attractive when beginning a design, since they are small enough to compile and simulate easily, sometimes by hand. They are especially tempting when designers are working on a novel computer because compilers may not be available until much later in the design. Although the use of such small benchmarks early in the design process may be justified, there is no valid rationale for using them to evaluate working computer systems.

As mentioned earlier, different classes and applications of computers will require different types of benchmarks. For desktop computers, the most common benchmarks are either measures of CPU performance or benchmarks focusing on a specific task, such as DVD playback or graphics performance for games. In Section 4.4, we will examine the SPEC CPU benchmarks, which focus on CPU performance and measure response time to complete a benchmark. For servers, the decision of which benchmark to use depends heavily on the nature of the intended application. For scientific servers, CPU-oriented benchmarks with scientific applications are typically used, and response time to complete a benchmark is the metric. For other server environments, benchmarks of Web serving, file serving, and databases are commonly used. These server benchmarks usually emphasize throughput, albeit with possible requirements on response time to individual events, such as a database query or Web page request. Section 4.4 examines the SPECweb99 benchmark designed to test Web server performance. In embedded computing, good benchmarks are much more rare. Often customers use their specific embedded application or a segment of it for benchmarking purposes. The one major benchmark suite developed for embedded computers is EEMBC, and we discuss those benchmarks in the "In More Depth" section on the CD.

Once we have selected a set of suitable benchmarks and obtained performance measurements, we can write a performance report. The guiding principle in reporting performance measurements should be *reproducibility*—we should list everything another experimenter would need to duplicate the results. This list must include the version of the operating system, compilers, and the input, as well as the computer configuration. As an example, the system description section of a SPEC CPU2000 benchmark report is in Figure 4.3.

One important element of reproducibility is the choice of input. Different inputs can generate quite different behavior. For example, an input can trigger certain execution paths that may be typical, or it may exercise rarely used, and

Hardware	
Hardware vendor	Dell
Model number	Precision WorkStation 360 (3.2 GHz Pentium 4 Extreme Edition)
CPU	Intel Pentium 4 (800 MHz system bus)
CPU MHz	3200
FPU	Integrated
CPU(s) enabled	1
CPU(s) orderable	1
Parallel	No
Primary cache	12 K(I) micro-ops + 8 KB(D) on chip
Secondary cache	512 KB(I+D) on chip
L3 cache	2048 KB(I+D) on chip
Other cache	N/A
Memory	4 x 512 MB ECC DDR400 SDRAM CL3
Disk subsystem	1x 80 GB ATA/100 7200 RPM
Other hardware	

Software	
Operating system	Windows XP Professional SP1
Compiler	Intel C++ Compiler 7.1 (20030402Z)
	Microsoft Visual Studio.NET (7.0.9466)
	MicroQuill SmartHeap Library 6.01
File system type	NTFS
System state	Default

FIGURE 4.3   System description of a desktop system using the fastest Pentium 4 available in 2003. In addition to this formatted mandatory description, there are 23 lines of notes describing special flag settings used for portability (4), optimization (2), tuning (12), base timing (2), a special library (2), and BIOS setting (1).

hence less important, parts of an application. Some of the most important effects from the input set are in the memory system. Larger input sets tend to stress the memory system to a greater extent, and the use of realistically sized workloads in servers both for commercial and scientific applications is critical if a benchmark is intended to predict what real applications may see.

Comparing and Summarizing Performance

Once we have selected programs to use as benchmarks and agreed on whether we are measuring response time or throughput, you might think that performance comparison would be straightforward. However, we must still decide how to summarize the performance of a group of benchmarks. Although summarizing a set of

	Computer A	Computer B
Program 1 (seconds)	1	10
Program 2 (seconds)	1000	100
Total time (seconds)	1001	110

FIGURE 4.4   Execution times of two programs on two different computers. Taken from Figure 1 of Smith [1988].

measurements results in less information, marketers and even users often prefer to have a single number to compare performance. The key question is, How should a summary be computed? Figure 4.4, which is abstracted from an article about summarizing performance, illustrates some of the difficulties facing such efforts.

Using our definition of *faster*, the following statements hold for the program measurements in Figure 4.4:

- A is 10 times faster than B for program 1.

- B is 10 times faster than A for program 2.

Taken individually, each of these statements is true. Collectively, however, they present a confusing picture—the relative performance of computers A and B is unclear.

Total Execution Time: A Consistent Summary Measure

The simplest approach to summarizing relative performance is to use total execution time of the two programs. Thus

$$\frac{\text{Performance}_B}{\text{Performance}_A} = \frac{\text{Execution time}_A}{\text{Execution time}_B} = \frac{1001}{110} = 9.1$$

That is, B is 9.1 times as fast as A for programs 1 and 2 together.

This summary is directly proportional to execution time, our final measure of performance. If the workload consists of running programs 1 and 2 an equal number of times, this statement would predict the relative execution times for the workload on each computer.

The average of the execution times that is directly proportional to total execution time is the **arithmetic mean** (AM):

$$\text{AM} = \frac{1}{n}\sum_{i=1}^{n}\text{Time}_i$$

arithmetic mean (AM) The average of the execution times that is directly proportional to total execution time.

where Time$_i$ is the execution time for the ith program of a total of n in the workload. Since it is the mean of execution times, a smaller mean indicates a smaller average execution time and thus improved performance.

The arithmetic mean is proportional to execution time, assuming that the programs in the workload are each run an equal number of times. Is that the right workload? If not, we can assign a weighting factor w_i to each program to indicate the frequency of the program in that workload. If, for example, 20% of the tasks in the workload were program 1 and 80% of the tasks in the workload were program 2, then the weighting factors would be 0.2 and 0.8. By summing the products of weighting factors and execution times, we can obtain a clear picture of the performance of the workload. This sum is called the **weighted arithmetic mean**. One method of weighting programs is to choose weights so that the execution time of each benchmark is equal on the computer used as the base. The standard arithmetic mean is a special case of the weighted arithmetic mean where all weights are equal. We explore the weighted mean in more detail in Exercises 4.15 and 4.16.

weighted arithmetic mean
An average of the execution time of a workload with weighting factors designed to reflect the presence of the programs in a workload; computed as the sum of the products of weighting factors and execution times.

Check Yourself

1. Suppose you are choosing between four different desktop computers: one is an Apple MacIntosh and the other three are PC-compatible computers that use a Pentium 4, an AMD processor (using the same compiler as the Pentium 4), and a Pentium 5 (which does not yet exist in 2004 but has the same architecture as the Pentium 4 and uses the same compiler). Which of the following statements are true?

   a. The fastest computer will be the one with the highest clock rate.

   b. Since all PCs use the same Intel-compatible instruction set and execute the same number of instructions for a program, the fastest PC will be the one with the highest clock rate.

   c. Since AMD uses different techniques than Intel to execute instructions, they may have different CPIs. But, you can still tell which of the two Pentium-based PCs is fastest by looking at the clock rate.

   d. Only by looking at the results of benchmarks for tasks similar to your workload can you get an accurate picture of likely performance.

2. Assume the following measurements of execution time were taken:

Program	Computer A	Computer B
1	2 sec	4 sec
2	5 sec	2 sec

Which of the following statements is true?

a. A is faster than B for program 1.

b. A is faster than B for program 2.

c. A is faster than B for a workload with equal numbers of executions of programs 1 and 2.

d. A is faster than B for a workload with twice as many executions of program 1 as of program 2.

4.4 Real Stuff: Two SPEC Benchmarks and the Performance of Recent Intel Processors

SPEC (System Performance Evaluation Cooperative) is an effort funded and supported by a number of computer vendors to create standard sets of benchmarks for modern computer systems. It began in 1989 focusing on benchmarking workstations and servers using CPU-intensive benchmarks. (A more detailed history is contained in Section 4.7.) Today, SPEC offers a dozen different benchmark sets designed to test a wide variety of computing environments using real applications and strictly specified execution rules and reporting requirements. The SPEC benchmark sets include benchmarks for CPU performance, graphics, high-performance computing, object-oriented computing, Java applications, client-server models, mail systems, file systems, and Web servers. In this section, we examine the performance of a variety of Dell computer systems that use Pentium III and Pentium 4 processors using a CPU performance benchmark and a Web-oriented system benchmark.

Performance with SPEC CPU Benchmarks

The latest release of the **SPEC CPU benchmarks** is the SPEC CPU2000 suite, which consists of 12 integer and 14 floating-point programs, as shown in Figure 4.5. The SPEC CPU benchmarks are intended to measure CPU performance, although wall clock time is the reported measurement. Separate summaries are reported for the integer and floating-point benchmark sets. The execution time measurements are first normalized by dividing the execution time on a Sun Ultra 5_10 with a 300 MHz processor by the execution time on the measured computer; this normalization yields a measure, called the *SPEC ratio*, which has the advantage that bigger numeric results indicate faster performance (i.e., SPEC ratio is the inverse of execution time). A CINT2000 or CFP2000 summary measurement is obtained by taking the geometric mean of the SPEC ratios. (See the "In More Depth" section on the CD for a discussion of trade-offs in using geometric mean.)

system performance evaluation cooperative (SPEC) benchmark A set of standard CPU-intensive, integer and floating-point benchmarks based on real programs.

Integer benchmarks		FP benchmarks	
Name	**Description**	**Name**	**Type**
gzip	Compression	wupwise	Quantum chromodynamics
vpr	FPGA circuit placement and routing	swim	Shallow water model
gcc	The Gnu C compiler	mgrid	Multigrid solver in 3-D potential field
mcf	Combinatorial optimization	applu	Parabolic/elliptic partial differential equation
crafty	Chess program	mesa	Three-dimensional graphics library
parser	Word processing program	galgel	Computational fluid dynamics
eon	Computer visualization	art	Image recognition using neural networks
perlbmk	perl application	equake	Seismic wave propagation simulation
gap	Group theory, interpreter	facerec	Image recognition of faces
vortex	Object-oriented database	ammp	Computational chemistry
bzip2	Compression	lucas	Primality testing
twolf	Place and rote simulator	fma3d	Crash simulation using finite-element method
		sixtrack	High-energy nuclear physics accelerator design
		apsi	Meteorology: pollutant distribution

FIGURE 4.5   The SPEC CPU2000 benchmarks. The 12 integer benchmarks in the left half of the table are written in C and C++, while the floating-point benchmarks in the right half are written in Fortran (77 or 90) and C. For more information on SPEC and on the SPEC benchmarks, see *www.spec.org*. The SPEC CPU benchmarks use wall clock time as the metric, but because there is little I/O, they measure CPU performance.

For a given instruction set architecture, increases in CPU performance can come from three sources:

1. Increases in clock rate

2. Improvements in processor organization that lower the CPI

3. Compiler enhancements that lower the instruction count or generate instructions with a lower average CPI (e.g., by using simpler instructions)

To illustrate such performance improvements, Figure 4.6 shows the SPEC CINT2000 and CFP2000 measurements for a series of Intel Pentium III and Pentium 4 processors measured using the Dell Precision desktop computers. Since SPEC requires that the benchmarks be run on real hardware and the memory system has a significant effect on performance, other systems with these processors may produce different performance levels. In addition to the clock rate differences, the Pentium III and Pentium 4 use different pipeline structures, which we describe in more detail in Chapter 6.

There are several important observations from these two performance graphs. First, observe that the performance of each of these processors scales almost linearly with clock rate increases. Often this is not the case, since losses in the mem-

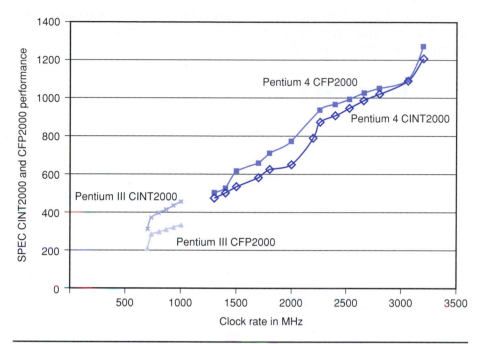

FIGURE 4.6 The SPEC CINT2000 and CFP2000 ratings for the Intel Pentium III and Pentium 4 processors at different clock speeds. SPEC requires two sets of measurements: one that allows aggressive optimization with benchmark-specific switches, and one that allows only the standard optimization switches (called the "base" measurements). This chart contains base measurements; for the integer benchmarks the differences are small. For more details on SPEC, see *www.spec.org*. The Pentium 4 Extreme (a version of the Pentium 4 introduced in late 2003) is not included in these results, since it uses a different cache architecture than the rest of the Pentium 4 processors.

ory system, which we discuss in Chapter 7, often worsen with higher clock rates. The strong performance of these processors is due both to the aggressive cache systems used in these processors and to the inability of many of the SPEC benchmarks to stress such a memory system.

Comparing the Pentium III and Pentium 4 performances yields even more interesting insights. In particular, note the relative positions of the CINT2000 and CFP2000 curves for the Pentium III versus the Pentium 4. One can quickly draw the inference that the Pentium 4 is either relatively better than the Pentium III on floating-point benchmarks or relatively worse on integer benchmarks. But, which is the case?

The Pentium 4 uses a more advanced integrated circuit technology as well as a more aggressive pipeline structure, both of which allow for a significant clock rate increase. One comparison that is particularly interesting is the SPEC CINT2000 and CFP2000 measurement divided by the clock rate in MHz. The following table summarizes the average value of this ratio across different clock rates for each processor:

Ratio	Pentium III	Pentium 4
CINT2000 / Clock rate in MHz	0.47	0.36
CFP2000 / Clock rate in MHz	0.34	0.39

Metrics such as benchmark performance divided by clock rate are sometimes thought of as measurements of implementation efficiency, although, as we have seen, one cannot separate the interaction of clock rate and other improvements.

These measurements are particularly interesting because of the differences between the integer and floating-point benchmarks. The CINT2000 performance ratios are typical: when a faster version of a processor is introduced it may sacrifice one aspect of a design (such as CPI) to enhance another (such as clock rate). Assuming one compiler for both processors, and hence identical code, the CINT2000 ratios tell us that the CPI of the Pentium 4 is 1.3 (0.47/0.36) times that of the Pentium III.

How then can these numbers be reversed for the floating-point benchmarks? The answer is that the Pentium 4 furnishes a set of new instructions (called the Streaming SIMD Extensions 2; see Chapter 3) that provide a significant boost for floating point. Thus, both the instruction count and the CPI for the Pentium 4 will differ from that of the Pentium III, producing improved performance.

SPECweb99: A Throughput Benchmark for Web Servers

In 1996, SPEC introduced its first benchmark designed to measure Web server performance; the benchmark was superseded by a new version in 1999. SPECweb99 differs from SPEC CPU in a number of ways:

- SPECweb99 focuses on throughput, measuring the maximum number of connections that a system running as a Web server can support. The system must provide response to a client request within a bounded time and with a bounded number of errors.

- Because SPECweb99 measures throughput, multiprocessors (systems with more than one CPU) are often used in benchmarks.

- SPECweb99 provides only a program to generate Web server requests; the Web server software becomes part of the system being measured.

- SPECweb99 performance depends on a wide measure of system characteristics, including the disk system and the network.

System	Processor	Number of disk drives	Number of CPUs	Number of networks	Clock rate (GHz)	Result
1550/1000	Pentium III	2	2	2	1	2765
1650	Pentium III	3	2	1	1.4	1810
2500	Pentium III	8	2	4	1.13	3435
2550	Pentium III	1	2	1	1.26	1454
2650	Pentium 4 Xeon	5	2	4	3.06	5698
4600	Pentium 4 Xeon	10	2	4	2.2	4615
6400/700	Pentium III Xeon	5	4	4	0.7	4200
6600	Pentium 4 Xeon MP	8	4	8	2	6700
8450/700	Pentium III Xeon	7	8	8	0.7	8001

FIGURE 4.7 **SPECweb99 performance for a variety of Dell PowerEdge systems using the Xeon versions of the Pentium III and Pentium 4 microprocessors.**

To show how these characteristics produce a remarkably varied picture of Web server performance, we selected the SPECweb99 results for a series of Dell Power-Edge servers that use the Xeon versions of the Pentium III and Pentium 4 processors. The Xeon processors are built using the basic structure of the Pentium III or Pentium 4, but support multiprocessing. In addition the Xeon MP supports a third level of off-chip cache and can support more than two processors. The results for a variety of these Dell systems are shown in Figure 4.7.

Looking at the data in Figure 4.7, we can see that the clock rate of the processors is clearly not the most important factor in determining Web server performance. In fact, the 8400 has twice as many slow processors as the 6600 and yet offers better performance. We expect these systems to be configured to achieve the best performance. That is, for a given set of CPUs, disks and additional networks are added until the processor becomes the bottleneck.

Performance, Power, and Energy Efficiency

As mentioned in Chapter 1, power is increasingly becoming the key limitation in processor performance. In the embedded market, where many processors go into environments that rely solely on passive cooling or on battery power, power consumption is often a constraint that is as important as performance and cost.

No doubt, many readers will have encountered power limitations when using their laptops. Indeed, between the challenges of removing excess heat and the limitations of battery life, power consumption has become a critical factor in the design of processors for laptops. Battery capacity has improved only slightly over time, with the major improvements coming from new materials. Hence, the ability of the processor to operate efficiently and conserve power is crucial. To save power, techniques ranging from putting parts of the computer to sleep, to reducing clock rate and voltage, have all been used. In fact, power consumption is so important that Intel has designed a line of processors, the Pentium M series, specifically for mobile, battery-powered applications.

As we discussed in Chapter 1, for CMOS technology, we can reduce power by reducing frequency. Hence, recent processors intended for laptop use all have the ability to adapt frequency to reduce power consumption, simultaneously, of course, reducing performance. Thus, adequately evaluating the energy efficiency of a processor requires examining its performance at maximum power, at an intermediate level that conserves battery life, and at a level that maximizes battery life. In the Intel Mobile Pentium and Pentium M lines, there are two available clock rates: maximum and reduced clock rate. The best performance is obtained by running at maximum speed, the best battery life by running always at the reduced rate, and the intermediate, performance-power optimized level by switching dynamically between these two clock rates.

Figure 4.8 shows the performance of three Intel Pentium processors designed for use in mobile applications running SPEC CINT2000 and SPEC CFP2000 as benchmarks. As we can see, the newest processor, the Pentium M, has the best performance when run at full clock speed, as well as with the adaptive clock rate mode. The Pentium M's 600 MHz clock makes it slower when run in minimum power mode than the Pentium 4-M, but still faster than the older Pentium III-M design.

For power-limited applications, the most important metric is probably energy efficiency, which is computed by taking performance and dividing by average power consumption when running the benchmark. Figure 4.9 shows the relative energy efficiency for these processors running the SPEC2000 benchmarks. This data clearly shows the energy efficiency advantage of the newer Pentium M design. In all three modes, it has a significant advantage in energy efficiency over the mobile versions of the Pentium III and Pentium 4. Notice that the Pentium 4-M has only a slight efficiency advantage over the Pentium III-M. This data clearly shows the advantage of a processor like the Pentium M, which is designed for reduced power usage from the start, as opposed to a design like the Pentium III-M or Pentium 4-M, which are modified versions of the standard processors. Of course, adequately measuring energy efficiency also requires the use of additional benchmarks designed to reflect how users employ battery-powered computers. Both PC review magazines and Intel's technical journal regularly undertake such studies.

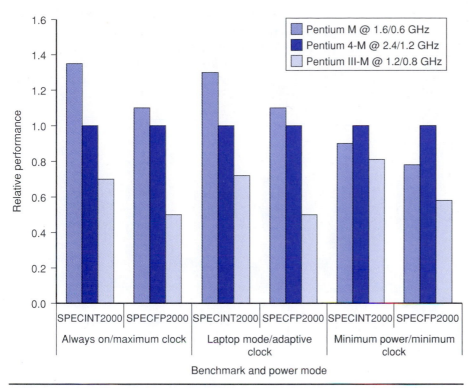

FIGURE 4.8 Relative performance of three Intel processors on SPECINT2000 and SPECFP2000 in three different modes. Each processor operates at two different clock rates, listed in the legend.

Which of the following one-processor Pentium III configurations is likely to produce the best performance on SPECweb99 based on the data in Figure 4.7?

Check Yourself

    a. 1.26 GHz processor, 1 disk, 1 network connection

    b. 1 GHz processor, 6 disks, 3 network connections

    c. 1.1 GHz processor, 2 disks, 2 network connections

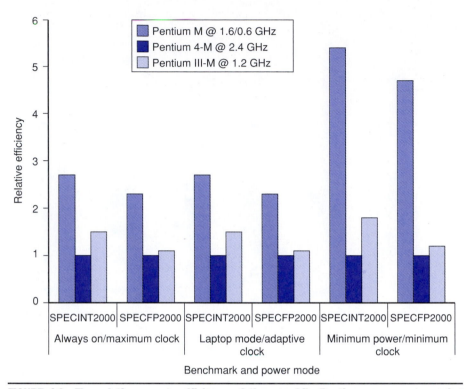

FIGURE 4.9   The relative energy efficiency of three mobile Pentium processors running SPEC2000 in three modes. Energy efficiency is measured as the inverse of joules consumed per benchmark, which is computed by dividing the inverse of the execution time for a benchmark by the watts dissipated.

4.5   Fallacies and Pitfalls

Cost/performance fallacies and pitfalls have ensnared many a computer architect, including us. Accordingly, this section suffers no shortage of relevant examples. We start with a pitfall that has trapped many designers and reveals an important relationship in computer design.

Pitfall: Expecting the improvement of one aspect of a computer to increase performance by an amount proportional to the size of the improvement.

This pitfall has visited designers of both hardware and software. A simple design problem illustrates it well. Suppose a program runs in 100 seconds on a computer, with multiply operations responsible for 80 seconds of this time. How much do I have to improve the speed of multiplication if I want my program to run five times faster?

The execution time of the program after I make the improvement is given by the following simple equation known as **Amdahl's law**:

$$\text{Execution time after improvement} =$$

$$\frac{\text{Execution time affected by improvement}}{\text{Amount of improvement}} + \text{Execution time unaffected}$$

Amdahl's law A rule stating that the performance enhancement possible with a given improvement is limited by the amount that the improved feature is used.

For this problem:

$$\text{Execution time after improvement} = \frac{80 \text{ seconds}}{n} + (100 - 80 \text{ seconds})$$

Since we want the performance to be five times faster, the new execution time should be 20 seconds, giving

$$20 \text{ seconds} = \frac{80 \text{ seconds}}{n} + 20 \text{ seconds}$$

$$0 = \frac{80 \text{ seconds}}{n}$$

That is, there is *no amount* by which we can enhance-multiply to achieve a fivefold increase in performance, if multiply accounts for only 80% of the workload. The performance enhancement possible with a given improvement is limited by the amount that the improved feature is used.

This concept also yields what we call the law of diminishing returns in everyday life. We can use Amdahl's law to estimate performance improvements when we know the time consumed for some function and its potential speedup. Amdahl's law, together with the CPU performance equation, are handy tools for evaluating potential enhancements. Amdahl's law is explored in more detail in the exercises and in the ⊚ **In More Depth**: Amdahl's Law on the CD.

A common theme in hardware design is a corollary of Amdahl's law: *Make the common case fast.* This simple guideline reminds us that in many cases the frequency with which one event occurs may be much higher than another. Amdahl's law reminds us that the opportunity for improvement is affected by how much time the event consumes. Thus, making the common case fast will tend to enhance performance better than optimizing the rare case. Ironically, the common case is often simpler than the rare case and hence is often easier to enhance.

Pitfall: Using a subset of the performance equation as a performance metric.

We have already shown the fallacy of predicting performance based on simply one of clock rate, instruction count, or CPI. Another common mistake is to use two of the three factors to compare performance. Although using two of the three factors may be valid in a limited context, it is also easily misused. Indeed, nearly all proposed alternatives to the use of time as the performance metric have led eventually to misleading claims, distorted results, or incorrect interpretations.

million instructions per second (MIPS) A measurement of program execution speed based on the number of millions of instructions. MIPS is computed as the instruction count divided by the product of the execution time and 10^6.

One alternative to time as the metric is **MIPS (million instructions per second)**. For a given program, MIPS is simply

$$\text{MIPS} = \frac{\text{Instruction count}}{\text{Execution time} \times 10^6}$$

This MIPS measurement is also called *native MIPS* to distinguish it from some alternative definitions of MIPS that we discuss in ⊚ **Section 4.7** on the CD.

Since MIPS is an instruction execution rate, MIPS specifies performance inversely to execution time; faster computers have a higher MIPS rating. The good news about MIPS is that it is easy to understand, and faster computers mean bigger MIPS, which matches intuition.

There are three problems with using MIPS as a measure for comparing computers. First, MIPS specifies the instruction execution rate but does not take into account the capabilities of the instructions. We cannot compare computers with different instruction sets using MIPS, since the instruction counts will certainly differ. In our earlier example examining the SPEC CFP2000 performance, using MIPS to compare the performance of the Pentium III and Pentium 4 would yield misleading results. Second, MIPS varies between programs on the same computer; thus a computer cannot have a single MIPS rating for all programs. Finally and most importantly, MIPS can vary inversely with performance! There are many examples of this anomalous behavior; one is given below.

MIPS as a Performance Measure

EXAMPLE

Consider the computer with three instruction classes and CPI measurements from the last example on page 252. Now suppose we measure the code for the same program from two different compilers and obtain the following data:

Code from	Instruction counts (in billions) for each instruction class		
	A	B	C
Compiler 1	5	1	1
Compiler 2	10	1	1

Assume that the computer's clock rate is 4 GHz. Which code sequence will execute faster according to MIPS? According to execution time?

First we find the execution time for the two different compilers using the following equation:

$$\text{Execution time} = \frac{\text{CPU clock cycles}}{\text{Clock rate}}$$

We can use an earlier formula for CPU clock cycles:

$$\text{CPU clock cycles} = \sum_{i=1}^{n} (\text{CPI}_i \times \text{C}_i)$$

$$\text{CPU clock cycles}_1 = (5 \times 1 + 1 \times 2 + 1 \times 3) \times 10^9 = 10 \times 10^9$$

$$\text{CPU clock cycles}_2 = (10 \times 1 + 1 \times 2 + 1 \times 3) \times 10^9 = 15 \times 10^9$$

Now, we find the execution time for the two compilers:

$$\text{Execution time}_1 = \frac{10 \times 10^9}{4 \times 10^9} = 2.5 \text{ seconds}$$

$$\text{Execution time}_2 = \frac{15 \times 10^9}{4 \times 10^9} = 3.75 \text{ seconds}$$

So, we conclude that compiler 1 generates the faster program, according to execution time. Now, let's compute the MIPS rate for each version of the program, using

$$\text{MIPS} = \frac{\text{Instruction count}}{\text{Execution time} \times 10^6}$$

$$\text{MIPS}_1 = \frac{(5 + 1 + 1) \times 10^9}{2.5 \times 10^6} = 2800$$

$$\text{MIPS}_2 = \frac{(10 + 1 + 1) \times 10^9}{3.75 \times 10^6} = 3200$$

So, the code from compiler 2 has a higher MIPS rating, but the code from compiler 1 runs faster!

As examples such as this show, MIPS can fail to give a true picture of performance—even when comparing two versions of the same program on the same computer. In Section 2.7, we discuss other uses of the term *MIPS*, and how such usages can also be misleading.

Check Yourself

Consider the following performance measurements for a program:

Measurement	Computer A	Computer B
Instruction count	10 billion	8 billion
Clock rate	4 GHz	4 GHz
CPI	1.0	1.1

a. Which computer has the higher MIPS rating?

b. Which computer is faster?

4.6   Concluding Remarks

Although we have focused on performance and how to evaluate it in this chapter, designing only for performance without considering cost, functionality, and other requirements is unrealistic. All computer designers must balance performance and cost. Of course, there exists a domain of *high-performance design,* in which performance is the primary goal and cost is secondary. Much of the supercomputer and high-end server industry designs in this fashion. At the other extreme is *low-cost design,* typified by the embedded market, where cost and power take precedence over performance. In the middle are most desktop designs, as well as low-end servers; these computers require *cost/performance design,* in which the designer balances cost against performance. Examples from the desktop computer industry typify the kinds of trade-offs that designers in this region must live with.

We have seen in this chapter that there is a reliable method of determining and reporting performance, using the execution time of real programs as the metric. This execution time is related to other important measurements we can make by the following equation:

$$\frac{\text{Seconds}}{\text{Program}} = \frac{\text{Instructions}}{\text{Program}} \times \frac{\text{Clock cycles}}{\text{Instruction}} \times \frac{\text{Seconds}}{\text{Clock cycle}}$$

We will use this equation and its constituent factors many times. Remember, though, that individually the factors do not determine performance: only the product, which equals execution time, is a reliable measure of performance.

> Execution time is the only valid and unimpeachable measure of performance. Many other metrics have been proposed and found wanting. Sometimes these metrics are flawed from the start by not reflecting execution time; other times a metric that is valid in a limited context is extended and used beyond that context or without the additional clarification needed to make it valid.
>
> Similarly, any measure that summarizes performance should reflect execution time. Weighted arithmetic means summarize performance while tracking execution time. Through the use of weights, a weighted arithmetic mean can adjust for different running times, balancing the contribution of each benchmark to the summary.

The BIG Picture

Of course, simply knowing this equation is not enough to guide the design or evaluation of a computer. We must understand how the different aspects of a design affect each of these key parameters. This insight involves a wide variety of issues, from the effectiveness of the compiler, to the effects of instruction set design on instruction count, to the impact of pipelining and memory systems on CPI, to the interaction between the technology and organization that determine the clock rate. The art of computer design and evaluation lies not in plugging numbers into a performance equation, but in accurately determining how alternatives will affect performance and cost.

Most computer users care about both cost and performance. While understanding the relationship among aspects of a design and its performance is challenging, determining the cost of various design features is often a more difficult problem. The cost of a computer is affected not only by the cost of the components, but by the costs of labor to assemble the computer, of research and development overhead, of sales and marketing, and by the profit margin. Finally, because of the rapid change in implementation technologies, the most cost-effective choice today is often suboptimal in six months or a year.

Computer designs will always be measured by cost and performance, as well as other important factors such as power, reliability, cost of ownership, and scalability. Although this chapter has focused on performance, the best designs will strike the appropriate balance for a given market among all these factors.

Historical Perspective and Further Reading

This section, which reviews the history of performance measurement and benchmarking, appears as **Section 4.7** on the ⊙ CD.

4.8   Exercises

4.1 [5] <§4.1> We wish to compare the performance of two different computers: M1 and M2. The following measurements have been made on these computers:

Program	Time on M1	Time on M2
1	2.0 seconds	1.5 seconds
2	5.0 seconds	10.0 seconds

Which computer is faster for each program, and how many times as fast is it?

4.2 [5] <§4.1> Consider the two computers and programs in Exercise 4.1. The following additional measurements were made:

Program	Instructions executed on M1	Instructions executed on M2
1	5×10^9	6×10^9

Find the instruction execution rate (instructions per second) for each computer when running program 1.

4.3 [5] <§4.1> Suppose that M1 in Exercise 4.1 costs $500 and M2 costs $800. If you needed to run program 1 a large number of times, which computer would you buy in large quantities? Why?

4.4 [10] <§4.1> ⊙ **For More Practice:** Cost-Effective Computing

4.5 [5] <§4.1> ⊙ **For More Practice:** Cost-Effective Computing

4.6 [5] <§4.1> Another user has the following requirements for the computers discussed in Exercise 4.1: P1 must be executed 1600 times each hour. Any remaining time is used to run P2. If the computer has enough performance to execute program 1 the required number of times per hour, then performance is measured by the throughput for program 2. Which computer is faster for this workload? Which computer is more cost-effective?

4.7 [10] <§4.2> Suppose you wish to run a program P with 7.5×10^9 instructions on a 5 GHz machine with a CPI of 0.8.

a. What is the expected CPU time?

b. When you run P, it takes 3 seconds of wall clock time to complete. What is the percentage of the CPU time P received?

4.8 [10] <§4.2> Consider two different implementations, P1 and P2, of the same instruction set. There are five classes of instructions (A, B, C, D, and E) in the instruction set.

P1 has a clock rate of 4 GHz. P2 has a clock rate of 6 GHz. The average number of cycles for each instruction class for P1 and P2 is as follows:

Class	CPI on P1	CPI on P2
A	1	2
B	2	2
C	3	2
D	4	4
E	3	4

Assume that peak performance is defined as the fastest rate that a computer can execute any instruction sequence. What are the peak performances of P1 and P2 expressed in instructions per second?

4.9 [5] <§§4.1–4.2> If the number of instructions executed in a certain program is divided equally among the classes of instructions in Exercise 4.8 except for class A, which occurs twice as often as each of the others, how much faster is P2 than P1?

4.10 [12] <§4.2> Consider two different implementations, I1 and I2, of the same instruction set. There are three classes of instructions (A, B, and C) in the instruction set. I1 has a clock rate of 6 GHz, and I2 has a clock rate of 3 GHz. The average number of cycles for each instruction class on I1 and I2 is given in the following table:

Class	CPI on I1	CPI on I2	C1 Usage	C2 Usage	C3 Usage
A	2	1	40%	40%	50%
B	3	2	40%	20%	25%
C	5	2	20%	40%	25%

The table also contains a summary of average proportion of instruction classes generated by three different compilers. C1 is a compiler produced by the makers of I1,

C2 is produced by the makers of I2, and the other compiler is a third-party product. Assume that each compiler uses the same number of instructions for a given program but that the instruction mix is as described in the table. Using C1 on both I1 and I2, how much faster can the makers of I1 claim I1 is compared to I2? Using C2, how much faster can the makers of I2 claim that I2 is compared to I1? If you purchased I1, which compiler would you use? If you purchased I2, which compiler would you use? Which computer and compiler would you purchase if all other criteria were identical, including cost?

4.11 [5] <§4.2> Consider program P, which runs on a 1 GHz machine M in 10 seconds. An optimization is made to P, replacing all instances of multiplying a value by 4 (mult X, X,4) with two instructions that set x to $x + x$ twice (add X,X; add X,X). Call this new optimized program P′. The CPI of a multiply instruction is 4, and the CPI of an add is 1. After recompiling, the program now runs in 9 seconds on machine M. How many multiplies were replaced by the new compiler?

4.12 [5] <§4.2> Your company could speed up a Java program on their new computer by adding hardware support for garbage collection. Garbage collection currently comprises 20% of the cycles of the program. You have two possible changes to the machine. The first one would be to automatically handle garbage collection in hardware. This causes an increase in cycle time by a factor of 1.2. The second would be to provide for new hardware instructions to be added to the ISA that could be used during garbage collection. This would halve the number of instruction needed for garbage collections but increase the cycle time by 1.1. Which of these two options, if either, should you choose?

4.13 [5] <§4.2> For the following set of variables, identify all of the subsets that can be used to calculate execution time. Each subset should be minimal; that is, it should not contain any variable that is not needed.

{CPI, clock rate, cycle time, MIPS, number of instructions in program, number of cycles in program}

4.14 [5] <§4.2> The table below shows the number of floating-point operations executed in three different programs and the runtime for those programs on three different computers:

Program	Floating-point operations	Execution time in seconds		
		Computer A	Computer B	Computer C
Program 1	5×10^9	2	5	10
Program 2	20×10^9	20	20	20
Program 3	40×10^9	200	50	15

Which computer is fastest according to total execution time? How many times as fast is it compared to the other two computers?

4.15 [15] <§§4.2, 4.3> One user has told you that the three programs in Exercise 4.14 constitute the bulk of his workload, but he does not run them equally. The user wants to determine how the three computers compare when the workload consists of different mixes of these three programs. (You know you can use the arithmetic mean to find the relative performance.)

Suppose the total number of floating-point operations (FLOPS) executed in the workload is equally divided among the three programs. That is, program 1 runs 8 times for every time program 3 runs, and program 2 runs twice for every time program 3 runs. Find which computer is fastest for this workload and by what factor. How does this compare with the total execution time with equal numbers of program executions?

4.16 [15] <§§4.2, 4.3> An alternative weighting to that of Exercise 4.15 is to assume that equal amounts of time will be spent running each program on one of the computers. Which computer is fastest using the data given for Exercise 4.14 and assuming a weighting that generates equal execution time for each of the benchmark programs on computer A? Which computer is fastest if we assume a weighting that generates equal execution time on computer B? Computer C? Explain the results.

4.17 [5] <§§4.2–4.3> If the clock rates of computers M1 and M2 in Exercise 4.1 are 4 GHz and 6 GHz, respectively, find the clock cycles per instruction (CPI) for program 1 on both computers using the data in Exercises 4.1 and 4.2.

4.18 [5] <§§4.2–4.3> Assuming the CPI for program 2 on each computer in Exercise 4.1 is the same as the CPI for program 1 found in Exercise 4.17, find the instruction count for program 2 running on each computer using the execution times from Exercise 4.1.

4.19 [5] <§4.3> ◉ **In More Depth:** Amdahl's Law

4.20 [10] <§4.3> ◉ **In More Depth:** Amdahl's Law

4.21 [10] <§4.3> ◉ **In More Depth:** Amdahl's Law

4.22 [5] <§4.3> ◉ **In More Depth:** Amdahl's Law

4.23 [5] <§4.3> ◉ **In More Depth:** Amdahl's Law

4.24 [20] <§4.3> ◉ **In More Depth:** Amdahl's Law

4.25 [5] <§4.3> ◉ **In More Depth:** Choosing the Right Mean

4.26 [15] <§4.3> ◉ **In More Depth:** Choosing the Right Mean

4.27 [3 hours] <§4.3> ◉ **In More Depth:** Synthetic Benchmarks

4.28 [3 hours] <§4.3> ◉ **In More Depth:** Synthetic Benchmarks

4.29 [4 hours] <§4.3> ⊙ **In More Depth:** MIPS, MOPS, and Other FLOPS

4.30 [5] <§4.3> ⊙ **In More Depth:** MFLOPS as a Performance Metric

4.31 [15] <§4.3> ⊙ **In More Depth:** MFLOPS as a Performance Metric

4.32 [4 hours] <§4.3> ⊙ **In More Depth:** MFLOPS as a Performance Metric

4.33 [5] <§4.3> ⊙ **In More Depth:** Embedded Benchmarks

4.34 [5] <§§4.2, 4.3> ⊙ **In More Depth:** Using Hardware-Independent Metrics

4.35 [10] <§§4.2, 4.3> ⊙ **For More Practice:** Analyzing a Processor with Floating Point Implemented in Hardware or Software

4.36 [10] <§4.2> ⊙ **For More Practice:** Analyzing a Processor with Floating Point Implemented in Hardware or Software

4.37 [5] <§§4.2, 4.3> ⊙ **For More Practice:** Analyzing a Processor with Floating Point Implemented in Hardware or Software

4.38 [10] <§§4.2, 4.3> ⊙ **For More Practice:** Analyzing Enhancements to a Processor

4.39 [5] <§§4.2, 4.3> ⊙ **For More Practice:** Analyzing Enhancements to a Processor

4.40 [10] <§§4.2, 4.3> ⊙ **For More Practice:** Analyzing Enhancements to a Processor

4.41 [5] <§§4.2, 4.3> ⊙ **For More Practice:** Analyzing Enhancements to a Processor

4.42 [5] <§§4.2, 4.3> ⊙ **For More Practice:** Analyzing Enhancements to a Processor

4.43 [10] <§§4.2, 4.3> ⊙ **For More Practice:** Analyzing Enhancements to a Processor

4.44 [10] <§§4.2, 4.3> ⊙ **For More Practice:** Analyzing Enhancements to a Processor

4.45 [5] <§4.3> Assume that multiply instructions take 12 cycles and account for 15% of the instructions in a typical program, and the other 85% of the instructions require an average of 4 cycles for each instruction. What percentage of time does the CPU spend doing multiplication?

4.46 [5] <§4.3> Your hardware engineering team has indicated that it would be possible to reduce the number of cycles required for multiplication to 8 in Exercise

4.45, but this would require a 20% increase in the cycle time. Nothing else would be affected by the change. Should they proceed with the modification?

4.47 [10] <§4.4> Look at the current list of SPEC programs in Figure 4.5 on page 260. Does it include applications that match the ways you typically use your computer? What classes of programs are irrelevant or missing? Why do you think they were or were not included in SPEC? What would have to be done to include/exclude such programs in the next SPEC release?

4.48 [5] <§4.4> If benchmark suites are designed to provide a real-world metric for a specific computing task, explain why benchmark suites need to be updated.

4.49 [5] <§§4.2, 4.3, 4.4> **In More Depth:** The Difficulty with Kernel Benchmarks

4.50 [15] <§§4.2, 4.3, 4.4> ◉ **In More Depth:** The Difficulty with Kernel Benchmarks

4.51 [10] <§§4.1–4.5> Consider the following hypothetical news release:

"The company will unveil the industry's first 5 GHz version of the chip, which offers a 25% performance boost over the company's former speed champ, which runs at 4 GHz. The new chip can be plugged into system boards for the older original chip (which ran at 1 GHz) to provide a 70% performance boost."

Comment on the definition (or definitions) of performance that you believe the company used. Do you think the news release is misleading?

4.52 [indefinite] <§§4.1–4.5> Collect a set of articles that you believe contain incorrect analyses of performance or use misleading performance metrics to try to persuade readers. For example, an article in the *New York Times* (April 20, 1994, p. D1) described a video game player "that will surpass the computing power of even the most powerful personal computers" and presented the following chart to support the argument that "video game computers may be the supercomputers of tomorrow":

Computer	Approximate number of instructions per second	Price
1975 IBM mainframe	10,000,000	$10,000,000
1976 Cray-1	160,000,000	$20,000,000
1979 Digital VAX	1,000,000	$200,000
1981 IBM PC	250,000	$3,000
1984 Sun 2	1,000,000	$10,000
1994 Pentium-chip PC	66,000,000	$3,000
1995 Sony PCX video game	500,000,000	$500
1995 Microunity set-top	1,000,000,000	$500

The article never discussed how the nature of the instructions should impact the definition of "powerful." For each article you collect, describe why you think it is misleading or incorrect. Good places to look for material include the business or technology sections of newspapers, magazines (both articles and ads), and the Internet (newsgroups and the Web).

Answers to Check Yourself

§4.1, page 246: 1. a: both, b: latency, c: neither. 2. 7 sec.
§4.2, page 253: b.
§4.3, page 258: 1. F, F, F, T. 2. T, F, F, T
§4.4, page 265: b.
§4.5, page 270: a. Computer A. b. Computer B.

Computers in the Real World

Problem: Find ways to help transport people quickly while maintaining safety, comfort, and efficiency.

Solution: For more than 20 years, computers have played an increasingly important role in the control of transportation systems, including planes, trains, automobiles, and even ships. Essentially all modern transportation systems rely on computers to enhance their safety, comfort, and efficiency. Computers also play a critical role in improving fuel consumption and reducing air pollution. In these two pages, we examine some of the uses of computers in trains and automobiles.

In designing pipelines we must prevent hazards, at all costs, and we try to avoid pipeline delays. Computer-controlled trains try to do the same: hazards are life-threatening and can never be permitted, and delays are to be avoided!

The French TGV (*Train à Grande Vitesse*) is one of the fastest train systems in the world, with a typical top speed of 300 km/hour. Traditionally, trains were controlled by an engineer, using a set of track-side lights and signals that tell the engineer to proceed, slow down, or stop. At 300 km/hour, it is difficult to read such signals, and easy to miss one completely, leading to a possible disaster. In addition, some tracks, such as those containing tight curves, can be unsafe at the higher speeds; since the TGV was designed to run on existing track, finding a fail-safe method to communicate track conditions was critical.

The TGV designers solved this problem by a clever signaling system, called TVM (*Transmission Voie-Machine*), that runs through the rails and is picked up by antennas in the locomotive. The track is divided into blocks, which are typically about 1.5 km in length. Shorter blocks are used when track conditions change quickly or where a higher degree of safety is critical, such as in the Chunnel, where the block length is about one-tenth as long. Transmitters at the beginning of each block are used to communicate instructions to the cab, where they are carried out by an engineer; a computer also watches the communications, and implements the commands if the engineer fails to.

The Eurostar TGV train in Nice, France.

The interior of a Eurostar TGV cab.

One challenge is that the stopping distance for the TGV is nominally four blocks (somewhat shorter in an absolute emergency). The time to travel four blocks is 1.2 minutes, and with the newest signaling system trains are run at a 3-minute headway, even in fog! So the system must monitor the presence of all trains and ensure the most important property: only one train ever occupies a block of track at the same time! The system constantly communicates the maximum safe speed for the current block, improving performance and safety.

The TVM system has been built with extensive attention to safety, which means heavy use of redundancy to ensure the operation of the system in the face of failure of a component. The failure rate of TVM has been estimated at less than 1 failure in a million years. This attention to safety has paid off: in over two decades of service, there have been no fatal accidents caused by a TVM failure.

Computers have also played a key role in making cars safer, more efficient, and less polluting. The modern automobile has dozens of microprocessors controlling everything from braking, to ignition, to air bag deployment.

In the area of safety, air bags and antilock brakes have been two of the most important innovations since the seat belt. Antilock brakes preserve the ability to steer during the severe braking that might occur in emergency conditions. By detecting wheel lockup and alternately applying and releasing the brakes under computer control, an antilock brake system can avoid wheel lockup.

Air bags use a force sensor to detect severe deacceleration, which occurs during a collision. The air bags are deployed by a computer that reads the sensor. The new generation of air bags uses a two-stage deployment: when the deacceleration indicates a collision of moderate severity, the air bag inflates more slowly, reducing the possibility of passenger injury from rapid deployment in a moderate collision. Reliability of these safety systems has been enhanced by a computer-controlled test that is run every time the vehicle is started.

Modern ignition systems in automobiles aim to enhance mileage while reducing pollution. Happily, these two goals are doubly congruent: enhancing mileage reduces pollution through the use of less fuel, and mileage is enhanced by more effective combustion, which also reduces the emission of partially combusted fuel. Computers control the injection of fuel, the amount of air injected, and the spark timing, which must change as the engine runs faster. Careful control of these elements over the full operating range from 1000 to 6000 rpm and different temperature conditions has helped improve mileage and reduce pollution.

To learn more, see this reference on the library:

"An investigation of the Therac-25 accidents," Nancy G. Leveson and Clark S. Turner. *IEEE Computer*, 26(7): 18–41, July 1993

The Processor: Datapath and Control

In a major matter,
no details are small.

French Proverb

The Five Classic Components of a Computer

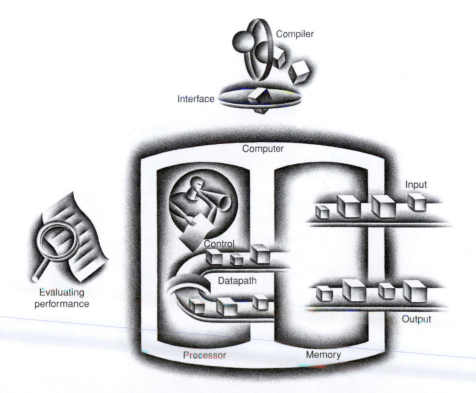

5.1 Introduction

In Chapter 4, we saw that the performance of a machine was determined by three key factors: instruction count, clock cycle time, and clock cycles per instruction (CPI). The compiler and the instruction set architecture, which we examined in Chapters 2 and 3, determine the instruction count required for a given program. However, both the clock cycle time and the number of clock cycles per instruction are determined by the implementation of the processor. In this chapter, we construct the datapath and control unit for two different implementations of the MIPS instruction set.

This chapter contains an explanation of the principles and techniques used in implementing a processor, starting with a highly abstract and simplified overview in this section, followed by sections that build up a datapath and construct a simple version of a processor sufficient to implement instructions sets like MIPS, and finally, developing the concepts necessary to implement more complex instruction sets, like the IA-32.

For the reader interested in understanding the high-level interpretation of instructions and its impact on program performance, this initial section provides enough background to understand these concepts as well as the basic concepts of pipelining, which are explained in Section 6.1 of the next chapter.

For those readers desiring an understanding of how hardware implements instructions, Sections 5.3 and 5.4 are all the additional material that is needed. Furthermore, these two sections are sufficient to understand all the material in Chapter 6 on pipelining. Only those readers with an interest in hardware design should go further.

The remaining sections of this chapter cover how modern hardware—including more complex processors such as the Intel Pentium series—is usually implemented. The basic principles of finite-state control are explained, and different methods of implementation, including microprogramming, are examined. For the reader interested in understanding the processor and its performance in more depth, Sections 5.4 and 5.5 will be useful. For readers with an interest in modern hardware design, Section 5.7 covers microprogramming, a technique used to implement more complex control such as that present in IA-32 processors, and Section 5.8 describes how hardware design languages and CAD tools are used to implement hardware.

A Basic MIPS Implementation

We will be examining an implementation that includes a subset of the core MIPS instruction set:

- ■ The memory-reference instructions load word (`lw`) and store word (`sw`)

- ■ The arithmetic-logical instructions add, sub, and, or, and slt

- ■ The instructions branch equal (`beq`) and jump (`j`), which we add last

This subset does not include all the integer instructions (for example, shift, multiply, and divide are missing), nor does it include any floating-point instructions. However, the key principles used in creating a datapath and designing the control will be illustrated. The implementation of the remaining instructions is similar.

In examining the implementation, we will have the opportunity to see how the instruction set architecture determines many aspects of the implementation, and how the choice of various implementation strategies affects the clock rate and CPI for the machine. Many of the key design principles introduced in Chapter 4 can be illustrated by looking at the implementation, such as the guidelines *Make the common case fast* and *Simplicity favors regularity*. In addition, most concepts used to implement the MIPS subset in this chapter and the next are the same basic ideas that are used to construct a broad spectrum of computers, from high-performance servers to general-purpose microprocessors to embedded processors, which are used increasingly in products ranging from VCRs to automobiles.

An Overview of the Implementation

In Chapters 2 and 3, we looked at the core MIPS instructions, including the integer arithmetic-logical instructions, the memory reference instructions, and the branch instructions. Much of what needs to be done to implement these instructions is the same, independent of the exact class of instruction. For every instruction, the first two steps are identical:

1. Send the program counter (PC) to the memory that contains the code and fetch the instruction from that memory.

2. Read one or two registers, using fields of the instruction to select the registers to read. For the load word instruction, we need to read only one register, but most other instructions require that we read two registers.

After these two steps, the actions required to complete the instruction depend on the instruction class. Fortunately, for each of the three instruction classes (memory reference, arithmetic-logical, and branches), the actions are largely the same, independent of the exact opcode.

Even across different instruction classes there are some similarities. For example, all instruction classes, except jump, use the arithmetic-logical unit (ALU) after reading the registers. The memory reference instructions use the ALU for an address calculation, the arithmetic-logical instructions for the operation execution, and branches for comparison. As we can see, the simplicity and regularity of the instruction set simplifies the implementation by making the execution of many of the instruction classes similar.

After using the ALU, the actions required to complete various instruction classes differ. A memory reference instruction will need to access the memory either to write data for a store or read data for a load. An arithmetic-logical instruction must write the data from the ALU back into a register. Lastly, for a branch instruction, we may need to change the next instruction address based on the comparison; otherwise the PC should be incremented by 4 to get the address of the next instruction.

Figure 5.1 shows the high-level view of a MIPS implementation, focusing on the various functional units and their interconnection. Although this figure shows most of the flow of data through the processor, it omits two important aspects of instruction execution.

First, in several places, Figure 5.1 shows data going to a particular unit as coming from two different sources. For example, the value written into the PC can come from one of two adders, and the data written into the register file can come from either the ALU or the data memory. In practice, these data lines cannot simply be wired together; we must add an element that chooses from among the multiple sources and steers one of those sources to its destination. This selection is commonly done with a device called a *multiplexor*, although this device might better be called a *data selector*. The multiplexor, which is described in detail in ⊙ **Appendix B**, selects from among several inputs based on the setting of its control lines. The control lines are set based primarily on information taken from the instruction being executed.

Second, several of the units must be controlled depending on the type of instruction. For example, the data memory must read on a load and write on a store. The register file must be written on a load and an arithmetic-logical instruction. And, of course, the ALU must perform one of several operations, as we saw in Chapter 3. (⊙ **Appendix B** describes the detailed logic design of the ALU.) Like the muxes, these operations are directed by control lines that are set on the basis of various fields in the instruction.

Figure 5.2 shows the datapath of Figure 5.1 with the three required multiplexors added, as well as control lines for the major functional units. A control unit that has the instruction as an input is used to determine how to set the control lines for the functional units and two of the multiplexors. The third multiplexor, which determines whether PC + 4 or the branch destination address is written

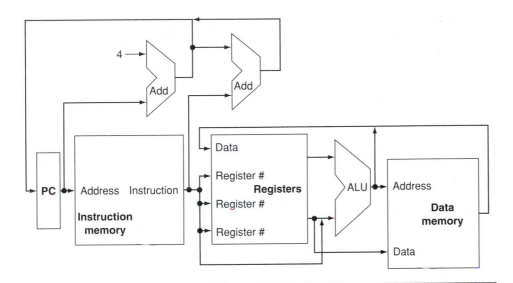

FIGURE 5.1   An abstract view of the implementation of the MIPS subset showing the major functional units and the major connections between them. All instructions start by using the program counter to supply the instruction address to the instruction memory. After the instruction is fetched, the register operands used by an instruction are specified by fields of that instruction. Once the register operands have been fetched, they can be operated on to compute a memory address (for a load or store), to compute an arithmetic result (for an integer arithmetic-logical instruction), or a compare (for a branch). If the instruction is an arithmetic-logical instruction, the result from the ALU must be written to a register. If the operation is a load or store, the ALU result is used as an address to either store a value from the registers or load a value from memory into the registers. The result from the ALU or memory is written back into the register file. Branches require the use of the ALU output to determine the next instruction address, which comes either from the ALU (where the PC and branch offset are summed) or from an adder that increments the current PC by 4. The thick lines interconnecting the functional units represent buses, which consist of multiple signals. The arrows are used to guide the reader in knowing how information flows. Since signal lines may cross, we explicitly show when crossing lines are connected by the presence of a dot where the lines cross.

into the PC, is set based on the Zero output of the ALU, which is used to perform the comparison of a beq instruction. The regularity and simplicity of the MIPS instruction set means that a simple decoding process can be used to determine how to set the control lines.

In the remainder of the chapter, we refine this view to fill in the details, which requires that we add further functional units, increase the number of connections between units, and, of course, add a control unit to control what actions are taken for different instruction classes. Sections 5.3 and 5.4 describe a simple implementation that uses a single long clock cycle for every instruction and follows the general form of Figures 5.1 and 5.2. In this first design, every instruction begins execution on one clock edge and completes execution on the next clock edge.

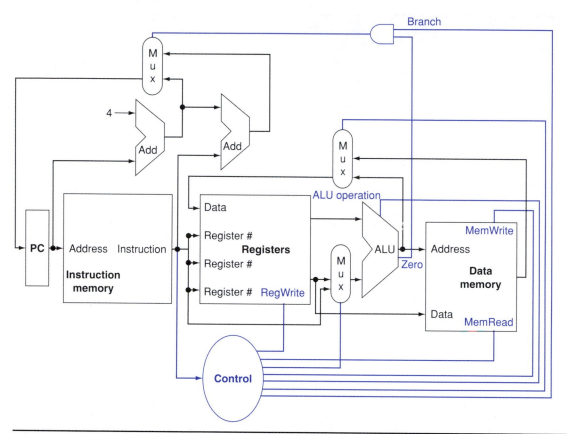

FIGURE 5.2   The basic implementation of the MIPS subset including the necessary multiplexors and control lines. The top multiplexor controls what value replaces the PC (PC + 4 or the branch destination address); the multiplexor is controlled by the gate that "ands" together the Zero output of the ALU and a control signal that indicates that the instruction is a branch. The multiplexor whose output returns to the register file is used to steer the output of the ALU (in the case of an arithmetic-logical instruction) or the output of the data memory (in the case of a load) for writing into the register file. Finally, the bottommost multiplexor is used to determine whether the second ALU input is from the registers (for a nonimmediate arithmetic-logical instruction) or from the offset field of the instruction (for an immediate operation, a load or store, or a branch). The added control lines are straightforward and determine the operation performed at the ALU, whether the data memory should read or write, and whether the registers should perform a write operation. The control lines are shown in color to make them easier to see.

While easier to understand, this approach is not practical, since it would be slower than an implementation that allows different instruction classes to take different numbers of clock cycles, each of which could be much shorter. After designing the control for this simple machine, we will look at an implementation that uses multiple clock cycles for each instruction. This multicycle design is used when we discuss more advanced control concepts, handling exceptions, and the use of hardware design languages in Sections 5.5 through 5.8.

The single-cycle datapath conceptually described in this section *must* have separate instruction and data memories because

1. the format of data and instructions is different in MIPS and hence different memories are needed.

2. having separate memories is less expensive.

3. the processor operates in one cycle and cannot use a single-ported memory for two different accesses within that cycle.

5.2 Logic Design Conventions

To discuss the design of a machine, we must decide how the logic implementing the machine will operate and how the machine is clocked. This section reviews a few key ideas in digital logic that we will use extensively in this chapter. If you have little or no background in digital logic, you will find it helpful to read through ◉ **Appendix B** before continuing.

The functional units in the MIPS implementation consist of two different types of logic elements: elements that operate on data values and elements that contain state. The elements that operate on data values are all *combinational*, which means that their outputs depend only on the current inputs. Given the same input, a combinational element always produces the same output. The ALU shown in Figure 5.1 and discussed in Chapter 3 and ◉ **Appendix B** is a combinational element. Given a set of inputs, it always produces the same output because it has no internal storage.

Other elements in the design are not combinational, but instead contain *state*. An element contains state if it has some internal storage. We call these elements **state elements** because, if we pulled the plug on the machine, we could restart it by loading the state elements with the values they contained before we pulled the plug. Furthermore, if we saved and restored the state elements, it would be as if the machine had never lost power. Thus, these state elements completely characterize the machine. In Figure 5.1, the instruction and data memories as well as the registers are all examples of state elements.

A state element has at least two inputs and one output. The required inputs are the data value to be written into the element and the clock, which determines

state element A memory element.

when the data value is written. The output from a state element provides the value that was written in an earlier clock cycle. For example, one of the logically simplest state elements is a D-type flip-flop (see ⊙ **Appendix B**), which has exactly these two inputs (a value and a clock) and one output. In addition to flip-flops, our MIPS implementation also uses two other types of state elements: memories and registers, both of which appear in Figure 5.1. The clock is used to determine when the state element should be written; a state element can be read at any time.

Logic components that contain state are also called *sequential* because their outputs depend on both their inputs and the contents of the internal state. For example, the output from the functional unit representing the registers depends both on the register numbers supplied and on what was written into the registers previously. The operation of both the combinational and sequential elements and their construction are discussed in more detail in ⊙ **Appendix B**.

We will use the word *asserted* to indicate a signal that is logically high and *assert* to specify that a signal should be driven logically high, and *deassert* or *deasserted* to represent logically low.

Clocking Methodology

clocking methodology The approach used to determine when data is valid and stable relative to the clock.

A **clocking methodology** defines when signals can be read and when they can be written. It is important to specify the timing of reads and writes because, if a signal is written at the same time it is read, the value of the read could correspond to the old value, the newly written value, or even some mix of the two! Needless to say, computer designs cannot tolerate such unpredictability. A clocking methodology is designed to prevent this circumstance.

edge-triggered clocking A clocking scheme in which all state changes occur on a clock edge.

For simplicity, we will assume an **edge-triggered clocking** methodology. An edge-triggered clocking methodology means that any values stored in a sequential logic element are updated only on a clock edge. Because only state elements can store a data value, any collection of combinational logic must have its inputs coming from a set of state elements and its outputs written into a set of state elements. The inputs are values that were written in a previous clock cycle, while the outputs are values that can be used in a following clock cycle.

Figure 5.3 shows the two state elements surrounding a block of combinational logic, which operates in a single clock cycle: all signals must propagate from state element 1, through the combinational logic, and to state element 2 in the time of one clock cycle. The time necessary for the signals to reach state element 2 defines the length of the clock cycle.

control signal A signal used for multiplexor selection or for directing the operation of a functional unit; contrasts with a data signal, which contains information that is operated on by a functional unit.

For simplicity, we do not show a write **control signal** when a state element is written on every active clock edge. In contrast, if a state element is not updated on every clock, then an explicit write control signal is required. Both the clock signal and the write control signal are inputs, and the state element is changed only when the write control signal is asserted and a clock edge occurs.

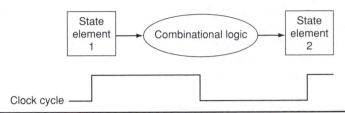

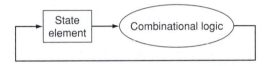

FIGURE 5.3 Combinational logic, state elements, and the clock are closely related. In a synchronous digital system, the clock determines when elements with state will write values into internal storage. Any inputs to a state element must reach a stable value (that is, have reached a value from which they will not change until after the clock edge) before the active clock edge causes the state to be updated. All state elements, including memory, are assumed to be edge-triggered.

FIGURE 5.4 An edge-triggered methodology allows a state element to be read and written in the same clock cycle without creating a race that could lead to indeterminate data values. Of course, the clock cycle still must be long enough so that the input values are stable when the active clock edge occurs. Feedback cannot occur within one clock cycle because of the edge-triggered update of the state element. If feedback were possible, this design could not work properly. Our designs in this chapter and the next rely on the edge-triggered timing methodology and structures like the one shown in this figure.

An edge-triggered methodology allows us to read the contents of a register, send the value through some combinational logic, and write that register in the same clock cycle, as shown in Figure 5.4. It doesn't matter whether we assume that all writes take place on the rising clock edge or on the falling clock edge, since the inputs to the combinational logic block cannot change except on the chosen clock edge. With an edge-triggered timing methodology, there is *no* feedback within a single clock cycle, and the logic in Figure 5.4 works correctly. In 🔵 **Appendix B** we briefly discuss additional timing constraints (such as setup and hold times) as well as other timing methodologies.

Nearly all of these state and logic elements will have inputs and outputs that are 32 bits wide, since that is the width of most of the data handled by the processor. We will make it clear whenever a unit has an input or output that is other than 32 bits in width. The figures will indicate *buses*, which are signals wider than 1 bit, with thicker lines. At times we will want to combine several buses to form a wider bus; for example, we may want to obtain a 32-bit bus by combining two 16-bit buses. In such cases, labels on the bus lines will make it clear that we are concatenating buses to form a wider bus. Arrows are also added to help clarify the direction of the flow of data between elements. Finally, color indicates a control signal as opposed to a signal that carries data; this distinction will become clearer as we proceed through this chapter.

Check Yourself

True or false: Because the register file is both read and written on the same clock cycle, any MIPS datapath using edge-triggered writes must have more than one copy of the register file.

5.3   Building a Datapath

datapath element A functional unit used to operate on or hold data within a processor. In the MIPS implementation the datapath elements include the instruction and data memories, the register file, the arithmetic logic unit (ALU), and adders.

program counter (PC) The register containing the address of the instruction in the program being executed.

A reasonable way to start a datapath design is to examine the major components required to execute each class of MIPS instruction. Let's start by looking at which **datapath elements** each instruction needs. When we show the datapath elements, we will also show their control signals.

Figure 5.5 shows the first element we need: a memory unit to store the instructions of a program and supply instructions given an address. Figure 5.5 also shows a register, which we call the **program counter (PC)**, that is used to hold the address of the current instruction. Lastly, we will need an adder to increment the PC to the address of the next instruction. This adder, which is combinational, can be built from the ALU we described in Chapter 3 and designed in detail in Ⓔ **Appendix B**, simply by wiring the control lines so that the control always specifies an add operation. We will draw such an ALU with the label *Add*, as in Figure 5.5, to indicate that it has been permanently made an adder and cannot perform the other ALU functions.

To execute any instruction, we must start by fetching the instruction from memory. To prepare for executing the next instruction, we must also increment the program counter so that it points at the next instruction, 4 bytes later. Figure 5.6 shows how the three elements from Figure 5.5 are combined to form a datapath that fetches instructions and increments the PC to obtain the address of the next sequential instruction.

Now let's consider the R-format instructions (see Figure 2.7 on page 67). They all read two registers, perform an ALU operation on the contents of the registers, and write the result. We call these instructions either *R-type instructions* or *arithmetic-logical instructions* (since they perform arithmetic or logical operations). This instruction class includes add, sub, and, or, and slt, which were

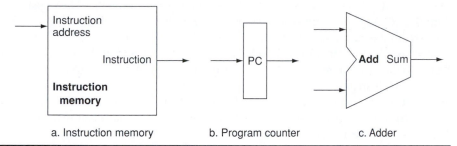

a. Instruction memory   b. Program counter   c. Adder

FIGURE 5.5 Two state elements are needed to store and access instructions, and an adder is needed to compute the next instruction address. The state elements are the instruction memory and the program counter. The instruction memory need only provide read access because the datapath does not write instructions. Since the instruction memory only reads, we treat it as combinational logic: the output at any time reflects the contents of the location specified by the address input, and no read control signal is needed. (We will need to write the instruction memory when we load the program; this is not hard to add, and we ignore it for simplicity.) The program counter is a 32-bit register that will be written at the end of every clock cycle and thus does not need a write control signal. The adder is an ALU wired to always perform an add of its two 32-bit inputs and place the result on its output.

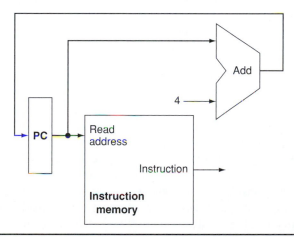

FIGURE 5.6 A portion of the datapath used for fetching instructions and incrementing the program counter. The fetched instruction is used by other parts of the datapath.

introduced in Chapter 2. Recall that a typical instance of such an instruction is add $t1,$t2,$t3, which reads $t2 and $t3 and writes $t1.

The processor's 32 general-purpose registers are stored in a structure called a **register file**. A register file is a collection of registers in which any register can be

register file A state element that consists of a set of registers that can be read and written by supplying a register number to be accessed.

read or written by specifying the number of the register in the file. The register file contains the register state of the machine. In addition, we will need an ALU to operate on the values read from the registers.

Because the R-format instructions have three register operands, we will need to read two data words from the register file and write one data word into the register file for each instruction. For each data word to be read from the registers, we need an input to the register file that specifies the register number to be read and an output from the register file that will carry the value that has been read from the registers. To write a data word, we will need two inputs: one to specify the *register number* to be written and one to supply the *data* to be written into the register. The register file always outputs the contents of whatever register numbers are on the Read register inputs. Writes, however, are controlled by the write control signal, which must be asserted for a write to occur at the clock edge. Thus, we need a total of four inputs (three for register numbers and one for data) and two outputs (both for data), as shown in Figure 5.7. The register number inputs are 5 bits wide to specify one of 32 registers ($32 = 2^5$), whereas the data input and two data output buses are each 32 bits wide.

Figure 5.7 shows the ALU, which takes two 32-bit inputs and produces a 32-bit result, as well as a 1-bit signal if the result is 0. The four-bit control signal of the ALU is described in detail in ⊙ **Appendix B**; we will review the ALU control shortly when we need to know how to set it.

Next, consider the MIPS load word and store word instructions, which have the general form `lw  $t1,offset_value($t2)` or `sw  $t1,offset_value ($t2)`. These instructions compute a memory address by adding the base register, which is `$t2`, to the 16-bit signed offset field contained in the instruction. If the instruction is a store, the value to be stored must also be read from the register file where it resides in `$t1`. If the instruction is a load, the value read from memory must be written into the register file in the specified register, which is `$t1`. Thus, we will need both the register file and the ALU from Figure 5.7.

In addition, we will need a unit to **sign-extend** the 16-bit offset field in the instruction to a 32-bit signed value, and a data memory unit to read from or write to. The data memory must be written on store instructions; hence, it has both read and write control signals, an address input, and an input for the data to be written into memory. Figure 5.8 shows these two elements.

The `beq` instruction has three operands, two registers that are compared for equality and a 16-bit offset used to compute the **branch target address** relative to the branch instruction address. Its form is `beq $t1,$t2,offset`. To implement this instruction, we must compute the branch target address by adding the sign-extended offset field of the instruction to the PC. There are two details in the definition of branch instructions (see Chapter 2) to which we must pay attention:

sign-extend To increase the size of a data item by replicating the high-order sign bit of the original data item in the high-order bits of the larger, destination data item.

branch target address The address specified in a branch, which becomes the new program counter (PC) if the branch is taken. In the MIPS architecture the branch target is given by the sum of the offset field of the instruction and the address of the instruction following the branch.

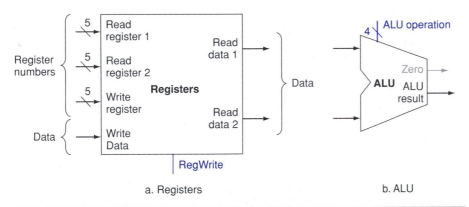

FIGURE 5.7   The two elements needed to implement R-format ALU operations are the register file and the ALU. The register file contains all the registers and has two read ports and one write port. The design of multiported register files is discussed in Section B.8 of ⊙ **Appendix B**. The register file always outputs the contents of the registers corresponding to the Read register inputs on the outputs; no other control inputs are needed. In contrast, a register write must be explicitly indicated by asserting the write control signal. Remember that writes are edge-triggered, so that all the write inputs (i.e., the value to be written, the register number, and the write control signal) must be valid at the clock edge. Since writes to the register file are edge-triggered, our design can legally read and write the same register within a clock cycle: the read will get the value written in an earlier clock cycle, while the value written will be available to a read in a subsequent clock cycle. The inputs carrying the register number to the register file are all 5 bits wide, whereas the lines carrying data values are 32 bits wide. The operation to be performed by the ALU is controlled with the ALU operation signal, which will be 4 bits wide, using the ALU designed in ⊙ **Appendix B**. We will use the Zero detection output of the ALU shortly to implement branches. The overflow output will not be needed until Section 5.6, when we discuss exceptions; we omit it until then.

■ The instruction set architecture specifies that the base for the branch address calculation is the address of the instruction following the branch. Since we compute PC + 4 (the address of the next instruction) in the instruction fetch datapath, it is easy to use this value as the base for computing the branch target address.

■ The architecture also states that the offset field is shifted left 2 bits so that it is a word offset; this shift increases the effective range of the offset field by a factor of 4.

To deal with the latter complication, we will need to shift the offset field by 2.

In addition to computing the branch target address, we must also determine whether the next instruction is the instruction that follows sequentially or the instruction at the branch target address. When the condition is true (i.e., the operands are equal), the branch target address becomes the new PC, and we say that the **branch** is **taken**. If the operands are not equal, the incremented PC should replace the current PC (just as for any other normal instruction); in this case, we say that the **branch** is **not taken**.

branch taken A branch where the branch condition is satisfied and the program counter (PC) becomes the branch target. All unconditional branches are taken branches.

branch not taken A branch where the branch condition is false and the program counter (PC) becomes the address of the instruction that sequentially follows the branch.

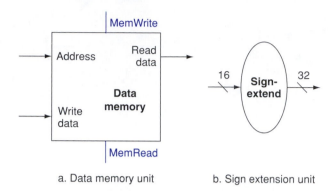

a. Data memory unit   b. Sign extension unit

FIGURE 5.8   The two units needed to implement loads and stores, in addition to the register file and ALU of Figure 5.7, are the data memory unit and the sign extension unit. The memory unit is a state element with inputs for the address and the write data, and a single output for the read result. There are separate read and write controls, although only one of these may be asserted on any given clock. The memory unit needs a read signal, since, unlike the register file, reading the value of an invalid address can cause problems, as we will see in Chapter 7. The sign extension unit has a 16-bit input that is sign-extended into a 32-bit result appearing on the output (see Chapter 3). We assume the data memory is edge-triggered for writes. Standard memory chips actually have a write enable signal that is used for writes. Although the write enable is not edge-triggered, our edge-triggered design could easily be adapted to work with real memory chips. See Section B.8 of ⊙ **Appendix B** for further discussion of how real memory chips work.

Thus, the branch datapath must do two operations: compute the branch target address and compare the register contents. (Branches also affect the instruction fetch portion of the datapath, as we will deal with shortly.) Because of the complexity of handling branches, we show the structure of the datapath segment that handles branches in Figure 5.9. To compute the branch target address, the branch datapath includes a sign extension unit, just like that in Figure 5.8, and an adder. To perform the compare, we need to use the register file shown in Figure 5.7 to supply the two register operands (although we will not need to write into the register file). In addition, the comparison can be done using the ALU we designed in ⊙ **Appendix B**. Since that ALU provides an output signal that indicates whether the result was 0, we can send the two register operands to the ALU with the control set to do a subtract. If the Zero signal out of the ALU unit is asserted, we know that the two values are equal. Although the Zero output always signals if the result is 0, we will be using it only to implement the equal test of branches. Later, we will show exactly how to connect the control signals of the ALU for use in the datapath.

The jump instruction operates by replacing the lower 28 bits of the PC with the lower 26 bits of the instruction shifted left by 2 bits. This shift is accomplished simply by concatenating 00 to the jump offset, as described in Chapter 2.

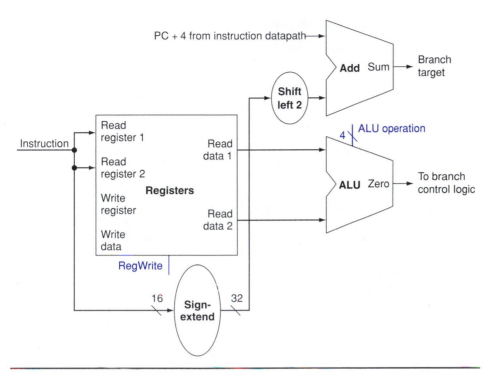

FIGURE 5.9 The datapath for a branch uses the ALU to evaluate the branch condition and a separate adder to compute the branch target as the sum of the incremented PC and the sign-extended, lower 16 bits of the instruction (the branch displacement), shifted left 2 bits. The unit labeled *Shift left 2* is simply a routing of the signals between input and output that adds 00_{two} to the low-order end of the sign-extended offset field; no actual shift hardware is needed, since the amount of the "shift" is constant. Since we know that the offset was sign-extended from 16 bits, the shift will throw away only "sign bits." Control logic is used to decide whether the incremented PC or branch target should replace the PC, based on the Zero output of the ALU.

Elaboration: In the MIPS instruction set, branches are delayed, meaning that the instruction immediately following the branch is always executed, *independent* of whether the branch condition is true or false. When the condition is false, the execution looks like a normal branch. When the condition is true, a delayed branch first executes the instruction immediately following the branch in sequential instruction order before jumping to the specified branch target address. The motivation for delayed branches arises from how pipelining affects branches (see Section 6.6). For simplicity, we ignore delayed branches in this chapter and implement a nondelayed beq instruction.

delayed branch A type of branch where the instruction immediately following the branch is always executed, independent of whether the branch condition is true or false.

Creating a Single Datapath

Now that we have examined the datapath components needed for the individual instruction classes, we can combine them into a single datapath and add the control to complete the implementation. The simplest datapath might attempt to execute all instructions in one clock cycle. This means that no datapath resource can be used more than once per instruction, so any element needed more than once must be duplicated. We therefore need a memory for instructions separate from one for data. Although some of the functional units will need to be duplicated, many of the elements can be shared by different instruction flows.

To share a datapath element between two different instruction classes, we may need to allow multiple connections to the input of an element, using a multiplexor and control signal to select among the multiple inputs.

EXAMPLE

Building a Datapath

The operations of arithmetic-logical (or R-type) instructions and the memory instructions datapath are quite similar. The key differences are the following:

- The arithmetic-logical instructions use the ALU with the inputs coming from the two registers. The memory instructions can also use the ALU to do the address calculation, although the second input is the sign-extended 16-bit offset field from the instruction.

- The value stored into a destination register comes from the ALU (for an R-type instruction) or the memory (for a load).

Show how to build a datapath for the operational portion of the memory reference and arithmetic-logical instructions that uses a single register file and a single ALU to handle both types of instructions, adding any necessary multiplexors.

ANSWER

To create a datapath with only a single register file and a single ALU, we must support two different sources for the second ALU input, as well as two different sources for the data stored into the register file. Thus, one multiplexor is placed at the ALU input and another at the data input to the register file. Figure 5.10 shows the operational portion of the combined datapath.

Now we can combine all the pieces to make a simple datapath for the MIPS architecture by adding the datapath for instruction fetch (Figure 5.6 on page 293),

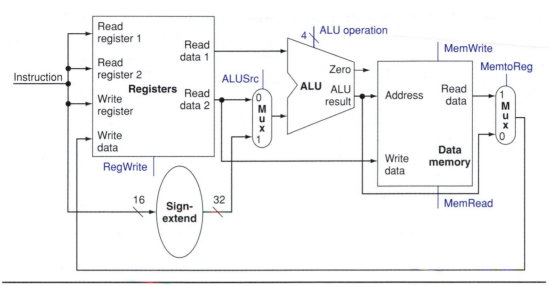

FIGURE 5.10   The datapath for the memory instructions and the R-type instructions. This example shows how a single datapath can be assembled from the pieces in Figures 5.7 and 5.8 by adding multiplexors. Two multiplexors are needed, as described as in the example.

the datapath from R-type and memory instructions (Figure 5.10), and the datapath for branches (Figure 5.9 on page 297). Figure 5.11 shows the datapath we obtain by composing the separate pieces. The branch instruction uses the main ALU for comparison of the register operands, so we must keep the adder in Figure 5.9 for computing the branch target address. An additional multiplexor is required to select either the sequentially following instruction address (PC + 4) or the branch target address to be written into the PC.

Now that we have completed this simple datapath, we can add the control unit. The control unit must be able to take inputs and generate a write signal for each state element, the selector control for each multiplexor, and the ALU control. The ALU control is different in a number of ways, and it will be useful to design it first before we design the rest of the control unit.

Which of the following is correct for a load instruction?

Check Yourself

a. MemtoReg should be set to cause the data from memory to be sent to the register file.

b. MemtoReg should be set to cause the correct register destination to be sent to the register file.

c. We do not care about the setting of MemtoReg.

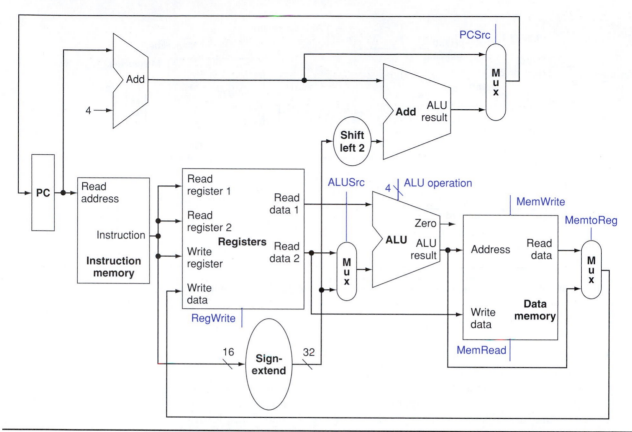

FIGURE 5.11   The simple datapath for the MIPS architecture combines the elements required by different instruction classes. This datapath can execute the basic instructions (load-store word, ALU operations, and branches) in a single clock cycle. An additional multiplexor is needed to integrate branches. The support for jumps will be added later.

5.4 A Simple Implementation Scheme

In this section, we look at what might be thought of as the simplest possible implementation of our MIPS subset. We build this simple implementation using the datapath of the last section and adding a simple control function. This simple implementation covers load word (lw), store word (sw), branch equal (beq), and the arithmetic-logical instructions add, sub, and, or, and set on less than. We will later enhance the design to include a jump instruction (j).

The ALU Control

As can be seen in 🔘 **Appendix B**, the ALU has 4 control inputs. These bits were not encoded; hence, only 6 of the possible 16 possible input combinations are used in this subset. The MIPS ALU in 🔘 **Appendix B** shows the 6 following combinations:

ALU control lines	Function
0000	AND
0001	OR
0010	add
0110	subtract
0111	set on less than
1100	NOR

Depending on the instruction class, the ALU will need to perform one of these first five functions. (NOR is needed for other parts of the MIPS instruction set.) For load word and store word instructions, we use the ALU to compute the memory address by addition. For the R-type instructions, the ALU needs to perform one of the five actions (AND, OR, subtract, add, or set on less than), depending on the value of the 6-bit funct (or function) field in the low-order bits of the instruction (see Chapter 2). For branch equal, the ALU must perform a subtraction.

We can generate the 4-bit ALU control input using a small control unit that has as inputs the function field of the instruction and a 2-bit control field, which we call ALUOp. ALUOp indicates whether the operation to be performed should be add (00) for loads and stores, subtract (01) for beq, or determined by the operation encoded in the funct field (10). The output of the ALU control unit is a 4-bit signal that directly controls the ALU by generating one of the 4-bit combinations shown previously.

In Figure 5.12, we show how to set the ALU control inputs based on the 2-bit ALUOp control and the 6-bit function code. For completeness, the relationship between the ALUOp bits and the instruction opcode is also shown. Later in this chapter we will see how the ALUOp bits are generated from the main control unit.

This style of using multiple levels of decoding—that is, the main control unit generates the ALUOp bits, which then are used as input to the ALU control that generates the actual signals to control the ALU unit—is a common implementation technique. Using multiple levels of control can reduce the size of the main control unit. Using several smaller control units may also potentially increase the speed of the control unit. Such optimizations are important, since the control unit is often performance-critical.

There are several different ways to implement the mapping from the 2-bit ALUOp field and the 6-bit funct field to the three ALU operation control bits.

Instruction opcode	ALUOp	Instruction operation	Funct field	Desired ALU action	ALU control input
LW	00	load word	XXXXXX	add	0010
SW	00	store word	XXXXXX	add	0010
Branch equal	01	branch equal	XXXXXX	subtract	0110
R-type	10	add	100000	add	0010
R-type	10	subtract	100010	subtract	0110
R-type	10	AND	100100	and	0000
R-type	10	OR	100101	or	0001
R-type	10	set on less than	101010	set on less than	0111

FIGURE 5.12   How the ALU control bits are set depends on the ALUOp control bits and the different function codes for the R-type instruction. The opcode, listed in the first column, determines the setting of the ALUOp bits. All the encodings are shown in binary. Notice that when the ALUOp code is 00 or 01, the desired ALU action does not depend on the function code field; in this case, we say that we "don't care" about the value of the function code, and the funct field is shown as XXXXXX. When the ALUOp value is 10, then the function code is used to set the ALU control input.

ALUOp		Funct field						Operation
ALUOp1	ALUOp0	F5	F4	F3	F2	F1	F0	
0	0	X	X	X	X	X	X	0010
X	1	X	X	X	X	X	X	0110
1	X	X	X	0	0	0	0	0010
1	X	X	X	0	0	1	0	0110
1	X	X	X	0	1	0	0	0000
1	X	X	X	0	1	0	1	0001
1	X	X	X	1	0	1	0	0111

FIGURE 5.13   The truth table for the 4 ALU control bits (called Operation). The inputs are the ALUOp and function code field. Only the entries for which the ALU control is asserted are shown. Some don't-care entries have been added. For example, the ALUOp does not use the encoding 11, so the truth table can contain entries 1X and X1, rather than 10 and 01. Also, when the function field is used, the first 2 bits (F5 and F4) of these instructions are always 10, so they are don't-care terms and are replaced with XX in the truth table.

Because only a small number of the 64 possible values of the function field are of interest and the function field is used only when the ALUOp bits equal 10, we can use a small piece of logic that recognizes the subset of possible values and causes the correct setting of the ALU control bits.

As a step in designing this logic, it is useful to create a truth table for the interesting combinations of the function code field and the ALUOp bits, as we've done in Figure 5.13; this truth table shows how the 4-bit ALU control is set depending on these two input fields. Since the full truth table is very large ($2^8 = 256$ entries) and we don't care about the value of the ALU control for many of these input combinations, we show only the truth table entries for which the ALU control must have a specific value. Throughout this chapter, we will use this practice of showing only the truth table entries that must be asserted and not showing those that are all zero or don't care. (This practice has a disadvantage, which we discuss in Section C.2 of ⊙ **Appendix C.**)

Because in many instances we do not care about the values of some of the inputs and to keep the tables compact, we also include **don't-care terms**. A don't-care term in this truth table (represented by an X in an input column) indicates that the output does not depend on the value of the input corresponding to that column. For example, when the ALUOp bits are 00, as in the first line of the table in Figure 5.13, we always set the ALU control to 010, independent of the function code. In this case, then, the function code inputs will be don't cares in this line of the truth table. Later, we will see examples of another type of don't-care term. If you are unfamiliar with the concept of don't-care terms, see ⊙ **Appendix B** for more information.

Once the truth table has been constructed, it can be optimized and then turned into gates. This process is completely mechanical. Thus, rather than show the final steps here, we describe the process and the result in Section C.2 of ⊙ **Appendix C.**

don't-care term An element of a logical function in which the output does not depend on the values of all the inputs. Don't-care terms may be specified in different ways.

Designing the Main Control Unit

Now that we have described how to design an ALU that uses the function code and a 2-bit signal as its control inputs, we can return to looking at the rest of the control. To start this process, let's identify the fields of an instruction and the control lines that are needed for the datapath we constructed in Figure 5.11 on page 300. To understand how to connect the fields of an instruction to the datapath, it is useful to review the formats of the three instruction classes: the R-type, branch, and load-store instructions. Figure 5.14 shows these formats.

There are several major observations about this instruction format that we will rely on:

- The op field, also called the **opcode**, is always contained in bits 31:26. We will refer to this field as Op[5:0].

- The two registers to be read are always specified by the rs and rt fields, at positions 25:21 and 20:16. This is true for the R-type instructions, branch equal, and store.

- The base register for load and store instructions is always in bit positions 25:21 (rs).

opcode The field that denotes the operation and format of an instruction.

Field	0	rs	rt	rd	shamt	funct
Bit positions	31:26	25:21	20:16	15:11	10:6	5:0

a. R-type instruction

Field	35 or 43	rs	rt	address
Bit positions	31:26	25:21	20:16	15:0

b. Load or store instruction

Field	4	rs	rt	address
Bit positions	31:26	25:21	20:16	15:0

c. Branch instruction

FIGURE 5.14   The three instruction classes (R-type, load and store, and branch) use two different instruction formats. The jump instructions use another format, which we will discuss shortly. (a) Instruction format for R-format instructions, which all have an opcode of 0. These instructions have three register operands: rs, rt, and rd. Fields rs and rt are sources, and rd is the destination. The ALU function is in the funct field and is decoded by the ALU control design in the previous section. The R-type instructions that we implement are add, sub, and, or, and slt. The shamt field is used only for shifts; we will ignore it in this chapter. (b) Instruction format for load (opcode = 35_{ten}) and store (opcode = 43_{ten}) instructions. The register rs is the base register that is added to the 16-bit address field to form the memory address. For loads, rt is the destination register for the loaded value. For stores, rt is the source register whose value should be stored into memory. (c) Instruction format for branch equal (opcode = 4). The registers rs and rt are the source registers that are compared for equality. The 16-bit address field is sign-extended, shifted, and added to the PC to compute the branch target address.

- The 16-bit offset for branch equal, load, and store is always in positions 15:0.

- The destination register is in one of two places. For a load it is in bit positions 20:16 (rt), while for an R-type instruction it is in bit positions 15:11 (rd). Thus we will need to add a multiplexor to select which field of the instruction is used to indicate the register number to be written.

Using this information, we can add the instruction labels and extra multiplexor (for the Write register number input of the register file) to the simple datapath. Figure 5.15 shows these additions plus the ALU control block, the write signals for state elements, the read signal for the data memory, and the control signals for the multiplexors. Since all the multiplexors have two inputs, they each require a single control line.

Figure 5.15 shows seven single-bit control lines plus the 2-bit ALUOp control signal. We have already defined how the ALUOp control signal works, and it is useful to define what the seven other control signals do informally before we determine how to set these control signals during instruction execution. Figure 5.16 describes the function of these seven control lines.

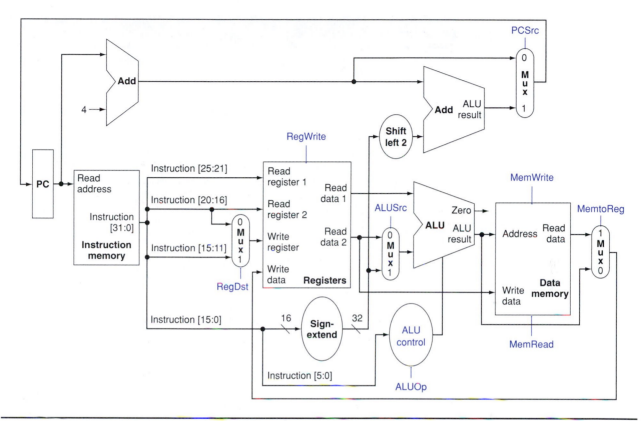

FIGURE 5.15 The datapath of Figure 5.12 with all necessary multiplexors and all control lines identified. The control lines are shown in color. The ALU control block has also been added. The PC does not require a write control, since it is written once at the end of every clock cycle; the branch control logic determines whether it is written with the incremented PC or the branch target address.

Now that we have looked at the function of each of the control signals, we can look at how to set them. The control unit can set all but one of the control signals based solely on the opcode field of the instruction. The PCSrc control line is the exception. That control line should be set if the instruction is branch on equal (a decision that the control unit can make) *and* the Zero output of the ALU, which is used for equality comparison, is true. To generate the PCSrc signal, we will need to AND together a signal from the control unit, which we call *Branch*, with the Zero signal out of the ALU.

These nine control signals (seven from Figure 5.16 and two for ALUOp) can now be set on the basis of six input signals to the control unit, which are the opcode bits. Figure 5.17 shows the datapath with the control unit and the control signals.

Signal name	Effect when deasserted	Effect when asserted
RegDst	The register destination number for the Write register comes from the rt field (bits 20:16).	The register destination number for the Write register comes from the rd field (bits 15:11).
RegWrite	None.	The register on the Write register input is written with the value on the Write data input.
ALUSrc	The second ALU operand comes from the second register file output (Read data 2).	The second ALU operand is the sign-extended, lower 16 bits of the instruction.
PCSrc	The PC is replaced by the output of the adder that computes the value of PC + 4.	The PC is replaced by the output of the adder that computes the branch target.
MemRead	None.	Data memory contents designated by the address input are put on the Read data output.
MemWrite	None.	Data memory contents designated by the address input are replaced by the value on the Write data input.
MemtoReg	The value fed to the register Write data input comes from the ALU.	The value fed to the register Write data input comes from the data memory.

FIGURE 5.16   The effect of each of the seven control signals. When the 1-bit control to a two-way multiplexor is asserted, the multiplexor selects the input corresponding to 1. Otherwise, if the control is deasserted, the multiplexor selects the 0 input. Remember that the state elements all have the clock as an implicit input and that the clock is used in controlling writes. The clock is never gated externally to a state element, since this can create timing problems. (See ⊙ **Appendix B** for further discussion of this problem.)

Before we try to write a set of equations or a truth table for the control unit, it will be useful to try to define the control function informally. Because the setting of the control lines depends only on the opcode, we define whether each control signal should be 0, 1, or don't care (X), for each of the opcode values. Figure 5.18 defines how the control signals should be set for each opcode; this information follows directly from Figures 5.12, 5.16, and 5.17.

Operation of the Datapath

With the information contained in Figures 5.16 and 5.18, we can design the control unit logic, but before we do that, let's look at how each instruction uses the datapath. In the next few figures, we show the flow of three different instruction classes through the datapath. The asserted control signals and active datapath elements are highlighted in each of these. Note that a multiplexor whose control is 0 has a definite action, even if its control line is not highlighted. Multiple-bit control signals are highlighted if any constituent signal is asserted.

Figure 5.19 shows the operation of the datapath for an R-type instruction, such as add $t1,$t2,$t3. Although everything occurs in one clock cycle, we can think of four steps to execute the instruction; these steps are ordered by the flow of information:

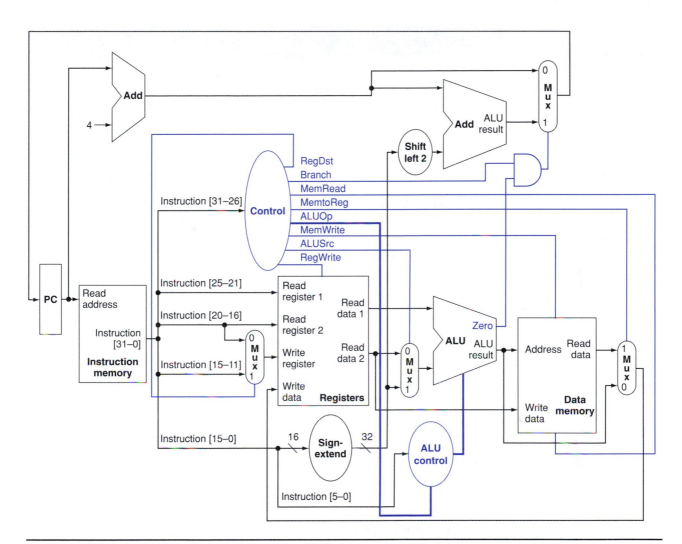

FIGURE 5.17 The simple datapath with the control unit. The input to the control unit is the 6-bit opcode field from the instruction. The outputs of the control unit consist of three 1-bit signals that are used to control multiplexors (RegDst, ALUSrc, and MemtoReg), three signals for controlling reads and writes in the register file and data memory (RegWrite, MemRead, and MemWrite), a 1-bit signal used in determining whether to possibly branch (Branch), and a 2-bit control signal for the ALU (ALUOp). An AND gate is used to combine the branch control signal and the Zero output from the ALU; the AND gate output controls the selection of the next PC. Notice that PCSrc is now a derived signal, rather than one coming directly from the control unit. Thus we drop the signal name in subsequent figures.

Instruction	RegDst	ALUSrc	Memto-Reg	Reg Write	Mem Read	Mem Write	Branch	ALUOp1	ALUOp0
R-format	1	0	0	1	0	0	0	1	0
lw	0	1	1	1	1	0	0	0	0
sw	X	1	X	0	0	1	0	0	0
beq	X	0	X	0	0	0	1	0	1

FIGURE 5.18   The setting of the control lines is completely determined by the opcode fields of the instruction. The first row of the table corresponds to the R-format instructions (add, sub, and, or, and slt). For all these instructions, the source register fields are rs and rt, and the destination register field is rd; this defines how the signals ALUSrc and RegDst are set. Furthermore, an R-type instruction writes a register (Reg-Write = 1), but neither reads nor writes data memory. When the Branch control signal is 0, the PC is unconditionally replaced with PC + 4; otherwise, the PC is replaced by the branch target if the Zero output of the ALU is also high. The ALUOp field for R-type instructions is set to 10 to indicate that the ALU control should be generated from the funct field. The second and third rows of this table give the control signal settings for lw and sw. These ALUSrc and ALUOp fields are set to perform the address calculation. The MemRead and MemWrite are set to perform the memory access. Finally, RegDst and RegWrite are set for a load to cause the result to be stored into the rt register. The branch instruction is similar to an R-format operation, since it sends the rs and rt registers to the ALU. The ALUOp field for branch is set for a subtract (ALU control = 01), which is used to test for equality. Notice that the MemtoReg field is irrelevant when the RegWrite signal is 0: since the register is not being written, the value of the data on the register data write port is not used. Thus, the entry MemtoReg in the last two rows of the table is replaced with X for don't care. Don't cares can also be added to RegDst when RegWrite is 0. This type of don't care must be added by the designer, since it depends on knowledge of how the datapath works.

1. The instruction is fetched, and the PC is incremented.

2. Two registers, $t2 and $t3, are read from the register file, and the main control unit computes the setting of the control lines during this step also.

3. The ALU operates on the data read from the register file, using the function code (bits 5:0, which is the funct field, of the instruction) to generate the ALU function.

4. The result from the ALU is written into the register file using bits 15:11 of the instruction to select the destination register ($t1).

Similarly, we can illustrate the execution of a load word, such as

```
lw $t1, offset($t2)
```

in a style similar to Figure 5.19. Figure 5.20 shows the active functional units and asserted control lines for a load. We can think of a load instruction as operating in five steps (similar to the R-type executed in four):

1. An instruction is fetched from the instruction memory, and the PC is incremented.

2. A register ($t2) value is read from the register file.

3. The ALU computes the sum of the value read from the register file and the sign-extended, lower 16 bits of the instruction (offset).

4. The sum from the ALU is used as the address for the data memory.

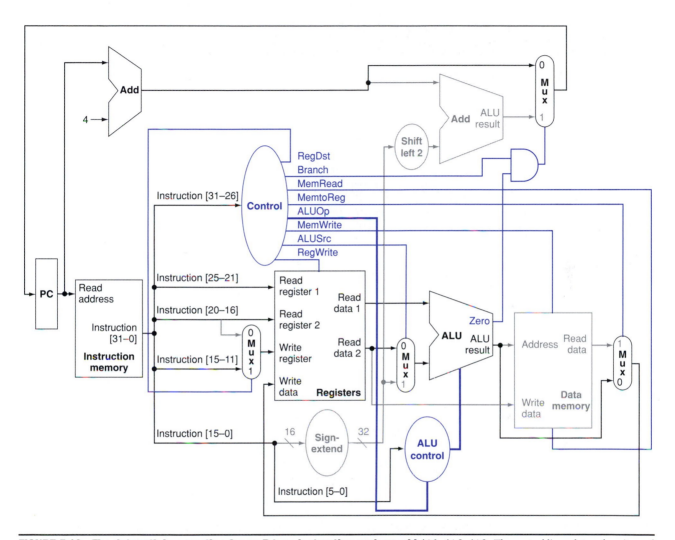

FIGURE 5.19   The datapath in operation for an R-type instruction such as add $t1,$t2,$t3. The control lines, datapath units, and connections that are active are highlighted.

5. The data from the memory unit is written into the register file; the register destination is given by bits 20:16 of the instruction ($t1).

Finally, we can show the operation of the branch-on-equal instruction, such as beq $t1,$t2,offset, in the same fashion. It operates much like an R-format

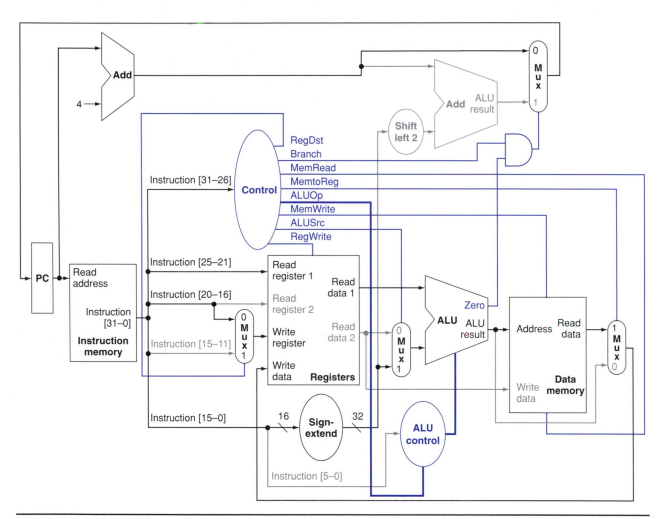

FIGURE 5.20 The datapath in operation for a load instruction. The control lines, datapath units, and connections that are active are highlighted. A store instruction would operate very similarly. The main difference would be that the memory control would indicate a write rather than a read, the second register value read would be used for the data to store, and the operation of writing the data memory value to the register file would not occur.

instruction, but the ALU output is used to determine whether the PC is written with PC + 4 or the branch target address. Figure 5.21 shows the four steps in execution:

1. An instruction is fetched from the instruction memory, and the PC is incremented.

2. Two registers, $t1 and $t2, are read from the register file.

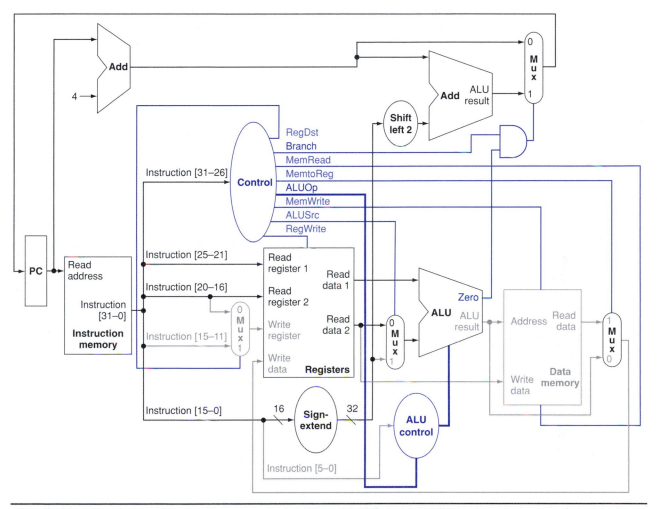

FIGURE 5.21 The datapath in operation for a branch-on-equal instruction. The control lines, datapath units, and connections that are active are highlighted. After using the register file and ALU to perform the compare, the Zero output is used to select the next program counter from between the two candidates.

3. The ALU performs a subtract on the data values read from the register file. The value of PC + 4 is added to the sign-extended, lower 16 bits of the instruction (`offset`) shifted left by two; the result is the branch target address.

4. The Zero result from the ALU is used to decide which adder result to store into the PC.

In the next section, we will examine machines that are truly sequential, namely, those in which each of these steps is a distinct clock cycle.

Finalizing the Control

Now that we have seen how the instructions operate in steps, let's continue with the control implementation. The control function can be precisely defined using the contents of Figure 5.18 on page 308. The outputs are the control lines, and the input is the 6-bit opcode field, Op [5:0]. Thus, we can create a truth table for each of the outputs based on the binary encoding of the opcodes.

Figure 5.22 shows the logic in the control unit as one large truth table that combines all the outputs and that uses the opcode bits as inputs. It completely specifies the control function, and we can implement it directly in gates in an automated fashion. We show this final step in Section C.2 in ◉ **Appendix C**.

Input or output	Signal name	R-format	lw	sw	beq
Inputs	Op5	0	1	1	0
	Op4	0	0	0	0
	Op3	0	0	1	0
	Op2	0	0	0	1
	Op1	0	1	1	0
	Op0	0	1	1	0
Outputs	RegDst	1	0	X	X
	ALUSrc	0	1	1	0
	MemtoReg	0	1	X	X
	RegWrite	1	1	0	0
	MemRead	0	1	0	0
	MemWrite	0	0	1	0
	Branch	0	0	0	1
	ALUOp1	1	0	0	0
	ALUOp0	0	0	0	1

single-cycle implementation Also called single clock cycle implementation. An implementation in which an instruction is executed in one clock cycle.

FIGURE 5.22   The control function for the simple single-cycle implementation is completely specified by this truth table. The top half of the table gives the combinations of input signals that correspond to the four opcodes that determine the control output settings. (Remember that Op [5:0] corresponds to bits 31:26 of the instruction, which is the op field.) The bottom portion of the table gives the outputs. Thus, the output RegWrite is asserted for two different combinations of the inputs. If we consider only the four opcodes shown in this table, then we can simplify the truth table by using don't cares in the input portion. For example, we can detect an R-format instruction with the expression $\overline{Op5} \cdot \overline{Op2}$, since this is sufficient to distinguish the R-format instructions from lw, sw, and beq. We do not take advantage of this simplification, since the rest of the MIPS opcodes are used in a full implementation.

Now, let's add the jump instruction to show how the basic datapath and control can be extended to handle other instructions in the instruction set.

Implementing Jumps

Figure 5.17 on page 307 shows the implementation of many of the instructions we looked at in Chapter 2. One class of instructions missing is that of the jump instruction. Extend the datapath and control of Figure 5.17 to include the jump instruction. Describe how to set any new control lines.

EXAMPLE

The jump instruction looks somewhat like a branch instruction but computes the target PC differently and is not conditional. Like a branch, the low-order 2 bits of a jump address are always 00_{two}. The next lower 26 bits of this 32-bit address come from the 26-bit immediate field in the instruction, as shown in Figure 5.23. The upper 4 bits of the address that should replace the PC come from the PC of the jump instruction plus 4. Thus, we can implement a jump by storing into the PC the concatenation of

ANSWER

- the upper 4 bits of the current PC + 4 (these are bits 31:28 of the sequentially following instruction address)
- the 26-bit immediate field of the jump instruction
- the bits 00_{two}

Figure 5.24 shows the addition of the control for jump added to Figure 5.17. An additional multiplexor is used to select the source for the new PC value, which is either the incremented PC (PC + 4), the branch target PC, or the jump target PC. One additional control signal is needed for the additional multiplexor. This control signal, called *Jump*, is asserted only when the instruction is a jump—that is, when the opcode is 2.

Field	000010	address
Bit positions	31:26	25:0

FIGURE 5.23 Instruction format for the jump instruction (opcode = 2). The destination address for a jump instruction is formed by concatenating the upper 4 bits of the current PC + 4 to the 26-bit address field in the jump instruction and adding 00 as the 2 low-order bits.

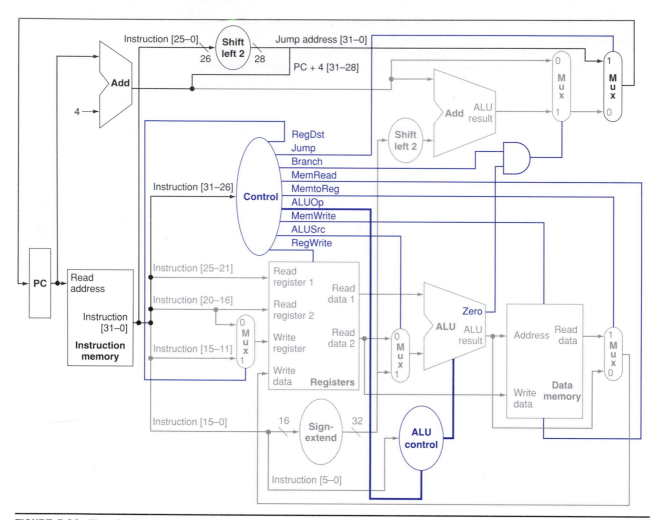

FIGURE 5.24 The simple control and datapath are extended to handle the jump instruction. An additional multiplexor (at the upper right) is used to choose between the jump target and either the branch target or the sequential instruction following this one. This multiplexor is controlled by the jump control signal. The jump target address is obtained by shifting the lower 26 bits of the jump instruction left 2 bits, effectively adding 00 as the low-order bits, and then concatenating the upper 4 bits of PC + 4 as the high-order bits, thus yielding a 32-bit address.

Why a Single-Cycle Implementation Is Not Used Today

Although the single-cycle design will work correctly, it would not be used in modern designs because it is inefficient. To see why this is so, notice that the clock cycle must have the same length for every instruction in this single-cycle design, and the CPI (see Chapter 4) will therefore be 1. Of course, the clock cycle is determined by the longest possible path in the machine. This path is almost certainly a load instruction, which uses five functional units in series: the instruction memory, the register file, the ALU, the data memory, and the register file. Although the CPI is 1, the overall performance of a single-cycle implementation is not likely to be very good, since several of the instruction classes could fit in a shorter clock cycle.

Performance of Single-Cycle Machines

Assume that the operation times for the major functional units in this implementation are the following:

- Memory units: 200 picoseconds (ps)
- ALU and adders: 100 ps
- Register file (read or write): 50 ps

EXAMPLE

Assuming that the multiplexors, control unit, PC accesses, sign extension unit, and wires have no delay, which of the following implementations would be faster and by how much?

1. An implementation in which every instruction operates in 1 clock cycle of a fixed length.

2. An implementation where every instruction executes in 1 clock cycle using a variable-length clock, which for each instruction is only as long as it needs to be. (Such an approach is not terribly practical, but it will allow us to see what is being sacrificed when all the instructions must execute in a single clock of the same length.)

To compare the performance, assume the following instruction mix: 25% loads, 10% stores, 45% ALU instructions, 15% branches, and 5% jumps.

Let's start by comparing the CPU execution times. Recall from Chapter 4 that

ANSWER

CPU execution time = Instruction count × CPI × Clock cycle time

Since CPI must be 1, we can simplify this to

CPU execution time = Instruction count × Clock cycle time

We need only find the clock cycle time for the two implementations, since the instruction count and CPI are the same for both implementations. The critical path for the different instruction classes is as follows:

Instruction class	Functional units used by the instruction class				
R-type	Instruction fetch	Register access	ALU	Register access	
Load word	Instruction fetch	Register access	ALU	Memory access	Register access
Store word	Instruction fetch	Register access	ALU	Memory access	
Branch	Instruction fetch	Register access	ALU		
Jump	Instruction fetch				

Using these critical paths, we can compute the required length for each instruction class:

Instruction class	Instruction memory	Register read	ALU operation	Data memory	Register write	Total
R-type	200	50	100	0	50	400 ps
Load word	200	50	100	200	50	600 ps
Store word	200	50	100	200		550 ps
Branch	200	50	100	0		350 ps
Jump	200					200 ps

The clock cycle for a machine with a single clock for all instructions will be determined by the longest instruction, which is 600 ps. (This timing is approximate, since our timing model is quite simplistic. In reality, the timing of modern digital systems is complex.)

A machine with a variable clock will have a clock cycle that varies between 200 ps and 600 ps. We can find the average clock cycle length for a machine with a variable-length clock using the information above and the instruction frequency distribution.

Thus, the average time per instruction with a variable clock is

$$\text{CPU clock cycle} = 600 \times 25\% + 550 \times 10\% + 400 \times 45\% + 350 \times 15\% + 200 \times 5\%$$

$$= 447.5 \text{ ps}$$

Since the variable clock implementation has a shorter average clock cycle, it is clearly faster. Let's find the performance ratio:

$$\frac{\text{CPU performance}_{\text{variable clock}}}{\text{CPU performance}_{\text{single clock}}} = \frac{\text{CPU execution time}_{\text{single clock}}}{\text{CPU execution time}_{\text{variable clock}}}$$

$$= \left(\frac{\text{IC} \times \text{CPU clock cycle}_{\text{single clock}}}{\text{IC} \times \text{CPU clock cycle}_{\text{variable clock}}} = \frac{\text{CPU clock cycle}_{\text{single clock}}}{\text{CPU clock cycle}_{\text{variable clock}}} \right)$$

$$= \frac{600}{447.5} = 1.34$$

The variable clock implementation would be 1.34 times faster. Unfortunately, implementing a variable-speed clock for each instruction class is extremely difficult, and the overhead for such an approach could be larger than any advantage gained. As we will see in the next section, an alternative is to use a shorter clock cycle that does less work and then vary the number of clock cycles for the different instruction classes.

The penalty for using the single-cycle design with a fixed clock cycle is significant, but might be considered acceptable for this small instruction set. Historically, early machines with very simple instruction sets did use this implementation technique. However, if we tried to implement the floating-point unit or an instruction set with more complex instructions, this single-cycle design wouldn't work well at all. An example of this is shown in the ⊙ **For More Practice** Exercise 5.4.

Because we must assume that the clock cycle is equal to the worst-case delay for all instructions, we can't use implementation techniques that reduce the delay of the common case but do not improve the worst-case cycle time. A single-cycle implementation thus violates our key design principle of making the common case fast. In addition, in this single-cycle implementation, each functional unit can be used only once per clock; therefore, some functional units must be duplicated, raising the cost of the implementation. A single-cycle design is inefficient both in its performance and in its hardware cost!

We can avoid these difficulties by using implementation techniques that have a shorter clock cycle—derived from the basic functional unit delays—and that require multiple clock cycles for each instruction. The next section explores this alternative implementation scheme. In Chapter 6, we'll look at another implementation technique, called pipelining, that uses a datapath very similar to the single-cycle datapath, but is much more efficient. Pipelining gains efficiency by overlapping the execution of multiple instructions, increasing hardware utilization and improving performance. For those readers interested primarily in the high-level concepts used in processors, the material of this section is sufficient to read the introductory sections of Chapter 6 and understand the basic functionality of a pipelined processor. For those, who want to understand how the hardware really implements the control, forge ahead!

Check Yourself

Look at the control signal in Figure 5.22 on page 312. Can any control signal in the figure be replaced by the inverse of another? (Hint: Take into account the don't cares.) If so, can you use one signal for the other without adding an inverter?

5.5   A Multicycle Implementation

In an earlier example, we broke each instruction into a series of steps corresponding to the functional unit operations that were needed. We can use these steps to create a **multicycle implementation**. In a multicycle implementation, each *step* in the execution will take 1 clock cycle. The multicycle implementation allows a functional unit to be used more than once per instruction, as long as it is used on different clock cycles. This sharing can help reduce the amount of hardware required. The ability to allow instructions to take different numbers of clock cycles and the ability to share functional units within the execution of a single instruction are the major advantages of a multicycle design. Figure 5.25 shows the abstract version of the mul-

multicycle implementation Also called multiple clock cycle implementation. An implementation in which an instruction is executed in multiple clock cycles.

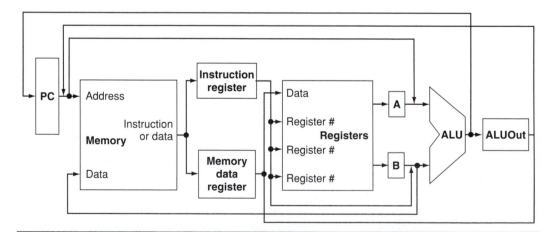

FIGURE 5.25   The high-level view of the multicycle datapath. This picture shows the key elements of the datapath: a shared memory unit, a single ALU shared among instructions, and the connections among these shared units. The use of shared functional units requires the addition or widening of multiplexors as well as new temporary registers that hold data between clock cycles of the same instruction. The additional registers are the Instruction register (IR), the Memory data register (MDR), A, B, and ALUOut.

ticycle datapath. If we compare Figure 5.25 to the datapath for the single-cycle version in Figure 5.11 on page 300, we can see the following differences:

- A single memory unit is used for both instructions and data.

- There is a single ALU, rather than an ALU and two adders.

- One or more registers are added after every major functional unit to hold the output of that unit until the value is used in a subsequent clock cycle.

At the end of a clock cycle, all data that is used in subsequent clock cycles must be stored in a state element. Data used by *subsequent instructions* in a later clock cycle is stored into one of the programmer-visible state elements: the register file, the PC, or the memory. In contrast, data used by the *same instruction* in a later cycle must be stored into one of these additional registers.

Thus, the position of the additional registers is determined by these two factors: what combinational units will fit in one clock cycle and what data is needed in later cycles implementing the instruction. In this multicycle design, we assume that the clock cycle can accommodate at most one of the following operations: a memory access, a register file access (two reads or one write), or an ALU operation. Hence, any data produced by one of these three functional units (the memory, the register file, or the ALU) must be saved into a temporary register for use on a later cycle. If it were not saved, then the possibility of a timing race could occur, leading to the use of an incorrect value.

The following temporary registers are added to meet these requirements:

- The Instruction register (IR) and the Memory data register (MDR) are added to save the output of the memory for an instruction read and a data read, respectively. Two separate registers are used, since, as will be clear shortly, both values are needed during the same clock cycle.

- The A and B registers are used to hold the register operand values read from the register file.

- The ALUOut register holds the output of the ALU.

All the registers except the IR hold data only between a pair of adjacent clock cycles and will thus not need a write control signal. The IR needs to hold the instruction until the end of execution of that instruction, and thus will require a write control signal. This distinction will become more clear when we show the individual clock cycles for each instruction.

Because several functional units are shared for different purposes, we need both to add multiplexors and to expand existing multiplexors. For example, since one memory is used for both instructions and data, we need a multiplexor to select between the two sources for a memory address, namely, the PC (for instruction access) and ALUOut (for data access).

Replacing the three ALUs of the single-cycle datapath by a single ALU means that the single ALU must accommodate all the inputs that used to go to the three different ALUs. Handling the additional inputs requires two changes to the datapath:

1. An additional multiplexor is added for the first ALU input. The multiplexor chooses between the A register and the PC.

2. The multiplexor on the second ALU input is changed from a two-way to a four-way multiplexor. The two additional inputs to the multiplexor are the constant 4 (used to increment the PC) and the sign-extended and shifted offset field (used in the branch address computation).

Figure 5.26 shows the details of the datapath with these additional multiplexors. By introducing a few registers and multiplexors, we are able to reduce the number of memory units from two to one and eliminate two adders. Since registers and multiplexors are fairly small compared to a memory unit or ALU, this could yield a substantial reduction in the hardware cost.

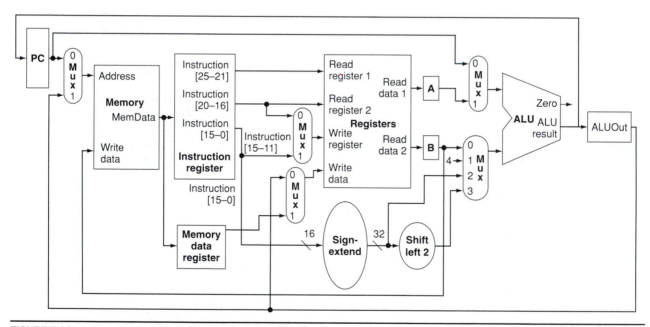

FIGURE 5.26   Multicycle datapath for MIPS handles the basic instructions. Although this datapath supports normal incrementing of the PC, a few more connections and a multiplexor will be needed for branches and jumps; we will add these shortly. The additions versus the single-clock datapath include several registers (IR, MDR, A, B, ALUOut), a multiplexor for the memory address, a multiplexor for the top ALU input, and expanding the multiplexor on the bottom ALU input into a four-way selector. These small additions allow us to remove two adders and a memory unit.

Because the datapath shown in Figure 5.26 takes multiple clock cycles per instruction, it will require a different set of control signals. The programmer-visible state units (the PC, the memory, and the registers) as well as the IR will need write control signals. The memory will also need a read signal. We can use the ALU control unit from the single-cycle datapath (see Figure 5.13 and ⊙ **Appendix C**) to control the ALU here as well. Finally, each of the two-input multiplexors requires a single control line, while the four-input multiplexor requires two control lines. Figure 5.27 shows the datapath of Figure 5.26 with these control lines added.

The multicycle datapath still requires additions to support branches and jumps; after these additions, we will see how the instructions are sequenced and then generate the datapath control.

With the jump instruction and branch instruction, there are three possible sources for the value to be written into the PC:

1. The output of the ALU, which is the value PC + 4 during instruction fetch. This value should be stored directly into the PC.

2. The register ALUOut, which is where we will store the address of the branch target after it is computed.

3. The lower 26 bits of the Instruction register (IR) shifted left by two and concatenated with the upper 4 bits of the incremented PC, which is the source when the instruction is a jump.

As we observed when we implemented the single-cycle control, the PC is written both unconditionally and conditionally. During a normal increment and for jumps, the PC is written unconditionally. If the instruction is a conditional branch, the incremented PC is replaced with the value in ALUOut only if the two designated registers are equal. Hence, our implementation uses two separate control signals: PCWrite, which causes an unconditional write of the PC, and PCWriteCond, which causes a write of the PC if the branch condition is also true.

We need to connect these two control signals to the PC write control. Just as we did in the single-cycle datapath, we will use a few gates to derive the PC write control signal from PCWrite, PCWriteCond, and the Zero signal of the ALU, which is used to detect if the two register operands of a beq are equal. To determine whether the PC should be written during a conditional branch, we AND together the Zero signal of the ALU with the PCWriteCond. The output of this AND gate is then ORed with PCWrite, which is the unconditional PC write signal. The output of this OR gate is connected to the write control signal for the PC.

Figure 5.28 shows the complete multicycle datapath and control unit, including the additional control signals and multiplexor for implementing the PC updating.

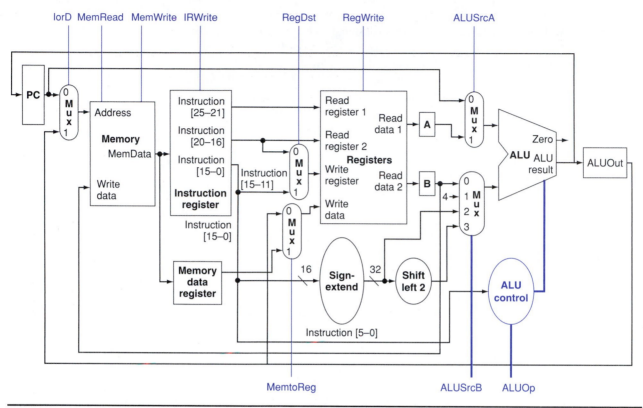

FIGURE 5.27   The multicycle datapath from Figure 5.26 with the control lines shown. The signals ALUOp and ALUSrcB are 2-bit control signals, while all the other control lines are 1-bit signals. Neither register A nor B requires a write signal, since their contents are only read on the cycle immediately after it is written. The memory data register has been added to hold the data from a load when the data returns from memory. Data from a load returning from memory cannot be written directly into the register file since the clock cycle cannot accommodate the time required for both the memory access and the register file write. The MemRead signal has been moved to the top of the memory unit to simplify the figures. The full set of datapaths and control lines for branches will be added shortly.

Before examining the steps to execute each instruction, let us informally examine the effect of all the control signals (just as we did for the single-cycle design in Figure 5.16 on page 306). Figure 5.29 shows what each control signal does when asserted and deasserted.

Elaboration: To reduce the number of signal lines interconnecting the functional units, designers can use *shared buses*. A shared bus is a set of lines that connect multiple units; in most cases, they include multiple sources that can place data on the bus

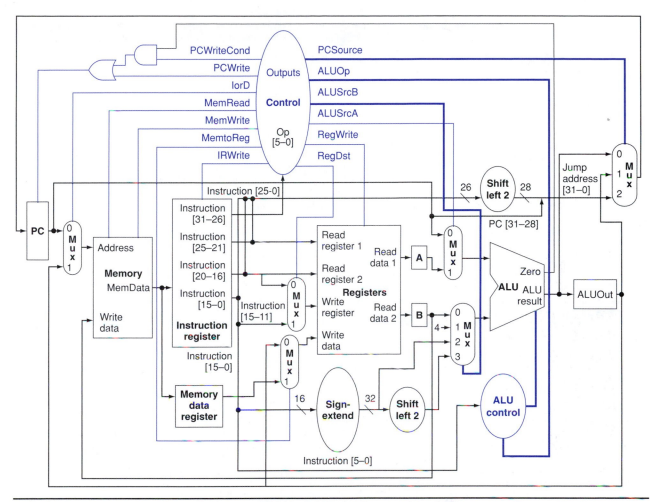

FIGURE 5.28 The complete datapath for the multicycle implementation together with the necessary control lines. The control lines of Figure 5.27 are attached to the control unit, and the control and datapath elements needed to effect changes to the PC are included. The major additions from Figure 5.27 include the multiplexor used to select the source of a new PC value; gates used to combine the PC write signals; and the control signals PCSource, PCWrite, and PCWriteCond. The PCWriteCond signal is used to decide whether a conditional branch should be taken. Support for jumps is included.

and multiple readers of the value. Just as we reduced the number of functional units for the datapath, we can reduce the number of buses interconnecting these units by sharing the buses. For example, there are six sources coming to the ALU; however, only two of them are needed at any one time. Thus, a pair of buses can be used to hold values that are being sent to the ALU. Rather than placing a large multiplexor in front of the

Actions of the 1-bit control signals

Signal name	Effect when deasserted	Effect when asserted
RegDst	The register file destination number for the Write register comes from the rt field.	The register file destination number for the Write register comes from the rd field.
RegWrite	None.	The general-purpose register selected by the Write register number is written with the value of the Write data input.
ALUSrcA	The first ALU operand is the PC.	The first ALU operand comes from the A register.
MemRead	None.	Content of memory at the location specified by the Address input is put on Memory data output.
MemWrite	None.	Memory contents at the location specified by the Address input is replaced by the value on the Write data input.
MemtoReg	The value fed to the register file Write data input comes from ALUOut.	The value fed to the register file Write data input comes from the MDR.
IorD	The PC is used to supply the address to the memory unit.	ALUOut is used to supply the address to the memory unit.
IRWrite	None.	The output of the memory is written into the IR.
PCWrite	None.	The PC is written; the source is controlled by PCSource.
PCWriteCond	None.	The PC is written if the Zero output from the ALU is also active.

Actions of the 2-bit control signals

Signal name	Value (binary)	Effect
ALUOp	00	The ALU performs an add operation.
	01	The ALU performs a subtract operation.
	10	The funct field of the instruction determines the ALU operation.
ALUSrcB	00	The second input to the ALU comes from the B register.
	01	The second input to the ALU is the constant 4.
	10	The second input to the ALU is the sign-extended, lower 16 bits of the IR.
	11	The second input to the ALU is the sign-extended, lower 16 bits of the IR shifted left 2 bits.
PCSource	00	Output of the ALU (PC + 4) is sent to the PC for writing.
	01	The contents of ALUOut (the branch target address) are sent to the PC for writing.
	10	The jump target address (IR[25:0] shifted left 2 bits and concatenated with PC + 4[31:28]) is sent to the PC for writing.

FIGURE 5.29   The action caused by the setting of each control signal in Figure 5.28 on page 323. The top table describes the 1-bit control signals, while the bottom table describes the 2-bit signals. Only those control lines that affect multiplexors have an action when they are deasserted. This information is similar to that in Figure 5.16 on page 306 for the single-cycle datapath, but adds several new control lines (IRWrite, PCWrite, PCWriteCond, ALUSrcB, and PCSource) and removes control lines that are no longer used or have been replaced (PCSrc, Branch, and Jump).

ALU, a designer can use a shared bus and then ensure that only one of the sources is driving the bus at any point. Although this saves signal lines, the same number of control lines will be needed to control what goes on the bus. The major drawback to using such bus structures is a potential performance penalty, since a bus is unlikely to be as fast as a point-to-point connection.

Breaking the Instruction Execution into Clock Cycles

Given the datapath in Figure 5.28, we now need to look at what should happen in each clock cycle of the multicycle execution, since this will determine what additional control signals may be needed, as well as the setting of the control signals. Our goal in breaking the execution into clock cycles should be to maximize performance. We can begin by breaking the execution of any instruction into a series of steps, each taking one clock cycle, attempting to keep the amount of work per cycle roughly equal. For example, we will restrict each step to contain at most one ALU operation, or one register file access, or one memory access. With this restriction, the clock cycle could be as short as the longest of these operations.

Recall that at the end of every clock cycle any data values that will be needed on a subsequent cycle must be stored into a register, which can be either one of the major state elements (e.g., the PC, the register file, or the memory), a temporary register written on every clock cycle (e.g., A, B, MDR, or ALUOut), or a temporary register with write control (e.g., IR). Also remember that because our design is edge-triggered, we can continue to read the current value of a register; the new value does not appear until the next clock cycle.

In the single-cycle datapath, each instruction uses a set of datapath elements to carry out its execution. Many of the datapath elements operate in series, using the output of another element as an input. Some datapath elements operate in parallel; for example, the PC is incremented and the instruction is read at the same time. A similar situation exists in the multicycle datapath. All the operations listed in one step occur in parallel within 1 clock cycle, while successive steps operate in series in different clock cycles. The limitation of one ALU operation, one memory access, and one register file access determines what can fit in one step.

Notice that we distinguish between reading from or writing into the PC or one of the stand-alone registers and reading from or writing into the register file. In the former case, the read or write is part of a clock cycle, while reading or writing a result into the register file takes an additional clock cycle. The reason for this distinction is that the register file has additional control and access overhead compared to the single stand-alone registers. Thus, keeping the clock cycle short motivates dedicating separate clock cycles for register file accesses.

The potential execution steps and their actions are given below. Each MIPS instruction needs from three to five of these steps:

1. Instruction fetch step

Fetch the instruction from memory and compute the address of the next sequential instruction:

```
IR <= Memory[PC];
PC <= PC + 4;
```

Operation: Send the PC to the memory as the address, perform a read, and write the instruction into the Instruction register (IR), where it will be stored. Also, increment the PC by 4. We use the symbol "<=" from Verilog; it indicates that all right-hand sides are evaluated and then all assignments are made, which is effectively how the hardware executes during the clock cycle.

To implement this step, we will need to assert the control signals MemRead and IRWrite, and set IorD to 0 to select the PC as the source of the address. We also increment the PC by 4, which requires setting the ALUSrcA signal to 0 (sending the PC to the ALU), the ALUSrcB signal to 01 (sending 4 to the ALU), and ALUOp to 00 (to make the ALU add). Finally, we will also want to store the incremented instruction address back into the PC, which requires setting PC source to 00 and setting PCWrite. The increment of the PC and the instruction memory access can occur in parallel. The new value of the PC is not visible until the next clock cycle. (The incremented PC will also be stored into ALUOut, but this action is benign.)

2. Instruction decode and register fetch step

In the previous step and in this one, we do not yet know what the instruction is, so we can perform only actions that are either applicable to all instructions (such as fetching the instruction in step 1) or not harmful, in case the instruction isn't what we think it might be. Thus, in this step we can read the two registers indicated by the rs and rt instruction fields, since it isn't harmful to read them even if it isn't necessary. The values read from the register file may be needed in later stages, so we read them from the register file and store the values into the temporary registers A and B.

We will also compute the branch target address with the ALU, which also is not harmful because we can ignore the value if the instruction turns out not to be a branch. The potential branch target is saved in ALUOut.

Performing these "optimistic" actions early has the benefit of decreasing the number of clock cycles needed to execute an instruction. We can do these optimistic actions early because of the regularity of the instruction formats. For instance, if the instruction has two register inputs, they are always in the rs and rt fields, and if the instruction is a branch, the offset is always the low-order 16 bits:

```
A <= Reg[IR[25:21]];
B <= Reg[IR[20:16]];
ALUOut <= PC + (sign-extend (IR[15-0]) << 2);
```

Operation: Access the register file to read registers rs and rt and store the results into registers A and B. Since A and B are overwritten on every cycle, the register file can be read on every cycle with the values stored into A and B. This step also computes the branch target address and stores the address in ALUOut, where it will be used on the next clock cycle if the instruction is a branch. This requires setting ALUSrcA to 0 (so that the PC is sent to the ALU), ALUSrcB to the value 11 (so that the sign-extended and shifted offset field is sent to the ALU), and ALUOp to 00 (so the ALU adds). The register file accesses and computation of branch target occur in parallel.

After this clock cycle, determining the action to take can depend on the instruction contents.

3. Execution, memory address computation, or branch completion

This is the first cycle during which the datapath operation is determined by the instruction class. In all cases, the ALU is operating on the operands prepared in the previous step, performing one of four functions, depending on the instruction class. We specify the action to be taken depending on the instruction class.

Memory reference:

```
ALUOut <= A + sign-extend (IR[15:0]);
```

Operation: The ALU is adding the operands to form the memory address. This requires setting ALUSrcA to 1 (so that the first ALU input is register A) and setting ALUSrcB to 10 (so that the output of the sign extension unit is used for the second ALU input). The ALUOp signals will need to be set to 00 (causing the ALU to add).

Arithmetic-logical instruction (R-type):

```
ALUOut <= A op B;
```

Operation: The ALU is performing the operation specified by the function code on the two values read from the register file in the previous cycle. This requires setting ALUSrcA = 1 and setting ALUSrcB = 00, which together cause the registers A and B to be used as the ALU inputs. The ALUOp signals will need to be set to 10 (so that the funct field is used to determine the ALU control signal settings).

Branch:

```
if (A == B) PC <= ALUOut;
```

Operation: The ALU is used to do the equal comparison between the two registers read in the previous step. The Zero signal out of the ALU is used to determine whether or not to branch. This requires setting ALUSrcA = 1 and setting ALUSrcB = 00 (so that the register file outputs are the ALU inputs). The ALUOp signals will need to be set to 01 (causing the ALU to subtract) for equality testing. The PCWriteCond signal will need to be asserted to update the PC if the Zero output of the ALU is asserted. By setting PCSource to 01, the value written into the PC will come from ALUOut, which holds the branch target address computed in the previous cycle. For conditional branches that are taken, we actually write the PC twice: once from the output of the ALU (during the Instruction decode/register fetch) and once from ALUOut (during the Branch completion step). The value written into the PC last is the one used for the next instruction fetch.

Jump:

```
# {x, y} is the Verilog notation for concatenation of
bit fields x and y
PC <= {PC [31:28], (IR[25:0]],2'b00)};
```

Operation: The PC is replaced by the jump address. PCSource is set to direct the jump address to the PC, and PCWrite is asserted to write the jump address into the PC.

4.   Memory access or R-type instruction completion step

During this step, a load or store instruction accesses memory and an arithmetic-logical instruction writes its result. When a value is retrieved from memory, it is stored into the memory data register (MDR), where it must be used on the next clock cycle.

Memory reference:

```
MDR <= Memory [ALUOut];
```

or

```
Memory [ALUOut] <= B;
```

Operation: If the instruction is a load, a data word is retrieved from memory and is written into the MDR. If the instruction is a store, then the data is written into memory. In either case, the address used is the one computed during the previous step and stored in ALUOut. For a store, the source operand is saved in B. (B is actually read twice, once in step 2 and once in step 3. Luckily, the same value is read both times, since the register number—which is stored in IR and used to read from the register file—does not change.) The signal MemRead (for a load) or MemWrite (for a store) will need to be asserted. In addition, for loads and stores, the signal IorD is set to 1 to force the memory address to come from the ALU, rather than the PC. Since MDR is written on every clock cycle, no explicit control signal need be asserted.

Arithmetic-logical instruction (R-type):

```
Reg[IR[15:11]] <= ALUOut;
```

Operation: Place the contents of ALUOut, which corresponds to the output of the ALU operation in the previous cycle, into the Result register. The signal RegDst must be set to 1 to force the rd field (bits 15:11) to be used to select the register file entry to write. RegWrite must be asserted, and MemtoReg must be set to 0 so that the output of the ALU is written, as opposed to the memory data output.

5. Memory read completion step

During this step, loads complete by writing back the value from memory.

Load:

```
Reg[IR[20:16]] <= MDR;
```

Operation: Write the load data, which was stored into MDR in the previous cycle, into the register file. To do this, we set MemtoReg = 1 (to write the result from memory), assert RegWrite (to cause a write), and we make RegDst = 0 to choose the rt (bits 20:16) field as the register number.

This five-step sequence is summarized in Figure 5.30. From this sequence we can determine what the control must do on each clock cycle.

Step name	Action for R-type instructions	Action for memory reference instructions	Action for branches	Action for jumps
Instruction fetch	IR <= Memory[PC] PC <= PC + 4			
Instruction decode/register fetch	A <= Reg [IR[25:21]] B <= Reg [IR[20:16]] ALUOut <= PC + (sign-extend (IR[15:0]) << 2)			
Execution, address computation, branch/jump completion	ALUOut <= A op B	ALUOut <= A + sign-extend (IR[15:0])	if (A == B) PC <= ALUOut	PC <= {PC [31:28], (IR[25:0]],2'b00)}
Memory access or R-type completion	Reg [IR[15:11]] <= ALUOut	Load: MDR <= Memory[ALUOut] or Store: Memory [ALUOut] <= B		
Memory read completion		Load: Reg[IR[20:16]] <= MDR		

FIGURE 5.30 Summary of the steps taken to execute any instruction class. Instructions take from three to five execution steps. The first two steps are independent of the instruction class. After these steps, an instruction takes from one to three more cycles to complete, depending on the instruction class. The empty entries for the Memory access step or the Memory read completion step indicate that the particular instruction class takes fewer cycles. In a multicycle implementation, a new instruction will be started as soon as the current instruction completes, so these cycles are not idle or wasted. As mentioned earlier, the register file actually reads every cycle, but as long as the IR does not change, the values read from the register file are identical. In particular, the value read into register B during the Instruction decode stage, for a branch or R-type instruction, is the same as the value stored into B during the Execution stage and then used in the Memory access stage for a store word instruction.

Defining the Control

Now that we have determined what the control signals are and when they must be asserted, we can implement the control unit. To design the control unit for the single-cycle datapath, we used a set of truth tables that specified the setting of the control signals based on the instruction class. For the multicycle datapath, the control is more complex because the instruction is executed in a series of steps. The control for the multicycle datapath must specify both the signals to be set in any step and the next step in the sequence.

In this subsection and in ◉ **Section 5.7**, we will look at two different techniques to specify the control. The first technique is based on finite-state machines that are usually represented graphically. The second technique, called **microprogramming**, uses a programming representation for control. Both of these techniques represent the control in a form that allows the detailed implementation—using gates, ROMs, or PLAs—to be synthesized by a CAD system. In this chapter, we will focus on the design of the control and its representation in these two forms.

◉ **Section 5.8** shows how hardware design languages are used to design modern processors with examples of both the multicycle datapath and the finite-state control. In modern digital systems design, the final step of taking a hardware description to actual gates is handled by logic and datapath synthesis tools. ◉ **Appendix C** shows how this process operates by translating the multicycle control unit to a detailed hardware implementation. The key ideas of control can be grasped from this chapter without examining the material in either ◉ **Section 5.8** or ◉ **Appendix C**. However, if you want to actually do some hardware design, Section 5.9 is useful, and ◉ **Appendix C** can show you what the implementations are likely to look like at the gate level.

Given this implementation, and the knowledge that each state requires 1 clock cycle, we can find the CPI for a typical instruction mix.

microprogram A symbolic representation of control in the form of instructions, called microinstructions, that are executed on a simple micromachine.

CPI in a Multicycle CPU

EXAMPLE

Using the SPECINT2000 instruction mix shown in Figure 3.26, what is the CPI, assuming that each state in the multicycle CPU requires 1 clock cycle?

ANSWER

The mix is 25% loads (1% load byte + 24% load word), 10% stores (1% store byte + 9% store word), 11% branches (6% beq, 5% bne), 2% jumps (1% jal + 1% jr), and 52% ALU (all the rest of the mix, which we assume to be ALU instructions). From Figure 5.30 on page 329, the number of clock cycles for each instruction class is the following:

- Loads: 5
- Stores: 4
- ALU instructions: 4
- Branches: 3
- Jumps: 3

The CPI is given by the following:

$$\text{CPI} = \frac{\text{CPU clock cycles}}{\text{Instruction count}} = \frac{\sum \text{Instruction count}_i \times \text{CPI}_i}{\text{Instruction count}}$$

$$= \sum \frac{\text{Instruction count}_i}{\text{Instruction count}} \times \text{CPI}_i$$

The ratio

$$\frac{\text{Instruction count}_i}{\text{Instruction count}}$$

is simply the instruction frequency for the instruction class i. We can therefore substitute to obtain

$$\text{CPI} = 0.25 \times 5 + 0.10 \times 4 + 0.52 \times 4 + 0.11 \times 3 + 0.02 \times 3 = 4.12$$

This CPI is better than the worst-case CPI of 5.0 when all the instructions take the same number of clock cycles. Of course, overheads in both designs may reduce or increase this difference. The multicycle design is probably also more cost-effective, since it uses fewer separate components in the datapath.

The first method we use to specify the multicycle control is a **finite-state machine**. A finite-state machine consists of a set of states and directions on how to change states. The directions are defined by a **next-state function**, which maps the current state and the inputs to a new state. When we use a finite-state machine for control, each state also specifies a set of outputs that are asserted when the machine is in that state. The implementation of a finite-state machine usually assumes that all outputs that are not explicitly asserted are deasserted. Similarly, the correct operation of the datapath depends on the fact that a signal that is not explicitly asserted is deasserted, rather than acting as a don't care. For example, the RegWrite signal should be asserted only when a register file entry is to be written; when it is not explicitly asserted, it must be deasserted.

finite-state machine A sequential logic function consisting of a set of inputs and outputs, a next-state function that maps the current state and the inputs to a new state, and an output function that maps the current state and possibly the inputs to a set of asserted outputs.

next-state function A combinational function that, given the inputs and the current state, determines the next state of a finite-state machine.

Multiplexor controls are slightly different, since they select one of the inputs whether they are 0 or 1. Thus, in the finite-state machine, we always specify the setting of all the multiplexor controls that we care about. When we implement the finite-state machine with logic, setting a control to 0 may be the default and thus may not require any gates. A simple example of a finite-state machine appears in ⊙ **Appendix B**, and if you are unfamiliar with the concept of a finite-state machine, you may want to examine ⊙ **Appendix B** before proceeding.

The finite-state control essentially corresponds to the five steps of execution shown on pages 325 through 329; each state in the finite-state machine will take 1 clock cycle. The finite-state machine will consist of several parts. Since the first two steps of execution are identical for every instruction, the initial two states of the finite-state machine will be common for all instructions. Steps 3 through 5 differ, depending on the opcode. After the execution of the last step for a particular instruction class, the finite-state machine will return to the initial state to begin fetching the next instruction.

Figure 5.31 shows this abstracted representation of the finite-state machine. To fill in the details of the finite-state machine, we will first expand the instruction fetch and decode portion, and then we will show the states (and actions) for the different instruction classes.

We show the first two states of the finite-state machine in Figure 5.32 using a traditional graphic representation. We number the states to simplify the explanation, though the numbers are arbitrary. State 0, corresponding to step 1, is the starting state of the machine.

The signals that are asserted in each state are shown within the circle representing the state. The arcs between states define the next state and are labeled with

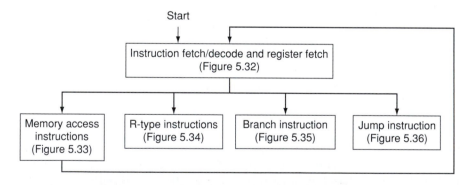

FIGURE 5.31   The high-level view of the finite-state machine control. The first steps are independent of the instruction class; then a series of sequences that depend on the instruction opcode are used to complete each instruction class. After completing the actions needed for that instruction class, the control returns to fetch a new instruction. Each box in this figure may represent one to several states. The arc labeled *Start* marks the state in which to begin when the first instruction is to be fetched.

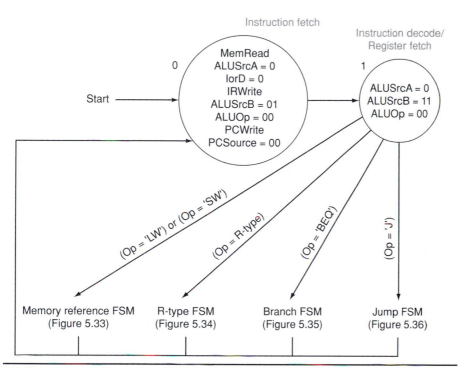

FIGURE 5.32 The instruction fetch and decode portion of every instruction is identical. These states correspond to the top box in the abstract finite-state machine in Figure 5.31. In the first state we assert two signals to cause the memory to read an instruction and write it into the Instruction register (MemRead and IRWrite), and we set IorD to 0 to choose the PC as the address source. The signals ALUSrcA, ALUSrcB, ALUOp, PCWrite, and PCSource are set to compute PC + 4 and store it into the PC. (It will also be stored into ALUOut, but never used from there.) In the next state, we compute the branch target address by setting ALUSrcB to 11 (causing the shifted and sign-extended lower 16 bits of the IR to be sent to the ALU), setting ALUSrcA to 0 and ALUOp to 00; we store the result in the ALUOut register, which is written on every cycle. There are four next states that depend on the class of the instruction, which is known during this state. The control unit input, called Op, is used to determine which of these arcs to follow. Remember that all signals not explicitly asserted are deasserted; this is particularly important for signals that control writes. For multiplexor controls, lack of a specific setting indicates that we do not care about the setting of the multiplexor.

conditions that select a specific next state when multiple next states are possible. After state 1, the signals asserted depend on the class of instruction. Thus, the finite-state machine has four arcs exiting state 1, corresponding to the four instruction classes: memory reference, R-type, branch on equal, and jump. This process of branching to different states depending on the instruction is called *decoding*, since the choice of the next state, and hence the actions that follow, depend on the instruction class.

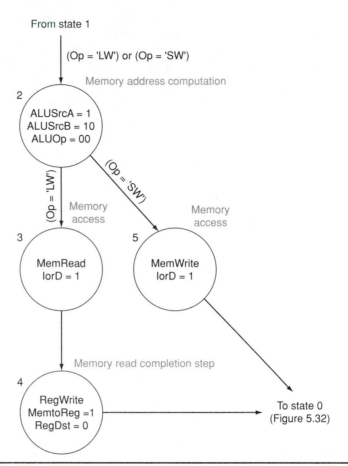

FIGURE 5.33   The finite-state machine for controlling memory reference instructions has four states. These states correspond to the box labeled "Memory access instructions" in Figure 5.31. After performing a memory address calculation, a separate sequence is needed for load and for store. The setting of the control signals ALUSrcA, ALUSrcB, and ALUOp is used to cause the memory address computation in state 2. Loads require an extra state to write the result from the MDR (where the result is written in state 3) into the register file.

Figure 5.33 shows the portion of the finite-state machine needed to implement the memory reference instructions. For the memory reference instructions, the first state after fetching the instruction and registers computes the memory address (state 2). To compute the memory address, the ALU input multiplexors must be set so that the first input is the A register, while the second input is the sign-extended displacement field; the result is written into the ALUOut register. After the memory address calculation, the memory should be read or written; this requires two different states. If the instruction opcode is lw, then state 3 (corresponding to the step Memory access) does the memory read (MemRead is asserted). The output of the memory is always written into MDR. If it is sw, state 5 does a memory write (MemWrite is asserted). In states 3 and 5, the signal IorD is set to 1 to force the memory address to come from the ALU. After performing a write, the instruction sw has completed execution, and the next state is state 0. If the instruction is a load, however, another state (state 4) is needed to write the result from the memory into the register file. Setting the multiplexor controls MemtoReg = 1 and RegDst = 0 will send the loaded value in the MDR to be written into the register file, using rt as the register number. After this state, corresponding to the Memory read completion step, the next state is state 0.

To implement the R-type instructions requires two states corresponding to steps 3 (Execute) and 4 (R-type completion). Figure 5.34 shows this two-state portion of the finite-state machine. State 6 asserts ALUSrcA and sets the ALUSrcB

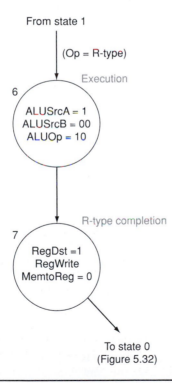

FIGURE 5.34 R-type instructions can be implemented with a simple two-state finite-state machine. These states correspond to the box labeled "R-type instructions" in Figure 5.31. The first state causes the ALU operation to occur, while the second state causes the ALU result (which is in ALUOut) to be written in the register file. The three signals asserted during state 7 cause the contents of ALUOut to be written into the register file in the entry specified by the rd field of the Instruction register.

signals to 00; this forces the two registers that were read from the register file to be used as inputs to the ALU. Setting ALUOp to 10 causes the ALU control unit to use the function field to set the ALU control signals. In state 7, RegWrite is asserted to cause the register file to write, RegDst is asserted to cause the rd field to be used as the register number of the destination, and MemtoReg is deasserted to select ALUOut as the source of the value to write into the register file.

For branches, only a single additional state is necessary because they complete execution during the third step of instruction execution. During this state, the control signals that cause the ALU to compare the contents of registers A and B must be set, and the signals that cause the PC to be written conditionally with the address in the ALUOut register are also set. To perform the comparison requires that we assert ALUSrcA and set ALUSrcB to 00, and set the ALUOp value to 01 (forcing a subtract). (We use only the Zero output of the ALU, not the result of the subtraction.) To control the writing of the PC, we assert PCWriteCond and set PCSource = 01, which will cause the value in the ALUOut register (containing the branch address calculated in state 1, Figure 5.32 on page 333) to be written into the PC if the Zero bit out of the ALU is asserted. Figure 5.35 shows this single state.

The last instruction class is jump; like branch, it requires only a single state (shown in Figure 5.36) to complete its execution. In this state, the signal PCWrite is asserted to cause the PC to be written. By setting PCSource to 10, the value supplied for writing will be the lower 26 bits of the Instruction register with 00_{two} added as the low-order bits concatenated with the upper 4 bits of the PC.

We can now put these pieces of the finite-state machine together to form a specification for the control unit, as shown in Figure 5.37. In each state, the signals that are asserted are shown. The next state depends on the opcode bits of the instruction, so we label the arcs with a comparison for the corresponding instruction opcodes.

A finite-state machine can be implemented with a temporary register that holds the current state and a block of combinational logic that determines both the datapath signals to be asserted and the next state. Figure 5.38 shows how such an implementation might look. ⊙ **Appendix C** describes in detail how the finite-state machine is implemented using this structure. In ⊙ **Section C.3**, the combinational control logic for the finite-state machine of Figure 5.37 is implemented both with a ROM (read-only memory) and a PLA (programmable logic array). (Also see ⊙ **Appendix B** for a description of these logic elements.) In the next section of this chapter, we consider another way to represent control. Both of these techniques are simply different representations of the same control information.

Pipelining, which is the subject of Chapter 6, is almost always used to accelerate the execution of instructions. For simple instructions, pipelining is capable of achieving the higher clock rate of a multicycle design and a single-cycle CPI of a single-clock design. In most pipelined processors, however, some instructions take longer than a single cycle and require multicycle control. Floating-point

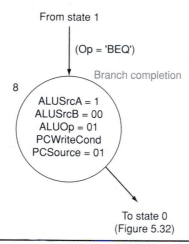

FIGURE 5.35 **The branch instruction requires a single state.** The first three outputs that are asserted cause the ALU to compare the registers (ALUSrcA, ALUSrcB, and ALUOp), while the signals PCSource and PCWriteCond perform the conditional write if the branch condition is true. Notice that we do not use the value written into ALUOut; instead, we use only the Zero output of the ALU. The branch target address is read from ALUOut, where it was saved at the end of state 1.

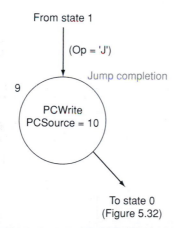

FIGURE 5.36 **The jump instruction requires a single state that asserts two control signals to write the PC with the lower 26 bits of the Instruction register shifted left 2 bits and concatenated to the upper 4 bits of the PC of this instruction.**

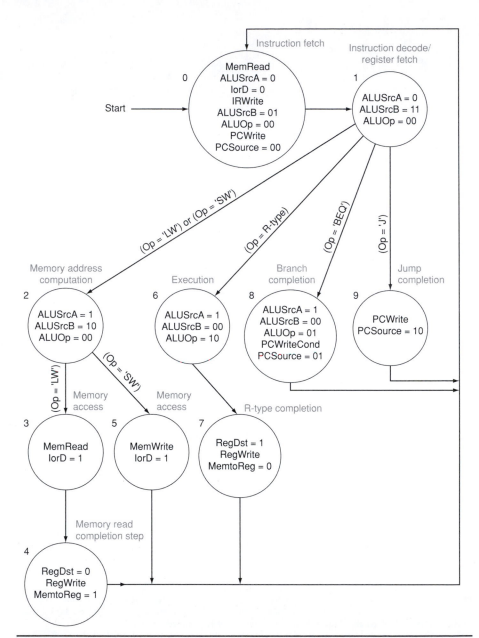

FIGURE 5.37 The complete finite-state machine control for the datapath shown in Figure 5.28. The labels on the arcs are conditions that are tested to determine which state is the next state; when the next state is unconditional, no label is given. The labels inside the nodes indicate the output signals asserted during that state; we always specify the setting of a multiplexor control signal if the correct operation requires it. Hence, in some states a multiplexor control will be set to 0.

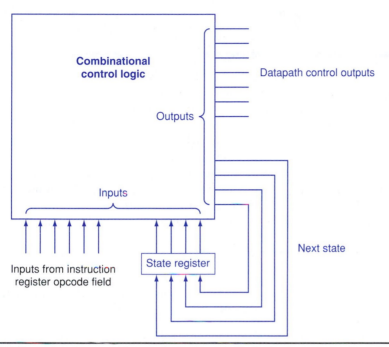

FIGURE 5.38 Finite-state machine controllers are typically implemented using a block of combinational logic and a register to hold the current state. The outputs of the combinational logic are the next-state number and the control signals to be asserted for the current state. The inputs to the combinational logic are the current state and any inputs used to determine the next state. In this case, the inputs are the instruction register opcode bits. Notice that in the finite-state machine used in this chapter, the outputs depend only on the current state, not on the inputs. The elaboration below explains this in more detail.

instructions are one universal example. There are many examples in the IA-32 architecture that require the use of multicycle control.

Elaboration: The style of finite-state machine in Figure 5.38 is called a Moore machine, after Edward Moore. Its identifying characteristic is that the output depends only on the current state. For a Moore machine, the box labeled Combinational control logic can be split into two pieces. One piece has the control output and only the state input, while the other has only the next-state output.

An alternative style of machine is a Mealy machine, named after George Mealy. The Mealy machine allows both the input and the current state to be used to determine the output. Moore machines have potential implementation advantages in speed and size of the control unit. The speed advantages arise because the control outputs, which are needed early in the clock cycle, do not depend on the inputs, but only on the current state. In 🔘 Appendix C, when the implementation of this finite-state machine is taken down to logic gates, the size advantage can be clearly seen. The potential disadvantage of a Moore machine is that it may require additional states. For example, in situations where there is a one-state difference between two sequences of states, the Mealy machine may unify the states by making the outputs depend on the inputs.

Understanding Program Performance

For a processor with a given clock rate, the relative performance between two code segments will be determined by the product of the CPI and the instruction count to execute each segment. As we have seen here, instructions can vary in their CPI, even for a simple processor. In the next two chapters, we will see that the introduction of pipelining and the use of caches create even larger opportunities for variation in the CPI. Although many factors that affect the CPI are controlled by the hardware designer, the programmer, the compiler, and software system dictate what instructions are executed, and it is this process that determines what the effective CPI for the program will be. Programmers seeking to improve performance must understand the role of CPI and the factors that affect it.

Check Yourself

1. True or false: Since the jump instruction does not depend on the register values or on computing the branch target address, it can be completed during the second state, rather than waiting until the third.

2. True, false, or maybe: The control signal PCWriteCond can be replaced by PCSource[0].

5.6   Exceptions

exception Also called interrupt. An unscheduled event that disrupts program execution; used to detect overflow.

interrupt An exception that comes from outside of the processor. (Some architectures use the term *interrupt* for all exceptions.)

Control is the most challenging aspect of processor design: it is both the hardest part to get right and the hardest part to make fast. One of the hardest parts of control is implementing **exceptions** and **interrupts**—events other than branches or jumps that change the normal flow of instruction execution. An exception is an unexpected event from within the processor; arithmetic overflow is an example of an exception. An interrupt is an event that also causes an unexpected change in control flow but comes from outside of the processor. Interrupts are used by I/O devices to communicate with the processor, as we will see in Chapter 8.

Many architectures and authors do not distinguish between interrupts and exceptions, often using the older name *interrupt* to refer to both types of events. We follow the MIPS convention, using the term *exception* to refer to *any* unexpected change in control flow without distinguishing whether the cause is internal or external; we use the term *interrupt* only when the event is externally caused. The Intel IA-32 architecture uses the word *interrupt* for all these events.

Interrupts were initially created to handle unexpected events like arithmetic overflow and to signal requests for service from I/O devices. The same basic mechanism was extended to handle internally generated exceptions as well. Here are some examples showing whether the situation is internally generated by the processor or externally generated:

Type of event	From where?	MIPS terminology
I/O device request	External	Interrupt
Invoke the operating system from user program	Internal	Exception
Arithmetic overflow	Internal	Exception
Using an undefined instruction	Internal	Exception
Hardware malfunctions	Either	Exception or interrupt

Many of the requirements to support exceptions come from the specific situation that causes an exception to occur. Accordingly, we will return to this topic in Chapter 7, when we discuss memory hierarchies, and in Chapter 8, when we discuss I/O, and we better understand the motivation for additional capabilities in the exception mechanism. In this section, we deal with the control implementation for detecting two types of exceptions that arise from the portions of the instruction set and implementation that we have already discussed.

Detecting exceptional conditions and taking the appropriate action is often on the critical timing path of a machine, which determines the clock cycle time and thus performance. Without proper attention to exceptions during design of the control unit, attempts to add exceptions to a complicated implementation can significantly reduce performance, as well as complicate the task of getting the design correct.

How Exceptions Are Handled

The two types of exceptions that our current implementation can generate are execution of an undefined instruction and an arithmetic overflow. The basic action that the machine must perform when an exception occurs is to save the address of the offending instruction in the exception program counter (EPC) and then transfer control to the operating system at some specified address.

The operating system can then take the appropriate action, which may involve providing some service to the user program, taking some predefined action in response to an overflow, or stopping the execution of the program and reporting an error. After performing whatever action is required because of the exception, the operating system can terminate the program or may continue its execution, using the EPC to determine where to restart the execution

vectored interrupt An interrupt for which the address to which control is transferred is determined by the cause of the exception.

of the program. In Chapter 7, we will look more closely at the issue of restarting the execution.

For the operating system to handle the exception, it must know the reason for the exception, in addition to the instruction that caused it. There are two main methods used to communicate the reason for an exception. The method used in the MIPS architecture is to include a status register (called the *Cause register*), which holds a field that indicates the reason for the exception.

A second method is to use **vectored interrupts**. In a vectored interrupt, the address to which control is transferred is determined by the cause of the exception. For example, to accommodate the two exception types listed above, we might define the following two exception vector addresses:

Exception type	Exception vector address (in hex)
Undefined instruction	C000 0000$_{hex}$
Arithmetic overflow	C000 0020$_{hex}$

The operating system knows the reason for the exception by the address at which it is initiated. The addresses are separated by 32 bytes or 8 instructions, and the operating system must record the reason for the exception and may perform some limited processing in this sequence. When the exception is not vectored, a single entry point for all exceptions can be used, and the operating system decodes the status register to find the cause.

We can perform the processing required for exceptions by adding a few extra registers and control signals to our basic implementation and by slightly extending the finite-state machine. Let's assume that we are implementing the exception system used in the MIPS architecture. (Implementing vectored exceptions is no more difficult.) We will need to add two additional registers to the datapath:

■ *EPC:* A 32-bit register used to hold the address of the affected instruction. (Such a register is needed even when exceptions are vectored.)

■ *Cause:* A register used to record the cause of the exception. In the MIPS architecture, this register is 32 bits, although some bits are currently unused. Assume that the low-order bit of this register encodes the two possible exception sources mentioned above: undefined instruction = 0 and arithmetic overflow = 1.

We will need to add two control signals to cause the EPC and Cause registers to be written; call these *EPCWrite* and *CauseWrite*. In addition, we will need a 1-bit control signal to set the low-order bit of the Cause register appropriately; call this signal *IntCause*. Finally, we will need to be able to write the *exception address*, which is the operating system entry point for exception handling, into the PC; in the MIPS architecture, this address is 8000 0180$_{hex}$. Currently, the PC is fed from the output of a three-way multiplexor, which is controlled by the signal PCSource (see Figure 5.28 on page 323). We can change this to a four-way multiplexor, with additional input wired to the constant value 8000 0180$_{hex}$. Then PCSource can be set to 11$_{two}$ to select this value to be written into the PC.

Because the PC is incremented during the first cycle of every instruction, we cannot just write the value of the PC into the EPC, since the value in the PC will be the instruction address plus 4. However, we can use the ALU to subtract 4 from the PC and write the output into the EPC. This requires no additional control signals or paths, since we can use the ALU to subtract, and the constant 4 is already a selectable ALU input. The data write port of the EPC, therefore, is connected to the ALU output. Figure 5.39 shows the multicycle datapath with these additions needed for implementing exceptions.

Using the datapath of Figure 5.39, the action to be taken for each different type of exception can be handled in one state apiece. In each case, the state sets the Cause register, computes and saves the original PC into the EPC, and writes the exception address into the PC. Thus, to handle the two exception types we are considering, we will need to add only the two states, but before we add them we must determine how to check for exceptions, since these checks will control the arcs to the new states.

How Control Checks for Exceptions

Now we have to design a method to detect these exceptions and to transfer control to the appropriate state in the exception states. Figure 5.40 shows the two new states (10 and 11) as well as their connection to the rest of the finite-state control. Each of the two possible exceptions is detected differently:

- *Undefined instruction:* This is detected when no next state is defined from state 1 for the op value. We handle this exception by defining the next-state value for all op values other than lw, sw, 0 (R-type), j, and beq as state 10. We show this by symbolically using *other* to indicate that the op field does not match any of the opcodes that label arcs out of state 1 to the new state 10, which is used for this exception.

- *Arithmetic overflow:* The ALU, designed in ◉ **Appendix B**, included logic to detect overflow, and a signal called *Overflow* is provided as an output from the ALU. This signal is used in the modified finite-state machine to specify an additional possible next state (state 11) for state 7, as shown in Figure 5.40.

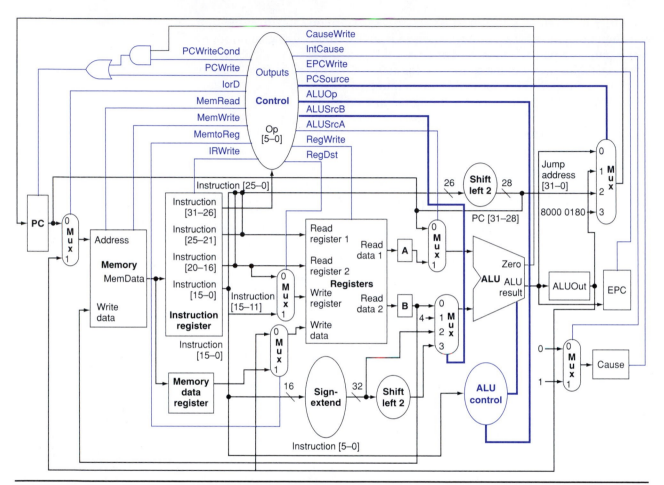

FIGURE 5.39   The multicycle datapath with the addition needed to implement exceptions. The specific additions include the Cause and EPC registers, a multiplexor to control the value sent to the Cause register, an expansion of the multiplexor controlling the value written into the PC, and control lines for the added multiplexor and registers. For simplicity, this figure does not show the ALU overflow signal, which would need to be stored in a 1-bit register and delivered as an additional input to the control unit (see Figure 5.40 to see how it is used).

Figure 5.40 represents a complete specification of the control for this MIPS subset with two types of exceptions. Remember that the challenge in designing the control of a real machine is to handle the variety of different interactions between instructions and other exception-causing events in such a way that the control logic remains both small and fast. The complex interactions that are possible are what make the control unit the most challenging aspect of hardware design.

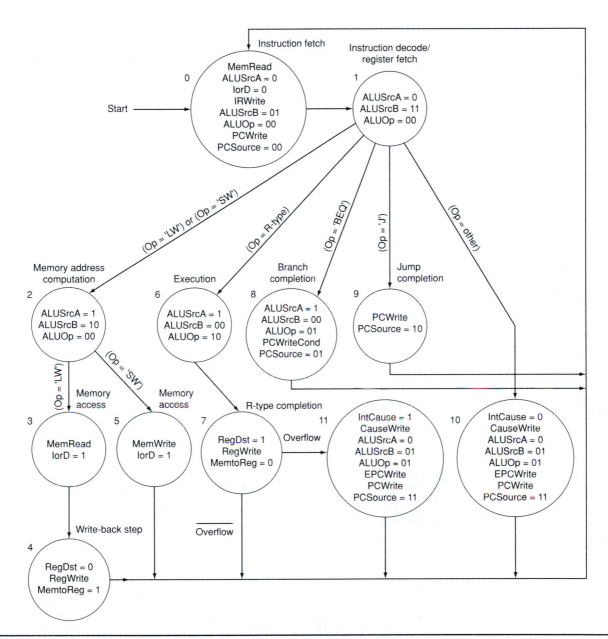

FIGURE 5.40 The finite-state machine with the additions to handle exception detection. States 10 and 11 are the new states that generate the appropriate control for exceptions. The branch out of state 1 labeled (*Op = other*) indicates the next state when the input does not match the opcode of any of lw, sw, 0 (R-type), j, or beq. The branch out of state 7 labeled *Overflow* indicates the action to be taken when the ALU signals an overflow.

Elaboration: If you examine the finite-state machine in Figure 5.40 closely, you can see that some problems could occur in the way the exceptions are handled. For example, in the case of arithmetic overflow, the instruction causing the overflow completes writing its result because the overflow branch is in the state when the write completes. However, it's possible that the architecture defines the instruction as having no effect if the instruction causes an exception; this is what the MIPS instruction set architecture specifies. In Chapter 7, we will see that certain classes of exceptions require us to prevent the instruction from changing the machine state, and that this aspect of handling exceptions becomes complex and potentially limits performance.

Check Yourself

Is this optimization proposed in the Check Yourself on page 340 concerning PCSource still valid in the extended control for exceptions shown in Figure 5.40 on page 345? Why or why not?

5.7 Microprogramming: Simplifying Control Design

Microprogramming is a technique for designing complex control units. It uses a very simple hardware engine that can then be programmed to implement a more complex instruction set. Microprogramming is used today to implement some parts of a complex instruction set, such as a Pentium, as well as in special-purpose processors. This section, which appears on the CD, explains the basic concepts and shows how they can be used to implement the MIPS multicycle control.

5.8 An Introduction to Digital Design Using a Hardware Design Language

Modern digital design is done using hardware description languages and modern computer-aided synthesis tools that can create detailed hardware designs from the descriptions using both libraries and logic synthesis. Entire books are written on such languages and their use in digital design. This section, which appears on the CD, gives a brief introduction and shows how a hardware design language, Verilog in this case, can be used to describe the MIPS multicycle control both behaviorally and in a form suitable for hardware synthesis.

5.9 Real Stuff: The Organization of Recent Pentium Implementations

The techniques described in this chapter for building datapaths and control units are at the heart of every computer. All recent computers, however, go beyond the techniques of this chapter and use pipelining. *Pipelining*, which is the subject of the next chapter, improves performance by overlapping the execution of multiple instructions, achieving throughput close to one instruction per clock cycle (like our single-cycle implementation) with a clock cycle time determined by the delay of individual functional units rather than the entire execution path of an instruction (like our multicycle design). The last Intel IA-32 processor without pipelining was the 80386, introduced in 1985; the very first MIPS processor, the R2000, also introduced in 1985, was pipelined.

Recent Intel IA-32 processors (the Pentium II, III, and 4) employ sophisticated pipelining approaches. These processors, however, are still faced with the challenge of implementing control for the complex IA-32 instruction set, described in Chapter 2. The basic functional units and datapaths in use in modern processors, while significantly more complex than those described in this chapter, have the same basic functionality and similar types of control signals. Thus the task of designing a control unit builds on the same principles used in this chapter.

Challenges Implementing More Complex Architectures

Unlike the MIPS architecture, the IA-32 architecture contains instructions that are very complex and can take tens, if not hundreds, of cycles to execute. For example, the string move instruction (MOVS) requires calculating and updating two different memory addresses as well as loading and storing a byte of the string. The larger number and greater complexity of addressing modes in the IA-32 architecture complicates implementation of even simple instructions similar to those on MIPS. Fortunately, a multicycle datapath is well structured to adapt to variations in the amount of work required per instruction that are inherent in IA-32 instructions. This adaptability comes from two capabilities:

1. A multicycle datapath allows instructions to take varying numbers of clock cycles. Simple IA-32 instructions that are similar to those in the MIPS architecture can execute in 3 or 4 clock cycles, while more complex instructions can take tens of cycles.

2. A multicycle datapath can use the datapath components more than once per instruction. This is critical to handling more complex addressing modes, as well as implementing more complex operations, both of which are present in the IA-32 architecture. Without this capability, the datapath

would need to be extended to handle the demands of the more complex instructions without reusing components, which would be completely impractical. For example, a single-cycle datapath, which doesn't reuse components, for the IA-32 would require several data memories and a very large number of ALUs.

microprogrammed control A method of specifying control that uses microcode rather than a finite-state representation.

Using the multicycle datapath and a **microprogrammed controller** provides a framework for implementing the IA-32 instruction set. The challenging task, however, is creating a high-performance implementation, which requires dealing with the diversity of the requirements arising from different instructions. Simply put, a high-performance implementation needs to ensure that the simple instructions execute quickly, and that the burden of the complexities of the instruction set penalize primarily the complex, less frequently used, instructions.

hardwired control An implementation of finite-state machine control typically using programmable logic arrays (PLAs) or collections of PLAs and random logic.

microcode The set of microinstructions that control a processor.

To accomplish this goal, every Intel implementation of the IA-32 architecture since the 486 has used a combination of **hardwired control** to handle simple instructions, and **microcoded** control to handle the more complex instructions. For those instructions that can be executed in a single pass through the datapath—those with complexity similar to a MIPS instruction—the hardwired control generates the control information and executes the instruction in one pass through the datapath that takes a small number of clock cycles. Those instructions that require multiple datapath passes and complex sequencing are handled by the microcoded controller that takes a larger number of cycles and multiple passes through the datapath to complete the execution of the instruction. The benefit of this approach is that it enables the designer to achieve low cycle counts for the simple instructions without having to build the enormously complex datapath that would be required to handle the full generality of the most complex instructions.

The Structure of the Pentium 4 Implementation

superscalar An advanced pipelining technique that enables the processor to execute more than one instruction per clock cycle.

Recent Pentium processors are capable of executing more than one instruction per clock, using an advanced pipelining technique, called **superscalar**. We describe how a superscalar processor works in the next chapter. The important thing to understand here is that executing more than one instruction per clock cycle requires duplicating the datapath resources. The simplest way to think about this is that the processor has multiple datapaths, although these are tailored to handle one class of instructions; say, loads and stores, ALU operations, or branches. In this way, the processor is able to execute a load or store in the same clock cycle that it is also executing a branch and an ALU operation. The Pentium III and 4 allow up to three IA-32 instructions to execute in a clock cycle.

microinstruction A representation of control using low-level instructions, each of which asserts a set of control signals that are active on a given clock cycle as well as specifies what microinstruction to execute next.

micro-operations The RISC-like instructions directly executed by the hardware in recent Pentium implementations.

The Pentium III and Pentium 4 execute simple **microinstructions** similar to MIPS instructions, called **micro-operations** in Intel terminology. These microinstructions are fully self-contained operations that are initially about 70 bits wide. The control of the datapath to implement these microinstructions is completely hardwired. This last level of control expands up to three microinstructions into about 120 control lines for the integer datapaths and 275 to over 400 control lines for the floating-point datapath—the latter number for the new SSE2 instructions included in the Pentium 4. This last step of expanding the microinstructions into control lines is very similar to the control generation for the single-cycle datapath or for the ALU control.

How is the translation between IA-32 instructions and microinstructions performed? In earlier Pentium implementations (i.e., the Pentium Pro, Pentium II, and Pentium III), the instruction decode unit would look at up to three IA-32 instructions at a time and use a set of PLAs to generate up to six microinstructions per cycle. With the significantly higher clock rate introduced in the Pentium 4, this solution was no longer adequate and an entirely new method of generating microinstructions was needed.

The solution adopted in the Pentium 4 is to include a **trace cache** of microinstructions, which is accessed by the IA-32 program counter. A trace cache is a sophisticated form of instruction cache, which we explain in detail in Chapter 7. For now, think of it as a buffer that holds the microinstructions that implement a given IA-32 instruction. When the trace cache is accessed with the address of the next IA-32 instruction to be executed, one of several events occurs:

trace cache   An instruction cache that holds a sequence of instructions with a given starting address; in recent Pentium implementations the trace cache holds micro-operations rather than IA-32 instructions.

- The translation of the IA-32 instruction is in the trace cache. In this case, up to three microinstructions are produced from the trace cache. These three microinstructions represent from one to three IA-32 instructions. The IA-32 PC is advanced one to three instructions depending on how many fit in the three-microinstruction sequence.

- The translation of the IA-32 instruction is in the trace cache, but it requires more than four microinstructions to implement. For such complex IA-32 instructions, there is a microcode ROM; the control unit transfers control to the microprogram residing in the ROM. Microinstructions are produced from the microprogram until the more complex IA-32 instruction has been completed. The microcode ROM provides a total of more than 8000 microinstructions, with a number of sequences being shared among IA-32 instructions. Control then transfers back to fetching instructions from the trace cache.

- The translation of the designated IA-32 instruction is not in the trace cache. In this case, an IA-32 instruction decoder is used to decode the IA-32 instruction. If the number of microinstructions is four or less, the decoded microinstructions are placed in the trace cache, where they may be found on the next execution of this instruction. Otherwise, the microcode ROM is used to complete the sequence.

From one to three microinstructions are sent from the trace cache to the Pentium 4 microinstruction pipeline, which we describe in detail at the end of Chapter 6. The use of simple, low-level, hardwired control and simple datapaths for handling the microinstructions together with the trace cache of decoded instructions allows the Pentium 4 to achieve impressive clock rates, similar to those for microprocessors implementing simpler instruction set architectures. Furthermore, the translation process, which combines direct hardwired control for simple instructions with microcoded control for complex instructions, allows the Pentium 4 to execute the simple, high-frequency instructions in the IA-32 instruction set at a high rate, yielding a low, and very competitive, CPI.

Understanding Program Performance

dispatch An operation in a microprogrammed control unit in which the next microinstruction is selected on the basis of one or more fields of a macroinstruction, usually by creating a table containing the addresses of the target microinstructions and indexing the table using a field of the macroinstruction. The dispatch tables are typically implemented in ROM or programmable logic array (PLA). The term *dispatch* is also used in dynamically scheduled processors to refer to the process of sending an instruction to a queue.

Although most of the Pentium 4 performance, ignoring the memory system, depends on the efficiency of the pipelined micro-operations, the effectiveness of the front end in decoding IA-32 instructions can have a significant effect on performance. In particular, because of the structure of the decoder, using simpler IA-32 instructions that require four or fewer micro-operations, and hence, avoiding a microcode **dispatch**, is likely to lead to better performance. Because of this implementation strategy (and a similar one on the Pentium III), compiler writers and assembly language programmers should try to make use of sequences of simple IA-32 instructions rather than more complex alternatives.

5.10 Fallacies and Pitfalls

Pitfall: Adding a complex instruction implemented with microprogramming may not be faster than a sequence using simpler instructions.

Most machines with a large and complex instruction set are implemented, at least in part, using microcode stored in ROM. Surprisingly, on such machines, sequences of individual simpler instructions are sometimes as fast as or even faster than the custom microcode sequence for a particular instruction.

How can this possibly be true? At one time, microcode had the advantage of being fetched from a much faster memory than instructions in the program. Since caches came into use in 1968, microcode no longer has such a consistent edge in fetch time. Microcode does, however, still have the advantage of using internal temporary registers in the computation, which can be helpful on machines with few general-purpose registers. The disadvantage of microcode is that the algorithms must be selected before the machine is announced and can't be changed until the next model of the architecture. The instructions in a program, on the other hand, can utilize improvements in its algorithms at any time during the life of the machine. Along the same lines, the microcode sequence is probably not optimal for all possible combinations of operands.

One example of such an instruction in the IA-32 implementations is the move string instruction (MOVS) used with a repeat prefix that we discussed in Chapter 2. This instruction is often slower than a loop that moves words at a time.

Another example involves the LOOP instruction, which decrements a register and branches to the specified label if the decremented register is not equal to zero. This instruction is designed to be used as the branch at the bottom of loops that have a fixed number of iterations (e.g., many *for* loops). Such an instruction, in addition to packing in some extra work, has benefits in minimizing the potential losses from the branch in pipelined machines (as we will see when we discuss branches in the next chapter).

Unfortunately, on all recent Intel IA-32 implementations, the LOOP instruction is always slower than the macrocode sequence consisting of simpler individual instructions (assuming that the small code size difference is not a factor). Thus, optimizing compilers focusing on speed never generate the LOOP instruction. This, in turn, makes it hard to motivate making LOOP fast in future implementations, since it is so rarely used!

Fallacy: *If there is space in the control store, new instructions are free of cost.*

One of the benefits of a microprogrammed approach is that control store implemented in ROM is not very expensive, and as transistor budgets grew, extra ROM was practically free. The analogy here is that of building a house and discovering, near completion, that you have enough land and materials left to add a room. This room wouldn't be free, however, since there would be the costs of labor and maintenance for the life of the home. The temptation to add "free" instructions can occur only when the instruction set is not fixed, as is likely to be the case in the first model of a computer. Because upward compatibility of binary programs is a highly desirable feature, all future models of this machine will be forced to include these so-called free instructions, even if space is later at a premium.

During the design of the 80286, many instructions were added to the instruction set. The availability of more silicon resource and the use of microprogrammed implementation made such additions seem painless. Possibly the largest addition was a sophisticated protection mechanism, which is largely unused today, but still must be implemented in newer implementations. This addition was motivated by a perceived need for such a mechanism and the desire to enhance microprocessor architectures to provide functionality equal to that of larger computers. Likewise, a number of decimal instructions were added to provide decimal arithmetic on bytes. Such instructions are rarely used today because using binary arithmetic on 32 bits and converting back and forth to decimal representation is considerably faster. Like the protection mechanisms, the decimal instructions must be implemented in newer processors even if only rarely used.

5.11   Concluding Remarks

As we have seen in this chapter, both the datapath and control for a processor can be designed starting with the instruction set architecture and an understanding of the basic characteristics of the technology. In Section 5.3, we saw how the datapath for a MIPS processor could be constructed based on the architecture and the decision to build a single-cycle implementation. Of course, the underlying technology also affects many design decisions by dictating what components can be used in the datapath, as well as whether a single-cycle implementation even makes sense. Along the same lines, in the first portion of Section 5.5, we saw how the decision to break the clock cycle into a series of steps led to the revised multicycle datapath. In both cases, the top-level organization—a single-cycle or multicycle machine—together with the instruction set, prescribed many characteristics of the datapath design.

Control may be designed using one of several initial representations. The choice of sequence control, and how logic is represented, can then be determined independently; the control can then be implemented with one of several methods using a structured logic technique. Figure 5.41 shows the variety of methods for specifying the control and moving from the specification to an implementation using some form of structured logic.

Similarly, the control is largely defined by the instruction set architecture, the organization, and the datapath design. In the single-cycle organization, these three aspects essentially define how the control signals must be set. In the multicycle design, the exact decomposition of the instruction execution into cycles, which is based on the instruction set architecture, together with the datapath, defines the requirements on the control.

Control is one of the most challenging aspects of computer design. A major reason is that designing the control requires an understanding of how all the com-

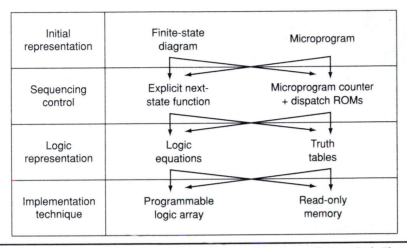

FIGURE 5.41 Alternative methods for specifying and implementing control. The arrows indicate possible design paths: any path from the initial representation to the final implementation technology is viable. Traditionally, "hardwired control" means that the techniques on the left-hand side are used, and "microprogrammed control" means that the techniques on the right-hand side are used.

ponents in the processor operate. To help meet this challenge, we examined two techniques for specifying control: finite-state diagrams and microprogramming. These control representations allow us to abstract the specification of the control from the details of how to implement it. Using abstraction in this fashion is the major method we have to cope with the complexity of computer designs.

Once the control has been specified, we can map it to detailed hardware. The exact details of the control implementation will depend on both the structure of the control and the underlying technology used to implement it. Abstracting the specification of control is also valuable because the decisions of how to implement the control are technology dependent and likely to change over time.

Historical Perspective and Further Reading

The rise of microprogramming and its effect on instruction set design and computer development is one of the more interesting interactions in the first few decades of the electronic computer. This story is the focus of the historical perspectives section on the CD.

5.13   Exercises

5.1 [6] <§5.2> Do we need combinational logic, sequential logic, or a combination of the two to implement each of the following:

a. multiplexor

b. comparator

c. incrementer/decrementer

d. barrel shifter

e. multiplier with shifters and adders

f. register

g. memory

h. ALU (the ones in single-cycle and multiple-cycle datapaths)

i. carry-lookahead adder

j. latch

k. general finite-state machine (FSM)

5.2 [10] <§5.4> Describe the effect that a single stuck-at-0 fault (i.e., regardless of what it should be, the signal is always 0) would have for the signals shown below, in the single-cycle datapath in Figure 5.17 on page 307. Which instructions, if any, will not work correctly? Explain why.

Consider each of the following faults separately:

    a.   RegWrite = 0

    b.   ALUOp0 = 0

    c.   ALUOp1 = 0

    d.   Branch = 0

    e.   MemRead = 0

    f.   MemWrite = 0

5.3 [5] <§5.4> This exercise is similar to Exercise 5.2, but this time consider stuck-at-1 faults (the signal is always 1).

5.4 [5] <§5.4> 🔘 **For More Practice:** Single-Cycle Datapaths with Floating Point

5.5 [5] <§5.4> 🔘 **For More Practice:** Single-Cycle Datapaths with Floating Point

5.6 [10] <§5.4> 🔘 **For More Practice:** Single-Cycle Datapaths with Floating Point

5.7 [2–3 months] <§§5.1–5.4> Using standard parts, build a machine that implements the single-cycle machine in this chapter.

5.8 [15] <§5.4> We wish to add the instruction jr (jump register) to the single-cycle datapath described in this chapter. Add any necessary datapaths and control signals to the single-cycle datapath of Figure 5.17 on page 307 and show the necessary additions to Figure 5.18 on page 308. You can photocopy these figures to make it faster to show the additions.

5.9 [10] <§5.4> This question is similar to Exercise 5.8 except that we wish to add the instruction sll (shift left logical), which is described in Section 2.5.

5.10 [15] <§5.4> This question is similar to Exercise 5.8 except that we wish to add the instruction lui (load upper immediate), which is described in Section 2.9.

5.11 [20] <§5.4> This question is similar to Exercise 5.8 except that we wish to add a variant of the lw (load word) instruction, which increments the index register after loading word from memory. This instruction (l_inc) corresponds to the following two instructions:

```
lw   $rt,L($rs)
addi $rs,$rs,4
```

5.12 [5] <§5.4> Explain why it is not possible to modify the single-cycle implementation to implement the load with increment instruction described in Exercise 5.11 without modifying the register file.

5.13 [7] <§5.4> Consider the single-cycle datapath in Figure 5.17 on page 307. A friend is proposing to modify this single-cycle datapath by eliminating the control signal MemtoReg. The multiplexor that has MemtoReg as an input will instead use either the ALUSrc or the MemRead control signal. Will your friend's modification work? Can one of the two signals (MemRead and ALUSrc) substitute for the other? Explain.

5.14 [10] <§5.4> MIPS chooses to simplify the structure of its instructions. The way we implement complex instructions through the use of MIPS instructions is to decompose such complex instructions into multiple simpler MIPS ones. Show how MIPS can implement the instruction swap $rs, $rt, which swaps the contents of registers $rs and $rt. Consider the case in which there is an available register that may be destroyed as well as the case in which no such register exists.

If the implementation of this instruction in hardware will increase the clock period of a single-instruction implementation by 10%, what percentage of swap operations in the instruction mix would recommend implementing it in hardware?

5.15 [5] <§5.4> 🔘 **For More Practice:** Effects of Faults in Control Multiplexors

5.16 [5] <§5.4> ⊙ **For More Practice:** Effects of Faults in Control Multiplexors

5.17 [5] <§5.5> ⊙ **For More Practice:** Effects of Faults in Control Multiplexors

5.18 [5] <§5.5> ⊙ **For More Practice:** Effects of Faults in Control Multiplexors

5.19 [15] <§5.4> ⊙ **For More Practice:** Adding Instructions to the Datapath

5.20 [15] <§5.4> ⊙ **For More Practice:** Adding Instructions to the Datapath

5.21 [8] <§5.4> ⊙ **For More Practice:** Adding Instructions to the Datapath

5.22 [15] <§5.4> ⊙ **For More Practice:** Adding Instructions to the Datapath

5.23 [5] <§5.4> ⊙ **For More Practice:** Adding Instructions to the Datapath

5.24 [15] <§5.4> ⊙ **For More Practice:** Modifying the Datapath and Control

5.25 [8] <§5.4> Repeat Exercise 5.14, but apply your solution to the instruction load with increment: `l_incr $rt,Address($rs)`.

5.26 [5] <§5.4> The concept of the "critical path," the longest possible path in the machine, was introduced in Section 5.4 on page 315. Based on your understanding of the single-cycle implementation, show which units can tolerate more delays (i.e., are not on the critical path), and which units can benefit from hardware optimization. Quantify your answers taking the same numbers presented on page 315 ("Example: Performance of Single-Cycle Machines").

5.27 [5] <§5.5> This exercise is similar to Exercise 5.2, but this time consider the effect that the stuck-at-0 faults would have on the *multiple-cycle* datapath in Figure 5.28. Consider each of the following faults:

    a.   RegWrite = 0

    b.   MemRead = 0

    c.   MemWrite = 0

    d.   IRWrite = 0

    e.   PCWrite = 0

    f.   PCWriteCond = 0

5.28 [5] <§5.5> This exercise is similar to Exercise 5.27, but this time consider stuck-at-1 faults (the signal is always 1).

5.29 [15] <§§5.4, 5.5> This exercise is similar to Exercise 5.13 but more general. Determine whether any of the control signals in the single-cycle implementation can be eliminated and replaced by another existing control signal, or its inverse. Note that such redundancy is there because we have a very small set of instructions at this point, and it will disappear (or be harder to find) when we implement a larger number of instructions.

5.30 [15] <§5.5> We wish to add the instruction `lui` (load upper immediate) described in Chapter 3 to the multicycle datapath described in this chapter. Use the same structure of the multicycle datapath of Figure 5.28 on page 323 and show the necessary modifications to the finite-state machine of Figure 5.37 on page 338. You may find it helpful to examine the execution steps shown on pages 325 through 329 and consider the steps that will need to be performed to execute the new instruction. How many cycles are required to implement this instruction?

5.31 [15] <§5.5> You are asked to modify the implementation of `lui` in Exercise 5.30 in order to cut the execution time by 1 cycle. Add any necessary datapaths and control signals to the multicycle datapath of Figure 5.28 on page 323. You can photocopy existing figures to make it easier to show your modifications. You have to maintain the assumption that you don't know what the instruction is before the end of state 1 (end of second cycle). Please explicitly state how many cycles it takes to execute the new instruction on your modified datapath and finite-state machine.

5.32 [20] <§5.5> This question is similar to Exercise 5.30 except that we wish to implement a new instruction `ldi` (load immediate) that loads a 32-bit immediate value from the memory location following the instruction address.

5.33 [15] <§5.5> Consider a change to the multiple-cycle implementation that alters the register file so that it has only one read port. Describe (via a diagram) any additional changes that will need to be made to the datapath in order to support this modification. Modify the finite-state machine to indicate how the instructions will work, given your new datapath.

5.34 [15] <§5.5> Two important parameters control the performance of a processor: cycle time and cycles per instruction. There is an enduring trade-off between these two parameters in the design process of microprocessors. While some designers prefer to increase the processor frequency at the expense of large CPI, other designers follow a different school of thought in which reducing the CPI comes at the expense of lower processor frequency.

Consider the following machines, and compare their performance using the SPEC CPUint 2000 data from Figure 3.26 on page 228.

M1: The multicycle datapath of Chapter 5 with a 4 GHz clock.

M2: A machine like the multicycle datapath of Chapter 5, except that register updates are done in the same clock cycle as a memory read or ALU operation. Thus, in Figure 5.37 on page 338, states 6 and 7 and states 3 and 4 are combined.

This machine has a 3.2 GHz clock, since the register update increases the length of the critical path.

M3: A machine like M2 except that effective address calculations are done in the same clock cycle as a memory access. Thus states 2, 3, and 4 can be combined, as can 2 and 5, as well as 6 and 7. This machine has a 2.8 GHz clock because of the long cycle created by combining address calculation and memory access.

Find out which of the machines is fastest. Are there instruction mixes that would make another machine faster, and if so, what are they?

5.35 [20] <§5.5> Your friends at C^3 (Creative Computer Corporation) have determined that the critical path that sets the clock cycle length of the multicycle datapath is memory access for loads and stores (not for fetching instructions). This has caused their newest implementation of the MIPS 30000 to run at a clock rate of 4.8 GHz rather than the target clock rate of 5.6 GHz. However, Clara at C^3 has a solution. If all the cycles that access memory are broken into two clock cycles, then the machine can run at its target clock rate.

Using the SPEC CPUint 2000 mixes shown in Chapter 3 (Figure 3.26 on page 228), determine how much faster the machine with the two-cycle memory accesses is compared with the 4.8 GHz machine with single-cycle memory access. Assume that all jumps and branches take the same number of cycles and that the set instructions and arithmetic-immediate instructions are implemented as R-type instructions. Would you consider the further step of splitting instruction fetch into two cycles if it would raise the clock rate to 6.4 GHz? Why?

5.36 [20] <§5.5> Suppose there were a MIPS instruction, called bcmp, that compares two blocks of words in two memory addresses. Assume that this instruction requires that the starting address of the first block is in register $t1 and the starting address of the second block is in $t2, and that the number of words to compare is in $t3 (which is $t3≥0). Assume the instruction can leave the result (the address of the first mismatch or zero if a complete match) in $t1 and/or $t2. Furthermore, assume that the values of these registers as well as registers $t4 and t5 can be destroyed in executing this instruction (so that the registers can be used as temporaries to execute the instruction).

Write the MIPS assembly language program to implement (emulate the behavior of) block compare. How many instructions will be executed to compare two 100-word blocks? Using the CPI of the instructions in the multicycle implementation, how many cycles are needed for the 100-word block compare?

5.37 [2–3 months] <§§5.1–5.5> Using standard parts, build a machine that implements the multicycle machine in this chapter.

5.38 [10] <§5.5> ⊙ **For More Practice:** Adding Instructions to the Datapath

5.39 [15] <§§5.1–5.5> ⊙ **For More Practice:** Comparing Processor Performance

5.40 [20] <§5.5> ⊙ **For More Practice:** Implementing Instructions in MIPS

5.41 [30] <§5.6> We wish to add the instruction eret (exception return) to the multicycle datapath described in this chapter. A primary task of the eret instruction is to reload the PC with the return address at which an exception, or error trap, occurred. Suppose that if the processor is serving an error trap, then the PC has to be loaded from a register ErrorPC. Otherwise the processor is serving an exception and the PC has to be loaded from EPC. Suppose that there is a bit in the cause register called trap to encode an error trap when it occurs and to save the PC in the ErrorPC register. Add any necessary datapaths and control signals to the multicycle datapath of Figure 5.39 on page 344 to accommodate the trap/exception call and return, and show the necessary modifications to the finite-state machine of Figure 5.40 on page 345 to implement the eret instruction. You can photocopy the figures to make it easier to show your modifications.

5.42 [6] <§5.6> Exceptions occur when a control flow change is required to handle an unexpected event in the processor. How can the cause and the instruction that caused the exception be represented by the hardware in a MIPS machine? Give two examples for conditions that a processor can handle by restarting execution of instructions after handling the exception, and two others for exceptions that lead to program termination.

5.43 [6] <§5.6> Exception detection is an important aspect of exception handling. Try to identify the cycle in which the following exceptions can be detected for the multicycle datapath in Figure 5.28 on page 323.

Consider the following exceptions:

a. Divide by zero exception (suppose we use the same ALU for division in one cycle, and that it is recognized by the rest of the control)

b. Overflow exception

c. Invalid instruction

d. External interrupt

e. Invalid instruction memory address

f. Invalid data memory address

5.44 [15] <§5.6> ⊙ **For More Practice:** Adding Instructions to the Datapath

5.45 [30] <§5.7> Microcode has been used to add more powerful instructions to an instruction set; let's explore the potential benefits of this approach. Devise a strategy for implementing the bcmp instruction described in Exercise 5.36 using the multicycle datapath and microcode. You will probably need to make some changes to the datapath in order to efficiently implement the bcmp instruction. Provide a description of your proposed changes and describe how the bcmp instruction will work. Are there any advantages that can be obtained by adding internal registers to the datapath to help support the bcmp instruction? Estimate the improvement in performance that you can achieve by implementing the instruction in hardware (as opposed to the software solution you obtained in Exercise 5.36) and explain where the performance increase comes from.

5.46 [30] <§5.7> ◉ **For More Practice:** Microcode

5.47 [5] <§5.7> ◉ **For More Practice:** Microcode

5.48 [30] <§5.7> ◉ **For More Practice:** Microcode

5.49 [30] <§5.8> Using the strategy you developed in Exercise 5.45, modify the MIPS microinstruction format described in ◉ Figure 5.7.1 and provide the complete microprogram for the bcmp instruction. Describe in detail how you extended the microcode so as to support the creation of more complex control structures (such as a loop) within the microcode. Has support for the bcmp instruction changed the size of the microcode? Will other instructions besides bcmp be affected by the change in the microinstruction format?

5.50 [5] <§5.8> A and B are registers defined through the following Verilog initialization code:

```
   reg A,B
   initial begin
      A = 1;
      B = 2;
   end
```

Analyze the following two segments of Verilog description lines, and compare the results of variables A and B, and the operation done in each example.

```
a)      always @(negedge clock) begin
        A = B;
        B = A;
     end
```

```
b)    always @(negedge clock) begin
          A <= B;
          B <= A;
      end
```

5.51 [15] <§§5.4, 5.8> Write the ALUControl module in combinational Verilog using the following form as the basis:

```
module ALUControl (ALUOp, FuncCode, ALUCtl);

              input ALUOp[1:0], FuncCode[5:0];

              output ALUCtl[3:0];

              . . . .

              endmodule
```

5.52 [1 week] <§§5.3, 5.4, 5.8> Using a hardware simulation language such as Verilog, implement a functional simulator for the single-cycle version. Build your simulator using an existing library of parts, if such a library is available. If the parts contain timing information, determine what the cycle time of your implementation will be.

5.53 [2–4 hours] <§§4.7, 5.5, 5.8, 5.9> Extend the multicycle Verilog description in ◉ Section 5.8 by adding an implementation of the unsigned MIPS multiply instruction; assume it is implemented using the MIPS ALU and a shift and add operation.

5.54 [2–4 hours] <§§4.7, 5.5, 5.8, 5.9> Extend the multicycle Verilog description in ◉ Section 5.8 by adding an implementation of the unsigned MIPS divide instruction; assume it is implemented using the MIPS ALU with a one-bit-at-a-time algorithm.

5.55 [1 week] <§§5.5, 5.8> Using a hardware simulation language such as Verilog, implement a functional simulator for a multicycle implementation of the design of a PowerPC processor. Build your simulator using an existing library of parts, if such a library is available. If the parts contain timing information, determine what the cycle time of your implementation will be.

Like MIPS, the PowerPC instructions are 32 bits each. Assume that your instruction set supports the following instruction formats:

R-type

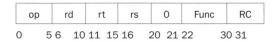

op	rd	rt	rs	0	Func	RC

0   5 6   10 11   15 16   20 21 22   30 31

Load-store & immediate

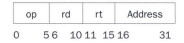

op	rd	rt	Address

0   5 6   10 11   15 16   31

Branch conditional

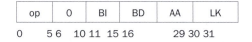

op	0	BI	BD	AA	LK

0   5 6   10 11   15 16   29 30 31

Jump

op	Address	AA	LK

0   5 6   10 11   15 16   29 30 31

RC-reg

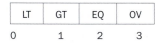

LT	GT	EQ	OV

0   1   2   3

Func field (22:30): Similar to MIPS, identifies function code.

RC bit(31): IF set (1), update the RC-reg control bits to reflect the results of the instruction (all R-type).

AA(30): 1 indicates that the given address is an absolute address; 0 indicates relative address.

LK: IF 1, updates LNKR (the link register), which can be used later for subroutine return implementation.

BI: Encodes the branch condition (e.g., beg -> BI = 2, blt -> BI = 0, etc.)

BD: Branch relative destination.

Your simplified PowerPC implementation should be able to implement the following instructions:

```
add:          add $Rd, $Rt, $Rs      ($Rd <- $Rt + $Rs)
              addi $Rd, $Rt, #n       ($Rd <- $Rt + #n)
subtract:     sub $Rd, $Rt, $Rs      ($Rd <- $Rt - $Rs)
              subi $Rd, $Rt, #n      ($Rd <- $Rt - #n)
load:        lw $Rd, Addr($Rt)       ($Rd <- Memory[$Rt + Addr])
store:       sw $Rd, Addr($Rt)       (Memory[$Rt + Addr] <- $Rd)
AND, OR:      and/or $Rd, $Rt, $Rs      ($Rd <- $Rt AND/OR $Rs)
              andi/ori $Rd, $Rt, #n       ($Rd <- $Rt AND/OR #n)
Jump:         jmp Addr  (PC <- Addr)
Branch conditional:  Beq Addr    (CR[2]==1? PC<- PC+BD : PC <-
    PC+4)
subroutine call:  jal Addr (LNKR <- PC+4; PC<- Addr)
subroutine restore: Ret     (PC <- LNKR)
```

5.56 [Discussion] <§§5.7, 5.10, 5.11> Hypothesis: If the first implementation of an architecture uses microprogramming, it affects the instruction set architecture. Why might this be true? Can you find an architecture that will probably always use microcode? Why? Which machines will never use microcode? Why? What control implementation do you think the architect had in mind when designing the instruction set architecture?

5.57 [Discussion] <§§5.7, 5.12> Wilkes invented microprogramming in large part to simplify construction of control. Since 1980, there has been an explosion of computer-aided design software whose goal is also to simplify construction of control. This has made control design much easier. Can you find evidence, based either on the tools or on real designs, that supports or refutes this hypothesis?

5.58 [Discussion] <§5.12> The MIPS instructions and the MIPS microinstructions have many similarities. What would make it difficult for a compiler to produce MIPS microcode rather than macrocode? What changes to the microarchitecture would make the microcode more useful for this application?

Answers to Check Yourself

§5.1, page 289: 3.

§5.2, page 292: false.

§5.3, page 299: A.

§5.4, page 318: Yes, MemtoReg and RegDst are inverses of one another. Yes, simply use the other signal and flip the order of the inputs to the multiplexor!

§5.5, page 340: 1. False. 2. Maybe: If the signal PCSource[0] is always set to zero when it is a don't care (which is most states), then it is identical to PCWriteCond.

§5.6, page 346: No, since the value of 11, which was formerly unused, is now used!

§ ⊙ 5.7, page 5.7-13: 4 tables with 55 entries (don't forget the primary dispatch!)

§5.8, page 5.8-6: 1. 0, 1, 1, X, 0. 2. No, since state is not assigned on every path.

Computers in the Real World

Empowering the Disabled

Problem: To overcome the obstacles faced by disabled people.

Solution: Use robotics, sensors, and computer control to replace or supplement damaged limbs and organs.

Firefighter Ken Whitten (right) has an artificial arm that is equipped with such computer technology. Sensors in latex fingers instantly register hot and cold, and an electronic interface in his artificial limb stimulates the nerve endings in his upper arm, which then pass the information to his brain. The $3000 system allows his hand to feel pressure and weight, so for the first time since losing his arms in a 1986 accident, he can pick up a can of soda without crushing it or having it slip through his fingers. The main enabling device is an electronic interface that can transmit signals to nerve endings in Whitten's upper arm, which then pass this information to his brain.

Harvey Fishman and Mark Peterman of Stanford have taken steps toward information technology that might someday treat age-related blindness. Their approach is to

Firefighter Ken Whitten proudly displays his new bionic arm.

bypass the photoreceptors of the eye with a signal from a digital camera that connects directly to the visual system. They are developing a neural interface to the visual system called the artificial synapse chip. The challenge is to turn electrical signals into the chemicals that cells use to communicate. This chip is attached to cells, and from the cell's perspective the artificial synapse is simply a hole in the silicon. This hole is connected to a reservoir of neurotransmitters. When an electric field is applied to the chip, the neurotransmitter is pumped through the hole, stimulating nearby cells. In 2003 they have created four artificial synapses on a chip one centimeter on a side.

Although this work is in its early stages, the potential is not limited to eye problems. According to Fishman, "Anywhere there's a severing of a nerve connection, there's a potential for us to reconnect it."

To learn more, see these references on the ⊙ library:

- Rick Smolan and Jennifer Erwitt, *One Digital Day: How the Microchip Is Changing Our World*, Times Publishing, 1998

- Peterman et al., "The artificial synapse chip: A flexible retinal interface based on directed retinal cell growth and neurotransmitter stimulation," *Artificial Organs: 27(11)*, November 18, 2003

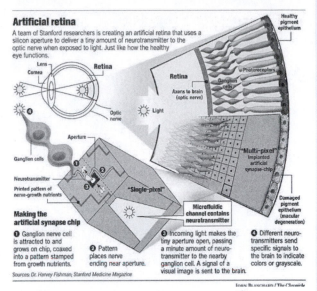

Artificial retina using artificial synapse chips. From *The San Francisco Chronicle*, January 5, 2004.

6

Enhancing
Performance
with Pipelining

Thus times do shift,
each thing his turn does hold;
New things succeed,
as former things grow old.

Robert Herrick
Hesperides: Ceremonies for Christmas Eve, 1648

The Five Classic Components of a Computer

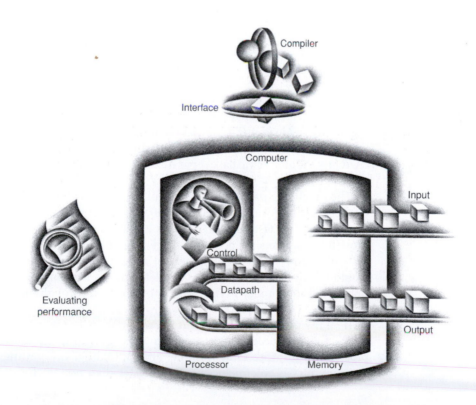

pipelining An implementation technique in which multiple instructions are overlapped in execution, much like an assembly line.

6.1 An Overview of Pipelining

Pipelining is an implementation technique in which multiple instructions are overlapped in execution. Today, pipelining is key to making processors fast.

This section relies heavily on one analogy to give an overview of the pipelining terms and issues. If you are interested in just the big picture, you should concentrate on this section and then skip to Sections 6.9 and 6.10 to see an introduction to the advanced pipelining techniques used in recent processors such as the Pentium III and 4. If you are interested in exploring the anatomy of a pipelined computer, this section is a good introduction to Sections 6.2 through 6.8.

Anyone who has done a lot of laundry has intuitively used pipelining. The *nonpipelined* approach to laundry would be

1. Place one dirty load of clothes in the washer.

2. When the washer is finished, place the wet load in the dryer.

3. When the dryer is finished, place the dry load on a table and fold.

4. When folding is finished, ask your roommate to put the clothes away.

When your roommate is done, then start over with the next dirty load.

The *pipelined* approach takes much less time, as Figure 6.1 shows. As soon as the washer is finished with the first load and placed in the dryer, you load the washer with the second dirty load. When the first load is dry, you place it on the table to start folding, move the wet load to the dryer, and the next dirty load into the washer. Next you have your roommate put the first load away, you start folding the second load, the dryer has the third load, and you put the fourth load into the washer. At this point all steps—called *stages* in pipelining—are operating concurrently. As long as we have separate resources for each stage, we can pipeline the tasks.

The pipelining paradox is that the time from placing a single dirty sock in the washer until it is dried, folded, and put away is not shorter for pipelining; the reason pipelining is faster for many loads is that everything is working in parallel, so more loads are finished per hour. Pipelining improves throughput of our laundry system without improving the time to complete a single load. Hence, pipelining would not decrease the time to complete one load of laundry, but when we have many loads of laundry to do, the improvement in throughput decreases the total time to complete the work.

If all the stages take about the same amount of time and there is enough work to do, then the speedup due to pipelining is equal to the number of stages in the pipeline, in this case four: washing, drying, folding, and putting away. So, pipelined laundry is potentially four times faster than nonpipelined: 20 loads would

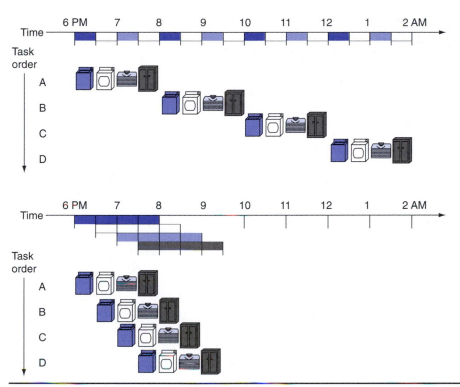

FIGURE 6.1 The laundry analogy for pipelining. Ann, Brian, Cathy, and Don each have dirty clothes to be washed, dried, folded, and put away. The washer, dryer, "folder," and "storer" each take 30 minutes for their task. Sequential laundry takes 8 hours for four loads of wash, while pipelined laundry takes just 3.5 hours. We show the pipeline stage of different loads over time by showing copies of the four resources on this two-dimensional time line, but we really have just one of each resource.

take about 5 times as long as 1 load, while 20 loads of sequential laundry takes 20 times as long as 1 load. It's only 2.3 times faster in Figure 6.1 because we only show 4 loads. Notice that at the beginning and end of the workload in the pipelined version in Figure 6.1, the pipeline is not completely full; this start-up and wind-down affects performance when the number of tasks is not large compared to the number of stages in the pipeline. If the number of loads is much larger than 4, then the stages will be full most of the time and the increase in throughput will be very close to 4.

The same principles apply to processors where we pipeline instruction execution. MIPS instructions classically take five steps:

1. Fetch instruction from memory.

2. Read registers while decoding the instruction. The format of MIPS instructions allows reading and decoding to occur simultaneously.

3. Execute the operation or calculate an address.

4. Access an operand in data memory.

5. Write the result into a register.

Hence, the MIPS pipeline we explore in this chapter has five stages. The following example shows that pipelining speeds up instruction execution just as it speeds up the laundry.

EXAMPLE

Single-Cycle versus Pipelined Performance

To make this discussion concrete, let's create a pipeline. In this example, and in the rest of this chapter, we limit our attention to eight instructions: load word (lw), store word (sw), add (add), subtract (sub), and (and), or (or), set less than (slt), and branch on equal (beq).

Compare the average time between instructions of a single-cycle implementation, in which all instructions take 1 clock cycle, to a pipelined implementation. The operation times for the major functional units in this example are 200 ps for memory access, 200 ps for ALU operation, and 100 ps for register file read or write. As we said in Chapter 5, in the single-cycle model every instruction takes exactly 1 clock cycle, so the clock cycle must be stretched to accommodate the slowest instruction.

ANSWER

Figure 6.2 shows the time required for each of the eight instructions. The single-cycle design must allow for the slowest instruction—in Figure 6.2 it is lw—so the time required for every instruction is 800 ps. Similarly to Figure 6.1, Figure 6.3 compares nonpipelined and pipelined execution of three load word instructions. Thus, the time between the first and fourth instructions in the nonpipelined design is 3 × 800 ns or 2400 ps.

All the pipeline stages take a single clock cycle, so the clock cycle must be long enough to accommodate the slowest operation. Just as the single-cycle design must take the worst-case clock cycle of 800 ps even though some instructions can be as fast as 500 ps, the pipelined execution clock cycle must have the worst-case clock cycle of 200 ps even though some stages take only 100 ps. Pipelining still offers a fourfold performance improvement: the time between the first and fourth instructions is 3 × 200 ps or 600 ps.

Instruction class	Instruction fetch	Register read	ALU operation	Data access	Register write	Total time
Load word (lw)	200 ps	100 ps	200 ps	200 ps	100 ps	800 ps
Store word (sw)	200 ps	100 ps	200 ps	200 ps		700 ps
R-format (add, sub, and, or, slt)	200 ps	100 ps	200 ps		100 ps	600 ps
Branch (beq)	200 ps	100 ps	200 ps			500 ps

FIGURE 6.2 Total time for each instruction calculated from the time for each component. This calculation assumes that the multiplexors, control unit, PC accesses, and sign extension unit have no delay.

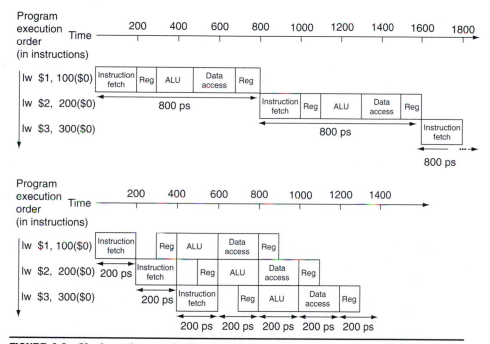

FIGURE 6.3 Single-cycle, nonpipelined execution in top versus pipelined execution in bottom. Both use the same hardware components, whose time is listed in Figure 6.2. In this case we see a fourfold speedup on average time between instructions, from 800 ps down to 200 ps. Compare this figure to Figure 6.1. For the laundry, we assumed all stages were equal. If the dryer were slowest, then the dryer stage would set the stage time. The computer pipeline stage times are limited by the slowest resource, either the ALU operation or the memory access. We assume the write to the register file occurs in the first half of the clock cycle and the read from the register file occurs in the second half. We use this assumption throughout this chapter.

We can turn the pipelining speedup discussion above into a formula. If the stages are perfectly balanced, then the time between instructions on the pipelined processor—assuming ideal conditions—is equal to

$$\text{Time between instructions}_{\text{pipelined}} = \frac{\text{Time between instructions}_{\text{nonpipelined}}}{\text{Number of pipe stages}}$$

Under ideal conditions and with a large number of instructions, the speedup from pipelining is approximately equal to the number of pipe stages; a five-stage pipeline is nearly five times faster.

The formula suggests that a five-stage pipeline should offer nearly a fivefold improvement over the 800 ps nonpipelined time, or a 160 ps clock cycle. The example shows, however, that the stages may be imperfectly balanced. In addition, pipelining involves some overhead, the source of which will be more clear shortly. Thus, the time per instruction in the pipelined processor will exceed the minimum possible, and speedup will be less than the number of pipeline stages.

Moreover, even our claim of fourfold improvement for our example is not reflected in the total execution time for the three instructions: it's 1400 ps versus 2400 ps. Of course, this is because the number of instructions is not large. What would happen if we increased the number of instructions? We could extend the previous figures to 1,000,003 instructions. We would add 1,000,000 instructions in the pipelined example; each instruction adds 200 ps to the total execution time. The total execution time would be 1,000,000 × 200 ps + 1400 ps, or 200,001,400 ps. In the nonpipelined example, we would add 1,0000,000 instructions, each taking 800 ps, so total execution time would be 1,000,000 × 800 ps + 2400 ps, or 800,002,400 ps. Under these ideal conditions, the ratio of total execution times for real programs on nonpipelined to pipelined processors is close to the ratio of times between instructions:

$$\frac{800{,}002{,}400 \text{ ps}}{200{,}001{,}400 \text{ ps}} \approx 4.00 \approx \frac{800 \text{ ps}}{200 \text{ ps}}$$

Pipelining improves performance by *increasing instruction throughput, as opposed to decreasing the execution time of an individual instruction,* but instruction throughput is the important metric because real programs execute billions of instructions.

Designing Instruction Sets for Pipelining

Even with this simple explanation of pipelining, we can get insight into the design of the MIPS instruction set, which was designed for pipelined execution.

First, all MIPS instructions are the same length. This restriction makes it much easier to fetch instructions in the first pipeline stage and to decode them in the second stage. In an instruction set like the IA-32, where instructions vary from 1 byte to 17 bytes, pipelining is considerably more challenging. As we saw in Chapter 5, all recent implementations of the IA-32 architecture actually translate IA-32 instructions into simple micro-operations that look like MIPS instructions. As we will see in Section 6.10, the Pentium 4 actually pipelines the micro-operations rather than the native IA-32 instructions!

Second, MIPS has only a few instruction formats, with the source register fields being located in the same place in each instruction. This symmetry means that the second stage can begin reading the register file at the same time that the hardware is determining what type of instruction was fetched. If MIPS instruction formats were not symmetric, we would need to split stage 2, resulting in six pipeline stages. We will shortly see the downside of longer pipelines.

Third, memory operands only appear in loads or stores in MIPS. This restriction means we can use the execute stage to calculate the memory address and then access memory in the following stage. If we could operate on the operands in memory, as in the IA-32, stages 3 and 4 would expand to an address stage, memory stage, and then execute stage.

Fourth, as discussed in Chapter 2, operands must be aligned in memory. Hence, we need not worry about a single data transfer instruction requiring two data memory accesses; the requested data can be transferred between processor and memory in a single pipeline stage.

Pipeline Hazards

There are situations in pipelining when the next instruction cannot execute in the following clock cycle. These events are called *hazards*, and there are three different types.

Structural Hazards

The first hazard is called a **structural hazard**. It means that the hardware cannot support the combination of instructions that we want to execute in the same clock cycle. A structural hazard in the laundry room would occur if we used a washer-dryer combination instead of a separate washer and dryer, or if our roommate was busy doing something else and wouldn't put clothes away. Our carefully scheduled pipeline plans would then be foiled.

As we said above, the MIPS instruction set was designed to be pipelined, making it fairly easy for designers to avoid structural hazards when designing a pipeline. Suppose, however, that we had a single memory instead of two memories. If the pipeline in Figure 6.3 had a fourth instruction, we would see that in the same clock cycle the first instruction is accessing data from memory while the fourth instruction is fetching an instruction from that same memory. Without two memories, our pipeline could have a structural hazard.

structural hazard An occurrence in which a planned instruction cannot execute in the proper clock cycle because the hardware cannot support the combination of instructions that are set to execute in the given clock cycle.

data hazard Also called pipeline data hazard. An occurrence in which a planned instruction cannot execute in the proper clock cycle because data that is needed to execute the instruction is not yet available.

Data Hazards

Data hazards occur when the pipeline must be stalled because one step must wait for another to complete. Suppose you found a sock at the folding station for which no match existed. One possible strategy is to run down to your room and search through your clothes bureau to see if you can find the match. Obviously, while you are doing the search, loads that have completed drying and are ready to fold and those that have finished washing and are ready to dry must wait.

In a computer pipeline, data hazards arise from the dependence of one instruction on an earlier one that is still in the pipeline (a relationship that does not really exist when doing laundry). For example, suppose we have an add instruction followed immediately by a subtract instruction that uses the sum ($s0):

```
add     $s0, $t0, $t1
sub     $t2, $s0, $t3
```

Without intervention, a data hazard could severely stall the pipeline. The add instruction doesn't write its result until the fifth stage, meaning that we would have to add three bubbles to the pipeline.

Although we could try to rely on compilers to remove all such hazards, the results would not be satisfactory. These dependences happen just too often and the delay is just too long to expect the compiler to rescue us from this dilemma.

forwarding Also called **bypassing**. A method of resolving a data hazard by retrieving the missing data element from internal buffers rather than waiting for it to arrive from programmer-visible registers or memory.

The primary solution is based on the observation that we don't need to wait for the instruction to complete before trying to resolve the data hazard. For the code sequence above, as soon as the ALU creates the sum for the add, we can supply it as an input for the subtract. Adding extra hardware to retrieve the missing item early from the internal resources is called **forwarding** or **bypassing**.

EXAMPLE

Forwarding with Two Instructions

For the two instructions above, show what pipeline stages would be connected by forwarding. Use the drawing in Figure 6.4 to represent the datapath during the five stages of the pipeline. Align a copy of the datapath for each instruction, similar to the laundry pipeline in Figure 6.1.

ANSWER

Figure 6.5 shows the connection to forward the value in $s0 after the execution stage of the add instruction as input to the execution stage of the sub instruction.

In this graphical representation of events, forwarding paths are valid only if the destination stage is later in time than the source stage. For example, there cannot be a valid forwarding path from the output of the memory access stage in the first

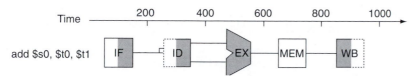

FIGURE 6.4   Graphical representation of the instruction pipeline, similar in spirit to the laundry pipeline in Figure 6.1 on page 371. Here we use symbols representing the physical resources with the abbreviations for pipeline stages used throughout the chapter. The symbols for the five stages: *IF* for the instruction fetch stage, with the box representing instruction memory; *ID* for the instruction decode/register file read stage, with the drawing showing the register file being read; *EX* for the execution stage, with the drawing representing the ALU; *MEM* for the memory access stage, with the box representing data memory; and *WB* for the write back stage, with the drawing showing the register file being written. The shading indicates the element is used by the instruction. Hence, MEM has a white background because add does not access the data memory. Shading on the right half of the register file or memory means the element is read in that stage, and shading of the left half means it is written in that stage. Hence the right half of ID is shaded in the second stage because the register file is read, and the left half of WB is shaded in the fifth stage because the register file is written.

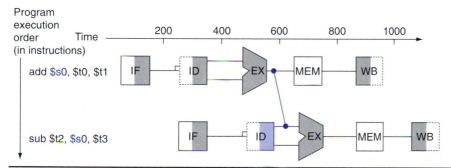

FIGURE 6.5   Graphical representation of forwarding. The connection shows the forwarding path from the output of the EX stage of add to the input of the EX stage for sub, replacing the value from register $s0 read in the second stage of sub.

instruction to the input of the execution stage of the following, since that would mean going backwards in time.

Forwarding works very well and is described in detail in Section 6.4. It cannot prevent all pipeline stalls, however. For example, suppose the first instruction was a load of $s0 instead of an add. As we can imagine from looking at Figure 6.5, the desired data would be available only *after* the fourth stage of the first instruction in the dependence, which is too late for the *input* of the third stage of sub. Hence, even with forwarding, we would have to stall one stage for a **load-use data hazard**, as Figure 6.6 shows. This figure shows an important pipeline concept, officially called a **pipeline stall**, but often given the nickname *bubble*. We shall see stalls elsewhere in the pipeline. Section 6.5 shows how we can handle hard cases like these, using either hardware detection and stalls or software that treats the load delay like a branch delay.

load-use data hazard A specific form of data hazard in which the data requested by a load instruction has not yet become available when it is requested.

pipeline stall Also called bubble. A stall initiated in order to resolve a hazard.

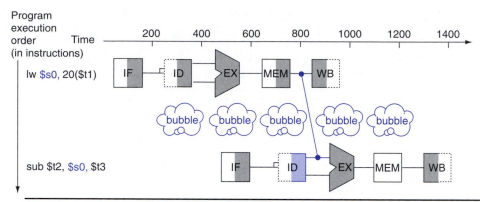

FIGURE 6.6   We need a stall even with forwarding when an R-format instruction following a load tries to use the data. Without the stall, the path from memory access stage output to execution stage input would be going backwards in time, which is impossible. This figure is actually a simplification, since we cannot know until after the subtract instruction is fetched and decoded whether or not a stall will be necessary. Section 6.5 shows the details of what really happens in the case of a hazard.

EXAMPLE

Reordering Code to Avoid Pipeline Stalls

Consider the following code segment in C:

```
A = B + E;
C = B + F;
```

Here is the generated MIPS code for this segment, assuming all variables are in memory and are addressable as offsets from $t0:

```
lw      $t1, 0($t0)
lw      $t2, 4($t0)
add     $t3, $t1,$t2
sw      $t3, 12($t0)
lw      $t4, 8($t0)
add     $t5, $t1,$t4
sw      $t5, 16($t0)
```

Find the hazards in the following code segment and reorder the instructions to avoid any pipeline stalls.

Both `add` instructions have a hazard because of their respective dependence on the immediately preceding `lw` instruction. Notice that bypassing eliminates several other potential hazards including the dependence of the first `add` on the first `lw` and any hazards for store instructions. Moving up the third `lw` instruction eliminates both hazards:

```
lw      $t1, 0($t0)
lw      $t2, 4($t0)
lw      $t4, 8($t0)
add     $t3, $t1,$t2
sw      $t3, 12($t0)
add     $t5, $t1,$t4
sw      $t5, 16($t0)
```

On a pipelined processor with forwarding, the reordered sequence will complete in two fewer cycles than the original version.

ANSWER

Forwarding yields another insight into the MIPS architecture, in addition to the four mentioned on pages 374–375. Each MIPS instruction writes at most one result and does so near the end of the pipeline. Forwarding is harder if there are multiple results to forward per instruction or they need to write a result early on in instruction execution.

Elaboration: The name "forwarding" comes from the idea that the result is passed forward from an earlier instruction to a later instruction. "Bypassing" comes from passing the result by the register file to the desired unit.

Control Hazards

The third type of hazard is called a **control hazard**, arising from the need to make a decision based on the results of one instruction while others are executing.

Suppose our laundry crew was given the happy task of cleaning the uniforms of a football team. Given how filthy the laundry is, we need to determine whether the detergent and water temperature setting we select is strong enough to get the uniforms clean but not so strong that the uniforms wear out sooner. In our laundry pipeline, we have to wait until the second stage to examine the dry uniform to see if we need to change the washer setup or not. What to do?

Here is the first of two solutions to control hazards in the laundry room and its computer equivalent.

Stall: Just operate sequentially until the first batch is dry and then repeat until you have the right formula. This conservative option certainly works, but it is slow.

control hazard Also called **branch hazard**. An occurrence in which the proper instruction cannot execute in the proper clock cycle because the instruction that was fetched is not the one that is needed; that is, the flow of instruction addresses is not what the pipeline expected.

The equivalent decision task in a computer is the branch instruction. Notice that we must begin fetching the instruction following the branch on the very next clock cycle. But, the pipeline cannot possibly know what the next instruction should be, since it *only just received* the branch instruction from memory! Just as with laundry, one possible solution is to stall immediately after we fetch a branch, waiting until the pipeline determines the outcome of the branch and knows what instruction address to fetch from.

Let's assume that we put in enough extra hardware so that we can test registers, calculate the branch address, and update the PC during the second stage of the pipeline (see Section 6.6 for details). Even with this extra hardware, the pipeline involving conditional branches would look like Figure 6.7. The `lw` instruction, executed if the branch fails, is stalled one extra 200 ps clock cycle before starting.

Performance of "Stall on Branch"

EXAMPLE

Estimate the impact on the clock cycles per instruction (CPI) of stalling on branches. Assume all other instructions have a CPI of 1.

ANSWER

Figure 3.26 on page 228 in Chapter 3 shows that branches are 13% of the instructions executed in SPECint2000. Since other instructions run have a CPI of 1 and branches took one extra clock cycle for the stall, then we would see a CPI of 1.13 and hence a slowdown of 1.13 versus the ideal case. Notice that this includes only branches and that jumps might also incur a stall.

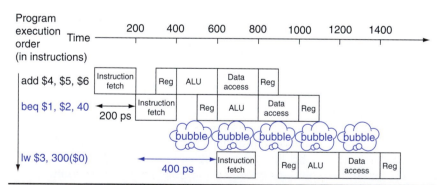

FIGURE 6.7   Pipeline showing stalling on every conditional branch as solution to control hazards. There is a one-stage pipeline stall, or bubble, after the branch. In reality, the process of creating a stall is slightly more complicated, as we will see in Section 6.6. The effect on performance, however, is the same as would occur if a bubble were inserted.

If we cannot resolve the branch in the second stage, as is often the case for longer pipelines, then we'd see an even larger slowdown if we stall on branches. The cost of this option is too high for most computers to use and motivates a second solution to the control hazard:

Predict: If you're pretty sure you have the right formula to wash uniforms, then just predict that it will work and wash the second load while waiting for the first load to dry. This option does not slow down the pipeline when you are correct. When you are wrong, however, you need to redo the load that was washed while guessing the decision.

Computers do indeed use *prediction* to handle branches. One simple approach is to always predict that branches will be **untaken**. When you're right, the pipeline proceeds at full speed. Only when branches are taken does the pipeline stall. Figure 6.8 shows such an example.

untaken branch One that falls through to the successive instruction. A taken branch is one that causes transfer to the branch target.

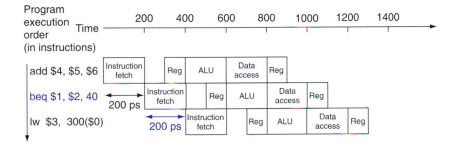

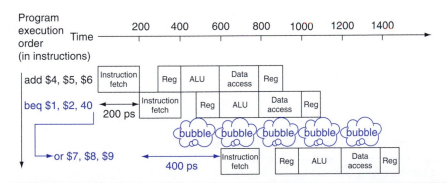

FIGURE 6.8   Predicting that branches are not taken as a solution to control hazard. The top drawing shows the pipeline when the branch is not taken. The bottom drawing shows the pipeline when the branch is taken. As we noted in Figure 6.7, the insertion of a bubble in this fashion simplifies what actually happens, at least during the first clock cycle immediately following the branch. Section 6.6 will reveal the details.

branch prediction A method of resolving a branch hazard that assumes a given outcome for the branch and proceeds from that assumption rather than waiting to ascertain the actual outcome.

A more sophisticated version of **branch prediction** would have some branches predicted as taken and some as untaken. In our analogy, the dark or home uniforms might take one formula while the light or road uniforms might take another. As a computer example, at the bottom of loops are branches that jump back to the top of the loop. Since they are likely to be taken and they branch backwards, we could always predict taken for branches that jump to an earlier address.

Such rigid approaches to branch prediction rely on stereotypical behavior and don't account for the individuality of a specific branch instruction. *Dynamic* hardware predictors, in stark contrast, make their guesses depending on the behavior of each branch and may change predictions for a branch over the life of a program. Following our analogy, in dynamic prediction a person would look at how dirty the uniform was and guess at the formula, adjusting the next guess depending on the success of recent guesses. One popular approach to dynamic prediction of branches is keeping a history for each branch as taken or untaken, and then using the recent past behavior to predict the future. As we will see later, the amount and type of history kept have become extensive, with the result being that dynamic branch predictors can correctly predict branches with over 90% accuracy (see Section 6.6). When the guess is wrong, the pipeline control must ensure that the instructions following the wrongly guessed branch have no effect and must restart the pipeline from the proper branch address. In our laundry analogy, we must stop taking new loads so that we can restart the load that we incorrectly predicted.

As in the case of all other solutions to control hazards, longer pipelines exacerbate the problem, in this case by raising the cost of misprediction. Solutions to control hazards are described in more detail in Section 6.6.

Elaboration: There is a third approach to the control hazard, called *delayed decision*. In our analogy, whenever you are going to make such a decision about laundry, just place a load of nonfootball clothes in the washer while waiting for football uniforms to dry. As long as you have enough dirty clothes that are not affected by the test, this solution works fine.

Called the *delayed branch* in computers, this is the solution actually used by the MIPS architecture. The delayed branch always executes the next sequential instruction, with the branch taking place *after* that one instruction delay. It is hidden from the MIPS assembly language programmer because the assembler can automatically arrange the instructions to get the branch behavior desired by the programmer. MIPS software will place an instruction immediately after the delayed branch instruction that is not affected by the branch, and a taken branch changes the address of the instruction that *follows* this safe instruction. In our example, the add instruction before the branch in Figure 6.7 does not affect the branch and can be moved after the branch to fully hide the branch delay. Since delayed branches are useful when the branches are short, no processor uses a delayed branch of more than 1 cycle. For longer branch delays, hardware-based branch prediction is usually used.

Pipeline Overview Summary

Pipelining is a technique that exploits parallelism among the instructions in a sequential instruction stream. It has the substantial advantage that, unlike some speedup techniques (see ⊙ **Chapter 9**), it is fundamentally invisible to the programmer.

In the next sections of this chapter, we cover the concept of pipelining using the MIPS instruction subset lw, sw, add, sub, and, or, slt, and beq (same as Chapter 5) and a simplified version of its pipeline. We then look at the problems that pipelining introduces and the performance attainable under typical situations.

If you wish to focus more on the software and the performance implications of pipelining, you now have sufficient background to skip to Section 6.9. Section 6.9 introduces advanced pipelining concepts, such as superscalar and dynamic scheduling, and Section 6.10 examines the pipeline of the Pentium 4 microprocessor.

Alternatively, if you are interested in understanding how pipelining is implemented and the challenges of dealing with hazards, you can proceed to examine the design of a pipelined datapath, explained in Section 6.2, and the basic control, explained in Section 6.3. You can then use this understanding to explore the implementation of forwarding in Section 6.4, and the implementation of stalls in Section 6.5. You can then read Section 6.6 to learn more about solutions to branch hazards, and then see how exceptions are handled in Section 6.8.

> Pipelining increases the number of simultaneously executing instructions and the rate at which instructions are started and completed. Pipelining does not reduce the time it takes to complete an individual instruction, also called the latency. For example, the five-stage pipeline still takes 5 clock cycles for the instruction to complete. In the terms used in Chapter 4, pipelining improves instruction *throughput* rather than individual instruction *execution time* or *latency*.
>
> Instruction sets can either simplify or make life harder for pipeline designers, who must already cope with structural, control, and data hazards. Branch prediction, forwarding, and stalls help make a computer fast while still getting the right answers.

The BIG Picture

latency (pipeline) The number of stages in a pipeline or the number of stages between two instructions during execution.

Outside of the memory system, the effective operation of the pipeline is usually the most important factor in determining the CPI of the processor and hence its performance. As we will see in Section 6.9, understanding the performance of a modern multiple-issue pipelined processor is complex and requires understanding more than just the issues that arise in a simple pipelined processor. Nonetheless, structural, data, and control hazards remain important in both simple pipelines and more sophisticated ones.

For modern pipelines, structural hazards usually revolve around the floating-point unit, which may not be fully pipelined, while control hazards are usually more of a problem in integer programs, which tend to have higher branch frequencies as well as less predictable branches. Data hazards can be performance bottlenecks in both integer and floating-point programs. Often it is easier to deal with data hazards in floating-point programs because the lower branch frequency and more regular access patterns allow the compiler to try to schedule instructions to avoid hazards. It is more difficult to perform such optimizations in integer programs that have less regular access involving more use of pointers. As we will see in Section 6.9, there are more ambitious compiler and hardware techniques for reducing data dependences through scheduling.

**Check
Yourself**

For each code sequence below, state whether it must stall, can avoid stalls using only forwarding, or can execute without stalling or forwarding.

Sequence 1	Sequence 2	Sequence 3

`lw    $t0,0($t0)`
`add   $t1,$t0,$t0`
	`add   $t1,$t0,$t0`
	`addi  $t2,$t0,#5`
	`addi  $t4,$t1,#5`
		`addi  $t1,$t0,#1`
		`addi  $t2,$t0,#2`
		`addi  $t3,$t0,#2`
		`addi  $t3,$t0,#4`
		`addi  $t5,$t0,#5`

*There is less in this than
meets the eye.*

Tallulah Bankhead, remark to
Alexander Wollcott, 1922

6.2   A Pipelined Datapath

Figure 6.9 shows the single-cycle datapath from Chapter 5. The division of an instruction into five stages means a five-stage pipeline, which in turn means that up to five instructions will be in execution during any single clock cycle. Thus, we

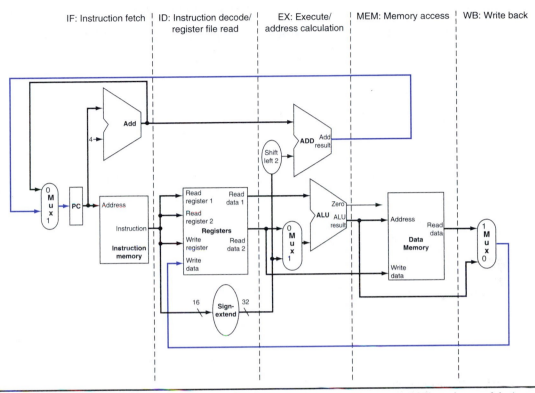

IF: Instruction fetch | ID: Instruction decode/register file read | EX: Execute/address calculation | MEM: Memory access | WB: Write back

FIGURE 6.9 The single-cycle datapath from Chapter 5 (similar to Figure 5.17 on page 307). Each step of the instruction can be mapped onto the datapath from left to right. The only exceptions are the update of the PC and the write-back step, shown in color, which sends either the ALU result or the data from memory to the left to be written into the register file. (Normally we use color lines for control, but these are data lines.)

must separate the datapath into five pieces, with each piece named corresponding to a stage of instruction execution:

1. IF: Instruction fetch

2. ID: Instruction decode and register file read

3. EX: Execution or address calculation

4. MEM: Data memory access

5. WB: Write back

In Figure 6.9, these five components correspond roughly to the way the datapath is drawn; instructions and data move generally from left to right through the five stages as they complete execution. Going back to our laundry analogy, clothes get cleaner, drier, and more organized as they move through the line, and they never move backwards.

There are, however, two exceptions to this left-to-right flow of instructions:

■ The write-back stage, which places the result back into the register file in the middle of the datapath

■ The selection of the next value of the PC, choosing between the incremented PC and the branch address from the MEM stage

Data flowing from right to left does not affect the current instruction; only later instructions in the pipeline are influenced by these reverse data movements. Note that the first right-to-left arrow can lead to data hazards and the second leads to control hazards.

One way to show what happens in pipelined execution is to pretend that each instruction has its own datapath, and then to place these datapaths on a time line to show their relationship. Figure 6.10 shows the execution of the instructions in Figure 6.3 by displaying their private datapaths on a common time line. We use a stylized version of the datapath in Figure 6.9 to show the relationships in Figure 6.10.

Figure 6.10 seems to suggest that three instructions need three datapaths. In Chapter 5, we added registers to hold data so that portions of the datapath could be shared during instruction execution; we use the same technique here to share the multiple datapaths. For example, as Figure 6.10 shows, the instruction memory is used during only one of the five stages of an instruction, allowing it to be shared by other instructions during the other four stages.

To retain the value of an individual instruction for its other four stages, the value read from instruction memory must be saved in a register. Similar arguments apply to every pipeline stage, so we must place registers wherever there are dividing lines between stages in Figure 6.9. This change is similar to the registers added in Chapter 5 when we went from a single-cycle to a multicycle datapath. Returning to our laundry analogy, we might have a basket between each pair of stages to hold the clothes for the next step.

Figure 6.11 shows the pipelined datapath with the pipeline registers highlighted. All instructions advance during each clock cycle from one pipeline register to the next. The registers are named for the two stages separated by that register. For example, the pipeline register between the IF and ID stages is called IF/ID.

Notice that there is no pipeline register at the end of the write-back stage. All instructions must update some state in the processor—the register file, memory, or the PC—so a separate pipeline register is redundant to the state that is updated. For example, a load instruction will place its result in 1 of the 32 registers, and any later instruction that needs that data will simply read the appropriate register.

Of course, every instruction updates the PC, whether by incrementing it or by setting it to a branch destination address. The PC can be thought of as a pipeline register: one that feeds the IF stage of the pipeline. Unlike the shaded pipeline reg-

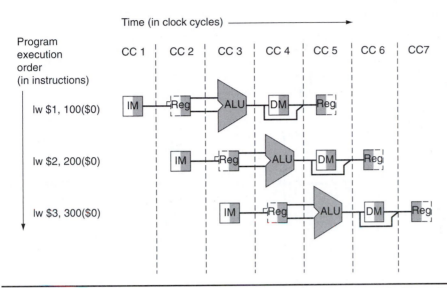

FIGURE 6.10 Instructions being executed using the single-cycle datapath in Figure 6.9, assuming pipelined execution. Similar to Figures 6.4 through 6.6, this figure pretends that each instruction has its own datapath, and shades each portion according to use. Unlike those figures, each stage is labeled by the physical resource used in that stage, corresponding to the portions of the datapath in Figure 6.9. *IM* represents the instruction memory and the PC in the instruction fetch stage, *Reg* stands for the register file and sign extender in the instruction decode/register file read stage (ID), and so on. To maintain proper time order, this stylized datapath breaks the register file into two logical parts: registers read during register fetch (ID) and registers written during write back (WB). This dual use is represented by drawing the unshaded left half of the register file using dashed lines in the ID stage, when it is not being written, and the unshaded right half in dashed lines in the WB stage, when it is not being read. As before, we assume the register file is written in the first half of the clock cycle and the register file is read during the second half.

isters in Figure 6.11, however, the PC is part of the visible architectural state; its contents must be saved when an exception occurs, while the contents of the pipeline registers can be discarded. In the laundry analogy, you could think of the PC as corresponding to the basket that holds the load of dirty clothes before the wash step!

To show how the pipelining works, throughout this chapter we show sequences of figures to demonstrate operation over time. These extra pages would seem to require much more time for you to understand. Fear not; the sequences take much less time than it might appear because you can compare them to see what changes occur in each clock cycle. Sections 6.4 and 6.5 describe what happens when there are data hazards between pipelined instructions; ignore them for now.

Figures 6.12 through 6.14, our first sequence, show the active portions of the datapath highlighted as a load instruction goes through the five stages of pipelined

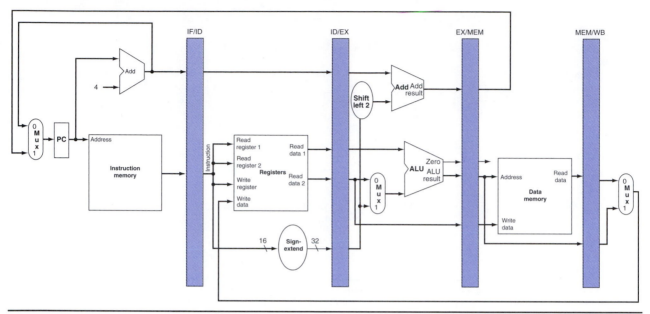

FIGURE 6.11   The pipelined version of the datapath in Figure 6.9. The pipeline registers, in color, separate each pipeline stage. They are labeled by the stages that they separate; for example, the first is labeled *IF/ID* because it separates the instruction fetch and instruction decode stages. The registers must be wide enough to store all the data corresponding to the lines that go through them. For example, the IF/ID register must be 64 bits wide because it must hold both the 32-bit instruction fetched from memory and the incremented 32-bit PC address. We will expand these registers over the course of this chapter, but for now the other three pipeline registers contain 128, 97, and 64 bits, respectively.

execution. We show a load first because it is active in all five stages. As in Figures 6.4 through 6.11, we highlight the *right half* of registers or memory when they are being *read* and highlight the *left half* when they are being *written*. We show the instruction abbreviation lw with the name of the pipe stage that is active in each figure. The five stages are the following:

1. *Instruction fetch:* The top portion of Figure 6.12 shows the instruction being read from memory using the address in the PC and then being placed in the IF/ID pipeline register. The IF/ID pipeline register is similar to the Instruction register in Figure 5.26 on page 320. The PC address is incremented by 4 and then written back into the PC to be ready for the next clock cycle. This incremented address is also saved in the IF/ID pipeline register in case it is needed later for an instruction, such as beq. The computer cannot know which type of instruction is being fetched, so it must prepare for any instruction, passing potentially needed information down the pipeline.

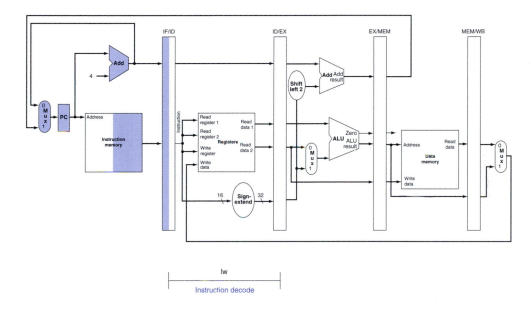

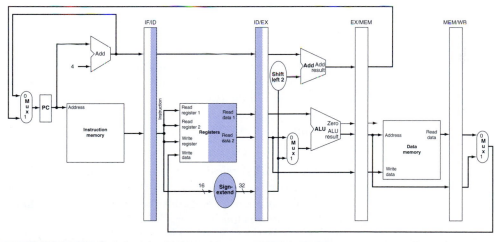

FIGURE 6.12 IF and ID: First and second pipe stages of an instruction, with the active portions of the datapath in Figure 6.11 highlighted. The highlighting convention is the same as that used in Figure 6.4. As in Chapter 5, there is no confusion when reading and writing registers because the contents change only on the clock edge. Although the load needs only the top register in stage 2, the processor doesn't know what instruction is being decoded, so it sign-extends the 16-bit constant and reads both registers into the ID/EX pipeline register. We don't need all three operands, but it simplifies control to keep all three.

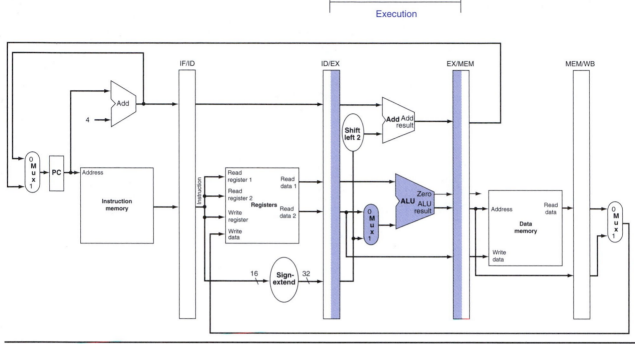

FIGURE 6.13   EX: The third pipe stage of a load instruction, highlighting the portions of the datapath in Figure 6.11 used in this pipe stage. The register is added to the sign-extended immediate, and the sum is placed in the EX/MEM pipeline register.

2. *Instruction decode and register file read:* The bottom portion of Figure 6.12 shows the instruction portion of the IF/ID pipeline register supplying the 16-bit immediate field, which is sign-extended to 32 bits, and the register numbers to read the two registers. All three values are stored in the ID/EX pipeline register, along with the incremented PC address. We again transfer everything that might be needed by any instruction during a later clock cycle.

3. *Execute or address calculation:* Figure 6.13 shows that the load instruction reads the contents of register 1 and the sign-extended immediate from the ID/EX pipeline register and adds them using the ALU. That sum is placed in the EX/MEM pipeline register.

4. *Memory access:* The top portion of Figure 6.14 shows the load instruction reading the data memory using the address from the EX/MEM pipeline register and loading the data into the MEM/WB pipeline register.

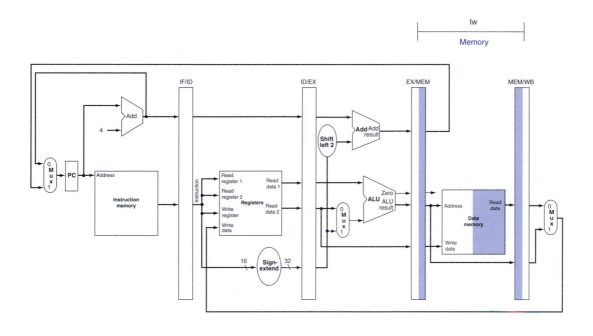

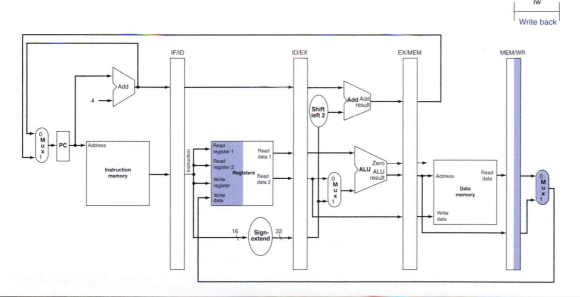

FIGURE 6.14 MEM and WB: The fourth and fifth pipe stages of a load instruction, highlighting the portions of the datapath in Figure 6.11 used in this pipe stage. Data memory is read using the address in the EX/MEM pipeline registers, and the data is placed in the MEM/WB pipeline register. Next, data is read from the MEM/WB pipeline register and written into the register file in the middle of the datapath.

5. *Write back:* The bottom portion of Figure 6.14 shows the final step: reading the data from the MEM/WB pipeline register and writing it into the register file in the middle of the figure.

This walk-through of the load instruction shows that any information needed in a later pipe stage must be passed to that stage via a pipeline register. Walking through a store instruction shows the similarity of instruction execution, as well as passing the information for later stages. Here are the five pipe stages of the store instruction:

1. *Instruction fetch:* The instruction is read from memory using the address in the PC and then is placed in the IF/ID pipeline register. This stage occurs before the instruction is identified, so the top portion of Figure 6.12 works for store as well as load.

2. *Instruction decode and register file read:* The instruction in the IF/ID pipeline register supplies the register numbers for reading two registers and extends the sign of the 16-bit immediate. These three 32-bit values are all stored in the ID/EX pipeline register. The bottom portion of Figure 6.12 for load instructions also shows the operations of the second stage for stores. These first two stages are executed by all instructions, since it is too early to know the type of the instruction.

3. *Execute and address calculation:* Figure 6.15 shows the third step; the effective address is placed in the EX/MEM pipeline register.

4. *Memory access:* The top portion of Figure 6.16 shows the data being written to memory. Note that the register containing the data to be stored was read in an earlier stage and stored in ID/EX. The only way to make the data available during the MEM stage is to place the data into the EX/MEM pipeline register in the EX stage, just as we stored the effective address into EX/MEM.

5. *Write back:* The bottom portion of Figure 6.16 shows the final step of the store. For this instruction, nothing happens in the write-back stage. Since every instruction behind the store is already in progress, we have no way to accelerate those instructions. Hence, an instruction passes through a stage even if there is nothing to do because later instructions are already progressing at the maximum rate.

The store instruction again illustrates that to pass something from an early pipe stage to a later pipe stage, the information must be placed in a pipeline register; otherwise, the information is lost when the next instruction enters that pipeline stage. For the store instruction we needed to pass one of the registers read in the ID stage to the MEM stage, where it is stored in memory. The data was first placed in the ID/EX pipeline register and then passed to the EX/MEM pipeline register.

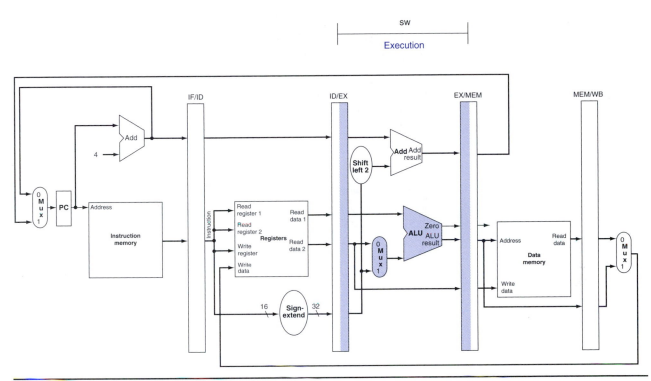

FIGURE 6.15 EX: The third pipe stage of a store instruction. Unlike the third stage of the load instruction in Figure 6.13, the second register value is loaded into the EX/MEM pipeline register to be used in the next stage. Although it wouldn't hurt to always write this second register into the EX/MEM pipeline register, we write the second register only on a store instruction to make the pipeline easier to understand.

Load and store illustrate a second key point: each logical component of the datapath—such as instruction memory, register read ports, ALU, data memory, and register write port—can be used only within a *single* pipeline stage. Otherwise we would have a *structural hazard* (see page 375). Hence these components, and their control, can be associated with a single pipeline stage.

Now we can uncover a bug in the design of the load instruction. Did you see it? Which register is changed in the final stage of the load? More specifically, which instruction supplies the write register number? The instruction in the IF/ID pipeline register supplies the write register number, yet this instruction occurs considerably *after* the load instruction!

Hence, we need to preserve the destination register number in the load instruction. Just as store passed the register *contents* from the ID/EX to the EX/MEM pipeline registers for use in the MEM stage, load must pass the register *number* from the ID/EX through EX/MEM to the MEM/WB pipeline register for use in

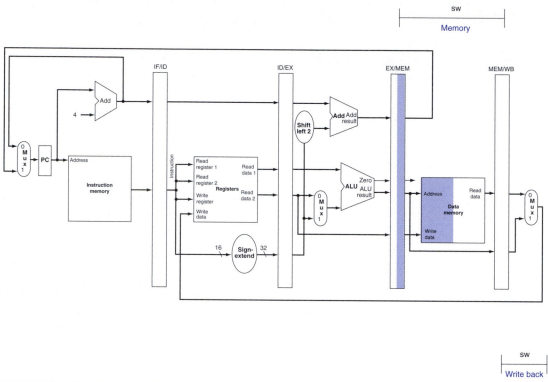

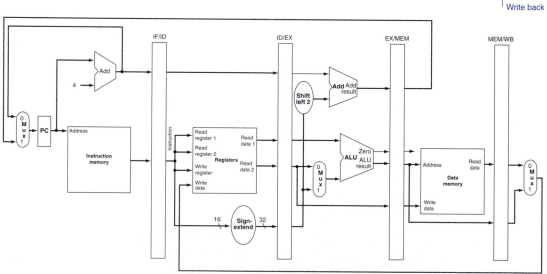

FIGURE 6.16 MEM and WB: The fourth and fifth pipe stages of a store instruction. In the fourth stage, the data is written into data memory for the store. Note that the data comes from the EX/MEM pipeline register and that nothing is changed in the MEM/WB pipeline register. Once the data is written in memory, there is nothing left for the store instruction to do, so nothing happens in stage 5.

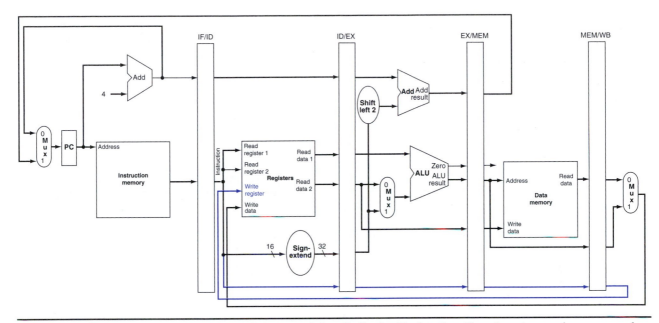

FIGURE 6.17   The corrected pipelined datapath to properly handle the load instruction. The write register number now comes from the MEM/WB pipeline register along with the data. The register number is passed from the ID pipe stage until it reaches the MEM/WB pipeline register, adding 5 more bits to the last three pipeline registers. This new path is shown in color.

the WB stage. Another way to think about the passing of the register number is that, in order to share the pipelined datapath, we need to preserve the instruction read during the IF stage, so each pipeline register contains a portion of the instruction needed for that stage and later stages.

Figure 6.17 shows the correct version of the datapath, passing the write register number first to the ID/EX register, then to the EX/MEM register, and finally to the MEM/WB register. The register number is used during the WB stage to specify the register to be written. Figure 6.18 is a single drawing of the corrected datapath, highlighting the hardware used in all five stages of the load word instruction in Figures 6.12 through 6.14. See Section 6.6 for an explanation of how to make the branch instruction work as expected.

Graphically Representing Pipelines

Pipelining can be difficult to understand, since many instructions are simultaneously executing in a single datapath in every clock cycle. To aid understanding, there are two basic styles of pipeline figures: *multiple-clock-cycle pipeline diagrams*, such as Figure 6.10 on page 387, and *single-clock-cycle pipeline diagrams*,

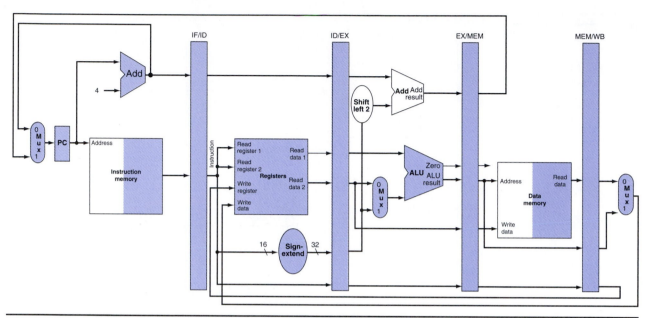

FIGURE 6.18   The portion of the datapath in Figure 6.17 that is used in all five stages of a load instruction.

such as Figures 6.12 through 6.16. The multiple-clock-cycle diagrams are simpler but do not contain all the details. For example, consider the following five-instruction sequence:

```
lw      $10, 20($1)
sub     $11, $2, $3
add     $12, $3, $4
lw      $13, 24($1)
add     $14, $5, $6
```

Figure 6.19 shows the multiple-clock-cycle pipeline diagram for these instructions. Time advances from left to right across the page in these diagrams, and instructions advance from the top to the bottom of the page, similar to the laundry pipeline in Figure 6.1 on page 371. A representation of the pipeline stages is placed in each portion along the instruction axis, occupying the proper clock cycles. These stylized datapaths represent the five stages of our pipeline, but a rectangle naming each pipe stage works just as well. Figure 6.20 shows the more traditional version of the multiple-clock-cycle pipeline diagram. Note that Figure 6.19 shows the physical resources used at each stage, while Figure 6.20 uses the *name* of each stage. We use multiple-clock-cycle diagrams to give overviews of pipelining situations.

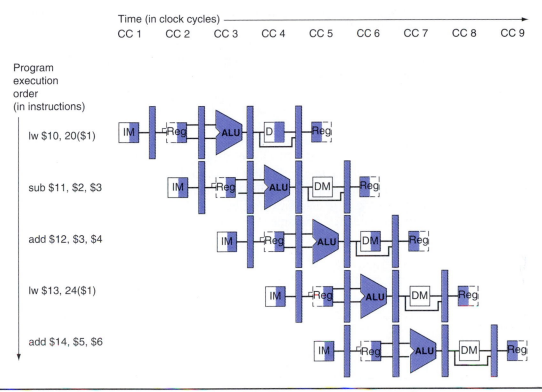

FIGURE 6.19 Multiple-clock-cycle pipeline diagram of five instructions. This style of pipeline representation shows the complete execution of instructions in a single figure. Instructions are listed in instruction execution order from top to bottom, and clock cycles move from left to right. Unlike Figure 6.4, here we show the pipeline registers between each stage. Figure 6.20 shows the traditional way to draw this diagram.

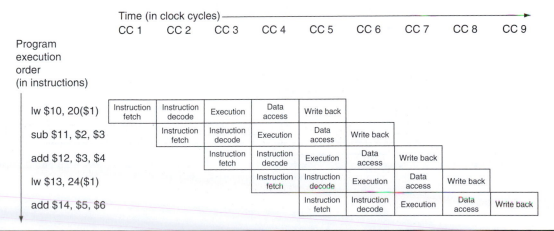

FIGURE 6.20 Traditional multiple-clock-cycle pipeline diagram of five instructions in Figure 6.19.

Single-clock-cycle pipeline diagrams show the state of the entire datapath during a single clock cycle, and usually all five instructions in the pipeline are identified by labels above their respective pipeline stages. We use this type of figure to show the details of what is happening within the pipeline during each clock cycle; typically, the drawings appear in groups to show pipeline operation over a sequence of clock cycles. A single-clock-cycle diagram represents a vertical slice through a set of multiple-clock-cycle diagrams, showing the usage of the datapath by each of the instructions in the pipeline at the designated clock cycle. For example, Figure 6.21 shows the single-clock-cycle diagram corresponding to clock cycle 5 of Figures 6.19 and 6.20. Obviously, the single-clock-cycle diagrams have more detail and take significantly more space to show the same number of clock cycles. The "For More Practice" section included on the CD includes the corresponding single-clock-cycle diagrams for these two instructions as well as exercises asking you to create such diagrams for another code sequence.

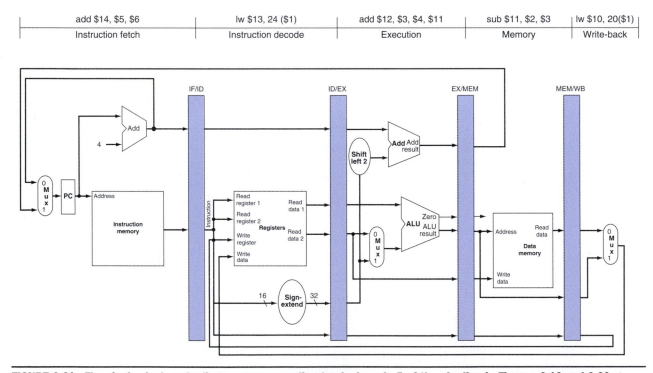

FIGURE 6.21   The single-clock-cycle diagram corresponding to clock cycle 5 of the pipeline in Figures 6.19 and 6.20. As you can see, a single-clock-cycle figure is a vertical slice through a multiple-clock-cycle diagram.

Check Yourself

A group of students were debating the efficiency of the five-stage pipeline when one student pointed out that not all instructions are active in every stage of the pipeline. After deciding to ignore the effects of hazards, they made the following five statements. Which ones are correct?

1. Allowing jumps, branches, and ALU instructions to take fewer stages than the five required by the load instruction will increase pipeline performance under all circumstances.

2. Trying to allow some instructions to take fewer cycles does not help, since the throughput is determined by the clock cycle; the number of pipe stages per instruction affects latency, not throughput.

3. Allowing jumps, branches, and ALU operations to take fewer cycles only helps when no loads or stores are in the pipeline, so the benefits are small.

4. You cannot make ALU instructions take fewer cycles because of the write-back of the result, but branches and jumps can take fewer cycles, so there is some opportunity for improvement.

5. Instead of trying to make instructions take fewer cycles, we should explore making the pipeline longer, so that instructions take more cycles, but the cycles are shorter. This could improve performance.

6.3 Pipelined Control

In the 6600 Computer, perhaps even more than in any previous computer, the control system is the difference.

James Thornton,
*Design of a Computer:
The Control Data 6600,* 1970

Just as we added control to the simple datapath in Section 5.4, we now add control to the pipelined datapath. We start with a simple design that views the problem through rose-colored glasses; in Sections 6.4 through 6.8, we remove these glasses to reveal the hazards of the real world.

The first step is to label the control lines on the existing datapath. Figure 6.22 shows those lines. We borrow as much as we can from the control for the simple datapath in Figure 5.17 on page 307. In particular, we use the same ALU control logic, branch logic, destination-register-number multiplexor, and control lines. These functions are defined in Figure 5.12 on page 302, Figure 5.16 on page 306, and Figure 5.18 on page 308. We reproduce the key information in Figures 6.23 through 6.25 to make the remaining text easier to follow.

As for the single-cycle implementation discussed in Chapter 5, we assume that the PC is written on each clock cycle, so there is no separate write signal for the

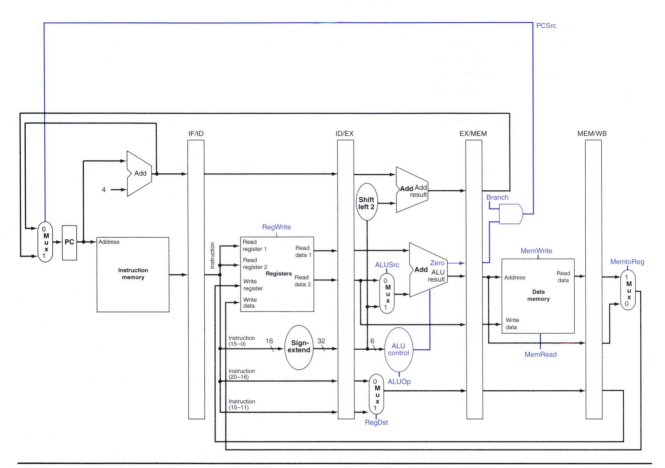

FIGURE 6.22   The pipelined datapath of Figure 6.17 with the control signals identified. This datapath borrows the control logic for PC source, register destination number, and ALU control from Chapter 5. Note that we now need the 6-bit funct field (function code) of the instruction in the EX stage as input to ALU control, so these bits must also be included in the ID/EX pipeline register. Recall that these 6 bits are also the 6 least significant bits of the immediate field in the instruction, so the ID/EX pipeline register can supply them from the immediate field since sign extension leaves these bits unchanged.

PC. By the same argument, there are no separate write signals for the pipeline registers (IF/ID, ID/EX, EX/MEM, and MEM/WB), since the pipeline registers are also written during each clock cycle.

To specify control for the pipeline, we need only set the control values during each pipeline stage. Because each control line is associated with a component active in only a single pipeline stage, we can divide the control lines into five groups according to the pipeline stage.

1. *Instruction fetch:* The control signals to read instruction memory and to write the PC are always asserted, so there is nothing special to control in this pipeline stage.

Instruction opcode	ALUOp	Instruction operation	Function code	Desired ALU action	ALU control input
LW	00	load word	XXXXXX	add	0010
SW	00	store word	XXXXXX	add	0010
Branch equal	01	branch equal	XXXXXX	subtract	0110
R-type	10	add	100000	add	0010
R-type	10	subtract	100010	subtract	0110
R-type	10	AND	100100	and	0000
R-type	10	OR	100101	or	0001
R-type	10	set on less than	101010	set on less than	0111

FIGURE 6.23 A copy of Figure 5.12 on page 302. This figure shows how the ALU control bits are set depending on the ALUOp control bits and the different function codes for the R-type instruction.

Signal name	Effect when deasserted (0)	Effect when asserted (1)
RegDst	The register destination number for the Write register comes from the rt field (bits 20:16).	The register destination number for the Write register comes from the rd field (bits 15:11).
RegWrite	None.	The register on the Write register input is written with the value on the Write data input.
ALUSrc	The second ALU operand comes from the second register file output (Read data 2).	The second ALU operand is the sign-extended, lower 16 bits of the instruction.
PCSrc	The PC is replaced by the output of the adder that computes the value of PC + 4.	The PC is replaced by the output of the adder that computes the branch target.
MemRead	None.	Data memory contents designated by the address input are put on the Read data output.
MemWrite	None.	Data memory contents designated by the address input are replaced by the value on the Write data input.
MemtoReg	The value fed to the register Write data input comes from the ALU.	The value fed to the register Write data input comes from the data memory.

FIGURE 6.24 A copy of Figure 5.16 on page 306. The function of each of seven control signals is defined. The ALU control lines (ALUOp) are defined in the second column of Figure 6.23. When a 1-bit control to a two-way multiplexor is asserted, the multiplexor selects the input corresponding to 1. Otherwise, if the control is deasserted, the multiplexor selects the 0 input. Note that PCSrc is controlled by an AND gate in Figure 6.22. If the Branch signal and the ALU Zero signal are both set, then PCSrc is 1; otherwise, it is 0. Control sets the Branch signal only during a beq instruction; otherwise, PCSrc is set to 0.

Instruction	Execution/address calculation stage control lines				Memory access stage control lines			Write-back stage control lines	
	Reg Dst	ALU Op1	ALU Op0	ALU Src	Branch	Mem Read	Mem Write	Reg Write	Mem to Reg
R-format	1	1	0	0	0	0	0	1	0
lw	0	0	0	1	0	1	0	1	1
sw	X	0	0	1	0	0	1	0	X
beq	X	0	1	0	1	0	0	0	X

FIGURE 6.25 The values of the control lines are the same as in Figure 5.18 on page 308, but they have been shuffled into three groups corresponding to the last three pipeline stages.

2. *Instruction decode/register file read:* As in the previous stage, the same thing happens at every clock cycle, so there are no optional control lines to set.

3. *Execution/address calculation:* The signals to be set are RegDst, ALUOp, and ALUSrc (see Figures 6.23 and 6.24). The signals select the Result register, the ALU operation, and either Read data 2 or a sign-extended immediate for the ALU.

4. *Memory access:* The control lines set in this stage are Branch, MemRead, and MemWrite. These signals are set by the branch equal, load, and store instructions, respectively. Recall that PCSrc in Figure 6.24 selects the next sequential address unless control asserts Branch and the ALU result was zero.

5. *Write back:* The two control lines are MemtoReg, which decides between sending the ALU result or the memory value to the register file, and Reg-Write, which writes the chosen value.

Since pipelining the datapath leaves the meaning of the control lines unchanged, we can use the same control values as before. Figure 6.25 has the same values as in Chapter 5, but now the nine control lines are grouped by pipeline stage.

Implementing control means setting the nine control lines to these values in each stage for each instruction. The simplest way to do this is to extend the pipeline registers to include control information.

Since the control lines start with the EX stage, we can create the control information during instruction decode. Figure 6.26 shows that these control signals are then used in the appropriate pipeline stage as the instruction moves down the pipeline, just as the destination register number for loads moves down the pipeline in Figure 6.17 on page 395. Figure 6.27 shows the full datapath with the extended pipeline registers and with the control lines connected to the proper stage.

What do you mean, why's it got to be built? It's a bypass. You've got to build bypasses.

Douglas Adams, *Hitchhikers Guide to the Galaxy,* 1979

6.4   Data Hazards and Forwarding

The examples in the previous section show the power of pipelined execution and how the hardware performs the task. It's now time to take off the rose-colored glasses and look at what happens with real programs. The instructions in Figures 6.19 through 6.21 were independent; none of them used the results calculated by any of the others. Yet in Section 6.1 we saw that data hazards are obstacles to pipelined execution.

Let's look at a sequence with many dependences, shown in color:

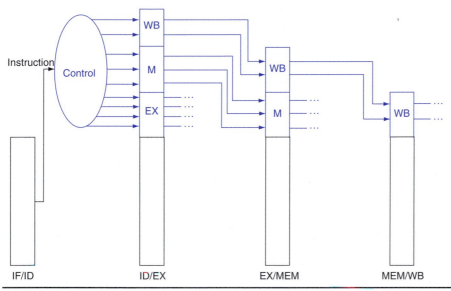

FIGURE 6.26 The control lines for the final three stages. Note that four of the nine control lines are used in the EX phase, with the remaining five control lines passed on to the EX/MEM pipeline register extended to hold the control lines; three are used during the MEM stage, and the last two are passed to MEM/WB for use in the WB stage.

```
sub   $2, $1,$3      # Register $2 written by sub
and   $12,$2,$5      # 1st operand($2) depends on sub
or    $13,$6,$2      # 2nd operand($2) depends on sub
add   $14,$2,$2      # 1st($2) & 2nd($2) depend on sub
sw    $15,100($2)    # Base ($2) depends on sub
```

The last four instructions are all dependent on the result in register $2 of the first instruction. If register $2 had the value 10 before the subtract instruction and −20 afterwards, the programmer intends that −20 will be used in the following instructions that refer to register $2.

How would this sequence perform with our pipeline? Figure 6.28 illustrates the execution of these instructions using a multiple-clock-cycle pipeline representation. To demonstrate the execution of this instruction sequence in our current pipeline, the top of Figure 6.28 shows the value of register $2, which changes during the middle of clock cycle 5, when the sub instruction writes its result.

One potential hazard can be resolved by the design of the register file hardware: What happens when a register is read and written in the same clock cycle? We assume that the write is in the first half of the clock cycle and the read is in the second half, so the read delivers what is written. As is the case for many implementations of register files, we have no data hazard in this case.

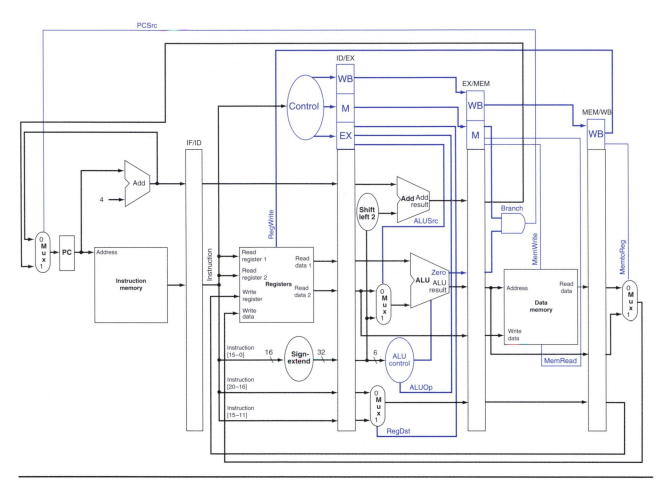

FIGURE 6.27   The pipelined datapath of Figure 6.22, with the control signals connected to the control portions of the pipeline registers. The control values for the last three stages are created during the instruction decode stage and then placed in the ID/EX pipeline register. The control lines for each pipe stage are used, and remaining control lines are then passed to the next pipeline stage.

Figure 6.28 shows that the values read for register $2 would *not* be the result of the sub instruction unless the read occurred during clock cycle 5 or later. Thus, the instructions that would get the correct value of –20 are add and sw; the and and or instructions would get the incorrect value 10! Using this style of drawing, such problems become apparent when a dependence line goes backwards in time.

But, look carefully at Figure 6.28: When is the data from the sub instruction actually produced? The result is available at the end of the EX stage or clock cycle 3. When is the data actually needed by the and and or instructions? At the beginning of the EX stage, or clock cycles 4 and 5, respectively. Thus, we can execute this

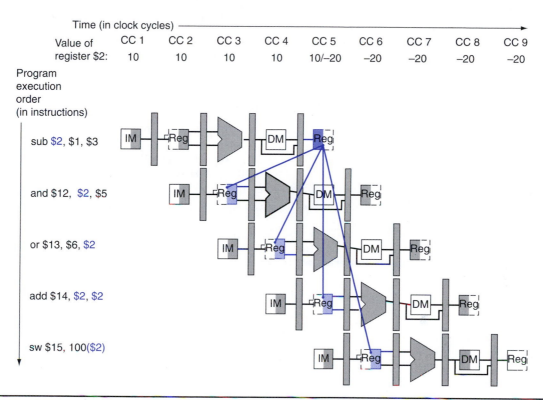

FIGURE 6.28 Pipelined dependences in a five-instruction sequence using simplified datapaths to show the dependences. All the dependent actions are shown in color, and "CC 1" at the top of the figure means clock cycle 1. The first instruction writes into $2, and all the following instructions read $2. This register is written in clock cycle 5, so the proper value is unavailable before clock cycle 5. (A read of a register during a clock cycle returns the value written at the end of the first half of the cycle, when such a write occurs.) The colored lines from the top datapath to the lower ones show the dependences. Those that must go backwards in time are *pipeline data hazards.*

segment without stalls if we simply *forward* the data as soon as it is available to any units that need it before it is available to read from the register file.

How does forwarding work? For simplicity in the rest of this section, we consider only the challenge of forwarding to an operation in the EX stage, which may be either an ALU operation or an effective address calculation. This means that when an instruction tries to use a register in its EX stage that an earlier instruction intends to write in its WB stage, we actually need the values as inputs to the ALU.

A notation that names the fields of the pipeline registers allows for a more precise notation of dependences. For example, "ID/EX.RegisterRs" refers to the number of one register whose value is found in the pipeline register ID/EX; that is, the one from the first read port of the register file. The first part of the name, to the left of the period, is the name of the pipeline register; the second part is the name of the field in that register. Using this notation, the two pairs of hazard conditions are

1a. EX/MEM.RegisterRd = ID/EX.RegisterRs

1b. EX/MEM.RegisterRd = ID/EX.RegisterRt

2a. MEM/WB.RegisterRd = ID/EX.RegisterRs

2b. MEM/WB.RegisterRd = ID/EX.RegisterRt

The first hazard in the sequence on page 403 is on register $2, between the result of `sub $2,$1,$3` and the first read operand of `and $12,$2,$5`. This hazard can be detected when the `and` instruction is in the EX stage and the prior instruction is in the MEM stage, so this is hazard 1a:

EX/MEM.RegisterRd = ID/EX.RegisterRs = $2

Dependence Detection

EXAMPLE

Classify the dependences in this sequence from page 403:

```
sub     $2,   $1, $3   # Register $2 set by sub
and     $12,  $2, $5   # 1st operand($2) set by sub
or      $13,  $6, $2   # 2nd operand($2) set by sub
add     $14,  $2, $2   # 1st($2) & 2nd($2) set by sub
sw      $15,  100($2)  # Index($2) set by sub
```

ANSWER

As mentioned above, the `sub-and` is a type 1a hazard. The remaining hazards are as follows:

- The `sub-or` is a type 2b hazard:

  MEM/WB.RegisterRd = ID/EX.RegisterRt = $2

- The two dependences on `sub-add` are not hazards because the register file supplies the proper data during the ID stage of `add`.

- There is no data hazard between `sub` and `sw` because `sw` reads $2 the clock cycle *after* `sub` writes $2.

Because some instructions do not write registers, this policy is inaccurate; sometimes it would forward when it was unnecessary. One solution is simply to check to see if the RegWrite signal will be active: examining the WB control field of the pipeline register during the EX and MEM stages determines if RegWrite is asserted. Also, MIPS requires that every use of $0 as an operand must yield an operand value of zero. In the event that an instruction in the pipeline has $0 as its destination (for example, sll $0, $1, 2), we want to avoid forwarding its possibly nonzero result value. Not forwarding results destined for $0 frees the assembly programmer and the compiler of any requirement to avoid using $0 as a destination. The conditions above thus work properly as long we add EX/MEM.RegisterRd ≠ 0 to the first hazard condition and MEM/WB.RegisterRd ≠ 0 to the second.

Now that we can detect hazards, half of the problem is resolved—but we must still forward the proper data.

Figure 6.29 shows the dependences between the pipeline registers and the inputs to the ALU for the same code sequence as in Figure 6.28. The change is that the dependence begins from a *pipeline* register rather than waiting for the WB stage to write the register file. Thus the required data exists in time for later instructions, with the pipeline registers holding the data to be forwarded.

If we can take the inputs to the ALU from *any* pipeline register rather than just ID/EX, then we can forward the proper data. By adding multiplexors to the input of the ALU and with the proper controls, we can run the pipeline at full speed in the presence of these data dependences.

For now, we will assume the only instructions we need to forward are the four R-format instructions: add, sub, and, and or. Figure 6.30 shows a close-up of the ALU and pipeline register before and after adding forwarding. Figure 6.31 shows the values of the control lines for the ALU multiplexors that select either the register file values or one of the forwarded values.

This forwarding control will be in the EX stage because the ALU forwarding multiplexors are found in that stage. Thus, we must pass the operand register numbers from the ID stage via the ID/EX pipeline register to determine whether to forward values. We already have the rt field (bits 20–16). Before forwarding, the ID/EX register had no need to include space to hold the rs field. Hence, rs (bits 25–21) is added to ID/EX.

Let's now write both the conditions for detecting hazards and the control signals to resolve them:

1. EX hazard:

```
if (EX/MEM.RegWrite
and (EX/MEM.RegisterRd ≠ 0)
and (EX/MEM.RegisterRd = ID/EX.RegisterRs)) ForwardA = 10

if (EX/MEM.RegWrite
and (EX/MEM.RegisterRd ≠ 0)
and (EX/MEM.RegisterRd = ID/EX.RegisterRt)) ForwardB = 10
```

Note that the EX/MEM.RegisterRd field is the register destination for either an ALU instruction (which comes from the RD field of the instruction) or a load (which comes from the Rt field).

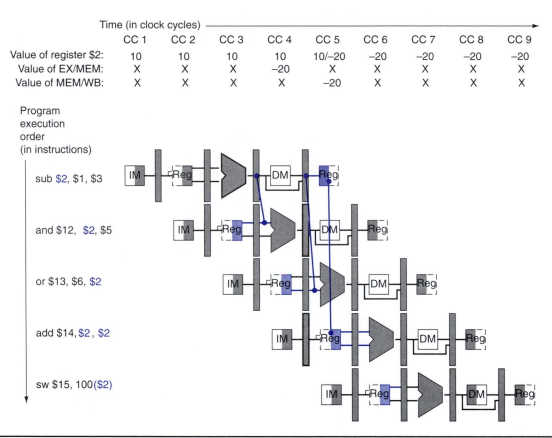

FIGURE 6.29   The dependences between the pipeline registers move forward in time, so it is possible to supply the inputs to the ALU needed by the and instruction and or instruction by forwarding the results found in the pipeline registers. The values in the pipeline registers show that the desired value is available before it is written into the register file. We assume that the register file forwards values that are read and written during the same clock cycle, so the add does not stall, but the values come from the register file instead of a pipeline register. Register file "forwarding"—that is, the read gets the value of the write in that clock cycle—is why clock cycle 5 shows register $2 having the value 10 at the beginning and −20 at the end of the clock cycle. As in the rest of this section, we handle all forwarding except for the value to be stored by a store instruction.

This case forwards the result from the previous instruction to either input of the ALU. If the previous instruction is going to write to the register file and the write register number matches the read register number of ALU inputs A or B, provided it is not register 0, then steer the multiplexor to pick the value instead from the pipeline register EX/MEM.

2.   MEM hazard:

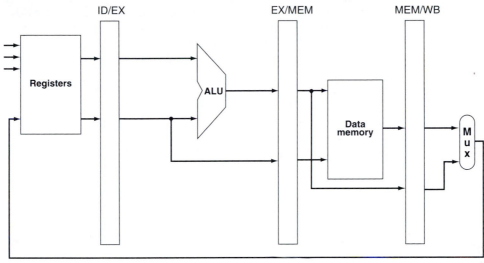

a. No forwarding

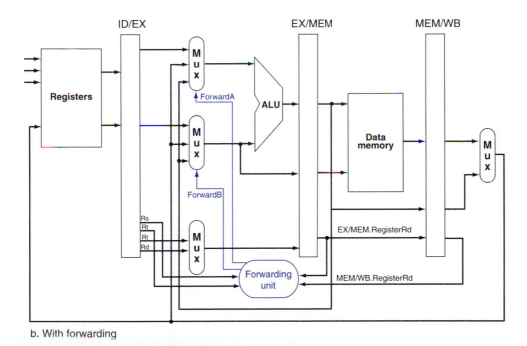

b. With forwarding

FIGURE 6.30 On the top are the ALU and pipeline registers before adding forwarding. On the bottom, the multiplexors have been expanded to add the forwarding paths, and we show the forwarding unit. The new hardware is shown in color. This figure is a stylized drawing, however, leaving out details from the full datapath such as the sign extension hardware. Note that the ID/EX.RegisterRt field is shown twice, once to connect to the mux and once to the forwarding unit, but it is a single signal. As in the earlier discussion, this ignores forwarding of a store value to a store instruction. Also note that this mechanism works for SIT instructions as well.

Mux control	Source	Explanation
ForwardA = 00	ID/EX	The first ALU operand comes from the register file.
ForwardA = 10	EX/MEM	The first ALU operand is forwarded from the prior ALU result.
ForwardA = 01	MEM/WB	The first ALU operand is forwarded from data memory or an earlier ALU result.
ForwardB = 00	ID/EX	The second ALU operand comes from the register file.
ForwardB = 10	EX/MEM	The second ALU operand is forwarded from the prior ALU result.
ForwardB = 01	MEM/WB	The second ALU operand is forwarded from data memory or an earlier ALU result.

FIGURE 6.31   The control values for the forwarding multiplexors in Figure 6.30. The signed immediate that is another input to the ALU is described in the elaboration at the end of this section.

```
if (MEM/WB.RegWrite
and (MEM/WB.RegisterRd ≠ 0)
and (MEM/WB.RegisterRd = ID/EX.RegisterRs)) ForwardA = 01

if (MEM/WB.RegWrite
and (MEM/WB.RegisterRd ≠ 0)
and (MEM/WB.RegisterRd = ID/EX.RegisterRt)) ForwardB = 01
```

As mentioned above, there is no hazard in the WB stage because we assume that the register file supplies the correct result if the instruction in the ID stage reads the same register written by the instruction in the WB stage. Such a register file performs another form of forwarding, but it occurs within the register file.

One complication is potential data hazards between the result of the instruction in the WB stage, the result of the instruction in the MEM stage, and the source operand of the instruction in the ALU stage. For example, when summing a vector of numbers in a single register, a sequence of instructions will all read and write to the same register:

```
add $1,$1,$2
add $1,$1,$3
add $1,$1,$4
 . . .
```

In this case, the result is forwarded from the MEM stage because the result in the MEM stage is the more recent result. Thus the control for the MEM hazard would be (with the additions highlighted)

```
if (MEM/WB.RegWrite
and (MEM/WB.RegisterRd ≠ 0)
```

```
and (EX/MEM.RegisterRd ≠ ID/EX.RegisterRs)
and (MEM/WB.RegisterRd = ID/EX.RegisterRs)) ForwardA = 01

if (MEM/WB.RegWrite
and (MEM/WB.RegisterRd ≠ 0)
and (EX/MEM.RegisterRd ≠ ID/EX.RegisterRt)
and (MEM/WB.RegisterRd = ID/EX.RegisterRt)) ForwardB = 01
```

Figure 6.32 shows the hardware necessary to support forwarding for operations that use results during the EX stage. Note that the EX/MEM.RegisterRd field is the register destination for either an ALU instruction (which comes from the Rd field of the instruction) or a load (which comes from the Rt field).

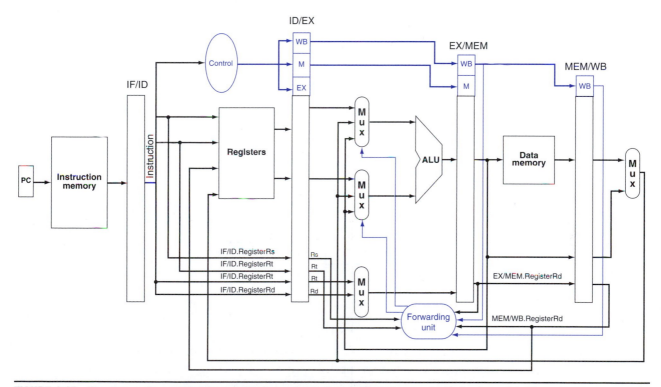

FIGURE 6.32 The datapath modified to resolve hazards via forwarding. Compared with the datapath in Figure 6.27 on page 404, the additions are the multiplexors to the inputs to the ALU. This figure is a more stylized drawing, however, leaving out details from the full datapath such as the branch hardware and the sign extension hardware.

Elaboration: Forwarding can also help with hazards when store instructions are dependent on other instructions. Since they use just one data value during the MEM stage, forwarding is easy. But consider loads immediately followed by stores. We need to add more forwarding hardware to make memory-to-memory copies run faster. If we were to redraw Figure 6.29 on page 408, replacing the sub and and instructions by lw and sw, we would see that it is possible to avoid a stall, since the data exists in the MEM/WB register of a load instruction in time for its use in the MEM stage of a store instruction. We would need to add forwarding into the memory access stage for this option. We leave this modification as an exercise.

In addition, the signed-immediate input to the ALU, needed by loads and stores, is missing from the datapath in Figure 6.32 on page 411. Since central control decides between register and immediate, and since the forwarding unit chooses the pipeline register for a register input to the ALU, the easiest solution is to add a 2:1 multiplexor that chooses between the ForwardB multiplexor output and the signed immediate. Figure 6.33 shows this addition. Note that this solution differs from what we learned in Chapter 5, where the multiplexor controlled by line ALUSrcB was expanded to include the immediate input.

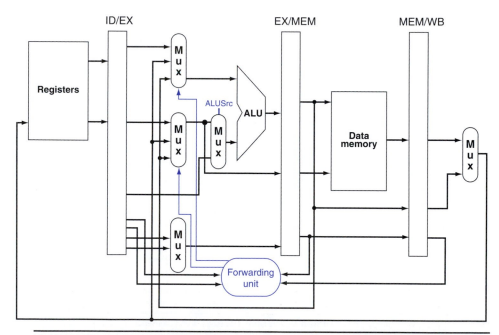

FIGURE 6.33   A close-up of the datapath in Figure 6.30 on page 409 shows a 2:1 multiplexor, which has been added to select the signed immediate as an ALU input.

6.5 Data Hazards and Stalls

As we said in Section 6.1, one case where forwarding cannot save the day is when an instruction tries to read a register following a load instruction that writes the same register. Figure 6.34 illustrates the problem. The data is still being read from memory in clock cycle 4 while the ALU is performing the operation for the following instruction. Something must stall the pipeline for the combination of load followed by an instruction that reads its result.

Hence, in addition to a forwarding unit, we need a *hazard detection unit*. It operates during the ID stage so that it can insert the stall between the load and its use. Checking for load instructions, the control for the hazard detection unit is this single condition:

```
if (ID/EX.MemRead and
    ((ID/EX.RegisterRt = IF/ID.RegisterRs) or
     (ID/EX.RegisterRt = IF/ID.RegisterRt)))
       stall the pipeline
```

The first line tests to see if the instruction is a load: the only instruction that reads data memory is a load. The next two lines check to see if the destination register field of the load in the EX stage matches either source register of the instruction in the ID stage. If the condition holds, the instruction stalls 1 clock cycle. After this 1-cycle stall, the forwarding logic can handle the dependence and execution proceeds. (If there were no forwarding, then the instructions in Figure 6.34 would need another stall cycle.)

If the instruction in the ID stage is stalled, then the instruction in the IF stage must also be stalled; otherwise, we would lose the fetched instruction. Preventing these two instructions from making progress is accomplished simply by preventing the PC register and the IF/ID pipeline register from changing. Provided these registers are preserved, the instruction in the IF stage will continue to be read using the same PC, and the registers in the ID stage will continue to be read using the same instruction fields in the IF/ID pipeline register. Returning to our favorite analogy, it's as if you restart the washer with the same clothes and let the dryer continue tumbling empty. Of course, like the dryer, the back half of the pipeline starting with the EX stage must be doing something; what it is doing is executing instructions that have no effect: **nops**.

How can we insert these nops, which act like bubbles, into the pipeline? In Figure 6.25 on page 401, we see that deasserting all nine control signals (setting them to 0) in the EX, MEM, and WB stages will create a "do nothing" or nop instruction. By identifying the hazard in the ID stage, we can insert a bubble into

nop An instruction that does no operation to change state.

Time (in clock cycles)

| CC 1 | CC 2 | CC 3 | CC 4 | CC 5 | CC 6 | CC 7 | CC 8 | CC 9 |

Program
execution
order
(in instructions)

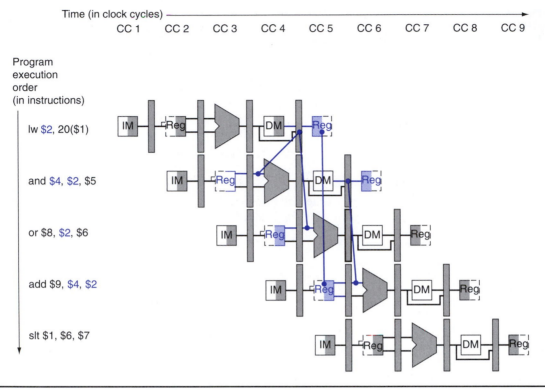

lw $2, 20($1)

and $4, $2, $5

or $8, $2, $6

add $9, $4, $2

slt $1, $6, $7

FIGURE 6.34   A pipelined sequence of instructions. Since the dependence between the load and the following instruction (and) goes backwards in time, this hazard cannot be solved by forwarding. Hence, this combination must result in a stall by the hazard detection unit.

the pipeline by changing the EX, MEM, and WB control fields of the ID/EX pipeline register to 0. These benign control values are percolated forward at each clock cycle with the proper effect: no registers or memories are written if the control values are all 0.

Figure 6.35 shows what really happens in the hardware: the pipeline execution slot associated with the and instruction is turned into a nop and all instructions beginning with the and instruction are delayed one cycle. The hazard forces the and and or instructions to repeat in clock cycle 4 what they did in clock cycle 3: and reads registers and decodes, and or is refetched from instruction memory. Such repeated work is what a stall looks like, but its effect is to stretch the time of the and and or instructions and delay the fetch of the add instruction. Like an air bubble in a water pipe, a stall bubble delays everything behind it and proceeds down the instruction pipe one stage each cycle until it exits at the end.

Figure 6.36 highlights the pipeline connections for both the hazard detection unit and the forwarding unit. As before, the forwarding unit controls the ALU multiplexors to replace the value from a general-purpose register with the value

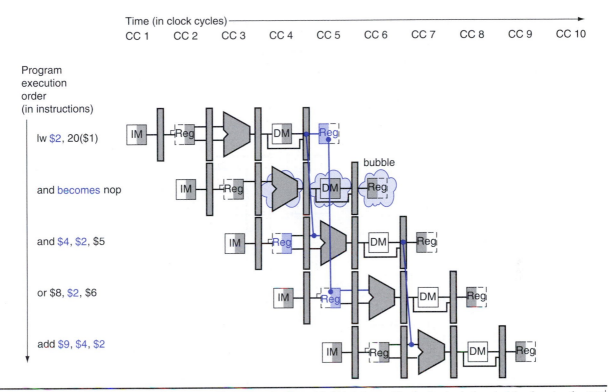

FIGURE 6.35 The way stalls are really inserted into the pipeline. A bubble is inserted beginning in clock cycle 4, by changing the and instruction to a nop. Note that the and instruction is really fetched and decoded in clock cycles 2 and 3, but its EX stage is delayed until clock cycle 5 (versus the unstalled position in clock cycle 4). Likewise the or instruction is fetched in clock cycle 3, but its IF stage is delayed until clock cycle 5 (versus the unstalled clock cycle 4 position). After insertion of the bubble, all the dependences go forward in time and no further hazards occur.

from the proper pipeline register. The hazard detection unit controls the writing of the PC and IF/ID registers plus the multiplexor that chooses between the real control values and all 0s. The hazard detection unit stalls and deasserts the control fields if the load-use hazard test above is true. We show the single-clock-cycle diagrams in the  **For More Practice** section on the CD.

> Although the hardware may or may not rely on the compiler to resolve hazard dependences to ensure correct execution, the compiler must understand the pipeline to achieve the best performance. Otherwise, unexpected stalls will reduce the performance of the compiled code.

The BIG Picture

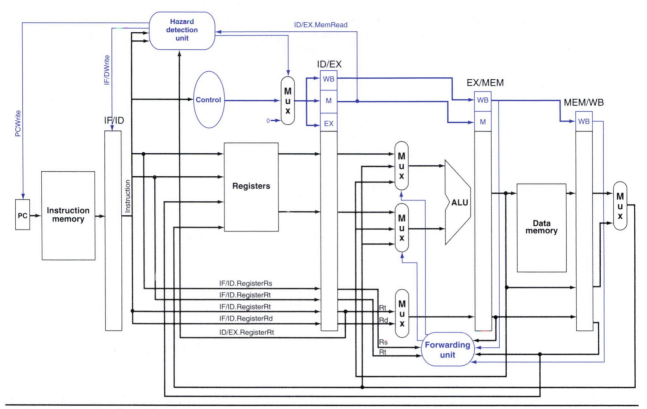

FIGURE 6.36 Pipelined control overview, showing the two multiplexors for forwarding, the hazard detection unit, and the forwarding unit. Although the ID and EX stages have been simplified—the sign-extended immediate and branch logic are missing—this drawing gives the essence of the forwarding hardware requirements.

Elaboration: Regarding the remark earlier about setting control lines to 0 to avoid writing registers or memory: only the signals RegWrite and MemWrite need be 0, while the other control signals can be don't cares.

There are a thousand hacking at the branches of evil to one who is striking at the root.

Henry David Thoreau, *Walden*, 1854

6.6   Control Hazards

Thus far we have limited our concern to hazards involving arithmetic operations and data transfers. But as we saw in Section 6.1, there are also pipeline hazards involving branches. Figure 6.37 shows a sequence of instructions and indicates

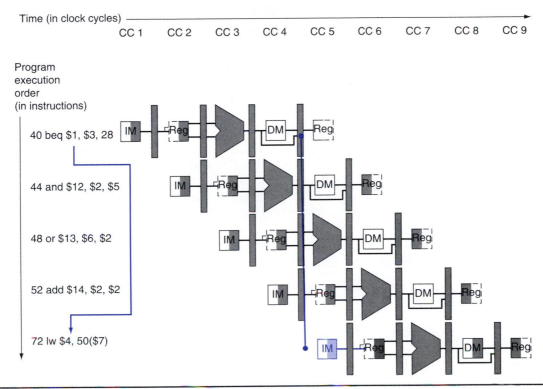

FIGURE 6.37 The impact of the pipeline on the branch instruction. The numbers to the left of the instruction (40, 44, . . .) are the addresses of the instructions. Since the branch instruction decides whether to branch in the MEM stage—clock cycle 4 for the `beq` instruction above—the three sequential instructions that follow the branch will be fetched and begin execution. Without intervention, those three following instructions will begin execution before `beq` branches to `lw` at location 72. (Figure 6.7 on page 380 assumed extra hardware to reduce the control hazard to 1 clock cycle; this figure uses the nonoptimized datapath.)

when the branch would occur in this pipeline. An instruction must be fetched at every clock cycle to sustain the pipeline, yet in our design the decision about whether to branch doesn't occur until the MEM pipeline stage. As mentioned in Section 6.1, this delay in determining the proper instruction to fetch is called a *control hazard* or *branch hazard*, in contrast to the *data hazards* we have just examined.

This section on control hazards is shorter than the previous sections on data hazards. The reasons are that control hazards are relatively simple to understand, they occur less frequently than data hazards, and there is nothing as effective against control hazards as forwarding is for data hazards. Hence, we use simpler schemes. We look at two schemes for resolving control hazards and one optimization to improve these schemes.

Assume Branch Not Taken

As we saw in Section 6.1, stalling until the branch is complete is too slow. A common improvement over branch stalling is to assume that the branch will not be taken and thus continue execution down the sequential instruction stream. If the branch is taken, the instructions that are being fetched and decoded must be discarded. Execution continues at the branch target. If branches are untaken half the time, and if it costs little to discard the instructions, this optimization halves the cost of control hazards.

To discard instructions, we merely change the original control values to 0s, much as we did to stall for a load-use data hazard. The difference is that we must also change the three instructions in the IF, ID, and EX stages when the branch reaches the MEM stage; for load-use stalls, we just changed control to 0 in the ID stage and let them percolate through the pipeline. Discarding instructions, then, means we must be able to **flush instructions** in the IF, ID, and EX stages of the pipeline.

flush (instructions) To discard instructions in a pipeline, usually due to an unexpected event.

Reducing the Delay of Branches

One way to improve branch performance is to reduce the cost of the taken branch. Thus far we have assumed the next PC for a branch is selected in the MEM stage, but if we move the branch execution earlier in the pipeline, then fewer instructions need be flushed. The MIPS architecture was designed to support fast single-cycle branches that could be pipelined with a small branch penalty. The designers observed that many branches rely only on simple tests (equality or sign, for example) and that such tests do not require a full ALU operation but can be done with at most a few gates. When a more complex branch decision is required, a separate instruction that uses an ALU to perform a comparison is required—a situation that is similar to the use of condition codes for branches.

Moving the branch decision up requires two actions to occur earlier: computing the branch target address and evaluating the branch decision. The easy part of this change is to move up the branch address calculation. We already have the PC value and the immediate field in the IF/ID pipeline register, so we just move the branch adder from the EX stage to the ID stage; of course, the branch target address calculation will be performed for all instructions, but only used when needed.

The harder part is the branch decision itself. For branch equal, we would compare the two registers read during the ID stage to see if they are equal. Equality can be tested by first exclusive ORing their respective bits and then ORing all the results. Moving the branch test to the ID stage implies additional forwarding and hazard detection hardware, since a branch dependent on a result still in the pipeline must still work properly with this optimization. For example, to implement branch on equal (and its inverse), we will need to forward results to the equality test logic that operates during ID. There are two complicating factors:

1. During ID, we must decode the instruction, decide whether a bypass to the equality unit is needed, and complete the equality comparison so that if the

instruction is a branch, we can set the PC to the branch target address. Forwarding for the operands of branches was formerly handled by the ALU forwarding logic, but the introduction of the equality test unit in ID will require new forwarding logic. Note that the bypassed source operands of a branch can come from either the ALU/MEM or MEM/WB pipeline latches.

2. Because the values in a branch comparison are needed during ID but may be produced later in time, it is possible that a data hazard can occur and a stall will be needed. For example, if an ALU instruction immediately preceding a branch produces one of the operands for the comparison in the branch, a stall will be required, since the EX stage for the ALU instruction will occur after the ID cycle of the branch. By extension, if a load is immediately followed by a conditional branch that on the load result, two stall cycles will be needed since the result from the load appears at the end of the MEM cycle but is needed at the beginning of ID for the branch.

Despite these difficulties, moving the branch execution to the ID stage is an improvement since it reduces the penalty of a branch to only one instruction if the branch is taken, namely, the one currently being fetched. The exercises explore the details of implementing the forwarding path and detecting the hazard.

To flush instructions in the IF stage, we add a control line, called IF.Flush, that zeros the instruction field of the IF/ID pipeline register. Clearing the register transforms the fetched instruction into a `nop`, an instruction that has no action and changes no state.

Pipelined Branch

Show what happens when the branch is taken in this instruction sequence, assuming the pipeline is optimized for branches that are not taken and that we moved the branch execution to the ID stage:

EXAMPLE

```
36 sub $10, $4, $8
40 beq  $1, $3, 7 # PC-relative branch to 40 + 4
+ 7 * 4 = 72
44 and $12, $2, $5
48 or  $13, $2, $6
52 add $14, $4, $2
56 slt $15, $6, $7
   . . .
72 lw  $4,  50($7)
```

Figure 6.38 shows what happens when a branch is taken. Unlike Figure 6.37, there is only one pipeline bubble on a taken branch.

ANSWER

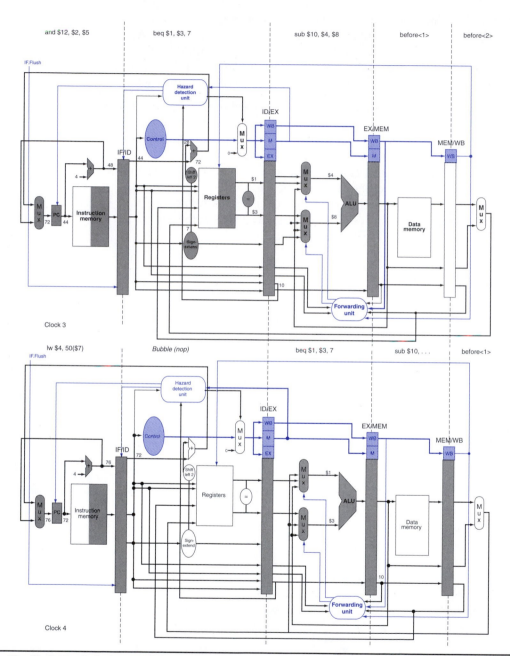

FIGURE 6.38   The ID stage of clock cycle 3 determines that a branch must be taken, so it selects 72 as the next PC address and zeros the instruction fetched for the next clock cycle. Clock cycle 4 shows the instruction at location 72 being fetched and the single bubble or nop instruction in the pipeline as a result of the taken branch. (Since the nop is really sll $0, $0, 0, it's arguable whether or not the ID stage in clock 4 should be highlighted.)

Dynamic Branch Prediction

Assuming a branch is not taken is one simple form of *branch prediction*. In that case, we predict that branches are untaken, flushing the pipeline when we are wrong. For the simple five-stage pipeline, such an approach, possibly coupled with compiler-based prediction, is probably adequate. With deeper pipelines, the branch penalty increases when measured in clock cycles. Similarly, with multiple issue, the branch penalty increases in terms of instructions lost. This combination means that in an aggressive pipeline, a simple static prediction scheme will probably waste too much performance. As we mentioned in Section 6.1, with more hardware it is possible to try to predict branch behavior during program execution.

One approach is to look up the address of the instruction to see if a branch was taken the last time this instruction was executed, and, if so, to begin fetching new instructions from the same place as the last time. This technique is called **dynamic branch prediction**.

One implementation of that approach is a **branch prediction buffer** or **branch history table**. A branch prediction buffer is a small memory indexed by the lower portion of the address of the branch instruction. The memory contains a bit that says whether the branch was recently taken or not.

This is the simplest sort of buffer; we don't know, in fact, if the prediction is the right one—it may have been put there by another branch that has the same low-order address bits. But this doesn't affect correctness. Prediction is just a hint that is assumed to be correct, so fetching begins in the predicted direction. If the hint turns out to be wrong, the incorrectly predicted instructions are deleted, the prediction bit is inverted and stored back, and the proper sequence is fetched and executed.

This simple 1-bit prediction scheme has a performance shortcoming: even if a branch is almost always taken, we will likely predict incorrectly twice, rather than once, when it is not taken. The following example shows this dilemma.

dynamic branch prediction Prediction of branches at runtime using runtime information.

branch prediction buffer Also called **branch history table**. A small memory that is indexed by the lower portion of the address of the branch instruction and that contains one or more bits indicating whether the branch was recently taken or not.

Loops and Prediction

EXAMPLE

Consider a loop branch that branches nine times in a row, then is not taken once. What is the prediction accuracy for this branch, assuming the prediction bit for this branch remains in the prediction buffer?

ANSWER

The steady-state prediction behavior will mispredict on the first and last loop iterations. Mispredicting the last iteration is inevitable since the prediction bit will say taken: the branch has been taken nine times in a row at that point. The misprediction on the first iteration happens because the bit is flipped on prior execution of the last iteration of the loop, since the branch was not taken on that exiting iteration. Thus, the prediction accuracy for this branch that is taken 90% of the time is only 80% (two incorrect predictions and eight correct ones).

Ideally, the accuracy of the predictor would match the taken branch frequency for these highly regular branches. To remedy this weakness, 2-bit prediction schemes are often used. In a 2-bit scheme, a prediction must be wrong twice before it is changed. Figure 6.39 shows the finite-state machine for a 2-bit prediction scheme.

A branch prediction buffer can be implemented as a small, special buffer accessed with the instruction address during the IF pipe stage. If the instruction is predicted as taken, fetching begins from the target as soon as the PC is known; as mentioned on page 418, it can be as early as the ID stage. Otherwise, sequential

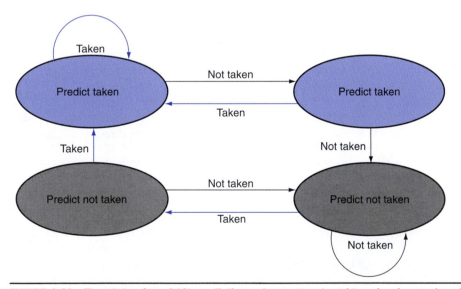

FIGURE 6.39   The states in a 2-bit prediction scheme. By using 2 bits rather than 1, a branch that strongly favors taken or not taken—as many branches do—will be mispredicted only once. The 2 bits are used to encode the four states in the system. The 2-bit scheme is a general instance of a counter-based predictor, which is incremented when the prediction is accurate and decremented otherwise, and uses the midpoint of its range as the division between taken and not taken.

fetching and executing continue. If the prediction turns out to be wrong, the prediction bits are changed as shown in Figure 6.39.

Elaboration: As we described in Section 6.1, in a five-stage pipeline we can make the control hazard a feature by redefining the branch. A delayed branch always executes the following instruction, but the second instruction following the branch will be affected by the branch.

Compilers and assemblers try to place an instruction that always executes after the branch in the **branch delay slot**. The job of the software is to make the successor instructions valid and useful. Figure 6.40 shows the three ways in which the branch delay slot can be scheduled.

The limitations on delayed branch scheduling arise from (1) the restrictions on the instructions that are scheduled into the delay slots and (2) our ability to predict at compile time whether a branch is likely to be taken or not.

Delayed branching was a simple and effective solution for a five-stage pipeline issuing one instruction each clock cycle. As processors go to both longer pipelines and issuing multiple instructions per clock cycle (see Section 6.9), the branch delay becomes longer and a single delay slot is insufficient. Hence, delayed branching has lost popularity compared to more expensive but more flexible dynamic approaches. Simultaneously, the growth in available transistors per chip has made dynamic prediction relatively cheaper.

Elaboration: A branch predictor tells us whether or not a branch is taken, but still requires the calculation of the branch target. In the five-stage pipeline, this calculation takes 1 cycle, meaning that taken branches will have a 1-cycle penalty. Delayed branches are one approach to eliminate that penalty. Another approach is to use a cache to hold the destination program counter or destination instruction, using a **branch target buffer**.

Elaboration: The 2-bit dynamic prediction scheme uses only information about a particular branch. Researchers noticed that using information about both a local branch and the global behavior of recently executed branches together yields greater prediction accuracy for the same number of prediction bits. Such predictors are called **correlating predictors**. A typical correlating predictor might have two 2-bit predictors for each branch with the choice between predictors made on the basis of whether the last executed branch was taken or not taken. Thus, the global branch behavior can be thought of as adding additional index bits for the prediction lookup.

A more recent innovation in branch prediction is the use of tournament predictors. A **tournament predictor** uses multiple predictors, tracking, for each branch, which predictor yields the best results. A typical tournament predictor might contain two predictions for each branch index: one based on local information and one based on global branch behavior. A selector would choose which predictor to use for any given prediction. The selector can operate similarly to a 1- or 2-bit predictor favoring whichever of the two predictors has been more accurate. Many recent advanced microprocessors make use of such elaborate predictors.

branch delay slot The slot directly after a delayed branch instruction, which in the MIPS architecture is filled by an instruction that does not affect the branch.

branch target buffer A structure that caches the destination PC or destination instruction for a branch. It is usually organized as a cache with tags, making it more costly than a simple prediction buffer.

correlating predictor A branch predictor that combines local behavior of a particular branch and global information about the behavior of some recent number of executed branches.

tournament branch predictor A branch predictor with multiple predictions for each branch and a selection mechanism that chooses which predictor to enable for a given branch.

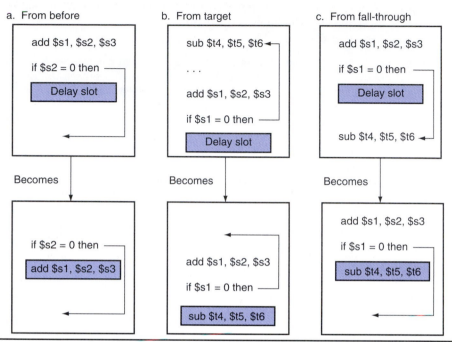

FIGURE 6.40   Scheduling the branch delay slot. The top box in each pair shows the code before scheduling; the bottom box shows the scheduled code. In (a), the delay slot is scheduled with an independent instruction from before the branch. This is the best choice. Strategies (b) and (c) are used when (a) is not possible. In the code sequences for (b) and (c), the use of $s1 in the branch condition prevents the add instruction (whose destination is $s1) from being moved into the branch delay slot. In (b) the branch delay slot is scheduled from the target of the branch; usually the target instruction will need to be copied because it can be reached by another path. Strategy (b) is preferred when the branch is taken with high probability, such as a loop branch. Finally, the branch may be scheduled from the not-taken fall-through as in (c). To make this optimization legal for (b) or (c), it must be OK to execute the sub instruction when the branch goes in the unexpected direction. By "OK" we mean that the work is wasted, but the program will still execute correctly. This is the case, for example, if $t4 were an unused temporary register when the branch goes in the unexpected direction.

Pipeline Summary

Thus far, we have seen three models of execution: single cycle, multicycle, and pipelined. Pipelined control strives for 1 clock cycle per instruction, like single cycle, but also for a fast clock cycle, like multicycle. Let's revisit the example comparison of single-cycle and multicycle processors.

Comparing Performance of Several Control Schemes

Compare performance for single cycle, multicycle, and pipelined control using the SPECint2000 instruction mix (see examples on pages 315 and 330) and assuming the same cycle times per unit as the example on page 315. For pipelined execution, assume that half of the load instructions are immediately followed by an instruction that uses the result, that the branch delay on misprediction is 1 clock cycle, and that one-quarter of the branches are mispredicted. Assume that jumps always pay 1 full clock cycle of delay, so their average time is 2 clock cycles. Ignore any other hazards.

EXAMPLE

From the example on page 315 ("Performance of Single-Cycle Machines"), we get the following functional unit times:

ANSWER

- 200 ps for memory access
- 100 ps for ALU operation
- 50 ps for register file read or write

For the single-cycle datapath, this leads to a clock cycle of

$$200 + 50 + 100 + 200 + 50 = 600 \text{ ps}$$

The example on page 330 ("CPI in a Multicycle CPU") has the following instruction frequencies:

- 25% loads
- 10% stores
- 11% branches
- 2% jumps
- 52% ALU instructions

Furthermore, the example on page 330 showed that the CPI for the multiple design was 4.12. The clock cycle for the multicycle datapath and the pipelined design must be the same as the longest functional unit: 200 ps.

For the pipelined design, loads take 1 clock cycle when there is no load-use dependence and 2 when there is. Hence, the average clock cycles per load instruction is 1.5. Stores take 1 clock cycle, as do the ALU instructions. Branches take 1 when predicted correctly and 2 when not, so the average clock cycles per branch instruction is 1.25. The jump CPI is 2. Hence the average CPI is

$$1.5 \times 25\% + 1 \times 10\% + 1 \times 52\% + 1.25 \times 11\% + 2 \times 2\% = 1.17$$

Let's compare the three designs by the average instruction time. For the single-cycle design, it is fixed at 600 ps. For the multicycle design, it is 200 × 4.12 = 824 ps. For the pipelined design, the average instruction time is 1.17 × 200 = 234 ps, making it almost twice as fast as either approach.

The clever reader will notice that the long cycle time of the memory is a performance bottleneck for both the pipelined and multicycle designs. Breaking memory accesses into two clock cycles and thereby allowing the clock cycle to be 100 ps would improve the performance in both cases. We explore this in the exercises.

This chapter started in the laundry room, showing principles of pipelining in an everyday setting. Using that analogy as a guide, we explained instruction pipelining step-by-step, starting with the single-cycle datapath and then adding pipeline registers, forwarding paths, data hazard detection, branch prediction, and flushing instructions on exceptions. Figure 6.41 shows the final evolved datapath and control.

Check Yourself

Consider three branch prediction schemes: branch not taken, predict taken, and dynamic prediction. Assume that they all have zero penalty when they predict correctly and 2 cycles when they are wrong. Assume that the average predict accuracy of the dynamic predictor is 90%. Which predictor is the best choice for the following branches?

1. A branch that is taken with 5% frequency

2. A branch that is taken with 95% frequency

3. A branch that is taken with 70% frequency

6.7 Using a Hardware Description Language to Describe and Model a Pipeline

This section, which appears on the CD, provides a behavioral model in Verilog of the MIPS five-stage pipeline. The initial model ignores hazards, and additions to the model highlight the changes for forwarding, data hazards, and branch hazards.

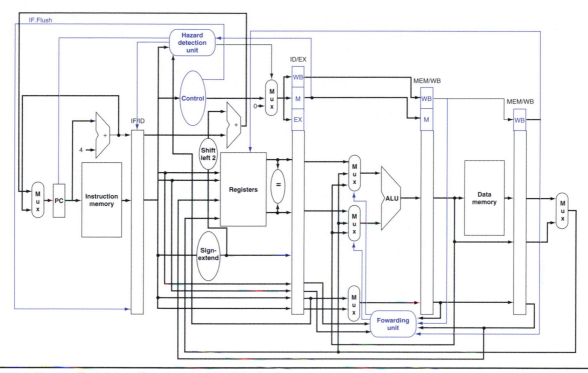

FIGURE 6.41 The final datapath and control for this chapter.

6.8 Exceptions

Another form of control hazard involves exceptions. For example, suppose the following instruction,

```
add    $1,$2,$1
```

has an arithmetic overflow. We need to transfer control to the exception routine immediately after this instruction because we wouldn't want this invalid value to contaminate other registers or memory locations.

Just as we did for the taken branch in the previous section, we must flush the instructions that follow the add instruction from the pipeline and begin fetching instructions from the new address. We will use the same mechanism we used for taken branches, but this time the exception causes the deasserting of control lines.

When we dealt with branch mispredict, we saw how to flush the instruction in the IF stage by turning it into a nop. To flush instructions in the ID stage, we use the multiplexor already in the ID stage that zeros control signals for stalls. A new

To make a computer with automatic program-interruption facilities behave [sequentially] was not an easy matter, because the number of instructions in various stages of processing when an interrupt signal occurs may be large.

Fred Brooks, Jr., *Planning a Computer System: Project Stretch*, 1962

control signal, called ID.Flush, is ORed with the stall signal from the hazard detection unit to flush during ID. To flush the instruction in the EX phase, we use a new signal called EX.Flush to cause new multiplexors to zero the control lines. To start fetching instructions from location $8000\ 0180_{hex}$, which is the exception location for an arithmetic overflow, we simply add an additional input to the PC multiplexor that sends $8000\ 0180_{hex}$ to the PC. Figure 6.42 shows these changes.

This example points out a problem with exceptions: if we do not stop execution in the middle of the instruction, the programmer will not be able to see the original value of register $1 that helped cause the overflow because it will be clobbered as the destination register of the add instruction. Because of careful planning, the overflow exception is detected during the EX stage; hence, we can use the EX.Flush signal to prevent the instruction in the EX stage from writing its result in the WB stage. Many exceptions require that we eventually complete the instruction that caused the exception as if it executed normally. The easiest way to do this

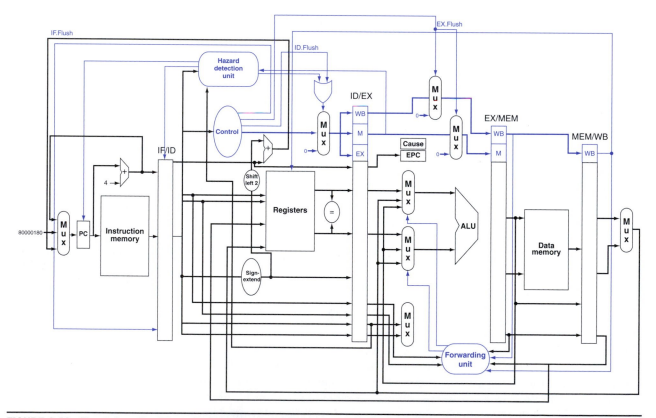

FIGURE 6.42 The datapath with controls to handle exceptions. The key additions include a new input, with the value $8000\ 0180_{hex}$, in the multiplexor that supplies the new PC value; a Cause register to record the cause of the exception; and an Exception PC register to save the address of the instruction that caused the exception. The $8000\ 0180_{hex}$ input to the multiplexor is the initial address to begin fetching instructions in the event of an exception. Although not shown, the ALU overflow signal is an input to the control unit.

is to flush the instruction and restart it from the beginning after the exception is handled.

The final step is to save the address of the offending instruction in the Exception Program Counter (EPC), as we did in Chapter 5. In reality, we save the address + 4, so the exception handling routine must first subtract 4 from the saved value. Figure 6.42 shows a stylized version of the datapath, including the branch hardware and necessary accommodations to handle exceptions.

Exception in a Pipelined Computer

Given this instruction sequence,

40_{hex}	sub	$11, $2, $4
44_{hex}	and	$12, $2, $5
48_{hex}	or	$13, $2, $6
$4C_{hex}$	add	$1, $2, $1
50_{hex}	slt	$15, $6, $7
54_{hex}	lw	$16, 50($7)

. . .

assume the instructions to be invoked on an exception begin like this:

40000040_{hex}	sw	$25, 1000($0)
40000044_{hex}	sw	$26, 1004($0)

. . .

Show what happens in the pipeline if an overflow exception occurs in the add instruction.

EXAMPLE

ANSWER

Figure 6.43 shows the events, starting with the add instruction in the EX stage. The overflow is detected during that phase, and $4000\ 0040_{hex}$ is forced into the PC. Clock cycle 7 shows that the add and following instructions are flushed, and the first instruction of the exception code is fetched. Note that the address of the instruction *following* the add is saved: $4C_{hex} + 4 = 50_{hex}$.

Chapter 5 lists some other causes of exceptions:

■ I/O device request

■ Invoking an operating system service from a user program

■ Using an undefined instruction

■ Hardware malfunction

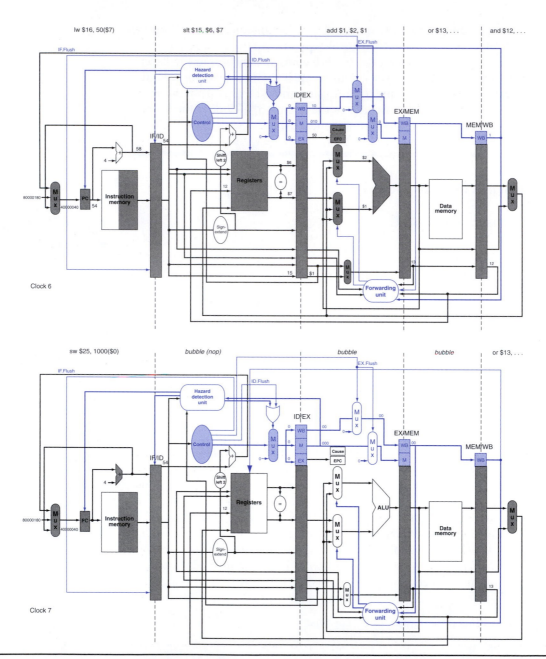

FIGURE 6.43 The result of an exception due to arithmetic overflow in the add instruction. The overflow is detected during the EX stage of clock 6, saving the address following the add in the EPC register ($4C + 4 = 50_{hex}$). Overflow causes all the Flush signals to be set near the end of this clock cycle, deasserting control values (setting them to 0) for the add. Clock cycle 7 shows the instructions converted to bubbles in the pipeline plus the fetching of the first instruction of the exception routine—sw $25,1000($0)—from instruction location 4000 0040$_{hex}$. Note that the and and or instructions, which are prior to the add, still complete. Although not shown, the ALU overflow signal is an input to the control unit.

With five instructions active in any clock cycle, the challenge is to associate an exception with the appropriate instruction. Moreover, multiple exceptions can occur simultaneously in a single clock cycle. The normal solution is to prioritize the exceptions so that it is easy to determine which is serviced first; this strategy works for pipelined processors as well. In most MIPS implementations, the hardware sorts exceptions so that the earliest instruction is interrupted.

I/O device requests and hardware malfunctions are not associated with a specific instruction, so the implementation has some flexibility as to when to interrupt the pipeline. Hence, using the mechanism used for other exceptions works just fine.

The EPC captures the address of the interrupted instructions, and the MIPS Cause register records all possible exceptions in a clock cycle, so the exception software must match the exception to the instruction. An important clue is knowing in which pipeline stage a type of exception can occur. For example, an undefined instruction is discovered in the ID stage, and invoking the operating system occurs in the EX stage. Exceptions are collected in the Cause register so that the hardware can interrupt based on later exceptions, once the earliest one has been serviced.

Hardware/ Software Interface

The hardware and the operating system must work in conjunction so that exceptions behave as you would expect. The hardware contract is normally to stop the offending instruction in midstream, let all prior instructions complete, flush all following instructions, set a register to show the cause of the exception, save the address of the offending instruction, and then jump to a prearranged address. The operating system contract is to look at the cause of the exception and act appropriately. For an undefined instruction, hardware failure, or arithmetic overflow exception, the operating system normally kills the program and returns an indicator of the reason. For an I/O device request or an operating system service call, the operating system saves the state of the program, performs the desired task, and, at some point in the future, restores the program to continue execution. In the case of I/O device requests, we may often choose to run another task before resuming the task that requested the I/O, since that task may often not be able to proceed until the I/O is complete. This is why the ability to save and restore the state of any task is critical. One of the most important and frequent uses of exceptions is handling page faults and TLB exceptions; Chapter 7 describes these exceptions and their handling in more detail.

imprecise interrupt Also called **imprecise exception**. Interrupts or exceptions in pipelined computers that are not associated with the exact instruction that was the cause of the interrupt or exception.

precise interrupt Also called **precise exception**. An interrupt or exception that is always associated with the correct instruction in pipelined computers.

The difficulty of always associating the correct exception with the correct instruction in pipelined computers has led some computer designers to relax this requirement in noncritical cases. Such processors are said to have **imprecise interrupts** or **imprecise exceptions**. In the example above, PC would normally have 58_{hex} at the start of the clock cycle after the exception is detected, even though the offending instruction is at address $4C_{hex}$. A processor with imprecise exceptions might put 58_{hex} into EPC and leave it up to the operating system to determine which instruction caused the problem. MIPS and the vast majority of computers today support **precise interrupts** or **precise exceptions**. (One reason is to support virtual memory, which we shall see in Chapter 7.)

Check Yourself

The MIPS designers wanted the integer multiply and divide instructions to operate in parallel with other integer instructions. Since multiply and divide take multiple clock cycles, a group of students are arguing over whether it is possible to implement precise exceptions. Which of the following arguments are completely accurate?

1. It is impossible to implement precise exceptions, since a multiply or divide can raise an exception after instructions that follow it.

2. It is trivial to implement precise exceptions since multiply and divide cannot raise an exception once they start, and so the timing of all exceptions is obviously precise.

3. It does not matter whether multiply or divide can raise an exception. The fact that they could still be executing and not completed when some other instruction raised an exception makes it impossible to implement precise exceptions.

4. Although it is true that a multiply or divide could still be executing, it is guaranteed to complete shortly, and when it does, any exception raised for an instruction following a multiply or divide will then be precise.

6.9 Advanced Pipelining: Extracting More Performance

Be forewarned that Sections 6.9 and 6.10 are brief overviews of fascinating but advanced topics. If you want to learn more details, you should consult our more advanced book, *Computer Architecture: A Quantitative Approach*, fourth edition, where the material covered in the next 18 pages is expanded to over 200 pages (including Appendices)!

Pipelining exploits the potential parallelism among instructions. This parallelism is called **instruction-level parallelism** (ILP). There are two primary methods for increasing the potential amount of instruction-level parallelism. The first is increasing the depth of the pipeline to overlap more instructions. Using our laundry analogy and assuming that the washer cycle was longer than the others, we could divide our washer into three machines that perform the wash, rinse, and spin steps of a traditional washer. We would then move from a four-stage to a six-stage pipeline. To get the full speedup, we need to rebalance the remaining steps so they are the same length, in processors or in laundry. The amount of parallelism being exploited is higher, since there are more operations being overlapped. Performance is potentially greater since the clock cycle can be shorter.

Another approach is to replicate the internal components of the computer so that it can launch multiple instructions in every pipeline stage. The general name for this technique is **multiple issue**. A multiple-issue laundry would replace our household washer and dryer with, say, three washers and three dryers. You would also have to recruit more assistants to fold and put away three times as much laundry in the same amount of time. The downside is the extra work to keep all the machines busy and transferring the loads to the next pipeline stage.

Launching multiple instructions per stage allows the instruction execution rate to exceed the clock rate or, stated alternatively, the CPI to be less than 1. It is sometimes useful to flip the metric, and use *IPC*, or *instructions per clock cycle*, particularly as values become less than 1! Hence, a 6 GHz four-way multiple-issue microprocessor can execute a peak rate of 24 billion instructions per second and have a best-case CPI of 0.25, or an IPC of 4. Assuming a five-stage pipeline, such a processor would have 20 instructions in execution at any given time. Today's high-end microprocessors attempt to issue from three to eight instructions in every clock cycle. There are typically, however, many constraints on what types of instructions may be executed simultaneously and what happens when dependences arise.

There are two major ways to implement a multiple-issue processor, with the major difference being the division of work between the compiler and the hardware. Because the division of work dictates whether decisions are being made statically (that is, at compile time) or dynamically (that is, during execution), the approaches are sometimes called **static multiple issue** and **dynamic multiple issue**. As we will see, both approaches have other, more commonly used names, which may be less precise or more restrictive.

instruction-level parallelism The parallelism among instructions.

multiple issue A scheme whereby multiple instructions are launched in 1 clock cycle.

static multiple issue An approach to implementing a multiple-issue processor where many decisions are made by the compiler before execution.

dynamic multiple issue An approach to implementing a multiple-issue processor where many decisions are made during execution by the processor.

There are two primary and distinct responsibilities that must be dealt with in a multiple-issue pipeline:

issue slots The positions from which instructions could issue in a given clock cycle; by analogy these correspond to positions at the starting blocks for a sprint.

1. Packaging instructions into **issue slots**: How does the processor determine how many instructions and which instructions can be issued in a given clock cycle? In most static issue processors, this process is at least partially handled by the compiler; in dynamic issue designs, it is normally dealt with at runtime by the processor, although the compiler will often have already tried to help improve the issue rate by placing the instructions in a beneficial order.

2. Dealing with data and control hazards: In static issue processors, some or all of the consequences of data and control hazards are handled statically by the compiler. In contrast, most dynamic issue processors attempt to alleviate at least some classes of hazards using hardware techniques operating at execution time.

Although we describe these as distinct approaches, in reality techniques from one approach are often borrowed by the other, and neither approach can claim to be perfectly pure.

The Concept of Speculation

One of the most important methods for finding and exploiting more ILP is speculation. **Speculation** is an approach that allows the compiler or the processor to "guess" about the properties of an instruction, so as to enable execution to begin for other instructions that may depend on the speculated instruction. For example, we might speculate on the outcome of a branch, so that instructions after the branch could be executed earlier. Or, we might speculate that a store that precedes a load does not refer to the same address, which would allow the load to be executed before the store. The difficulty with speculation is that it may be wrong. So, any speculation mechanism must include both a method to check if the guess was right and a method to unroll or back out the effects of the instructions that were executed speculatively. The implementation of this back-out capability adds complexity to any processor supporting speculation.

speculation An approach whereby the compiler or processor guesses the outcome of an instruction to remove it as a dependence in executing other instructions.

Speculation may be done in the compiler or by the hardware. For example, the compiler can use speculation to reorder instructions, moving an instruction across a branch or a load across a store. The processor hardware can perform the same transformation at runtime using techniques we discuss later in this section.

The recovery mechanisms used for incorrect speculation are rather different. In the case of speculation in software, the compiler usually inserts additional instructions that check the accuracy of the speculation and provide a fix-up routine to use when the speculation is incorrect. In hardware speculation, the processor usually buffers the speculative results until it knows they are no longer speculative. If the speculation is correct, the instructions are completed by allowing the contents of the buffers to be written to the registers or memory. If the speculation is incorrect, the hardware flushes the buffers and reexecutes the correct instruction sequence.

Speculation introduces one other possible problem: speculating on certain instructions may introduce exceptions that were formerly not present. For example, suppose a load instruction is moved in a speculative manner, but the address it uses is not legal when the speculation is incorrect. The result would be that an exception that should not have occurred will occur. The problem is complicated by the fact that if the load instruction were not speculative, then the exception must occur! In compiler-based speculation, such problems are avoided by adding special speculation support that allows such exceptions to be ignored until it is clear that they really should occur. In hardware-based speculation, exceptions are simply buffered until it is clear that the instruction causing them is no longer speculative and is ready to complete; at that point the exception is raised, and normal exception handling proceeds.

Since speculation can improve performance when done properly and decrease performance when done carelessly, significant effort goes into deciding when it is appropriate to speculate. Later in this section, we will examine both static and dynamic techniques for speculation.

Static Multiple Issue

Static multiple-issue processors all use the compiler to assist with packaging instructions and handling hazards. In a static issue processor, you can think of the set of instructions that issue in a given clock cycle, which is called an **issue packet**, as one large instruction with multiple operations. This view is more than an analogy. Since a static multiple-issue processor usually restricts what mix of instructions can be initiated in a given clock cycle, it is useful to think of the issue packet as a single instruction allowing several operations in certain predefined fields. This view led to the original name for this approach: Very Long Instruction Word (VLIW). The Intel IA-64 architecture uses this approach, which it calls by its own name: Explicitly Parallel Instruction Computer (EPIC). The Itanium and Itanium 2 processors, available in 2000 and 2002, respectively, are the first implementations of the IA-64 architecture.

Most static issue processors also rely on the compiler to take on some responsibility for handling data and control hazards. The compiler's responsibilities may include static branch prediction and code scheduling to reduce or prevent all hazards.

issue packet The set of instructions that issues together in 1 clock cycle; the packet may be determined statically by the compiler or dynamically by the processor.

Let's look at a simple static issue version of a MIPS processor, before we describe the use of these techniques in more aggressive processors. After using this simple example to review the comments, we discuss the highlights of the Intel IA-64 architecture.

An Example: Static Multiple Issue with the MIPS ISA

To give a flavor of static multiple issue, we consider a simple two-issue MIPS processor, where one of the instructions can be an integer ALU operation or branch, and the other can be a load or store. Such a design is like that used in some embedded MIPS processors. Issuing two instructions per cycle will require fetching and decoding 64 bits of instructions. In many static multiple-issue processors, and essentially all VLIW processors, the layout of simultaneously issuing instructions is restricted to simplify the decoding and instruction issue. Hence, we will require that the instructions be paired and aligned on a 64-bit boundary, with the ALU or branch portion appearing first. Furthermore, if one instruction of the pair cannot be used, we require that it be replaced with a no-op. Thus, the instructions always issue in pairs, possibly with a nop in one slot. Figure 6.44 shows how the instructions look as they go into the pipeline in pairs.

Static multiple-issue processors vary in how they deal with potential data and control hazards. In some designs, the compiler takes full responsibility for removing *all* hazards, scheduling the code and inserting no-ops so that the code executes without any need for hazard detection or hardware-generated stalls. In others, the hardware detects data hazards and generates stalls between two issue packets, while requiring that the compiler avoid all dependences within an instruction pair. Even so, a hazard generally forces the entire issue packet containing the dependent instruction to stall. Whether the software must handle all hazards or

Instruction type	Pipe stages							
ALU or branch instruction	IF	ID	EX	MEM	WB			
Load or store instruction	IF	ID	EX	MEM	WB			
ALU or branch instruction		IF	ID	EX	MEM	WB		
Load or store instruction		IF	ID	EX	MEM	WB		
ALU or branch instruction			IF	ID	EX	MEM	WB	
Load or store instruction			IF	ID	EX	MEM	WB	
ALU or branch instruction				IF	ID	EX	MEM	WB
Load or store instruction				IF	ID	EX	MEM	WB

FIGURE 6.44   Static two-issue pipeline in operation. The ALU and data transfer instructions are issued at the same time. Here we have assumed the same five-stage structure as used for the single-issue pipeline. Although this is not strictly necessary, it does have some advantages. In particular, keeping the register writes at the end of the pipeline simplifies the handling of exceptions and the maintenance of a precise exception model, which become more difficult in multiple-issue processors.

only try to reduce the fraction of hazards between separate issue packets, the appearance of having a large single instruction with multiple operations is reinforced. We will assume the second approach for this example.

To issue an ALU and a data transfer operation in parallel, the first need for additional hardware—beyond the usual hazard detection and stall logic—is extra ports in the register file (see Figure 6.45). In 1 clock cycle we may need to read two registers for the ALU operation and two more for a store, and also one write port for an ALU operation and one write port for a load. Since the ALU is tied up for the ALU operation, we also need a separate adder to calculate the effective address for data transfers. Without these extra resources, our two-issue pipeline would be hindered by structural hazards.

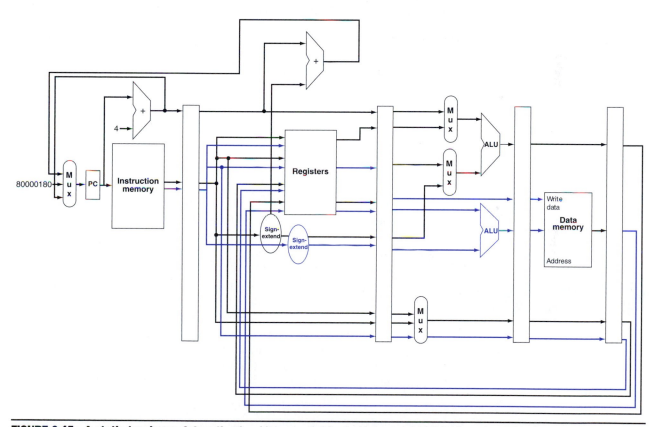

FIGURE 6.45 A static two-issue datapath. The additions needed for double issue are highlighted: another 32 bits from instruction memory, two more read ports and one more write port on the register file, and another ALU. Assume the bottom ALU handles address calculations for data transfers and the top ALU handles everything else.

Clearly, this two-issue processor can improve performance by up to a factor of 2. Doing so, however, requires that twice as many instructions be overlapped in execution, and this additional overlap increases the relative performance loss from data and control hazards. For example, in our simple five-stage pipeline, loads have a use latency of 1 clock cycle, which prevents one instruction from using the result without stalling. In the two-issue, five-stage pipeline the result of a load instruction cannot be used on the next *clock cycle*. This means that the next *two* instructions cannot use the load result without stalling. Furthermore, ALU instructions that had no use latency in the simple five-stage pipeline now have a one-instruction use latency, since the results cannot be used in the paired load or store. To effectively exploit the parallelism available in a multiple-issue processor, more ambitious compiler or hardware scheduling techniques are needed, and static multiple issue requires that the compiler take on this role.

EXAMPLE

Simple Multiple-Issue Code Scheduling

How would this loop be scheduled on a static two-issue pipeline for MIPS?

```
Loop:    lw      $t0, 0($s1)     # $t0=array element
         addu    $t0,$t0,$s2     # add scalar in $s2
         sw      $t0, 0($s1)     # store result
         addi    $s1,$s1,-4      # decrement pointer
         bne     $s1,$zero,Loop  # branch $s1!=0
```

Reorder the instructions to avoid as many pipeline stalls as possible. Assume branches are predicted, so that control hazards are handled by the hardware.

ANSWER

The first three instructions have data dependences, and so do the last two. Figure 6.46 shows the best schedule for these instructions. Notice that just one pair of instructions has both issue slots used. It takes 4 clocks per loop iteration; at 4 clocks to execute 5 instructions, we get the disappointing CPI of 0.8 versus the best case of 0.5., or an IPC of 1.25 versus 2.0. Notice that in computing CPI or IPC, we do not count any nops executed as useful instructions. Doing so would improve CPI, but not performance!

loop unrolling A technique to get more performance from loops that access arrays, in which multiple copies of the loop body are made and instructions from different iterations are scheduled together.

An important compiler technique to get more performance from loops is **loop unrolling**, where multiple copies of the loop body are made. After unrolling, there is more ILP available by overlapping instructions from different iterations.

	ALU or branch instruction	Data transfer instruction	Clock cycle
Loop:		`lw     $t0, 0($s1)`	1
	`addi    $s1,$s1,-4`		2
	`addu    $t0,$t0,$s2`		3
	`bne     $s1,$zero,Loop`	`sw     $t0, 4($s1)`	4

FIGURE 6.46 The scheduled code as it would look on a two-issue MIPS pipeline. The empty slots are nops.

Loop Unrolling for Multiple-Issue Pipelines

See how well loop unrolling and scheduling work in the example above. Assume that the loop index is a multiple of four, for simplicity.

EXAMPLE

ANSWER

To schedule the loop without any delays, it turns out that we need to make four copies of the loop body. After unrolling and eliminating the unnecessary loop overhead instructions, the loop will contain four copies each of `lw`, `add`, and `sw`, plus one `addi` and one `bne`. Figure 6.47 shows the unrolled and scheduled code.

During the unrolling process, the compiler introduced additional registers ($t1, $t2, $t3). The goal of this process, called **register renaming**, is to eliminate dependences that are not true data dependences, but could either lead to potential hazards or prevent the compiler from flexibly scheduling the code. Consider how the unrolled code would look using only $t0. There would be repeated instances of `lw  $t0,0($$s1)`, `addu  $t0,$t0,$s2` followed by `sw t0,4($s1)`, but these sequences, despite using $t0, are actually completely independent—no data values flow between one pair of these instructions and the next pair. This is what is called an **antidependence** or **name dependence**, which is an ordering forced purely by the reuse of a name, rather than a real data dependence.

Renaming the registers during the unrolling process allows the compiler to subsequently move these independent instructions so as to better schedule the code. The renaming process eliminates the name dependences, while preserving the true dependences.

Notice now that 12 of the 14 instructions in the loop execute as a pair. It takes 8 clocks for four loop iterations, or 2 clocks per iteration, which yields a CPI of 8/14 = 0.57. Loop unrolling and scheduling with dual issue gave us a factor of 2 improvement, partly from reducing the loop control instructions and partly from dual issue execution. The cost of this performance improvement is using four temporary registers rather than one, as well as a significant increase in code size.

register renaming The renaming of registers, by the compiler or hardware, to remove antidependences.

antidependence Also called **name dependence**. An ordering forced by the reuse of a name, typically a register, rather than by a true dependence that carries a value between two instructions.

	ALU or branch instruction		Data transfer instruction		Clock cycle
Loop:	addi	$s1,$s1,-16	lw	$t0, 0($s1)	1
			lw	$t1,12($s1)	2
	addu	$t0,$t0,$s2	lw	$t2, 8($s1)	3
	addu	$t1,$t1,$s2	lw	$t3, 4($s1)	4
	addu	$t2,$t2,$s2	sw	$t0, 16($s1)	5
	addu	$t3,$t3,$s2	sw	$t1,12($s1)	6
			sw	$t2, 8($s1)	7
	bne	$s1,$zero,Loop	sw	$t3, 4($s1)	8

FIGURE 6.47   The unrolled and scheduled code of Figure 6.46 as it would look on a static two-issue MIPS pipeline. The empty slots are nops. Since the first instruction in the loop decrements $s1 by 16, the addresses loaded are the original value of $s1, then that address minus 4, minus 8, and minus 12.

The Intel IA-64 Architecture

The IA-64 architecture is a register-register, RISC-style instruction set like the 64-bit version of the MIPS architecture (called MIPS-64), but with several unique features to support explicit, compiler-driven exploitation of ILP. Intel calls the approach EPIC (Explicitly Parallel Instruction Computer). The major differences between IA-64 and the MIPS architecture are the following:

1. IA-64 has many more registers than MIPS, including 128 integer and 128 floating-point registers, as well as 8 special registers for branches and 64 1-bit condition registers. In addition, IA-64 supports register windows in a fashion similar to the original Berkeley RISC and Sun SPARC architectures.

2. IA-64 places instructions into bundles that have a fixed format and explicit designation of dependences.

3. IA-64 includes special instructions and capabilities for speculation and for branch elimination, which increase the amount of ILP that can be exploited.

The IA-64 architecture is designed to achieve the major benefits of a VLIW—implicit parallelism among operations in an instruction and fixed formatting of the operation fields—while maintaining greater flexibility than a VLIW normally allows. The IA-64 architecture uses two different concepts to achieve this flexibility: instruction groups and bundles.

instruction group In IA-64, a sequence of consecutive instructions with no register data dependences among them.

stop In IA-64, an explicit indicator of a break between independent and dependent instructions.

An **instruction group** is a sequence of consecutive instructions with no register data dependences among them. All the instructions in a group could be executed in parallel if sufficient hardware resources existed and if any dependences through memory were preserved. An instruction group can be arbitrarily long, but the compiler must *explicitly* indicate the boundary between one instruction group and another. This boundary is indicated by placing a **stop** between two instructions that belong to different groups.

IA-64 instructions are encoded in *bundles,* which are 128 bits wide. Each bundle consists of a 5-bit template field and three instructions, each 41 bits in length. To simplify the decoding and instruction issue process, the template field of a bundle specifies which of five different execution units each instruction in the bundle requires. The five different execution units are integer ALU, noninteger ALU (includes shifters and multimedia operations), memory unit, floating-point unit, and branch unit.

The 5-bit template field within each bundle describes *both* the presence of any stops associated with the bundle and the execution unit type required by each instruction within the bundle. The bundle formats can specify only a subset of all possible combinations of instruction types and stops.

To enhance the amount of ILP that can be exploited, IA-64 provides extensive support for predication and for speculation (see the elaboration on page 442). **Predication** is a technique that can be used to eliminate branches by making the execution of an instruction dependent on a predicate, rather than dependent on a branch. As we saw earlier, branches reduce the opportunity to exploit ILP by restricting the movement of code. Loop unrolling works well to eliminate loop branches, but a branch within a loop—arising, for example, from an *if-then-else* statement—cannot be eliminated by loop unrolling. Predication, however, provides a method to eliminate the branch, allowing more flexible exploitation of parallelism.

For example, suppose we had a code sequence like

```
if (p) {statement 1} else {statement 2}
```

Using normal compilation methods, this segment would compile using two branches: one after the condition branching to the else portion and one after statement 1 branching to the next sequential statement. With predication, it could be compiled as

```
(p) statement 1
(~p) statement 2
```

where the use of (condition) indicates that the statement is executed only if condition is true, and otherwise becomes a no-op. Notice that predication can be used as a way to speculate, as well as a method to eliminate branches.

The IA-64 architecture provides comprehensive support for predication: nearly every instruction in the IA-64 architecture can be predicated by specifying a predicate register, whose identity is placed in the lower 6 bits of an instruction field. One consequence of full predication is that a conditional branch is simply a branch with a guarding predicate!

IA-64 is the most sophisticated example of an instruction set with support for compiler-based exploitation of ILP. Intel's Itanium and Itanium 2 processors implement this architecture. A brief summary of the characteristics of these processors is given in Figure 6.48.

predication A technique to make instructions dependent on predicates rather than on branches.

Processor	Maximum instr. issues / clock	Functional units	Maximum ops. per clock	Maximum clock rate	Transistors (millions)	Power (watts)	SPEC int2000	SPEC fp2000
Itanium	6	4 integer/media 2 memory 3 branch 2 FP	9	0.8 GHz	25	130	379	701
Itanium 2	6	6 integer/media 4 memory 3 branch 2 FP	11	1.5 Ghz	221	130	810	1427

FIGURE 6.48   A summary of the characteristics of the Itanium and Itanium 2, Intel's first two implementations of the IA-64 architecture. In addition to higher clock rates and more functional units, the Itanium 2 includes an on-chip level 3 cache, versus an off-chip level 3 cache in the Itanium.

Elaboration: Speculation support in the IA-64 architecture consists of separate support for control speculation, which deals with deferring exceptions for speculated instructions, and memory reference speculation, which supports speculation of load instructions. Deferred exception handling is supported by adding speculative load instructions, which, when an exception occurs, tag the result as **poison**. When a poisoned result is used by an instruction, the result is also poison. The software can then check for a poisoned result when it knows that the execution is no longer speculative.

In IA-64, we can also speculate on memory references by moving loads earlier than stores on which they may depend. This is done with an advanced load instruction. An **advanced load** executes normally, but uses a special table to track the address that the processor loaded from. All subsequent stores check that table and generate a flag in the entry if the store address matches the load address. A subsequent instruction must be used to check the status of the entry after the load is no longer speculative. If a store to the same address has intervened, the check instruction specifies a fix-up routine that reexecutes the load and any other dependent instructions before continuing execution; if no such store has occurred, the table entry is simply cleared, indicating that the load is no longer speculative.

poison A result generated when a speculative load yields an exception, or an instruction uses a poisoned operand.

advanced load In IA-64, a speculative load instruction with support to check for aliases that could invalidate the load.

Dynamic Multiple-Issue Processors

superscalar An advanced pipelining technique that enables the processor to execute more than one instruction per clock cycle.

Dynamic multiple-issue processors are also known as **superscalar** processors, or simply superscalars. In the simplest superscalar processors, instructions issue in order, and the processor decides whether zero, one, or more instructions can issue in a given clock cycle. Obviously, achieving good performance on such a processor still requires the compiler to try to schedule instructions to move dependences apart and thereby improve the instruction issue rate. Even with such compiler scheduling, there is an important difference between this simple superscalar and a VLIW processor: the code, whether scheduled or not, is guaranteed by the hardware to execute correctly. Furthermore, compiled code will always run correctly independent of the issue rate or pipeline structure of the processor. In some VLIW designs, this has not been the case, and recompilation was required when moving across different processor models; in other static issue processors, code would run correctly across different implementations, but often so poorly as to make compilation effectively required.

Many superscalars extend the basic framework of dynamic issue decisions to include **dynamic pipeline scheduling**. Dynamic pipeline scheduling chooses which instructions to execute in a given clock cycle while trying to avoid hazards and stalls. Let's start with a simple example of avoiding a data hazard. Consider the following code sequence:

```
lw      $t0, 20($s2)
addu    $t1, $t0, $t2
sub     $s4, $s4, $t3
slti    $t5, $s4, 20
```

Even though the sub instruction is ready to execute, it must wait for the lw and addu to complete first, which might take many clock cycles if memory is slow. (Chapter 7 explains caches, the reason that memory accesses are sometimes very slow.) Dynamic pipeline scheduling allows such hazards to be avoided either fully or partially.

Dynamic Pipeline Scheduling

Dynamic pipeline scheduling chooses which instructions to execute next, possibly reordering them to avoid stalls. In such processors, the pipeline is divided into three major units: an instruction fetch and issue unit, multiple functional units (a dozen or more in high-end designs in 2007), and a **commit unit.** Figure 6.49 shows the model. The first unit fetches instructions, decodes them, and sends each instruction to a corresponding functional unit for execution. Each functional unit has buffers, called **reservation stations**, that hold the operands and the operation. (In the next section, we will discuss an alternative to reservation stations used by many recent processors.) As soon as the buffer contains all its operands and the functional unit is ready to execute, the result is calculated. When the result is completed, it is sent to any reservation stations waiting for this particular result as well as to the commit unit, which buffers the result until it is safe to put the result into the register file or, for a store, into memory. The buffer in the commit unit, often called the **reorder buffer**, is also used to supply operands, in much the same way as forwarding logic does in a statically scheduled pipeline. Once a result is committed to the register file, it can be fetched directly from there, just as in a normal pipeline.

The combination of buffering operands in the reservation stations and results in the reorder buffer provides a form of register renaming, just like that used by

dynamic pipeline scheduling Hardware support for reordering the order of instruction execution so as to avoid stalls.

commit unit The unit in a dynamic or out-of-order execution pipeline that decides when it is safe to release the result of an operation to programmer-visible registers and memory.

reservation station A buffer within a functional unit that holds the operands and the operation.

reorder buffer The buffer that holds results in a dynamically scheduled processor until it is safe to store the results to memory or a register.

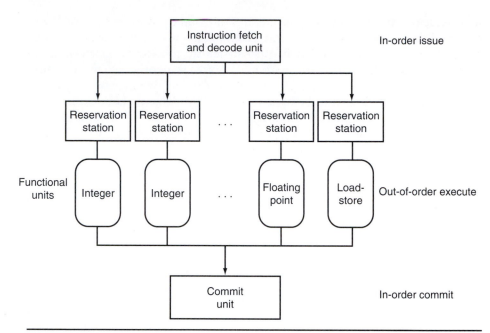

FIGURE 6.49   The three primary units of a dynamically scheduled pipeline. The final step of updating the state is also called retirement or graduation.

the compiler in our earlier loop unrolling example on page 439. To see how this conceptually works, consider the following steps:

1. When an instruction issues, if either of its operands is in the register file or the reorder buffer, it is copied to the reservation station immediately, where it is buffered until all the operands and an execution unit are available. For the issuing instruction, the register copy of the operand is no longer required, and if a write to that register occurred, the value could be overwritten.

2. If an operand is not in the register file or reorder buffer, it must be waiting to be produced by a functional unit. The name of the functional unit that will produce the result is tracked. When that unit eventually produces the result, it is copied directly into the waiting reservation station from the functional unit bypassing the registers.

These steps effectively use the reorder buffer and the reservation stations to implement register renaming.

Conceptually, you can think of a dynamically scheduled pipeline as analyzing the data flow structure of a program, as we saw when we discussed data flow analysis within a compiler in Chapter 2. The processor then executes the instructions in some order that preserves the data flow order of the program. To make programs behave as if they were running on a simple in-order pipeline, the instruction fetch and decode unit is required to issue instructions in order, which allows dependences to be tracked, and the commit unit is required to write results to registers and memory in program execution order. This conservative mode is called in-order completion. Hence, if an exception occurs, the computer can point to the last instruction executed, and the only registers updated will be those written by instructions before the instruction causing the exception. Although, the front end (fetch and issue) and the back end (commit) of the pipeline run in order, the functional units are free to initiate execution whenever the data they need is available. Today, all dynamically scheduled pipelines use in-order completion, although this was not always true.

Dynamic scheduling is often extended by including hardware-based speculation, especially for branch outcomes. By predicting the direction of a branch, a dynamically scheduled processor can continue to fetch and execute instructions along the predicted path. Because the instructions are **committed in order**, we know whether or not the branch was correctly predicted before any instructions from the predicted path are committed. A speculative, dynamically scheduled pipeline can also support speculation on load addresses, allowing load-store reordering, and using the commit unit to avoid incorrect speculation. In the next section we will look at the use of dynamic scheduling with speculation in the Pentium 4 design.

in-order commit A commit in which the results of pipelined execution are written to the programmer-visible state in the same order that instructions are fetched.

Elaboration: A commit unit controls updates to the register file *and* memory. Some dynamically scheduled processors update the register file immediately during execution using extra registers to implement the renaming function and preserving the older copy of a register until the instruction updating the register is no longer speculative. Other processors buffer the result, typically in a structure called a reorder buffer, and the actual update to the register file occurs later as part of the commit. Stores to memory must be buffered until commit time either in a *store buffer* (see Chapter 7) or in the reorder buffer. The commit unit allows the store to write to memory from the buffer when the buffer has a valid address and valid data, and when the store is no longer dependent on predicted branches.

out-of-order execution A situation in pipelined execution when an instruction blocked from executing does not cause the following instructions to wait.

Elaboration: Memory accesses benefit from *nonblocking caches,* which continue servicing cache accesses during a cache miss (see Chapter 7). **Out-of-order execution** processors need nonblocking caches to allow instructions to execute during a miss.

**Hardware/
Software
Interface**

Given that compilers can also schedule code around data dependences, you might ask, Why would a superscalar processor use dynamic scheduling? There are three major reasons. First, not all stalls are predictable. In particular, cache misses (see Chapter 7) cause unpredictable stalls. Dynamic scheduling allows the processor to hide some of those stalls by continuing to execute instructions while waiting for the stall to end.

Second, if the processor speculates on branch outcomes using dynamic branch prediction, it cannot know the exact order of instructions at compile time, since it depends on the predicted and actual behavior of branches. Incorporating dynamic speculation to exploit more ILP without incorporating dynamic scheduling would significantly restrict the benefits of such speculation.

Third, as the pipeline latency and issue width change from one implementation to another, the best way to compile a code sequence also changes. For example, how to schedule a sequence of dependent instructions is affected by both issue width and latency. The pipeline structure affects both the number of times a loop must be unrolled to avoid stalls as well as the process of compiler-based register renaming. Dynamic scheduling allows the hardware to hide most of these details. Thus, users and software distributors do not need to worry about having multiple versions of a program for different implementations of the same instruction set. Similarly, old legacy code will get much of the benefit of a new implementation without the need for recompilation.

**The BIG
Picture**

Both pipelining and multiple-issue execution increase peak instruction throughput and attempt to exploit ILP. Data and control dependences in programs, however, offer an upper limit on sustained performance because the processor must sometimes wait for a dependence to be resolved. Software-centric approaches to exploiting ILP rely on the ability of the compiler to find and reduce the effects of such dependences, while hardware-centric approaches rely on extensions to the pipeline and issue mechanisms. Speculation, performed by the compiler or the hardware, can increase the amount of ILP that can be exploited, although care must be taken since speculating incorrectly is likely to reduce performance.

Understanding Program Performance

Modern, high-performance microprocessors are capable of issuing several instructions per clock; unfortunately, sustaining that issue rate is very difficult. For example, despite the existence of processors with four to six issues per clock, very few applications can sustain more than two instructions per clock. There are two primary reasons for this.

First, within the pipeline, the major performance bottlenecks arise from dependences that cannot be alleviated, thus reducing the parallelism among instructions and the sustained issue rate. Although little can be done about true data dependences, often the compiler or hardware does not know precisely whether a dependence exists or not, and so must conservatively assume the dependence exists. For example, code that makes use of pointers, particularly in ways that create more aliasing, will lead to more implied potential dependences. In contrast, the greater regularity of array accesses often allows a compiler to deduce that no dependences exist. Similarly, branches that cannot be accurately predicted whether at runtime or compile time will limit the ability to exploit ILP. Often additional ILP is available, but the ability of the compiler or the hardware to find ILP that may be widely separated (sometimes by the execution of thousands of instructions) is limited.

Second, losses in the memory system (the topic of Chapter 7) also limit the ability to keep the pipeline full. Some memory system stalls can be hidden, but limited amounts of ILP also limit the extent to which such stalls can be hidden.

Check Yourself

State whether the following techniques or components are associated primarily with a software- or hardware-based approach to exploiting ILP. In some cases, the answer may be both.

1. Branch prediction

2. Multiple issue

3. VLIW

4. Superscalar

5. Dynamic scheduling

6. Out-of-order execution

7. Speculation

8. EPIC

9. Reorder buffer

10. Register renaming

11. Predication

6.10   Real Stuff: The Pentium 4 Pipeline

In the last chapter, we discussed how the Pentium 4 fetched and translated IA-32 instructions into micro-operations. The micro-operations are then executed by a sophisticated, dynamically scheduled, speculative pipeline capable of sustaining an execution rate of three micro-operations per clock cycle. This section focuses on that micro-operation pipeline. The Pentium 4 combines multiple issue with deep pipelining so as to achieve both a low CPI and a high clock rate.

When we consider the design of sophisticated, dynamically scheduled processors, the design of the functional units, the cache and register file, instruction issue, and overall pipeline control become intermingled, making it difficult to separate the datapath from the pipeline. Because of this, many engineers and researchers have adopted the term **microarchitecture** to refer to the detailed internal architecture of a processor. Figure 6.50 shows the microarchitecture of the Pentium 4, focusing on the structures for executing the micro-operations.

Another way to look at the Pentium 4 is to see the pipeline stages that a typical instruction goes through. Figure 6.51 shows the pipeline structure and the typical number of clock cycles spent in each; of course, the number of clock cycles varies due to the nature of dynamic scheduling as well as the requirements of individual micro-operations.

The Pentium 4, and the earlier Pentium III and Pentium Pro, all use the technique of decoding IA-32 instructions into micro-operations and executing those micro-operations using a speculative pipeline with multiple functional units. In fact, the basic microarchitecture is similar, and all these processors can complete up to three microoperations per cycle. The Pentium 4 gains its performance advantage over the Pentium III through several enhancements:

1. A pipeline that is roughly twice as deep (approximately 20 cycles versus 10) and can run almost twice as fast in the same technology

2. More functional units (7 versus 5)

3. Support for a larger number of outstanding operations (126 versus 40)

4. The use of a trace cache (see Chapter 7) and a much better branch predictor (4K entries versus 512)

5. Other enhancements to the memory system, which we discuss in Chapter 7

microarchitecture The organization of the processor, including the major functional units, their interconnection, and control.

architectural registers The instruction set visible registers of a processor; for example, in MIPS, these are the 32 integer and 16 floating-point registers.

Elaboration: The Pentium 4 uses a scheme for resolving antidependences and incorrect speculation that uses a reorder buffer together with register renaming. Register renaming explicitly renames the **architectural registers** in a processor (8 in the case of IA-32) to a larger set of physical registers (128 in the Pentium 4). The Pentium 4 uses

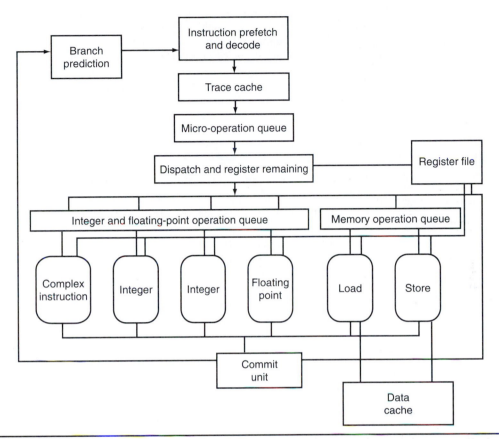

FIGURE 6.50 The microarchitecture of the Intel Pentium 4. The extensive queues allow up to 126 micro-operations to be outstanding at any point in time, including 48 loads and 24 stores. There are actually seven functional units, since the FP unit includes a separate dedicated unit for floating-point moves. The load and store units are actually separated into two parts, with the first part handling address calculation and the second part responsible for the actual memory reference. The integer ALUs operate at twice the clock frequency, allowing two integer ALU operations to be completed by each of the two integer units in a single clock cycle. As we described in Chapter 5, the Pentium 4 uses a special cache, called the trace cache, to hold predecoded sequences of micro-operations, corresponding to IA-32 instructions. The operation of a trace cache is explained in more detail in Chapter 7. The FP unit also handles the MMX multimedia and SSE2 instructions. There is an extensive bypass network among the functional units; since the pipeline is dynamic rather than static, bypassing is done by tagging results and tracking source operands, so as to allow a match when a result is produced for an instruction in one of the queues that needs the result.

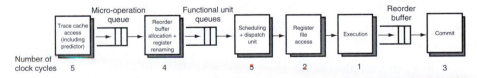

FIGURE 6.51 The Pentium 4 pipeline showing the pipeline flow for a typical instruction and the number of clock cycles for the major steps in the pipeline. The major buffers where instructions wait are also shown.

register renaming to remove antidependences. Register renaming requires the processor to maintain a map between the architectural registers and the physical registers, indicating which physical register is the most current copy of an architectural register. By keeping track of the renamings that have occurred, register renaming offers another approach to recovery in the event of incorrect speculation: simply undo the mappings that have occurred since the first incorrectly speculated instruction. This will cause the state of the processor to return to the last correctly executed instruction, keeping the correct mapping between the architectural and physical registers.

Understanding Program Performance

The Pentium 4 combines a deep pipeline (averaging 20 or more pipe stages per instruction) and aggressive multiple issue to achieve high performance. By keeping the latencies for back-to-back operations low (0 for ALU operations and 2 for loads), the impact of data dependences is reduced. What are the most serious potential performance bottlenecks for programs running on this processor? The following list includes some potential performance problems, the last three of which can apply in some form to any high-performance pipelined processor.

- The use of IA-32 instructions that do not map to three or fewer simple micro-operations

- Branches that are difficult to predict, causing misprediction stalls and restarts when speculation fails

- Poor instruction locality, which causes the trace cache not to function effectively

- Long dependences—typically caused by long-running instructions or data cache misses—which lead to stalls

- Performance delays arising in accessing memory (see Chapter 7) that cause the processor to stall

Check Yourself

Are the following statements true or false?

1. The Pentium 4 can issue more instructions per clock than the Pentium III.

2. The Pentium 4 multiple-issue pipeline directly executes IA-32 instructions.

3. The Pentium 4 uses dynamic scheduling but no speculation.

4. The Pentium 4 microarchitecture has many more registers than IA-32 requires.

5. The Pentium 4 pipeline has fewer stages than the Pentium III.

6. The trace cache in the Pentium 4 is exactly the same as an instruction cache.

6.11 Fallacies and Pitfalls

Fallacy: Pipelining is easy.

Our books testify to the subtlety of correct pipeline execution. Our advanced book had a pipeline bug in its first edition, despite its being reviewed by more than 100 people and being class-tested at 18 universities. The bug was uncovered only when someone tried to build the computer in that book. The fact that the Verilog to describe a pipeline like that in the Pentium 4 will be thousands of lines is an indication of the complexity. Beware!

Fallacy: Pipelining ideas can be implemented independent of technology.

When the number of transistors on-chip and speed of transistors made a five-stage pipeline the best solution, then the delayed branch (see the first elaboration on page 423) was a simple solution to control hazards. With longer pipelines, superscalar execution, and dynamic branch prediction, it is now redundant. In the early 1990s, dynamic pipeline scheduling took too many resources and was not required for high performance, but as transistor budgets continued to double and logic became much faster than memory, then multiple functional units and dynamic pipelining made more sense. Today, all high-end processors use multiple issue, and most choose to implement aggressive speculation as well.

Pitfall: Failure to consider instruction set design can adversely impact pipelining.

Many of the difficulties of pipelining arise because of instruction set complications. Here are some examples:

- Widely variable instruction lengths and running times can lead to imbalance among pipeline stages and severely complicate hazard detection in a design pipelined at the instruction set level. This problem was overcome, initially in the DEC VAX 8500 in the late 1980s, using the micropipelined scheme that the Pentium 4 employs today. Of course, the overhead of translation and maintaining correspondence between the micro-operations and the actual instructions remains.

- Sophisticated addressing modes can lead to different sorts of problems. Addressing modes that update registers, such as update addressing (see Chapter 3), complicate hazard detection. Other addressing modes that require multiple memory accesses substantially complicate pipeline control and make it difficult to keep the pipeline flowing smoothly.

Perhaps the best example is the DEC Alpha and the DEC NVAX. In comparable technology, the newer instruction set architecture of the Alpha allowed an implementation whose performance is more than twice as fast as NVAX. In another example, Bhandarkar and Clark [1991] compared the MIPS M/2000 and the DEC VAX 8700 by counting clock cycles of the SPEC benchmarks; they concluded that, although the MIPS M/2000 executes more instructions, the VAX on average executes 2.7 times as many clock cycles, so the MIPS is faster.

Nine-tenths of wisdom consists of being wise in time.

American proverb

6.12 Concluding Remarks

Pipelining improves the average execution time per instruction. Depending on whether you start with a single-cycle or multiple-cycle datapath, this reduction can be thought of as decreasing the clock cycle time or as decreasing the number of clock cycles per instruction (CPI). We started with the simple single-cycle datapath, so pipelining was presented as reducing the clock cycle time of the simple datapath. Multiple issue, in comparison, clearly focuses on reducing CPI (or increasing IPC). Figure 6.52 shows the effect on CPI and clock rate for each of the microarchitectures from Chapter 5 and this chapter. Performance is increased by moving up and to the right, since it is the product of IPC and clock rate that determines performance for a given instruction set.

Pipelining improves throughput, but not the inherent execution time, or *latency*, of instructions; the latency is similar in length to the multicycle approach. Unlike that approach, which uses the same hardware repeatedly during instruction execution, pipelining starts an instruction every clock cycle by having dedicated hardware. Similarly, multiple issue adds additional datapath hardware to allow multiple instructions to begin every clock cycle, but at an increase in effective latency. Figure 6.53 shows the datapaths from Figure 6.52 placed according to the amount of sharing of hardware and **instruction latency**.

instruction latency The inherent execution time for an instruction.

Pipelining and multiple issue both attempt to exploit instruction-level parallelism. The presence of data and control dependences, which can become hazards, are the primary limitations on how much parallelism can be exploited. Scheduling and speculation, both in hardware and software, are the primary techniques used to reduce the performance impact of dependences.

The switch to longer pipelines, multiple instruction issue, and dynamic scheduling in the mid-1990s has helped sustain the 60% per year processor performance increase that we have benefited from since the early 1980s. In the past, it appeared that the choice was between the highest clock rate processors and the most sophisticated superscalar processors. As we have seen, the Pentium 4 combines both and achieves remarkable performance.

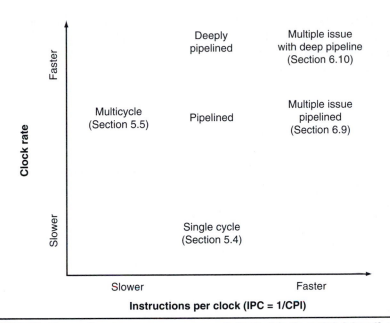

FIGURE 6.52 The performance consequences of simple (single-cycle) datapath and multicycle datapath from Chapter 5 and the pipelined execution model in this chapter. Remember that CPU performance is a function of IPC times clock rate, and hence moving to the upper right increases performance. Although the instructions per clock cycle is slightly larger in the simple datapath, the pipelined datapath is close, and it uses a clock rate as fast as the multicycle datapath.

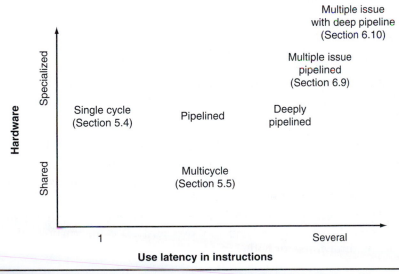

FIGURE 6.53 The basic relationship between the datapaths in Figure 6.52. Notice that the *x*-axis is use latency in instructions, which is what determines the ease of keeping the pipeline full. The pipelined datapath is shown as multiple clock cycles for instruction latency because the execution time of an instruction is not shorter; it's the instruction throughput that is improved.

With remarkable advances in processing, Amdahl's law suggests that another part of the system will become the bottleneck. That bottleneck is the topic of the next chapter: the memory system.

An alternative to pushing uniprocessors to automatically exploit parallelism at the instruction level is trying multiprocessors, which exploit parallelism at much coarser levels. Parallel processing is the topic of **Chapter 9**, which appears on the CD.

6.13   Historical Perspective and Further Reading

This section, which appears on the CD, discusses the history of the first pipelined processors, the earliest superscalars, and the development of out-of-order and speculative techniques, as well as important developments in the accompanying compiler technology.

6.14   Exercises

6.1 [5] <§6.1> If the time for an ALU operation can be shortened by 25% (compared to the description in Figure 6.2 on page 373):

a. Will it affect the speedup obtained from pipelining? If yes, by how much? Otherwise, why?

b. What if the ALU operation now takes 25% more time?

6.2 [10] <§6.1> A computer architect needs to design the pipeline of a new microprocessor. She has an example workload program core with 10^6 instructions. Each instruction takes 100 ps to finish.

a. How long does it take to execute this program core on a nonpipelined processor?

b. The current state-of-the-art microprocessor has about 20 pipeline stages. Assume it is perfectly pipelined. How much speedup will it achieve compared to the nonpipelined processor?

c. Real pipelining isn't perfect, since implementing pipelining introduces some overhead per pipeline stage. Will this overhead affect instruction latency, instruction throughput, or both?

6.3 [5] <§6.1> Using a drawing similar to Figure 6.5 on page 377, show the forwarding paths needed to execute the following four instructions:

```
add $3, $4, $6
sub $5, $3, $2
lw  $7, 100($5)
add $8, $7, $2
```

6.4 [10] <§6.1> Identify all of the data dependences in the following code. Which dependences are data hazards that will be resolved via forwarding? Which dependences are data hazards that will cause a stall?

```
add $3, $4, $2
sub $5, $3, $1
lw  $6, 200($3)
add $7, $3, $6
```

6.5 [5] <§6.1> ⊙ **For More Practice:** Delayed Branches

6.6 [10] <§6.2> Using Figure 6.22 on page 400 as a guide, use colored pens or markers to show which portions of the datapath are active and which are inactive in each of the five stages of the sw instruction. We suggest that you use five photocopies of Figure 6.22 to answer this exercise. (We hereby grant you permission to violate the Copyright Protection Act in doing the exercises in Chapter 5 and this chapter!) Be sure to include a legend to explain your color scheme.

6.7 [5] <§6.2> ⊙ **For More Practice:** Understanding Pipelines by Drawing Them

6.8 [5] <§6.2> ⊙ **For More Practice:** Understanding Pipelines by Drawing Them

6.9 [15] <§6.2> ⊙ **For More Practice:** Understanding Pipelines by Drawing Them

6.10 [5] <§6.2> ⊙ **For More Practice:** Pipeline Registers

6.11 [15] <§§3.6, 6.2> ⊙ **For More Practice:** Pipelining Floating Point

6.12 [15] <§6.3> Figure 6.37 on page 417 and Figure 6.35 on page 415 are two styles of drawing pipelines. To make sure you understand the relationship between these two styles, draw the information in Figures 6.31 through 6.35 on pages 410 through 415 using the style of Figure 6.37 on page 417. Highlight the active portions of the datapaths in the figure.

6.13 [20] <§6.3> Figure 6.14.10 on page 6.14.12 is similar to Figure 6.14.7 on page 6.14.9 in the ⊙ **For More Practice** section, but the instructions are unidentified. Determine as much as you can about the five instructions in the five pipeline stages. If you cannot fill in a field of an instruction, state why. For some fields it will be easier to decode the machine instructions into assembly language, using Figure

3.18 on page 205 and Figure A.10.2 on page A-49 as references. For other fields it will be easier to look at the values of the control signals, using Figures 6.26 through 6.28 on pages 403 through 405 as references. You may need to carefully examine Figures 6.14.5 through 6.14.9 to understand how collections of control values are presented (i.e., the leftmost bit in one cycle will become the uppermost bit in another cycle). For example, the EX control value for the subtract instruction, 1100, computed during the ID stage of cycle 3 in Figure 6.14.6 becomes three separate values specifying RegDst (1), ALUOp (10), and ALUSrc (0) in cycle 4.

6.14 [40] <§6.3> The following piece of code is executed using the pipeline shown in Figure 6.30 on page 409:

```
lw   $5, 40($2)
add  $6, $3, $2
or   $7, $2, $1
and  $8, $4, $3
sub  $9, $2, $1
```

At cycle 5, right before the instructions are executed, the processor state is as follows:

 a. The PC has the value 100_{ten}, the address of the `sub_instruction`.

 b. Every register has the initial value 10_{ten} plus the register number (e.g., register $8 has the initial value 18_{ten}).

 c. Every memory word accessed as data has the initial value 1000_{ten} plus the byte address of the word (e.g., Memory[8] has the initial value 1008_{ten}).

Determine the value of every field in the four pipeline registers in cycle 5.

6.15 [20] <§6.3> ◉ **For More Practice:** Labeling Pipeline Diagrams with Control

6.16 [20] <§6.4> ◉ **For More Practice:** Illustrating Pipelines with Forwarding

6.17 [5] <§§6.4, 6.5> Consider executing the following code on the pipelined datapath of Figure 6.36 on page 416:

```
add   $2, $3, $1
sub   $4, $3, $5
add   $5, $3, $7
add   $7, $6, $1
add   $8, $2, $6
```

At the end of the fifth cycle of execution, which registers are being read and which register will be written?

6.18 [5] <§§6.4, 6.5> With regard to the program in Exercise 6.17, explain what the forwarding unit is doing during the fifth cycle of execution. If any comparisons are being made, mention them.

6.19 [5] <§§6.4, 6.5> With regard to the program in Exercise 6.17, explain what the hazard detection unit is doing during the fifth cycle of execution. If any comparisons are being made, mention them.

6.20 [20] <§§6.4, 6.5> ⊙ **For More Practice:** Forwarding in Memory

6.21 [5] <§6.5> We have a program of 10^3 instructions in the format of "lw, add, lw, add,..." The add instruction depends (and only depends) on the lw instruction right before it. The lw instruction also depends (and only depends) on the add instruction right before it. If the program is executed on the pipelined datapath of Figure 6.36 on page 416:

  a. What would be the actual CPI?

  b. Without forwarding, what would be the actual CPI?

6.22 [5] <§§6.4, 6.5> Consider executing the following code on the pipelined datapath of Figure 6.36 on page 416:

```
lw    $4, 100($2)
sub   $6, $4, $3
add   $2, $3, $5
```

How many cycles will it take to execute this code? Draw a diagram like that of Figure 6.34 on page 414 that illustrates the dependences that need to be resolved, and provide another diagram like that of Figure 6.35 on page 415 that illustrates how the code will actually be executed (incorporating any stalls or forwarding) so as to resolve the identified problems.

6.23 [15] <§6.5> List all the inputs and outputs of the forwarding unit in Figure 6.36 on page 416. Give the names, the number of bits, and brief usage for each input and output.

6.24 [20] <§6.5> ⊙ **For More Practice:** Illustrating Pipelines with Stalls and Forwarding

6.25 [20] <§6.5> ⊙ **For More Practice:** Impact on Forwarding of Moving It to ID Stage

6.26 [15] <§§6.2–6.5> ⊙ **For More Practice:** Impact of Memory-Addressing Mode on Pipeline

6.27 [10] <§§6.2–6.5> ⊙ **For More Practice:** Impact of Arithmetic Operations with Memory Operands on Pipeline

6.28 [30] <§6.5, Appendix C> ⊙ **For More Practice:** Forwarding Unit Hardware Design

6.29 [1 week] <§§6.4, 6.5> Using the simulator provided with this book, collect statistics on data hazards for a C program (supplied by either the instructor or with the software). You will write a subroutine that is passed the instruction to be executed, and this routine must model the five-stage pipeline in this chapter. Have your program collect the following statistics:

- Number of instructions executed.

- Number of data hazards not resolved by forwarding and number resolved by forwarding.

- If the MIPS C compiler that you are using issues nop instructions to avoid hazards, count the number of nop instructions as well.

Assuming that the memory accesses always take 1 clock cycle, calculate the average number of clock cycles per instruction. Classify nop instructions as stalls inserted by software, then subtract them from the number of instructions executed in the CPI calculation.

6.30 [7] <§§6.4, 6.5> In the example on page 425, we saw that the performance advantage of the multicycle design was limited by the longer time required to access memory versus use the ALU. Suppose the memory access became 2 clock cycles long. Find the relative performance of the single-cycle and multicycle designs. In the next few exercises, we extend this to the pipelined design, which requires lots more work!

6.31 [10] <§6.6> ⊙ **For More Practice:** Coding with Conditional Moves

6.32 [10] <§6.6> ⊙ **For More Practice:** Performance Advantage of Conditional Move

6.33 [20] <§§6.2–6.6> In the example on page 425, we saw that the performance advantage of both the multicycle and the pipelined designs was limited by the longer time required to access memory versus use the ALU. Suppose the memory access became 2 clock cycles long. Draw the modified pipeline. List all the possible new forwarding situations and all possible new hazards and their length.

6.34 [20] <§§6.2–6.6> Redo the example on page 425 using the restructured pipeline of Exercise 6.33 to compare the single cycle and multicycle. For branches, assume the same prediction accuracy, but increase the penalty as appropriate. For loads, assume that the subsequent instructions depend on the load with a probability of $1/2$, $1/4$, $1/8$, $1/16$, and so on. That is, the instruction following a load by two has a 25% probability of using the load result as one of its sources. Ignoring any other data hazards, find the relative performance of the pipelined design to the single-cycle design with the restructured pipeline.

6.35 [10] <§§6.4–6.6> As pointed out on page 418, moving the branch comparison up to the ID stage introduces an opportunity for both forwarding and hazards that cannot be resolved by forwarding. Give a set of code sequences that show the possible forwarding paths required and hazard cases that must be detected, considering only one of the two operands. The number of cases should equal the maximum length of the hazard if no forwarding existed.

6.36 [15] <§6.6> We have a program core consisting of five conditional branches. The program core will be executed thousands of times. Below are the outcomes of each branch for one execution of the program core (T for taken, N for not taken).

Branch 1: T-T-T
Branch 2: N-N-N-N
Branch 3: T-N-T-N-T-N
Branch 4: T-T-T-N-T
Branch 5: T-T-N-T-T-N-T

Assume the behavior of each branch remains the same for each program core execution. For dynamic schemes, assume each branch has its own prediction buffer and each buffer is initialized to the same state before each execution. List the predictions for the following branch prediction schemes:

a. Always taken

b. Always not taken

c. 1-bit predictor, initialized to predict taken

d. 2-bit predictor, initialized to weakly predict taken

What are the prediction accuracies?

6.37 [10] <§§6.4–6.6> Sketch all the forwarding paths for the branch inputs and show when they must be enabled (as we did on page 411).

6.38 [10] <§§6.4–6.6> Write the logic to detect any hazards on the branch sources, as we did on page 413.

6.39 [10] <§§6.4–6.6> The example on page 378 shows how to *maximize* performance on our pipelined datapath with forwarding and stalls on a use following a load. Rewrite the following code to *minimize* performance on this datapath—that is, reorder the instructions so that this sequence takes the *most* clock cycles to execute while still obtaining the same result.

```
lw    $2, 100($6)
lw    $3, 200($7)
add   $4, $2, $3
add   $6, $3, $5
sub   $8, $4, $6
lw    $7, 300($8)
beq   $7, $8, Loop
```

6.40 [20] <§6.6> Consider the pipelined datapath in Figure 6.54 on page 461. Can an attempt to flush and an attempt to stall occur simultaneously? If so, do they result in conflicting actions and/or cooperating actions? If there are any cooperating actions, how do they work together? If there are any conflicting actions, which should take priority? Is there a simple change you can make to the datapath to ensure the necessary priority? You may want to consider the following code sequence to help you answer this question:

```
        beq $1, $2, TARGET    # assume that the branch is taken
        lw  $3, 40($4)
        add $2, $3, $4
        sw  $2, 40($4)
TARGET: or  $1, $1, $2
```

6.41 [15] <§§ 6.4, 6.7> The Verilog for implementing forwarding in Figure 6.7.2 on pages 6.7-4–6.7-5 did not consider forwarding of a result as the value to be stored by an SW instruction. Add this to the Verilog code.

6.42 [5] <§§6.5, 6.7> The Verilog for implementing stalls in Figure 6.7.3 on pages 6.7-6–6.7-7 did not consider forwarding of a result to use in an address calculation. Make this simple addition to the Verilog code.

6.43 [15] <§§6.6, 6.7> The Verilog code for implementing branch hazard detection and stalls in Figure 6.7.3 on pages 6.7-6–6.7-7 does not detect the possibility of data hazards for the two source registers of a BEQ instruction. Extend the Verilog in Figure 6.7.3 to handle all data hazards for branch operands. Write both the forwarding and stall logic needed for completing branches during ID.

6.44 [10] <§§6.6, 6.7> Rewrite the Verilog code in Figure 6.7.3 on pages 6.7-6–6.7-7 to implement a delayed branch strategy.

6.45 [20] <§§6.6, 6.7> Rewrite the Verilog code in Figure 6.7.3 on pages 6.7-6–6.7-7 to implement a branch target buffer. Assume the buffer is implemented with a module with the following definition:

```
module PredictPC (currentPC,nextPC,miss,update,destination);
   input currentPC,
      update, // true if previous prediction was unavailable or incorrect
      destination; / used with update to correct a prediction
   output nextPC, // returns the next PC if prediction is accurate
      miss; // true means no prediction in buffer
endmodule;
```

Make sure you accommodate all three possibilities: a correct prediction, a miss in the buffer (that is, miss = true), and an incorrect prediction. In the last two cases, you must also update the prediction.

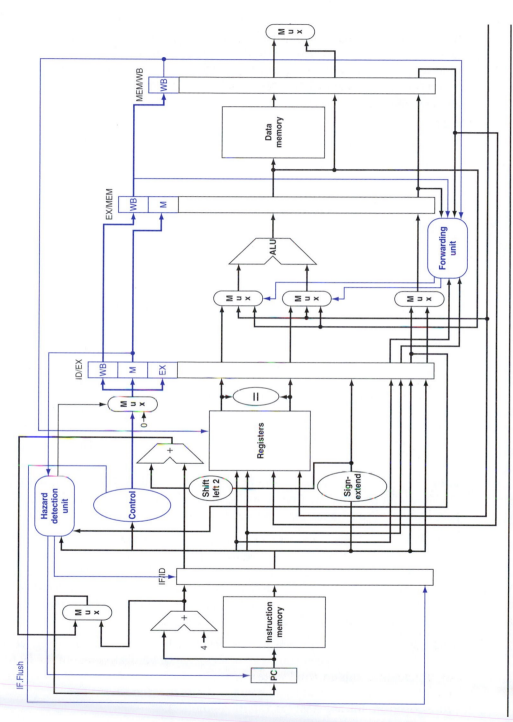

FIGURE 6.54 Datapath for branch, including hardware to flush the instruction that follows the branch. This optimization moves the branch decision from the fourth pipeline stage to the second; only one instruction that follows the branch will be in the pipe at that time. The control line IF.Flush turns the fetched instruction into a nop by zeroing the IF/ID pipeline register. Although the flush line is shown coming from the control unit in this figure, in reality it comes from hardware that determines if a branch is taken, labeled with an equal sign to the right of the registers in the ID stage. The forwarding muxes and paths must also be added to this stage, but are not shown to simplify the figure.

6.46 [1 month] <§§5.4, 6.3–6.8> If you have access to a simulation system such as Verilog or ViewLogic, first design the single-cycle datapath and control from Chapter 5. Then evolve this design into a pipelined organization, as we did in this chapter. Be sure to run MIPS programs at each step to ensure that your refined design continues to operate correctly.

6.47 [10] <§6.9> The following code has been unrolled once but not yet scheduled. Assume the loop index is a multiple of two (i.e., $10 is a multiple of eight):

```
Loop:     lw    $2,  0($10)
          sub   $4,  $2, $3
          sw    $4,  0($10)
          lw    $5,  4($10)
          sub   $6,  $5, $3
          sw    $6,  4($10)
          addi  $10, $10, 8
          bne   $10, $30, Loop
```

Schedule this code for fast execution on the standard MIPS pipeline (assume that it supports addi instruction). Assume initially $10 is 0 and $30 is 400 and that branches are resolved in the MEM stage. How does the scheduled code compare against the original unscheduled code?

6.48 [20] <§6.9> This exercise is similar to Exercise 6.47, except this time the code should be unrolled twice (creating three copies of the code). However, it is not known that the loop index is a multiple of three, and thus you will need to invent a means of ensuring that the code still executes properly. (Hint: Consider adding some code to the beginning or end of the loop that takes care of the cases not handled by the loop.)

6.49 [20] <§6.9> Using the code in Exercise 6.47, unroll the code four times and schedule it for the static multiple-issue version of the MIPS processor described on pages 436–439. You may assume that the loop executes for a multiple of four times.

6.50 [10] <§§6.1–6.9> As technology leads to smaller feature sizes, the wires become relatively slower (as compared to the logic). As logic becomes faster with the shrinking feature size and clock rates increase, wire delays consume more clock cycles. That is why the Pentium 4 has several pipeline stages dedicated to transferring data along wires from one part of the pipeline to another. What are the drawbacks to having to add pipe stages for wire delays?

6.51 [30] <§6.10> New processors are introduced more quickly than new versions of textbooks. To keep your textbook current, investigate some of the latest developments in this area and write a one-page elaboration to insert at the end of Section 6.10. Use the World Wide Web to explore the characteristics of the lastest processors from Intel or AMD as a starting point.

§6.1, page 384: 1. Stall on the LW result. 2. Bypass the ADD result. 3. No stall or bypass required.

§6.2, page 399: Statements 2 and 5 are correct; the rest are incorrect.

§6.6, page 426: 1. Predict not taken. 2. Predict taken. 3. Dynamic prediction.

§6.7, ⊙ page 6.7-3: Statements 1 and 3 are both true.

§6.7, ⊙ page 6.7-7: Only statement 3 is completely accurate.

§6.8, page 432: Only statement 4 is totally accurate. Statement 2 is partially accurate.

§6.9, page 447: 1. Both. 2. Both. 3. Software. 4. Hardware. 5. Hardware. 6. Hardware. 7. Both. 8. Both, since there is substantial hardware support. 9. Hardware. 10. Both. 11. Software.

§6.10, page 450: All the statements are false.

Computers in the Real World

Mass Communication without Gatekeepers

Problem: Offer society sources of news and opinion beyond those found in the traditional mass media.

Solution: Use the Internet and World Wide Web to select and publish nontraditional and nonlocal news sources.

The Internet holds the promise of allowing citizens to communicate without the information first being interpreted by traditional mass media like television, newspapers, and magazines. To see what the future might be, we could look at countries that have widespread, high-speed Internet access.

One place is South Korea. In 2002, 68% of South Korean households had broadband access, compared to 15% in the United States and 8% in Western Europe. (Broadband is generally digital subscriber loop or cable speeds, about 300 to 1000 Kbps.) The main reason for the greater penetration is that 70% of households are in large cities and almost half are found in apartments. Hence, the Korean telecommunications industry could afford to quickly offer broadband to 90% of the households.

What was the impact of widespread high-speed access on Korean society? Internet news sites became extremely popular. One example is OhMyNews, which publishes articles from *anyone* after first checking that the facts in the article are correct.

Many believe that Internet news services influenced the outcome of the 2002 Korean presidential election. First, they encouraged more young people to vote. Second, the winning candidate advocated politics that were

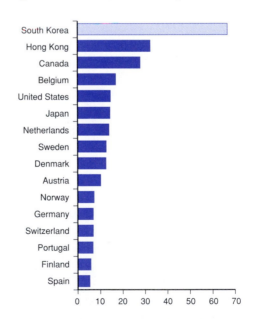

Percentage of households with broadband connections by country in 2002.
Source: The Yankee Group, Boston.

closer to those popular on the Internet news services. Together they overcame the disadvantage that most major media organizations endorsed his opponent.

Google News is another example of nontraditional access to news that goes beyond the mass media of one country. It searches international news services for topics, and then summarizes and displays them by popularity. Rather than leaving the decision of what articles should be on the front page to local newspaper editors, the worldwide media decides. In addition, by providing links to stories from many countries, the reader gets an international perspective rather than a local one. It also is updated many times a day unlike a daily newspaper. The figure below compares the *New York Times* front page to the Google News Web site on the same day.

The widespread impact of these technologies reminds us that computer engineers have responsibilities to their communities. We must be aware of societal values concerning privacy, security, free speech, and so on to ensure that new technological innovations enhance those values rather than inadvertently compromising them.

To learn more, see these references on the ◉ library:

- "Seriously wired," *The Economist*, April 17, 2003
- OhMyNews, *www.ohmynews.com*
- Google News, *www.news.google.com*

New York Times front page	Google News
Judge Rules Out a Death Penalty for 9/11 Suspect Rebuke for Justice Dept. **Poll Shows Drop in Confidence on Bush Skill in Handling Crises** Country on Wrong Track, Says Solid Majority **Revised Admission for High Schools** City Says Students Will Get First Preference **No Illicit Arms Found in Iraq, U.S. Inspector Tells Congress** **U.S. Practice How to Down Hijacked Jets** **Coetzee, Writer of Apartheid as Bleak Mirror, Wins Nobel** **Sexual Accusations Lead to an Apology by Schwarzenegger** **Interim Chief Accepts Stock Exchange Shift** **Yankees Even with Twins** Agency Warns of Fake Drugs Limbaugh Fallback Position	Top Stories More than 1000 rally behind Schwarzenegger AP - 5 minutes ago Maria Shriver defends husband CNN Can accusations hurt Arnold's campaign? KESQ and 1252 related Bush: Hussein 'A Danger to the World' ABC news - 5 hours ago Bush Stands By Decision Voice of America Hunt for weapons yields no evidence The Canberra Times and 598 related World Stories Defiant UN chief announces rival blueprint for Iraq The Times (UK) - 2 hours ago France, Russia Assail US Draft on Iraq Reuters and 782 related

***New York Times* versus Google News on October 3, 2003, at 6 PM PT.** The newspaper front page headlines must balance big stories with national news, local news, and sports. Google News has many stories per headline from around the world, with links the reader can follow. Google stories vary by time of day and hence are more recent.

7

Large and Fast: Exploiting Memory Hierarchy

*Ideally one would desire an indefinitely large memory
capacity such that any particular . . . word would be
immediately available. . . . We are . . . forced to
recognize the possibility of constructing a hierarchy of
memories, each of which has greater capacity than the
preceding but which is less quickly accessible.*

A. W. Burks, H. H. Goldstine, and J. von Neumann
Preliminary Discussion of the Logical Design of an Electronic Computing Instrument, 1946

The Five Classic Components of a Computer

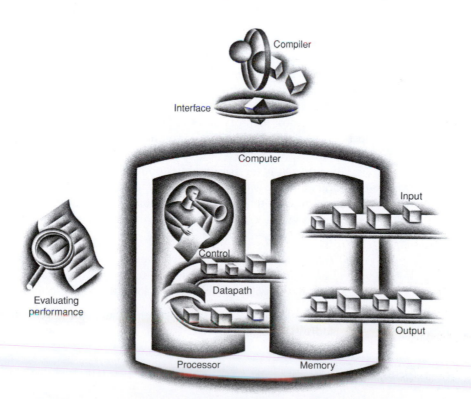

7.1   Introduction

From the earliest days of computing, programmers have wanted unlimited amounts of fast memory. The topics we will look at in this chapter aid programmers by creating the illusion of unlimited fast memory. Before we look at how the illusion is actually created, let's consider a simple analogy that illustrates the key principles and mechanisms that we use.

Suppose you were a student writing a term paper on important historical developments in computer hardware. You are sitting at a desk in a library with a collection of books that you have pulled from the shelves and are examining. You find that several of the important computers that you need to write about are described in the books you have, but there is nothing about the EDSAC. Therefore, you go back to the shelves and look for an additional book. You find a book on early British computers that covers the EDSAC. Once you have a good selection of books on the desk in front of you, there is a good probability that many of the topics you need can be found in them, and you may spend most of your time just using the books on the desk without going back to the shelves. Having several books on the desk in front of you saves time compared to having only one book there and constantly having to go back to the shelves to return it and take out another.

The same principle allows us to create the illusion of a large memory that we can access as fast as a very small memory. Just as you did not need to access all the books in the library at once with equal probability, a program does not access all of its code or data at once with equal probability. Otherwise, it would be impossible to make most memory accesses fast and still have large memory in computers, just as it would be impossible for you to fit all the library books on your desk and still find what you wanted quickly.

This *principle of locality* underlies both the way in which you did your work in the library and the way that programs operate. The principle of locality states that programs access a relatively small portion of their address space at any instant of time, just as you accessed a very small portion of the library's collection. There are two different types of locality:

■ **Temporal locality** (locality in time): If an item is referenced, it will tend to be referenced again soon. If you recently brought a book to your desk to look at, you will probably need to look at it again soon.

■ **Spatial locality** (locality in space): If an item is referenced, items whose addresses are close by will tend to be referenced soon. For example, when

temporal locality The principle stating that if a data location is referenced then it will tend to be referenced again soon.

spatial locality The locality principle stating that if a data location is referenced, data locations with nearby addresses will tend to be referenced soon.

you brought out the book on early English computers to find out about the EDSAC, you also noticed that there was another book shelved next to it about early mechanical computers, so you also brought back that book too and, later on, found something useful in that book. Books on the same topic are shelved together in the library to increase spatial locality. We'll see how spatial locality is used in memory hierarchies a little later in this chapter.

Just as accesses to books on the desk naturally exhibit locality, locality in programs arises from simple and natural program structures. For example, most programs contain loops, so instructions and data are likely to be accessed repeatedly, showing high amounts of temporal locality. Since instructions are normally accessed sequentially, programs show high spatial locality. Accesses to data also exhibit a natural spatial locality. For example, accesses to elements of an array or a record will naturally have high degrees of spatial locality.

We take advantage of the principle of locality by implementing the memory of a computer as a **memory hierarchy**. A memory hierarchy consists of multiple levels of memory with different speeds and sizes. The faster memories are more expensive per bit than the slower memories and thus smaller.

memory hierarchy A structure that uses multiple levels of memories; as the distance from the CPU increases, the size of the memories and the access time both increase.

Today, there are three primary technologies used in building memory hierarchies. Main memory is implemented from DRAM (dynamic random access memory), while levels closer to the processor (caches) use SRAM (static random access memory). DRAM is less costly per bit than SRAM, although it is substantially slower. The price difference arises because DRAM uses significantly less area per bit of memory, and DRAMs thus have larger capacity for the same amount of silicon; the speed difference arises from several factors described in Section B.8 of ⊙ **Appendix B**. The third technology, used to implement the largest and slowest level in the hierarchy, is magnetic disk. The access time and price per bit vary widely among these technologies, as the table below shows, using typical values for 2004:

Memory technology	Typical access time	$ per GB in 2004
SRAM	0.5–5 ns	$4000–$10,000
DRAM	50–70 ns	$100–$200
Magnetic disk	5,000,000–20,000,000 ns	$0.50–$2

Because of these differences in cost and access time, it is advantageous to build memory as a hierarchy of levels. Figure 7.1 shows the faster memory is close to the processor and the slower, less expensive memory is below it. The goal is to present the user with as much memory as is available in the cheapest technology, while providing access at the speed offered by the fastest memory.

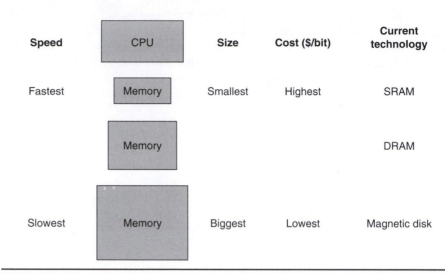

FIGURE 7.1   The basic structure of a memory hierarchy. By implementing the memory system as a hierarchy, the user has the illusion of a memory that is as large as the largest level of the hierarchy, but can be accessed as if it were all built from the fastest memory.

The memory system is organized as a hierarchy: a level closer to the processor is generally a subset of any level further away, and all the data is stored at the lowest level. By analogy, the books on your desk form a subset of the library you are working in, which is in turn a subset of all the libraries on campus. Furthermore, as we move away from the processor, the levels take progressively longer to access, just as we might encounter in a hierarchy of campus libraries.

A memory hierarchy can consist of multiple levels, but data is copied between only two adjacent levels at a time, so we can focus our attention on just two levels. The upper level—the one closer to the processor—is smaller and faster (since it uses more expensive technology) than the lower level. Figure 7.2 shows that the minimum unit of information that can be either present or not present in the two-level hierarchy is called a **block** or a *line*; in our library analogy, a block of information is one book.

If the data requested by the processor appears in some block in the upper level, this is called a *hit* (analogous to your finding the information in one of the books on your desk). If the data is not found in the upper level, the request is called a *miss*. The lower level in the hierarchy is then accessed to retrieve the block containing the requested data. (Continuing our analogy, you go from your desk to the shelves to find the desired book.) The **hit rate**, or *hit ratio*, is the fraction of memory accesses found in the upper level; it is often used as a measure of the perfor-

block The minimum unit of information that can be either present or not present in the two-level hierarchy.

hit rate The fraction of memory accesses found in a cache.

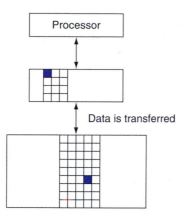

Data is transferred

FIGURE 7.2 Every pair of levels in the memory hierarchy can be thought of as having an upper and lower level. Within each level, the unit of information that is present or not is called a *block*. Usually we transfer an entire block when we copy something between levels.

mance of the memory hierarchy. The **miss rate** (1 − hit rate) is the fraction of memory accesses not found in the upper level.

Since performance is the major reason for having a memory hierarchy, the time to service hits and misses is important. **Hit time** is the time to access the upper level of the memory hierarchy, which includes the time needed to determine whether the access is a hit or a miss (that is, the time needed to look through the books on the desk). The **miss penalty** is the time to replace a block in the upper level with the corresponding block from the lower level, plus the time to deliver this block to the processor (or, the time to get another book from the shelves and place it on the desk). Because the upper level is smaller and built using faster memory parts, the hit time will be much smaller than the time to access the next level in the hierarchy, which is the major component of the miss penalty. (The time to examine the books on the desk is much smaller than the time to get up and get a new book from the shelves.)

As we will see in this chapter, the concepts used to build memory systems affect many other aspects of a computer, including how the operating system manages memory and I/O, how compilers generate code, and even how applications use the computer. Of course, because all programs spend much of their time accessing memory, the memory system is necessarily a major factor in determining performance. The reliance on memory hierarchies to achieve performance has meant that programmers, who used to be able to think of memory as a flat, random access storage device, now need to understand

miss rate The fraction of memory accesses not found in a level of the memory hierarchy.

hit time The time required to access a level of the memory hierarchy, including the time needed to determine whether the access is a hit or a miss.

miss penalty The time required to fetch a block into a level of the memory hierarchy from the lower level, including the time to access the block, transmit it from one level to the other, insert it in the level that experienced the miss, and then pass the block to the requestor.

memory hierarchies to get good performance. We show how important this understanding is with two examples.

Since memory systems are so critical to performance, computer designers have devoted a lot of attention to these systems and developed sophisticated mechanisms for improving the performance of the memory system. In this chapter, we will see the major conceptual ideas, although many simplifications and abstractions have been used to keep the material manageable in length and complexity. We could easily have written hundreds of pages on memory systems, as dozens of recent doctoral theses have demonstrated.

Check Yourself

Which of the following statements are generally true?

1. Caches take advantage of temporal locality.

2. On a read, the value returned depends on which blocks are in the cache.

3. Most of the cost of the memory hierarchy is at the highest level.

The BIG Picture

Programs exhibit both temporal locality, the tendency to reuse recently accessed data items, and spatial locality, the tendency to reference data items that are close to other recently accessed items. Memory hierarchies take advantage of temporal locality by keeping more recently accessed data items closer to the processor. Memory hierarchies take advantage of spatial locality by moving blocks consisting of multiple contiguous words in memory to upper levels of the hierarchy.

Figure 7.3 shows that a memory hierarchy uses smaller and faster memory technologies close to the processor. Thus, accesses that hit in the highest level of the hierarchy can be processed quickly. Accesses that miss go to lower levels of the hierarchy, which are larger but slower. If the hit rate is high enough, the memory hierarchy has an effective access time close to that of the highest (and fastest) level and a size equal to that of the lowest (and largest) level.

In most systems, the memory is a true hierarchy, meaning that data cannot be present in level i unless it is also present in level $i + 1$.

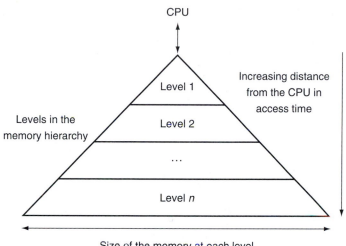

FIGURE 7.3 **This diagram shows the structure of a memory hierarchy: as the distance from the processor increases, so does the size.** This structure with the appropriate operating mechanisms allows the processor to have an access time that is determined primarily by level 1 of the hierarchy and yet have a memory as large as level *n*. Maintaining this illusion is the subject of this chapter. Although the local disk is normally the bottom of the hierarchy, some systems use tape or a file server over a local area network as the next levels of the hierarchy.

7.2 The Basics of Caches

Cache: a safe place for hiding or storing things.

Webster's New World Dictionary of the American Language, Third College Edition (1988)

In our library example, the desk acted as a cache—a safe place to store things (books) that we needed to examine. *Cache* was the name chosen to represent the level of the memory hierarchy between the processor and main memory in the first commercial computer to have this extra level. Today, although this remains the dominant use of the word *cache*, the term is also used to refer to any storage managed to take advantage of locality of access. Caches first appeared in research computers in the early 1960s and in production computers later in that same decade; every general-purpose computer built today, from servers to low-power embedded processors, includes caches.

In this section, we begin by looking at a very simple cache in which the processor requests are each one word and the blocks also consist of a single word. (Readers already familiar with cache basics may want to skip to Section 7.3 on page 492.)

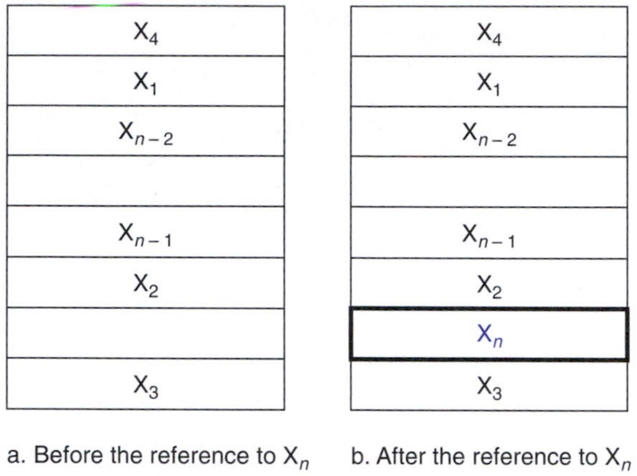

a. Before the reference to X_n b. After the reference to X_n

FIGURE 7.4   The cache just before and just after a reference to a word X_n that is not initially in the cache. This reference causes a miss that forces the cache to fetch X_n from memory and insert it into the cache.

Figure 7.4 shows such a simple cache, before and after requesting a data item that is not initially in the cache. Before the request, the cache contains a collection of recent references $X_1, X_2, \ldots, X_{n-1}$, and the processor requests a word X_n that is not in the cache. This request results in a miss, and the word X_n is brought from memory into the cache.

In looking at the scenario in Figure 7.4, there are two questions to answer: How do we know if a data item is in the cache? Moreover, if it is, how do we find it? The answers to these two questions are related. If each word can go in exactly one place in the cache, then it is straightforward to find the word if it is in the cache. The simplest way to assign a location in the cache for each word in memory is to assign the cache location based on the *address* of the word in mem-

direct-mapped cache A cache structure in which each memory location is mapped to exactly one location in the cache.

ory. This cache structure is called **direct mapped**, since each memory location is mapped directly to exactly one location in the cache. The typical mapping between addresses and cache locations for a direct-mapped cache is usually simple. For example, almost all direct-mapped caches use the mapping

(Block address) modulo (Number of cache blocks in the cache)

This mapping is attractive because if the number of entries in the cache is a power of 2, then modulo can be computed simply by using the low-order $\log_2$ (cache size in blocks) bits of the address; hence the cache may be accessed directly with the low-order bits. For example, Figure 7.5 shows how the memory addresses between

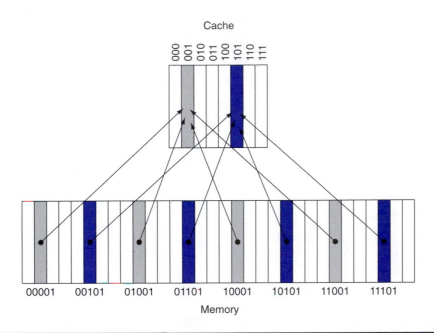

FIGURE 7.5 A direct-mapped cache with eight entries showing the addresses of memory words between 0 and 31 that map to the same cache locations. Because there are eight words in the cache, an address X maps to the cache word X modulo 8. That is, the low-order $\log_2(8) = 3$ bits are used as the cache index. Thus, addresses 00001_{two}, 01001_{two}, 10001_{two}, and 11001_{two} all map to entry 001_{two} of the cache, while addresses 00101_{two}, 01101_{two}, 10101_{two}, and 11101_{two} all map to entry 101_{two} of the cache.

1_{ten} (00001_{two}) and 29_{ten} (11101_{two}) map to locations 1_{ten} (001_{two}) and 5_{ten} (101_{two}) in a direct-mapped cache of eight words.

Because each cache location can contain the contents of a number of different memory locations, how do we know whether the data in the cache corresponds to a requested word? That is, how do we know whether a requested word is in the cache or not? We answer this question by adding a set of **tags** to the cache. The tags contain the address information required to identify whether a word in the cache corresponds to the requested word. The tag needs only to contain the upper portion of the address, corresponding to the bits that are not used as an index into the cache. For example, in Figure 7.5 we need only have the upper 2 of the 5 address bits in the tag, since the lower 3-bit index field of the address selects the block. We exclude the index bits because they are redundant, since by definition the index field of every address must have the same value.

We also need a way to recognize that a cache block does not have valid information. For instance, when a processor starts up, the cache does not have good data,

tag A field in a table used for a memory hierarchy that contains the address information required to identify whether the associated block in the hierarchy corresponds to a requested word.

and the tag fields will be meaningless. Even after executing many instructions, some of the cache entries may still be empty, as in Figure 7.4. Thus, we need to know that the tag should be ignored for such entries. The most common method is to add a **valid bit** to indicate whether an entry contains a valid address. If the bit is not set, there cannot be a match for this block.

valid bit A field in the tables of a memory hierarchy that indicates that the associated block in the hierarchy contains valid data.

For the rest of this section, we will focus on explaining how reads work in a cache and how the cache control works for reads. In general, handling reads is a little simpler than handling writes, since reads do not have to change the contents of the cache. After seeing the basics of how reads work and how cache misses can be handled, we'll examine the cache designs for real computers and detail how these caches handle writes.

Accessing a Cache

Figure 7.6 shows the contents of an eight-word direct-mapped cache as it responds to a series of requests from the processor. Since there are eight blocks in the cache, the low-order 3 bits of an address give the block number. Here is the action for each reference:

Decimal address of reference	Binary address of reference	Hit or miss in cache	Assigned cache block (where found or placed)
22	10110_{two}	miss (7.6b)	$(10110_{two} \bmod 8) = 110_{two}$
26	11010_{two}	miss (7.6c)	$(11010_{two} \bmod 8) = 010_{two}$
22	10110_{two}	hit	$(10110_{two} \bmod 8) = 110_{two}$
26	11010_{two}	hit	$(11010_{two} \bmod 8) = 010_{two}$
16	10000_{two}	miss (7.6d)	$(10000_{two} \bmod 8) = 000_{two}$
3	00011_{two}	miss (7.6e)	$(00011_{two} \bmod 8) = 011_{two}$
16	10000_{two}	hit	$(10000_{two} \bmod 8) = 000_{two}$
18	10010_{two}	miss (7.6f)	$(10010_{two} \bmod 8) = 010_{two}$

When the word at address 18 (10010_{two}) is brought into cache block 2 (010_{two}), the word at address 26 (11010_{two}), which was in cache block 2 (010_{two}), must be replaced by the newly requested data. This behavior allows a cache to take advantage of temporal locality: recently accessed words replace less recently referenced words. This situation is directly analogous to needing a book from the shelves and having no more space on your desk—some book already on your desk must be returned to the shelves. In a direct-mapped cache, there is only one place to put the newly requested item and hence only one choice of what to replace.

Index	V	Tag	Data
000	N		
001	N		
010	N		
011	N		
100	N		
101	N		
110	N		
111	N		

a. The initial state of the cache after power-on

Index	V	Tag	Data
000	N		
001	N		
010	N		
011	N		
100	N		
101	N		
110	Y	10_{two}	Memory(10110_{two})
111	N		

b. After handling a miss of address (10110_{two})

Index	V	Dlata	
000	N		
001	N		
010	Y	11_{two}	Memory (11010_{two})
011	N		
100	N		
101	N		
110	Y	10_{two}	Memorlly (10110_{two})
111	N		

c. After handling a miss of address (11010_{two})

Index	V	Tag	Data
000	Y	10_{two}	Memory (10000_{two})
001	N		
010	Y	11_{two}	Memory (11010_{two})
011	N		
100	N		
101	N		
110	Y	10_{two}	Memory (10110_{two})
111	N		

d. After handling a miss of address (10000_{two})

Index	V	Tag	Data
000	Y	10_{two}	Memory (10000_{two})
001	N		
010	Y	11_{two}	Memory (11010_{two})
011	Y	00_{two}	Memory (00011_{two})
100	N		
101	N		
110	Y	10_{two}	Memory (10110_{two})
111	N		

e. After handling a miss of address (00011_{two})

Index	V	Tag	Data
000	Y	10_{two}	Memory (10000_{two})
001	N		
010	Y	10_{two}	Memory (10010_{two})
011	Y	00_{two}	Memory (00011_{two})
100	N		
101	N		
110	Y	10_{two}	Memory (10110_{two})
111	N		

f. After handling a miss of address (10010_{two})

FIGURE 7.6 The cache contents are shown after each reference request that *misses,* with the index and tag fields shown in binary. The cache is initially empty, with all valid bits (V entry in cache) turned off (N). The processor requests the following addresses: 10110_{two} (miss), 11010_{two} (miss), 10110_{two} (hit), 11010_{two} (hit), 10000_{two} (miss), 00011_{two} (miss), 10000_{two} (hit), and 10010_{two} (miss). The figures show the cache contents after each miss in the sequence has been handled. When address 10010_{two} (18) is referenced, the entry for address 11010_{two} (26) must be replaced, and a reference to 11010_{two} will cause a subsequent miss. The tag field will contain only the upper portion of the address. The full address of a word contained in cache block i with tag field j for this cache is $j \times 8 + i$, or equivalently the concatenation of the tag field j and the index i. For example, in cache f above, index 010 has tag 10 and corresponds to address 10010.

We know where to look in the cache for each possible address: the low-order bits of an address can be used to find the unique cache entry to which the address could map. Figure 7.7 shows how a referenced address is divided into

- a cache index, which is used to select the block

- a tag field, which is used to compare with the value of the tag field of the cache

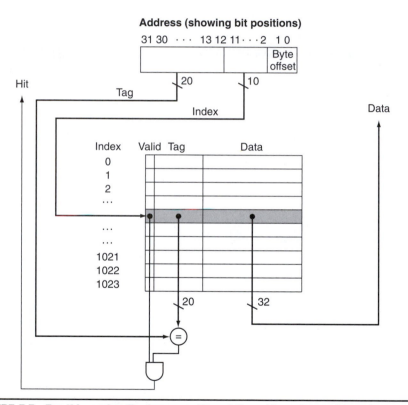

FIGURE 7.7   For this cache, the lower portion of the address is used to select a cache entry consisting of a data word and a tag. The tag from the cache is compared against the upper portion of the address to determine whether the entry in the cache corresponds to the requested address. Because the cache has 2^{10} (or 1024) words and a block size of 1 word, 10 bits are used to index the cache, leaving $32 - 10 - 2 = 20$ bits to be compared against the tag. If the tag and upper 20 bits of the address are equal and the valid bit is on, then the request hits in the cache, and the word is supplied to the processor. Otherwise, a miss occurs.

The index of a cache block, together with the tag contents of that block, uniquely specifies the memory address of the word contained in the cache block. Because the index field is used as an address to access the cache and because an n-bit field has 2^n values, the total number of entries in a direct-mapped cache must be a power of 2. In the MIPS architecture, since words are aligned to multiples of 4 bytes, the least significant 2 bits of every address specify a byte within a word and hence are ignored when selecting the word in the block.

The total number of bits needed for a cache is a function of the cache size and the address size because the cache includes both the storage for the data and the tags. The size of the block above was one word, but normally it is several. Assuming the 32-bit byte address, a direct-mapped cache of size 2^n blocks with 2^m-word (2^{m+2}-byte) blocks will require a tag field whose size is $32 - (n + m + 2)$ bits because n bits are used for the index, m bits are used for the word within the block, and 2 bits are used for the byte part of the address. The total number of bits in a direct-mapped cache is $2^n \times$ (block size + tag size + valid field size). Since the block size is 2^m words (2^{m+5} bits) and the address size is 32 bits, the number of bits in such a cache is $2^n \times (2m \times 32 + (32 - n - m - 2) + 1) = 2^n \times (2m \times 32 + 31 - n - m)$. However, the naming convention is to exclude the size of the tag and valid field and to count only the size of the data.

Bits in a Cache

How many total bits are required for a direct-mapped cache with 16 KB of data and 4-word blocks, assuming a 32-bit address?

EXAMPLE

We know that 16 KB is 4K words, which is 2^{12} words, and, with a block size of 4 words (2^2), 2^{10} blocks. Each block has 4×32 or 128 bits of data plus a tag, which is $32 - 10 - 2 - 2$ bits, plus a valid bit. Thus, the total cache size is

ANSWER

$$2^{10} \times (128 + (32 - 10 - 2 - 2) + 1) = 2^{10} \times 147 = 147 \text{ Kbits}$$

or 18.4 KB for a 16 KB cache. For this cache, the total number of bits in the cache is about 1.15 times as many as needed just for the storage of the data.

EXAMPLE

ANSWER

Mapping an Address to a Multiword Cache Block

Consider a cache with 64 blocks and a block size of 16 bytes. What block number does byte address 1200 map to?

We saw the formula on page 474. The block is given by

$$(\text{Block address}) \text{ modulo } (\text{Number of cache blocks})$$

where the address of the block is

$$\frac{\text{Byte address}}{\text{Bytes per block}}$$

Notice that this block address is the block containing all addresses between

$$\left\lfloor \frac{\text{Byte address}}{\text{Bytes per block}} \right\rfloor \times \text{Bytes per block}$$

and

$$\left\lfloor \frac{\text{Byte address}}{\text{Bytes per block}} \right\rfloor \times \text{Bytes per block} + (\text{Bytes per block} - 1)$$

Thus, with 16 bytes per block, byte address 1200 is block address

$$\left\lfloor \frac{1200}{16} \right\rfloor = 75$$

which maps to cache block number (75 modulo 64) = 11. In fact, this block maps all addresses between 1200 and 1215.

Larger blocks exploit spatial locality to lower miss rates. As Figure 7.8 shows, increasing the block size usually decreases the miss rate. The miss rate may go up eventually if the block size becomes a significant fraction of the cache size because the number of blocks that can be held in the cache will become small, and there will be a great deal of competition for those blocks. As a result, a block will be bumped out of the cache before many of its words are accessed. Stated alternatively, spatial locality among the words in a block decreases with a very large block; consequently, the benefits in the miss rate become smaller.

A more serious problem associated with just increasing the block size is that the cost of a miss increases. The miss penalty is determined by the time required to

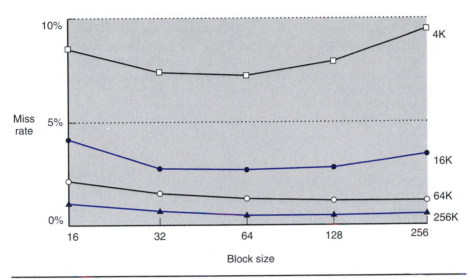

FIGURE 7.8 Miss rate versus block size. Note that miss rate actually goes up if the block size is too large relative to the cache size. Each line represents a cache of different size. (This figure is independent of associativity, discussed soon.) Unfortunately, SPEC2000 traces would take too long if block size were included, so this data is based on SPEC92.

fetch the block from the next lower level of the hierarchy and load it into the cache. The time to fetch the block has two parts: the latency to the first word and the transfer time for the rest of the block. Clearly, unless we change the memory system, the transfer time—and hence the miss penalty—will increase as the block size grows. Furthermore, the improvement in the miss rate starts to decrease as the blocks become larger. The result is that the increase in the miss penalty overwhelms the decrease in the miss rate for large blocks, and cache performance thus decreases. Of course, if we design the memory to transfer larger blocks more efficiently, we can increase the block size and obtain further improvements in cache performance. We discuss this topic in the next section.

Elaboration: The major disadvantage of increasing the block size is that the cache miss penalty increases. Although it is hard to do anything about the latency component of the miss penalty, we may be able to hide some of the transfer time so that the miss penalty is effectively smaller. The simplest method for doing this, called *early restart*, is simply to resume execution as soon as the requested word of the block is returned, rather than wait for the entire block. Many processors use this technique for instruction access, where it works best. Instruction accesses are largely sequential, so if the memory system can deliver a word every clock cycle, the processor may be able to restart operation when the requested word is returned, with the memory system delivering new instruction words just in time. This technique is usually less effective for data caches because it is likely that the words will be requested from the block in a less predictable way, and the probability that the processor will need another word from a different cache block before the transfer completes is high. If the processor cannot access the data cache because a transfer is ongoing, then it must stall.

An even more sophisticated scheme is to organize the memory so that the requested word is transferred from the memory to the cache first. The remainder of the block is then transferred, starting with the address after the requested word and wrapping around to the beginning of the block. This technique, called *requested word first*, or *critical word first*, can be slightly faster than early restart, but it is limited by the same properties that limit early restart.

Handling Cache Misses

cache miss A request for data from the cache that cannot be filled because the data is not present in the cache.

Before we look at the cache of a real system, let's see how the control unit deals with **cache misses**. The control unit must detect a miss and process the miss by fetching the requested data from memory (or, as we shall see, a lower-level cache). If the cache reports a hit, the computer continues using the data as if nothing happened. Consequently, we can use the same basic control that we developed in Chapter 5 and enhanced to accommodate pipelining in Chapter 6. The memories in the datapath in Chapters 5 and 6 are simply replaced by caches.

Modifying the control of a processor to handle a hit is trivial; misses, however, require some extra work. The cache miss handling is done with the processor control unit and with a separate controller that initiates the memory access and refills the cache. The processing of a cache miss creates a stall, similar to the pipeline stalls discussed in Chapter 6, as opposed to an interrupt, which would require saving the state of all registers. For a cache miss, we can stall the entire processor, essentially freezing the contents of the temporary and programmer-visible registers, while we wait for memory. In contrast, pipeline stalls, discussed in Chapter 6, are more complex because we must continue executing some instructions while we stall others.

Let's look a little more closely at how instruction misses are handled for either the multicycle or pipelined datapath; the same approach can be easily extended to handle data misses. If an instruction access results in a miss, then the content of the Instruction register is invalid. To get the proper instruction into the cache, we must be able to instruct the lower level in the memory hierarchy to perform a read. Since the program counter is incremented in the first clock cycle of execution in both the pipelined and multicycle processors, the address of the instruction that generates an instruction cache miss is equal to the value of the program counter minus 4. Once we have the address, we need to instruct the main memory to perform a read. We wait for the memory to respond (since the access will take multiple cycles), and then write the words into the cache.

We can now define the steps to be taken on an instruction cache miss:

1. Send the original PC value (current PC − 4) to the memory.

2. Instruct main memory to perform a read and wait for the memory to complete its access.

3. Write the cache entry, putting the data from memory in the data portion of the entry, writing the upper bits of the address (from the ALU) into the tag field, and turning the valid bit on.

4. Restart the instruction execution at the first step, which will refetch the instruction, this time finding it in the cache.

The control of the cache on a data access is essentially identical: on a miss, we simply stall the processor until the memory responds with the data.

Handling Writes

Writes work somewhat differently. Suppose on a store instruction, we wrote the data into only the data cache (without changing main memory); then, after the write into the cache, memory would have a different value from that in the cache. In such a case, the cache and memory are said to be *inconsistent*. The simplest way to keep the main memory and the cache consistent is to always write the data into both the memory and the cache. This scheme is called **write-through**.

The other key aspect of writes is what occurs on a write miss. We first fetch the words of the block from memory. After the block is fetched and placed into the cache, we can overwrite the word that caused the miss into the cache block. We also write the word to main memory using the full address.

Although this design handles writes very simply, it would not provide very good performance. With a write-through scheme, every write causes the data to be written to main memory. These writes will take a long time, likely at least 100 processor clock cycles, and could slow down the processor considerably. For the SPEC2000 integer benchmarks, for example, 10% of the instructions are stores. If the CPI without cache misses was 1.0, spending 100 extra cycles on every write would lead to a CPI of $1.0 + 100 \times 10\% = 11$, reducing performance by more than a factor of 10.

One solution to this problem is to use a **write buffer**. A write buffer stores the data while it is waiting to be written to memory. After writing the data into the cache and into the write buffer, the processor can continue execution. When a write to main memory completes, the entry in the write buffer is freed. If the write buffer is full when the processor reaches a write, the processor must stall until there is an empty position in the write buffer. Of course, if the rate at which the memory can complete writes is less than the rate at which the processor is gener-

write-through A scheme in which writes always update both the cache and the memory, ensuring that data is always consistent between the two.

write buffer A queue that holds data while the data is waiting to be written to memory.

write-back A scheme that handles writes by updating values only to the block in the cache, then writing the modified block to the lower level of the hierarchy when the block is replaced.

ating writes, no amount of buffering can help because writes are being generated faster than the memory system can accept them.

The rate at which writes are generated may also be *less* than the rate at which the memory can accept them, and yet stalls may still occur. This can happen when the writes occur in bursts. To reduce the occurrence of such stalls, processors usually increase the depth of the write buffer beyond a single entry.

The alternative to a write-through scheme is a scheme called **write-back.** In a write-back scheme, when a write occurs, the new value is written only to the block in the cache. The modified block is written to the lower level of the hierarchy when it is replaced. Write-back schemes can improve performance, especially when processors can generate writes as fast or faster than the writes can be handled by main memory; a write-back scheme is, however, more complex to implement than write-through.

In the rest of this section, we describe caches from real processors, and we examine how they handle both reads and writes. In Section 7.5, we will describe the handling of writes in more detail.

Elaboration: Writes introduce several complications into caches that are not present for reads. Here we discuss two of them: the policy on write misses and efficient implementation of writes in write-back caches.

Consider a miss in a write-through cache. The strategy followed in most write-through cache designs, called *fetch-on-miss*, *fetch-on-write*, or sometimes *allocate-on-miss*, allocates a cache block to the address that missed and fetches the rest of the block into the cache before writing the data and continuing execution. Alternatively, we could either allocate the block in the cache but not fetch the data (called *no-fetch-on-write*), or even not allocate the block (called *no-allocate-on-write*). Another name for these strategies that do not place the written data into the cache is *write-around*, since the data is written around the cache to get to memory. The motivation for these schemes is the observation that sometimes programs write entire blocks of data before reading them. In such cases, the fetch associated with the initial write miss may be unnecessary. There are a number of subtle issues involved in implementing these schemes in multiword blocks, including complicating the handling of write hits by requiring mechanisms similar to those used for write-back caches.

Actually implementing stores efficiently in a cache that uses a write-back strategy is more complex than in a write-through cache. In a write-back cache, we must write the block back to memory if the data in the cache is dirty and we have a cache miss. If we simply overwrote the block on a store instruction before we knew whether the store had hit in the cache (as we could for a write-through cache), we would destroy the contents of the block, which is not backed up in memory. A write-through cache can write the data into the cache and read the tag; if the tag mismatches, then a miss occurs. Because the cache is write-through, the overwriting of the block in the cache is not catastrophic since memory has the correct value.

In a write-back cache, because we cannot overwrite the block, stores either require two cycles (a cycle to check for a hit followed by a cycle to actually perform the write) or require an extra buffer, called a *store buffer*, to hold that data—effectively allowing the store to take only one cycle by pipelining it. When a store buffer is used, the processor does the cache lookup and places the data in the store buffer during the normal cache access cycle. Assuming a cache hit, the new data is written from the store buffer into the cache on the next unused cache access cycle.

By comparison, in a write-through cache, writes can always be done in one cycle. There are some extra complications with multiword blocks, however, since we cannot simply overwrite the tag when we write the data. Instead, we read the tag and write the data portion of the selected block. If the tag matches the address of the block being written, the processor can continue normally, since the correct block has been updated. If the tag does not match, the processor generates a write miss to fetch the rest of the block corresponding to that address. Because it is always safe to overwrite the data, write hits still take one cycle.

Many write-back caches also include write buffers that are used to reduce the miss penalty when a miss replaces a dirty block. In such a case, the dirty block is moved to a write-back buffer associated with the cache while the requested block is read from memory. The write-back buffer is later written back to memory. Assuming another miss does not occur immediately, this technique halves the miss penalty when a dirty block must be replaced.

An Example Cache: The Intrinsity FastMATH Processor

The Intrinsity FastMATH is a fast embedded microprocessor that uses the MIPS architecture and a simple cache implementation. Near the end of the chapter, we will examine the more complex cache design of the Intel Pentium P4, but we start with this simple, yet real, example for pedagogical reasons. Figure 7.9 shows the organization of the Intrinsity FastMATH data cache.

This processor has a 12-stage pipeline, similar to that discussed in Chapter 6. When operating at peak speed, the processor can request both an instruction word and a data word on every clock. To satisfy the demands of the pipeline without stalling, separate instruction and data caches are used. Each cache is 16 KB, or 4K words, with 16-word blocks.

Read requests for the cache are straightforward. Because there are separate data and instruction caches, separate control signals will be needed to read and write each cache. (Remember that we need to update the instruction cache when a miss occurs.) Thus, the steps for a read request to either cache are as follows:

1. Send the address to the appropriate cache. The address comes either from the PC (for an instruction) or from the ALU (for data).

2. If the cache signals hit, the requested word is available on the data lines. Since there are 16 words in the desired block, we need to select the right

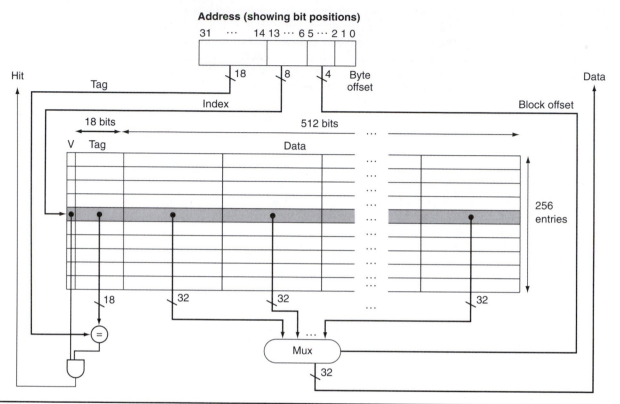

FIGURE 7.9   The 16 KB caches in the Intrinsity FastMATH each contain 256 blocks with 16 words per block. The tag field is 18 bits wide and the index field is 8 bits wide, while a 4-bit field (bits 5–2) is used to index the block and select the word from the block using a 16-to-1 multiplexor. In practice, to eliminate the multiplexor, caches use a separate large RAM for the data and a smaller RAM for the tags, with the block offset supplying the extra address bits for the large data RAM. In this case, the large RAM is 32 bits wide and must have 16 times as many words as blocks in the cache.

one. A block index field is used to control the multiplexor (shown at the bottom of the figure), which selects the requested word from the 16 words in the indexed block.

3. If the cache signals miss, we send the address to the main memory. When the memory returns with the data, we write it into the cache and then read it to fulfill the request.

For writes, the Intrinsity FastMATH offers both write-through and write-back, leaving it up to the operating system to decide which strategy to use for an application. It has a one-entry write buffer.

Instruction miss rate	Data miss rate	Effective combined miss rate
0.4%	11.4%	3.2%

FIGURE 7.10 Approximate instruction and data miss rates for the Intrinsity FastMATH processor for SPEC2000 benchmarks. The combined miss rate is the effective miss rate seen for the combination of the 16 KB instruction cache and 16 KB data cache. It is obtained by weighting the instruction and data individual miss rates by the frequency of instruction and data references.

What cache miss rates are attained with a cache structure like that used by the Intrinsity FastMATH? Figure 7.10 shows the miss rates for the instruction and data caches for the SPEC2000 integer benchmarks. The combined miss rate is the effective miss rate per reference for each program after accounting for the differing frequency of instruction and data accesses.

Although miss rate is an important characteristic of cache designs, the ultimate measure will be the effect of the memory system on program execution time; we'll see how miss rate and execution time are related shortly.

Elaboration: A combined cache with a total size equal to the sum of the two split caches will usually have a better hit rate. This higher rate occurs because the combined cache does not rigidly divide the number of entries that may be used by instructions from those that may be used by data. Nonetheless, many processors use a split instruction and data cache to increase cache *bandwidth*.

Here are miss rates for caches the size of those found in the Intrinsity FastMATH processor, and for a combined cache whose size is equal to the total of the two caches:

- Total cache size: 32 KB
- Split cache effective miss rate: 3.24%
- Combined cache miss rate: 3.18%

The miss rate of the split cache is only slightly worse.

The advantage of doubling the cache bandwidth, by supporting both an instruction and data access simultaneously, easily overcomes the disadvantage of a slightly increased miss rate. This observation is another reminder that we cannot use miss rate as the sole measure of cache performance, as Section 7.3 shows.

split cache A scheme in which a level of the memory hierarchy is composed of two independent caches that operate in parallel with each other, with one handling instructions and one handling data.

Designing the Memory System to Support Caches

Cache misses are satisfied from main memory, which is constructed from DRAMs. In Section 7.1, we saw that DRAMs are designed with the primary emphasis on density rather than access time. Although it is difficult to reduce the latency to fetch the first word from memory, we can reduce the miss penalty if we increase the bandwidth from the memory to the cache. This reduction allows larger block sizes to be used while still maintaining a low miss penalty, similar to that for a smaller block.

The processor is typically connected to memory over a bus. The clock rate of the bus is usually much slower than the processor, by as much as a factor of 10. The speed of this bus affects the miss penalty.

To understand the impact of different organizations of memory, let's define a set of hypothetical memory access times. Assume

- 1 memory bus clock cycle to send the address

- 15 memory bus clock cycles for each DRAM access initiated

- 1 memory bus clock cycle to send a word of data

If we have a cache block of four words and a one-word-wide bank of DRAMs, the miss penalty would be $1 + 4 \times 15 + 4 \times 1 = 65$ memory bus clock cycles. Thus, the number of bytes transferred per bus clock cycle for a single miss would be

$$\frac{4 \times 4}{65} = 0.25$$

Figure 7.11 shows three options for designing the memory system. The first option follows what we have been assuming: memory is one word wide, and all accesses are made sequentially. The second option increases the bandwidth to memory by widening the memory and the buses between the processor and memory; this allows parallel access to all the words of the block. The third option increases the bandwidth by widening the memory but not the interconnection bus. Thus, we still pay a cost to transmit each word, but we can avoid paying the cost of the access latency more than once. Let's look at how much these other two options improve the 65-cycle miss penalty that we would see for the first option [Figure 7.11(a)].

Increasing the width of the memory and the bus will increase the memory bandwidth proportionally, decreasing both the access time and transfer time portions of the miss penalty. With a main memory width of two words, the miss penalty drops from 65 memory bus clock cycles to $1 + (2 \times 15) + 2 \times 1 = 33$ memory bus clock cycles. With a four-word-wide memory, the miss penalty is just 17 memory bus clock cycles. The bandwidth for a single miss is then 0.48 (almost twice as high) bytes per bus clock cycle for a memory that is two words wide, and 0.94 bytes per bus clock cycle when the memory is four words wide (almost four times higher). The major costs of this enhancement are the wider bus and the potential increase in cache access time due to the multiplexor and control logic between the processor and cache.

Instead of making the entire path between the memory and cache wider, the memory chips can be organized in banks to read or write multiple words in one

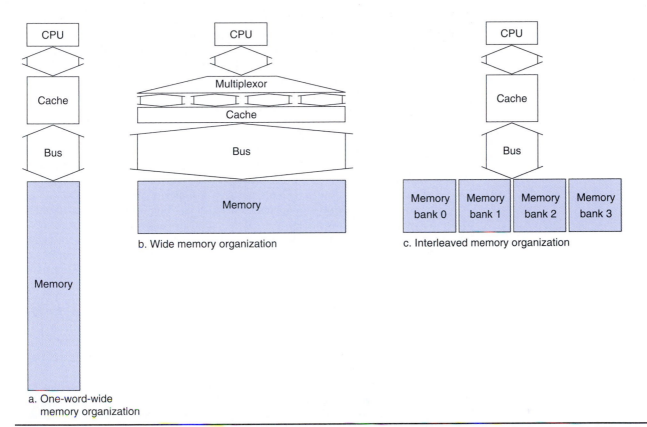

FIGURE 7.11 The primary method of achieving higher memory bandwidth is to increase the physical or logical width of the memory system. In this figure, memory bandwidth is improved two ways. The simplest design, (a), uses a memory where all components are one word wide; (b) shows a wider memory, bus, and cache; while (c) shows a narrow bus and cache with an interleaved memory. In (b), the logic between the cache and processor consists of a multiplexor used on reads and control logic to update the appropriate words of the cache on writes.

access time rather than reading or writing a single word each time. Each bank could be one word wide so that the width of the bus and the cache need not change, but sending an address to several banks permits them all to read simultaneously. This scheme, which is called *interleaving*, retains the advantage of incurring the full memory latency only once. For example, with four banks, the time to get a four-word block would consist of 1 cycle to transmit the address and read request to the banks, 15 cycles for all four banks to access memory, and 4 cycles to send the four words back to the cache. This yields a miss penalty of $1 + (1 \times 15) + 4 \times 1 = 20$ memory bus clock cycles. This is an effective bandwidth per miss of 0.80 bytes per clock, or about three times the bandwidth for the one-word-wide memory and bus. Banks are also valuable on writes. Each bank can write independently, quadrupling the write bandwidth and leading to fewer stalls in a write-through cache. As we will see, an alternative strategy for writes makes interleaving even more attractive.

Elaboration: Memory chips are organized to produce a number of output bits, usually 4 to 32, with 16 being the most popular in 2006. We describe the organization of a RAM as $d \times w$, where d is the number of addressable locations (the depth) and w is the output (or width of each location). One path to improving the rate at which we transfer data from the memory to the caches is to take advantage of the structure of DRAMs. DRAMs are logically organized as rectangular arrays, and access time is divided into row access and column access. DRAMs buffer a row of bits inside the DRAM for column access. They also come with optional timing signals that allow repeated accesses to the buffer without a row access time. This capability, originally called *page mode*, has gone through a series of enhancements. In page mode, the buffer acts like an SRAM; by changing column address, random bits can be accessed in the buffer until the next row access. This capability changes the access time significantly, since the access time to bits in the row is much lower. Figure 7.12 shows how the density, cost, and access time of DRAMs have changed over the years.

The newest development is DDR SDRAMs (double data rate synchronous DRAMs). SDRAMs provide for a burst access to data from a series of sequential locations in the DRAM. An SDRAM is supplied with a starting address and a burst length. The data in the burst is transferred under control of a clock signal, which in 2006 can run at up to

Year introduced	Chip size	$ per MB	Total access time to a new row/column	Column access time to existing row
1980	64 Kbit	$1500	250 ns	150 ns
1983	256 Kbit	$500	185 ns	100 ns
1985	1 Mbit	$200	135 ns	40 ns
1989	4 Mbit	$50	110 ns	40 ns
1992	16 Mbit	$15	90 ns	30 ns
1996	64 Mbit	$10	60 ns	12 ns
1998	128 Mbit	$4	60 ns	10 ns
2000	256 Mbit	$1	55 ns	7 ns
2004	512 Mbit	$0.25	50 ns	5 ns
2006	512 Mbit	$0.20	40 ns	2.5 ns

FIGURE 7.12   DRAM size increased by multiples of four approximately once every three years until 1996, and thereafter considerably slower. The improvements in access time have been slower but continuous, and cost almost tracks density improvements, although cost is often affected by other issues, such as availability and demand. The cost per megabyte is not adjusted for inflation.

400 MHz. The two key advantages of SDRAMs are the use of a clock that eliminates the need to synchronize and the elimination of the need to supply successive addresses in the burst. The DDR part of the name means data transfers on both the leading and falling edge of the clock, thereby getting twice as much bandwidth as you might expect based on the clock rate and the data width. To deliver such high bandwidth, the internal DRAM is organized as interleaved memory banks.

The advantage of these optimizations is that they use the circuitry already largely on the DRAMs, adding little cost to the system while achieving a significant improvement in bandwidth. The internal architecture of DRAMs and how these optimizations are implemented are described in Section B.8 of ⊙ Appendix B.

Summary

We began the previous section by examining the simplest of caches: a direct-mapped cache with a one-word block. In such a cache, both hits and misses are simple, since a word can go in exactly one location and there is a separate tag for every word. To keep the cache and memory consistent, a write-through scheme can be used, so that every write into the cache also causes memory to be updated. The alternative to write-through is a write-back scheme that copies a block back to memory when it is replaced; we'll discuss this scheme further in upcoming sections.

To take advantage of spatial locality, a cache must have a block size larger than one word. The use of a larger block decreases the miss rate and improves the efficiency of the cache by reducing the amount of tag storage relative to the amount of data storage in the cache. Although a larger block size decreases the miss rate, it can also increase the miss penalty. If the miss penalty increased linearly with the block size, larger blocks could easily lead to lower performance. To avoid this, the bandwidth of main memory is increased to transfer cache blocks more efficiently. The two common methods for doing this are making the memory wider and interleaving. In both cases, we reduce the time to fetch the block by minimizing the number of times we must start a new memory access to fetch a block, and, with a wider bus, we can also decrease the time needed to send the block from the memory to the cache.

Check Yourself

The speed of the memory system affects the designer's decision on the size of the cache block. Which of the following cache designer guidelines are generally valid?

1. The shorter the memory latency, the smaller the cache block.

2. The shorter the memory latency, the larger the cache block.

3. The higher the memory bandwidth, the smaller the cache block.

4. The higher the memory bandwidth, the larger the cache block.

7.3   Measuring and Improving Cache Performance

In this section, we begin by looking at how to measure and analyze cache performance; we then explore two different techniques for improving cache performance. One focuses on reducing the miss rate by reducing the probability that two different memory blocks will contend for the same cache location. The second technique reduces the miss penalty by adding an additional level to the hierarchy. This technique, called *multilevel caching*, first appeared in high-end computers selling for over $100,000 in 1990; since then it has become common on desktop computers selling for less than $1000!

CPU time can be divided into the clock cycles that the CPU spends executing the program and the clock cycles that the CPU spends waiting for the memory system. Normally, we assume that the costs of cache accesses that are hits are part of the normal CPU execution cycles. Thus,

$$\text{CPU time} = (\text{CPU execution clock cycles} + \text{Memory-stall clock cycles}) \times \text{Clock cycle time}$$

The memory-stall clock cycles come primarily from cache misses, and we make that assumption here. We also restrict the discussion to a simplified model of the memory system. In real processors, the stalls generated by reads and writes can be quite complex, and accurate performance prediction usually requires very detailed simulations of the processor and memory system.

Memory-stall clock cycles can be defined as the sum of the stall cycles coming from reads plus those coming from writes:

$$\text{Memory-stall clock cycles} = \text{Read-stall cycles} + \text{Write-stall cycles}$$

The read-stall cycles can be defined in terms of the number of read accesses per program, the miss penalty in clock cycles for a read, and the read miss rate:

$$\text{Read-stall cycles} = \frac{\text{Reads}}{\text{Program}} \times \text{Read miss rate} \times \text{Read miss penalty}$$

Writes are more complicated. For a write-through scheme, we have two sources of stalls: write misses, which usually require that we fetch the block before continuing the write (see the elaboration on page 484 for more details on dealing with writes), and write buffer stalls, which occur when the write buffer is full when a write occurs. Thus, the cycles stalled for writes equals the sum of these two:

$$\text{Write-stall cycles} = \left(\frac{\text{Writes}}{\text{Program}} \times \text{Write miss rate} \times \text{Write miss penalty} \right)$$

$$+ \text{ Write buffer stalls}$$

Because the write buffer stalls depend on the timing of writes, and not just the frequency, it is not possible to give a simple equation to compute such stalls. Fortunately, in systems with a reasonable write buffer depth (e.g., four or more words) and a memory capable of accepting writes at a rate that significantly exceeds the average write frequency in programs (e.g., by a factor of 2), the write buffer stalls will be small, and we can safely ignore them. If a system did not meet these criteria, it would not be well designed; instead, the designer should have used either a deeper write buffer or a write-back organization.

Write-back schemes also have potential additional stalls arising from the need to write a cache block back to memory when the block is replaced. We will discuss this more in Section 7.5.

In most write-through cache organizations, the read and write miss penalties are the same (the time to fetch the block from memory). If we assume that the write buffer stalls are negligible, we can combine the reads and writes by using a single miss rate and the miss penalty:

$$\text{Memory-stall clock cycles} = \frac{\text{Memory accesses}}{\text{Program}} \times \text{Miss rate} \times \text{Miss penalty}$$

We can also factor this as

$$\text{Memory-stall clock cycles} = \frac{\text{Instructions}}{\text{Program}} \times \frac{\text{Misses}}{\text{Instruction}} \times \text{Miss penalty}$$

Let's consider a simple example to help us understand the impact of cache performance on processor performance.

Calculating Cache Performance

Assume an instruction cache miss rate for a program is 2% and a data cache miss rate is 4%. If a processor has a CPI of 2 without any memory stalls and the miss penalty is 100 cycles for all misses, determine how much faster a processor would run with a perfect cache that never missed. Use the instruction frequencies for SPECint2000 from Chapter 3, Figure 3.26, on page 228.

EXAMPLE

ANSWER

The number of memory miss cycles for instructions in terms of the Instruction count (I) is

$$\text{Instruction miss cycles} = I \times 2\% \times 100 = 2.00 \times I$$

Assume the frequency of all loads and stores in SPECint2000 is 36%. Therefore, we can find the number of memory miss cycles for data references:

$$\text{Data miss cycles} = I \times 36\% \times 4\% \times 100 = 1.44 \times I$$

The total number of memory-stall cycles is 2.00 I + 1.44 I = 3.44 I. This is more than 3 cycles of memory stall per instruction. Accordingly, the CPI with memory stalls is 2 + 3.44 = 5.44. Since there is no change in instruction count or clock rate, the ratio of the CPU execution times is

$$\frac{\text{CPU time with stalls}}{\text{CPU time with perfect cache}} = \frac{I \times CPI_{\text{stall}} \times \text{Clock cycle}}{I \times CPI_{\text{perfect}} \times \text{Clock cycle}}$$

$$= \frac{CPI_{\text{stall}}}{CPI_{\text{perfect}}} = \frac{5.44}{2}$$

The performance with the perfect cache is better by $\frac{5.44}{2} = 2.72$.

What happens if the processor is made faster, but the memory system is not? The amount of time spent on memory stalls will take up an increasing fraction of the execution time; Amdahl's law, which we examined in Chapter 4, reminds us of this fact. A few simple examples show how serious this problem can be. Suppose we speed up the computer in the previous example by reducing its CPI from 2 to 1 without changing the clock rate, which might be done with an improved pipeline. The system with cache misses would then have a CPI of 1 + 3.44 = 4.44, and the system with the perfect cache would be

$$\frac{4.44}{1} = 4.44 \text{ times faster}$$

The amount of execution time spent on memory stalls would have risen from

$$\frac{3.44}{5.44} = 63\%$$

to

$$\frac{3.44}{4.44} = 77\%$$

Similarly, increasing clock rate without changing the memory system also increases the performance lost due to cache misses, as the next example shows.

Cache Performance with Increased Clock Rate

Suppose we increase the performance of the computer in the previous example by doubling its clock rate. Since the main memory speed is unlikely to change, assume that the absolute time to handle a cache miss does not change. How much faster will the computer be with the faster clock, assuming the same miss rate as the previous example?

EXAMPLE

Measured in the faster clock cycles, the new miss penalty will be twice as many clock cycles, or 200 clock cycles. Hence:

ANSWER

Total miss cycles per instruction $= (2\% \times 200) + 36\% \times (4\% \times 200) = 6.88$

Thus, the faster computer with cache misses will have a CPI of $2 + 6.88 = 8.88$, compared to a CPI with cache misses of 5.44 for the slower computer.

Using the formula for CPU time from the previous example, we can compute the relative performance as

$$\frac{\text{Performance with fast clock}}{\text{Performance with slow clock}} = \frac{\text{Execution time with slow clock}}{\text{Execution time with fast clock}}$$

$$= \frac{IC \times CPI_{\text{slow clock}} \times \text{Clock cycle}}{IC \times CPI_{\text{fast clock}} \times \dfrac{\text{Clock cycle}}{2}}$$

$$= \frac{5.44}{8.88 \times \frac{1}{2}} = 1.23$$

Thus, the computer with the faster clock is about 1.2 times faster rather than 2 times faster, which it would have been if we ignored cache misses.

As these examples illustrate, relative cache penalties increase as a processor becomes faster. Furthermore, if a processor improves both clock rate and CPI, it suffers a double hit:

1. The lower the CPI, the more pronounced the impact of stall cycles.

2. The main memory system is unlikely to improve as fast as processor cycle time, primarily because the performance of the underlying DRAM is not getting much faster. When calculating CPI, the cache miss penalty is measured in processor clock cycles needed for a miss. Therefore, if the main memories of two processors have the same absolute access times, a higher processor clock rate leads to a larger miss penalty.

Thus, the importance of cache performance for processors with low CPI and high clock rates is greater, and consequently the danger of neglecting cache behavior in assessing the performance of such processors is greater. As we will see in Section 7.6, the use of fast, pipelined processors in desktop PCs and workstations has led to the use of sophisticated cache systems even in computers selling for less than $1000.

The previous examples and equations assume that the hit time is not a factor in determining cache performance. Clearly, if the hit time increases, the total time to access a word from the memory system will increase, possibly causing an increase in the processor cycle time. Although we will see additional examples of what can increase hit time shortly, one example is increasing the cache size. A larger cache could clearly have a longer access time, just as if your desk in the library was very large (say, 3 square meters), it would take longer to locate a book on the desk. With pipelines deeper than five stages, an increase in hit time likely adds another stage to the pipeline, since it may take multiple cycles for a cache hit. Although it is more complex to calculate the performance impact of a deeper pipeline, at some point the increase in hit time for a larger cache could dominate the improvement in hit rate, leading to a decrease in processor performance.

The next subsection discusses alternative cache organizations that decrease miss rate but may sometimes increase hit time; additional examples appear in "Fallacies and Pitfalls" (Section 7.7).

Reducing Cache Misses by More Flexible Placement of Blocks

So far, when we place a block in the cache, we have used a simple placement scheme: A block can go in exactly one place in the cache. As mentioned earlier, it is called *direct mapped* because there is a direct mapping from any block address in memory to a single location in the upper level of the hierarchy. There is actually a whole range of schemes for placing blocks. At one extreme is direct mapped, where a block can be placed in exactly one location.

At the other extreme is a scheme where a block can be placed in *any* location in the cache. Such a scheme is called **fully associative** because a block in memory may be associated with any entry in the cache. To find a given block in a fully associative cache, all the entries in the cache must be searched because a block can be placed in any one. To make the search practical, it is done in parallel with a comparator associated with each cache entry. These comparators significantly increase the hardware cost, effectively making fully associative placement practical only for caches with small numbers of blocks.

fully associative cache A cache structure in which a block can be placed in any location in the cache.

The middle range of designs between direct mapped and fully associative is called **set associative**. In a set-associative cache, there are a fixed number of locations (at least two) where each block can be placed; a set-associative cache with n locations for a block is called an n-way set-associative cache. An n-way set-associative cache consists of a number of sets, each of which consists of n blocks. Each block in the memory maps to a unique *set* in the cache given by the index field, and a block can be placed in *any* element of that set. Thus, a set-associative placement combines direct-mapped placement and fully associative placement: a block is directly mapped into a set, and then all the blocks in the set are searched for a match.

set-associative cache A cache that has a fixed number of locations (at least two) where each block can be placed.

Remember that in a direct-mapped cache, the position of a memory block is given by

$$(\text{Block number}) \bmod (\text{Number of cache blocks})$$

In a set-associative cache, the set containing a memory block is given by

$$(\text{Block number}) \bmod (\text{Number of sets in the cache})$$

Since the block may be placed in any element of the set, *all the tags of all the elements of the set* must be searched. In a fully associative cache, the block can go anywhere and *all tags of all the blocks in the cache* must be searched. For example, Figure 7.13 shows where block 12 may be placed in a cache with eight blocks total, according to the block placement policy for direct-mapped, two-way set-associative, and fully associative caches.

We can think of every block placement strategy as a variation on set associativity. Figure 7.14 shows the possible associativity structures for an eight-block cache. A direct-mapped cache is simply a one-way set-associative cache: each

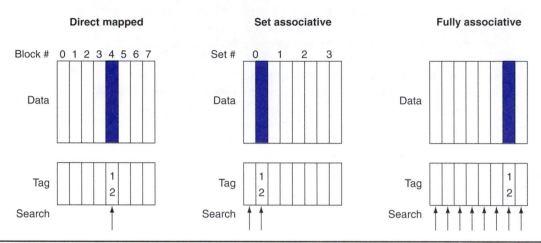

FIGURE 7.13   The location of a memory block whose address is 12 in a cache with eight blocks varies for direct-mapped, set-associative, and fully associative placement. In direct-mapped placement, there is only one cache block where memory block 12 can be found, and that block is given by (12 modulo 8) = 4. In a two-way set-associative cache, there would be four sets, and memory block 12 must be in set (12 mod 4) = 0; the memory block could be in either element of the set. In a fully associative placement, the memory block for block address 12 can appear in any of the eight cache blocks.

cache entry holds one block and each set has one element. A fully associative cache with m entries is simply an m-way set-associative cache; it has one set with m blocks, and an entry can reside in any block within that set.

The advantage of increasing the degree of associativity is that it usually decreases the miss rate, as the next example shows. The main disadvantage, which we discuss in more detail shortly, is an increase in the hit time.

Misses and Associativity in Caches

EXAMPLE

Assume there are three small caches, each consisting of four one-word blocks. One cache is fully associative, a second is two-way set associative, and the third is direct mapped. Find the number of misses for each cache organization given the following sequence of block addresses: 0, 8, 0, 6, 8.

One-way set associative
(direct mapped)

Block	Tag	Data
0		
1		
2		
3		
4		
5		
6		
7		

Two-way set associative

Set	Tag	Data	Tag	Data
0				
1				
2				
3				

Four-way set associative

Set	Tag	Data	Tag	Data	Tag	Data	Tag	Data
0								
1								

Eight-way set associative (fully associative)

Tag	Data	Tag	Data	Tag	Data	Tag	Data	Tag	Data	Tag	Data	Tag	Data	Tag	Data

FIGURE 7.14 An eight-block cache configured as direct mapped, two-way set associative, four-way set associative, and fully associative. The total size of the cache in blocks is equal to the number of sets times the associativity. Thus, for a fixed cache size, increasing the associativity decreases the number of sets, while increasing the number of elements per set. With eight blocks, an eight-way set-associative cache is the same as a fully associative cache.

The direct-mapped case is easiest. First, let's determine to which cache block each block address maps:

ANSWER

Block address	Cache block
0	(0 modulo 4) = 0
6	(6 modulo 4) = 2
8	(8 modulo 4) = 0

Now we can fill in the cache contents after each reference, using a blank entry to mean that the block is invalid, colored text to show a new entry added to the cache for the associate reference, and plain text to show an old entry in the cache:

Address of memory block accessed	Hit or miss	Contents of cache blocks after reference			
		0	1	2	3
0	miss	Memory[0]			
8	miss	Memory[8]			
0	miss	Memory[0]			
6	miss	Memory[0]		Memory[6]	
8	miss	Memory[8]		Memory[6]	

The direct-mapped cache generates five misses for the five accesses.

The set-associative cache has two sets (with indices 0 and 1) with two elements per set. Let's first determine to which set each block address maps:

Block address	Cache set
0	(0 modulo 2) = 0
6	(6 modulo 2) = 0
8	(8 modulo 2) = 0

Because we have a choice of which entry in a set to replace on a miss, we need a replacement rule. Set-associative caches usually replace the least recently used block within a set; that is, the block that was used furthest in the past is replaced. (We will discuss replacement rules in more detail shortly.) Using this replacement rule, the contents of the set-associative cache after each reference looks like this:

Address of memory block accessed	Hit or miss	Contents of cache blocks after reference			
		Set 0	Set 0	Set 1	Set 1
0	miss	Memory[0]			
8	miss	Memory[0]	Memory[8]		
0	hit	Memory[0]	Memory[8]		
6	miss	Memory[0]	Memory[6]		
8	miss	Memory[8]	Memory[6]		

Notice that when block 6 is referenced, it replaces block 8, since block 8 has been less recently referenced than block 0. The two-way set-associative cache has four misses, one less than the direct-mapped cache.

The fully associative cache has four cache blocks (in a single set); any memory block can be stored in any cache block. The fully associative cache has the best performance, with only three misses:

Address of memory block accessed	Hit or miss	Contents of cache blocks after reference			
		Block 0	Block 1	Block 2	Block 3
0	miss	Memory[0]			
8	miss	Memory[0]	Memory[8]		
0	hit	Memory[0]	Memory[8]		
6	miss	Memory[0]	Memory[8]	Memory[6]	
8	hit	Memory[0]	Memory[8]	Memory[6]	

For this series of references, three misses is the best we can do because three unique block addresses are accessed. Notice that if we had eight blocks in the cache, there would be no replacements in the two-way set-associative cache (check this for yourself), and it would have the same number of misses as the fully associative cache. Similarly, if we had 16 blocks, all three caches would have the same number of misses. This change in miss rate shows us that cache size and associativity are not independent in determining cache performance.

How much of a reduction in the miss rate is achieved by associativity? Figure 7.15 shows the improvement for the SPEC2000 benchmarks for a 64 KB data cache with a 16-word block, and associativity ranging from direct mapped to eight-way. Going from one-way to two-way associativity decreases the miss rate by about 15%, but there is little further improvement in going to higher associativity.

Associativity	Data miss rate
1	10.3%
2	8.6%
4	8.3%
8	8.1%

FIGURE 7.15 The data cache miss rates for an organization like the Intrinsity FastMATH processor for SPEC2000 benchmarks with associativity varying from one-way to eight-way. These results for 10 SPEC2000 programs are from Hennessy and Patterson [2003].

Locating a Block in the Cache

Now, let's consider the task of finding a block in a cache that is set associative. Just as in a direct-mapped cache, each block in a set-associative cache includes an address tag that gives the block address. The tag of every cache block within the appropriate set is checked to see if it matches the block address from the processor. Figure 7.16 shows how the address is decomposed. The index value is used to select the set containing the address of interest, and the tags of all the blocks in the set must be searched. Because speed is of the essence, all the tags in the selected set are searched in parallel. As in a fully associative cache, a sequential search would make the hit time of a set-associative cache too slow.

If the total cache size is kept the same, increasing the associativity increases the number of blocks per set, which is the number of simultaneous compares needed to perform the search in parallel: each increase by a factor of 2 in associativity doubles the number of blocks per set and halves the number of sets. Accordingly, each factor-of-2 increase in associativity decreases the size of the index by 1 bit and increases the size of the tag by 1 bit. In a fully associative cache, there is effectively only one set, and all the blocks must be checked in parallel. Thus, there is no index, and the entire address, excluding the block offset, is compared against the tag of every block. In other words, we search the entire cache without any indexing.

In a direct-mapped cache, such as in Figure 7.7 on page 478, only a single comparator is needed, because the entry can be in only one block, and we access the cache simply by indexing. Figure 7.17 shows that in a four-way set-associative cache, four comparators are needed, together with a 4-to-1 multiplexor to choose among the four potential members of the selected set. The cache access consists of indexing the appropriate set and then searching the tags of the set. The costs of an associative cache are the extra comparators and any delay imposed by having to do the compare and select from among the elements of the set.

The choice among direct-mapped, set-associative, or fully associative mapping in any memory hierarchy will depend on the cost of a miss versus the cost of implementing associativity, both in time and in extra hardware.

Tag	Index	Block offset

FIGURE 7.16   The three portions of an address in a set-associative or direct-mapped cache. The index is used to select the set, then the tag is used to choose the block by comparison with the blocks in the selected set. The block offset is the address of the desired data within the block.

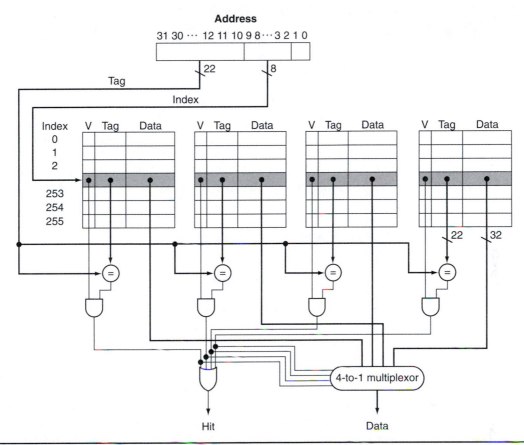

FIGURE 7.17 The implementation of a four-way set-associative cache requires four comparators and a 4-to-1 multiplexor. The comparators determine which element of the selected set (if any) matches the tag. The output of the comparators is used to select the data from one of the four blocks of the indexed set, using a multiplexor with a decoded select signal. In some implementations, the Output enable signals on the data portions of the cache RAMs can be used to select the entry in the set that drives the output. The Output enable signal comes from the comparators, causing the element that matches to drive the data outputs. This organization eliminates the need for the multiplexor.

Size of Tags versus Set Associativity

Increasing associativity requires more comparators, and more tag bits per cache block. Assuming a cache of 4K blocks, a four-word block size, and a 32-bit address, find the total number of sets and the total number of tag bits for caches that are direct mapped, two-way and four-way set associative, and fully associative.

EXAMPLE

ANSWER

Since there are 16 (= 2^4) bytes per block, a 32-bit address yields 32 − 4 = 28 bits to be used for index and tag. The direct-mapped cache has the same number of sets as blocks, and hence 12 bits of index, since $\log_2(4K) = 12$; hence, the total number of tag bits is (28 − 12) × 4K = 16 × 4K = 64 Kbits.

Each degree of associativity decreases the number of sets by a factor of 2 and thus decreases the number of bits used to index the cache by 1 and increases the number of bits in the tag by 1. Thus, for a two-way set-associative cache, there are 2K sets, and the total number of tag bits is (28 − 11) × 2 × 2K = 34 × 2K = 68 Kbits. For a four-way set-associative cache, the total number of sets is 1K, and the total number of tag bits is (28 − 10) × 4 × 1K = 72 × 1K = 72 Kbits.

For a fully associative cache, there is only one set with 4K blocks, and the tag is 28 bits, leading to a total of 28 × 4K × 1 = 112K tag bits.

Choosing Which Block to Replace

When a miss occurs in a direct-mapped cache, the requested block can go in exactly one position, and the block occupying that position must be replaced. In an associative cache, we have a choice of where to place the requested block, and hence a choice of which block to replace. In a fully associative cache, all blocks are candidates for replacement. In a set-associative cache, we must choose among the blocks in the selected set.

least recently used (LRU) A replacement scheme in which the block replaced is the one that has been unused for the longest time.

The most commonly used scheme is **least recently used** (LRU), which we used in the previous example. In an LRU scheme, the block replaced is the one that has been unused for the longest time. LRU replacement is implemented by keeping track of when each element in a set was used relative to the other elements in the set. For a two-way set-associative cache, tracking when the two elements were used can be implemented by keeping a single bit in each set and setting the bit to indicate an element whenever that element is referenced. As associativity increases, implementing LRU gets harder; in Section 7.5, we will see an alternative scheme for replacement.

Reducing the Miss Penalty Using Multilevel Caches

All modern computers make use of caches. In most cases, these caches are implemented on the same die as the microprocessor that forms the processor. To further close the gap between the fast clock rates of modern processors and the relatively long time required to access DRAMs, many microprocessors support an additional level of caching. This second-level cache, which can be on the same chip or off-chip in a separate set of SRAMs, is accessed whenever a miss occurs in the primary cache. If the second-level cache contains the desired data, the miss penalty for the first-level cache will be the access time of the second-level cache, which will be much less than the access time of main memory. If neither the primary nor secondary cache contains the data, a main memory access is required, and a larger miss penalty is incurred.

How significant is the performance improvement from the use of a secondary cache? The next example shows us.

Performance of Multilevel Caches

Suppose we have a processor with a base CPI of 1.0, assuming all references hit in the primary cache, and a clock rate of 5 GHz. Assume a main memory access time of 100 ns, including all the miss handling. Suppose the miss rate per instruction at the primary cache is 2%. How much faster will the processor be if we add a secondary cache that has a 5 ns access time for either a hit or a miss and is large enough to reduce the miss rate to main memory to 0.5%?

EXAMPLE

The miss penalty to main memory is

$$\frac{100 \text{ ns}}{0.2\frac{\text{ns}}{\text{clock cycle}}} = 500 \text{ clock cycles}$$

ANSWER

The effective CPI with one level of caching is given by

Total CPI = Base CPI + Memory-stall cycles per instruction

For the processor with one level of caching,

Total CPI = 1.0 + Memory-stall cycles per instruction = 1.0 + 2% × 500 = 11.0

With two levels of caching, a miss in the primary (or first-level) cache can be satisfied either by the secondary cache or by main memory. The miss penalty for an access to the second-level cache is

$$\frac{5 \text{ ns}}{0.2 \dfrac{\text{ns}}{\text{clock cycle}}} = 25 \text{ clock cycles}$$

If the miss is satisfied in the secondary cache, then this is the entire miss penalty. If the miss needs to go to main memory, then the total miss penalty is the sum of the secondary cache access time and the main memory access time.

Thus, for a two-level cache, total CPI is the sum of the stall cycles from both levels of cache and the base CPI:

$$\begin{aligned}
\text{Total CPI} &= 1 + \text{Primary stalls per instruction} \\
&\quad + \text{Secondary stalls per instruction} \\
&= 1 + 2\% \times 25 + 0.5\% \times 500 = 1 + 0.5 + 2.5 = 4.0
\end{aligned}$$

Thus, the processor with the secondary cache is faster by

$$\frac{11.0}{4.0} = 2.8$$

Alternatively, we could have computed the stall cycles by summing the stall cycles of those references that hit in the secondary cache ($(2\% - 0.5\%) \times 25 = 0.4$) and those references that go to main memory, which must include the cost to access the secondary cache as well as the main memory access time ($0.5\% \times (25 + 500) = 2.6$). The sum, $1.0 + 0.4 + 2.6$, is again 4.0.

The design considerations for a primary and secondary cache are significantly different because the presence of the other cache changes the best choice versus a single-level cache. In particular, a two-level cache structure allows the primary cache to focus on minimizing hit time to yield a shorter clock cycle, while allowing the secondary cache to focus on miss rate to reduce the penalty of long memory access times.

The interaction of the two caches permits such a focus. The miss penalty of the primary cache is significantly reduced by the presence of the secondary cache, allowing the primary to be smaller and have a higher miss rate. For the secondary cache, access time becomes less important with the presence of the primary cache, since the access time of the secondary cache affects the miss penalty of the primary cache, rather than directly affecting the primary cache hit time or the processor cycle time.

The effect of these changes on the two caches can be seen by comparing each cache to the optimal design for a single level of cache. In comparison to a single-level cache, the primary cache of a **multilevel cache** is often smaller. Furthermore, the primary cache often uses a smaller block size, to go with the smaller cache size and reduced miss penalty. In comparison, the secondary cache will often be larger than in a single-level cache, since the access time of the secondary cache is less critical. With a larger total size, the secondary cache often will use a larger block size than appropriate with a single-level cache.

multilevel cache A memory hierarchy with multiple levels of caches, rather than just a cache and main memory.

Understanding Program Performance

In Chapter 2, we saw that Quicksort had an algorithmic advantage over Bubble Sort that could not be overcome by language or compiler optimization. Figure 7.18(a) shows instructions executed by item searched for Radix Sort versus Quicksort. Indeed, for large arrays, Radix Sort has an algorithmic advantage over Quicksort in terms of number of operations. Figure 7.18(b) shows time per key instead of instructions executed. We see that the lines start on the same trajectory as Figure 7.18(a), but then the Radix Sort line diverges as the data to sort increases. What is going on? Figure 7.18(c) answers by looking at the cache misses per item sorted: Quicksort consistently has many fewer misses per item to be sorted.

Alas, standard algorithmic analysis ignores the impact of the memory hierarchy. As faster clock rates and Moore's law allow architects to squeeze all of the performance out of a stream of instructions, using the memory hierarchy well is critical to high performance. As we said in the introduction, understanding the behavior of the memory hierarchy is critical to understanding the performance of programs on today's computers.

Elaboration: Multilevel caches create several complications. First, there are now several different types of misses and corresponding miss rates. In the example on page 498, we saw the primary cache miss rate and the global miss rate—the fraction of references that missed in all cache levels. There is also a miss rate for the secondary cache, which is the ratio of all misses in the secondary cache divided by the number of accesses. This miss rate is called the local miss rate of the secondary cache. Because the primary cache filters accesses, especially those with good spatial and temporal locality, the local miss rate of the secondary cache is much higher than the global miss rate. For the example on page 498, we can compute the local miss rate of the secondary cache as 0.5%/2% = 25%! Luckily, the global miss rate dictates how often we must access the main memory.

global miss rate The fraction of references that miss in all levels of a multilevel cache.

local miss rate The fraction of references to one level of a cache that miss; used in multilevel hierarchies.

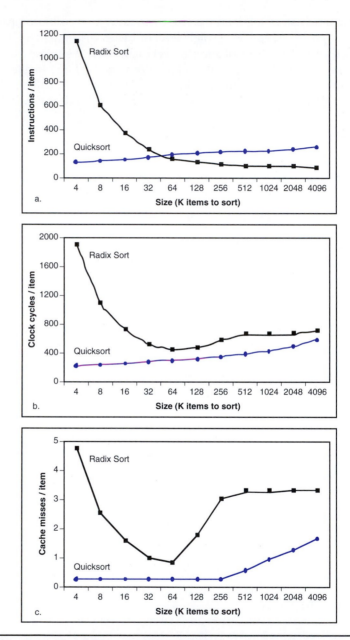

FIGURE 7.18 Comparing Quicksort and Radix Sort by (a) instructions executed per item sorted, (b) time per item sorted, and (c) cache misses per item sorted. This data is from a paper by LaMarca and Ladner [1996]. Although the numbers would change for newer computers, the idea still holds. Due to such results, new versions of Radix Sort have been invented that take memory hierarchy into account, to regain its algorithmic advantages (see Section 7.7). The basic idea of cache optimizations is to use all the data in a block repeatedly before it is replaced on a miss.

Additional complications arise because the caches may have different block sizes to match the larger or smaller total size. Likewise, the associativity of the cache may change. On-chip caches are often built with associativity of four or higher, while off-chip caches rarely have associativity of greater than two. On-chip L1 caches tend to have lower associativity than on-chip L2 caches since fast hit time is more important for L1 caches. These changes in block size and associativity introduce complications in the modeling of the caches, which typically means that all levels need to be simulated together to understand the behavior.

Elaboration: With out-of-order processors, performance is more complex, since they execute instructions during the miss penalty. Instead of instruction miss rates and data miss rates, we use misses per instruction, and this formula:

$$\frac{\text{Memory-stall cycles}}{\text{Instruction}} = \frac{\text{Misses}}{\text{Instruction}} \times (\text{Total miss latency} - \text{Overlapped miss latency})$$

There is no general way to calculate overlapped miss latency, so evaluations of memory hierarchies for out-of-order processors inevitably require simulation of the processor and memory hierarchy. Only by seeing the execution of the processor during each miss can we see if the processor stalls waiting for data or simply finds other work to do. A guideline is that the processor often hides the miss penalty for an L1 cache miss that hits in the L2 cache, but it rarely hides a miss to the L2 cache.

Elaboration: The performance challenge for algorithms is that the memory hierarchy varies between different implementations of the same architecture in cache size, associativity, block size, and number of caches. To copy with such variability, some recent numerical libraries parameterize their algorithms and then search the parameter space at runtime to find the best combination for a particular computer.

Which of the following is generally true about a design with multiple levels of caches?

Check Yourself

1. First-level caches are more concerned about hit time, and second-level caches are more concerned about miss rate.

2. First-level caches are more concerned about miss rate, and second-level caches are more concerned about hit time.

Summary

In this section, we focused on three topics: cache performance, using associativity to reduce miss rates, and the use of multilevel cache hierarchies to reduce miss penalties.

Since the total number of cycles spent on a program is the sum of the processor cycles and the memory-stall cycles, the memory system can have a significant effect on program execution time. In fact, as processors get faster (by lowering CPI or by increasing the clock rate or both), the relative effect of the memory-stall cycles increases, making good memory systems critical to achieving high performance. The number of memory-stall cycles depends on both the miss rate and the miss penalty. The challenge, as we will see in Section 7.5, is to reduce one of these factors without significantly affecting other critical factors in the memory hierarchy.

To reduce the miss rate, we examined the use of associative placement schemes. Such schemes can reduce the miss rate of a cache by allowing more flexible placement of blocks within the cache. Fully associative schemes allow blocks to be placed anywhere, but also require that every block in the cache be searched to satisfy a request. This search is usually implemented by having a comparator per cache block and searching the tags in parallel. The cost of the comparators makes large fully associative caches impractical. Set-associative caches are a practical alternative, since we need only search among the elements of a unique set that is chosen by indexing. Set-associative caches have higher miss rates but are faster to access. The amount of associativity that yields the best performance depends on both the technology and the details of the implementation.

Finally, we looked at multilevel caches as a technique to reduce the miss penalty by allowing a larger secondary cache to handle misses to the primary cache. Second-level caches have become commonplace as designers find that limited silicon and the goals of high clock rates prevent primary caches from becoming large. The secondary cache, which is often 10 or more times larger than the primary cache, handles many accesses that miss in the primary cache. In such cases, the miss penalty is that of the access time to the secondary cache (typically < 10 processor cycles) versus the access time to memory (typically > 100 processor cycles). As with associativity, the design trade-offs between the size of the secondary cache and its access time depend on a number of aspects of the implementation.

7.4 Virtual Memory

In the previous section, we saw how caches provided fast access to recently used portions of a program's code and data. Similarly, the main memory can act as a "cache" for the secondary storage, usually implemented with magnetic disks. This technique is called **virtual memory**. Historically, there were two major motivations for virtual memory: to allow efficient and safe sharing of memory among multiple programs, and to remove the programming burdens of a small, limited amount of main memory. Four decades after its invention, it's the former reason that reigns today.

Consider a collection of programs running at once on a computer. The total memory required by all the programs may be much larger than the amount of main memory available on the computer, but only a fraction of this memory is actively being used at any point in time. Main memory need contain only the active portions of the many programs, just as a cache contains only the active portion of one program. Thus, the principle of locality enables virtual memory as well as caches, and virtual memory allows us to efficiently share the processor as well as the main memory. Of course, to allow multiple programs to share the same memory, we must be able to protect the programs from each other, ensuring that a program can only read and write the portions of main memory that have been assigned to it.

We cannot know which programs will share the memory with other programs when we compile them. In fact, the programs sharing the memory change dynamically while the programs are running. Because of this dynamic interaction, we would like to compile each program into its own *address space*— a separate range of memory locations accessible only to this program. Virtual memory implements the translation of a program's address space to **physical addresses**. This translation process enforces **protection** of a program's address space from other programs.

The second motivation for virtual memory is to allow a single user program to exceed the size of primary memory. Formerly, if a program became too large for memory, it was up to the programmer to make it fit. Programmers divided programs into pieces and then identified the pieces that were mutually exclusive. These *overlays* were loaded or unloaded under user program control during execution, with the programmer ensuring that the program never tried to access an overlay that was not loaded and that the overlays loaded never exceeded the total size of the memory. Overlays were traditionally organized as modules, each containing both code and data. Calls between procedures in different modules would lead to overlaying of one module with another.

. . . a system has been devised to make the core drum combination appear to the programmer as a single level store, the requisite transfers taking place automatically.

Kilburn et al., "One-level storage system," 1962

virtual memory A technique that uses main memory as a "cache" for secondary storage.

physical address An address in main memory.

protection A set of mechanisms for ensuring that multiple processes sharing the processor, memory, or I/O devices cannot interfere, intentionally or unintentionally, with one another by reading or writing each other's data. These mechanisms also isolate the operating system from a user process.

As you can well imagine, this responsibility was a substantial burden on programmers. Virtual memory, which was invented to relieve programmers of this difficulty, automatically manages the two levels of the memory hierarchy represented by main memory (sometimes called *physical memory* to distinguish it from virtual memory) and secondary storage.

Although the concepts at work in virtual memory and in caches are the same, their differing historical roots have led to the use of different terminology. A virtual memory block is called a *page*, and a virtual memory miss is called a **page fault**. With virtual memory, the processor produces a **virtual address**, which is translated by a combination of hardware and software to a *physical address*, which in turn can be used to access main memory. Figure 7.19 shows the virtually addressed memory with pages mapped to main memory. This process is called *address mapping* or **address translation**. Today, the two memory hierarchy levels controlled by virtual memory are DRAMs

page fault An event that occurs when an accessed page is not present in main memory.

virtual address An address that corresponds to a location in virtual space and is translated by address mapping to a physical address when memory is accessed.

address translation Also called address mapping. The process by which a virtual address is mapped to an address used to access memory.

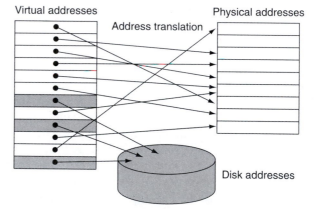

FIGURE 7.19   In virtual memory, blocks of memory (called *pages*) are mapped from one set of addresses (called *virtual addresses*) to another set (called *physical addresses*). The processor generates virtual addresses while the memory is accessed using physical addresses. Both the virtual memory and the physical memory are broken into pages, so that a virtual page is really mapped to a physical page. Of course, it is also possible for a virtual page to be absent from main memory and not be mapped to a physical address, residing instead on disk. Physical pages can be shared by having two virtual addresses point to the same physical address. This capability is used to allow two different programs to share data or code.

and magnetic disks (see Chapter 1, page 23). If we return to our library analogy, we can think of a virtual address as the title of a book and a physical address as the location of that book in the library, such as might be given by the Library of Congress call number.

Virtual memory also simplifies loading the program for execution by providing *relocation*. Relocation maps the virtual addresses used by a program to different physical addresses before the addresses are used to access memory. This relocation allows us to load the program anywhere in main memory. Furthermore, all virtual memory systems in use today relocate the program as a set of fixed-size blocks (pages), thereby eliminating the need to find a contiguous block of memory to allocate to a program; instead, the operating system need only find a sufficient number of pages in main memory. Formerly, relocation problems required special hardware and special support in the operating system; today, virtual memory also provides this function.

In virtual memory, the address is broken into a *virtual page number* and a *page offset*. Figure 7.20 shows the translation of the virtual page number to a *physical page number*. The physical page number constitutes the upper portion of the physical address, while the page offset, which is not changed, constitutes the lower

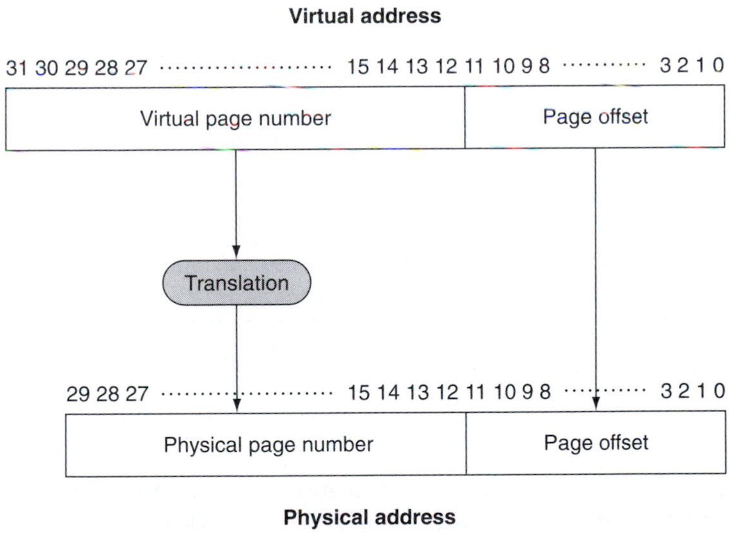

Virtual address

Physical address

FIGURE 7.20   Mapping from a virtual to a physical address. The page size is 2^{12} = 4 KB. The number of physical pages allowed in memory is 2^{18}, since the physical page number has 18 bits in it. Thus, main memory can have at most 1 GB, while the virtual address space is 4 GB.

portion. The number of bits in the page offset field determines the page size. The number of pages addressable with the virtual address need not match the number of pages addressable with the physical address. Having a larger number of virtual pages than physical pages is the basis for the illusion of an essentially unbounded amount of virtual memory.

Many design choices in virtual memory systems are motivated by the high cost of a miss, which in virtual memory is traditionally called a *page fault*. A page fault will take millions of clock cycles to process. (The table on page 469 shows that main memory is about 100,000 times faster than disk.) This enormous miss penalty, dominated by the time to get the first word for typical page sizes, leads to several key decisions in designing virtual memory systems:

- Pages should be large enough to try to amortize the high access time. Sizes from 4 KB to 16 KB are typical today. New desktop and server systems are being developed to support 32 KB and 64 KB pages, but new embedded systems are going in the other direction, to 1 KB pages.

- Organizations that reduce the page fault rate are attractive. The primary technique used here is to allow fully associative placement of pages in memory.

- Page faults can be handled in software because the overhead will be small compared to the disk access time. In addition, software can afford to use clever algorithms for choosing how to place pages because even small reductions in the miss rate will pay for the cost of such algorithms.

- Write-through will not work for virtual memory, since writes take too long. Instead, virtual memory systems use write-back.

The next few subsections address these factors in virtual memory design.

Elaboration: Although we normally think of virtual addresses as much larger than physical addresses, the opposite can occur when the processor address size is small relative to the state of the memory technology. No single program can benefit, but a collection of programs running at the same time can benefit from not having to be swapped to memory or by running on parallel processors. Given that Moore's law applies to DRAM, 32-bit processors are already problematic for servers and soon for desktops.

segmentation A variable-size address mapping scheme in which an address consists of two parts: a segment number, which is mapped to a physical address, and a segment offset.

Elaboration: The discussion of virtual memory in this book focuses on paging, which uses fixed-size blocks. There is also a variable-size block scheme called segmentation. In segmentation, an address consists of two parts: a segment number and a segment offset. The segment register is mapped to a physical address, and the offset is *added* to find the actual physical address. Because the segment can vary in size, a bounds check is also needed to make sure that the offset is within the segment. The major use of segmentation is to support more powerful methods of protection and sharing in an address space. Most operating system textbooks contain extensive discussions of segmentation compared to paging and of the use of segmentation to logically share the address space. The major disadvantage of segmentation is that it splits the address space into logically separate pieces that must be manipulated as a two-part address: the segment number and the offset. Paging, in contrast, makes the boundary between page number and offset invisible to programmers and compilers.

Segments have also been used as a method to extend the address space without changing the word size of the computer. Such attempts have been unsuccessful because of the awkwardness and performance penalties inherent in a two-part address of which programmers and compilers must be aware.

Many architectures divide the address space into large fixed-size blocks that simplify protection between the operating system and user programs and increase the efficiency of implementing paging. Although these divisions are often called "segments," this mechanism is much simpler than variable block size segmentation and is not visible to user programs; we discuss it in more detail shortly.

Placing a Page and Finding It Again

Because of the incredibly high penalty for a page fault, designers reduce page fault frequency by optimizing page placement. If we allow a virtual page to be mapped to any physical page, the operating system can then choose to replace any page it wants when a page fault occurs. For example, the operating system can use a sophisticated algorithm and complex data structures, which track page usage, to try to choose a page that will not be needed for a long time. The ability to use a clever and flexible replacement scheme reduces the page fault rate and simplifies the use of fully associative placement of pages.

As mentioned in Section 7.3, the difficulty in using fully associative placement is in locating an entry, since it can be anywhere in the upper level of the hierarchy. A full search is impractical. In virtual memory systems, we locate pages by using a table that indexes the memory; this structure is called a **page table** and resides in memory. A page table is indexed with the page number from the virtual address to discover the corresponding physical page number. Each program has its own page table, which maps the virtual address space of that program to main memory. In our library analogy, the page table corresponds to a mapping between book titles and library locations. Just as the card catalog may contain entries for books in another library on campus rather than the local branch library, we will see that the page table may contain entries for pages not present in memory. To indicate the location of the page table in memory, the hardware includes a register that points to the start of the page table; we call this the *page table register*. Assume for now that the page table is in a fixed and contiguous area of memory.

page table The table containing the virtual to physical address translations in a virtual memory system. The table, which is stored in memory, is typically indexed by the virtual page number; each entry in the table contains the physical page number for that virtual page if the page is currently in memory.

The page table, together with the program counter and the registers, specifies the *state* of a program. If we want to allow another program to use the processor, we must save this state. Later, after restoring this state, the program can continue execution. We often refer to this state as a *process*. The process is considered *active* when it is in possession of the processor; otherwise, it is considered *inactive*. The operating system can make a process active by loading the process's state, including the program counter, which will initiate execution at the value of the saved program counter.

The process's address space, and hence all the data it can access in memory, is defined by its page table, which resides in memory. Rather than save the entire page table, the operating system simply loads the page table register to point to the page table of the process it wants to make active. Each process has its own page table, since different processes use the same virtual addresses. The operating system is responsible for allocating the physical memory and updating the page tables, so that the virtual address spaces of different processes do not collide. As we will see shortly, the use of separate page tables also provides protection of one process from another.

Figure 7.21 uses the page table register, the virtual address, and the indicated page table to show how the hardware can form a physical address. A valid bit is used in each page table entry, just as we did in a cache. If the bit is off, the page is not present in main memory and a page fault occurs. If the bit is on, the page is in memory and the entry contains the physical page number.

Because the page table contains a mapping for every possible virtual page, no tags are required. In cache terminology, the index that is used to access the page table consists of the full block address, which is the virtual page number.

Page Faults

If the valid bit for a virtual page is off, a page fault occurs. The operating system must be given control. This transfer is done with the exception mechanism, which we discuss later in this section. Once the operating system gets control, it must find the page in the next level of the hierarchy (usually magnetic disk) and decide where to place the requested page in main memory.

The virtual address alone does not immediately tell us where the page is on disk. Returning to our library analogy, we cannot find the location of a library book on the shelves just by knowing its title. Instead, we go to the catalog and look up the book, obtaining an address for the location on the shelves, such as the Library of Congress call number. Likewise, in a virtual memory system, we must keep track of the location on disk of each page in virtual address space.

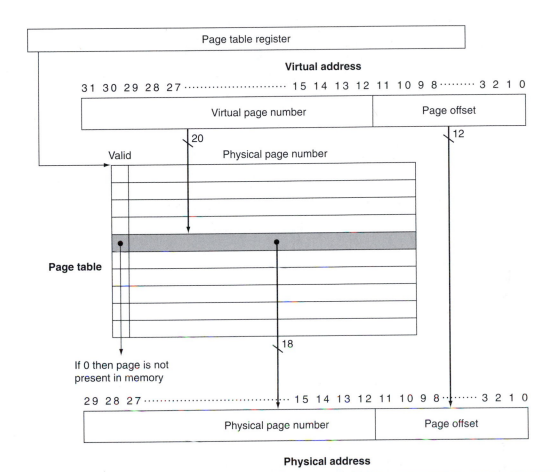

FIGURE 7.21 The page table is indexed with the virtual page number to obtain the corresponding portion of the physical address. The starting address of the page table is given by the page table pointer. In this figure, the page size is 2^{12} bytes, or 4 KB. The virtual address space is 2^{32} bytes, or 4 GB, and the physical address space is 2^{30} bytes, which allows main memory of up to 1 GB. The number of entries in the page table is 2^{20}, or 1 million entries. The valid bit for each entry indicates whether the mapping is legal. If it is off, then the page is not present in memory. Although the page table entry shown here need only be 19 bits wide, it would typically be rounded up to 32 bits for ease of indexing. The extra bits would be used to store additional information that needs to be kept on a per-page basis, such as protection.

Because we do not know ahead of time when a page in memory will be chosen to be replaced, the operating system usually creates the space on disk for all the pages of a process when it creates the process. This disk space is called the **swap space**. At that time, it also creates a data structure to record where each virtual page is stored on disk. This data structure may be part of the page table or may be an auxiliary data structure indexed in the same way as the page table. Figure 7.22

swap space The space on the disk reserved for the full virtual memory space of a process.

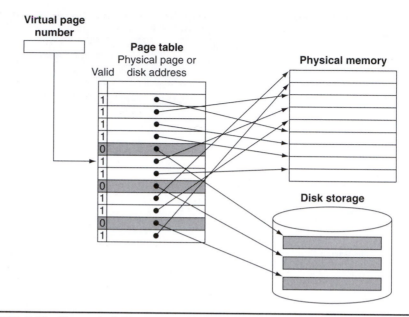

FIGURE 7.22   The page table maps each page in virtual memory to either a page in main memory or a page stored on disk, which is the next level in the hierarchy. The virtual page number is used to index the page table. If the valid bit is on, the page table supplies the physical page number (i.e., the starting address of the page in memory) corresponding to the virtual page. If the valid bit is off, the page currently resides only on disk, at a specified disk address. In many systems, the table of physical page addresses and disk page addresses, while logically one table, is stored in two separate data structures. Dual tables are justified in part because we must keep the disk addresses of all the pages, even if they are currently in main memory. Remember that the pages in main memory and the pages on disk are identical in size.

shows the organization when a single table holds either the physical page number or the disk address.

The operating system also creates a data structure that tracks which processes and which virtual addresses use each physical page. When a page fault occurs, if all the pages in main memory are in use, the operating system must choose a page to replace. Because we want to minimize the number of page faults, most operating systems try to choose a page that they hypothesize will not be needed in the near future. Using the past to predict the future, operating systems follow the least recently used (LRU) replacement scheme, which we mentioned in Section 7.3. The operating system searches for the least recently used page, making the assumption that a page that has not been used in a long time is less likely to be needed than a more recently accessed page. The replaced pages are written to swap space on the disk. In case you are wondering, the operating system is just another process, and these tables controlling memory are in memory; the details of this seeming contradiction will be explained shortly.

For example, suppose the page references (in order) were 10, 12, 9, 7, 11, 10, and then we referenced page 8, which was not present in memory. The LRU page is 12; in LRU replacement, we would replace page 12 in main memory with page 8. If the next reference also generated a page fault, we would replace page 9, since it would then be the LRU among the pages present in memory.

Implementing a completely accurate LRU scheme is too expensive, since it requires updating a data structure on *every* memory reference. Instead, most operating systems approximate LRU by keeping track of which pages have and which pages have not been recently used. To help the operating system estimate the LRU pages, some computers provide a **use bit** or **reference bit**, which is set whenever a page is accessed. The operating system periodically clears the reference bits and later records them so it can determine which pages were touched during a particular time period. With this usage information, the operating system can select a page that is among the least recently referenced (detected by having its reference bit off). If this bit is not provided by the hardware, the operating system must find another way to estimate which pages have been accessed.

Hardware/ Software Interface

reference bit Also called **use bit**. A field that is set whenever a page is accessed and that is used to implement LRU or other replacement schemes.

Elaboration: With a 32-bit virtual address, 4 KB pages, and 4 bytes per page table entry, we can compute the total page table size:

$$\text{Number of page table entries} = \frac{2^{32}}{2^{12}} = 2^{20}$$

$$\text{Size of page table} = 2^{20} \text{ page table entries} \times 2^2 \frac{\text{bytes}}{\text{page table entry}} = 4 \text{ MB}$$

That is, we would need to use 4 MB of memory for each program in execution at any time. On a computer with tens to hundreds of active programs and a fixed-size page table, most or all of the memory would be tied up in page tables!

A range of techniques is used to reduce the amount of storage required for the page table. The five techniques below aim at reducing the total maximum storage required as well as minimizing the main memory dedicated to page tables:

1. The simplest technique is to keep a limit register that restricts the size of the page table for a given process. If the virtual page number becomes larger than the contents of the limit register, entries must be added to the page table. This technique

allows the page table to grow as a process consumes more space. Thus, the page table will only be large if the process is using many pages of virtual address space. This technique requires that the address space expand in only one direction.

2. Allowing growth in only one direction is not sufficient, since most languages require two areas whose size is expandable: one area holds the stack and the other area holds the heap. Because of this duality, it is convenient to divide the page table and let it grow from the highest address down, as well as from the lowest address up. This means that there will be two separate page tables and two separate limits. The use of two page tables breaks the address space into two segments. The high-order bit of an address usually determines which segment and thus which page table to use for that address. Since the segment is specified by the high-order address bit, each segment can be as large as one-half of the address space. A limit register for each segment specifies the current size of the segment, which grows in units of pages. This type of segmentation is used by many architectures, including MIPS. Unlike the type of segmentation discussed in the second elaboration on page 514, this form of segmentation is invisible to the application program, although not to the operating system. The major disadvantage of this scheme is that it does not work well when the address space is used in a sparse fashion rather than as a contiguous set of virtual addresses.

3. Another approach to reducing the page table size is to apply a hashing function to the virtual address so that the page table data structure need be only the size of the number of *physical* pages in main memory. Such a structure is called an *inverted page table*. Of course, the lookup process is slightly more complex with an inverted page table because we can no longer just index the page table.

4. Multiple levels of page tables can also be used to reduce the total amount of page table storage. The first level maps large fixed-size blocks of virtual address space, perhaps 64 to 256 pages in total. These large blocks are sometimes called segments, and this first-level mapping table is sometimes called a segment table, though the segments are invisible to the user. Each entry in the segment table indicates whether any pages in that segment are allocated and, if so, points to a page table for that segment. Address translation happens by first looking in the segment table, using the highest-order bits of the address. If the segment address is valid, the next set of high-order bits is used to index the page table indicated by the segment table entry. This scheme allows the address space to be used in a sparse fashion (multiple noncontiguous segments can be active) without having to allocate the entire page table. Such schemes are particularly useful with very large address spaces and in software systems that require noncontiguous allocation. The primary disadvantage of this two-level mapping is the more complex process for address translation.

5. To reduce the actual main memory tied up in page tables, most modern systems also allow the page tables to be paged. Although this sounds tricky, it works by using the same basic ideas of virtual memory and simply allowing the page tables to reside in the virtual address space. In addition, there are some small but critical

problems, such as a never-ending series of page faults, which must be avoided. How these problems are overcome is both very detailed and typically highly processor specific. In brief, these problems are avoided by placing all the page tables in the address space of the operating system and placing at least some of the page tables for the system in a portion of main memory that is physically addressed and is always present and thus never on disk.

What about Writes?

The difference between the access time to the cache and main memory is tens to hundreds of cycles, and write-through schemes can be used, although we need a write buffer to hide the latency of the write from the processor. In a virtual memory system, writes to the next level of the hierarchy (disk) take millions of processor clock cycles; therefore, building a write buffer to allow the system to write through to disk would be completely impractical. Instead, virtual memory systems must use write-back, performing the individual writes into the page in memory and copying the page back to disk when it is replaced in the memory. This copying back to the lower level in the hierarchy is the source of the other name for this technique of handling writes, namely, *copy-back*.

A write-back scheme has another major advantage in a virtual memory system. Because the disk transfer time is small compared with its access time, copying back an entire page is much more efficient than writing individual words back to the disk. A write-back operation, although more efficient than transferring individual words, is still costly. Thus, we would like to know whether a page *needs* to be copied back when we choose to replace it. To track whether a page has been written since it was read into the memory, a *dirty bit* is added to the page table. The dirty bit is set when any word in a page is written. If the operating system chooses to replace the page, the dirty bit indicates whether the page needs to be written out before its location in memory can be given to another page.

Hardware/ Software Interface

Making Address Translation Fast: The TLB

Since the page tables are stored in main memory, every memory access by a program can take at least twice as long: one memory access to obtain the physical address and a second access to get the data. The key to improving access performance is to rely on locality of reference to the page table. When a translation for a virtual page number is used, it will probably be needed again in the near future because the references to the words on that page have both temporal and spatial locality.

translation-lookaside buffer (TLB) A cache that keeps track of recently used address mappings to avoid an access to the page table.

Accordingly, modern processors include a special cache that keeps track of recently used translations. This special address translation cache is traditionally referred to as a **translation-lookaside buffer** (TLB), although it would be more accurate to call it a translation cache. The TLB corresponds to that little piece of paper we typically use to record the location of a set of books we look up in the card catalog; rather than continually searching the entire catalog, we record the location of several books and use the scrap of paper as a cache of Library of Congress call numbers.

Figure 7.23 shows that each tag entry in the TLB holds a portion of the virtual page number, and each data entry of the TLB holds a physical page number. Because we will no longer access the page table on every reference, instead accessing the TLB, the TLB will need to include other bits, such as the dirty and the reference bit.

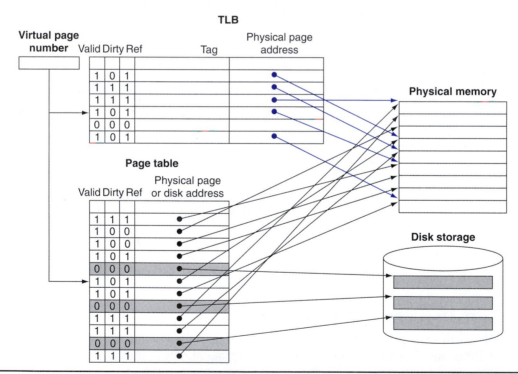

FIGURE 7.23   The TLB acts as a cache on the page table for the entries that map to physical pages only. The TLB contains a subset of the virtual-to-physical page mappings that are in the page table. The TLB mappings are shown in color. Because the TLB is a cache, it must have a tag field. If there is no matching entry in the TLB for a page, the page table must be examined. The page table either supplies a physical page number for the page (which can then be used to build a TLB entry) or indicates that the page resides on disk, in which case a page fault occurs. Since the page table has an entry for every virtual page, no tag field is needed; in other words, it is *not* a cache.

On every reference, we look up the virtual page number in the TLB. If we get a hit, the physical page number is used to form the address, and the corresponding reference bit is turned on. If the processor is performing a write, the dirty bit is also turned on. If a miss in the TLB occurs, we must determine whether it is a page fault or merely a TLB miss. If the page exists in memory, then the TLB miss indicates only that the translation is missing. In such cases, the processor can handle the TLB miss by loading the translation from the page table into the TLB and then trying the reference again. If the page is not present in memory, then the TLB miss indicates a true page fault. In this case, the processor invokes the operating system using an exception. Because the TLB has many fewer entries than the number of pages in main memory, TLB misses will be much more frequent than true page faults.

TLB misses can be handled either in hardware or in software. In practice, with care there can be little performance difference between the two approaches because the basic operations are the same in either case.

After a TLB miss occurs and the missing translation has been retrieved from the page table, we will need to select a TLB entry to replace. Because the reference and dirty bits are contained in the TLB entry, we need to copy these bits back to the page table entry when we replace an entry. These bits are the only portion of the TLB entry that can be changed. Using write-back—that is, copying these entries back at miss time rather than when they are written—is very efficient, since we expect the TLB miss rate to be small. Some systems use other techniques to approximate the reference and dirty bits, eliminating the need to write into the TLB except to load a new table entry on a miss.

Some typical values for a TLB might be

- TLB size: 16–512 entries

- Block size: 1–2 page table entries (typically 4–8 bytes each)

- Hit time: 0.5–1 clock cycle

- Miss penalty: 10–100 clock cycles

- Miss rate: 0.01%–1%

Designers have used a wide variety of associativities in TLBs. Some systems use small, fully associative TLBs because a fully associative mapping has a lower miss rate; furthermore, since the TLB is small, the cost of a fully associative mapping is not too high. Other systems use large TLBs, often with small associativity. With a fully associative mapping, choosing the entry to replace becomes tricky since implementing a hardware LRU scheme is too expensive. Furthermore, since TLB misses are much more frequent than page faults and thus must be handled more cheaply, we cannot afford an expensive software algorithm, as we can for page faults. As a result, many systems provide some support for randomly choosing an entry to replace. We'll examine replacement schemes in a little more detail in Section 7.5.

The Intrinsity FastMATH TLB

To see these ideas in a real processor, let's take a closer look at the TLB of the Intrinsity FastMATH. The memory system uses 4 KB pages and a 32-bit address space; thus, the virtual page number is 20 bits long, as in the top of Figure 7.24. The physical address is the same size as the virtual address. The TLB contains 16 entries, is fully associative, and is shared between the instruction and data references. Each entry is 64 bits wide and contains a 20-bit tag (which is the virtual page number for that TLB entry), the corresponding physical page number (also 20 bits), a valid bit, a dirty bit, and other bookkeeping bits.

Figure 7.24 shows the TLB and one of the caches, while Figure 7.25 shows the steps in processing a read or write request. When a TLB miss occurs, the MIPS hardware saves the page number of the reference in a special register and generates an exception. The exception invokes the operating system, which handles the miss in software. To find the physical address for the missing page, the TLB miss routine indexes the page table using the page number of the virtual address and the page table register, which indicates the starting address of the active process page table. Using a special set of system instructions that can update the TLB, the operating system places the physical address from the page table into the TLB. A TLB miss takes about 13 clock cycles, assuming the code and the page table entry are in the instruction cache and data cache, respectively. (We will see the MIPS TLB code on page 534.) A true page fault occurs if the page table entry does not have a valid physical address. The hardware maintains an index that indicates the recommended entry to replace; the recommended entry is chosen randomly.

There is an extra complication for write requests: namely, the write access bit in the TLB must be checked. This bit prevents the program from writing into pages for which it has only read access. If the program attempts a write and the write access bit is off, an exception is generated. The write access bit forms part of the protection mechanism, which we discuss shortly.

Integrating Virtual Memory, TLBs, and Caches

Our virtual memory and cache systems work together as a hierarchy, so that data cannot be in the cache unless it is present in main memory. The operating system plays an important role in maintaining this hierarchy by flushing the contents of any page from the cache, when it decides to migrate that page to disk. At the same time, the OS modifies the page tables and TLB, so that an attempt to access any data on the page will generate a page fault.

Under the best of circumstances, a virtual address is translated by the TLB and sent to the cache where the appropriate data is found, retrieved, and sent back to the processor. In the worst case, a reference can miss in all three components of

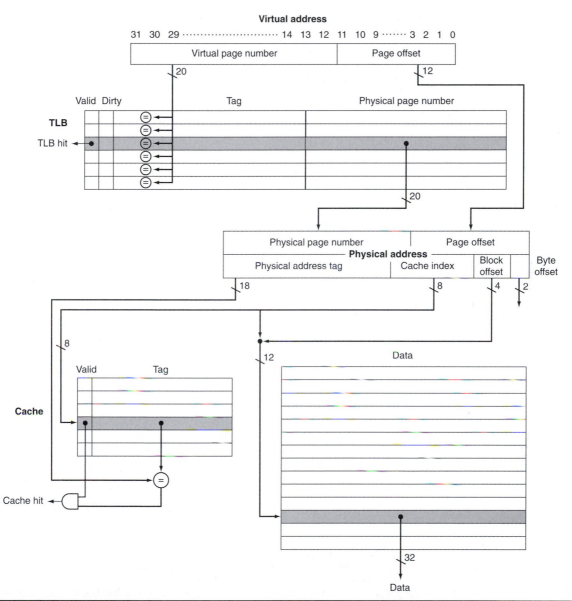

FIGURE 7.24 The TLB and cache implement the process of going from a virtual address to a data item in the Intrinsity Fast-MATH. This figure shows the organization of the TLB and the data cache assuming a 4 KB page size. This diagram focuses on a read; Figure 7.25 describes how to handle writes. Note that unlike Figure 7.9 on page 486, the tag and data RAMs are split. By addressing the long but narrow data RAM with the cache index concatenated with the block offset, we select the desired word in the block without a 16:1 multiplexor. While the cache is direct mapped, the TLB is fully associative. Implementing a fully associative TLB requires that every TLB tag be compared against the virtual page number, since the entry of interest can be anywhere in the TLB. If the valid bit of the matching entry is on, the access is a TLB hit, and bits from the physical page number together with bits from the page offset form the index that is used to access the cache. (The Intrinsity actually has a 16 KB page size; the elaboration on page 528 explains how it works.)

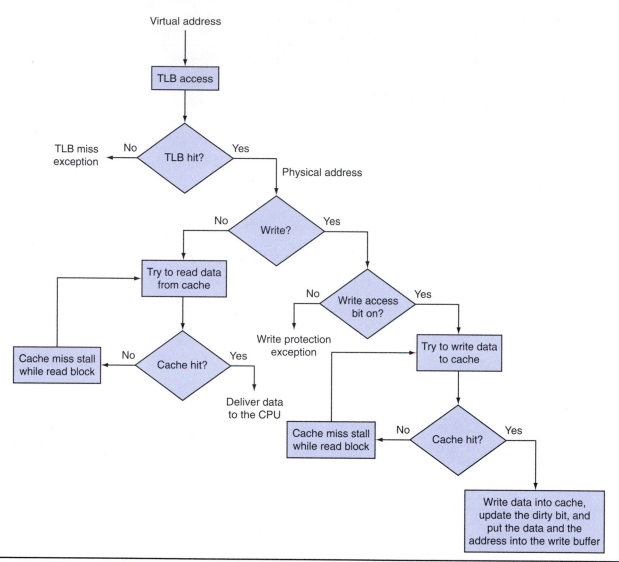

FIGURE 7.25   Processing a read or a write-through in the Intrinsity FastMATH TLB and cache. If the TLB generates a hit, the cache can be accessed with the resulting physical address. For a read, the cache generates a hit or miss and supplies the data or causes a stall while the data is brought from memory. If the operation is a write, a portion of the cache entry is overwritten for a hit and the data is sent to the write buffer if we assume write-through. A write miss is just like a read miss except that the block is modified after it is read from memory. Write-back requires writes to set a dirty bit for the cache block, and a write buffer is loaded with the whole block only on a read miss or write miss if the block to be replaced is dirty. Notice that a TLB hit and a cache hit are independent events, but a cache hit can only occur after a TLB hit occurs, which means that the data must be present in memory. The relationship between TLB misses and cache misses is examined further in the following example and the exercises at the end of this chapter.

the memory hierarchy: the TLB, the page table, and the cache. The following example illustrates these interactions in more detail.

Overall Operation of a Memory Hierarchy

In a memory hierarchy like that of Figure 7.24 that includes a TLB and a cache organized as shown, a memory reference can encounter three different types of misses: a TLB miss, a page fault, and a cache miss. Consider all the combinations of these three events with one or more occurring (seven possibilities). For each possibility, state whether this event can actually occur and under what circumstances.

EXAMPLE

Figure 7.26 shows the possible circumstances and whether they can arise in practice or not.

ANSWER

Elaboration: Figure 7.26 assumes that all memory addresses are translated to physical addresses before the cache is accessed. In this organization, the cache is *physically indexed* and *physically tagged* (both the cache index and tag are physical, rather than virtual, addresses). In such a system, the amount of time to access memory, assuming a cache hit, must accommodate both a TLB access and a cache access; of course, these accesses can be pipelined.

Alternatively, the processor can index the cache with an address that is completely or partially virtual. This is called a virtually addressed cache, and it uses tags that are virtual addresses; hence, such a cache is *virtually indexed* and *virtually tagged*. In such caches, the address translation hardware (TLB) is unused during the normal cache access, since the cache is accessed with a virtual address that has not been translated to a physical address. This takes the TLB out of the critical path, reducing cache

virtually addressed cache A cache that is accessed with a virtual address rather than a physical address.

TLB	Page table	Cache	Possible? If so, under what circumstance?
Hit	Hit	Miss	Possible, although the page table is never really checked if TLB hits.
Miss	Hit	Hit	TLB misses, but entry found in page table; after retry, data is found in cache.
Miss	Hit	Miss	TLB misses, but entry found in page table; after retry, data misses in cache.
Miss	Miss	Miss	TLB misses and is followed by a page fault; after retry, data must miss in cache.
Hit	Miss	Miss	Impossible: cannot have a translation in TLB if page is not present in memory.
Hit	Miss	Hit	Impossible: cannot have a translation in TLB if page is not present in memory.
Miss	Miss	Hit	Impossible: data cannot be allowed in cache if the page is not in memory.

FIGURE 7.26 The possible combinations of events in the TLB, virtual memory system, and cache. Three of these combinations are impossible, and one is possible (TLB hit, virtual memory hit, cache miss) but never detected.

aliasing A situation in which the same object is accessed by two addresses; can occur in virtual memory when there are two virtual addresses for the same physical page.

latency. When a cache miss occurs, however, the processor needs to translate the address to a physical address so that it can fetch the cache block from main memory.

When the cache is accessed with a virtual address and pages are shared between programs (which may access them with different virtual addresses), there is the possibility of aliasing. Aliasing occurs when the same object has two names—in this case, two virtual addresses for the same page. This ambiguity creates a problem because a word on such a page may be cached in two different locations, each corresponding to different virtual addresses. This ambiguity would allow one program to write the data without the other program being aware that the data had changed. Completely virtually addressed caches either introduce design limitations on the cache and TLB to reduce aliases or require the operating system, and possibly the user, to take steps to ensure that aliases do not occur.

Figure 7.24 assumed a 4 KB page size, but it's really 16 KB. The Intrinsity Fast-MATH uses such a memory system organization. The cache and TLB are still accessed in parallel, so the upper 2 bits of the cache index must be virtual. Hence, up to four cache entries could be aliased to the same physical memory address. As the L2 cache on the chip includes all entries in the L1 caches, on an L1 miss it checks the other three possible cache locations in the L2 cache for aliases. If it finds one, it flushes it from the caches to prevent aliases from occurring.

A common compromise between these two design points is caches that are virtually indexed (sometimes using just the page offset portion of the address, which is really a physical address since it is untranslated), but use physical tags. These designs, which are *virtually indexed but physically tagged*, attempt to achieve the performance advantages of virtually indexed caches with the architecturally simpler advantages of a physically addressed cache. For example, there is no alias problem in this case. The L1 data cache of the Pentium 4 is an example, as would the Intrinsity L1 data cache if the page size was 4 KB. To pull off this trick, there must be careful coordination between the minimum page size, the cache size, and associativity.

physically addressed cache A cache that is addressed by a physical address.

Elaboration: The FastMATH TLB is a bit more complicated than in Figure 7.24. MIPS includes two physical page mappings per virtual page number, thereby mapping an even-odd pair of virtual page numbers into two physical page numbers. Hence, the tag is 1 bit narrower since each entry corresponds to two pages. The least significant bit of the virtual page number selects between the two physical pages. There are separate bookkeeping bits for each physical page. This optimization doubles the amount of memory mapped per TLB entry. As the elaboration on page 530 explains, the tag field actually includes an 8-bit address space ID field to reduce the cost of context switches. To support the variable page sizes mentioned on page 537, there is also a 32-bit mask field that determines the dividing line between the virtual page address and the page offset.

Implementing Protection with Virtual Memory

One of the most important functions for virtual memory is to allow sharing of a single main memory by multiple processes, while providing memory protection among these processes and the operating system. The protection mechanism must ensure that although multiple processes are sharing the same main memory, one renegade process cannot write into the address space of another user process or into the operating system either intentionally or unintentionally. For example, if the program that maintains student grades were running on a computer at the same time as the programs of the students in the first programming course, we wouldn't want the errant program of a beginner to write over someone's grades. The write access bit in the TLB can protect a page from being written. Without this level of protection, computer viruses would be even more widespread.

To enable the operating system to implement protection in the virtual memory system, the hardware must provide at least the three basic capabilities summarized below.

1. Support at least two modes that indicate whether the running process is a user process or an operating system process, variously called a **supervisor** process, a **kernel** process, or an *executive* process.

2. Provide a portion of the processor state that a user process can read but not write. This includes the user/supervisor mode bit, which dictates whether the processor is in user or supervisor mode, the page table pointer, and the TLB. To write these elements, the operating system uses special instructions that are only available in supervisor mode.

3. Provide mechanisms whereby the processor can go from user mode to supervisor mode, and vice versa. The first direction is typically accomplished by a **system call** exception, implemented as a special instruction (*syscall* in the MIPS instruction set) that transfers control to a dedicated location in supervisor code space. As with any other exception, the program counter from the point of the system call is saved in the exception PC (EPC), and the processor is placed in supervisor mode. To return to user mode from the exception, use the *return from exception* (ERET) instruction, which resets to user mode and jumps to the address in EPC.

By using these mechanisms and storing the page tables in the operating system's address space, the operating system can change the page tables while preventing a user process from changing them, ensuring that a user process can access only the storage provided to it by the operating system.

We also want to prevent a process from reading the data of another process. For example, we wouldn't want a student program to read the grades while they were in the processor's memory. Once we begin sharing main memory, we must provide the ability for a process to protect its data from both reading and writing by another process; otherwise, sharing the main memory will be a mixed blessing!

Hardware/ Software Interface

kernel mode Also called **supervisor mode**. A mode indicating that a running process is an operating system process.

system call A special instruction that transfers control from user mode to a dedicated location in supervisor code space, invoking the exception mechanism in the process.

Remember that each process has its own virtual address space. Thus, if the operating system keeps the page tables organized so that the independent virtual pages map to disjoint physical pages, one process will not be able to access another's data. Of course, this also requires that a user process be unable to change the page table mapping. The operating system can assure safety if it prevents the user process from modifying its own page tables. Yet, the operating system must be able to modify the page tables. Placing the page tables in the protected address space of the operating system satisfies both requirements.

When processes want to share information in a limited way, the operating system must assist them, since accessing the information of another process requires changing the page table of the accessing process. The write access bit can be used to restrict the sharing to just read sharing, and, like the rest of the page table, this bit can be changed only by the operating system. To allow another process, say, P1, to read a page owned by process P2, P2 would ask the operating system to create a page table entry for a virtual page in P1's address space that points to the same physical page that P2 wants to share. The operating system could use the write protection bit to prevent P1 from writing the data, if that was P2's wish. Any bits that determine the access rights for a page must be included in both the page table and the TLB because the page table is accessed only on a TLB *miss*.

context switch A changing of the internal state of the processor to allow a different process to use the processor that includes saving the state needed to return to the currently executing process.

Elaboration: When the operating system decides to change from running process P1 to running process P2 (called a context switch or *process switch*), it must ensure that P2 cannot get access to the page tables of P1 because that would compromise protection. If there is no TLB, it suffices to change the page table register to point to P2's page table (rather than to P1's); with a TLB, we must clear the TLB entries that belong to P1—both to protect the data of P1 and to force the TLB to load the entries for P2. If the process switch rate were high, this could be quite inefficient. For example, P2 might load only a few TLB entries before the operating system switched back to P1. Unfortunately, P1 would then find that all its TLB entries were gone and would have to pay TLB misses to reload them. This problem arises because the virtual addresses used by P1 and P2 are the same, and we must clear out the TLB to avoid confusing these addresses.

A common alternative is to extend the virtual address space by adding a *process identifier* or *task identifier*. The Intrinsity FastMATH has an 8-bit address space ID (ASID) field for this purpose. This small field identifies the currently running process; it is kept in a register loaded by the operating system when it switches processes. The process identifier is concatenated to the tag portion of the TLB, so that a TLB hit occurs only if both the page number *and* the process identifier match. This combination eliminates the need to clear the TLB, except on rare occasions.

Similar problems can occur for a cache, since on a process switch the cache will contain data from the running process. These problems arise in different ways for physically addressed and virtually addressed caches, and a variety of different solutions, such as process identifiers, are used to ensure that a process gets its own data.

Handling TLB Misses and Page Faults

Although the translation of virtual to physical addresses with a TLB is straightforward when we get a TLB hit, handling TLB misses and page faults is more complex. A TLB miss occurs when no entry in the TLB matches a virtual address. A TLB miss can indicate one of two possibilities:

1. The page is present in memory, and we need only create the missing TLB entry.

2. The page is not present in memory, and we need to transfer control to the operating system to deal with a page fault.

How do we know which of these two circumstances has occurred? When we process the TLB miss, we will look for a page table entry to bring into the TLB. If the matching page table entry has a valid bit that is turned off, then the corresponding page is not in memory and we have a page fault, rather than just a TLB miss. If the valid bit is on, we can simply retrieve the desired entry.

A TLB miss can be handled in software or hardware because it will require only a short sequence of operations to copy a valid page table entry from memory into the TLB. MIPS traditionally handles a TLB miss in software. It brings in the page table entry from memory and then reexecutes the instruction that caused the TLB miss. Upon reexecuting it will get a TLB hit. If the page table entry indicates the page is not in memory, this time it will get a page fault exception.

Handling a TLB miss or a page fault requires using the exception mechanism to interrupt the active process, transferring control to the operating system, and later resuming execution of the interrupted process. A page fault will be recognized sometime during the clock cycle used to access memory. To restart the instruction after the page fault is handled, the program counter of the instruction that caused the page fault must be saved. Just as in Chapters 5 and 6, the exception program counter (EPC) is used to hold this value.

In addition, a TLB miss or page fault exception must be asserted by the end of the same clock cycle that the memory access occurs, so that the next clock cycle will begin exception processing rather than continue normal instruction execution. If the page fault was not recognized in this clock cycle, a load instruction could overwrite a register, and this could be disastrous when we try to restart the instruction. For example, consider the instruction `lw $1,0($1)`: the computer must be able to prevent the write pipeline stage from occurring; otherwise, it could not properly restart the instruction, since the contents of `$1` would have been destroyed. A similar complication arises on stores. We must prevent the write into memory from actually completing when there is a page fault; this is usually done by deasserting the write control line to the memory.

Register	CP0 register number	Description
EPC	14	Where to restart after exception
Cause	13	Cause of exception
BadVAddr	8	Address that caused exception
Index	0	Location in TLB to be read or written
Random	1	Pseudorandom location in TLB
EntryLo	2	Physical page address and flags
EntryHi	10	Virtual page address
Context	4	Page table address and page number

FIGURE 7.27   MIPS control registers. These are considered to be in coprocessor 0, and hence are read using `mfc0` and written using `mtc0`.

Hardware/ Software Interface

exception enable Also called **interrupt enable**. A signal or action that controls whether the process responds to an exception or not; necessary for preventing the occurrence of exceptions during intervals before the processor has safely saved the state needed to restart.

Between the time we begin executing the exception handler in the operating system and the time that the operating system has saved all the state of the process, the operating system is particularly vulnerable. For example, if another exception occurred when we were processing the first exception in the operating system, the control unit would overwrite the exception program counter, making it impossible to return to the instruction that caused the page fault! We can avoid this disaster by providing the ability to disable and **enable exceptions**. When an exception first occurs, the processor sets a bit that disables all other exceptions; this could happen at the same time the processor sets the supervisor mode bit. The operating system will then save just enough state to allow it to recover if another exception occurs—namely, the exception program counter and Cause register. EPC and Cause are two of the special control registers that help with exceptions, TLB misses, and page faults; Figure 7.27 shows the rest. The operating system can then reenable exceptions. These steps make sure that exceptions will not cause the processor to lose any state and thereby be unable to restart execution of the interrupting instruction.

Once the operating system knows the virtual address that caused the page fault, it must complete three steps:

1. Look up the page table entry using the virtual address and find the location of the referenced page on disk.

2. Choose a physical page to replace; if the chosen page is dirty, it must be written out to disk before we can bring a new virtual page into this physical page.

3. Start a read to bring the referenced page from disk into the chosen physical page.

Of course, this last step will take millions of processor clock cycles (so will the second if the replaced page is dirty); accordingly, the operating system will usually select another process to execute in the processor until the disk access completes. Because the operating system has saved the state of the process, it can freely give control of the processor to another process.

When the read of the page from disk is complete, the operating system can restore the state of the process that originally caused the page fault and execute the instruction that returns from the exception. This instruction will reset the processor from kernel to user mode, as well as restore the program counter. The user process then reexecutes the instruction that faulted, accesses the requested page successfully, and continues execution.

Page fault exceptions for data accesses are difficult to implement properly in a processor because of a combination of three characteristics:

1. They occur in the middle of instructions, unlike instruction page faults.

2. The instruction cannot be completed before handling the exception.

3. After handling the exception, the instruction must be restarted as if nothing had occurred.

Making instructions **restartable**, so that the exception can be handled and the instruction later continued, is relatively easy in an architecture like the MIPS. Because each instruction writes only one data item and this write occurs at the end of the instruction cycle, we can simply prevent the instruction from completing (by not writing) and restart the instruction at the beginning.

For processors with much more complex instructions that may touch many memory locations and write many data items, making instructions restartable is much harder. Processing one instruction may generate a number of page faults in the middle of the instruction. For example, some processors have block move instructions that touch thousands of data words. In such processors, instructions often cannot be restarted from the beginning, as we do for MIPS instructions. Instead, the instruction must be interrupted and later continued midstream in its execution. Resuming an instruction in the middle of its execution usually requires saving some special state, processing the exception, and restoring that special state. Making this work properly requires careful and detailed coordination between the exception-handling code in the operating system and the hardware.

Let's look in more detail at MIPS. When a TLB miss occurs, the MIPS hardware saves the page number of the reference in a special register called `BadVAddr` and generates an exception.

The exception invokes the operating system, which handles the miss in software. Control is transferred to address $8000\ 0000_{hex}$, the location of the TLB miss **handler**. To find the physical address for the missing page, the TLB miss routine indexes

restartable instruction An instruction that can resume execution after an exception is resolved without the exception's affecting the result of the instruction.

handler Name of a software routine invoked to "handle" an exception or interrupt.

the page table using the page number of the virtual address and the page table register, which indicates the starting address of the active process page table. To make this indexing fast, MIPS hardware places everything you need in the special `Context` register: the upper 12 bits have the address of the base of the page table, and the next 18 bits have the virtual address of the missing page. Each page table entry is one word, so the last 2 bits are 0. Thus, the first two instructions copy the Context register into the kernel temporary register $k1 and then load the page table entry from that address into $k1. Recall that $k0 and $k1 are reserved for the operating system to use without saving; a major reason for this convention is to make the TLB miss handler fast. Below is the MIPS code for a typical TLB miss handler:

```
TLBmiss:
  mfc0  $k1,Context    # copy address of PTE into temp $k1
  lw    $k1, 0($k1)    # put PTE into temp $k1
  mtc0  $k1,EntryLo    # put PTE into special register EntryLo
  tlbwr                # put EntryLo into TLB entry at Random
  eret                 # return from TLB miss exception
```

As shown above, MIPS has a special set of system instructions to update the TLB. The instruction `tlbwr` copies from control register `EntryLo` into the TLB entry selected by the control register `Random`. `Random` implements random replacement, so it is basically a free-running counter. A TLB miss takes about a dozen clock cycles.

Note that the TLB miss handler does not check to see if the page table entry is valid. Because the exception for TLB entry missing is much more frequent than a page fault, the operating system loads the TLB from the page table without examining the entry and restarts the instruction. If the entry is invalid, another and different exception occurs, and the operating system recognizes the page fault. This method makes the frequent case of a TLB miss fast, at a slight performance penalty for the infrequent case of a page fault.

Once the process that generated the page fault has been interrupted, it transfers control to 8000 0180$_{hex}$, a different address than the TLB miss handler. This is the general address for exception; TLB miss has a special entry point to lower the penalty for a TLB miss. The operating system uses the exception Cause register to diagnose the cause of the exception. Because the exception is a page fault, the operating system knows that extensive processing will be required. Thus, unlike a TLB miss, it saves the entire state of the active process. This state includes all the general-purpose and floating-point registers, the page table address register, the EPC, and the exception Cause register. Since exception handlers do not usually use the floating-point registers, the general entry point does not save them, leaving that to the few handlers that need them.

Figure 7.28 sketches the MIPS code of an exception handler. Note that we save and restore the state in MIPS code, taking care when we enable and disable exceptions, but we invoke C code to handle the particular exception.

Save state			
Save GPR	addi	$k1,$sp, -XCPSIZE	# save space on stack for state
	sw	$sp, XCT_SP($k1)	# save $sp on stack
	sw	$v0, XCT_V0($k1)	# save $v0 on stack
	...		# save $v1, $ai, $si, $ti,... on stack
	sw	$ra, XCT_RA($k1)	# save $ra on stack
Save hi, lo	mfhi	$v0	# copy Hi
	mflo	$v1	# copy Lo
	sw	$v0, XCT_HI($k1)	# save Hi value on stack
	sw	$v1, XCT_LI($k1)	# save Lo value on stack
Save exception registers	mfc0	$a0, $cr	# copy cause register
	sw	$a0, XCT_CR($k1)	# save $cr value on stack
	...		# save $v1,....
	mfc0	$a3, $sr	# copy status register
	sw	$a3, XCT_SR($k1)	# save $sr on stack
Set sp	move	$sp, $k1	# sp = sp - XCPSIZE
Enable nested exceptions			
	andi	$v0, $a3, MASK1	# $v0 = $sr & MASK1, enable exceptions
	mtc0	$v0, $sr	# $sr = value that enables exceptions
Call C exception handler			
Set $gp	move	$gp, GPINIT	# set $gp to point to heap area
Call C code	move	$a0, $sp	# arg1 = pointer to exception stack
	jal	xcpt_deliver	# call C code to handle exception
Restoring state			
Restore most GPR, hi, lo	move	$at, $sp	# temporary value of $sp
	lw	$ra, XCT_RA($at)	# restore $ra from stack
	...		# restore $t0,....., $a1
	lw	$a0, XCT_A0($k1)	# restore $a0 from stack
Restore status register	lw	$v0, XCT_SR($at)	# load old $sr from stack
	li	$v1, MASK2	# mask to disable exceptions
	and	$v0, $v0, $v1	# $v0 = $sr & MASK2, disenable exceptions
	mtc0	$v0, $sr	# set status register
Exception return			
Restore $sp and rest of GPR used as temporary registers	lw	$sp, XCT_SP($at)	# restore $sp from stack
	lw	$v0, XCT_V0($at)	# restore $v0 from stack
	lw	$v1, XCT_V1($at)	# restore $v1 from stack
	lw	$k1, XCT_EPC($at)	# copy old $epc from stack
	lw	$at, XCT_AT($at)	# restore $at from stack
Restore ERC and return	mtc0	$k1, $epc	# restore $epc
	eret	$ra	# return to interrupted instruction

FIGURE 7.28 MIPS code to save and restore state on an exception.

The virtual address that caused the fault depends on whether the fault was an instruction or data fault. The address of the instruction that generated the fault is in the EPC. If it was an instruction page fault, the EPC contains the virtual address of the faulting page; otherwise, the faulting virtual address can be computed by examining the instruction (whose address is in the EPC) to find the base register and offset field.

unmapped A portion of the address space that cannot have page faults.

Elaboration: This simplified version assumes that the stack pointer (sp) is valid. To avoid the problem of a page fault during this low-level exception code, MIPS sets aside a portion of its address space that cannot have page faults, called unmapped. The operating system places exception entry point code and the exception stack in unmapped memory. MIPS hardware translates virtual addresses 8000 0000$_{hex}$ to BFFF FFFF$_{hex}$ to physical addresses simply by ignoring the upper bits of the virtual address, thereby placing these addresses in the low part of physical memory. Thus, the operating system places exception entry points and exception stacks in unmapped memory.

Elaboration: The code in Figure 7.28 shows the MIPS-32 exception return sequence. MIPS-I uses `rfe` and `jr` instead of `eret`.

Summary

Virtual memory is the name for the level of memory hierarchy that manages caching between the main memory and disk. Virtual memory allows a single program to expand its address space beyond the limits of main memory. More importantly, in recent computer systems virtual memory supports sharing of the main memory among multiple, simultaneously active processes, which together require far more total physical main memory than exists. To support sharing, virtual memory also provides mechanisms for memory protection.

Managing the memory hierarchy between main memory and disk is challenging because of the high cost of page faults. Several techniques are used to reduce the miss rate:

1. Blocks, called pages, are made large to take advantage of spatial locality and to reduce the miss rate.

2. The mapping between virtual addresses and physical addresses, which is implemented with a page table, is made fully associative so that a virtual page can be placed anywhere in main memory.

3. The operating system uses techniques, such as LRU and a reference bit, to choose which pages to replace.

Writes to disk are expensive, so virtual memory uses a write-back scheme and also tracks whether a page is unchanged (using a dirty bit) to avoid writing unchanged pages back to disk.

The virtual memory mechanism provides address translation from a virtual address used by the program to the physical address space used for accessing memory. This address translation allows protected sharing of the main memory and provides several additional benefits, such as simplifying memory allocation. To ensure that processes are protected from each other requires that only the operating system can change the address translations, which is implemented by preventing user programs from changing the page tables. Controlled sharing of pages among processes can be implemented with the help of the operating system and access bits in the page table that indicate whether the user program has read or write access to a page.

If a processor had to access a page table resident in memory to translate every access, virtual memory would have too much overhead and caches would be pointless! Instead, a TLB acts as a cache for translations from the page table. Addresses are then translated from virtual to physical using the translations in the TLB.

Caches, virtual memory, and TLBs all rely on a common set of principles and policies. The next section discusses this common framework.

Understanding Program Performance

Although virtual memory was invented to enable a small memory to act as a large one, the performance difference between disk and memory means that if a program routinely accesses more virtual memory than it has physical memory it will run very slowly. Such a program would be continuously swapping pages between memory and disk, called *thrashing*. Thrashing is a disaster if it occurs, but it is rare. If your program thrashes, the easiest solution is to run it on a computer with more memory or buy more memory for your computer. A more complex choice is to reexamine your algorithm and data structures to see if you can change the locality and thereby reduce the number of pages that your program uses simultaneously. This set of pages is informally called the *working set*.

A more common performance problem is TLB misses. Since a TLB might handle only 32–64 page entries at a time, a program could easily see a high TLB miss rate, as the processor may access less than a quarter megabyte directly: $64 \times 4\ KB = 0.25\ MB$. For example, TLB misses are often a challenge for Radix Sort. To try to alleviate this problem, most computer architectures now support variable page sizes. For example, in addition to the standard 4 KB page, MIPS hardware supports 16 KB, 64 KB, 256 KB, 1 MB, 4 MB, 16 MB, 64 MB, and 256 MB pages. Hence, if a program uses large page sizes, it can access more memory directly without TLB misses.

The practical challenge is getting the operating system to allow programs to select these larger page sizes. Once again, the more complex solution to reducing TLB misses is to reexamine the algorithm and data structures to reduce the working set of pages.

Match the memory hierarchy element on the left with the closest phrase on the right:

1. L1 cache
2. L2 cache
3. Main memory
4. TLB

a. A cache for a cache
b. A cache for disks
c. A cache for a main memory
d. A cache for page table entries

7.5 A Common Framework for Memory Hierarchies

By now, you've recognized that the different types of memory hierarchies share a great deal in common. Although many of the aspects of memory hierarchies differ quantitatively, many of the policies and features that determine how a hierarchy functions are similar qualitatively. Figure 7.29 shows how some of the quantitative characteristics of memory hierarchies can differ. In the rest of this section, we will discuss the common operational aspects of memory hierarchies and how these determine their behavior. We will examine these policies as a series of four questions that apply between any two levels of a memory hierarchy, although for simplicity we will primarily use terminology for caches.

Question 1: Where Can a Block Be Placed?

We have seen that block placement in the upper level of the hierarchy can use a range of schemes, from direct mapped to set associative to fully associative. As mentioned above, this entire range of schemes can be thought of as variations on a set-associative scheme where the number of sets and the number of blocks per set varies:

Scheme name	Number of sets	Blocks per set
Direct mapped	Number of blocks in cache	1
Set associative	Number of blocks in cache Associativity	Associativity (typically 2–16)
Fully associative	1	Number of blocks in the cache

The advantage of increasing the degree of associativity is that it usually decreases the miss rate. The improvement in miss rate comes from reducing misses that compete for the same location. We will examine these in more detail shortly. First, let's look at how much improvement is gained. Figure 7.30 shows the data for a workload consisting of the SPEC2000 benchmarks with caches of 4

Feature	Typical values for L1 caches	Typical values for L2 caches	Typical values for paged memory	Typical values for a TLB
Total size in blocks	250–2000	15,000–50,000	16,000–250,000	40–1024
Total size in kilobytes	16–64	2000–3000	500,000–1,000,000,000	0.25–16
Block size in bytes	16–64	64–128	4000–64,000	4–32
Miss penalty in clocks	10–25	100–1000	10,000,000–100,000,000	10–1000
Miss rates (global for L2)	2%–5%	0.1%–2%	0.00001%–0.0001%	0.01%–2%

FIGURE 7.29 The key quantitative design parameters that characterize the major elements of memory hierarchy in a computer. These are typical values for these levels as of 2006. Although the range of values is wide, this is partially because many of the values that have shifted over time are related; for example, as caches become larger to overcome larger miss penalties, block sizes also grow.

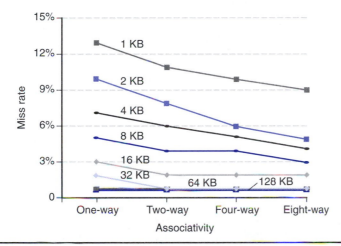

FIGURE 7.30 The data cache miss rates for each of eight cache sizes improve as the associativity increases. While the benefit of going from one-way (direct mapped) to two-way set associative is significant, the benefits of further associativity are smaller (e.g., 1%–10% improvement going from two-way to four-way versus 20%–30% improvement going from one-way to two-way). There is even less improvement in going from four-way to eight-way set associative, which, in turn, comes very close to the miss rates of a fully associative cache. Smaller caches obtain a significantly larger absolute benefit from associativity because the base miss rate of a small cache is larger. Figure 7.15 explains how this data was collected.

KB to 512 KB, varying from direct mapped to eight-way set associative. The largest gains are obtained in going from direct mapped to two-way set associative, which yields between a 20% and 30% reduction in the miss rate. As cache sizes grow, the relative improvement from associativity increases only slightly; since the overall miss rate of a larger cache is lower, the opportunity for improving the miss rate decreases and the absolute improvement in the miss rate from associativity shrinks significantly. The potential disadvantages of associativity, as we mentioned earlier, are increased cost and slower access time.

Question 2: How Is a Block Found?

The choice of how we locate a block depends on the block placement scheme, since that dictates the number of possible locations. We can summarize the schemes as follows:

Associativity	Location method	Comparisons required
Direct mapped	Index	1
Set associative	Index the set, search among elements	Degree of associativity
Full	Search all cache entries	Size of the cache
	Separate lookup table	0

The choice among direct-mapped, set-associative, or fully associative mapping in any memory hierarchy will depend on the cost of a miss versus the cost of implementing associativity, both in time and in extra hardware. Including the L2 cache on the chip enables much higher associativity, because the hit times are not as critical and the designer does not have to rely on standard SRAM chips as the building blocks. Fully associative caches are prohibitive except for small sizes, where the cost of the comparators is not overwhelming and where the absolute miss rate improvements are greatest.

In virtual memory systems, a separate mapping table (the page table) is kept to index the memory. In addition to the storage required for the table, using an index table requires an extra memory access. The choice of full associativity for page placement and the extra table is motivated by four facts:

1. Full associativity is beneficial, since misses are very expensive.

2. Full associativity allows software to use sophisticated replacement schemes that are designed to reduce the miss rate.

3. The full map can be easily indexed with no extra hardware and no searching required.

4. The large page size means the page table size overhead is relatively small. (The use of a separate lookup table, like a page table for virtual memory, is not practical for a cache because the table would be much larger than a page table and could not be accessed quickly.)

Therefore, virtual memory systems almost always use fully associative placement.

Set-associative placement is often used for caches and TLBs, where the access combines indexing and the search of a small set. A few systems have used direct-mapped caches because of their advantage in access time and simplicity. The advantage in access time occurs because finding the requested block does not depend on a comparison. Such design choices depend on many details of the implementation, such as whether the cache is on-chip, the technology used for implementing the cache, and the critical role of cache access time in determining the processor cycle time.

Question 3: Which Block Should Be Replaced on a Cache Miss?

When a miss occurs in an associative cache, we must decide which block to replace. In a fully associative cache, all blocks are candidates for replacement. If the cache is set associative, we must choose among the blocks in the set. Of course, replacement is easy in a direct-mapped cache because there is only one candidate.

We have already mentioned the two primary strategies for replacement in set-associative or fully associative caches:

- *Random:* Candidate blocks are randomly selected, possibly using some hardware assistance. For example, MIPS supports random replacement for TLB misses.

- *Least recently used* (LRU): The block replaced is the one that has been unused for the longest time.

In practice, LRU is too costly to implement for hierarchies with more than a small degree of associativity (two to four, typically), since tracking the usage information is costly. Even for four-way set associativity, LRU is often approximated— for example, by keeping track of which of a pair of blocks is LRU (which requires 1 bit), and then tracking which block in each pair is LRU (which requires 1 bit per pair).

For larger associativity, either LRU is approximated or random replacement is used. In caches, the replacement algorithm is in hardware, which means that the scheme should be easy to implement. Random replacement is simple to build in hardware, and for a two-way set-associative cache, random replacement has a miss rate about 1.1 times higher than LRU replacement. As the caches become larger, the miss rate for both replacement strategies falls, and the absolute difference becomes small. In fact, random replacement can sometimes be better than the simple LRU approximations that are easily implemented in hardware.

In virtual memory, some form of LRU is always approximated since even a tiny reduction in the miss rate can be important when the cost of a miss is enormous. Reference bits or equivalent functionality is often provided to make it easier for the operating system to track a set of less recently used pages. Because misses are so expensive and relatively infrequent, approximating this information primarily in software is acceptable.

Question 4: What Happens on a Write?

A key characteristic of any memory hierarchy is how it deals with writes. We have already seen the two basic options:

■ *Write-through*: The information is written to both the block in the cache and the block in the lower level of the memory hierarchy (main memory for a cache). The caches in Section 7.2 used this scheme.

■ *Write-back* (also called *copy-back*): The information is written only to the block in the cache. The modified block is written to the lower level of the hierarchy only when it is replaced. Virtual memory systems always use write-back, for the reasons discussed in Section 7.4.

Both write-back and write-through have their advantages. The key advantages of write-back are the following:

■ Individual words can be written by the processor at the rate that the cache, rather than the memory, can accept them.

■ Multiple writes within a block require only one write to the lower level in the hierarchy.

■ When blocks are written back, the system can make effective use of a high-bandwidth transfer, since the entire block is written.

Write-through has these advantages:

■ Misses are simpler and cheaper because they never require a block to be written back to the lower level.

■ Write-through is easier to implement than write-back, although to be practical in a high-speed system, a write-through cache will need to use a write buffer.

In virtual memory systems, only a write-back policy is practical because of the long latency of a write to the lower level of the hierarchy (disk). As processors continue to increase in performance at a faster rate than DRAM-based main memory, the rate at which writes are generated by a processor will exceed the rate at which the memory system can process them, even allowing for physically and logically wider memories. Consequently, more and more caches are using a write-back strategy.

While caches, TLBs, and virtual memory may initially look very different, they rely on the same two principles of locality and can be understood by looking at how they deal with four questions:

Question 1: Where can a block be placed?
Answer: One place (direct mapped), a few places (set associative), or any place (fully associative).

Question 2: How is a block found?
Answer: There are four methods: indexing (as in a direct-mapped cache), limited search (as in a set-associative cache), full search (as in a fully associative cache), and a separate lookup table (as in a page table).

Question 3: What block is replaced on a miss?
Answer: Typically, either the least recently used or a random block.

Question 4: How are writes handled?
Answer: Each level in the hierarchy can use either write-through or write-back.

The **BIG** Picture

three Cs model A cache model in which all cache misses are classified into one of three categories: compulsory misses, capacity misses, and conflict misses.

compulsory miss Also called **cold-start miss**. A cache miss caused by the first access to a block that has never been in the cache.

capacity miss A cache miss that occurs because the cache, even with full associativity, cannot contain all the blocks needed to satisfy the request.

conflict miss Also called **collision miss**. A cache miss that occurs in a set-associative or direct-mapped cache when multiple blocks compete for the same set and that are eliminated in a fully associative cache of the same size.

The Three Cs: An Intuitive Model for Understanding the Behavior of Memory Hierarchies

In this section, we look at a model that provides insight into the sources of misses in a memory hierarchy and how the misses will be affected by changes in the hierarchy. We will explain the ideas in terms of caches, although the ideas carry over directly to any other level in the hierarchy. In this model, all misses are classified into one of three categories (the **three Cs**):

- **Compulsory misses**: These are cache misses caused by the first access to a block that has never been in the cache. These are also called **cold-start misses**.

- **Capacity misses**: These are cache misses caused when the cache cannot contain all the blocks needed during execution of a program. Capacity misses occur when blocks are replaced and then later retrieved.

- **Conflict misses**: These are cache misses that occur in set-associative or direct-mapped caches when multiple blocks compete for the same set. Conflict misses are those misses in a direct-mapped or set-associative cache that are eliminated in a fully associative cache of the same size. These cache misses are also called **collision misses**.

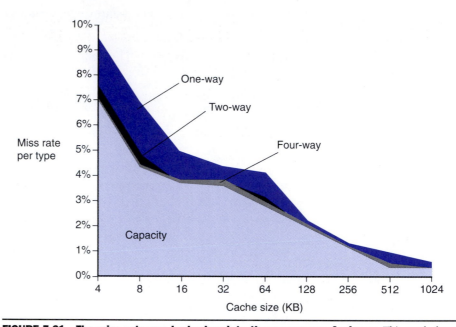

FIGURE 7.31 The miss rate can be broken into three sources of misses. This graph shows the total miss rate and its components for a range of cache sizes. This data is for the SPEC2000 integer and floating-point benchmarks and is from the same source as the data in Figure 7.30. The compulsory miss component is 0.006% and cannot be seen in this graph. The next component is the capacity miss rate, which depends on cache size. The conflict portion, which depends both on associativity and on cache size, is shown for a range of associativities from one-way to eight-way. In each case, the labeled section corresponds to the increase in the miss rate that occurs when the associativity is changed from the next higher degree to the labeled degree of associativity. For example, the section labeled *two-way* indicates the additional misses arising when the cache has associativity of two rather than four. Thus, the difference in the miss rate incurred by a direct-mapped cache versus a fully associative cache of the same size is given by the sum of the sections marked *eight-way, four-way, two-way,* and *one-way.* The difference between eight-way and four-way is so small that it is difficult to see on this graph.

Figure 7.31 shows how the miss rate divides into the three sources. These sources of misses can be directly attacked by changing some aspect of the cache design. Since conflict misses arise directly from contention for the same cache block, increasing associativity reduces conflict misses. Associativity, however, may slow access time, leading to lower overall performance.

Capacity misses can easily be reduced by enlarging the cache; indeed, second-level caches have been growing steadily larger for many years. Of course, when we make the cache larger, we must also be careful about increasing the access time, which could lead to lower overall performance. Thus, first-level caches have been growing slowly if at all.

Design change	Effect on miss rate	Possible negative performance effect
Increase cache size	Decreases capacity misses	May increase access time
Increase associativity	Decreases miss rate due to conflict misses	May increase access time
Increase block size	Decreases miss rate for a wide range of block sizes due to spatial locality	Increases miss penalty. Very large block could increase miss rate

FIGURE 7.32   Memory hierarchy design challenges.

Because compulsory misses are generated by the first reference to a block, the primary way for the cache system to reduce the number of compulsory misses is to increase the block size. This will reduce the number of references required to touch each block of the program once because the program will consist of fewer cache blocks. Increasing the block size too much can have a negative effect on performance because of the increase in the miss penalty.

The decomposition of misses into the three Cs is a useful qualitative model. In real cache designs, many of the design choices interact, and changing one cache characteristic will often affect several components of the miss rate. Despite such shortcomings, this model is a useful way to gain insight into the performance of cache designs.

The challenge in designing memory hierarchies is that every change that potentially improves the miss rate can also negatively affect overall performance, as Figure 7.32 summarizes. This combination of positive and negative effects is what makes the design of a memory hierarchy interesting.

The BIG Picture

Check Yourself

Which of the following statements (if any) are generally true?

1. There is no way to reduce compulsory misses.

2. Fully associative caches have no conflict misses.

3. In reducing misses, associativity is more important than capacity.

<table>
<tr><td>**7.6**</td></tr>
</table>

7.6   Real Stuff: The Pentium P4 and the AMD Opteron Memory Hierarchies

In this section, we will look at the memory hierarchy in two modern microprocessors: the Intel Pentium P4 and the AMD Opteron processor. In 2004, the P4 is used in a variety of PC desktops and small servers. The AMD Opteron processor is finding its way into higher-end servers and clusters.

Figure 7.33 shows the Opteron die photo, and Figure 1.9 on page 21 in Chapter 1 shows the P4 die photo. Both have secondary caches on the main processor die. Such integration reduces access time to the secondary cache and also reduces the number of pins on the chip, since there is no need for a bus to an external secondary cache.

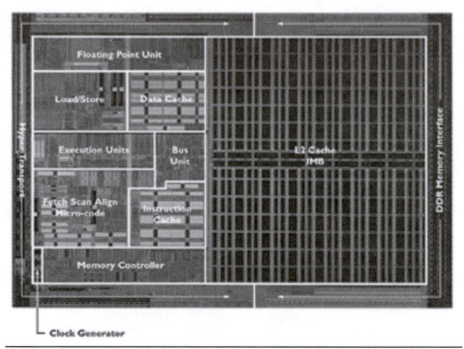

FIGURE 7.33   An AMD Opteron die processor photo with the components labeled. The L2 cache occupies 42% of the die. The remaining components in order of size are HyperTransport: 13%, DDR memory: 10%, Fetch/Scan/Align/Microcode: 6%, Memory controller: 4%, FPU: 4%, Instruction cache: 4%, Data cache: 4%, Execution units: 3%, Bus unit: 2%, and Clock generator: 0.2%. In a 0.13 technology, this die is 193 mm^2.

The Memory Hierarchies of the P4 and Opteron

Figure 7.34 summarizes the address sizes and TLBs of the two processors.

Note that the AMD Opteron has four TLBs while the P4 has two and that the virtual and physical addresses do not have to match the word size. AMD implements only 48 of the potential 64 bits of its virtual space and 40 of the potential 64 bits of its physical address space. Intel increases the physical address space to 36 bits, although no single program can address more than 32 bits.

Figure 7.35 shows their caches. Note that both the L1 data cache and the L2 cache are larger in the Opteron and that P4 uses a larger block size for its L2 cache than its L1 data cache.

Although the Opteron runs the same IA-32 programs as the Pentium P4, its biggest difference is that it has added a 64-bit addressing mode. Just as the 80386 added a flat 32-bit address space and 32-bit registers to the prior 16-bit 80286 architecture, Opteron added a new mode with flat 64-bit address space and 64-bit registers to the IA-32 architecture, called *AMD64*. It increases the program counter to 64 bits, extends eight 32-bit registers to 64 bits, adds eight new 64-bit registers, and doubles the number of SSE2 registers. In 2004 Intel announced that future IA-32 processors would include their 64-bit address extension.

Techniques to Reduce Miss Penalties

Both the Pentium P4 and the AMD Opteron have additional optimizations that allow them to reduce the miss penalty. The first of these is the return of the

Characteristic	Intel Pentium P4	AMD Opteron
Virtual address	32 bits	48 bits
Physical address	36 bits	40 bits
Page size	4 KB, 2/4 MB	4 KB, 2/4 MB
TLB organization	1 TLB for instructions and 1 TLB for data Both are four-way set associative Both use pseudo-LRU replacement Both have 128 entries TLB misses handled in hardware	2 TLBs for instructions and 2 TLBs for data Both L1 TLBs fully associative, LRU replacement Both L2 TLBs are four-way set associativity, round-robin LRU Both L1 TLBs have 40 entries Both L2 TLBs have 512 entries TLB misses handled in hardware

FIGURE 7.34 Address translation and TLB hardware for the Intel Pentium P4 and AMD Opteron. The word size sets the maximum size of the virtual address, but a processor need not use all bits. The physical address size is independent of word size. The P4 has one TLB for instructions and a separate identical TLB for data, while the Opteron has both an L1 TLB and an L2 TLB for instructions and identical L1 and L2 TLBs for data. Both processors provide support for large pages, which are used for things like the operating system or mapping a frame buffer. The large-page scheme avoids using a large number of entries to map a single object that is always present.

Characteristic	Intel Pentium P4	AMD Opteron
L1 cache organization	Split instruction and data caches	Split instruction and data caches
L1 cache size	8 KB for data, 96 KB trace cache for RISC instructions (12K RISC operations)	64 KB each for instructions/data
L1 cache associativity	4-way set associative	2-way set associative
L1 replacement	Approximated LRU replacement	LRU replacement
L1 block size	64 bytes	64 bytes
L1 write policy	Write-through	Write-back
L2 cache organization	Unified (instruction and data)	Unified (instruction and data)
L2 cache size	512 KB	1024 KB (1 MB)
L2 cache associativity	8-way set associative	16-way set associative
L2 replacement	Approximated LRU replacement	Approximated LRU replacement
L2 block size	128 bytes	64 bytes
L2 write policy	Write-back	Write-back

FIGURE 7.35   First-level and second-level caches in the Intel Pentium P4 and AMD Opteron. The primary caches in the P4 are physically indexed and tagged; for a discussion of the alternatives, see the elaboration on page 527.

nonblocking cache A cache that allows the processor to make references to the cache while the cache is handling an earlier miss.

requested word first on a miss, as described in the elaboration on page 490. Both allow the processor to continue to execute instructions that access the data cache during a cache miss. This technique, called a **nonblocking cache**, is commonly used as designers attempt to hide the cache miss latency by using out-of-order processors. They implement two flavors of nonblocking. *Hit under miss* allows additional cache hits during a miss, while *miss under miss* allows multiple outstanding cache misses. The aim of the first of these two is hiding some miss latency with other work, while the aim of the second is overlapping the latency of two different misses.

Overlapping a large fraction of miss times for multiple outstanding misses requires a high-bandwidth memory system capable of handling multiple misses in parallel. In desktop systems, the memory may only be able to take limited advantage of this capability, but large servers and multiprocessors often have memory systems capable of handling more than one outstanding miss in parallel.

Both microprocessors prefetch instructions and have a built-in hardware prefetch mechanism for data accesses. They look at a pattern of data misses and use this information to try to predict the next address to start fetching the data before the miss occurs. Such techniques generally work best when accessing arrays in loops.

A significant challenge facing cache designers is to support processors like the P4 and Opteron that can execute more than one memory instruction per clock cycle. Multiple requests can be supported in the first-level cache by two different techniques. The cache can be multiported, allowing more than one simultaneous access to the same cache block. Multiported caches, however, are often too expensive, since the RAM cells in a multiported memory must be much larger than single-ported cells. The alternative scheme is to break the cache into banks and allow multiple, independent accesses, provided the accesses are to different banks. The technique is similar to interleaved main memory (see Figure 7.11 on page 489).

To reduce the memory traffic in a multiprocessor configuration, Intel has other versions of the P4 with much larger on-chip caches in 2004. For example, the Intel Pentium P4 Xeon comes with a *third*-level cache *on-chip* of 1 MB and is intended for dual-processor servers. A more radical example is the Intel Pentium P4 Extreme Edition, which comes with 2 MB of L3 cache but no support for multiprocessing. These two chips are much larger and more expensive. For example, in 2004 a Precision Workstation 360 with a 3.2 GHz P4 cost about $1900. Upgrading to the Extreme Edition processor added $500 to the price. The Dell Precision Workstation 450, which allows dual processors, cost about $2000 for a 3.2 GHz Xeon with 1 MB of L3 cache. Adding a second processor like that one added $1500 to the price.

The sophisticated memory hierarchies of these chips and the large fraction of the dies dedicated to caches and TLBs show the significant design effort expended to try to close the gap between processor cycle times and memory latency. Future advances in processor pipeline designs, together with the increased use of multiprocessing that presents its own problems in memory hierarchies, provide many new challenges for designers.

Elaboration: Perhaps the largest difference between the AMD and Intel chips is the use of a trace cache for the P4 instruction cache, while the AMD Opteron uses a more traditional instruction cache.

Instead of organizing the instructions in a cache block sequentially to promote spatial locality, a *trace cache* finds a dynamic sequence of instructions *including taken branches* to load into a cache block. Thus, the cache blocks contain dynamic *traces* of the executed instructions as determined by the CPU rather than static sequences of instructions as determined by memory layout. It folds branch prediction (Chapter 6) into the cache, so the branches must be validated along with the addresses in order to have a valid fetch. In addition, the P4 caches the micro-operations (see Chapter 5) rather than the IA-32 instructions as in the Opteron.

Clearly, trace caches have much more complicated address mapping mechanisms, since the addresses are no longer aligned to power-of-2 multiples of the word size.

Trace caches can improve utilization of cache blocks, however. For example, very long blocks in conventional caches may be entered from a taken branch, and hence the first portion of the block occupies space in the cache that might not be fetched. Similarly, such blocks may be exited by taken branches, so the last portion of the block might be wasted. Given that taken branches or jumps occur every 5–10 instructions, effective block utilization is a real problem for processors like the Opteron, whose 64-byte block would likely include 16–24 8086 instructions. Trace caches store instructions only from the branch entry point to the exit of the trace, thereby avoiding such header and trailer overhead. A downside of trace caches is that they potentially store the same instructions multiple times in the cache: conditional branches making different choices result in the same instructions being part of separate traces, which each appear in the cache.

To account for both the larger size of the micro-operations and the redundancy inherent in a trace cache, Intel claims that the miss rate of the 96 KB trace cache of the P4, which holds 12K micro-operations, is about that of an 8 KB cache, which holds about 2K–3K IA-32 instructions.

7.7 Fallacies and Pitfalls

As one of the most naturally quantitative aspects of computer architecture, the memory hierarchy would seem to be less vulnerable to fallacies and pitfalls. Not only have there been many fallacies propagated and pitfalls encountered, but some have led to major negative outcomes. We start with a pitfall that often traps students in exercises and exams.

Pitfall: Forgetting to account for byte addressing or the cache block size in simulating a cache.

When simulating a cache (by hand or by computer), we need to make sure we account for the effect of byte addressing and multiword blocks in determining which cache block a given address maps into. For example, if we have a 32-byte direct-mapped cache with a block size of 4 bytes, the byte address 36 maps into block 1 of the cache, since byte address 36 is block address 9 and (9 modulo 8) = 1. On the other hand, if address 36 is a word address, then it maps into block (36 mod 8) = 4. Make sure the problem clearly states the base of the address.

In like fashion, we must account for the block size. Suppose we have a cache with 256 bytes and a block size of 32 bytes. Which block does the byte address 300 fall into? If we break the address 300 into fields, we can see the answer:

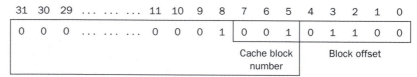

Block address

Byte address 300 is block address

$$\left\lfloor \frac{300}{32} \right\rfloor = 9$$

The number of blocks in the cache is

$$\left\lfloor \frac{256}{32} \right\rfloor = 8$$

Block number 9 falls into cache block number (9 modulo 8) = 1.

This mistake catches many people, including the authors (in earlier drafts) and instructors who forget whether they intended the addresses to be in words, bytes, or block numbers. Remember this pitfall when you tackle the exercises.

Pitfall: Ignoring memory system behavior when writing programs or when generating code in a compiler.

This could easily be written as a fallacy: "Programmers can ignore memory hierarchies in writing code." We illustrate with an example using matrix multiply, to complement the sort comparison in Figure 7.18 on page 508.

Here is the inner loop of the version of matrix multiply from Chapter 3:

```
for (i=0; i!=500; i=i+1)
    for (j=0; j!=500; j=j+1)
        for (k=0; k!=500; k=k+1)
            x[i][j] = x[i][j] + y[i][k] * z[k][j];
```

When run with inputs that are 500 × 500 double precision matrices, the CPU runtime of the above loop on a MIPS CPU with a 1 MB secondary cache was about half the speed compared to when the loop order is changed to k,j,i (so i is innermost)! The only difference is how the program accesses memory and the ensuing effect on the memory hierarchy. Further compiler optimizations using a technique called *blocking* can result in a runtime that is another four times faster for this code!

Pitfall: Using average memory access time to evaluate the memory hierarchy of an out-of-order processor.

If a processor stalls during a cache miss, then you can separately calculate the memory-stall time and the processor execution time, and hence evaluate the memory hierarchy independently using average memory access time.

If the processor continues to execute instructions, and may even sustain more cache misses during a cache miss, then the only accurate assessment of the memory hierarchy is to simulate the out-of-order processor along with the memory hierarchy.

Pitfall: Extending an address space by adding segments on top of an unsegmented address space.

During the 1970s, many programs grew so large that not all the code and data could be addressed with just a 16-bit address. Computers were then revised to offer 32-bit addresses, either through an unsegmented 32-bit address space (also called a *flat address space*) or by adding 16 bits of segment to the existing 16-bit address. From a marketing point of view, adding segments that were programmer-visible and that forced the programmer and compiler to decompose programs into segments could solve the addressing problem. Unfortunately, there is trouble any time a programming language wants an address that is larger than one segment, such as indices for large arrays, unrestricted pointers, or reference parameters. Moreover, adding segments can turn every address into two words—one for the segment number and one for the segment offset—causing problems in the use of addresses in registers. Given the size of DRAMs and Moore's law, many of today's 32-bit systems are facing similar problems.

7.8　Concluding Remarks

The difficulty of building a memory system to keep pace with faster processors is underscored by the fact that the raw material for main memory, DRAMs, is essentially the same in the fastest computers as it is in the slowest and cheapest. Figure 7.36 compares the memory hierarchy of microprocessors aimed at desktop, server, and embedded applications. The L1 caches are similar across applications, with the primary differences being L2 cache size, die size, processor clock rate, and instructions issued per clock.

It is the principle of locality that gives us a chance to overcome the long latency of memory access—and the soundness of this strategy is demonstrated at all levels of the memory hierarchy. Although these levels of the hierarchy look quite different in quantitative terms, they follow similar strategies in their operation and exploit the same properties of locality.

Because processor speeds continue to improve faster than either DRAM access times or disk access times, memory will increasingly be the factor that limits performance. Processors increase in performance at a high rate, and DRAMs are now doubling their density about every two years. The *access time* of DRAMs, however, is improving at a much slower rate—less than 10% per year. Figure 7.37 plots processor performance against a 7% annual performance improvement in DRAM latency. While latency improves slowly, recent enhancements in DRAM technology (double data rate DRAMs and related techniques) have led to greater

MPU	AMD Opteron	Intrinsity FastMATH	Intel Pentium 4	Intel PXA250	Sun UltraSPARC IV
Instruction set architecture	IA-32, AMD64	MIPS-32	IA-32	ARM	SPARC v9
Intended application	Server	Embedded	Desktop	Low-power embedded	Server
Die size (mm^2) (2004)	193	122	217		356
Instructions issued/clock	3	2	3 RISC ops	1	4 × 2
Clock rate (2004)	2.0 GHz	2.0 GHz	3.2 GHz	0.4 GHz	1.2 GHz
Instruction cache	64 KB, 2-way set associative	16 KB, direct mapped	12000 RISC op trace cache (~96 KB)	32 KB, 32-way set associative	32 KB, 4-way set associative
Latency (clocks)	3?	4	4	1	2
Data cache	64 KB, 2-way set associative	16 KB, 1-way set associative	8 KB, 4-way set associative	32 KB, 32-way set associative	64 KB, 4-way set associative
Latency (clocks)	3	3	2	1	2
TLB entries (I/D/L2 TLB)	40/40/512/512	16	128/128	32/32	128/512
Minimum page size	4 KB	4 KB	4 KB	1 KB	8 KB
On-chip L2 cache	1024 KB, 16-way set associative	1024 KB, 4-way set associative	512 KB, 8-way set associative	—	—
Off-chip L2 cache	—	—	—	—	16 MB, 2-way set associative
Block size (L1/L2, bytes)	64	64	64/128	32	32

FIGURE 7.36 Desktop, embedded, and server microprocessors in 2004. From a memory hierarchy perspective, the primary differences between categories is the L2 cache. There is no L2 cache for the low-power embedded, a large on-chip L2 for the embedded and desktop, and 16 MB off-chip for the server. The processor clock rates also vary: 0.4 GHz for low-power embedded, 1 GHz or higher for the rest. Note that UltraSPARC IV has two processors on the chip.

increases in memory bandwidth. This potentially higher memory bandwidth has enabled designers to increase cache block sizes with smaller increases in the miss penalty.

Recent Trends

The challenge in designing memory hierarchies to close this growing gap, as we noted in the Big Picture on page 545, is that all the hardware design choices for memory hierarchies have both a positive and negative effect on performance. This means that for each level of the hierarchy there is an optimal performance point per program, which must include some misses. If this is the case, how can we overcome the growing gap between processor speeds and lower levels of the hierarchy? This question is currently the topic of much research.

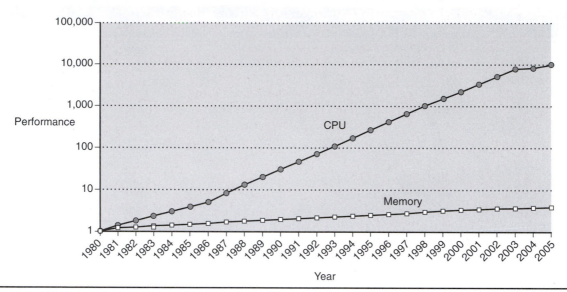

FIGURE 7.37   Using their 1980 performance as a baseline, the access time of DRAMs versus the performance of processors is plotted over time. Note that the vertical axis must be on a logarithmic scale to record the size of the processor-DRAM performance gap. The memory baseline is 64 KB DRAM in 1980, with three years to the next generation until 1996 and two years thereafter, with a 7% per year performance improvement in latency. The processor line assumes a 35% improvement per year until 1986, and a 55% improvement until 2003. It slows thereafter.

On-chip first-level caches initially helped close the gap that was growing between processor clock cycle time and off-chip SRAM cycle time. To narrow the gap between the small on-chip caches and DRAM, second-level caches became widespread. Today, all desktop computers use second-level caches on-chip, and third-level caches are becoming popular in some segments. Multilevel caches also make it possible to use other optimizations more easily for two reasons. First, the design parameters of a second- or third-level cache are different from a first-level cache. For example, because a second- or third-level cache will be much larger, it is possible to use larger block sizes. Second, a second- or third-level cache is not constantly being used by the processor, as a first-level cache is. This allows us to consider having the second- or third-level cache do something when it is idle that may be useful in preventing future misses.

Another possible direction is to seek software help. Efficiently managing the memory hierarchy using a variety of program transformations and hardware facilities is a major focus of compiler enhancements. Two different ideas are being explored. One idea is to reorganize the program to enhance its spatial and temporal locality. This approach focuses on loop-oriented programs that use large arrays as the major data structure; large linear algebra problems are a typical example. By restructuring the loops that access the arrays, substantially improved locality—and, therefore, cache performance—can be obtained. The discussion on page 551 showed how effective even a simple change of loop structure could be.

Another direction is to try to use compiler-directed **prefetching**. In prefetching, a block of data is brought into the cache before it is actually referenced. The compiler tries to identify data blocks needed in the future and, using special instructions, tells the memory hierarchy to move the blocks into the cache. When the block is actually referenced, it is found in the cache, rather than causing a cache miss. The use of secondary caches has made prefetching even more attractive, since the secondary cache can be involved in a prefetch, while the primary cache continues to service processor requests.

As we will see in ⊙ **Chapter 9**, memory systems are also a central design issue for parallel processors. The growing importance of the memory hierarchy in determining system performance in both uniprocessor and multiprocessor systems means that this important area will continue to be a focus of both designers and researchers for some years to come.

prefetching A technique in which data blocks needed in the future are brought into the cache early by the use of special instructions that specify the address of the block.

7.9 Historical Perspective and Further Reading

This history section ⊙ gives an overview of memory technologies, from mercury delay lines to DRAM, the invention of the memory hierarchy, and protection mechanisms, and concludes with a brief history of operating systems, including CTSS, MULTICS, Unix, BSD Unix, MS-DOS, Windows, and Linux.

7.10 Exercises

7.1 [5] <§7.1> SRAM is commonly used to implement small, fast, on-chip caches while DRAM is used for larger, slower main memory. In the past, a common design for supercomputers was to build machines with no caches and main memories made entirely out of SRAM (the Cray C90, for example, a very fast computer in its day). If cost were no object, would you still want to design a system this way?

7.2 [10] <§7.2> Describe the general characteristics of a program that would exhibit very little temporal and spatial locality with regard to data accesses. Provide an example program (pseudocode is fine).

7.3 [10] <§7.2> Describe the general characteristics of a program that would exhibit very high amounts of temporal locality but very little spatial locality with regard to data accesses. Provide an example program (pseudocode is fine).

7.4 [10] <§7.2> Describe the general characteristics of a program that would exhibit very little temporal locality but very high amounts of spatial locality with regard to data accesses. Provide an example program (pseudocode is fine).

7.5 [3/3] <§7.2> A new processor can use either a write-through or write-back cache selectable through software.

   a. Assume the processor will run data-intensive applications with a large number of load and store operations. Explain which cache write policy should be used.

   b. Consider the same question but this time for a safety-critical system in which data integrity is more important than memory performance.

7.6 [10] <§7.2> 🔵 **For More Practice:** Locality

7.7 [10] <§7.2> 🔵 **For More Practice:** Locality

7.8 [10] <§7.2> 🔵 **For More Practice:** Locality

7.9 [10] <§7.2> Here is a series of address references given as word addresses: 2, 3, 11, 16, 21, 13, 64, 48, 19, 11, 3, 22, 4, 27, 6, and 11. Assuming a direct-mapped cache with 16 one-word blocks that is initially empty, label each reference in the list as a hit or a miss and show the final contents of the cache.

7.10 [10] <§7.2> Using the series of references given in Exercise 7.9, show the hits and misses and final cache contents for a direct-mapped cache with four-word blocks and a *total size* of 16 words.

7.11 [15] <§7.2> Given the following pseudocode:

```
int array[10000,100000];
for each element array[i][j] {
        array[i][j] = array[i][j]*2;


}
```

write two C programs that implement this algorithm: one should access the elements of the array in row-major order, and the other should access them in column-major order. Compare the execution times of the two programs. What does this tell you about the effects of memory layout on cache performance?

7.12 [10] <§7.2> Compute the total number of bits required to implement the cache in Figure 7.9 on page 486. This number is different from the size of the cache, which usually refers to the number of bytes of data stored in the cache. The number of bits needed to implement the cache represents the total amount of memory needed for storing all the data, tags, and valid bits.

7.13 [10] <§7.2> Find a method to eliminate the AND gate on the valid bit in Figure 7.7 on page 478. (Hint: You need to change the comparison.)

7.14 [10] <§7.2> Consider a memory hierarchy using one of the three organizations for main memory shown in Figure 7.11 on page 489. Assume that the cache block size is 16 words, that the width of organization (b) of the figure is four words, and that the number of banks in organization (c) is four. If the main memory latency for a new access is 10 memory bus clock cycles and the transfer time is 1 memory bus clock cycle, what are the miss penalties for each of these organizations?

7.15 [10] <§7.2> ◉ **For More Practice:** Cache Performance

7.16 [15] <§7.2> Cache C1 is direct mapped with 16 one-word blocks. Cache C2 is direct mapped with 4 four-word blocks. Assume that the miss penalty for C1 is 8 memory bus clock cycles and the miss penalty for C2 is 11 memory bus clock cycles. Assuming that the caches are initially empty, find a reference string for which C2 has a lower miss rate but spends more memory bus clock cycles on cache misses than C1. Use word addresses.

7.17 [5] <§7.2> ◉ **In More Depth:** Average Memory Access Time

7.18 [5] <§7.2> ◉ **In More Depth:** Average Memory Access Time

7.19 [10] <§7.2> ◉ **In More Depth:** Average Memory Access Time

7.20 [10] <§7.2> Assume a memory system that supports interleaving either four reads or four writes. Given the following memory addresses in order as they appear on the memory bus: 3, 9, 17, 2, 51, 37, 13, 4, 8, 41, 67, 10, which ones will result in a bank conflict?

7.21 [3 hours] <§7.3> Use a cache simulator to simulate several different cache organizations for the first 1 million references in a trace of gcc. Both dinero (a cache simulator) and the gcc traces are available—see the Preface of this book for information on how to obtain them. Assume an instruction cache of 32 KB and a data cache of 32 KB using the same organization. You should choose at least two kinds of associativity and two block sizes. Draw a diagram like that in Figure 7.17 on page 503 that shows the data cache organization with the best hit rate.

7.22 [1 day] <§7.3> You are commissioned to design a cache for a new system. It has a 32-bit physical byte address and requires separate instruction and data caches. The SRAMs have an access time of 1.5 ns and a size of 32K × 8 bits, and you have a total of 16 SRAMs to use. The miss penalty for the memory system is 8 + 2

× Block size in words. Using set associativity adds 0.2 ns to the cache access time. Using the first 1 million references of gcc, find the best I and D cache organizations, given the available SRAMs.

7.23 [10] <§§7.2, B.5> ⊙ **For More Practice:** Cache Configurations

7.24 [10] <§§7.2, B.5> ⊙ **For More Practice:** Cache Configurations

7.25 [10] <§7.3> ⊙ **For More Practice:** Cache Operation

7.26 [10] <§7.3> ⊙ **For More Practice:** Cache Operation

7.27 [10] <§7.3> ⊙ **For More Practice:** Cache Operation

7.28 [5] <§7.3> Associativity usually improves the miss ratio, but not always. Give a short series of address references for which a two-way set-associative cache with LRU replacement would experience more misses than a direct-mapped cache of the same size.

7.29 [15] <§7.3> Suppose a computer's address size is k bits (using byte addressing), the cache size is S bytes, the block size is B bytes, and the cache is A-way set-associative. Assume that B is a power of 2, so $B = 2^b$. Figure out what the following quantities are in terms of S, B, A, b, and k: the number of sets in the cache, the number of index bits in the address, and the number of bits needed to implement the cache (see Exercise 7.12).

7.30 [10] <§7.3> ⊙ **For More Practice:** Unusual Cache Configurations

7.31 [10] <§7.3> ⊙ **For More Practice:** Unusual Cache Configurations

7.32 [20] <§7.3> Consider three processors with different cache configurations:

- *Cache 1:* Direct mapped with one-word blocks
- *Cache 2:* Direct mapped with four-word blocks
- *Cache 3:* Two-way set associative with four-word blocks

The following miss rate measurements have been made:

- *Cache 1:* Instruction miss rate is 4%; data miss rate is 6%.
- *Cache 2:* Instruction miss rate is 2%; data miss rate is 4%.
- *Cache 3:* Instruction miss rate is 2%; data miss rate is 3%.

For these processors, one-half of the instructions contain a data reference. Assume that the cache miss penalty is 6 + Block size in words. The CPI for this workload was measured on a processor with cache 1 and was found to be 2.0. Determine which processor spends the most cycles on cache misses.

7.33 [5] <§7.3> The cycle times for the processors in Exercise 7.32 are 420 ps for the first and second processors and 310 ps for the third processor. Determine which processor is the fastest and which is the slowest.

7.34 [15] <§7.3> Assume that the cache for the system described in Exercise 7.32 is two-way set associative and has eight-word blocks and a total size of 16 KB. Show the cache organization and access using the same format as Figure 7.17 on page 503.

7.35 [10] <§§7.2, 7.4> The following C program is run (with no optimizations) on a processor with a cache that has eight-word (32-byte) blocks and holds 256 bytes of data:

```
int i,j,c,stride,array[512];
...
for (i=0; i<10000; i++)
    for (j=0; j<512; j=j+stride)
      c = array[j]+17;
```

If we consider only the cache activity generated by references to the array and we assume that integers are words, what is the expected miss rate when the cache is direct mapped and stride = 256? How about if stride = 255? Would either of these change if the cache were two-way set associative?

7.36 [10] <§§7.3, B.5> ◉ **For More Practice:** Unusual Cache Configurations

7.37 [5] <§§7.2–7.4> ◉ **For More Practice:** Memory Hierarchy Interactions

7.38 [4 hours] <§§7.2–7.4> We want to use a cache simulator to simulate several different TLB and virtual memory organizations. Use the first 1 million references of gcc for this evaluation. We want to know the TLB miss rate for each of the following TLBs and page sizes:

1. 64-entry TLB with full associativity and 4 KB pages

2. 32-entry TLB with full associativity and 8 KB pages

3. 64-entry TLB with eight-way associativity and 4 KB pages

4. 128-entry TLB with four-way associativity and 4 KB pages

7.39 [15] <§7.4> Consider a virtual memory system with the following properties:

■ 40-bit virtual byte address

■ 16 KB pages

■ 36-bit physical byte address

What is the total size of the page table for each process on this processor, assuming that the valid, protection, dirty, and use bits take a total of 4 bits and that all the virtual pages are in use? (Assume that disk addresses are not stored in the page table.)

7.40 [15] <§7.4> Assume that the virtual memory system of Exercise 7.39 is implemented with a two-way set-associative TLB with a total of 256 TLB entries. Show the virtual-to-physical mapping with a figure like Figure 7.24 on page 525. Make sure to label the width of all fields and signals.

7.41 [10] <§7.4> A processor has a 16-entry TLB and uses 4 KB pages. What are the performance consequences of this memory system if a program accesses at least 2 MB of memory at a time? Can anything be done to improve performance?

7.42 [10] <§7.4> Buffer overflows are a common exploit used to gain control of a system. If a buffer is allocated on the stack, a hacker could overflow the buffer and insert a sequence of malicous instructions compromising the system. Can you think of a hardware mechanism that could be used to prevent this?

7.43 [15] <§7.4> ⊙ **For More Practice:** Memory Hierarchy Interactions

7.44 [15] <§7.4> ⊙ **For More Practice:** Hierarchical Page Tables

7.45 [5] <§7.5> If all misses are classified into one of three categories—compulsory, capacity, or conflict (as discussed on page 543)—which misses are likely to be reduced when a program is rewritten so as to require less memory? How about if the clock rate of the processor that the program is running on is increased? How about if the associativity of the existing cache is increased?

7.46 [5] <§7.5> The following C program could be used to help construct a cache simulator. Many of the data types have not been defined, but the code accurately describes the actions that take place during a read access to a direct-mapped cache.

```
word ReadDirectMappedCache(address a)
  static Entry cache[CACHE_SIZE_IN_WORDS];
  Entry e = cache[a.index];
  if (e.valid == FALSE !! e.tag != a.tag) {
    e.valid = true;
    e.tag = a.tag;
    e.data = load_from_memory(a);
  }
  return e.data;
```

Your task is to modify this code to produce an accurate description of the actions that take place during a read access to a direct-mapped cache with multiple-word blocks.

7.47 [8] <§7.5> This exercise is similar to Exercise 7.46, except this time write the code for read accesses to an *n*-way set-associative cache with one-word blocks. Note that your code will likely suggest that the comparisons are sequential in nature when in fact they would be performed in parallel by actual hardware.

7.48 [8] <§7.5> Extend your solution to Exercise 7.46 by including the specification of a new procedure for handling write accesses, assuming a write-through policy. Be sure to consider whether or not your solution for handling read accesses needs to be modified.

7.49 [8] <§7.5> Extend your solution to Exercise 7.46 by including the specification of a new procedure for handling write accesses, assuming a write-back policy. Be sure to consider whether or not your solution for handling read accesses needs to be modified.

7.50 [8] <§7.5> This exercise is similar to Exercise 7.48, but this time extend your solution to Exercise 7.47. Assume that the cache uses random replacement.

7.51 [8] <§7.5> This exercise is similar to Exercise 7.49, but this time extend your solution to Exercise 7.47. Assume that the cache uses random replacement.

7.52 [5] <§§7.7–7.8> Why might a compiler perform the following optimization?

```
/* Before */

for (j = 0; j < 20; j++)
  for (i = 0; i < 200; i++)
    x[i][j] = x[i][j] + 1;

/* After */

for (i = 0; i < 200; i++)
  for (j = 0; j < 20; j++)
    x[i][j] = x[i][j] + 1;
```

Answers to Check Yourself

§7.1, page 472: 1.
§7.2, page 491: 1 and 4: A lower miss penalty can lead to smaller blocks, yet higher memory bandwidth usually leads to larger blocks, since the miss penalty is only slightly larger.
§7.3, page 509: 1.
§7.4, page 538: 1-a, 2-c, 3-b, 4-d.
§7.5, page 545: 2.

Computers in the Real World

Saving the World's Art Treasures

Problem: Find a way to help conserve artwork threatened by environmental factors and aging or damaged by earlier attempts at restoration without causing further harm to irreplaceable artworks.

Solution: Use computers and scientific instrumentation to analyze the artwork and its setting, enabling art conservators and restorers to undertake a more informed and successful preservation of an artwork.

Art conservation and restoration have developed into high-technology fields that make extensive use of computing and scientific instrumentation. For example, one of the most challenging forms of art to restore and maintain are frescoes, which are painted in the wet plaster of a wall or ceiling. Moisture and heat change the surface and cause deterioration; similarly, air pollution, smoke from candles, and other contaminants directly attack the paint as well as add dirt and grime that cover the original artwork.

During the restoration of Michelangelo's frescoes in the Sistine Chapel, computers were used to survey the ceiling, finding cracks and precisely mapping the surface and the frescoes.

Since the width of the ceiling and walls varies from about three feet to almost six feet, there are significant differences in thermal behavior, which in turn affects the surface painting. Computers were used to model the entire structure, including the high humidity generated when a thousand people stand inside the chapel on a warm day! This led to a computer-controlled climate system that uses sensors placed in strategic locations. The goal is to keep the visitors cool while preserving Michelangelo's masterpiece for generations to come.

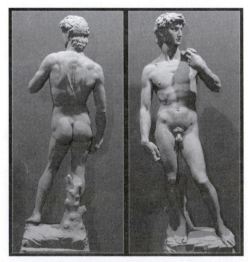

A laser scan of Michelangelo's statue of David.

Perhaps the area of art conservation that has been most affected by the availability of low-cost, high-performance computation has been painting restoration. Three techniques—infrared reflectography, ultraviolet imaging, and X-radiography—have found the heaviest use. Because of the need for highly precise, high-resolution imaging, computer-controlled cameras or X-ray scanners are used in all these techniques. This results in a patchwork of images, which are then stitched together by a computer. The combination of computer-controlled motion of a camera or X-ray scanner and subsequent computer composition of tens to thousands of images permits that scanning of large surfaces at very high resolution.

Infrared reflectography uses light in the near-infrared spectrum and a digital camera to detect the intensity of reflection of the light from the surface of a painting, mural, or fresco. This technique is useful for finding the underdrawing that most artists use to initially sketch out the forms in a painting. The underdrawing, typically done in black, often using charcoal, absorbs the infrared light. In the figure below are two images of a painting: one shown in normal light (on the left) and one using the infrared reflectography technique (on the right).

Restorers use ultraviolet imaging to look at the original colors of a painting that has been retouched. X-radiography provides similar information, since white and yellow pigments that were covered or painted over appear darker due to their lead content.

Scanning technologies have also been applied to three-dimensional art objects, such as sculpture. Michelangelo's David was scanned using a laser range finder by a group led by Professor Marc Levoy at Stanford. The resulting database for a scan with 0.29 mm resolution consists of over 2 billion polygons and 32 gigabytes of data. The Digital Michelangelo project has created a detailed model of the famous sculpture useful both for conservation and as an educational tool for students around the world. Two of the many images that can be derived from the three-dimensional scan as shown on the opposite page.

To learn more, see these references on the ⊙ library:

Conserving paintings, a site dedicated to Harvard University's digital imaging lab

Sistine Chapel, a short background on the Sistine Chapel

The Digital Michelangelo project

An image from the Sistine Chapel in normal light (left) and in infrared (right).

Storage, Networks, and Other Peripherals

Combining bandwidth and storage . . .
enables swift and reliable access to
the ever-expanding troves of content
on the proliferating disks and . . .
repositories of the Internet.

George Gilder
The End Is Drawing Nigh, 2000

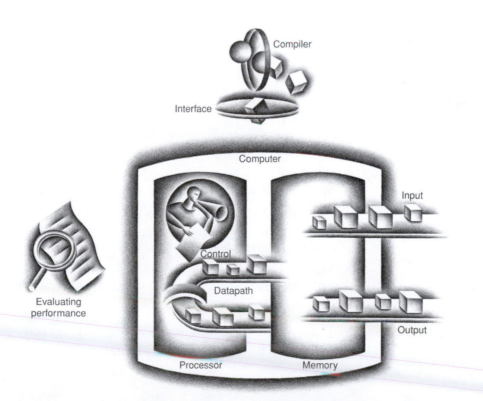
The Five Classic Components of a Computer

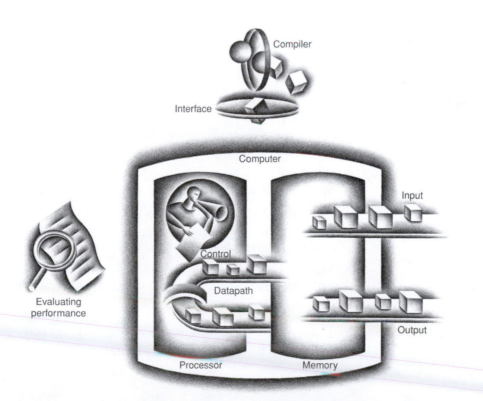

8.1 Introduction

Although users can get frustrated if their computer hangs and must be rebooted, they become apoplectic if their storage system crashes and they lose information. Thus, the bar for dependability is much higher for storage than for computation. Networks also plan for failures in communication, including several mechanisms to detect and recover from such failures. Hence, I/O systems generally place much greater emphasis on dependability and cost, while processors and memory focus on performance and cost.

I/O systems must also plan for expandability and for diversity of devices, which is not a concern for processors. Expandability is related to storage capacity, which is another design parameter for I/O systems; systems may need a lower bound of storage capacity to fulfill their role.

Although performance plays a smaller role for I/O, it is more complex. For example, with some devices we may care primarily about access latency, while with others throughput is crucial. Furthermore, performance depends on many aspects of the system: the device characteristics, the connection between the device and the rest of the system, the memory hierarchy, and the operating system. Figure 8.1 shows the structure of a simple system with its I/O. All of the components, from the individual I/O devices to the processor to the system software, will affect the dependability, expandability, and performance of tasks that include I/O.

I/O devices are incredibly diverse. Three characteristics are useful in organizing this wide variety:

- *Behavior:* Input (read once), output (write only, cannot be read), or storage (can be reread and usually rewritten).

- *Partner:* Either a human or a machine is at the other end of the I/O device, either feeding data on input or reading data on output.

- *Data rate:* The peak rate at which data can be transferred between the I/O device and the main memory or processor. It is useful to know what maximum demand the device may generate.

For example, a keyboard is an *input* device used by a *human* with a *peak data rate* of about 10 bytes per second. Figure 8.2 shows some of the I/O devices connected to computers.

In Chapter 1, we briefly discussed four important and characteristic I/O devices: mice, graphics displays, disks, and networks. In this chapter we go into much more depth on disk storage and networks.

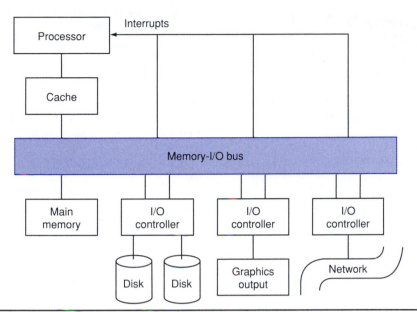

FIGURE 8.1 A typical collection of I/O devices. The connections between the I/O devices, processor, and memory are usually called *buses*. Communication among the devices and the processor uses both interrupts and protocols on the bus, as we will see in this chapter. Figure 8.11 on page 585 shows the organization for a desktop PC.

How we should assess I/O performance often depends on the application. In some environments, we may care primarily about system throughput. In these cases, I/O bandwidth will be most important. Even I/O bandwidth can be measured in two different ways:

1. How much data can we move through the system in a certain time?

2. How many I/O operations can we do per unit of time?

Which performance measurement is best may depend on the environment. For example, in many multimedia applications, most I/O requests are for long streams of data, and transfer bandwidth is the important characteristic. In another environment, we may wish to process a large number of small, unrelated accesses to an I/O device. An example of such an environment might be a tax-processing office of the National Income Tax Service (NITS). NITS mostly cares about processing a large number of forms in a given time; each tax form is stored separately and is fairly small. A system oriented toward large file transfer may be satisfactory, but an I/O system that can support the simultaneous transfer of many small files may be cheaper and faster for processing millions of tax forms.

Device	Behavior	Partner	Data rate (Mbit/sec)
Keyboard	Input	Human	0.0001
Mouse	Input	Human	0.0038
Voice input	Input	Human	0.2640
Sound input	Input	Machine	3.0000
Scanner	Input	Human	3.2000
Voice output	Output	Human	0.2640
Sound output	Output	Human	8.0000
Laser printer	Output	Human	3.2000
Graphics display	Output	Human	800.0000–8000.0000
Modem	Input or output	Machine	0.0160–0.0640
Network/LAN	Input or output	Machine	100.0000–1000.0000
Network/wireless LAN	Input or output	Machine	11.0000–54.0000
Optical disk	Storage	Machine	80.0000
Magnetic tape	Storage	Machine	32.0000
Magnetic disk	Storage	Machine	240.0000–2560.0000

FIGURE 8.2   The diversity of I/O devices. I/O devices can be distinguished by whether they serve as input, output, or storage devices; their communication partner (people or other computers); and their peak communication rates. The data rates span eight orders of magnitude. Note that a network can be an input or an output device, but cannot be used for storage. Transfer rates for devices are always quoted in base 10, so that 10 Mbit/sec = 10,000,000 bits/sec.

I/O requests Reads or writes to I/O devices.

In other applications, we care primarily about response time, which you will recall is the total elapsed time to accomplish a particular task. If the **I/O requests** are extremely large, response time will depend heavily on bandwidth, but in many environments most accesses will be small, and the I/O system with the lowest latency per access will deliver the best response time. On single-user machines such as desktop computers and laptops, response time is the key performance characteristic.

A large number of applications, especially in the vast commercial market for computing, require both high throughput and short response times. Examples include automatic teller machines (ATMs), order entry and inventory tracking systems, file servers, and Web servers. In such environments, we care about both how long each task takes *and* how many tasks we can process in a second. The number of ATM requests you can process per hour doesn't matter if each one takes 15 minutes—you won't have any customers left! Similarly, if you can process each ATM request quickly but can only handle a small number of requests at once, you won't be able to support many ATMs, or the cost of the computer per ATM will be very high.

In summary, the three classes of desktop, server, and embedded computers are sensitive to I/O dependability and cost. Desktop and embedded systems are more focused on response time and diversity of I/O devices, while server systems are more focused on throughput and expandability of I/O devices.

8.2   Disk Storage and Dependability

As mentioned in Chapter 1, magnetic disks rely on a rotating platter coated with a magnetic surface and use a moveable read/write head to access the disk. Disk storage is **nonvolatile**—the data remains even when power is removed. A magnetic disk consists of a collection of platters (1–4), each of which has two recordable disk surfaces. The stack of platters is rotated at 5400 to 15,000 RPM and has a diameter from an inch to just over 3.5 inches. Each disk surface is divided into concentric circles, called **tracks**. There are typically 10,000 to 50,000 tracks per surface. Each track is in turn divided into **sectors** that contain the information; each track may have 100 to 500 sectors. Sectors are typically 512 bytes in size, although there is an initiative to increase the sector size to 4096 bytes. The sequence recorded on the magnetic media is a sector number, a gap, the information for that sector including error correction code (see ⊙ **Appendix B**, page B-65), a gap, the sector number of the next sector, and so on. Originally, all tracks had the same number of sectors and hence the same number of bits, but with the introduction of zone bit recording (ZBR) in the early 1990s, disk drives changed to a varying number of sectors (and hence bits) per track, instead keeping the spacing between bits constant. ZBR increases the number of bits on the outer tracks and thus increases the drive capacity.

As we saw in Chapter 1, to read and write information the read/write heads must be moved so that they are over the correct location. The disk heads for each surface are connected together and move in conjunction, so that every head is over the same track of every surface. The term *cylinder* is used to refer to all the tracks under the heads at a given point on all surfaces.

To access data, the operating system must direct the disk through a three-stage process. The first step is to position the head over the proper track. This operation is called a **seek**, and the time to move the head to the desired track is called the *seek time*.

Disk manufacturers report minimum seek time, maximum seek time, and average seek time in their manuals. The first two are easy to measure, but the average is open to wide interpretation because it depends on the seek distance. The industry has decided to calculate average seek time as the sum of the time for all possible seeks divided by the number of possible seeks. Average seek times are usually advertised as 3 ms to 14 ms, but, depending on the application and scheduling of disk requests, the actual average seek time may be only 25% to 33% of the

nonvolatile Storage device where data retains its value even when power is removed.

track One of thousands of concentric circles that makes up the surface of a magnetic disk.

sector One of the segments that make up a track on a magnetic disk; a sector is the smallest amount of information that is read or written on a disk.

seek The process of positioning a read/write head over the proper track on a disk.

advertised number because of locality of disk references. This locality arises both because of successive accesses to the same file and because the operating system tries to schedule such accesses together.

Once the head has reached the correct track, we must wait for the desired sector to rotate under the read/write head. This time is called the **rotational latency** or **rotational delay**. The average latency to the desired information is halfway around the disk. Because the disks rotate at 5400 RPM to 15,000 RPM, the average rotational latency is between

rotational latency Also called **rotational delay**. The time required for the desired sector of a disk to rotate under the read/write head; usually assumed to be half the rotation time.

$$\text{Average rotational latency} \ = \ \frac{0.5 \text{ rotation}}{5400 \text{ RPM}} \ = \ \frac{0.5 \text{ rotation}}{5400 \text{ RPM}/\left(60 \frac{\text{seconds}}{\text{minute}}\right)}$$

$$= \ 0.0056 \text{ seconds} \ = \ 5.6 \text{ ms}$$

and

$$\text{Average rotational latency} \ = \ \frac{0.5 \text{ rotation}}{15,000 \text{ RPM}} \ = \ \frac{0.5 \text{ rotation}}{15,000 \text{ RPM}/\left(60 \frac{\text{seconds}}{\text{minute}}\right)}$$

$$= \ 0.0020 \text{ seconds} \ = \ 2.0 \text{ ms}$$

The last component of a disk access, *transfer time,* is the time to transfer a block of bits. The transfer time is a function of the sector size, the rotation speed, and the recording density of a track. Transfer rates in 2004 were between 30 and 80 MB/sec. The one complication is that most disk controllers have a built-in cache that stores sectors as they are passed over; transfer rates from the cache are typically higher and may be up to 320 MB/sec in 2004. Today, most disk transfers are multiple sectors in length.

A *disk controller* usually handles the detailed control of the disk and the transfer between the disk and the memory. The controller adds the final component of disk access time, *controller time*, which is the overhead the controller imposes in performing an I/O access. The average time to perform an I/O operation will consist of these four times plus any wait time incurred because other processes are using the disk.

EXAMPLE

Disk Read Time

What is the average time to read or write a 512-byte sector for a typical disk rotating at 10,000 RPM? The advertised average seek time is 6 ms, the transfer rate is 50 MB/sec, and the controller overhead is 0.2 ms. Assume that the disk is idle so that there is no waiting time.

Average disk access time is equal to Average seek time + Average rotational delay + Transfer time + Controller overhead. Using the advertised average seek time, the answer is

$$6.0 \text{ ms} + \frac{0.5 \text{ rotation}}{10{,}000 \text{ RPM}} + \frac{0.5 \text{ KB}}{50 \text{ MB/sec}} + 0.2 \text{ ms} = 6.0 + 3.0 + 0.01 + 0.2 = 9.2 \text{ ms}$$

If the measured average seek time is 25% of the advertised average time, the answer is

$$1.5 \text{ ms} + 3.0 \text{ ms} + 0.01 \text{ ms} + 0.2 \text{ ms} = 4.7 \text{ ms}$$

Notice that when we consider measured average seek time, as opposed to advertised average seek time, the rotational latency can be the largest component of the access time.

Disk densities have continued to increase for more than 50 years. The impact of this compounded improvement in density and the reduction in physical size of a disk drive has been amazing, as Figure 8.3 shows. The aims of different disk designers have led to a wide variety of drives being available at any particular time. Figure 8.4 shows the characteristics of three magnetic disks. In 2004, these disks from a single manufacturer cost between $0.50 and $5 per gigabyte, depending on size, interface, and performance. The smaller drive has advantages in power and volume per byte.

Elaboration: Most disk controllers include caches. Such caches allow for fast access to data that was recently read between transfers requested by the CPU. They use write-through and do not update on a write miss. They often also include prefetch algorithms to try to anticipate demand. Of course, such capabilities complicate the measurement of disk performance and increase the importance of workload choice.

Dependability, Reliability, and Availability

Users crave dependable storage, but how do you define it? In the computer industry, it is harder than looking it up in the dictionary. After considerable debate, the following is considered the standard definition (Laprie 1985):

Computer system dependability is the quality of delivered service such that reliance can justifiably be placed on this service. The service delivered by a system is its observed actual behavior as perceived by other system(s) interacting with this system's users. Each module also has an ideal specified behavior, where a service specification is an agreed description of the expected behavior. A system failure occurs when the actual behavior deviates from the specified behavior.

FIGURE 8.3   Six magnetic disks, varying in diameter from 14 inches down to 1.8 inches.
The IBM microdrive, not shown, has a 1-inch diameter. The pictured disks were introduced over more than
15 years ago and hence are not intended to be representative of the best capacity of modern disks of these
diameters. This photograph does, however, accurately portray their relative physical sizes. The widest disk is
the DEC R81, containing four 14-inch diameter platters and storing 456 MB. It was manufactured in 1985.
The 8-inch diameter disk comes from Fujitsu, and this 1984 disk stores 130 MB on six platters. The Microp-
olis RD53 has five 5.25-inch platters and stores 85 MB. The IBM 0361 also has five platters, but these are just
3.5 inches in diameter. This 1988 disk holds 320 MB. In 2004, the most dense 3.5-inch disk had 2 platters
and held 200 GB in the same space, yielding an increase in density of about 600 times! The Conner CP 2045
has two 2.5-inch platters containing 40 MB and was made in 1990. The smallest disk in this photograph is
the Integral 1820. This single 1.8-inch platter contains 20 MB and was made in 1992. Figure 8.11 on page
585 shows a 10-inch drive that holds 340 MB.

Thus, you need a reference specification of expected behavior to be able to
determine dependability. Users can then see a system alternating between two
states of delivered service with respect to the service specification:

1. *Service accomplishment,* where the service is delivered as specified

2. *Service interruption,* where the delivered service is different from the specified service

Transitions from state 1 to state 2 are caused by failures, and transitions from state
2 to state 1 are called *restorations.* Failures can be permanent or intermittent. The
latter is the more difficult case to diagnose when a system oscillates between the
two states; permanent failures are much easier to diagnose. This definition leads
to two related terms: reliability and availability.

Characteristics	Seagate ST373453	Seagate ST3200822	Seagate ST94811A
Disk diameter (inches)	3.50	3.50	2.50
Formatted data capacity (GB)	73.4	200.0	40.0
Number of disk surfaces (heads)	8	4	2
Rotation speed (RPM)	15,000	7200	5400
Internal disk cache size (MB)	8	8	8
External interface, bandwidth (MB/sec)	Ultra320 SCSI, 320	Serial ATA, 150	ATA, 100
Sustained transfer rate (MB/sec)	57–86	32–58	34
Minimum seek (read/write) (ms)	0.2/0.4	1.0/1.2	1.5/2.0
Average seek read/write (ms)	3.6/3.9	8.5/9.5	12.0/14.0
Mean time to failure (MTTF) (hours)	1,200,000 @ 25°C	600,000 @ 25°C	330,000 @ 25°C
Warranty (years)	5	3	—
Nonrecoverable read errors per bits read	<1 per 10^{15}	< 1 per 10^{14}	< 1 per 10^{14}
Temperature, vibration limits (operating)	5°–55°C, 400 Hz @ 0.5 G	0°–60°C, 350 Hz @ 0.5 G	5°–55°C, 400 Hz @ 1 G
Size: dimensions (in.), weight (pounds)	1.0" × 4.0" × 5.8", 1.9 lbs	1.0" × 4.0" × 5.8", 1.4 lbs	0.4" × 2.7" × 3.9", 0.2 lbs
Power: operating/idle/standby (watts)	20?/12/—	12/8/1	2.4/1.0/0.4
GB/cu. in., GB/watt	3 GB/cu.in., 4 GB/W	9 GB/cu.in., 16 GB/W	10 GB/cu.in., 17 GB/W
Price in 2004, $/GB	≈ $400, ≈ $5/GB	≈ $100, ≈ $0.5/GB	≈ $100, ≈ $2.50/GB

FIGURE 8.4   Characteristics of three magnetic disks by a single manufacturer in 2004. The disks shown here either interface to SCSI, a standard I/O bus for many systems, or ATA, a standard I/O bus for PCs. The first disk is intended for file servers, the second for desktop PCs, and the last for laptop computers. Each disk has an 8 MB cache. The transfer rate from the cache is 3–6 times faster than the transfer rate from the disk surface. The much lower cost of the ATA 3.5-inch drive is primarily due to the hypercompetitive PC market, although there are differences in performance and reliability between it and the SCSI drive. The service life for these disks is 5 years, although Seagate offers a 5-year guarantee only on the SCSI drive, with a 1-year guarantee on the other two. Note that the quoted MTTF assumes nominal power and temperature. Disk lifetimes can be much shorter if temperature and vibration are not controlled. See the link to Seagate at *www.seagate.com* for more information on these drives.

Reliability is a measure of the continuous service accomplishment—or, equivalently, of the time to failure—from a reference point. Hence, the mean time to failure (MTTF) of disks in Figure 8.4 is a reliability measure. Service interruption is measured as mean time to repair (MTTR). *Mean time between failures* (MTBF) is simply the sum of MTTF + MTTR. Although MTBF is widely used, MTTF is often the more appropriate term.

Availability is a measure of the service accomplishment with respect to the alternation between the two states of accomplishment and interruption. Availability is statistically quantified as

$$\text{Availability} = \frac{\text{MTTF}}{(\text{MTTF} + \text{MTTR})}$$

Note that reliability and availability are quantifiable measures, rather than just synonyms for dependability.

What is the cause of failures? Figure 8.5 summarizes many papers that have collected data on reasons for computer systems and telecommunications systems to fail. Clearly, human operators are a significant source of failures.

small computer systems interface (SCSI) A bus used as a standard for I/O devices.

Operator	Software	Hardware	System	Year data collected
42%	25%	18%	Data center (Tandem)	1985
15%	55%	14%	Data center (Tandem)	1989
18%	44%	39%	Data center (DEC VAX)	1985
50%	20%	30%	Data center (DEC VAX)	1993
50%	14%	19%	U.S. public telephone network	1996
54%	7%	30%	U.S. public telephone network	2000
60%	25%	15%	Internet services	2002

FIGURE 8.5   Summary of studies of reasons for failures. Although it is difficult to collect data to determine if operators are the cause of errors, since operators often record the reasons for failures, these studies did capture that data. There were often other categories, such as environmental reasons for outages, but they were generally small. The top two rows come from a classic paper by Jim Gray [1990], which is still widely quoted almost 20 years after the data was collected. The next two rows are from a paper by Murphy and Gent, who studied causes of outages in VAX systems over time ("Measuring system and software reliability using an automated data collection process," *Quality and Reliability Engineering International* 11:5, September–October 1995, 341–53). The fifth and sixth rows are studies of FCC failure data about the U.S. public switched telephone network by Kuhn ("Sources of failure in the public switched telephone network," *IEEE Computer* 30:4, April 1997, 31–36) and by Patty Enriquez. The most recent study of three Internet services is from Oppenheimer, Ganapath, and Patterson [2003].

To increase MTTF, you can improve the quality of the components or design systems to continue operation in the presence of components that have failed. Hence, failure needs to be defined with respect to a context. A failure in a component may not lead to a failure of the system. To make this distinction clear, the term *fault* is used to mean failure of a component. Here are three ways to improve MTTF:

1. *Fault avoidance:* preventing fault occurrence by construction

2. *Fault tolerance:* using redundancy to allow the service to comply with the service specification despite faults occurring, which applies primarily to hardware faults

3. *Fault forecasting:* predicting the presence and creation of faults, which applies to hardware and software faults

Shrinking MTTR can help availability as much as increasing MTTF. For example, tools for fault detection, diagnosis, and repair can help reduce the time to repair faults by people, software, and hardware.

RAID

redundant arrays of inexpensive disks (RAID) An organization of disks that uses an array of small and inexpensive disks so as to increase both performance and reliability.

Leveraging redundancy to improve the availability of disk storage is captured in the phrase **Redundant Arrays of Inexpensive Disks**, abbreviated **RAID**. At the time the term was coined, the alternative was large, expensive disks, such as the larger ones in Figure 8.3. The argument was that by replacing a few large disks with many small disks, performance would improve because there would be more read heads, and there would be advantages in cost, power, and floor space since smaller disks are much more efficient per gigabyte than larger disks. Redundancy was needed because the many more smaller disks had lower reliability than a few large disks.

By having many small disks, the cost of extra redundancy to improve dependability is small relative to the large disks. Thus, dependability was more affordable if you constructed a redundant array of inexpensive disks. In retrospect, this was the key advantage.

How much redundancy do you need? Do you need extra information to find the faults? Does it matter how you organize the data and the extra check information on these disks? The paper that coined the term gave an evolutionary answer to these questions, starting with the simplest but most expensive solution. Figure 8.6 shows the evolution and example cost in number of extra check disks. To keep track of the evolution, the authors numbered the stages of RAID, and they are still used today.

No Redundancy (RAID 0)

Simply spreading data over multiple disks, called **striping**, automatically forces accesses to several disks. Striping across a set of disks makes the collection appear to software as a single large disk, which simplifies storage management. It also improves performance for large accesses, since many disks can operate at once. Video-editing systems, for example, often stripe their data and may not worry about dependability as much as, say, databases.

RAID 0 is something of a misnomer as there is no redundancy. However, RAID levels are often left to the operator to set when creating a storage system, and RAID 0 is often listed as one of the options. Hence, the term *RAID 0* has become widely used.

striping Allocation of logically sequential blocks to separate disks to allow higher performance than a single disk can deliver.

Mirroring (RAID 1)

This traditional scheme for tolerating disk failure, called **mirroring** or *shadowing*, uses twice as many disks as does RAID 0. Whenever data is written to one disk, that data is also written to a redundant disk, so that there are always two copies of the information. If a disk fails, the system just goes to the "mirror" and reads its contents to get the desired information. Mirroring is the most expensive RAID solution, since it requires the most disks.

mirroring Writing the identical data to multiple disks to increase data availability.

Error Detecting and Correcting Code (RAID 2)

RAID 2 borrows an error detection and correction scheme most often used for memories (see ⊙ **Appendix B**). Since RAID 2 has fallen into disuse, we'll not describe it here.

FIGURE 8.6 RAID for an example of four data disks showing extra check disks per RAID level and companies that use each level. Figures 8.7 and 8.8 explain the difference between RAID 3, RAID 4, and RAID 5.

Bit-Interleaved Parity (RAID 3)

The cost of higher availability can be reduced to $1/N$, where N is the number of disks in a **protection group**. Rather than have a complete copy of the original data for each disk, we need only add enough redundant information to restore the lost information on a failure. Reads or writes go to all disks in the group, with one extra disk to hold the check information in case there is a failure. RAID 3 is popular in applications with large data sets, such as multimedia and some scientific codes.

Parity is one such scheme. Readers unfamiliar with parity can think of the redundant disk as having the sum of all the data in the other disks. When a disk fails, then you subtract all the data in the good disks from the parity disk; the remaining information must be the missing information. Parity is simply the sum modulo two.

protection group The group of data disks or blocks that share a common check disk or block.

Unlike RAID 1, many disks must be read to determine the missing data. The assumption behind this technique is that taking longer to recover from failure but spending less on redundant storage is a good trade-off.

Block-Interleaved Parity (RAID 4)

RAID 4 uses the same ratio of data disks and check disks as RAID 3, but they access data differently. The parity is stored as blocks and associated with a set of data blocks.

In RAID 3, every access went to all disks. However, some applications prefer smaller accesses, allowing independent accesses to occur in parallel. That is the purpose of the RAID levels 4 to 6. Since error detection information in each sector is checked on reads to see if the data is correct, such "small reads" to each disk can occur independently as long as the minimum access is one sector. In the RAID context, a small access goes to just one disk in a protection group while a large access goes to all the disks in a protection group.

Writes are another matter. It would seem that each small write would demand that all other disks be accessed to read the rest of the information needed to recalculate the new parity, as in Figure 8.7. A "small write" would require reading the old data and old parity, adding the new information, and then writing the new parity to the parity disk and the new data to the data disk.

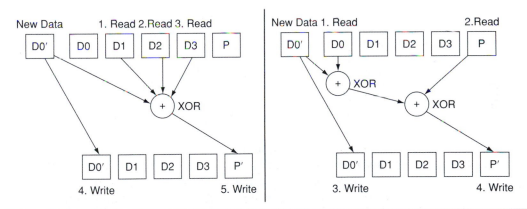

FIGURE 8.7 Small write update on RAID 3 versus RAID 4. This optimization for small writes reduces the number of disk accesses as well as the number of disks occupied. This figure assumes we have four blocks of data and one block of parity. The straightforward RAID 3 parity calculation in the left of the figure reads blocks D1, D2, and D3 before adding block D0′ to calculate the new parity P′. (In case you were wondering, the new data D0′ comes directly from the CPU, so disks are not involved in reading it.) The RAID 4 shortcut on the right reads the old value D0 and compares it to the new value D0′ to see which bits will change. You then read to old parity P and then change the corresponding bits to form P′. The logical function exclusive OR does exactly what we want. This example replaces three disk reads (D1, D2, D3) and two disk writes (D0′, P′) involving all the disks for two disk reads (D0, P) and two disk writes (D0′, P′), which involve just two disks. Increasing the size of the parity group increases the savings of the shortcut. RAID 5 uses the same shortcut.

The key insight to reduce this overhead is that parity is simply a sum of information; by watching which bits change when we write the new information, we need only change the corresponding bits on the parity disk. Figure 8.7 shows the shortcut. We must read the old data from the disk being written, compare old data to the new data to see which bits change, read the old parity, change the corresponding bits, then write the new data and new parity. Thus, the small write involves four disk accesses to two disks instead of accessing all disks. This organization is RAID 4.

Distributed Block-Interleaved Parity (RAID 5)

RAID 4 efficiently supports a mixture of large reads, large writes, and small reads, plus it allows small writes. One drawback to the system is that the parity disk must be updated on every write, so the parity disk is the bottleneck for back-to-back writes.

To fix the parity-write bottleneck, the parity information can be spread throughout all the disks so that there is no single bottleneck for writes. The distributed parity organization is RAID 5.

Figure 8.8 shows how data is distributed in RAID 4 versus RAID 5. As the organization on the right shows, in RAID 5 the parity associated with each row of data blocks is no longer restricted to a single disk. This organization allows multiple writes to occur simultaneously as long as the parity blocks are not located to the same disk. For example, a write to block 8 on the right must also access its parity block P2, thereby occupying the first and third disks. A second write to block 5 on the right, implying an update to its parity block P1, accesses the second and fourth disks and thus could occur concurrently with the write to block 8. Those same writes to the organization on the left result in changes to blocks P1 and P2, both on the fifth disk, which is a bottleneck.

P + Q Redundancy (RAID 6)

Parity-based schemes protect against a single self-identifying failure. When a single failure correction is not sufficient, parity can be generalized to have a second calculation over the data and another check disk of information. This second check block allows recovery from a second failure. Thus, the storage overhead is twice that of RAID 5. The small write shortcut of Figure 8.7 works as well, except now there are six disk accesses instead of four to update both P and Q information.

RAID Summary

RAID 1 and RAID 5 are widely used in servers; one estimate is 80% of disks in servers are found in some RAID system.

One weakness of the RAID systems is repair. First, to avoid making the data unavailable during repair, the array must be designed to allow the failed disks to

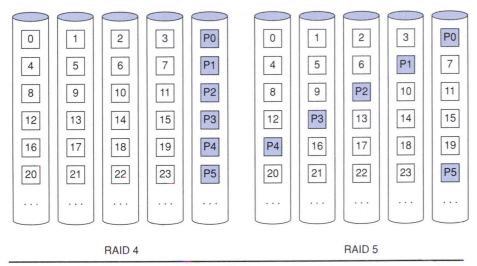

RAID 4   RAID 5

FIGURE 8.8 Block-interleaved parity (RAID 4) versus distributed block-interleaved parity (RAID 5). By distributing parity blocks to all disks, some small writes can be performed in parallel.

be replaced without having to turn off the system. RAIDs have enough redundancy to allow continuous operation, but **hot-swapping** disks places demands on the physical and electrical design of the array and the disk interfaces. Second, another failure could occur during repair, so the repair time affects the chances of losing data: the longer the repair time, the greater the chances of another failure that will lose data. Rather than having to wait for the operator to bring in a good disk, some systems include **standby spares** so that the data can be reconstructed immediately upon discovery of the failure. The operator can then replace the failed disks in a more leisurely fashion. Third, although disk manufacturers quote very high MTTF for their products, those numbers are under nominal conditions. If a particular disk array has been subject to temperature cycles due to, say, the failure of the air conditioning system, or to shaking due to a poor rack design, construction, or installation, the failure rates will be much higher. The calculation of RAID reliability assumes independence between disk failures, but disk failures could be correlated because such damage due to the environment would likely happen to all the disks in the array. Finally, a human operator ultimately determines which disks to remove. As Figure 8.5 shows, operators are only human, so they occasionally remove the good disk instead of the broken disk, leading to an unrecoverable disk failure.

Although RAID 6 is rarely used today, a cautious operator might want its extra redundancy to protect against expected hardware failures plus a safety margin to protect against human error and correlated failures due to problems with the environment.

hot-swapping Replacing a hardware component while the system is running.

standby spares Reserve hardware resources that can immediately take the place of a failed component.

**Check
Yourself**

Which of the following are true about dependability?

1. If a system is up, then all its components are accomplishing their expected service.

2. Availability is a quantitative measure of the percentage of time a system is accomplishing its expected service.

3. Reliability is a quantitative measure of continuous service accomplishment by a system.

4. The major source of outages today is software.

Which of the following are true about RAID levels 1, 3, 4, 5, and 6?

1. RAID systems rely on redundancy to achieve high availability.

2. RAID 1 (mirroring) has the highest check disk overhead.

3. For small writes, RAID 3 (bit-interleaved parity) has the worst throughput.

4. For large writes, RAID 3, 4, and 5 have the same throughput.

Elaboration: One issue is how mirroring interacts with striping. Suppose you had, say, four disks' worth of data to store and eight physical disks to use. Would you create four pairs of disks—each organized as RAID 1—and then stripe data across the four RAID 1 pairs? Alternatively, would you create two sets of four disks—each organized as RAID 0—and then mirror writes to both RAID 0 sets? The RAID terminology has evolved to call the former RAID 1 + 0 or RAID 10 ("striped mirrors") and the latter RAID 0 + 1 or RAID 01 ("mirrored stripes").

Networks

Networks are growing in popularity over time, and unlike other I/O devices, there are many books and courses on them. For readers who have not taken courses or read books on networking, **Section 8.3** on the ⊙ **CD** gives a quick overview of the topics and terminology, including internetworking, the OSI model, protocol families such as TCP/IP, long-haul networks such as ATM, local area networks such as Ethernet, and wireless networks such as IEEE 802.11.

8.4 Buses and Other Connections between Processors, Memory, and I/O Devices

In a computer system, the various subsystems must have interfaces to one another. For example, the memory and processor need to communicate, as do the processor and the I/O devices. For many years, this has been done with a *bus*. A bus is a shared communication link, which uses one set of wires to connect multiple subsystems. The two major advantages of the bus organization are versatility and low cost. By defining a single connection scheme, new devices can easily be added, and peripherals can even be moved between computer systems that use the same kind of bus. Furthermore, buses are cost-effective because a single set of wires is shared in multiple ways.

The major disadvantage of a bus is that it creates a communication bottleneck, possibly limiting the maximum I/O throughput. When I/O must pass through a single bus, the bandwidth of that bus limits the maximum I/O throughput. Designing a bus system capable of meeting the demands of the processor as well as connecting large numbers of I/O devices to the machine presents a major challenge.

One reason bus design is so difficult is that the maximum bus speed is largely limited by physical factors: the length of the bus and the number of devices. These physical limits prevent us from running the bus arbitrarily fast. In addition, the need to support a range of devices with widely varying latencies and data transfer rates also makes bus design challenging.

As it becomes difficult to run many parallel wires at high speed due to clock skew and reflection, the industry is in transition from parallel shared buses to high-speed serial point-to-point interconnections with switches. Thus, such networks are gradually replacing buses in our systems.

As a result of this transition, this section has been revised in this edition to emphasize the general problem of connecting I/O devices, processors, and memory rather than focusing exclusively on buses.

Bus Basics

Classically, a bus generally contains a set of control lines and a set of data lines. The control lines are used to signal requests and acknowledgments, and to indicate what type of information is on the data lines. The data lines of the bus carry information between the source and the destination. This information may consist of data, complex commands, or addresses. For example, if a disk wants to write some data into memory from a disk sector, the data lines will be used to indicate the address in memory in which to place the data as well as to carry the

bus transaction A sequence of bus operations that includes a request and may include a response, either of which may carry data. A transaction is initiated by a single request and may take many individual bus operations.

processor-memory bus A bus that connects processor and memory and that is short, generally high speed, and matched to the memory system so as to maximize memory-processor bandwidth.

backplane bus A bus that is designed to allow processors, memory, and I/O devices to coexist on a single bus.

synchronous bus A bus that includes a clock in the control lines and a fixed protocol for communicating that is relative to the clock.

asynchronous bus A bus that uses a handshaking protocol for coordinating usage rather than a clock; can accommodate a wide variety of devices of differing speeds.

actual data from the disk. The control lines will be used to indicate what type of information is contained on the data lines of the bus at each point in the transfer. Some buses have two sets of signal lines to separately communicate both data and address in a single bus transmission. In either case, the control lines are used to indicate what the bus contains and to implement the bus protocol. And because the bus is shared, we also need a protocol to decide who uses it next; we will discuss this problem shortly.

Let's consider a typical **bus transaction**. A bus transaction includes two parts: sending the address and receiving or sending the data. Bus transactions are typically defined by what they do to memory. A *read* transaction transfers data *from* memory (to either the processor or an I/O device), and a *write* transaction writes data *to* the memory. Clearly, this terminology is confusing. To avoid this, we'll try to use the terms *input* and *output*, which are always defined from the perspective of the processor: an input operation is inputting data from the device to memory, where the processor can read it, and an output operation is outputting data to a device from memory where the processor wrote it.

Buses are traditionally classified as **processor-memory buses** or *I/O buses*. Processor-memory buses are short, generally high speed, and matched to the memory system so as to maximize memory-processor bandwidth. I/O buses, by contrast, can be lengthy, can have many types of devices connected to them, and often have a wide range in the data bandwidth of the devices connected to them. I/O buses do not typically interface directly to the memory but use either a processor-memory or a **backplane bus** to connect to memory. Other buses with different characteristics have emerged for special functions, such as graphics buses.

The I/O bus serves as a way of expanding the machine and connecting new peripherals. To make this easier, the computer industry has developed several standards. The standards serve as a specification for the computer manufacturer and for the peripheral manufacturer. A standard ensures the computer designer that peripherals will be available for a new machine, and it ensures the peripheral builder that users will be able to hook up their new equipment. Figure 8.9 summarizes the key characteristics of the two dominant I/O bus standards: Firewire and USB. They connect a variety of devices to the desktop computer, from keyboards to cameras to disks.

The two basic schemes for communication on the bus are **synchronous** and **asynchronous**. If a bus is synchronous, it includes a clock in the control lines and a fixed protocol for communicating that is relative to the clock. For example, for a processor-memory bus performing a read from memory, we might have a protocol that transmits the address and read command on the first clock cycle, using the control lines to indicate the type of request. The memory might then be required to respond with the data word on the fifth clock. This type of protocol can be implemented easily in a small finite-state machine. Because the protocol is predetermined and involves little logic, the bus can run very fast and the interface logic will be small.

Characteristic	Firewire (1394)	USB 2.0
Bus type	I/O	I/O
Basic data bus width (signals)	4	2
Clocking	Asynchronous	Asynchronous
Theoretical peak bandwidth	50 MB/sec (Firewire 400) or 100 MB/sec (Firewire 800)	0.2 MB/sec (low speed), 1.5 MB/sec (full speed), or 60 MB/sec (high speed)
Hot pluggable	Yes	Yes
Maximum number of devices	63	127
Maximum bus length (copper wire)	4.5 meters	5 meters
Standard name	IEEE 1394, 1394b	USB Implementors Forum

FIGURE 8.9 Key characteristics of two dominant I/O bus standards.

Synchronous buses have two major disadvantages, however. First, every device on the bus must run at the same clock rate. Second, because of clock skew problems, synchronous buses cannot be long if they are fast (see ⊚ **Appendix B** for a discussion of clock skew). Processor-memory buses are often synchronous because the devices communicating are close, small in number, and prepared to operate at high clock rates.

An asynchronous bus is not clocked. Because it is not clocked, an asynchronous bus can accommodate a wide variety of devices, and the bus can be lengthened without worrying about clock skew or synchronization problems. Both Firewire and USB 2.0 are asynchronous. To coordinate the transmission of data between sender and receiver, an asynchronous bus uses a **handshaking protocol**. A handshaking protocol consists of a series of steps in which the sender and receiver proceed to the next step only when both parties agree. The protocol is implemented with an additional set of control lines.

A simple example will illustrate how asynchronous buses work. Let's consider a device requesting a word of data from the memory system. Assume that there are three control lines:

1. *ReadReq:* Used to indicate a read request for memory. The address is put on the data lines at the same time.

2. *DataRdy:* Used to indicate that the data word is now ready on the data lines. In an output transaction, the memory would assert this signal since it is providing the data. In an input transaction, an I/O device would assert this signal, since it would provide data. In either case, the data is placed on the data lines at the same time.

3. *Ack:* Used to acknowledge the ReadReq or the DataRdy signal of the other party.

handshaking protocol A series of steps used to coordinate asynchronous bus transfers in which the sender and receiver proceed to the next step only when both parties agree that the current step has been completed.

In an asynchronous protocol, the control signals ReadReq and DataRdy are asserted until the other party (the memory or the device) indicates that the control lines have been seen and the data lines have been read; this indication is made by asserting the Ack line. This complete process is called *handshaking*. Figure 8.10 shows how such a protocol operates by depicting the steps in the communication.

Although much of the bandwidth of a bus is decided by the choice of a synchronous or asynchronous protocol and the timing characteristics of the bus, several other factors affect the bandwidth that can be attained by a single transfer. The most important of these is the data bus width, and whether it supports block transfers or it transfers a word at a time.

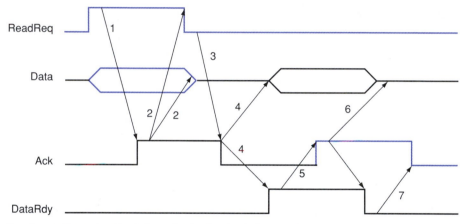

The steps in the protocol begin immediately after the device signals a request by raising ReadReq and putting the address on the data lines:

1. When memory sees the ReadReq line, it reads the address from the data bus and raises Ack to indicate it has been seen.
2. I/O device sees the Ack line high and releases the ReadReq and data lines.
3. Memory sees that ReadReq is low and drops the Ack line to acknowledge the ReadReq signal.
4. This step starts when the memory has the data ready. It places the data from the read request on the data lines and raises DataRdy.
5. The I/O device sees DataRdy, reads the data from the bus, and signals that it has the data by raising Ack.
6. The memory sees the Ack signal, drops DataRdy, and releases the data lines.
7. Finally, the I/O device, seeing DataRdy go low, drops the Ack line, which indicates that the transmission is completed.

A new bus transaction can now begin.

FIGURE 8.10   The asynchronous handshaking protocol consists of seven steps to read a word from memory and receive it in an I/O device. The signals in color are those asserted by the I/O device, while the memory asserts the signals shown in black. The arrows label the seven steps and the event that triggers each step. The symbol showing two lines (high and low) at the same time on the data lines indicates that the data lines have valid data at this point. (The symbol indicates that the data is valid, but the value is not known.)

Elaboration: Another method for increasing the effective bus bandwidth is to release the bus when it is not being used for transmitting information. This type of protocol is called a split transaction protocol. The advantage of such a protocol is that, by freeing the bus during the time data is not being transmitted, the protocol allows another requestor to use the bus. This can improve the effective bus bandwidth for the entire system if the memory is sophisticated enough to handle multiple overlapping transactions. Multiprocessors sharing a memory bus may use split transaction protocols.

split transaction protocol A protocol in which the bus is released during a bus transaction while the requestor is waiting for the data to be transmitted, which frees the bus for access by another requestor.

The Buses and Networks of the Pentium 4

Figure 8.11 shows the I/O system of a PC based on the Pentium 4. The processor connects to peripherals via two main chips. The chip next to the processor is the memory controller hub, commonly called the *north bridge*, and the one connected to it is the I/O controller hub, called the *south bridge*.

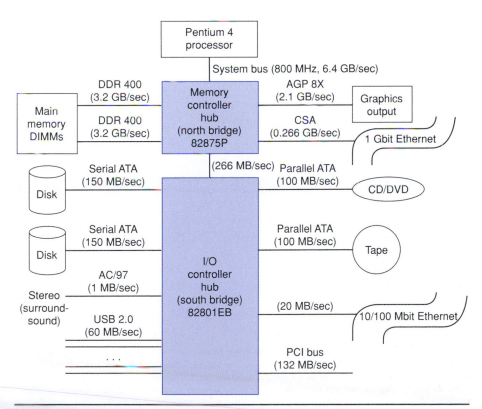

FIGURE 8.11 Organization of the I/O system on a Pentium 4 PC using the Intel 875 chip set. Note that the maximum transfer rate between the north bridge (memory hub) and south bridge (I/O hub) is 266 MB/sec, which is why Intel put the AGP bus and Gigabit Ethernet on the north bridge.

The north bridge is basically a DMA controller, connecting the processor to memory, the AGP graphic bus, and the south bridge chip. The south bridge connects the north bridge to a cornucopia of I/O buses. Intel and others offer a wide variety of these chip sets to connect the Pentium 4 to the outside world. To give a flavor of the options, Figure 8.12 shows two of the chip sets.

As Moore's law continues, an increasing number of I/O controllers that were formerly available as optional cards that connected to I/O buses have been co-opted into these chip sets. For example, the south bridge chip of the Intel 875 includes a striping RAID controller, and the north bridge chip of the Intel 845GL includes a graphics controller.

	875P chip set	**845GL chip set**
Target segment	Performance PC	Value PC
System bus (64 bit)	800/533 MHz	400 MHz
Memory controller hub ("north bridge")		
Package size, pins	42.5 × 42.5 mm, 1005	37.5 × 37.5 mm, 760
Memory speed	DDR 400/333/266 SDRAM	DDR 266/200, PC133 SDRAM
Memory buses, widths	2 × 72	1 × 64
Number of DIMMs, DRAM Mbit support	4, 128/256/512 Mbits	2, 128/256/512 Mbits
Maximum memory capacity	4 GB	2 GB
Memory error correction available?	Yes	No
AGP graphics bus, speed	Yes, 8X or 4X	No
Graphics controller	External	Internal (Extreme Graphics)
CSA Gigabit Ethernet interface	Yes	No
South bridge interface speed (8 bit)	266 MHz	266 MHz
I/O controller hub ("south bridge")		
Package size, pins	31 × 31 mm, 460	31 × 31 mm, 421
PCI bus: width, speed, masters	32-bit, 33 MHz, 6 masters	32-bit, 33 MHz, 6 masters
Ethernet MAC controller, interface	100/10 Mbit	100/10 Mbit
USB 2.0 ports, controllers	8, 4	6, 3
ATA 100 ports	2	2
Serial ATA 150 controller, ports	Yes, 2	No
RAID 0 controller	Yes	No
AC-97 audio controller, interface	Yes	Yes
I/O management	SMbus 2.0, GPIO	SMbus 2.0, GPIO

FIGURE 8.12   Two Pentium 4 I/O chip sets from Intel. The 845GL north bridge uses many fewer pins than the 875 by having just one memory bus and by omitting the AGP bus and the Gigabit Ethernet interface. Note that the serial nature of USB and Serial ATA means that two more USB ports and two more Serial ATA ports need just 39 more pins in the south bridge of the 875 versus the 845GL chip sets.

These two chips demonstrate the gradual evolution from parallel shared buses to high-speed serial point-to-point interconnections with switches via the past and future versions of ATA and PCI.

Serial ATA is a serial successor to the parallel ATA bus used by magnetic and optical disks in PCs. The first generation transfers at 150 MB/sec compared to 100 MB/sec for the parallel ATA-100 bus. Its distance is 1 meter, twice the maximum length of ATA-100. It uses just 7 wires, with one 2-wire data channel in each direction, compared to 80 for ATA-100.

The south bridge in Figure 8.11 demonstrates the transitory period between parallel buses and serial networks by providing both parallel and serial ATA buses.

PCI Express is a serial successor to the popular PCI bus. Rather than 32–64 shared wires operating at 33 MHz–133 MHz with a peak bandwidth of 132–1064 MB/sec, PCI Express uses just 4 wires in each direction operating at 625 MHz to offer 300 MB/sec per direction. The bandwidth per pin of PCI Express is 5–10 times its predecessors. A computer can then afford to have several PCI Express interfaces to get even higher bandwidth.

Although the chips in Figure 8.11 only show the parallel PCI bus, Intel plans to replace the AGP graphics bus and the bus between the north bridge and the south bridge with PCI Express in the next generation of these chips.

Buses and networks provide electrical interconnection among I/O devices, processors, and memory, and also define the lowest-level protocol for communication. Above this basic level, we must define hardware and software protocols for controlling data transfers between I/O devices and memory, and for the processor to specify commands to the I/O devices. These topics are covered in the next section.

Both networks and buses connect components together. Which of the following are true about them?

Check Yourself

1. Networks and I/O buses are almost always standardized.

2. Shared media networks and multimaster buses need an arbitration scheme.

3. Local area networks and processor-memory buses are almost always synchronous.

4. High-performance networks and buses use similar techniques compared to their lower-performance alternatives: they are wider, send many words per transaction, and have separate address and data lines.

8.5   Interfacing I/O Devices to the Processor, Memory, and Operating System

A bus or network protocol defines how a word or block of data should be communicated on a set of wires. This still leaves several other tasks that must be performed to actually cause data to be transferred from a device and into the memory address space of some user program. This section focuses on these tasks and will answer such questions as the following:

- How is a user I/O request transformed into a device command and communicated to the device?

- How is data actually transferred to or from a memory location?

- What is the role of the operating system?

As we will see in answering these questions, the operating system plays a major role in handling I/O, acting as the interface between the hardware and the program that requests I/O.

The responsibilities of the operating system arise from three characteristics of I/O systems:

1. Multiple programs using the processor share the I/O system.

2. I/O systems often use interrupts (externally generated exceptions) to communicate information about I/O operations. Because interrupts cause a transfer to kernel or supervisor mode, they must be handled by the operating system (OS).

3. The low-level control of an I/O device is complex because it requires managing a set of concurrent events and because the requirements for correct device control are often very detailed.

Hardware/ Software Interface

The three characteristics of I/O systems above lead to several different functions the OS must provide:

- The OS guarantees that a user's program accesses only the portions of an I/O device to which the user has rights. For example, the OS must not allow a program to read or write a file on disk if the owner of the file has not granted access to this program. In a system with shared I/O devices, protection could not be provided if user programs could perform I/O directly.

- The OS provides abstractions for accessing devices by supplying routines that handle low-level device operations.

■ The OS handles the interrupts generated by I/O devices, just as it handles the exceptions generated by a program.

■ The OS tries to provide equitable access to the shared I/O resources, as well as schedule accesses in order to enhance system throughput.

To perform these functions on behalf of user programs, the operating system must be able to communicate with the I/O devices and to prevent the user program from communicating with the I/O devices directly. Three types of communication are required:

1. The OS must be able to give commands to the I/O devices. These commands include not only operations like read and write, but also other operations to be done on the device, such as a disk seek.

2. The device must be able to notify the OS when the I/O device has completed an operation or has encountered an error. For example, when a disk completes a seek, it will notify the OS.

3. Data must be transferred between memory and an I/O device. For example, the block being read on a disk read must be moved from disk to memory.

In the next few sections, we will see how these communications are performed.

Giving Commands to I/O Devices

To give a command to an I/O device, the processor must be able to address the device and to supply one or more command words. Two methods are used to address the device: memory-mapped I/O and special I/O instructions. In **memory-mapped I/O**, portions of the address space are assigned to I/O devices. Reads and writes to those addresses are interpreted as commands to the I/O device.

For example, a write operation can be used to send data to an I/O device where the data will be interpreted as a command. When the processor places the address and data on the memory bus, the memory system ignores the operation because the address indicates a portion of the memory space used for I/O. The device controller, however, sees the operation, records the data, and transmits it to the device as a command. User programs are prevented from issuing I/O operations directly because the OS does not provide access to the address space assigned to the I/O devices and thus the addresses are protected by the address translation. Memory-mapped I/O can also be used to transmit data by writing or reading to select addresses. The device uses the address to determine the type of command, and the data may be provided by a write or obtained by a read. In any event, the address encodes both the device identity and the type of transmission between processor and device.

memory-mapped I/O An I/O scheme in which portions of address space are assigned to I/O devices and reads and writes to those addresses are interpreted as commands to the I/O device.

Actually performing a read or write of data to fulfill a program request usually requires several separate I/O operations. Furthermore, the processor may have to interrogate the status of the device between individual commands to determine whether the command completed successfully. For example, a simple printer has two I/O device registers—one for status information and one for data to be printed. The Status register contains a *done bit*, set by the printer when it has printed a character, and an *error bit*, indicating that the printer is jammed or out of paper. Each byte of data to be printed is put into the Data register. The processor must then wait until the printer sets the done bit before it can place another character in the buffer. The processor must also check the error bit to determine if a problem has occurred. Each of these operations requires a separate I/O device access.

I/O instruction A dedicated instruction that is used to give a command to an I/O device and that specifies both the device number and the command word (or the location of the command word in memory).

Elaboration: The alternative to memory-mapped I/O is to use dedicated I/O instructions in the processor. These I/O instructions can specify both the device number and the command word (or the location of the command word in memory). The processor communicates the device address via a set of wires normally included as part of the I/O bus. The actual command can be transmitted over the data lines in the bus. Examples of computers with I/O instructions are the Intel IA-32 and the IBM 370 computers. By making the I/O instructions illegal to execute when not in kernel or supervisor mode, user programs can be prevented from accessing the devices directly.

Communicating with the Processor

The process of periodically checking status bits to see if it is time for the next I/O operation, as in the previous example, is called **polling**. Polling is the simplest way for an I/O device to communicate with the processor. The I/O device simply puts the information in a Status register, and the processor must come and get the information. The processor is totally in control and does all the work.

polling The process of periodically checking the status of an I/O device to determine the need to service the device.

Polling can be used in several different ways. Real-time embedded applications poll the I/O devices since the I/O rates are predetermined and it makes I/O overhead more predictable, which is helpful for real time. As we will see, this allows polling to be used even when the I/O rate is somewhat higher.

The disadvantage of polling is that it can waste a lot of processor time because processors are so much faster than I/O devices. The processor may read the Status register many times, only to find that the device has not yet completed a comparatively slow I/O operation, or that the mouse has not budged since the last time it was polled. When the device completes an operation, we must still read the status to determine whether it was successful.

interrupt-driven I/O An I/O scheme that employs interrupts to indicate to the processor that an I/O device needs attention.

The overhead in a polling interface was recognized long ago, leading to the invention of interrupts to notify the processor when an I/O device requires attention from the processor. **Interrupt-driven I/O**, which is used by almost all systems for at least some devices, employs I/O interrupts to indicate to the processor that an I/O device needs attention. When a device wants to notify the processor that it has completed some operation or needs attention, it causes the processor to be interrupted.

An I/O interrupt is just like the exceptions we saw in Chapters 5, 6, and 7, with two important distinctions:

1. An I/O interrupt is asynchronous with respect to the instruction execution. That is, the interrupt is not associated with any instruction and does not prevent the instruction completion. This is very different from either page fault exceptions or exceptions such as arithmetic overflow. Our control unit need only check for a pending I/O interrupt at the time it starts a new instruction.

2. In addition to the fact that an I/O interrupt has occurred, we would like to convey further information such as the identity of the device generating the interrupt. Furthermore, the interrupts represent devices that may have different priorities and whose interrupt requests have different urgencies associated with them.

To communicate information to the processor, such as the identity of the device raising the interrupt, a system can use either vectored interrupts or an exception Cause register. When the processor recognizes the interrupt, the device can send either the vector address or a status field to place in the Cause register. As a result, when the OS gets control, it knows the identity of the device that caused the interrupt and can immediately interrogate the device. An interrupt mechanism eliminates the need for the processor to poll the device and instead allows the processor to focus on executing programs.

Interrupt Priority Levels

To deal with the different priorities of the I/O devices, most interrupt mechanisms have several levels of priority; Unix operating systems use four to six levels. These priorities indicate the order in which the processor should process interrupts. Both internally generated exceptions and external I/O interrupts have priorities; typically, I/O interrupts have lower priority than internal exceptions. There may be multiple I/O interrupt priorities, with high-speed devices associated with the higher priorities.

To support priority levels for interrupts, MIPS provides the primitives that let the operating system implement the policy, similar to how MIPS handles TLB misses. Figure 8.13 shows the key registers, and Section A.7 in Appendix A gives more details.

The Status register determines who can interrupt the computer. If the interrupt enable bit is 0, then none can interrupt. A more refined blocking of interrupts is available in the interrupt mask field. There is a bit in the mask corresponding to

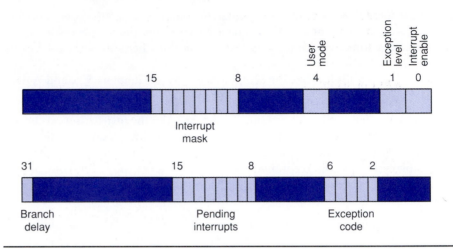

FIGURE 8.13   The Cause and Status registers. This version of the Cause register corresponds to the MIPS-32 architecture. The earlier MIPS I architecture had three nested sets of kernel/user and interrupt enable bits to support nested interrupts. Section A.7 in Appendix A has more detials about these registers.

each bit in the pending interrupt field of the Cause register. To enable the corresponding interrupt, there must be a 1 in the mask field at that bit position. Once an interrupt occurs, the operating system can find the reason in the exception code field of the Status register: 0 means an interrupt occurred, with other values for the exceptions mentioned in Chapter 7.

Here are the steps that must occur in handling an interrupt:

1. Logically AND the pending interrupt field and the interrupt mask field to see which enabled interrupts could be the culprit. Copies are made of these two registers using the `mfc0` instruction.

2. Select the higher priority of these interrupts. The software convention is that the leftmost is the highest priority.

3. Save the interrupt mask field of the Status register.

4. Change the interrupt mask field to disable all interrupts of equal or lower priority.

5. Save the processor state needed to handle the interrupt.

6. To allow higher-priority interrupts, set the interrupt enable bit of the Cause register to 1.

7. Call the appropriate interrupt routine.

8. Before restoring state, set the interrupt enable bit of the Cause register to 0. This allows you to restore the interrupt mask field.

Appendix A shows an exception handler for a simple I/O task on pages A-36 to A-37.

How do the *interrupt priority levels* (IPL) correspond to these mechanisms? The IPL is an operating system invention. It is stored in the memory of the process, and every process is given an IPL. At the lowest IPL, all interrupts are permitted. Conversely, at the highest IPL, all interrupts are blocked. Raising and lowering the IPL involves changes to the interrupt mask field of the Status register.

Elaboration: The two least significant bits of the pending interrupt and interrupt mask fields are for software interrupts, which are lower priority. These are typically used by higher-priority interrupts to leave work for lower-priority interrupts to do once the immediate reason for the interrupt is handled. Once the higher-priority interrupt is finished, the lower-priority tasks will be noticed and handled.

Transferring the Data between a Device and Memory

We have seen two different methods that enable a device to communicate with the processor. These two techniques—polling and I/O interrupts—form the basis for two methods of implementing the transfer of data between the I/O device and memory. Both these techniques work best with lower-bandwidth devices, where we are more interested in reducing the cost of the device controller and interface than in providing a high-bandwidth transfer. Both polling and interrupt-driven transfers put the burden of moving data and managing the transfer on the processor. After looking at these two schemes, we will examine a scheme more suitable for higher-performance devices or collections of devices.

We can use the processor to transfer data between a device and memory based on polling. In real-time applications, the processor loads data from I/O device registers and stores them into memory.

An alternative mechanism is to make the transfer of data interrupt driven. In this case, the OS would still transfer data in small numbers of bytes from or to the device. But because the I/O operation is interrupt driven, the OS simply works on other tasks while data is being read from or written to the device. When the OS recognizes an interrupt from the device, it reads the status to check for errors. If there are none, the OS can supply the next piece of data, for example, by a sequence of memory-mapped writes. When the last byte of an I/O request has been transmitted and the I/O operation is completed, the OS can inform the program. The processor and OS do all the work in this process, accessing the device and memory for each data item transferred.

Interrupt-driven I/O relieves the processor from having to wait for every I/O event, although if we used this method for transferring data from or to a hard disk, the overhead could still be intolerable, since it could consume a large fraction of the processor when the disk was transferring. For high-bandwidth devices like hard disks, the transfers consist primarily of relatively large blocks of data

direct memory access (DMA)
A mechanism that provides a device controller the ability to transfer data directly to or from the memory without involving the processor.

bus master   A unit on the bus that can initiate bus requests.

(hundreds to thousands of bytes). Thus, computer designers invented a mechanism for offloading the processor and having the device controller transfer data directly to or from the memory without involving the processor. This mechanism is called **direct memory access** (DMA). The interrupt mechanism is still used by the device to communicate with the processor, but only on completion of the I/O transfer or when an error occurs.

DMA is implemented with a specialized controller that transfers data between an I/O device and memory independent of the processor. The DMA controller becomes the **bus master** and directs the reads or writes between itself and memory. There are three steps in a DMA transfer:

1.   The processor sets up the DMA by supplying the identity of the device, the operation to perform on the device, the memory address that is the source or destination of the data to be transferred, and the number of bytes to transfer.

2.   The DMA starts the operation on the device and arbitrates for the bus. When the data is available (from the device or memory), it transfers the data. The DMA device supplies the memory address for the read or the write. If the request requires more than one transfer on the bus, the DMA unit generates the next memory address and initiates the next transfer. Using this mechanism, a DMA unit can complete an entire transfer, which may be thousands of bytes in length, without bothering the processor. Many DMA controllers contain some memory to allow them to deal flexibly either with delays in transfer or with those incurred while waiting to become bus master.

3.   Once the DMA transfer is complete, the controller interrupts the processor, which can then determine by interrogating the DMA device or examining memory whether the entire operation completed successfully.

There may be multiple DMA devices in a computer system. For example, in a system with a single processor-memory bus and multiple I/O buses, each I/O bus controller will often contain a DMA processor that handles any transfers between a device on the I/O bus and the memory.

Unlike either polling or interrupt-driven I/O, DMA can be used to interface a hard disk without consuming all the processor cycles for a single I/O. Of course, if the processor is also contending for memory, it will be delayed when the memory is busy doing a DMA transfer. By using caches, the processor can avoid having to access memory most of the time, thereby leaving most of the memory bandwidth free for use by I/O devices.

Elaboration: To further reduce the need to interrupt the processor and occupy it in handling an I/O request that may involve doing several actual operations, the I/O controller can be made more intelligent. Intelligent controllers are often called *I/O proces-*

sors (as well as *I/O controllers* or *channel controllers*). These specialized processors basically execute a series of I/O operations, called an *I/O program*. The program may be stored in the I/O processor, or it may be stored in memory and fetched by the I/O processor. When using an I/O processor, the operating system typically sets up an I/O program that indicates the I/O operations to be done as well as the size and transfer address for any reads or writes. The I/O processor then takes the operations from the I/O program and interrupts the processor only when the entire program is completed. DMA processors are essentially special-purpose processors (usually single-chip and nonprogrammable), while I/O processors are often implemented with general-purpose microprocessors, which run a specialized I/O program.

Direct Memory Access and the Memory System

When DMA is incorporated into an I/O system, the relationship between the memory system and processor changes. Without DMA, all accesses to the memory system come from the processor and thus proceed through address translation and cache access as if the processor generated the references. With DMA, there is another path to the memory system—one that does not go through the address translation mechanism or the cache hierarchy. This difference generates some problems in both virtual memory systems and systems with caches. These problems are usually solved with a combination of hardware techniques and software support.

The difficulties in having DMA in a virtual memory system arise because pages have both a physical and a virtual address. DMA also creates problems for systems with caches because there can be two copies of a data item: one in the cache and one in memory. Because the DMA processor issues memory requests directly to the memory rather than through the processor cache, the value of a memory location seen by the DMA unit and the processor may differ. Consider a read from disk that the DMA unit places directly into memory. If some of the locations into which the DMA writes are in the cache, the processor will receive the old value when it does a read. Similarly, if the cache is write-back, the DMA may read a value directly from memory when a newer value is in the cache, and the value has not been written back. This is called the *stale data problem* or *coherence problem*.

In a system with virtual memory, should DMA work with virtual addresses or physical addresses? The obvious problem with virtual addresses is that the DMA unit will need to translate the virtual addresses to physical addresses. The major problem with the use of a physical address in a DMA transfer is that the transfer cannot easily cross a page boundary. If an I/O request crossed a page boundary, then the memory locations to which it was being transferred would not necessarily be contiguous in the virtual memory. Consequently, if we use physical addresses, we must constrain all DMA transfers to stay within one page.

Hardware/ Software Interface

One method to allow the system to initiate DMA transfers that cross page boundaries is to make the DMA work on virtual addresses. In such a system, the DMA unit has a small number of map entries that provide virtual-to-physical mapping for a transfer. The operating system provides the mapping when the I/O is initiated. By using this mapping, the DMA unit need not worry about the location of the virtual pages involved in the transfer.

Another technique is for the operating system to break the DMA transfer into a series of transfers, each confined within a single physical page. The transfers are then *chained* together and handed to an I/O processor or intelligent DMA unit that executes the entire sequence of transfers; alternatively, the operating system can individually request the transfers.

Whichever method is used, the operating system must still cooperate by not remapping pages while a DMA transfer involving that page is in progress.

We have looked at three different methods for transferring data between an I/O device and memory. In moving from polling to an interrupt-driven to a DMA interface, we shift the burden for managing an I/O operation from the processor to a progressively more intelligent I/O controller. These methods have the advantage of freeing up processor cycles. Their disadvantage is that they increase the cost of the I/O system. Because of this, a given computer system can choose which point along this spectrum is appropriate for the I/O devices connected to it.

Before discussing the design of I/O systems, let's look briefly at performance measures of them.

Hardware/ Software Interface

The coherency problem for I/O data is avoided by using one of three major techniques. One approach is to route the I/O activity through the cache. This ensures that reads see the latest value while writes update any data in the cache. Routing all I/O through the cache is expensive and potentially has a large negative performance impact on the processor, since the I/O data is rarely used immediately and may displace useful data that a running program needs. A second choice is to have the OS selectively invalidate the cache for an I/O read or force write-backs to occur for an I/O write (often called cache *flushing*). This approach requires some small amount of hardware support and is probably more efficient if the software can perform the function easily and efficiently. Because this flushing of large parts of the cache need only happen on DMA block accesses, it will be relatively infrequent. The third approach is to provide a hardware mechanism for selectively flushing (or invalidating) cache entries. Hardware invalidation to ensure cache coherence is typical in multiprocessor systems, and the same technique can be used for I/O; we discuss this topic in detail in Chapter 9.

In ranking the three ways of doing I/O, which statements are true?

1. If we want the lowest latency for an I/O operation to a single I/O device, the order is polling, DMA, and interrupt driven.

2. In terms of lowest impact on processor utilization from a single I/O device, the order is DMA, interrupt driven, and polling.

8.6 I/O Performance Measures: Examples from Disk and File Systems

How should we compare I/O systems? This is a complex question because I/O performance depends on many aspects of the system and different applications stress different aspects of the I/O system. Furthermore, a design can make complex trade-offs between response time and throughput, making it impossible to measure just one aspect in isolation. For example, handling a request as early as possible generally minimizes response time, although greater throughput can be achieved if we try to handle related requests together. Accordingly, we may increase throughput on a disk by grouping requests that access locations that are close together. Such a policy will increase the response time for some requests, probably leading to a larger variation in response time. Although throughput will be higher, some benchmarks constrain the maximum response time to any request, making such optimizations potentially problematic.

In this section, we give some examples of measurements proposed for determining the performance of disk systems. These benchmarks are affected by a variety of system features, including the disk technology, how disks are connected, the memory system, the processor, and the file system provided by the operating system.

Before we discuss these benchmarks, we need to address a confusing point about terminology and units. The performance of I/O systems depends on the rate at which the system transfers data. The transfer rate depends on the clock rate, which is typically given in GHz = 10^9 cycles per second. The transfer rate is usually quoted in GB/sec. In I/O systems, GBs are measured using base 10 (i.e., 1 GB = 10^9 = 1,000,000,000 bytes), unlike main memory where base 2 is used (i.e., 1 GB = 2^{30} = 1,073,741,824 bytes). In addition to adding confusion, this difference introduces the need to convert between base 10 (1K = 1000) and base 2 (1K = 1024) because many I/O accesses are for data blocks that have a size that is a power of 2. Rather than complicate all our examples by accurately converting one of the two measurements, we make note here of this distinction and the fact that treating the two measures as if the units were identical introduces a small error. We illustrate this error in Section 8.9.

Transaction Processing I/O Benchmarks

transaction processing A type of application that involves handling small short operations (called transactions) that typically require both I/O and computation. Transaction processing applications typically have both response time requirements and a performance measurement based on the throughput of transactions.

I/O rate Performance measure of I/Os per unit time, such as reads per second.

data rate Performance measure of bytes per unit time, such as GB/second.

Transaction processing (TP) applications involve both a response time requirement and a performance measurement based on throughput. Furthermore, most of the I/O accesses are small. Because of this, TP applications are chiefly concerned with **I/O rate**, measured as the number of disk accesses per second, as opposed to **data rate**, measured as bytes of data per second. TP applications generally involve changes to a large database, with the system meeting some response time requirements as well as gracefully handling certain types of failures. These applications are extremely critical and cost-sensitive. For example, banks normally use TP systems because they are concerned about a range of characteristics. These include making sure transactions aren't lost, handling transactions quickly, and minimizing the cost of processing each transaction. Although dependability in the face of failure is an absolute requirement in such systems, both response time and throughput are critical to building cost-effective systems.

A number of transaction processing benchmarks have been developed. The best-known set of benchmarks is a series developed by the Transaction Processing Council (TPC).

TPC-C, initially created in 1992, simulates a complex query environment. TPC-H models ad hoc decision support—the queries are unrelated and knowledge of past queries cannot be used to optimize future queries; the result is that query execution times can be very long. TPC-R simulates a business decision support system where users run a standard set of queries. In TPC-R, preknowledge of the queries is taken for granted, and the DBMS can be optimized to run these queries. TPC-W is a Web-based transaction benchmark that simulates the activities of a business-oriented transactional Web server. It exercises the database system as well as the underlying Web server software. The TPC benchmarks are described at *www.tpc.org*.

All the TPC benchmarks measure performance in transactions per second. In addition, they include a response time requirement, so that throughput performance is measured only when the response time limit is met. To model real-world systems, higher transaction rates are also associated with larger systems, both in terms of users and the size of the database that the transactions are applied to. Finally, the system cost for a benchmark system must also be included, allowing accurate comparisons of cost/performance.

File System and Web I/O Benchmarks

File systems, which are stored on disks, have a different access pattern. For example, measurements of Unix file systems in an engineering environment have found that 80% of accesses are to files of less than 10 KB and that 90% of all file accesses are to data with sequential addresses on the disk. Furthermore, 67% of the accesses were reads, 27% were writes, and 6% were read-modify-write accesses, which read data, modify it, and then rewrite the same location. Such measurements have led to the creation of synthetic file system benchmarks. One of the most popular of such benchmarks has five phases, using 70 files:

- *MakeDir:* Constructs a directory subtree that is identical in structure to the given directory subtree
- *Copy:* Copies every file from the source subtree to the target subtree
- *ScanDir:* Recursively traverses a directory subtree and examines the status of every file in it
- *ReadAll:* Scans every byte of every file in a subtree once
- *Make:* Compiles and links all the files in a subtree

As we will see in Section 8.7, the design of an I/O system involves knowing what the workload is.

In addition to processor benchmarks, SPEC offers both a file server benchmark (SPECSFS) and a Web server benchmark (SPECWeb). SPECSFS is a benchmark for measuring NFS (Network File System) performance using a script of file server requests; it tests the performance of the I/O system, including both disk and network I/O, as well as the processor. SPECSFS is a throughput-oriented benchmark but with important response time requirements. SPECWeb is a Web server benchmark that simulates multiple clients requesting both static and dynamic pages from a server, as well as clients posting data to the server.

I/O Performance versus Processor Performance

Amdahl's law in Chapter 2 reminds us that neglecting I/O is dangerous. A simple example demonstrates this.

Impact of I/O on System Performance

Suppose we have a benchmark that executes in 100 seconds of elapsed time, where 90 seconds is CPU time and the rest is I/O time. If CPU time improves by 50% per year for the next five years but I/O time doesn't improve, how much faster will our program run at the end of five years?

EXAMPLE

We know that

$$\text{Elapsed time} = \text{CPU time} + \text{I/O time}$$

$$100 = 90 + \text{I/O time}$$

$$\text{I/O time} = 10 \text{ seconds}$$

ANSWER

The new CPU times and the resulting elapsed times are computed in the following table.

After *n* years	CPU time	I/O time	Elapsed time	% I/O time
0	90 seconds	10 seconds	100 seconds	10%
1	$\frac{90}{1.5}$ = 60 seconds	10 seconds	70 seconds	14%
2	$\frac{60}{1.5}$ = 40 seconds	10 seconds	50 seconds	20%
3	$\frac{40}{1.5}$ = 27 seconds	10 seconds	37 seconds	27%
4	$\frac{27}{1.5}$ = 18 seconds	10 seconds	28 seconds	36%
5	$\frac{18}{1.5}$ = 12 seconds	10 seconds	22 seconds	45%

The improvement in CPU performance over five years is

$$\frac{90}{12} = 7.5$$

However, the improvement in elapsed time is only

$$\frac{100}{22} = 4.5$$

and the I/O time has increased from 10% to 45% of the elapsed time.

Check Yourself

Are the following true or false? Unlike processor benchmarks, I/O benchmarks

1. concentrate on throughput rather than latency.

2. can require that the data set scale in size or number of users to achieve performance milestones.

3. come from organizations rather than from individuals.

8.7 Designing an I/O System

There are two primary types of specifications that designers encounter in I/O systems: latency constraints and bandwidth constraints. In both cases, knowledge of the traffic pattern affects the design and analysis.

Latency constraints involve ensuring that the latency to complete an I/O operation is bounded by a certain amount. In the simple case, the system may be unloaded, and the designer must ensure that some latency bound is met either because it is critical to the application or because the device must receive certain guaranteed service to prevent errors. Examples of the latter are similar to the analysis we looked at in the previous section. Likewise, determining the latency on an unloaded system is relatively easy, since it involves tracing the path of the I/O operation and summing the individual latencies.

Finding the average latency (or distribution of latency) under a load is a much more complex problem. Such problems are tackled either by queuing theory (when the behavior of the workload requests and I/O service times can be approximated by simple distributions) or by simulation (when the behavior of I/O events is complex). Both topics are beyond the limits of this text.

Designing an I/O system to meet a set of bandwidth constraints given a workload is the other typical problem designers face. Alternatively, the designer may be given a partially configured I/O system and be asked to balance the system to maintain the maximum bandwidth achievable as dictated by the preconfigured portion of the system. This latter design problem is a simplified version of the first.

The general approach to designing such a system is as follows:

1. Find the weakest link in the I/O system, which is the component in the I/O path that will constrain the design. Depending on the workload, this component can be anywhere, including the CPU, the memory system, the backplane bus, the I/O controllers, or the devices. Both the workload and configuration limits may dictate where the weakest link is located.

2. Configure this component to sustain the required bandwidth.

3. Determine the requirements for the rest of the system and configure them to support this bandwidth.

The easiest way to understand this methodology is with an example.

I/O System Design

Consider the following computer system:

- A CPU that sustains 3 billion instructions per second and averages 100,000 instructions in the operating system per I/O operation

- A memory backplane bus capable of sustaining a transfer rate of 1000 MB/sec

- SCSI Ultra320 controllers with a transfer rate of 320 MB/sec and accommodating up to 7 disks

- Disk drives with a read/write bandwidth of 75 MB/sec and an average seek plus rotational latency of 6 ms

EXAMPLE

If the workload consists of 64 KB reads (where the block is sequential on a track) and the user program needs 200,000 instructions per I/O operation, find the maximum sustainable I/O rate and the number of disks and SCSI controllers required. Assume that the reads can always be done on an idle disk if one exists (i.e., ignore disk conflicts).

ANSWER

The two fixed components of the system are the memory bus and the CPU. Let's first find the I/O rate that these two components can sustain and determine which of these is the bottleneck. Each I/O takes 200,000 user instructions and 100,000 OS instructions, so

Maximum I/O rate of CPU =

$$\frac{\text{Instruction execution rate}}{\text{Instructions per I/O}} = \frac{3 \times 10^9}{(200 + 100) \times 10^3} = 10,000\frac{\text{I/Os}}{\text{second}}$$

Each I/O transfers 64 KB, so

$$\text{Maximum I/O rate of bus} = \frac{\text{Bus bandwidth}}{\text{Bytes per I/O}} = \frac{1000 \times 10^6}{64 \times 10^3} = 15,625\frac{\text{I/Os}}{\text{second}}$$

The CPU is the bottleneck, so we can now configure the rest of the system to perform at the level dictated by the CPU, 10,000 I/Os per second.

Let's determine how many disks we need to be able to accommodate 10,000 I/Os per second. To find the number of disks, we first find the time per I/O operation at the disk:

$$\text{Time per I/O at disk} = \text{Seek} + \text{rotational time} + \text{Transfer time}$$
$$= 6 \text{ ms} + \frac{64 \text{ KB}}{75 \text{ MB/sec}} = 6.9 \text{ ms}$$

Thus, each disk can complete 1000 ms/6.9 ms or 146 I/Os per second. To saturate the CPU requires 10,000 I/Os per second, or $10,000/146 \approx 69$ disks.

To compute the number of SCSI buses, we need to check the average transfer rate per disk to see if we can saturate the bus, which is given by

$$\text{Transfer rate} = \frac{\text{Transfer size}}{\text{Transfer time}} = \frac{64 \text{ KB}}{6.9 \text{ ms}} \approx 9.56 \text{ MB/sec}$$

The maximum number of disks per SCSI bus is 7, which won't saturate this bus. This means we will need 69/7, or 10 SCSI buses and controllers.

Notice the significant number of simplifying assumptions that are needed to do this example. In practice, many of these simplifications might not hold for critical I/O-intensive applications (such as databases). For this reason, simulation is often the only plausible way to predict the I/O performance of a realistic workload.

8.8 Real Stuff: A Digital Camera

Digital cameras are basically embedded computers with removable, writable, non-volatile storage, and interesting I/O devices. Figure 8.14 shows our example.

FIGURE 8.14 The Sanyo VPC-SX500 with Flash memory card and IBM Microdrive. Although newer cameras offer more pixels per picture, the principles are the same. This 1360 × 1024 pixel digital camera stores pictures either using CompactFlash memory or using an IBM Microdrive. This photo was taken using a 340 MB microdrive and an 8 MB CompactFlash memory. As Figure 8.15 shows, in 2004 the capacities were as large as 1 GB to 4 GB. It is 4.3 inches wide × 2.5 inches high × 1.6 inches deep, and it weighs 7.4 ounces. In addition to taking a still picture and converting it to JPEG format every 0.9 seconds, it can record a Quick Time video clip at VGA size (640 × 480). One technological advantage is the use of a custom system on a chip to reduce size and power, so the camera only needs two AA batteries to operate versus four in other digital cameras.

When powered on, the microprocessor first runs diagnostics on all components and writes any error messages to the liquid crystal display (LCD) on the back of the camera. This camera uses a 1.8-inch low-temperature polysilicon TFT color LCD. When photographers take pictures, they first hold the shutter halfway so that the microprocessor can take a light reading. The microprocessor then keeps the shutter open to get the necessary light, which is captured by a charged-couple device (CCD) as red, green, and blue pixels.

For the camera in Figure 8.14, the CCD is a $1/2$-inch, 1360 × 1024 pixel, progressive scan chip. The pixels are scanned out row by row and then passed through routines for white balance, color, and aliasing correction, and then stored in a 4 MB frame buffer. The next step is to compress the image into a standard format, such as JPEG, and store it in the removable Flash memory. The photographer picks the compression, in this camera called either fine or normal, with a compression ratio of 10 to 20 times. A fine-quality compressed image takes less than 0.5 MB, and a normal-quality compressed image takes about 0.25 MB. The microprocessor then updates the LCD display to show that there is room for one less picture.

Although the previous paragraph covers the basics of a digital camera, there are many more features that are included: showing the recorded images on the color LCD display; sleep mode to save battery life; monitoring battery energy; buffering to allow recording a rapid sequence of uncompressed images; and, in this camera, video recording using MPEG format and audio recording using WAV format.

This camera allows the photographer to use a Microdrive disk instead of CompactFlash memory. Figure 8.15 compares CompactFlash and the IBM Microdrive.

Characteristics	Sandisk Type I CompactFlash SDCFB-128-768	Sandisk Type II CompactFlash SDCFB-1000-768	Hitachi 4 GB Microdrive DSCM-10340
Formatted data capacity (MB)	128	1000	4000
Bytes per sector	512	512	512
Data transfer rate (MB/sec)	4 (burst)	4 (burst)	4–7
Link speed to buffer (MB/sec)	6	6	33
Power standby/operating (W)	0.15/0.66	0.15/0.66	0.07/0.83
Size: height × width × depth (inches)	1.43 × 1.68 × 0.13	1.43 × 1.68 × 0.13	1.43 × 1.68 × 0.16
Weight in grams (454 grams/pound)	11.4	13.5	16
Write cycles before sector wear-out	300,000	300,000	Not applicable
Mean time between failures (hours)	> 1,000,000	> 1,000,000	(see caption)
Best price (2004)	$40	$200	$480

FIGURE 8.15   Characteristics of three storage alternatives for digital cameras. Hitachi matches the Type II form factor in the Microdrive, while the CompactFlash card uses that space to include many more Flash chips. Hitachi does not quote MTTF for the 1.0-inch drives, but the service life is five years or 8800 powered-on hours, whichever is first. They rotate at 3600 RPM and have 12 ms seek times.

The CompactFlash standard package was proposed by Sandisk Corporation in 1994 for the PCMCIA-ATA cards of portable PCs. Because it follows the ATA interface, it simulates a disk interface including seek commands, logical tracks, and so on. It includes a built-in controller to support many types of Flash memory and to help with chip yield for Flash memories by mapping out bad blocks.

The electronic brain of this camera is an embedded computer with several special functions embedded on the chip. Figure 8.16 shows the block diagram of a chip similar to the one in the camera. Such chips have been called *systems on a chip* (SOC) because they essentially integrate into a single chip all the parts that were found on a small printed circuit board of the past. SOC generally reduces size and lowers power compared to less integrated solutions. The manufacturer claims the SOC enables the camera to operate on half the number of batteries and to offer a smaller form factor than competitors' cameras.

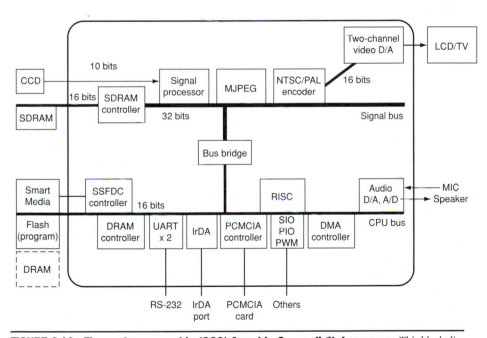

FIGURE 8.16   The system on a chip (SOC) found in Sanyo digital cameras. This block diagram is for the predecessor of the SOC in the camera in Figure 8.14. The successor SOC, called Super Advanced IC, uses three buses instead of two, operates at 60 MHz, consumes 800 mW, and fits 3.1M transistors in a 10.2 × 10.2 mm die using a 0.35-micron process. Note that this embedded system has twice as many transistors as the state-of-the-art, high-performance microprocessor in 1990! The SOC in the figure is limited to processing 1024 × 768 pixels, but its successor supports 1360 × 1024 pixels. (See Okada, Matsuda, Yamada, and Kobayashi [1999].)

For higher performance, it has two buses. The 16-bit bus is for the many slower I/O devices: Smart Media interface, program and data memory, and DMA. The 32-bit bus is for the SDRAM, the signal processor (which is connected to the CCD), the Motion JPEG encoder, and the NTSC/PAL encoder (which is connected to the LCD). Unlike desktop microprocessors, note the large variety of I/O buses that this chip must integrate. The 32-bit RISC MPU is a proprietary design and runs at 28.8 MHz, the same clock rate as the buses. This 700 mW chip contains 1.8M transistors in a 10.5 × 10.5 mm die implemented using a 0.35-micron process.

8.9   Fallacies and Pitfalls

Fallacy: The rated mean time to failure of disks is 1,200,000 hours or almost 140 years, so disks practically never fail.

The current marketing practices of disk manufacturers can mislead users. How is such an MTTF calculated? Early in the process manufacturers will put thousands of disks in a room, run them for a few months, and count the number that fail. They compute MTTF as the total number of hours that the disks were cumulatively up divided by the number that failed.

One problem is that this number far exceeds the lifetime of a disk, which is commonly assumed to be five years or 43,800 hours. For this large MTTF to make some sense, disk manufacturers argue that the calculation corresponds to a user who buys a disk, and then keeps replacing the disk every five years—the planned lifetime of the disk. The claim is that if many customers (and their great-grandchildren) did this for the next century, on average they would replace a disk 27 times before a failure, or about 140 years.

A more useful measure would be percentage of disks that fail. Assume 1000 disks with a 1,200,000-hour MTTF and that the disks are used 24 hours a day. If you replaced failed disks with a new one having the same reliability characteristics, the number that would fail over five years (43,800 hours) is

$$\text{Failed disks} = \frac{1000 \text{ drives} \times 43{,}800 \text{ hours/drive}}{1{,}200{,}000 \text{ hours/failure}} = 36$$

Stated alternatively, 3.6% would fail over the 5-year period.

Pitfall: Using the peak transfer rate of a portion of the I/O system to make performance projections or performance comparisons.

Many of the components of an I/O system, from the devices to the controllers to the buses, are specified using their peak bandwidths. In practice, these peak bandwidth measurements are often based on unrealistic assumptions about the system or are unattainable because of other system limitations. For example, in quoting bus performance, the peak transfer rate is sometimes specified using a memory system that is impossible to build. For networked systems, the software overhead of initiating communication is ignored.

The 32-bit, 33 MHz PCI bus has a peak bandwidth of about 133 MB/sec. In practice, even for long transfers, it is difficult to sustain more than about 80 MB/sec for realistic memory systems. As mentioned above, users of wireless networks typically achieve only about a third of the peak bandwidth.

Amdahl's law also reminds us that the throughput of an I/O system will be limited by the lowest-performance component in the I/O path.

Fallacy: Magnetic disk storage is on its last legs and will be replaced shortly.

This is both a fallacy and a pitfall. Such claims have been made constantly for the past 20 years, though the string of failed alternatives in recent years seems to have reduced the level of claims for the death of magnetic storage. Among the unsuccessful contenders are magnetic bubble memories, optical storage, and holographic storage. None of these systems has matched the combination of characteristics that favor magnetic disks: high reliability, nonvolatility, low cost, reasonable access time, and rapid improvement. Magnetic storage technology continues to improve at the same—or faster—pace that it has sustained over the past 25 years.

Pitfall: Using magnetic tapes to back up disks.

Once again, this is both a fallacy and a pitfall.

Magnetic tapes have been part of computer systems as long as disks because they use similar technology as disks, and hence historically have followed the same density improvements. The historic cost/performance difference between disks and tapes is based on a sealed, rotating disk having lower access time than sequential tape access; but removable spools of magnetic tape mean many tapes can be used per reader, and they can be very long and so have high capacity. Hence, in the past a single magnetic tape could hold the contents of many disks, and since it was 10 to 100 times cheaper per gigabyte than disks, it was a useful backup medium.

The claim was that magnetic tapes must track disks since innovations in disks must help tapes. This claim was important because tapes were a small market and could not afford a separate large research and development effort. One reason the market is small is that desktop owners generally do not back up disks onto tape, and so while desktops are by far the largest market for disks, desktops are a small market for tapes.

Alas, the larger market has led disks to improve much more quickly than tapes. Starting in 2000 to 2002, the largest popular disk was larger than the largest popular tape. In that same time frame, the price per gigabyte of ATA disks dropped below that of tapes. Tape apologists now claim that tapes have compatibility requirements that are not imposed on disks; tape readers must read or write the current and previous generation of tapes, and must read the last four generations of tapes. As disks are closed systems, disk heads need only read the platters enclosed with them, and this advantage explains why disks are improving much more rapidly.

Today, some organizations have dropped tapes altogether, using networks and remote disks to replicate the data geographically. The sites are picked so that disasters would not take out both sites, enabling instantaneous recovery time. (Long recovery time is another serious drawback to the serial nature of magnetic tapes.) Such a solution depends on advances in disk capacity and network bandwidth to make economic sense, but these two are getting much greater investment and hence have better recent records of accomplishment than tape.

Fallacy: A 100 MB/sec bus can transfer 100 MB of data in 1 second.

First, you generally cannot use 100% of any computer resource. For a bus, you would be fortunate to get 70% to 80% of the peak bandwidth. Time to send the address, time to acknowledge the signals, and stalls while waiting to use a busy bus are among the reasons you cannot use 100% of a bus.

Second, the definition of a megabyte of storage and a megabyte per second of bandwidth do not agree. As we discussed on page 597, I/O bandwidth measures are usually quoted in base 10 (i.e., 1 MB/sec = 10^6 bytes/sec), while 1 MB of data is typically a base 2 measure (i.e., 1 MB = 2^{20} bytes). How significant is this distinction? If we could use 100% of the bus for data transfer, the time to transfer 100 MB of data on a 100 MB/sec bus is actually

$$\frac{100 \times 2^{20}}{100 \times 10^6} = \frac{1,048,576}{1,000,000} = 1.048576 \approx 1.05 \text{ second}$$

A similar but larger error is introduced when we treat a gigabyte of data transferred or stored as equivalent, meaning 10^9 versus 2^{30} bytes.

Pitfall: Trying to provide features only within the network versus end to end.

The concern is providing at a lower level features that can only be accomplished at the highest level, thus only partially satisfying the communication demand. Saltzer, Reed, and Clark [1984] give the *end-to-end argument* as follows:

> *The function in question can completely and correctly be specified only with the knowledge and help of the application standing at the endpoints of the communication system. Therefore, providing that questioned function as a feature of the communication system itself is not possible.*

Their example of the pitfall was a network at MIT that used several gateways, each of which added a checksum from one gateway to the next. The programmers of the application assumed the checksum guaranteed accuracy, incorrectly believing that the message was protected while stored in the memory of each gateway. One gateway developed a transient failure that swapped one pair of bytes per million bytes transferred. Over time the source code of one operating system was repeatedly passed through the gateway, thereby corrupting the code. The only solution was to correct the infected source files by comparing to paper listings and repairing the code by hand! Had the checksums been calculated and checked by the application running on the end systems, safety would have been assured.

There is a useful role for intermediate checks, however, provided that end-to-end checking is available. End-to-end checking may show that *something* is broken between two nodes, but it doesn't point to where the problem is. Intermediate checks can discover *what* is broken. You need both for repair.

> *Pitfall: Moving functions from the CPU to the I/O processor, expecting to improve performance without a careful analysis.*

There are many examples of this pitfall trapping people, although I/O processors, when properly used, can certainly enhance performance. A frequent instance of this fallacy is the use of intelligent I/O interfaces, which, because of the higher overhead to set up an I/O request, can turn out to have worse latency than a processor-directed I/O activity (although if the processor is freed up sufficiently, system throughput may still increase). Frequently, performance falls when the I/O processor has much lower performance than the main processor. Consequently, a small amount of main processor time is replaced with a larger amount of I/O processor time. Workstation designers have seen both these phenomena repeatedly.

Myer and Sutherland [1968] wrote a classic paper on the trade-off of complexity and performance in I/O controllers. Borrowing the religious concept of the "wheel of reincarnation," they eventually noticed they were caught in a loop of continuously increasing the power of an I/O processor until it needed its own simpler coprocessor:

> We approached the task by starting with a simple scheme and then adding commands and features that we felt would enhance the power of the machine. Gradually the [display] processor became more complex.... Finally the display processor came to resemble a full-fledged computer with some special graphics features. And then a strange thing happened. We felt compelled to add to the processor a second, subsidiary processor, which, itself, began to grow in complexity. It was then that we discovered the disturbing truth. Designing a display processor can become a never-ending cyclical process. In fact, we found the process so frustrating that we have come to call it the "wheel of reincarnation."

8.10 Concluding Remarks

I/O systems are evaluated on several different characteristics: dependability; the variety of I/O devices supported; the maximum number of I/O devices; cost; and performance, measured both in latency and in throughput. These goals lead to widely varying schemes for interfacing I/O devices. In the low-end and midrange systems, buffered DMA is likely to be the dominant transfer mechanism. In the high-end systems, latency and bandwidth may both be important, and cost may be secondary. Multiple paths to I/O devices with limited buffering often characterize high-end I/O systems. Typically, being able to access the data on an I/O device at any time (high availability) becomes more important as systems grow. As a result, redundancy and error correction mechanisms become more and more prevalent as we enlarge the system.

Storage and networking demands are growing at unprecedented rates, in part because of increasing demands for all information to be at your fingertips. One estimate is that the amount of information created in 2002 was 5 exabytes—equivalent to 500,000 copies of the text in the U.S. Library of Congress—and that the total amount of information in the world doubled in the last three years [Lyman and Varian 2003].

Future directions of I/O include expanding the reach of wired and wireless networks, with nearly every device potentially having an IP address, and the continuing transformation from parallel buses to serial networks and switches. However, consolidation in the disk industry may lead to a slowdown in improvement in disk capacity to earlier rates, which have doubled every year between 2000 and 2004.

Understanding Program Performance

The performance of an I/O system, whether measured by bandwidth or latency, depends on all the elements in the path between the device and memory, including the operating system that generates the I/O commands. The bandwidth of the buses, the memory, and the device determine the maximum transfer rate from or to the device. Similarly, the latency depends on the device latency, together with any latency imposed by the memory system or buses. The effective bandwidth and response latency also depend on other I/O requests that may cause contention for some resource in the path. Finally, the operating system is a bottleneck. In some cases, the OS takes a long time to deliver an I/O request from a user program to an I/O device, leading to high latency. In other cases, the operating system effectively limits the I/O bandwidth because of limitations in the number of concurrent I/O operations it can support.

Keep in mind that while performance can help sell an I/O system, users overwhelmingly demand dependability and capacity from their I/O systems.

8.11 Historical Perspective and Further Reading

The history of I/O systems is a fascinating one. This ⊙ **Section 8.11** gives a brief history of magnetic disks, RAID, databases, the Internet, the World Wide Web, and how Ethernet continues to triumph over its challengers.

8.12 Exercises

8.1 [10] <§§8.1–8.2> Here are two different I/O systems intended for use in transaction processing:

- System A can support 1500 I/O operations per second.

- System B can support 1000 I/O operations per second.

The systems use the same processor that executes 500 million instructions per second. Assume that each transaction requires 5 I/O operations and that each I/O operation requires 10,000 instructions. Ignoring response time and assuming that transactions may be arbitrarily overlapped, what is the maximum transaction-per-second rate that each machine can sustain?

8.2 [15] <§§8.1–8.2> The latency of an I/O operation for the two systems in Exercise 8.1 differs. The latency for an I/O on system A is equal to 20 ms, while for system B the latency is 18 ms for the first 500 I/Os per second and 25 ms per I/O for each I/O between 500 and 1000 I/Os per second. In the workload, every 10th transaction depends on the immediately preceding transaction and must wait for its completion. What is the maximum transaction rate that still allows every transaction to complete in 1 second and that does not exceed the I/O bandwidth of the machine? (For simplicity, assume that all transaction requests arrive at the beginning of a 1-second interval.)

8.3 [5] <§§8.1–8.2> Suppose we want to use a laptop to send 100 files of approximately 40 MB each to another computer over a 5 Mbit/sec wireless connection. The laptop battery currently holds 100,000 joules of energy. The wireless networking card alone consumes 5 watts while transmitting, while the rest of the laptop always consumes 35 watts. Before each file transfer we need 10 seconds to choose which file to send. How many complete files can we transfer before the laptop's battery runs down to zero?

8.4 [10] <§§8.1–8.2> Consider the laptop's hard disk power consumption in Exercise 8.3. Assume that it is no longer constant, but varies between 6 watts when it is spinning and 1 watt when it is not spinning. The power consumed by the laptop apart from the hard disk and wireless card is a constant 32 watts. Suppose that the hard disk's transfer rate is 50 MB/sec, its delay before it can begin transfer is 20 ms, and at all other times it does not spin. How many complete files can we transfer before the laptop's battery runs down to zero? How much energy would we need to send all 100 files? (Consider that the wireless card cannot send data until it is in memory.)

8.5 [5] <§8.3> The following simplified diagram shows two potential ways of numbering the sectors of data on a disk (only two tracks are shown and each track has eight sectors). Assuming that typical reads are contiguous (e.g., all 16 sectors are read in order), which way of numbering the sectors will be likely to result in higher performance? Why?

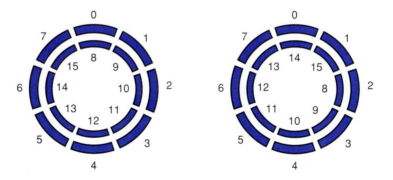

8.6 [20] <§8.3> In this exercise, we will run a program to evaluate the behavior of a disk drive. Disk sectors are addressed sequentially within a track, tracks sequentially within cylinders, and cylinders sequentially within the disk. Determining head switch time and cylinder switch time is difficult because of rotational effects. Even determining platter count, sectors/track, and rotational delay is difficult based on observation of typical disk workloads.

The key is to factor out disk rotational effects by making consecutive seeks to individual sectors with addresses that differ by a linearly increasing amount starting with 0, 1, 2, and so forth. The Skippy algorithm, from work by Nisha Talagala and colleagues of U.C. Berkeley [2000], is

```
fd = open("raw disk device");
for (i = 0; i < measurements; i++) {
    //time the following sequence, and output <i, time>
    lseek(fd, i * SINGLE_SECTOR, SEEK_CUR);
    write(fd, buffer, SINGLE_SECTOR);
}
close(fd);
```

The basic algorithm skips through the disk, increasing the distance of the seek by one sector before every write, and outputs the distance and time for each write. The raw device interface is used to avoid file system optimizations. SINGLE_SECTOR is the size of a single sector in bytes. The SEEK_CUR argument to lseek moves the file pointer an amount relative to the current pointer. A technical report describing Skippy and two other disk drive benchmarks (run in seconds or minutes rather than hours or days) is at *http://sunsite.berkeley.edu/Dienst/UI/2.0/Describe/ncstrl.ucb/CSD-99-1063*.

Run the Skippy algorithm on a disk drive of your choosing.

a. What is the number of heads?

b. The number of platters?

c. What is the rotational latency?

d. What is the head switch time (the time to switch the head that is reading from one disk surface to another without moving the arm; that is, in the same cylinder)?

e. What is the cylinder switch time? (It is the time to move the arm to the next sequential cylinder.)

8.7 [20] <§8.3> Figure 8.17 shows the output from running the benchmark Skippy on a disk.

a. What is the number of heads?

b. The number of platters?

c. What is the rotational latency?

d. What is the head switch time (the time to switch the head that is reading from one disk surface to another without moving the arm; that is, in the same cylinder)?

e. What is the cylinder switch time (the time to move the arm to the next sequential cylinder)?

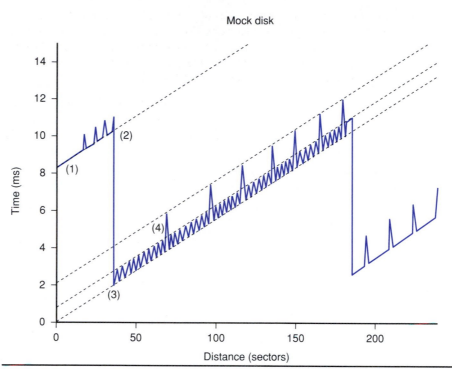

FIGURE 8.17   Example output of Skippy for a hypothetical disk.

8.8 [10] <§8.3> Consider two RAID disk systems that are meant to store 10 terabytes of data (not counting any redundancy). System A uses RAID 1 technology, and System B uses RAID 5 technology with four disks in a "protection group."

  a. How many more terabytes of storage are needed in System A than in System B?

  b. Suppose an application writes one block of data to the disk. If reading or writing a block takes 30 ms, how much time will the write take on System A in the worst case? How about on System B in the worst case?

  c. Is System A more reliable than System B? Why or why not?

8.9 [15] <§8.3> What can happen to a RAID 5 system if the power fails between the write update to the data block and the write update to the check block so that only one of the two is successfully written? What could be done to prevent this from happening?

8.10 [5] <§8.3> The speed of light is approximately 3×10^8 meters per second, and electrical signals travel at about 50% of this speed in a conductor. When the term *high speed* is applied to a network, it is the bandwidth that is higher, not necessarily the velocity of the electrical signals. How much of a factor is the actual "flight time" for the electrical signals? Consider two computers that are 20 meters apart and two computers that are 2000 kilometers apart. Compare your results to the latencies reported in the example on page 8.3-7 in ◉ **Section 8.3**.

8.11 [5] <§8.3> The number of bytes in transit on a network is defined as the flight time (described in Exercise 8.10) multiplied by the delivered bandwidth. Calculate the number of bytes in transit for the two networks described in Exercise 8.10, assuming a delivered bandwidth of 6 MB/sec.

8.12 [5] <§8.3> A secret agency simultaneously monitors 100 cellular phone conversations and multiplexes the data onto a network with a bandwidth of 5 MB/sec and an overhead latency of 150 μs per 1 KB message. Calculate the transmission time per message and determine whether there is sufficient bandwidth to support this application. Assume that the phone conversation data consists of 2 bytes sampled at a rate of 4 KHz.

8.13 [5] <§8.3> Wireless networking has a much higher bit error rate (BER) than wired networking. One way to cope with a higher BER is to use an error-correcting code (ECC) on the transmitted data. A very simple ECC is to triplicate each bit, encoding each zero as 000 and each one as 111. When an encoded 3-bit pattern is received, the system chooses the most likely original bit.

  a. If the system received 001, what is the most likely value of the original bit?

  b. If 000 was sent but a double-bit error causes it to be received as 110, what will the receiver believe was the original bit's value?

  c. How many bit errors can this simple ECC correct?

  d. How many bit errors can this ECC detect?

  e. If 1 out of every 100 bits sent over the network is incorrect, what percentage of bit errors would a receiver using this ECC not detect?

8.14 [5] <§8.3> There are two types of parity: even and odd. A binary word with even parity and no errors will have an even number of 1s in it, while a word with odd parity and no errors will have an odd number of 1s in it. Compute the parity bit for each of the following 8-bit words if even parity is used:

  a. 01100111

  b. 01010101

8.15 [10] <§8.3>

  a. If a system uses even parity, and the word 0111 is read from the disk, can we tell if there is a single-bit error?

b. If a system uses odd parity, and the word 0101 appears on the processor-memory bus, we suspect that a single-bit error has occurred. Can we tell which bit the error occurs in? Why or why not?

c. If a system uses even parity and the word 0101 appears on the processor-memory bus, can we tell if there is a double-bit error?

8.16 [10] <§8.3> A program repeatedly performs a three-step process: it reads in a 4 KB block of data from disk, does some processing on that data, and then writes out the result as another 4 KB block elsewhere on the disk. Each block is contiguous and randomly located on a single track on the disk. The disk drive rotates at 10,000 RPM, has an average seek time of 8 ms, and has a transfer rate of 50 MB/sec. The controller overhead is 2 ms. No other program is using the disk or processor, and there is no overlapping of disk operation with processing. The processing step takes 20 million clock cycles, and the clock rate is 5 GHz. What is the overall speed of the system in blocks processed per second?

8.17 [5] <§8.4> The OSI network protocol is a hierarchy of layers of abstraction, creating an interface between network applications and the physical wires. This is similar to the levels of abstraction used in the ISA interface between software and hardware. Name three advantages to using abstraction in network protocol design.

8.18 [5] <§§8.3, 8.5> Suppose we have a system with the following characteristics:

1. A memory and bus system supporting block access of 4 to 16 32-bit words.

2. A 64-bit synchronous bus clocked at 200 MHz, with each 64-bit transfer taking 1 clock cycle, and 1 clock cycle required to send an address to memory.

3. Two clock cycles needed between each bus operation. (Assume the bus is idle before an access.)

4. A memory access time for the first four words of 200 ns; each additional set of four words can be read in 20 ns.

Assume that the bus and memory systems described above are used to handle disk accesses from disks like the one described in the example on page 570. If the I/O is allowed to consume 100% of the bus and memory bandwidth, what is the maximum number of simultaneous disk transfers that can be sustained for the two block sizes?

8.19 [5] <§8.5> In the system described in Exercise 8.18, the memory system took 200 ns to read the first four words, and each additional four words required 20 ns. Assuming that the memory system takes 150 ns to read the first four words and 30 ns to read each additional four words, find the sustained bandwidth and the latency for a read of 256 words for transfers that use 4-word blocks and for transfers that use 16-word blocks. Also compute the effective number of bus transactions per second for each case.

8.20 [5] <§8.5> Exercise 8.19 demonstrates that using larger block sizes results in an increase in the maximum sustained bandwidth that can be achieved. Under what conditions might a designer tend to favor smaller block sizes? Specifically, why would a designer choose a block size of 4 instead of 16 (assuming all of the characteristics are as identified in Exercise 8.19)?

8.21 [15] <§8.5> This question examines in more detail how increasing the block size for bus transactions decreases the total latency required and increases the maximum sustainable bandwidth. In Exercise 8.19, two different block sizes are considered (4 words and 16 words). Compute the total latency and the maximum bandwidth for all of the possible block sizes (between 4 and 16) and plot your results. Summarize what you learn by looking at your graph.

8.22 [15] <§8.5> This exercise is similar to Exercise 8.21. This time fix the block size at 4 and 16 (as in Exercise 8.19), but compute latencies and bandwidths for reads of different sizes. Specifically, consider reads of from 4 to 256 words, and use as many data points as you need to construct a meaningful graph. Use your graph to help determine at what point block sizes of 16 result in a reduced latency when compared with block sizes of 4.

8.23 [10] <§8.5> This exercise examines a design alternative to the system described in Exercise 8.18 that may improve the performance of writes. For writes, assume all of the characteristics reported in Exercise 8.18 as well as the following:

> The first 4 words are written 200 ns after the address is available, and each new write takes 20 ns. Assume a bus transfer of the most recent data to write, and a write of the previous 4 words can be overlapped.

The performance analysis reported in the example would thus remain unchanged for writes (in actuality, some minor changes might exist due to the need to compute error correction codes, etc., but we'll ignore this). An alternative bus scheme relies on separate 32-bit address and data lines. This will permit an address and data to be transmitted in the same cycle. For this bus alternative, what will the latency of the entire 256-word transfer be? What is the sustained bandwidth? Consider block sizes of 4 and 8 words. When do you think the alternative scheme would be heavily favored?

8.24 <20> <§8.5> Consider an asynchronous bus used to interface an I/O device to the memory system described in Exercise 8.18. Each I/O request asks for 16 words of data from the memory, which, along with the I/O device, has a 4-word bus. Assume the same type of handshaking protocol as appears in Figure 8.10 on page 584, except that it is extended so that the memory can continue the transaction by sending additional blocks of data until the transaction is complete. Modify Figure 8.10 (both the steps and diagram) to indicate how such a transfer might take place. Assuming that each handshaking step takes 20 ns and memory access takes 60 ns, how long does it take to complete a transfer? What is the maximum sustained bandwidth for this asynchronous bus, and how does it compare to the synchronous bus in the example?

8.25 [1 day–1 week] <§§8.2–8.5> ⊙ **For More Practice:** Writing Code to Benchmark I/O Performance

8.26 [3 days–1 week] <§§8.3–8.5> ⊙ **In More Depth:** Ethernet

8.27 [15] <§8.5> We want to compare the maximum bandwidth for a synchronous and an asynchronous bus. The synchronous bus has a clock cycle time of 50 ns, and each bus transmission takes 1 clock cycle. The asynchronous bus requires 40 ns per handshake. The data portion of both buses is 32 bits wide. Find the bandwidth for each bus when performing one-word reads from a 200-ns memory.

8.28 [20] <§8.5> Suppose we have a system with the following characteristics:

1. A memory and bus system supporting block access of 4 to 16 32-bit words.

2. A 64-bit synchronous bus clocked at 200 MHz, with each 64-bit transfer taking 1 clock cycle, and 1 clock cycle required to send an address to memory.

3. Two clock cycles needed between each bus operation. (Assume the bus is idle before an access.)

4. A memory access time for the first four words of 200 ns; each additional set of four words can be read in 20 ns. Assume that a bus transfer of the most recently read data and a read of the next four words can be overlapped.

Find the sustained bandwidth and the latency for a read of 256 words for transfers that use 4-word blocks and for transfers that use 16-word blocks. Also compute the effective number of bus transactions per second for each case. Recall that a single bus transaction consists of an address transmission followed by data.

8.29 [10] <§8.5> Let's determine the impact of polling overhead for three different devices. Assume that the number of clock cycles for a polling operation—including transferring to the polling routine, accessing the device, and restarting the user program—is 400 and that the processor executes with a 500 MHz clock.

Determine the fraction of CPU time consumed for the following three cases, assuming that you poll often enough so that no data is ever lost and assuming that the devices are potentially always busy:

1. The mouse must be polled 30 times per second to ensure that we do not miss any movement made by the user.

2. The floppy disk transfers data to the processor in 16-bit units and has a data rate of 50 KB/sec. No data transfer can be missed.

3. The hard disk transfers data in four-word chunks and can transfer at 4 MB/sec. Again, no transfer can be missed.

8.30 [20] <§§8.3–8.6> ⊙ **In More Depth:** Disk Arrays

8.31 [10] <§§8.3–8.6> ⊙ **In More Depth:** Disk Arrays

8.32 [5] <§8.6> Suppose you are designing a microprocessor that uses special instructions to access I/O devices (instead of mapping the devices to memory addresses). What special instructions would you need to include? What additional bus lines would you need this microprocessor to support in order to address I/O devices?

8.33 <§8.6> An important advantage of interrupts over polling is the ability of the processor to perform other tasks while waiting for communication from an I/O device. Suppose that a 1 GHz processor needs to read 1000 bytes of data from a particular I/O device. The I/O device supplies 1 byte of data every 0.02 ms. The code to process the data and store it in a buffer takes 1000 cycles.

a. If the processor detects that a byte of data is ready through polling, and a polling iteration takes 60 cycles, how many cycles does the entire operation take?

b. If instead, the processor is interrupted when a byte is ready, and the processor spends the time between interrupts on another task, how many cycles of this other task can the processor complete while the I/O communication is taking place? The overhead for handling an interrupt is 200 cycles.

8.34 [20] <§§8.3–8.6> ⊙ **For More Practice:** Finding I/O Bandwidth Bottlenecks

8.35 [15] <§§8.3–8.6> ⊙ **For More Practice:** Finding I/O Bandwidth Bottlenecks

8.36 [15] <§§7.3, 7.5, 8.4, 8.5> ⊙ **For More Practice:** I/O System Operation

8.37 [10] <§8.6> Write a paragraph identifying some of the simplifying assumptions made in the analysis below:

Suppose we have a processor that executes with a 500 MHz clock and the number of clock cycles for a polling operation—including transferring to the polling routine, accessing the device, and restarting the user program—is 400. The hard disk transfers data in four-word chunks and can transfer at 4 MB/sec. Assume that you poll often enough that no data is ever lost and assume that the hard disk is potentially always busy. The initial setup of a DMA transfer takes 1000 clock cycles for the processor, and the handling of the interrupt at DMA completion requires 500 clock cycles for the processor. The hard disk has a transfer rate of 4 MB/sec and uses DMA. Ignore any impact from bus contention between the processor and the DMA controller. Therefore, if the average transfer from the disk is 8 KB, the fraction of the 500 MHz processor consumed if the disk is actively transferring 100% of the time is 0.2%.

8.38 [8] <§8.6> Suppose we have the same hard disk and processor we used in Exercise 8.37, but we use interrupt-driven I/O. The overhead for each transfer, including the interrupt, is 500 clock cycles. Find the fraction of the processor consumed if the hard disk is only transferring data 5% of the time.

8.39 [8] <§8.6> Suppose we have the same processor and hard disk as in Exercise 8.37. Assume that the initial setup of a DMA transfer takes 1000 clock cycles for the processor, and assume the handling of the interrupt at DMA completion requires 500 clock cycles for the processor. The hard disk has a transfer rate of 4 MB/sec and uses DMA. If the average transfer from the disk is 8 KB, what fraction of the 500 MHz processor is consumed if the disk is actively transferring 100% of the time? Ignore any impact from bus contention between the processor and DMA controller.

8.40 [2 days–1 week] <§8.5, Appendix A> ◉ **For More Practice:** Using SPIM to Explore I/O

8.41 [3 days–1 week] <§8.6, Appendix A> ◉ **For More Practice:** Writing Code to Perform I/O

8.42 [3 days–1 week] <§8.6, Appendix A> ◉ **For More Practice:** Writing Code to Perform I/O

8.43 [15] <§§8.3–8.7> Redo the example on page 601, but instead assume that the reads are random 8 KB reads. You can assume that the reads are always to an idle disk, if one is available.

8.44 [20] <§§8.3–8.7> Here are a variety of building blocks used in an I/O system that has a synchronous processor-memory bus running at 800 MHz and one or more I/O adapters that interface I/O buses to the processor-memory bus.

- *Memory system:* The memory system has a 32-bit interface and handles four-word transfers. The memory system has separate address and data lines and, for writes to memory, accepts a word every clock cycle for 4 clock cycles and then takes an additional 4 clock cycles before the words have been stored and it can accept another transaction.

- *DMA interfaces:* The I/O adapters use DMA to transfer the data between the I/O buses and the processor-memory bus. The DMA unit arbitrates for the processor-memory bus and sends/receives four-word blocks from/to the memory system. The DMA controller can accommodate up to eight disks. Initiating a new I/O operation (including the seek and access) takes

0.1 ms, during which another I/O cannot be initiated by this controller (but outstanding operations can be handled).

- *I/O bus:* The I/O bus is a synchronous bus with a sustainable bandwidth of 100 MB/sec; each transfer is one word long.

- *Disks:* The disks have a measured average seek plus rotational latency of 8 ms. The disks have a read/write bandwidth of 40 MB/sec, when they are transferring.

Find the time required to read a 16 KB sector from a disk to memory, assuming that this is the only activity on the bus.

8.45 [15] <§§8.3–8.6> For the I/O system described in Exercise 8.44, find the maximum instantaneous bandwidth at which data can be transferred from disk to memory using as many disks as needed. How many disks and I/O buses (the minimum of each) do you need to achieve the bandwidth? Since you need only achieve this bandwidth for an instant, latencies need not be considered.

8.46 [5] <§8.7> In order to perform a disk or network access, it is typically necessary for the user to have the operating system communicate with the disk or network controllers. Suppose that in a particular 5 GHz computer, it takes 10,000 cycles to trap to the OS, 20 ms for the OS to perform a disk access, and 25 µs for the OS to perform a network access. In a disk access, what percentage of the delay time is spent in trapping to the OS? How about in a network access?

8.47 [5] <§8.7> Suppose that in the computer in Exercise 8.46 we can somehow reduce the time for the OS to communicate with the disk controller by 60%, and we can reduce the time for the OS to communicate with the network by 40%. By what percentage can we reduce the total time for a network access? By what percentage can we reduce the total time for a disk access? Is it worthwhile for us to spend a lot of effort improving the OS trap latency in a computer that performs many disk accesses? How about in a computer that performs many network accesses?

§8.2, page 580: Dependability: 2 and 3. RAID: All are true.
§8.3, page 8.3-10: 1.
§8.4, page 587: 1 and 2.
§8.5, page 597: 1 and 2.
§8.6, page 600: 1 and 2.

Answers to Check Yourself

Computers in the Real World

Saving Lives through Better Diagnosis

Problem: Find a way to examine internal organs to diagnose psychological problems without the use of invasive surgery or harmful radiation.

Solution: The development of magnetic resonance imaging (MRI), a three-dimensional scanning technology, has been one of the most important breakthroughs in modern medical technology. MRI uses a combination of radio-frequency pulses and magnetic fields to scan tissue. The organ to be imaged is scanned in a series of two-dimensional slices, which are then composed to create a three-dimensional image.

In addition to this computationally intensive task of composing the slices to create a volumetric image, extensive computation is used to extract the initial two-dimensional images, since the signal-to-noise ratio is often low. The development of MRI has allowed the scanning of soft tissues, such as the brain, for which X-rays are not as effective and exploratory surgery is dangerous. Without a cost-effective computing capability, MRI would remain slow and expensive.

The two illustrations show a series of MRI images of the human brain; the images below represent two-dimensional slices, while those on the facing page show a three-dimensional reconstruction. Once an image is in digital form, a physician can manipulate the image, removing outer layers, examining the image from different viewpoints, or looking at the three-dimensional structure to help in diagnosis.

The major benefits of MRI are twofold:

■ It can reduce the need for unnecessary exploratory surgery. A physician may be able to determine whether a patient ex-

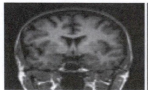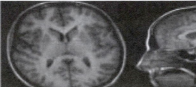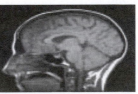

MRI images of a human brain, in two-dimensional view.

periencing headaches has a brain tumor, which requires surgery, or simply needs medication for a headache.

- By providing a surgeon with an accurate three-dimensional image, MRI can improve the surgical planning process and hence the outcome. For example, in operating on the brain to remove a tumor without accurate images of the tumor, the surgeon likely would have to enter the brain and then create a plan on the fly depending on the size and exact placement of the tumor. Furthermore, minimally invasive techniques (e.g., endoscopic surgery), which have become quite effective, would be impossible without accurate images.

There are many new interesting uses of MRI technology, which rely on faster and more cost-effective computing. Some of the most promising are as follows:

- Real-time imaging of the heart and blood vessels to enhance diagnosis of cardiac and cardiovascular disease.

- Combining real-time images and MRI images during surgery to help surgeons

accurately perform surgery, particularly when using minimally invasive techniques.

- Functional MRI (FMRI): a new type of application that uses MRI to examine brain function, primarily by analyzing blood flow in various portions of the brain. FMRI is being used for a number of applications, including exploring the physiological bases for cognitive problems such as dyslexia, pain management, planning for neurosurgery, and understanding neurological disorders.

To learn more, see these references on the ⊙ library:

MRI scans from the National Institutes of Health's Visible Human project

Principles of MRI and its application to medical imaging (long and reasonably detailed, but only a little mathematics)

Using MRI to do real-time cardiac imaging and angiography (imaging of blood vessels)

Functional MRI, *www.fmri.org/fmri.htm*

Visualization and imaging (including MRI and CT images): high-performance computing for complex images

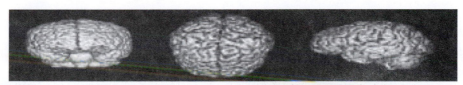

MRI images of a human brain in three dimensions.

Assemblers, Linkers, and the SPIM Simulator

James R. Larus
Microsoft Research
Microsoft

Fear of serious injury cannot alone justify suppression of free speech and assembly.

Louis Brandeis
Whitney v. California, 1927

A.1   Introduction

Encoding instructions as binary numbers is natural and efficient for computers. Humans, however, have a great deal of difficulty understanding and manipulating these numbers. People read and write symbols (words) much better than long sequences of digits. Chapter 2 showed that we need not choose between numbers and words because computer instructions can be represented in many ways. Humans can write and read symbols, and computers can execute the equivalent binary numbers. This appendix describes the process by which a human-readable program is translated into a form that a computer can execute, provides a few hints about writing assembly programs, and explains how to run these programs on SPIM, a simulator that executes MIPS programs. Unix, Windows, and Mac OS X versions of the SPIM simulator are available on the CD.

Assembly language is the symbolic representation of a computer's binary encoding—**machine language**. Assembly language is more readable than machine language because it uses symbols instead of bits. The symbols in assembly language name commonly occurring bit patterns, such as opcodes and register specifiers, so

machine language Binary representation used for communication within a computer system.

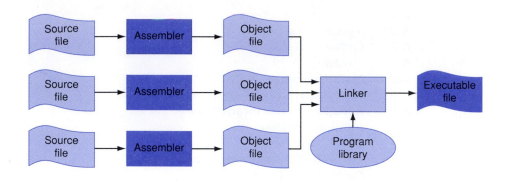

FIGURE A.1.1　The process that produces an executable file. An assembler translates a file of assembly language into an object file, which is linked with other files and libraries into an executable file.

people can read and remember them. In addition, assembly language permits programmers to use *labels* to identify and name particular memory words that hold instructions or data.

A tool called an **assembler** translates assembly language into binary instructions. Assemblers provide a friendlier representation than a computer's 0s and 1s that simplifies writing and reading programs. Symbolic names for operations and locations are one facet of this representation. Another facet is programming facilities that increase a program's clarity. For example, **macros**, discussed in Section A.2, enable a programmer to extend the assembly language by defining new operations.

An assembler reads a single assembly language *source file* and produces an *object file* containing machine instructions and bookkeeping information that helps combine several object files into a program. Figure A.1.1 illustrates how a program is built. Most programs consist of several files—also called *modules*—that are written, compiled, and assembled independently. A program may also use prewritten routines supplied in a *program library*. A module typically contains *references* to subroutines and data defined in other modules and in libraries. The code in a module cannot be executed when it contains **unresolved references** to labels in other object files or libraries. Another tool, called a **linker**, combines a collection of object and library files into an *executable file*, which a computer can run.

To see the advantage of assembly language, consider the following sequence of figures, all of which contain a short subroutine that computes and prints the sum of the squares of integers from 0 to 100. Figure A.1.2 shows the machine language that a MIPS computer executes. With considerable effort, you could use the opcode and instruction format tables in Chapter 2 to translate the instructions

assembler　A program that translates a symbolic version of instructions into the binary version.

macro　A pattern-matching and replacement facility that provides a simple mechanism to name a frequently used sequence of instructions.

unresolved reference　A reference that requires more information from an outside source in order to be complete.

linker　Also called **link editor**. A systems program that combines independently assembled machine language programs and resolves all undefined labels into an executable file.

```
00100111101111011111111111100000
10101111101111110000000000010100
10101111101001000000000000100000
10101111101001010000000000100100
10101111101000000000000000011000
10101111101000000000000000011100
10001111101011100000000000011100
10001111101110000000000000011000
00000001110011100000000000011001
00100101110010000000000000000001
00101001000000010000000001100101
10101111101010000000000000011100
00000000000000000111100000010010
00000011000011111100100000100001
00010100001000001111111111110111
10101111101110010000000000011000
00111000000010000001000000000000
10001111101001010000000000011000
00001100000100000000000011101100
00100100100010000001000011000000
10001111101111110000000000010100
00100111101111010000000000100000
00000011110000000000000000001000
00000000000000000001000000100001
```

FIGURE A.1.2   MIPS machine language code for a routine to compute and print the sum of the squares of integers between 0 and 100.

into a symbolic program similar to Figure A.1.3. This form of the routine is much easier to read because operations and operands are written with symbols, rather than with bit patterns. However, this assembly language is still difficult to follow because memory locations are named by their address, rather than by a symbolic label.

Figure A.1.4 shows assembly language that labels memory addresses with mnemonic names. Most programmers prefer to read and write this form. Names that begin with a period, for example, .data and .globl, are **assembler directives** that tell the assembler how to translate a program but do not produce machine instructions. Names followed by a colon, such as str: or main:, are labels that name the next memory location. This program is as readable as most assembly language programs (except for a glaring lack of comments), but it is still difficult to follow because many simple operations are required to accomplish simple tasks and because assembly language's lack of control flow constructs provides few hints about the program's operation.

By contrast, the C routine in Figure A.1.5 is both shorter and clearer since variables have mnemonic names and the loop is explicit rather than constructed with branches. In fact, the C routine is the only one that we wrote. The other forms of the program were produced by a C compiler and assembler.

assembler directive An operation that tells the assembler how to translate a program but does not produce machine instructions; always begins with a period.

```
addiu               $29, $29, -32
sw                  $31, 20($29)
sw                  $4,  32($29)
sw                  $5,  36($29)
sw                  $0,  24($29)
sw                  $0,  28($29)
lw                  $14, 28($29)
lw                  $24, 24($29)
multu               $14, $14
addiu               $8,  $14, 1
slti                $1,  $8, 101
sw                  $8,  28($29)
mflo                $15
addu                $25, $24, $15
bne                 $1,  $0, -9
sw                  $25, 24($29)
lui                 $4,  4096
lw                  $5,  24($29)
jal                 1048812
addiu               $4,  $4, 1072
lw                  $31, 20($29)
addiu               $29, $29, 32
jr                  $31
move                $2,  $0
```

FIGURE A.1.3 The routine from Figure A.1.2 written in assembly language. However, the code for the routine does not label registers or memory locations nor include comments.

source language The high-level language in which a program is originally written.

In general, assembly language plays two roles (see Figure A.1.6). The first role is the output language of compilers. A *compiler* translates a program written in a *high-level language* (such as C or Pascal) into an equivalent program in machine or assembly language. The high-level language is called the **source language**, and the compiler's output is its *target language.*

Assembly language's other role is as a language in which to write programs. This role used to be the dominant one. Today, however, because of larger main memories and better compilers, most programmers write in a high-level language and rarely, if ever, see the instructions that a computer executes. Nevertheless, assembly language is still important to write programs in which speed or size are critical or to exploit hardware features that have no analogues in high-level languages.

Although this appendix focuses on MIPS assembly language, assembly programming on most other machines is very similar. The additional instructions and address modes in CISC machines, such as the VAX, can make assembly programs shorter but do not change the process of assembling a program or provide assembly language with the advantages of high-level languages such as type-checking and structured control flow.

```
                    .text
                    .align      2
                    .globl      main
main:
                    subu        $sp, $sp, 32
                    sw          $ra, 20($sp)
                    sd          $a0, 32($sp)
                    sw          $0,  24($sp)
                    sw          $0,  28($sp)
loop:
                    lw          $t6, 28($sp)
                    mul         $t7, $t6, $t6
                    lw          $t8, 24($sp)
                    addu        $t9, $t8, $t7
                    sw          $t9, 24($sp)
                    addu        $t0, $t6, 1
                    sw          $t0, 28($sp)
                    ble         $t0, 100, loop
                    la          $a0, str
                    lw          $a1, 24($sp)
                    jal         printf
                    move        $v0, $0
                    lw          $ra, 20($sp)
                    addu        $sp, $sp, 32
                    jr          $ra


                    .data
                    .align      0
str:
                    .asciiz     "The sum from 0 .. 100 is %d\n"
```

FIGURE A.1.4 The same routine written in assembly language with labels, but no comments. The commands that start with periods are assembler directives (see pages A-46–A-48). .text indicates that succeeding lines contain instructions. .data indicates that they contain data. .align n indicates that the items on the succeeding lines should be aligned on a 2^n byte boundary. Hence, .align 2 means the next item should be on a word boundary. .globl main declares that main is a global symbol that should be visible to code stored in other files. Finally, .asciiz stores a null-terminated string in memory.

```
    #include <stdio.h>

int
main (int argc, char *argv[])
{
                    int i;
                    int sum = 0;

                    for (i = 0; i <= 100; i = i + 1) sum = sum + i * i;
                    printf ("The sum from 0 .. 100 is %d\n", sum);
}
```

FIGURE A.1.5 The routine written in the C programming language.

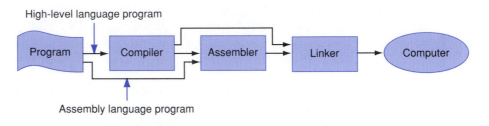

High-level language program

Assembly language program

FIGURE A.1.6   Assembly language either is written by a programmer or is the output of a compiler.

When to Use Assembly Language

The primary reason to program in assembly language, as opposed to an available high-level language, is that the speed or size of a program is critically important. For example, consider a computer that controls a piece of machinery, such as a car's brakes. A computer that is incorporated in another device, such as a car, is called an *embedded computer*. This type of computer needs to respond rapidly and predictably to events in the outside world. Because a compiler introduces uncertainty about the time cost of operations, programmers may find it difficult to ensure that a high-level language program responds within a definite time interval—say, 1 millisecond after a sensor detects that a tire is skidding. An assembly language programmer, on the other hand, has tight control over which instructions execute. In addition, in embedded applications, reducing a program's size, so that it fits in fewer memory chips, reduces the cost of the embedded computer.

A hybrid approach, in which most of a program is written in a high-level language and time-critical sections are written in assembly language, builds on the strengths of both languages. Programs typically spend most of their time executing a small fraction of the program's source code. This observation is just the principle of locality that underlies caches (see Section 7.2 in Chapter 7).

Program profiling measures where a program spends its time and can find the time-critical parts of a program. In many cases, this portion of the program can be made faster with better data structures or algorithms. Sometimes, however, significant performance improvements only come from recoding a critical portion of a program in assembly language.

This improvement is not necessarily an indication that the high-level language's compiler has failed. Compilers typically are better than programmers at producing uniformly high-quality machine code across an entire program. Programmers, however, understand a program's algorithms and behavior at a deeper level than a compiler and can expend considerable effort and ingenuity improving small sections of the program. In particular, programmers often consider several procedures simultaneously while writing their code. Compilers typically compile each procedure in isolation and must follow strict conventions governing the use of registers at procedure boundaries. By retaining commonly used values in registers, even across procedure boundaries, programmers can make a program run faster.

Another major advantage of assembly language is the ability to exploit specialized instructions, for example, string copy or pattern-matching instructions. Compilers, in most cases, cannot determine that a program loop can be replaced by a single instruction. However, the programmer who wrote the loop can replace it easily with a single instruction.

Currently, a programmer's advantage over a compiler has become difficult to maintain as compilation techniques improve and machines' pipelines increase in complexity (Chapter 6).

The final reason to use assembly language is that no high-level language is available on a particular computer. Many older or specialized computers do not have a compiler, so a programmer's only alternative is assembly language.

Drawbacks of Assembly Language

Assembly language has many disadvantages that strongly argue against its widespread use. Perhaps its major disadvantage is that programs written in assembly language are inherently machine-specific and must be totally rewritten to run on another computer architecture. The rapid evolution of computers discussed in Chapter 1 means that architectures become obsolete. An assembly language program remains tightly bound to its original architecture, even after the computer is eclipsed by new, faster, and more cost-effective machines.

Another disadvantage is that assembly language programs are longer than the equivalent programs written in a high-level language. For example, the C program in Figure A.1.5 is 11 lines long, while the assembly program in Figure A.1.4 is 31 lines long. In more complex programs, the ratio of assembly to high-level language (its *expansion factor*) can be much larger than the factor of 3 in this example. Unfortunately, empirical studies have shown that programmers write roughly the same number of lines of code per day in assembly as in high-level languages. This means that programmers are roughly x times more productive in a high-level language, where x is the assembly language expansion factor.

To compound the problem, longer programs are more difficult to read and understand and they contain more bugs. Assembly language exacerbates the problem because of its complete lack of structure. Common programming idioms, such as *if-then* statements and loops, must be built from branches and jumps. The resulting programs are hard to read because the reader must reconstruct every higher-level construct from its pieces and each instance of a statement may be slightly different. For example, look at Figure A.1.4 and answer these questions: What type of loop is used? What are its lower and upper bounds?

Elaboration: Compilers can produce machine language directly instead of relying on an assembler. These compilers typically execute much faster than those that invoke an assembler as part of compilation. However, a compiler that generates machine language must perform many tasks that an assembler normally handles, such as resolving addresses and encoding instructions as binary numbers. The trade-off is between compilation speed and compiler simplicity.

Elaboration: Despite these considerations, some embedded applications are written in a high-level language. Many of these applications are large and complex programs that must be extremely reliable. Assembly language programs are longer and more difficult to write and read than high-level language programs. This greatly increases the cost of writing an assembly language program and makes it extremely difficult to verify the correctness of this type of program. In fact, these considerations led the Department of Defense, which pays for many complex embedded systems, to develop Ada, a new high-level language for writing embedded systems.

A.2   Assemblers

An assembler translates a file of assembly language statements into a file of binary machine instructions and binary data. The translation process has two major parts. The first step is to find memory locations with labels so the relationship between symbolic names and addresses is known when instructions are translated. The second step is to translate each assembly statement by combining the numeric equivalents of opcodes, register specifiers, and labels into a legal instruction. As shown in Figure A.1.1, the assembler produces an output file, called an *object file*, which contains the machine instructions, data, and bookkeeping information.

An object file typically cannot be executed because it references procedures or data in other files. A **label** is **external** (also called **global**) if the labeled object can be referenced from files other than the one in which it is defined. A label is **local** if the object can be used only within the file in which it is defined. In most assemblers, labels are local by default and must be explicitly declared global. Subroutines and global variables require external labels since they are referenced from many files in a program. Local labels hide names that should not be visible to other modules—for example, static functions in C, which can only be called by other functions in the same file. In addition, compiler-generated names—for

external label Also called **global label**. A label referring to an object that can be referenced from files other than the one in which it is defined.

local label A label referring to an object that can be used only within the file in which it is defined.

example, a name for the instruction at the beginning of a loop—are local so the compiler need not produce unique names in every file.

Local and Global Labels

Consider the program in Figure A.1.4 on page A-7. The subroutine has an external (global) label `main`. It also contains two local labels—`loop` and `str`—that are only visible with this assembly language file. Finally, the routine also contains an unresolved reference to an external label `printf`, which is the library routine that prints values. Which labels in Figure A.1.4 could be referenced from another file?

Only global labels are visible outside of a file, so the only label that could be referenced from another file is `main`.

EXAMPLE

ANSWER

Since the assembler processes each file in a program individually and in isolation, it only knows the addresses of local labels. The assembler depends on another tool, the linker, to combine a collection of object files and libraries into an executable file by resolving external labels. The assembler assists the linker by providing lists of labels and unresolved references.

However, even local labels present an interesting challenge to an assembler. Unlike names in most high-level languages, assembly labels may be used before they are defined. In the example, in Figure A.1.4, the label `str` is used by the `la` instruction before it is defined. The possibility of a **forward reference**, like this one, forces an assembler to translate a program in two steps: first find all labels and then produce instructions. In the example, when the assembler sees the `la` instruction, it does not know where the word labeled `str` is located or even whether `str` labels an instruction or datum.

forward reference A label that is used before it is defined.

An assembler's first pass reads each line of an assembly file and breaks it into its component pieces. These pieces, which are called *lexemes*, are individual words, numbers, and punctuation characters. For example, the line

```
ble     $t0, 100, loop
```

contains 6 lexemes: the opcode `ble`, the register specifier `$t0`, a comma, the number `100`, a comma, and the symbol `loop`.

If a line begins with a label, the assembler records in its **symbol table** the name of the label and the address of the memory word that the instruction occupies. The assembler then calculates how many words of memory the instruction on the current line will occupy. By keeping track of the instructions' sizes, the assembler

symbol table A table that matches names of labels to the addresses of the memory words that instructions occupy.

can determine where the next instruction goes. To compute the size of a variable-length instruction, like those on the VAX, an assembler has to examine it in detail. Fixed-length instructions, like those on MIPS, on the other hand, require only a cursory examination. The assembler performs a similar calculation to compute the space required for data statements. When the assembler reaches the end of an assembly file, the symbol table records the location of each label defined in the file.

The assembler uses the information in the symbol table during a second pass over the file, which actually produces machine code. The assembler again examines each line in the file. If the line contains an instruction, the assembler combines the binary representations of its opcode and operands (register specifiers or memory address) into a legal instruction. The process is similar to the one used in Section 2.4 in Chapter 2. Instructions and data words that reference an external symbol defined in another file cannot be completely assembled (they are unresolved) since the symbol's address is not in the symbol table. An assembler does not complain about unresolved references since the corresponding label is likely to be defined in another file.

The **BIG** Picture

Assembly language is a programming language. Its principal difference from high-level languages such as BASIC, Java, and C is that assembly language provides only a few simple types of data and control flow. Assembly language programs do not specify the type of value held in a variable. Instead, a programmer must apply the appropriate operations (e.g., integer or floating-point addition) to a value. In addition, in assembly language, programs must implement all control flow with *go to*s. Both factors make assembly language programming for any machine—MIPS or 8086—more difficult and error-prone than writing in a high-level language.

backpatching A method for translating from assembly language to machine instructions in which the assembler builds a (possibly incomplete) binary representation of every instruction in one pass over a program and then returns to fill in previously undefined labels.

Elaboration: If an assembler's speed is important, this two-step process can be done in one pass over the assembly file with a technique known as backpatching. In its pass over the file, the assembler builds a (possibly incomplete) binary representation of every instruction. If the instruction references a label that has not yet been defined, the assembler records the label and instruction in a table. When a label is defined, the assembler consults this table to find all instructions that contain a forward reference to the label. The assembler goes back and corrects their binary representation to incorporate the address of the label. Backpatching speeds assembly because the assembler only reads its input once. However, it requires an assembler to hold the entire binary representation of a program in memory so instructions can be backpatched. This requirement can limit the size of programs that can be assembled. The process is complicated by machines with several types of branches that span different ranges of instruction. When the assembler first sees an unresolved label in a branch instruction, it must either use the largest possible branch or risk having to go back and readjust many instructions to make room for a larger branch.

Object File Format

Assemblers produce object files. An object file on Unix contains six distinct sections (see Figure A.2.1):

- The *object file* header describes the size and position of the other pieces of the file.

- The **text segment** contains the machine language code for routines in the source file. These routines may be unexecutable because of unresolved references.

- The **data segment** contains a binary representation of the data in the source file. The data also may be incomplete because of unresolved references to labels in other files.

- The **relocation information** identifies instructions and data words that depend on **absolute addresses**. These references must change if portions of the program are moved in memory.

- The *symbol table* associates addresses with external labels in the source file and lists unresolved references.

- The *debugging information* contains a concise description of the way in which the program was compiled, so a debugger can find which instruction addresses correspond to lines in a source file and print the data structures in readable form.

The assembler produces an object file that contains a binary representation of the program and data and additional information to help link pieces of a program. This relocation information is necessary because the assembler does not know which memory locations a procedure or piece of data will occupy after it is

text segment The segment of a Unix object file that contains the machine language code for routines in the source file.

data segment The segment of a Unix object or executable file that contains a binary representation of the initialized data used by the program.

relocation information The segment of a Unix object file that identifies instructions and data words that depend on absolute addresses.

absolute address A variable's or routine's actual address in memory.

Object file header	Text segment	Data segment	Relocation information	Symbol table	Debugging information

FIGURE A.2.1   Object file. A Unix assembler produces an object file with six distinct sections.

linked with the rest of the program. Procedures and data from a file are stored in a contiguous piece of memory, but the assembler does not know where this memory will be located. The assembler also passes some symbol table entries to the linker. In particular, the assembler must record which external symbols are defined in a file and what unresolved references occur in a file.

Elaboration: For convenience, assemblers assume each file starts at the same address (for example, location 0) with the expectation that the linker will *relocate* the code and data when they are assigned locations in memory. The assembler produces *relocation information*, which contains an entry describing each instruction or data word in the file that references an absolute address. On MIPS, only the subroutine call, load, and store instructions reference absolute addresses. Instructions that use PC-relative addressing, such as branches, need not be relocated.

Additional Facilities

Assemblers provide a variety of convenience features that help make assembler programs short and easier to write, but do not fundamentally change assembly language. For example, *data layout directives* allow a programmer to describe data in a more concise and natural manner than its binary representation.

In Figure A.1.4, the directive

```
.asciiz "The sum from 0 .. 100 is %d\n"
```

stores characters from the string in memory. Contrast this line with the alternative of writing each character as its ASCII value (Figure 2.21 in Chapter 2 on page 91 describes the ASCII encoding for characters):

```
.byte 84, 104, 101, 32, 115, 117, 109, 32
.byte 102, 114, 111, 109, 32, 48, 32, 46
.byte 46, 32, 49, 48, 48, 32, 105, 115
.byte 32, 37, 100, 10, 0
```

The .asciiz directive is easier to read because it represents characters as letters, not binary numbers. An assembler can translate characters to their binary representation much faster and more accurately than a human. Data layout directives specify data in a human-readable form that the assembler translates to binary. Other layout directives are described in Section A.10 on page A-46.

EXAMPLE

String Directive

Define the sequence of bytes produced by this directive:

```
.asciiz "The quick brown fox jumps over the lazy dog"
```

ANSWER

```
.byte 84,  104, 101, 32,  113, 117, 105, 99
.byte 107, 32,  98,  114, 111, 119, 110, 32
.byte 102, 111, 120, 32,  106, 117, 109, 112
.byte 115, 32,  111, 118, 101, 114, 32,  116
.byte 104, 101, 32,  108, 97,  122, 121, 32
.byte 100, 111, 103, 0
```

Macros are a pattern-matching and replacement facility that provide a simple mechanism to name a frequently used sequence of instructions. Instead of repeatedly typing the same instructions every time they are used, a programmer invokes the macro and the assembler replaces the macro call with the corresponding sequence of instructions. Macros, like subroutines, permit a programmer to create and name a new abstraction for a common operation. Unlike subroutines, however, macros do not cause a subroutine call and return when the program runs since a macro call is replaced by the macro's body when the program is assembled. After this replacement, the resulting assembly is indistinguishable from the equivalent program written without macros.

Macros

EXAMPLE

As an example, suppose that a programmer needs to print many numbers. The library routine `printf` accepts a format string and one or more values to print as its arguments. A programmer could print the integer in register $7 with the following instructions:

```
        .data
int_str: .asciiz "%d"
        .text
        la    $a0, int_str   # Load string address
                             # into first arg
```

```
        mov    $a1, $7  # Load value into
                        # second arg
        jal    printf  # Call the printf routine
```

The .data directive tells the assembler to store the string in the program's data segment, and the .text directive tells the assembler to store the instructions in its text segment.

However, printing many numbers in this fashion is tedious and produces a verbose program that is difficult to understand. An alternative is to introduce a macro, print_int, to print an integer:

```
        .data
int_str:.asciiz "%d"
        .text
        .macro print_int($arg)
        la     $a0, int_str # Load string address into
                            # first arg
        mov    $a1, $arg    # Load macro's parameter
                            # ($arg) into second arg
        jal    printf       # Call the printf routine
        .end_macro
print_int($7)
```

formal parameter A variable that is the argument to a procedure or macro; replaced by that argument once the macro is expanded.

The macro has a **formal parameter**, $arg, that names the argument to the macro. When the macro is expanded, the argument from a call is substituted for the formal parameter throughout the macro's body. Then the assembler replaces the call with the macro's newly expanded body. In the first call on print_int, the argument is $7, so the macro expands to the code

```
la  $a0, int_str
mov $a1, $7
jal printf
```

In a second call on print_int, say, print_int($t0), the argument is $t0, so the macro expands to

```
la  $a0, int_str
mov $a1, $t0
jal printf
```

What does the call print_int($a0) expand to?

```
la  $a0, int_str
mov $a1, $a0
jal printf
```

This example illustrates a drawback of macros. A programmer who uses this macro must be aware that `print_int` uses register $a0 and so cannot correctly print the value in that register.

Hardware/ Software Interface

Some assemblers also implement *pseudoinstructions,* which are instructions provided by an assembler but not implemented in hardware. Chapter 2 contains many examples of how the MIPS assembler synthesizes pseudoinstructions and addressing modes from the spartan MIPS hardware instruction set. For example, Section 2.6 in Chapter 2 describes how the assembler synthesizes the `blt` instruction from two other instructions: `slt` and `bne`. By extending the instruction set, the MIPS assembler makes assembly language programming easier without complicating the hardware. Many pseudoinstructions could also be simulated with macros, but the MIPS assembler can generate better code for these instructions because it can use a dedicated register ($at) and is able to optimize the generated code.

Elaboration: Assemblers *conditionally assemble* pieces of code, which permits a programmer to include or exclude groups of instructions when a program is assembled. This feature is particularly useful when several versions of a program differ by a small amount. Rather than keep these programs in separate files—which greatly complicates fixing bugs in the common code—programmers typically merge the versions into a single file. Code particular to one version is conditionally assembled, so it can be excluded when other versions of the program are assembled.

If macros and conditional assembly are useful, why do assemblers for Unix systems rarely, if ever, provide them? One reason is that most programmers on these systems write programs in higher-level languages like C. Most of the assembly code is produced by compilers, which find it more convenient to repeat code rather than define macros. Another reason is that other tools on Unix—such as `cpp`, the C preprocessor, or `m4`, a general macro processor—can provide macros and conditional assembly for assembly language programs.

A.3 **Linkers**

separate compilation Splitting a program across many files, each of which can be compiled without knowledge of what is in the other files.

Separate compilation permits a program to be split into pieces that are stored in different files. Each file contains a logically related collection of subroutines and data structures that form a *module* in a larger program. A file can be compiled and assembled independently of other files, so changes to one module do not require recompiling the entire program. As we discussed above, separate compilation necessitates the additional step of linking to combine object files from separate modules and fix their unresolved references.

The tool that merges these files is the *linker* (see Figure A.3.1). It performs three tasks:

- Searches the program libraries to find library routines used by the program

- Determines the memory locations that code from each module will occupy and relocates its instructions by adjusting absolute references

- Resolves references among files

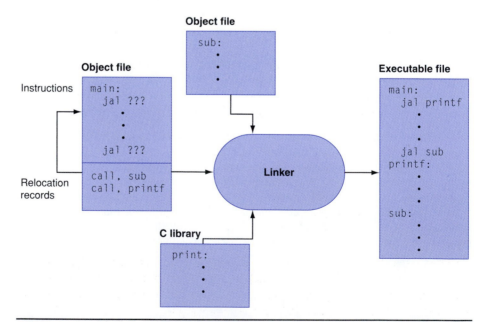

FIGURE A.3.1   The linker searches a collection of object files and program libraries to find nonlocal routines used in a program, combines them into a single executable file, and resolves references between routines in different files.

A linker's first task is to ensure that a program contains no undefined labels. The linker matches the external symbols and unresolved references from a program's files. An external symbol in one file resolves a reference from another file if both refer to a label with the same name. Unmatched references mean a symbol was used, but not defined anywhere in the program.

Unresolved references at this stage in the linking process do not necessarily mean a programmer made a mistake. The program could have referenced a library routine whose code was not in the object files passed to the linker. After matching symbols in the program, the linker searches the system's program libraries to find predefined subroutines and data structures that the program references. The basic libraries contain routines that read and write data, allocate and deallocate memory, and perform numeric operations. Other libraries contain routines to access a database or manipulate terminal windows. A program that references an unresolved symbol that is not in any library is erroneous and cannot be linked. When the program uses a library routine, the linker extracts the routine's code from the library and incorporates it into the program text segment. This new routine, in turn, may depend on other library routines, so the linker continues to fetch other library routines until no external references are unresolved or a routine cannot be found.

If all external references are resolved, the linker next determines the memory locations that each module will occupy. Since the files were assembled in isolation, the assembler could not know where a module's instructions or data will be placed relative to other modules. When the linker places a module in memory, all absolute references must be *relocated* to reflect its true location. Since the linker has relocation information that identifies all relocatable references, it can efficiently find and backpatch these references.

The linker produces an executable file that can run on a computer. Typically, this file has the same format as an object file, except that it contains no unresolved references or relocation information.

A.4 Loading

A program that links without an error can be run. Before being run, the program resides in a file on secondary storage, such as a disk. On Unix systems, the operating system kernel brings a program into memory and starts it running. To start a program, the operating system performs the following steps:

1. Reads the executable file's header to determine the size of the text and data segments.

2. Creates a new address space for the program. This address space is large enough to hold the text and data segments, along with a stack segment (see Section A.5).

3. Copies instructions and data from the executable file into the new address space.

4. Copies arguments passed to the program onto the stack.

5. Initializes the machine registers. In general, most registers are cleared, but the stack pointer must be assigned the address of the first free stack location (see Section A.5).

6. Jumps to a start-up routine that copies the program's arguments from the stack to registers and calls the program's `main` routine. If the `main` routine returns, the start-up routine terminates the program with the exit system call.

A.5   Memory Usage

The next few sections elaborate the description of the MIPS architecture presented earlier in the book. Earlier chapters focused primarily on hardware and its relationship with low-level software. These sections focus primarily on how assembly language programmers use MIPS hardware. These sections describe a set of conventions followed on many MIPS systems. For the most part, the hardware does not impose these conventions. Instead, they represent an agreement among programmers to follow the same set of rules so that software written by different people can work together and make effective use of MIPS hardware.

Systems based on MIPS processors typically divide memory into three parts (see Figure A.5.1). The first part, near the bottom of the address space (starting at address 400000_{hex}), is the *text segment*, which holds the program's instructions.

The second part, above the text segment, is the *data segment*, which is further divided into two parts. **Static data** (starting at address 10000000_{hex}) contains objects whose size is known to the compiler and whose lifetime—the interval during which a program can access them—is the program's entire execution. For example, in C, global variables are statically allocated since they can be referenced anytime during a program's execution. The linker both assigns static objects to locations in the data segment and resolves references to these objects.

static data The portion of memory that contains data whose size is known to the compiler and whose lifetime is the program's entire execution.

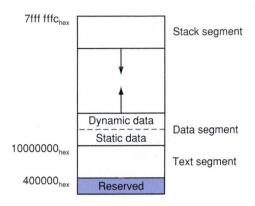

FIGURE A.5.1 Layout of memory.

Hardware/
Software
Interface Because the data segment begins far above the program at address 10000000_{hex}, load and store instructions cannot directly reference data objects with their 16-bit offset fields (see Section 2.4 in Chapter 2). For example, to load the word in the data segment at address 10010020_{hex} into register $v0 requires two instructions:

```
lui $s0, 0x1001 # 0x1001 means 1001 base 16
lw  $v0, 0x0020($s0) # 0x10010000 + 0x0020 = 0x10010020
```

(The *0x* before a number means that it is a hexadecimal value. For example, $0x8000$ is 8000_{hex} or $32,768_{ten}$.)

To avoid repeating the `lui` instruction at every load and store, MIPS systems typically dedicate a register ($gp) as a *global pointer* to the static data segment. This register contains address 10008000_{hex}, so load and store instructions can use their signed 16-bit offset fields to access the first 64 KB of the static data segment. With this global pointer, we can rewrite the example as a single instruction:

```
lw $v0, 0x8020($gp)
```

Of course, a global pointer register makes addressing locations 10000000_{hex}–10010000_{hex} faster than other heap locations. The MIPS compiler usually stores *global variables* in this area because these variables have fixed locations and fit better than other global data, such as arrays.

Immediately above static data is *dynamic data*. This data, as its name implies, is allocated by the program as it executes. In C programs, the `malloc` library routine finds and returns a new block of memory. Since a compiler cannot predict how much memory a program will allocate, the operating system expands the dynamic data area to meet demand. As the upward arrow in the figure indicates, `malloc` expands the dynamic area with the `sbrk` system call, which causes the operating system to add more pages to the program's virtual address space (see Section 7.4 in Chapter 7) immediately above the dynamic data segment.

stack segment The portion of memory used by a program to hold procedure call frames.

The third part, the program **stack segment**, resides at the top of the virtual address space (starting at address 7fffffff$_{hex}$). Like dynamic data, the maximum size of a program's stack is not known in advance. As the program pushes values on the stack, the operating system expands the stack segment down, toward the data segment.

This three-part division of memory is not the only possible one. However, it has two important characteristics: the two dynamically expandable segments are as far apart as possible, and they can grow to use a program's entire address space.

A.6   Procedure Call Convention

Conventions governing the use of registers are necessary when procedures in a program are compiled separately. To compile a particular procedure, a compiler must know which registers it may use and which registers are reserved for other procedures. Rules for using registers are called **register use** or **procedure call conventions**. As the name implies, these rules are, for the most part, conventions followed by software rather than rules enforced by hardware. However, most compilers and programmers try very hard to follow these conventions because violating them causes insidious bugs.

register use convention Also called **procedure call convention**. A software protocol governing the use of registers by procedures.

The calling convention described in this section is the one used by the gcc compiler. The native MIPS compiler uses a more complex convention that is slightly faster.

The MIPS CPU contains 32 general-purpose registers that are numbered 0–31. Register $0 always contains the hardwired value 0.

- Registers $at (1), $k0 (26), and $k1 (27) are reserved for the assembler and operating system and should not be used by user programs or compilers.

- Registers $a0–$a3 (4–7) are used to pass the first four arguments to routines (remaining arguments are passed on the stack). Registers $v0 and $v1 (2, 3) are used to return values from functions.

■ Registers $t0–$t9 (8–15, 24, 25) are **caller-saved registers** that are used to hold temporary quantities that need not be preserved across calls (see Section 2.7 in Chapter 2).

■ Registers $s0–$s7 (16–23) are **callee-saved registers** that hold long-lived values that should be preserved across calls.

■ Register $gp (28) is a global pointer that points to the middle of a 64K block of memory in the static data segment.

■ Register $sp (29) is the stack pointer, which points to the last location on the stack. Register $fp (30) is the frame pointer. The jal instruction writes register $ra (31), the return address from a procedure call. These two registers are explained in the next section.

> **caller-saved register** A register saved by the routine being called.

> **callee-saved register** A register saved by the routine making a procedure call.

The two-letter abbreviations and names for these registers—for example $sp for the stack pointer—reflect the registers' intended uses in the procedure call convention. In describing this convention, we will use the names instead of register numbers. Figure A.6.1 lists the registers and describes their intended uses.

Procedure Calls

This section describes the steps that occur when one procedure (the *caller*) invokes another procedure (the *callee*). Programmers who write in a high-level language (like C or Pascal) never see the details of how one procedure calls another because the compiler takes care of this low-level bookkeeping. However, assembly language programmers must explicitly implement every procedure call and return.

Most of the bookkeeping associated with a call is centered around a block of memory called a **procedure call frame**. This memory is used for a variety of purposes:

■ To hold values passed to a procedure as arguments

■ To save registers that a procedure may modify, but that the procedure's caller does not want changed

■ To provide space for variables local to a procedure

> **procedure call frame** A block of memory that is used to hold values passed to a procedure as arguments, to save registers that a procedure may modify but that the procedure's caller does not want changed, and to provide space for variables local to a procedure.

In most programming languages, procedure calls and returns follow a strict last-in, first-out (LIFO) order, so this memory can be allocated and deallocated on a stack, which is why these blocks of memory are sometimes called *stack frames*.

Figure A.6.2 shows a typical stack frame. The frame consists of the memory between the frame pointer ($fp), which points to the first word of the frame, and the stack pointer ($sp), which points to the last word of the frame. The stack grows down from higher memory addresses, so the frame pointer points above the stack pointer. The executing procedure uses the frame pointer to quickly

Register name	Number	Usage
$zero	0	Constant 0
$at	1	Reserved for assembler
$v0	2	Expression evaluation and results of a function
$v1	3	Expression evaluation and results of a function
$a0	4	Argument 1
$a1	5	Argument 2
$a2	6	Argument 3
$a3	7	Argument 4
$t0	8	Temporary (not preserved across call)
$t1	9	Temporary (not preserved across call)
$t2	10	Temporary (not preserved across call)
$t3	11	Temporary (not preserved across call)
$t4	12	Temporary (not preserved across call)
$t5	13	Temporary (not preserved across call)
$t6	14	Temporary (not preserved across call)
$t7	15	Temporary (not preserved across call)
$s0	16	Saved temporary (preserved across call)
$s1	17	Saved temporary (preserved across call)
$s2	18	Saved temporary (preserved across call)
$s3	19	Saved temporary (preserved across call)
$s4	20	Saved temporary (preserved across call)
$s5	21	Saved temporary (preserved across call)
$s6	22	Saved temporary (preserved across call)
$s7	23	Saved temporary (preserved across call)
$t8	24	Temporary (not preserved across call)
$t9	25	Temporary (not preserved across call)
$k0	26	Reserved for OS kernel
$k1	27	Reserved for OS kernel
$gp	28	Pointer to global area
$sp	29	Stack pointer
$fp	30	Frame pointer
$ra	31	Return address (used by function call)

FIGURE A.6.1   MIPS registers and usage convention.

access values in its stack frame. For example, an argument in the stack frame can be loaded into register $v0 with the instruction

```
lw $v0, 0($fp)
```

A stack frame may be built in many different ways; however, the caller and callee must agree on the sequence of steps. The steps below describe the calling convention used on most MIPS machines. This convention comes into play at

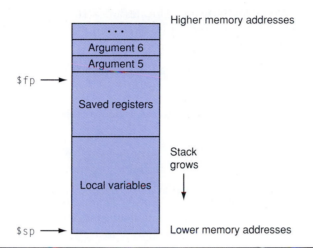

FIGURE A.6.2   Layout of a stack frame. The frame pointer ($fp) points to the first word in the currently executing procedure's stack frame. The stack pointer ($sp) points to the last word of the frame. The first four arguments are passed in registers, so the fifth argument is the first one stored on the stack.

three points during a procedure call: immediately before the caller invokes the callee, just as the callee starts executing, and immediately before the callee returns to the caller. In the first part, the caller puts the procedure call arguments in standard places and invokes the callee to do the following:

1. Pass arguments. By convention, the first four arguments are passed in registers $a0–$a3. Any remaining arguments are pushed on the stack and appear at the beginning of the called procedure's stack frame.

2. Save caller-saved registers. The called procedure can use these registers ($a0–$a3 and $t0–$t9) without first saving their value. If the caller expects to use one of these registers after a call, it must save its value before the call.

3. Execute a jal instruction (see Section 2.7 of Chapter 2), which jumps to the callee's first instruction and saves the return address in register $ra.

Before a called routine starts running, it must take the following steps to set up its stack frame:

1. Allocate memory for the frame by subtracting the frame's size from the stack pointer.

2. Save callee-saved registers in the frame. A callee must save the values in these registers ($s0–$s7, $fp, and $ra) before altering them since the caller expects to find these registers unchanged after the call. Register $fp is

saved by every procedure that allocates a new stack frame. However, register $ra only needs to be saved if the callee itself makes a call. The other callee-saved registers that are used also must be saved.

3. Establish the frame pointer by adding the stack frame's size minus four to $sp and storing the sum in register $fp.

**Hardware/
Software
Interface**

The MIPS register use convention provides callee- and caller-saved registers because both types of registers are advantageous in different circumstances. Callee-saved registers are better used to hold long-lived values, such as variables from a user's program. These registers are only saved during a procedure call if the callee expects to use the register. On the other hand, caller-saved registers are better used to hold short-lived quantities that do not persist across a call, such as immediate values in an address calculation. During a call, the callee can also use these registers for short-lived temporaries.

Finally, the callee returns to the caller by executing the following steps:

1. If the callee is a function that returns a value, place the returned value in register $v0.

2. Restore all callee-saved registers that were saved upon procedure entry.

3. Pop the stack frame by adding the frame size to $sp.

4. Return by jumping to the address in register $ra.

recursive procedures
Procedures that call themselves either directly or indirectly through a chain of calls.

Elaboration: A programming language that does not permit recursive procedures—procedures that call themselves either directly or indirectly through a chain of calls—need not allocate frames on a stack. In a nonrecursive language, each procedure's frame may be statically allocated since only one invocation of a procedure can be active at a time. Older versions of Fortran prohibited recursion because statically allocated frames produced faster code on some older machines. However, on load-store architectures like MIPS, stack frames may be just as fast because a frame pointer register points directly to the active stack frame, which permits a single load or store instruction to access values in the frame. In addition, recursion is a valuable programming technique.

Procedure Call Example

As an example, consider the C routine

```
main ()
{
    printf ("The factorial of 10 is %d\n", fact (10));
}

int fact (int n)
{
    if (n < 1)
            return (1);
    else
            return (n * fact (n - 1));
}
```

which computes and prints 10! (the factorial of 10, $10! = 10 \times 9 \times \ldots \times 1$). fact is a recursive routine that computes $n!$ by multiplying n times $(n-1)!$. The assembly code for this routine illustrates how programs manipulate stack frames.

Upon entry, the routine main creates its stack frame and saves the two callee-saved registers it will modify: $fp and $ra. The frame is larger than required for these two registers because the calling convention requires the minimum size of a stack frame to be 24 bytes. This minimum frame can hold four argument registers ($a0–$a3) and the return address $ra, padded to a doubleword boundary (24 bytes). Since main also needs to save $fp, its stack frame must be two words larger (remember: the stack pointer is kept doubleword aligned).

```
        .text
        .globl main
    main:
        subu    $sp,$sp,32      # Stack frame is 32 bytes long
        sw      $ra,20($sp)     # Save return address
        sw      $fp,16($sp)     # Save old frame pointer
        addiu   $fp,$sp,28      # Set up frame pointer
```

The routine main then calls the factorial routine and passes it the single argument 10. After fact returns, main calls the library routine printf and passes it both a format string and the result returned from fact:

```
        li      $a0,10          # Put argument (10) in $a0
        jal     fact            # Call factorial function

        la      $a0,$LC         # Put format string in $a0
        move    $a1,$v0         # Move fact result to $a1
        jal     printf          # Call the print function
```

Finally, after printing the factorial, main returns. But first, it must restore the registers it saved and pop its stack frame:

```
lw      $ra,20($sp)    # Restore return address
lw      $fp,16($sp)    # Restore frame pointer
addiu   $sp,$sp,32     # Pop stack frame
jr      $ra            # Return to caller

        .rdata
$LC:
        .ascii  "The factorial of 10 is %d\n\000"
```

The factorial routine is similar in structure to main. First, it creates a stack frame and saves the callee-saved registers it will use. In addition to saving $ra and $fp, fact also saves its argument ($a0), which it will use for the recursive call:

```
        .text
fact:
    subu    $sp,$sp,32    # Stack frame is 32 bytes long
    sw      $ra,20($sp)   # Save return address
    sw      $fp,16($sp)   # Save frame pointer
    addiu   $fp,$sp,28    # Set up frame pointer
    sw      $a0,0($fp)    # Save argument (n)
```

The heart of the fact routine performs the computation from the C program. It tests if the argument is greater than 0. If not, the routine returns the value 1. If the argument is greater than 0, the routine recursively calls itself to compute fact(n-1) and multiplies that value times *n:*

```
    lw      $v0,0($fp)    # Load n
    bgtz    $v0,$L2       # Branch if n > 0
    li      $v0,1         # Return 1
    jr      $L1           # Jump to code to return

$L2:
    lw      $v1,0($fp)    # Load n
    subu    $v0,$v1,1     # Compute n - 1
    move    $a0,$v0       # Move value to $a0
    jal     fact          # Call factorial function

    lw      $v1,0($fp)    # Load n
    mul     $v0,$v0,$v1   # Compute fact(n-1) * n
```

Finally, the factorial routine restores the callee-saved registers and returns the value in register $v0:

```
$L1:                              # Result is in $v0
    lw        $ra, 20($sp)        # Restore $ra
    lw        $fp, 16($sp)        # Restore $fp
    addiu     $sp, $sp, 32        # Pop stack
    jr        $ra                 # Return to caller
```

Stack in Recursive Procedure

Figure A.6.3 shows the stack at the call fact(7). main runs first, so its frame is deepest on the stack. main calls fact(10), whose stack frame is next on the stack. Each invocation recursively invokes fact to compute the next-lowest factorial. The stack frames parallel the LIFO order of these calls. What does the stack look like when the call to fact(10) returns?

EXAMPLE

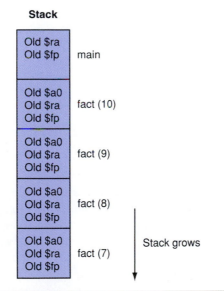

FIGURE A.6.3   Stack frames during the call of fact(7).

ANSWER

Elaboration: The difference between the MIPS compiler and the gcc compiler is that the MIPS compiler usually does not use a frame pointer, so this register is available as another callee-saved register, $s8. This change saves a couple of instructions in the procedure call and return sequence. However, it complicates code generation because a procedure must access its stack frame with $sp, whose value can change during a procedure's execution if values are pushed on the stack.

Another Procedure Call Example

As another example, consider the following routine that computes the tak function, which is a widely used benchmark created by Ikuo Takeuchi. This function does not compute anything useful, but is a heavily recursive program that illustrates the MIPS calling convention.

```
int tak (int x, int y, int z)
{
    if (y < x)
            return 1+ tak (tak (x - 1, y, z),
                            tak (y - 1, z, x),
                            tak (z - 1, x, y));
    else
            return z;
}

int main ()
{
    tak(18, 12, 6);
}
```

The assembly code for this program is shown below. The tak function first saves its return address in its stack frame and its arguments in callee-saved registers, since the routine may make calls that need to use registers $a0–$a2 and $ra. The function uses callee-saved registers since they hold values that persist over the lifetime of the function, which includes several calls that could potentially modify registers.

```
        .text
        .globl  tak

tak:
        subu    $sp, $sp, 40
        sw      $ra, 32($sp)

        sw      $s0, 16($sp)    # x
```

```
move      $s0, $a0
sw        $s1, 20($sp)    # y
move      $s1, $a1
sw        $s2, 24($sp)    # z
move      $s2, $a2
sw        $s3, 28($sp)    # temporary
```

The routine then begins execution by testing if $y < x$. If not, it branches to label L1, which is shown below.

```
bge       $s1, $s0, L1    # if (y < x)
```

If $y < x$, then it executes the body of the routine, which contains four recursive calls. The first call uses almost the same arguments as its parent:

```
addiu     $a0, $s0, -1
move      $a1, $s1
move      $a2, $s2
jal       tak             # tak (x - 1, y, z)
move      $s3, $v0
```

Note that the result from the first recursive call is saved in register $s3, so that it can be used later.

The function now prepares arguments for the second recursive call.

```
addiu     $a0, $s1, -1
move      $a1, $s2
move      $a2, $s0
jal       tak             # tak (y - 1, z, x)
```

In the instructions below, the result from this recursive call is saved in register $s0. But first we need to read, for the last time, the saved value of the first argument from this register.

```
addiu     $a0, $s2, -1
move      $a1, $s0
move      $a2, $s1
move      $s0, $v0
jal       tak             # tak (z - 1, x, y)
```

After the three inner recursive calls, we are ready for the final recursive call. After the call, the function's result is in $v0 and control jumps to the function's epilogue.

```
move      $a0, $s3
move      $a1, $s0
move      $a2, $v0
jal       tak       # tak (tak(...), tak(...), tak(...))
```

```
        addiu       $v0, $v0, 1
        j           L2
```

This code at label L1 is the consequent of the *if-then-else* statement. It just moves the value of argument z into the return register and falls into the function epilogue.

```
    L1:
        move        $v0, $s2
```

The code below is the function epilogue, which restores the saved registers and returns the function's result to its caller.

```
    L2:
        lw          $ra, 32($sp)
        lw          $s0, 16($sp)
        lw          $s1, 20($sp)
        lw          $s2, 24($sp)
        lw          $s3, 28($sp)
        addiu       $sp, $sp, 40
        jr          $ra
```

The main routine calls the tak function with its initial arguments, then takes the computed result (7) and prints it using SPIM's system call for printing integers.

```
        .globl      main
    main:
        subu        $sp, $sp, 24
        sw          $ra, 16($sp)

        li          $a0, 18
        li          $a1, 12
        li          $a2, 6
        jal         tak                 # tak(18, 12, 6)

        move        $a0, $v0
        li          $v0, 1              # print_int syscall
        syscall

        lw          $ra, 16($sp)
        addiu       $sp, $sp, 24
        jr          $ra
```

A.7   Exceptions and Interrupts

Section section 5.6 of Chapter 5 describes the MIPS exception facility, which responds both to exceptions caused by errors during an instruction's execution and to external interrupts caused by I/O devices. This section describes exception and **interrupt handling** in more detail.[1] In MIPS processors, a part of the CPU called *coprocessor 0* records the information the software needs to handle exceptions and interrupts. The MIPS simulator SPIM does not implement all of coprocessor 0's registers, since many are not useful in a simulator or are part of the memory system, which SPIM does not implement. However, SPIM does provide the following coprocessor 0 registers:

interrupt handler A piece of code that is run as a result of an exception or an interrupt.

Register name	Register number	Usage
BadVAddr	8	Memory address at which memory reference occurred
Count	9	Timer
Compare	11	Value compared against timer that causes interrupt when they match
Status	12	Interrupt mask and enable bits
Cause	13	Exception type and pending interrupt bits
EPC	14	Address of instruction that caused exception
Config	16	Configuration of machine

These seven registers are part of coprocessor 0's register set. They are accessed by the `mfc0 mtc0` instructions. After an exception, register EPC contains the address of the instruction that was executing when the exception occurred. If the exception was caused by an external interrupt, then the instruction will not have started executing. All other exceptions are caused by the execution of the instruction at EPC, except when the offending instruction is in the delay slot of a branch or jump. In that case, EPC points to the branch or jump instruction and the BD bit is set in the Cause register. When that bit is set, the exception handler must look at EPC + 4 for the offending instruction. However, in either case, an exception handler properly resumes the program by returning to the instruction at EPC.

---

1. This section discusses exceptions in the MIPS-32 architecture, which is what SPIM implements in version 7.0 and later. Earlier versions of SPIM implemented the MIPS-1 architecture, which handled exceptions slightly differently. Converting programs from these versions to run on MIP-32 should not be difficult, as the changes are limited to the Status and Cause register fields and the replacement of the `rfe` instruction by the `eret` instruction.

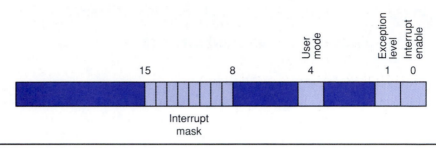

FIGURE A.7.1   The Status register.

If the instruction that caused the exception made a memory access, register BadVAddr contains the referenced memory location's address.

The Count register is a timer that increments at a fixed rated (by default, every 10 milliseconds) while SPIM is running. When the value in the Count register equals the value in the Compare register, a hardware interrupt at priority level 5 occurs.

Figure A.7.1 shows the subset of the Status register fields implemented by the MIPS simulator SPIM. The interrupt mask field contains a bit for each of the six hardware and two software interrupt levels. A mask bit that is 1 allows interrupts at that level to interrupt the processor. A mask bit that is 0 disables interrupts at that level. When an interrupt arrives, it sets its interrupt pending bit in the Cause register, even if the mask bit is disabled. When an interrupt is pending, it will interrupt the processor when its mask bit is subsequenntly enabled.

The user mode bit is 0 if the processor is running in kernel mode and 1 if it is running in user mode. On SPIM, this bit is fixed at 1, since the SPIM processor does not implement kernel mode. The exception level bit is normally 0, but is set to 1 after an exception occurs. When this bit is 1, interrups are disabled and the EPC is not updated if another exception occurs. This bit prevents an exception handler from being disturbed by an interrupt or exception, but it should be reset when the handler finishes. If the interrupt enable bit is 1, interrupts are allowed. If it is 0, they are disabled.

Figure A.7.2 shows the subset of Cause register fields that SPIM implements. The branch delay bit is 1 if the last exception occurred in an instruction executed in the delay slot of a branch. The interrupt pending bits become 1 when an interrupt is raised at a given hardware or software level. The exception code register describes the cause of an exception through the following codes:

Number	Name	Description
0	Int	Interrupt (hardware)
4	AdEL	Address error exception (load or instruction fetch)
5	AdES	Address error exception (store)
6	IBE	Bus error on instruction fetch
7	DBE	Bus error on data load or store
8	Sys	Syscall exception
9	Bp	Breakpoint exception
10	RI	Reserved instruction exception
11	CpU	Coprocessor unimplemented
12	Ov	Arithmetic overflow exception
13	Tr	Trap
15	FPE	Floating point

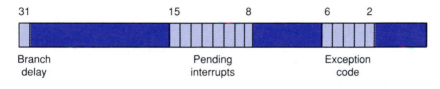

FIGURE A.7.2   The Cause register.

Exceptions and interrupts cause a MIPS processor to jump to a piece of code, at address 80000080_{hex} (in the kernel, not user address space), called an *exception handler*. This code examines the exception's cause and jumps to an appropriate point in the operating system. The operating system responds to an exception either by terminating the process that caused the exception or by performing some action. A process that causes an error, such as executing an unimplemented instruction, is killed by the operating system. On the other hand, other exceptions such as page faults are requests from a process to the operating system to perform a service, such as bringing in a page from disk. The operating system processes these requests and resumes the process. The final type of exceptions are interrupts from external devices. These generally cause the operating system to move data to or from an I/O device and resume the interrupted process.

The code in the example below is a simple exception handler, which invokes a routine to print a message at each exception (but not interrupts). This code is similar to the exception handler (exceptions.s) used by the SPIM simulator.

EXAMPLE

Exception Handler

The exception handler first saves register $a1, which is used in pseudoinstructions in the handler code, then saves $a0 and $a1, which it later uses to pass arguments. The exception handler cannot store the old values from these registers on the stack, as would an ordinary routine, because the cause of the exception might have been a memory reference that used a bad value (such as 0) in the stack pointer. Instead, the exception handler stores these registers in an exception handler register ($k1, since it can't access memory without using $at) and two memory locations (save0 and save1). If the exception routine itself could be interrupted, two locations would not be enough since the second exception would overwrite values saved during the first exception. However, this simple exception handler finishes running before it enables interrupts, so the problem does not arise.

```
.ktext 0x80000080
mov $k1, $at    # Save $at register
sw  $a0, save0  # Handler is not re-entrant and can't use
sw  $a1, save1  # stack to save $a0, $a1
                # Don't need to save $k0/$k1
```

The exception handler then moves the Cause and EPC registers into CPU registers. The Cause and EPC registers are not part of the CPU register set. Instead, they are registers in coprocessor 0, which is the part of the CPU that handles exceptions. The instruction mfc0 $k0, $13 moves coprocessor 0's register 13 (the Cause register) into CPU register $k0. Note that the exception handler need not save registers $k0 and $k1 because user programs are not supposed to use these registers. The exception handler uses the value from the Cause register to test if the exception was caused by an interrupt (see the preceding table). If so, the exception is ignored. If the exception was not an interrupt, the handler calls print_excp to print a warning message.

```
mfc0    $k0, $13        # Move Cause into $k0

srl     $a0, $k0, 2     # Extract ExcCode field
andi    $a0, $a0, 0xf

bgtz    $a0, done       # Branch if ExcCode is Int (0)

mov     $a0, $k0        # Move Cause into $a0
mfco    $a1, $14        # Move EPC into $a1
jal     print_excp      # Print exception error message
```

Before returning, the exception handler clears the Cause register; resets the Status register to enable interrupts and clear the EXL bit, which allows subsequent exceptions to change the EPC register; and restores registers $a0, $a1, and $at. It then executes the eret (exception return) instruction, which returns to the instruction pointed to by EPC. This exception handler returns to the instruction following the one that caused the exception, so as to not reexecute the faulting instruction and cause the same exception again.

```
done:   mfc0    $k0, $14        # Bump EPC
        addiu   $k0, $k0, 4     # Do not reexecute
                                # faulting instruction
        mtc0    $k0, $14        # EPC

        mtc0    $0, $13         # Clear Cause register

        mfc0    $k0, $12        # Fix Status register
        andi    $k0, 0xfffd     # Clear EXL bit
        or i    $k0, 0x1        # Enable interrupts
        mtc0    $k0, $12
        lw      $a0, save       # Restore registers
        lw      $a1, save1
        mov     $at, $k1

        eret                    # Return to EPC

        .kdata
save0:  .word 0
save1:  .word 0
```

Elaboration: On real MIPS processors, the return from an exception handler is more complex. The exception handler cannot always jump to the instruction following EPC. For example, if the instruction that caused the exception was in a branch instruction's delay slot (see Chapter 6), the next instruction may not be the following instruction in memory.

A.8   Input and Output

SPIM simulates one I/O device: a memory-mapped console on which a program can read and write characters. When a program is running, SPIM connects its own terminal (or a separate console window in the X-window version xspim or the Windows version PCSpim) to the processor. A MIPS program running on

SPIM can read the characters that you type. In addition, if the MIPS program writes characters to the terminal, they appear on SPIM's terminal or console window. One exception to this rule is control-C: this character is not passed to the program, but instead causes SPIM to stop and return to command mode. When the program stops running (for example, because you typed control-C or because the program hit a breakpoint), the terminal is reconnected to SPIM so you can type SPIM commands.

To use memory-mapped I/O (see below), `spim` or `xspim` must be started with the `-mapped_io` flag. `PCSpim` can enable memory-mapped I/O through a command line flag or the "Settings" dialog.

The terminal device consists of two independent units: a *receiver* and a *transmitter*. The receiver reads characters from the keyboard. The transmitter displays characters on the console. The two units are completely independent. This means, for example, that characters typed at the keyboard are not automatically echoed on the display. Instead, a program echoes a character by reading it from the receiver and writing it to the transmitter.

A program controls the terminal with four memory-mapped device registers, as shown in Figure A.8.1. "Memory-mapped" means that each register appears as

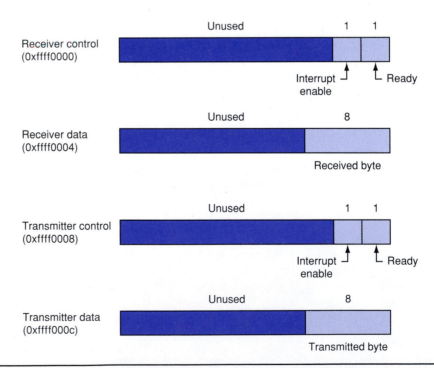

FIGURE A.8.1 The terminal is controlled by four device registers, each of which appears as a memory location at the given address. Only a few bits of these registers are actually used. The others always read as 0s and are ignored on writes.

a special memory location. The *Receiver Control register* is at location ffff0000$_{hex}$. Only two of its bits are actually used. Bit 0 is called "ready": if it is 1, it means that a character has arrived from the keyboard but has not yet been read from the Receiver Data register. The ready bit is read-only: writes to it are ignored. The ready bit changes from 0 to 1 when a character is typed at the keyboard, and it changes from 1 to 0 when the character is read from the Receiver Data register.

Bit 1 of the Receiver Control register is the keyboard "interrupt enable." This bit may be both read and written by a program. The interrupt enable is initially 0. If it is set to 1 by a program, the terminal requests an interrupt at hardware level 1 whenever a character is typed and the ready bit becomes 1. However, for the interrupt to affect the processor, interrupts must also be enabled in the Status register (see Section A.7). All other bits of the Receiver Control register are unused.

The second terminal device register is the *Receiver Data register* (at address ffff0004$_{hex}$). The low-order 8 bits of this register contain the last character typed at the keyboard. All other bits contain 0s. This register is read-only and changes only when a new character is typed at the keyboard. Reading the Receiver Data register resets the ready bit in the Receiver Control register to 0. The value in this register is undefined if the Receiver Control register is 0.

The third terminal device register is the *Transmitter Control register* (at address ffff0008$_{hex}$). Only the low-order 2 bits of this register are used. They behave much like the corresponding bits of the Receiver Control register. Bit 0 is called "ready" and is read-only. If this bit is 1, the transmitter is ready to accept a new character for output. If it is 0, the transmitter is still busy writing the previous character. Bit 1 is "interrupt enable" and is readable and writable. If this bit is set to 1, then the terminal requests an interrupt at hardware level 0 whenever the transmitter is ready for a new character and the ready bit becomes 1.

The final device register is the *Transmitter Data register* (at address ffff000c$_{hex}$). When a value is written into this location, its low-order 8 bits (i.e., an ASCII character as in Figure 2.21 in Chapter 2) are sent to the console. When the Transmitter Data register is written, the ready bit in the Transmitter Control register is reset to 0. This bit stays 0 until enough time has elapsed to transmit the character to the terminal; then the ready bit becomes 1 again. The Transmitter Data register should only be written when the ready bit of the Transmitter Control register is 1. If the transmitter is not ready, writes to the Transmitter Data register are ignored (the write appears to succeed but the character is not output).

Real computers require time to send characters to a console or terminal. These time lags are simulated by SPIM. For example, after the transmitter starts to write a character, the transmitter's ready bit becomes 0 for a while. SPIM measures time in instructions executed, not in real clock time. This means that the transmitter does not become ready again until the processor executes a certain number of instructions. If you stop the machine and look at the ready bit, it will not change. However, if you let the machine run, the bit eventually changes back to 1.

A.9   SPIM

SPIM is a software simulator that runs assembly language programs written for processors that implement the MIPS-32 architecture, specifically Release 1 of this architecture with a fixed memory mapping, no caches, and only coprocessors 0 and 1.[2] SPIM's name is just MIPS spelled backwards. SPIM can read and immediately execute assembly language files. SPIM is a self-contained system for running MIPS programs. It contains a debugger and provides a few operating system-like services. SPIM is much slower than a real computer (100 or more times). However, its low cost and wide availability cannot be matched by real hardware!

An obvious question is, Why use a simulator when most people have PCs that contain processors that run significantly faster than SPIM? One reason is that the processor in PCs are Intel 8086s, whose architecture is far less regular and far more complex to understand and program than MIPS processors. The MIPS architecture may be the epitome of a simple, clean RISC machine.

In addition, simulators can provide a better environment for assembly programming than an actual machine because they can detect more errors and provide more features than an actual computer.

Finally, simulators are a useful tool in studying computers and the programs that run on them. Because they are implemented in software, not silicon, simulators can be examined and easily modified to add new instructions, build new systems such as multiprocessors, or simply collect data.

Simulation of a Virtual Machine

The basic MIPS architecture is difficult to program directly because of delayed branches, delayed loads, and restricted address modes. This difficulty is tolerable since these computers were designed to be programmed in high-level languages and present an interface appropriate for compilers rather than assembly language programmers. A good part of the programming complexity results from delayed instructions. A *delayed branch* requires two cycles to execute (see the first elaboration on pages 382 and 423 of Chapter 6). In the second cycle, the instruction immediately following the branch executes. This instruction can perform useful work that normally would have been done before the branch. It can also be a nop (no operation) that does nothing. Similarly, *delayed loads* require 2 cycles to bring

---

2. Earlier versions of SPIM (before 7.0) implemented the MIPS-1 architecture used in the original MIPS R2000 processors. This architecture is almost a proper subset of the MIPS-32 architecture, with the difference being the manner in which exceptions are handled. MIPS-32 also introduced approximately 60 new instructions, which are supported by SPIM. Programs that ran on the earlier versions of SPIM and did not use exceptions should run unmodified on newer versions of SPIM. Programs that used exceptions will require minor changes.

a value from memory, so the instruction immediately following a load cannot use the value (see Section 6.2 of Chapter 6).

MIPS wisely chose to hide this complexity by having its assembler implement a **virtual machine.** This virtual computer appears to have nondelayed branches and loads and a richer instruction set than the actual hardware. The assembler *reorganizes* (rearranges) instructions to fill the delay slots. The virtual computer also provides *pseudoinstructions*, which appear as real instructions in assembly language programs. The hardware, however, knows nothing about pseudoinstructions, so the assembler must translate them into equivalent sequences of actual, machine instructions. For example, the MIPS hardware only provides instructions to branch when a register is equal to or not equal to 0. Other conditional branches, such as one that branches when one register is greater than another, are synthesized by comparing the two registers and branching when the result of the comparison is true (nonzero).

By default, SPIM simulates the richer virtual machine, since this is the machine that most programmers will find useful. However, SPIM can also simulate the delayed branches and loads in the actual hardware. Below, we describe the virtual machine and only mention in passing features that do not belong to the actual hardware. In doing so, we follow the convention of MIPS assembly language programmers (and compilers), who routinely use the extended machine as if it were implemented in silicon.

virtual machine A virtual computer that appears to have nondelayed branches and loads and a richer instruction set than the actual hardware.

Getting Started with SPIM

The rest of this appendix introduces SPIM and the MIPS R2000 assembly language. Many details should never concern you; however, the sheer volume of information can sometimes obscure the fact that SPIM is a simple, easy-to-use program. This section contains a quick tutorial on using SPIM, which should enable you to load, debug, and run simple MIPS programs.

SPIM comes in different versions for different types of computer systems. The one constant is the simplest version, called spim, is a command line–driven program that runs in a console window. It operates like most programs of this type: you type a line of text, hit the return key, and spim executes your command. Despite its lack of a fancy interface, spim can do everything that its fancy cousins can do.

There are two fancy cousins to spim. The version that runs in the X-windows environment of a Unix or Linus system is called xspim. xspim is an easier program to learn and use than spim because its commands are always visible on the screen and because it continually displays the machine's registers and memory. The other fancy version is called PCspim and runs on Microsoft Windows. The Unix and Windows versions of **SPIM** ⊙ are on the CD (click on Tutorials). Tutorials on xspim, pcSpim, spim, and **spim command line options** ⊙ are on the CD (click on Software).

If you are going to run SPIM on a PC running Microsoft Windows, you should first look at the tutorial on **PCSpim** ⊙ on the CD. If you are going to run SPIM on a computer running Unix or Linus, you should read the tutorial on **xspim** ⊙ (click on Tutorials).

Surprising Features

Although SPIM faithfully simulates the MIPS computer, SPIM is a simulator and certain things are not identical to an actual computer. The most obvious differences are that instruction timing and the memory systems are not identical. SPIM does not simulate caches or memory latency, nor does it accurately reflect floating-point operation or multiply and divide instruction delays. In addition, the floating-point instructions do not detect many error conditions, which would cause exceptions on a real machine.

Another surprise (which occurs on the real machine as well) is that a pseudoinstruction expands to several machine instructions. When you single-step or examine memory, the instructions that you see are different from the source program. The correspondence between the two sets of instructions is fairly simple since SPIM does not reorganize instructions to fill delay slots.

Byte Order

Processors can number bytes within a word so the byte with the lowest number is either the leftmost or rightmost one. The convention used by a machine is called its *byte order*. MIPS processors can operate with either *big-endian* or *little-endian* byte order. For example, in a big-endian machine, the directive .byte 0, 1, 2, 3 would result in a memory word containing

Byte #			
0	1	2	3

while in a little-endian machine, the word would contain

Byte #			
3	2	1	0

SPIM operates with both byte orders. SPIM's byte order is the same as the byte order of the underlying machine that runs the simulator. For example, on an Intel 8086, SPIM is little endian, while on a Macintosh or Sun SPARC, SPIM is big endian.

System Calls

SPIM provides a small set of operating-system-like services through the system call (`syscall`) instruction. To request a service, a program loads the system call code (see Figure A.9.1) into register $v0 and arguments into registers $a0–$a3 (or $f12 for floating-point values). System calls that return values put their results in register $v0 (or $f0 for floating-point results). For example, the following code prints "the answer = 5":

```
        .data
    str:
        .asciiz  "the answer = "
        .text
        li      $v0, 4      # system call code for print_str
        la      $a0, str    # address of string to print
        syscall             # print the string

        li      $v0, 1      # system call code for print_int
        li      $a0, 5      # integer to print
        syscall             # print it
```

Service	System call code	Arguments	Result
print_int	1	$a0 = integer	
print_float	2	$f12 = float	
print_double	3	$f12 = double	
print_string	4	$a0 = string	
read_int	5		integer (in $v0)
read_float	6		float (in $f0)
read_double	7		double (in $f0)
read_string	8	$a0 = buffer, $a1 = length	
sbrk	9	$a0 = amount	address (in $v0)
exit	10		
print_char	11	$a0 = char	
read_char	12		char (in $v0)
open	13	$a0 = filename (string), $a1 = flags, $a2 = mode	file descriptor (in $a0)
read	14	$a0 = file descriptor, $a1 = buffer, $a2 = length	num chars read (in $a0)
write	15	$a0 = file descriptor, $a1 = buffer, $a2 = length	num chars read (in $a0)
close	16	$a0 = file descriptor	
exit2	17	$a0 = result	

FIGURE A.9.1 System services.

The print_int system call is passed an integer and prints it on the console. print_float prints a single floating-point number; print_double prints a double precision number; and print_string is passed a pointer to a null-terminated string, which it writes to the console.

The system calls read_int, read_float, and read_double read an entire line of input up to and including the newline. Characters following the number are ignored. read_string has the same semantics as the Unix library routine fgets. It reads up to $n - 1$ characters into a buffer and terminates the string with a null byte. If fewer than $n - 1$ characters are on the current line, read_string reads up to and including the newline and again null-terminates the string. *Warning:* Programs that use these syscalls to read from the terminal should not use memory-mapped I/O (see Section A.8).

sbrk returns a pointer to a block of memory containing n additional bytes. exit stops the program SPIM from running. exit2 terminates the SPIM program, and the argument to exit2 becomes the value returned when the SPIM simulator itself terminates.

print_char and read_char write and read a single character. open, read, write, and close are the standard Unix library calls.

A.10   MIPS R2000 Assembly Language

A MIPS processor consists of an integer processing unit (the CPU) and a collection of coprocessors that perform ancillary tasks or operate on other types of data such as floating-point numbers (see Figure A.10.1). SPIM simulates two coprocessors. Coprocessor 0 handles exceptions, interrupts. Coprocessor 1 is the floating-point unit. SPIM simulates most aspects of this unit.

Addressing Modes

MIPS is a load-store architecture, which means that only load and store instructions access memory. Computation instructions operate only on values in registers. The bare machine provides only one memory-addressing mode: c(rx), which uses the sum of the immediate c and register rx as the address. The virtual machine provides the following addressing modes for load and store instructions:

Format	Address computation
(register)	Contents of register
imm	Immediate
imm (register)	Immediate + contents of register
label	Address of label
label ± imm	Address of label + or – immediate
label ± imm (register)	Address of label + or – (immediate + contents of register)

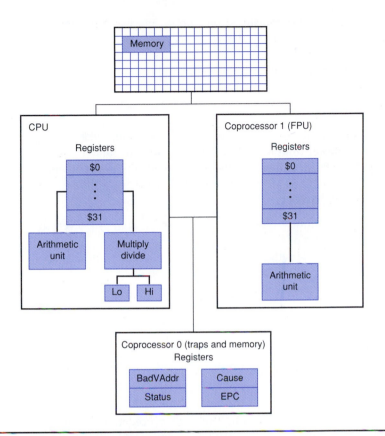

FIGURE A.10.1   MIPS R2000 CPU and FPU.

Most load and store instructions operate only on aligned data. A quantity is *aligned* if its memory address is a multiple of its size in bytes. Therefore, a half-word object must be stored at even addresses and a full word object must be stored at addresses that are a multiple of four. However, MIPS provides some instructions to manipulate unaligned data (lwl, lwr, swl, and swr).

Elaboration: The MIPS assembler (and SPIM) synthesizes the more complex addressing modes by producing one or more instructions before the load or store to compute a complex address. For example, suppose that the label table referred to memory location 0x10000004 and a program contained the instruction

```
ld $a0, table + 4($a1)
```

The assembler would translate this instruction into the instructions

```
lui $at, 4096
addu $at, $at, $a1
lw $a0, 8($at)
```

The first instruction loads the upper bits of the label's address into register $at, which the register that the assemble reserves for its own use. The second instruction adds the contents of register $a1 to the label's partial address. Finally, the load instruction uses the hardware address mode to add the sum of the lower bits of the label's address and the offset from the original instruction to the value in register $at.

Assembler Syntax

Comments in assembler files begin with a sharp sign (#). Everything from the sharp sign to the end of the line is ignored.

Identifiers are a sequence of alphanumeric characters, underbars (_), and dots (.) that do not begin with a number. Instruction opcodes are reserved words that *cannot* be used as identifiers. Labels are declared by putting them at the beginning of a line followed by a colon, for example:

```
        .data
item:   .word 1
        .text
        .globl main        # Must be global
main:   lw    $t0, item
```

Numbers are base 10 by default. If they are preceded by *0x*, they are interpreted as hexadecimal. Hence, 256 and 0x100 denote the same value.

Strings are enclosed in double quotes ("). Special characters in strings follow the C convention:

- newline   \n

- tab   \t

- quote   \"

SPIM supports a subset of the MIPS assembler directives:

.align n   Align the next datum on a 2^n byte boundary. For example, .align 2 aligns the next value on a word boundary. .align 0 turns off automatic alignment of .half, .word, .float, and .double directives until the next .data or .kdata directive.

.ascii str   Store the string *str* in memory, but do not null-terminate it.

`.asciiz str`	Store the string *str* in memory and null-terminate it.
`.byte b1,..., bn`	Store the *n* values in successive bytes of memory.
`.data <addr>`	Subsequent items are stored in the data segment. If the optional argument *addr* is present, subsequent items are stored starting at address *addr*.
`.double d1,..., dn`	Store the *n* floating-point double precision numbers in successive memory locations.
`.extern sym size`	Declare that the datum stored at *sym* is *size* bytes large and is a global label. This directive enables the assembler to store the datum in a portion of the data segment that is efficiently accessed via register $gp.
`.float f1,..., fn`	Store the *n* floating-point single precision numbers in successive memory locations.
`.globl sym`	Declare that label *sym* is global and can be referenced from other files.
`.half h1,..., hn`	Store the *n* 16-bit quantities in successive memory halfwords.
`.kdata <addr>`	Subsequent data items are stored in the kernel data segment. If the optional argument *addr* is present, subsequent items are stored starting at address *addr*.
`.ktext <addr>`	Subsequent items are put in the kernel text segment. In SPIM, these items may only be instructions or words (see the `.word` directive below). If the optional argument *addr* is present, subsequent items are stored starting at address *addr*.
`.set noat` and `.set at`	The first directive prevents SPIM from complaining about subsequent instructions that use register $at. The second directive reenables the warning. Since pseudoinstructions expand into code that uses register $at, programmers must be very careful about leaving values in this register.
`.space n`	Allocate *n* bytes of space in the current segment (which must be the data segment in SPIM).

`.text <addr>`	Subsequent items are put in the user text segment. In SPIM, these items may only be instructions or words (see the `.word` directive below). If the optional argument *addr* is present, subsequent items are stored starting at address *addr*.
`.word w1,..., wn`	Store the *n* 32-bit quantities in successive memory words.

SPIM does not distinguish various parts of the data segment (`.data`, `.rdata`, and `.sdata`).

Encoding MIPS Instructions

Figure A.10.2 explains how a MIPS instruction is encoded in a binary number. Each column contains instruction encodings for a field (a contiguous group of bits) from an instruction. The numbers at the left margin are values for a field. For example, the `j` opcode has a value of 2 in the opcode field. The text at the top of a column names a field and specifies which bits it occupies in an instruction. For example, the `op` field is contained in bits 26–31 of an instruction. This field encodes most instructions. However, some groups of instructions use additional fields to distinguish related instructions. For example, the different floating-point instructions are specified by bits 0–5. The arrows from the first column show which opcodes use these additional fields.

Instruction Format

The rest of this appendix describes both the instructions implemented by actual MIPS hardware and the pseudoinstructions provided by the MIPS assembler. The two types of instructions are easily distinguished. Actual instructions depict the fields in their binary representation. For example, in

Addition (with overflow)

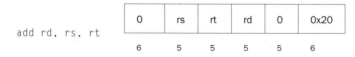

the `add` instruction consists of six fields. Each field's size in bits is the small number below the field. This instruction begins with 6 bits of 0s. Register specifiers begin with an *r*, so the next field is a 5-bit register specifier called `rs`. This is the same register that is the second argument in the symbolic assembly at the left of this line. Another common field is imm_{16}, which is a 16-bit immediate number.

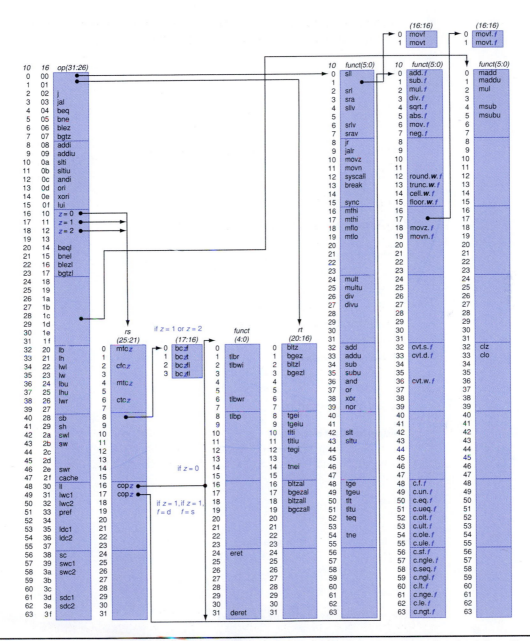

FIGURE A.10.2 MIPS opcode map. The values of each field are shown to its left. The first column shows the values in base 10 and the second shows base 16 for the op field (bits 31 to 26) in the third column. This op field completely specifies the MIPS operation except for 6 op values: 0, 1, 16, 17, 18, and 19. These operations are determined by other fields, identified by pointers. The last field (funct) uses "*f*" to mean "s" if rs = 16 and op = 17 or "d" if rs = 17 and op = 17. The second field (rs) uses "*z*" to mean "0","1","2", or "3" if op = 16, 17, 18, or 19, respectively. If rs = 16, the operation is specified elsewhere: if *z* = 0, the operations are specified in the fourth field (bits 4 to 0); if *z* = 1, then the operations are in the last field with *f* = s. If rs = 17 and *z* = 1, then the operations are in the last field with *f* = d.

Pseudoinstructions follow roughly the same conventions, but omit instruction encoding information. For example:

Multiply (without overflow)

```
mul rdest, rsrc1, src2      pseudoinstruction
```

In pseudoinstructions, `rdest` and `rsrc1` are registers and `src2` is either a register or an immediate value. In general, the assembler and SPIM translate a more general form of an instruction (e.g., `add $v1, $a0, 0x55`) to a specialized form (e.g., `addi $v1, $a0, 0x55`).

Arithmetic and Logical Instructions

Absolute value

```
abs rdest, rsrc      pseudoinstruction
```

Put the absolute value of register `rsrc` in register `rdest`.

Addition (with overflow)

```
add rd, rs, rt
```

0	rs	rt	rd	0	0x20
6	5	5	5	5	6

Addition (without overflow)

```
addu rd, rs, rt
```

0	rs	rt	rd	0	0x21
6	5	5	5	5	6

Put the sum of registers `rs` and `rt` into register `rd`.

Addition immediate (with overflow)

```
addi rt, rs, imm
```

8	rs	rt	imm
6	5	5	16

Addition immediate (without overflow)

```
addiu rt, rs, imm
```

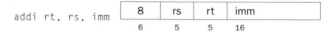

9	rs	rt	imm
6	5	5	16

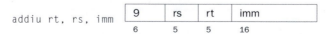

Put the sum of register `rs` and the sign-extended immediate into register `rt`.

AND

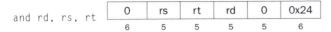

`and rd, rs, rt`

Put the logical AND of registers `rs` and `rt` into register `rd`.

AND immediate

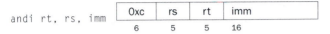

`andi rt, rs, imm`

Put the logical AND of register `rs` and the zero-extended immediate into register `rt`.

Count leading ones

`clo rd, rs`

Count leading zeros

`clz rd, rs`

Count the number of leading ones (zeros) in the word in register `rs` and put the result into register `rd`. If a word is all ones (zeros), the result is 32.

Divide (with overflow)

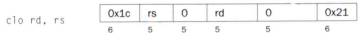

`div rs, rt`

Divide (without overflow)

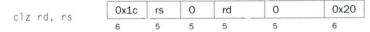

`divu rs, rt`

Divide register `rs` by register `rt`. Leave the quotient in register `lo` and the remainder in register `hi`. Note that if an operand is negative, the remainder is unspecified by the MIPS architecture and depends on the convention of the machine on which SPIM is run.

Divide (with overflow)

`div rdest, rsrc1, src2`   *pseudoinstruction*

Divide (without overflow)

```
divu rdest, rsrcl, src2      pseudoinstruction
```

Put the quotient of register `rsrcl` and `src2` into register `rdest`.

Multiply

`mult rs, rt`

Multiply registers `rs` and `rt`. Leave the low-order word of the product in register `lo` and the high-order word in register `hi`.

Unsigned multiply

`multu rs, rt`

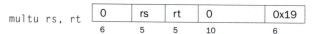

Multiply registers `rs` and `rt`. Leave the low-order word of the product in register `lo` and the high-order word in register `hi`.

Multiply (without overflow)

`mul rd, rs, rt`

0x1c	rs	rt	rd	0	2
6	5	5	5	5	6

Put the low-order 32 bits of the product `rs` and `rt` into register `rd`.

Multiply (with overflow)

```
mulo rdest, rsrcl, src2        pseudoinstruction
```

Unsigned multiply (with overflow)

```
mulou rdest, rsrcl, src2       pseudoinstruction
```

Put the low-order 32 bits of the product of register `rsrcl` and `src2` into register `rdest`.

Multiply add

`madd rs, rt`

0x1c	rs	rt	0	0
6	5	5	10	6

Unsigned multiply add

maddu rs, rt

0x1c	rs	rt	0	1
6	5	5	10	6

Multiply registers rs and rt and add the resulting 64-bit product to the 64-bit value in the concatenated registers lo and hi.

Multiply subtract

msub rs, rt

0x1c	rs	rt	0	4
6	5	5	10	6

Unsigned multiply subtract

msubu rs, rt

0x1c	rs	rt	0	5
6	5	5	10	6

Multiply registers rs and rt and subtract the resulting 64-bit product from the 64-bit value in the concatenated registers lo and hi.

Negate value (with overflow)

neg rdest, rsrc   *pseudoinstruction*

Negate value (without overflow)

negu rdest, rsrc   *pseudoinstruction*

Put the negative of register rsrc into register rdest.

NOR

nor rd, rs, rt

0	rs	rt	rd	0	0x27
6	5	5	5	5	6

Put the logical NOR of registers rs and rt into register rd.

NOT

not rdest, rsrc   *pseudoinstruction*

Put the bitwise logical negation of register rsrc into register rdest.

OR

```
or rd, rs, rt
```

0	rs	rt	rd	0	0x25
6	5	5	5	5	6

Put the logical OR of registers rs and rt into register rd.

OR immediate

```
ori rt, rs, imm
```

0xd	rs	rt	imm
6	5	5	16

Put the logical OR of register rs and the zero-extended immediate into register rt.

Remainder

```
rem rdest, rsrc1, rsrc2                 pseudoinstruction
```

Unsigned remainder

```
remu rdest, rsrc1, rsrc2                pseudoinstruction
```

Put the remainder of register rsrc1 divided by register rsrc2 into register rdest. Note that if an operand is negative, the remainder is unspecified by the MIPS architecture and depends on the convention of the machine on which SPIM is run.

Shift left logical

```
sll rd, rt, shamt
```

0	rs	rt	rd	shamt	0
6	5	5	5	5	6

Shift left logical variable

```
sllv rd, rt, rs
```

0	rs	rt	rd	0	4
6	5	5	5	5	6

Shift right arithmetic

```
sra rd, rt, shamt
```

0	rs	rt	rd	shamt	3
6	5	5	5	5	6

Shift right arithmetic variable

```
srav rd, rt, rs
```

0	rs	rt	rd	0	7
6	5	5	5	5	6

Shift right logical

```
srl rd, rt, shamt
```

0	rs	rt	rd	shamt	2
6	5	5	5	5	6

Shift right logical variable

```
srlv rd, rt, rs
```

0	rs	rt	rd	0	6
6	5	5	5	5	6

Shift register rt left (right) by the distance indicated by immediate shamt or the register rs and put the result in register rd. Note that argument rs is ignored for sll, sra, and srl.

Rotate left

```
rol rdest, rsrc1, rsrc2          pseudoinstruction
```

Rotate right

```
ror rdest, rsrc1, rsrc2          pseudoinstruction
```

Rotate register rsrc1 left (right) by the distance indicated by rsrc2 and put the result in register rdest.

Subtract (with overflow)

```
sub rd, rs, rt
```

0	rs	rt	rd	0	0x22
6	5	5	5	5	6

Subtract (without overflow)

```
subu rd, rs, rt
```

0	rs	rt	rd	0	0x23
6	5	5	5	5	6

Put the difference of registers rs and rt into register rd.

Exclusive OR

xor rd, rs, rt

0	rs	rt	rd	0	0x26
6	5	5	5	5	6

Put the logical XOR of registers rs and rt into register rd.

XOR immediate

xori rt, rs, imm

0xe	rs	rt	Imm
6	5	5	16

Put the logical XOR of register rs and the zero-extended immediate into register rt.

Constant-Manipulating Instructions

Load upper immediate

lui rt, imm

0xf	0	rt	imm
6	5	5	16

Load the lower halfword of the immediate imm into the upper halfword of register rt. The lower bits of the register are set to 0.

Load immediate

li rdest, imm   *pseudoinstruction*

Move the immediate imm into register rdest.

Comparison Instructions

Set less than

slt rd, rs, rt

0	rs	rt	rd	0	0x2a
6	5	5	5	5	6

Set less than unsigned

sltu rd, rs, rt

0	rs	rt	rd	0	0x2b
6	5	5	5	5	6

Set register rd to 1 if register rs is less than rt, and to 0 otherwise.

Set less than immediate

slti rt, rs, imm

0xa	rs	rt	imm
6	5	5	16

Set less than unsigned immediate

sltiu rt, rs, imm

0xb	rs	rt	imm
6	5	5	16

Set register rt to 1 if register rs is less than the sign-extended immediate, and to 0 otherwise.

Set equal

seq rdest, rsrc1, rsrc2   *pseudoinstruction*

Set register rdest to 1 if register rsrc1 equals rsrc2, and to 0 otherwise.

Set greater than equal

sge rdest, rsrc1, rsrc2   *pseudoinstruction*

Set greater than equal unsigned

sgeu rdest, rsrc1, rsrc2   *pseudoinstruction*

Set register rdest to 1 if register rsrc1 is greater than or equal to rsrc2, and to 0 otherwise.

Set greater than

sgt rdest, rsrc1, rsrc2   *pseudoinstruction*

Set greater than unsigned

sgtu rdest, rsrc1, rsrc2   *pseudoinstruction*

Set register rdest to 1 if register rsrc1 is greater than rsrc2, and to 0 otherwise.

Set less than equal

```
sle rdest, rsrc1, rsrc2
```
        pseudoinstruction

Set less than equal unsigned

```
sleu rdest, rsrc1, rsrc2
```
        pseudoinstruction

Set register `rdest` to 1 if register `rsrc1` is less than or equal to `rsrc2`, and to 0 otherwise.

Set not equal

```
sne rdest, rsrc1, rsrc2
```
        pseudoinstruction

Set register `rdest` to 1 if register `rsrc1` is not equal to `rsrc2`, and to 0 otherwise.

Branch Instructions

Branch instructions use a signed 16-bit instruction *offset* field; hence they can jump $2^{15} - 1$ *instructions* (not bytes) forward or 2^{15} instructions backward. The *jump* instruction contains a 26-bit address field. In actual MIPS processors, branch instructions are delayed branches, which do not transfer control until the instruction following the branch (its "delay slot") has executed (see Chapter 6). Delayed branches affect the offset calculation, since it must be computed relative to the address of the delay slot instruction (PC + 4), which is when the branch occurs. SPIM does not simulate this delay slot, unless the `-bare` or `-delayed_branch` flags are specified.

In assembly code, offsets are not usually specified as numbers. Instead, an instructions branch to a label, and the assembler computes the distance between the branch and target instructions.

In MIPS-32, all actual (not pseudo) conditional branch instructions have a "likely" variant (for example, `beq`'s likely variant is `beql`), which does *not* execute the instruction in the branch's delay slot if the branch is not taken. Do not use these instructions; they may be removed in subsequent versions of the architecture. SPIM implements these instructions, but they are not described further.

Branch instruction

```
b label
```
        pseudoinstruction

Unconditionally branch to the instruction at the label.

Branch coprocessor false

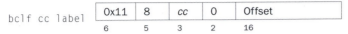

bclf cc label

Conditionally branch the number of instructions specified by the offset if the floating-point coprocessor's condition flag numbered *cc* is false (true). If *cc* is omitted from the instruction, condition code flag 0 is assumed.

Branch coprocessor true

bclt cc label

Branch on equal

4	rs	rt	Offset
6	5	5	16

beq rs, rt, label

Conditionally branch the number of instructions specified by the offset if register rs equals rt.

Branch on greater than equal zero

1	rs	1	Offset
6	5	5	16

bgez rs, label

Conditionally branch the number of instructions specified by the offset if register rs is greater than or equal to 0.

Branch on greater than equal zero and link

1	rs	0x11	Offset
6	5	5	16

bgezal rs, label

Conditionally branch the number of instructions specified by the offset if register rs is greater than or equal to 0. Save the address of the next instruction in register 31.

Branch on greater than zero

7	rs	0	Offset
6	5	5	16

bgtz rs, label

Conditionally branch the number of instructions specified by the offset if register rs is greater than 0.

Branch on less than equal zero

`blez rs, label`

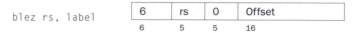

Conditionally branch the number of instructions specified by the offset if register rs is less than or equal to 0.

Branch on less than and link

`bltzal rs, label`

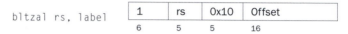

Conditionally branch the number of instructions specified by the offset if register rs is less than 0. Save the address of the next instruction in register 31.

Branch on less than zero

`bltz rs, label`

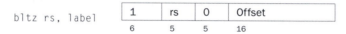

Conditionally branch the number of instructions specified by the offset if register rs is less than 0.

Branch on not equal

`bne rs, rt, label`

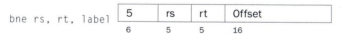

Conditionally branch the number of instructions specified by the offset if register rs is not equal to rt.

Branch on equal zero

`beqz rsrc, label`   *pseudoinstruction*

Conditionally branch to the instruction at the label if rsrc equals 0.

Branch on greater than equal

`bge rsrc1, rsrc2, label`   *pseudoinstruction*

Branch on greater than equal unsigned

```
bgeu rsrc1, rsrc2, label          pseudoinstruction
```

Conditionally branch to the instruction at the label if register rsrc1 is greater than or equal to rsrc2.

Branch on greater than

```
bgt rsrc1, src2, label            pseudoinstruction
```

Branch on greater than unsigned

```
bgtu rsrc1, src2, label           pseudoinstruction
```

Conditionally branch to the instruction at the label if register rsrc1 is greater than src2.

Branch on less than equal

```
ble rsrc1, src2, label            pseudoinstruction
```

Branch on less than equal unsigned

```
bleu rsrc1, src2, label           pseudoinstruction
```

Conditionally branch to the instruction at the label if register rsrc1 is less than or equal to src2.

Branch on less than

```
blt rsrc1, rsrc2, label           pseudoinstruction
```

Branch on less than unsigned

```
bltu rsrc1, rsrc2, label          pseudoinstruction
```

Conditionally branch to the instruction at the label if register rsrc1 is less than rsrc2.

Branch on not equal zero

```
bnez rsrc, label                        pseudoinstruction
```

Conditionally branch to the instruction at the label if register rsrc is not equal to 0.

Jump Instructions

Jump

Unconditionally jump to the instruction at target.

Jump and link

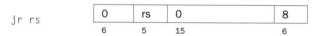

Unconditionally jump to the instruction at target. Save the address of the next instruction in register $ra.

Jump and link register

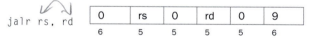

Unconditionally jump to the instruction whose address is in register rs. Save the address of the next instruction in register rd (which defaults to 31).

Jump register

Unconditionally jump to the instruction whose address is in register rs.

Trap Instructions

Trap if equal

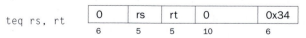

If register rs is equal to register rt, raise a Trap exception.

Trap if equal immediate

teqi rs, imm

1	rs	0xc	imm
6	5	5	16

If register rs is equal to the sign-extended value imm, raise a Trap exception.

Trap if not equal

teq rs, rt

0	rs	rt	0	0x36
6	5	5	10	6

If register rs is not equal to register rt, raise a Trap exception.

Trap if not equal immediate

teqi rs, imm

1	rs	0xe	imm
6	5	5	16

If register rs is not equal to the sign-extended value imm, raise a Trap exception.

Trap if greater equal

tge rs, rt

0	rs	rt	0	0x30
6	5	5	10	6

Unsigned trap if greater equal

tgeu rs, rt

0	rs	rt	0	0x31
6	5	5	10	6

If register rs is greater than or equal to register rt, raise a Trap exception.

Trap if greater equal immediate

tgei rs, imm

1	rs	8	imm
6	5	5	16

Unsigned trap if greater equal immediate

tgeiu rs, imm

1	rs	9	imm
6	5	5	16

If register rs is greater than or equal to the sign-extended value imm, raise a Trap exception.

Trap if less than

tlt rs, rt

0	rs	rt	0	0x32
6	5	5	10	6

Unsigned trap if less than

tltu rs, rt

0	rs	rt	0	0x33
6	5	5	10	6

If register rs is less than register rt, raise a Trap exception.

Trap if less than immediate

tlti rs, imm

1	rs	a	imm
6	5	5	16

Unsigned trap if less than immediate

tltiu rs, imm

1	rs	b	imm
6	5	5	16

If register rs is less than the sign-extended value imm, raise a Trap exception.

Load Instructions

Load address

la rdest, address   *pseudoinstruction*

Load computed *address*—not the contents of the location—into register rdest.

Load byte

lb rt, address

0x20	rs	rt	Offset
6	5	5	16

Load unsigned byte

lbu rt, address

0x24	rs	rt	Offset
6	5	5	16

Load the byte at *address* into register rt. The byte is sign-extended by lb, but not by lbu.

Load halfword

`lh rt, address`

0x21	rs	rt	Offset
6	5	5	16

Load unsigned halfword

`lhu rt, address`

0x25	rs	rt	Offset
6	5	5	16

Load the 16-bit quantity (halfword) at *address* into register `rt`. The halfword is sign-extended by `lh`, but not by `lhu`.

Load word

`lw rt, address`

0x23	rs	rt	Offset
6	5	5	16

Load the 32-bit quantity (word) at *address* into register `rt`.

Load word coprocessor 1

`lwc1 ft, address`

0x31	rs	rt	Offset
6	5	5	16

Load the word at *address* into register `ft` in the floating-point unit.

Load word left

`lwl rt, address`

0x22	rs	rt	Offset
6	5	5	16

Load word right

`lwr rt, address`

0x26	rs	rt	Offset
6	5	5	16

Load the left (right) bytes from the word at the possibly unaligned *address* into register `rt`.

Load doubleword

`ld rdest, address`   *pseudoinstruction*

Load the 64-bit quantity at *address* into registers `rdest` and `rdest + 1`.

Unaligned load halfword

```
ulh rdest, address
```
pseudoinstruction

Unaligned load halfword unsigned

```
ulhu rdest, address
```
pseudoinstruction

Load the 16-bit quantity (halfword) at the possibly unaligned *address* into register rdest. The halfword is sign-extended by ulh, but not ulhu.

Unaligned load word

```
ulw rdest, address
```
pseudoinstruction

Load the 32-bit quantity (word) at the possibly unaligned *address* into register rdest.

Load linked

`ll rt, address`

0x30	rs	rt	Offset
6	5	5	16

Store the 32-bit quantity (word) at *address* into register rt and start an atomic read-modify-write operation. This operation is completed by a store conditional (sc) instruction, which will fail if another processor writes into the block containing the loaded word. Since SPIM does not simulate multiple processors, the store conditional operation always succeeds.

Store Instructions

Store byte

`sb rt, address`

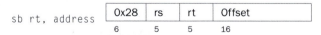

0x28	rs	rt	Offset
6	5	5	16

Store the low byte from register rt at *address*.

Store halfword

sh rt, address

0x29	rs	rt	Offset
6	5	5	16

Store the low halfword from register rt at *address.*

Store word

sw rt, address

0x2b	rs	rt	Offset
6	5	5	16

Store the word from register rt at *address.*

Store word coprocessor 1

swcl ft, address

0x31	rs	ft	Offset
6	5	5	16

Store the floating-point value in register ft of the floating-point coprocessor at *address.*

Store double coprocessor 1

sdcl ft, address

0x3d	rs	ft	Offset
6	5	5	16

Store the doubleword floating-point value in registers ft and ft + 1 of the floating-point coprocessor at *address.* Register ft must be even numbered.

Store word left

swl rt, address

0x2a	rs	rt	Offset
6	5	5	16

Store word right

swr rt, address

0x2e	rs	rt	Offset
6	5	5	16

Store the left (right) bytes from register rt at the possibly unaligned *address.*

Store doubleword

```
sd rsrc, address
```
                                              pseudoinstruction

Store the 64-bit quantity in registers `rsrc` and `rsrc + 1` at *address*.

Unaligned store halfword

```
ush rsrc, address
```
                                              pseudoinstruction

Store the low halfword from register `rsrc` at the possibly unaligned *address*.

Unaligned store word

```
usw rsrc, address
```
                                              pseudoinstruction

Store the word from register `rsrc` at the possibly unaligned *address*.

Store conditional

```
sc rt, address
```
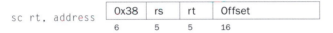

0x38	rs	rt	Offset
6	5	5	16

Store the 32-bit quantity (word) in register `rt` into memory at *address* and complete an atomic read-modify-write operation. If this atomic operation is successful, the memory word is modified and register `rt` is set to 1. If the atomic operation fails because another processor wrote to a location in the block containing the addressed word, this instruction does not modify memory and writes 0 into register `rt`. Since SPIM does not simulate multiple processors, the instruction always succeeds.

Data Movement Instructions

Move

```
move rdest, rsrc
```
                                              pseudoinstruction

Move register `rsrc` to `rdest`.

Move from hi

mfhi rd

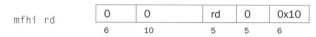

Move from lo

mflo rd

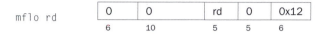

The multiply and divide unit produces its result in two additional registers, hi and lo. These instructions move values to and from these registers. The multiply, divide, and remainder pseudoinstructions that make this unit appear to operate on the general registers move the result after the computation finishes.

Move the hi (lo) register to register rd.

Move to hi

mthi rs

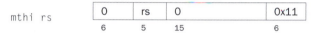

Move to lo

mtlo rs

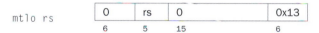

Move register rs to the hi (lo) register.

Move from coprocessor 0

mfc0 rt, rd

0x10	0	rt	rd	0
6	5	5	5	11

Move from coprocessor 1

mfc1 rt, rd

0x11	0	rt	fs	0
6	5	5	5	11

Coprocessors have their own register sets. These instructions move values between these registers and the CPU's registers.

Move register rd in a coprocessor (register fs in the FU) to CPU register rt. The floating-point unit is coprocessor 1.

Move double from coprocessor 1

```
mfc1.d rdest, frsrc1                pseudoinstruction
```

Move floating-point registers `frsrc1` and `frsrc1 + 1` to CPU registers `rdest` and `rdest + 1`.

Move to coprocessor 0

`mtc0 rd, rt`

0x10	4	rt	rd	0
6	5	5	5	11

Move to coprocessor 1

`mtc1 rd, fs`

0x11	4	rt	fs	0
6	5	5	5	11

Move CPU register `rt` to register `rd` in a coprocessor (register `fs` in the FPU).

Move conditional not zero

`movn rd, rs, rt`

0	rs	rt	rd	0xb
6	5	5	5	11

Move register `rs` to register `rd` if register `rt` is not 0.

Move conditional zero

`movz rd, rs, rt`

0	rs	rt	rd	0xa
6	5	5	5	11

Move register `rs` to register `rd` if register `rt` is 0.

Move conditional on FP false

`movf rd, rs, cc`

0	rs	cc	0	rd	0	1
6	5	3	2	5	5	6

Move CPU register `rs` to register `rd` if FPU condition code flag number *cc* is 0. If *cc* is omitted from the instruction, condition code flag 0 is assumed.

Move conditional on FP true

movt rd, rs, cc

0	rs	cc	1	rd	0	1
6	5	3	2	5	5	6

Move CPU register rs to register rd if FPU condition code flag number *cc* is 1. If *cc* is omitted from the instruction, condition code flag 0 is assumed.

Floating-Point Instructions

The MIPS has a floating-point coprocessor (numbered 1) that operates on single precision (32-bit) and double precision (64-bit) floating-point numbers. This coprocessor has its own registers, which are numbered $f0–$f31. Because these registers are only 32 bits wide, two of them are required to hold doubles, so only floating-point registers with even numbers can hold double precision values. The floating-point coprocessor also has 8 condition code (*cc*) flags, numbered 0–7, which are set by compare instructions and tested by branch (bclf or bclt) and conditional move instructions.

Values are moved in or out of these registers one word (32 bits) at a time by lwc1, swc1, mtc1, and mfc1 instructions or one double (64 bits) at a time by ldc1 and sdc1 described above, or by the l.s, l.d, s.s, and s.d pseudoinstructions described below.

In the actual instructions below, bits 21–26 are 0 for single precision and 1 for double precision. In the pseudoinstructions below, fdest is a floating-point register (e.g., $f2).

Floating-point absolute value double

abs.d fd, fs

0x11	1	0	fs	fd	5
6	5	5	5	5	6

Floating-point absolute value single

abs.s fd, fs

0x11	0	0	fs	fd	5

Compute the absolute value of the floating-point double (single) in register fs and put it in register fd.

Floating-point addition double

add.d fd, fs, ft

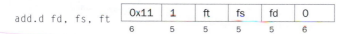

0x11	1	ft	fs	fd	0
6	5	5	5	5	6

Floating-point addition single

add.s fd, fs, ft

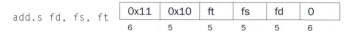

0x11	0x10	ft	fs	fd	0
6	5	5	5	5	6

Compute the sum of the floating-point doubles (singles) in registers fs and ft and put it in register fd.

Floating-point ceiling to word

ceil.w.d fd, fs

ceil.w.s fd, fs

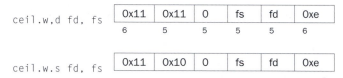

0x11	0x11	0	fs	fd	0xe
6	5	5	5	5	6

0x11	0x10	0	fs	fd	0xe

Compute the ceiling of the floating-point double (single) in register fs, convert to a 32-bit fixed-point value, and put the resulting word in register fd.

Compare equal double

c.eq.d fs, ft

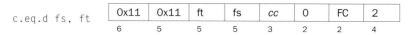

0x11	0x11	ft	fs	*cc*	0	FC	2
6	5	5	5	3	2	2	4

Compare equal single

c.eq.s cc fs, ft

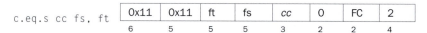

0x11	0x11	ft	fs	*cc*	0	FC	2
6	5	5	5	3	2	2	4

Compare the floating-point double in register fs against the one in ft and set the floating-point condition flag *cc* to 1 if they are equal. If *cc* is omitted, condition code flag 0 is assumed.

Compare less than equal double

c.le.d cc fs, ft

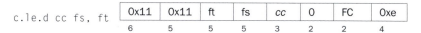

0x11	0x11	ft	fs	*cc*	0	FC	0xe
6	5	5	5	3	2	2	4

Compare less than equal single

c.le.s cc fs, ft

0x11	0x10	ft	fs	*cc*	0	FC	0xe
6	5	5	5	3	2	2	4

Compare the floating-point double (single) in register fs against the one in ft and set the floating-point condition flag *cc* to 1 if the first is less than or equal to the second. If *cc* is omitted, condition code flag 0 is assumed.

Compare less than double

`c.lt.d cc fs, ft`

0x11	0x11	ft	fs	*cc*	0	FC	0xc
6	5	5	5	3	2	2	4

Compare less than single

`c.lt. cc s fs, ft`

0x11	0x10	ft	fs	*cc*	0	FC	0xc
6	5	5	5	3	2	2	4

Compare the floating-point double (single) in register `fs` against the one in `ft` and set the condition flag *cc* to 1 if the first is less than the second. If *cc* is omitted, condition code flag 0 is assumed.

Convert single to double

`cvt.d.s fd, fs`

0x11	0x10	0	fs	fd	0x21
6	5	5	5	5	6

Convert integer to double

`cvt.d.w fd, fs`

0x11	0x14	0	fs	fd	0x21
6	5	5	5	5	6

Convert the single precision floating-point number or integer in register `fs` to a double (single) precision number and put it in register `fd`.

Convert double to single

`cvt.s.d fd, fs`

0x11	0x11	0	fs	fd	0x20
6	5	5	5	5	6

Convert integer to single

`cvt.s.w fd, fs`

0x11	0x14	0	fs	fd	0x20
6	5	5	5	5	6

Convert the double precision floating-point number or integer in register `fs` to a single precision number and put it in register `fd`.

Convert double to integer

`cvt.w.d fd, fs`

0x11	0x11	0	fs	fd	0x24
6	5	5	5	5	6

Convert single to integer

`cvt.w.s fd, fs`	0x11	0x10	0	fs	fd	0x24
	6	5	5	5	5	6

Convert the double or single precision floating-point number in register fs to an integer and put it in register fd.

Floating-point divide double

`div.d fd, fs, ft`	0x11	0x11	ft	fs	fd	3
	6	5	5	5	5	6

Floating-point divide single

`div.s fd, fs, ft`	0x11	0x10	ft	fs	fd	3
	6	5	5	5	5	6

Compute the quotient of the floating-point doubles (singles) in registers fs and ft and put it in register fd.

Floating-point floor to word

`floor.w.d fd, fs`	0x11	0x11	0	fs	fd	0xf
	6	5	5	5	5	6

`floor.w.s fd, fs`	0x11	0x10	0	fs	fd	0xf

Compute the floor of the floating-point double (single) in register fs and put the resulting word in register fd.

Load floating-point double

`l.d fdest, address`	*pseudoinstruction*

Load floating-point single

`l.s fdest, address`	*pseudoinstruction*

Load the floating-point double (single) at address into register fdest.

Move floating-point double

```
mov.d fd, fs
```

0x11	0x11	0	fs	fd	6
6	5	5	5	5	6

Move floating-point single

```
mov.s fd, fs
```

0x11	0x10	0	fs	fd	6
6	5	5	5	5	6

Move the floating-point double (single) from register fs to register fd.

Move conditional floating-point double false

```
movf.d fd, fs, cc
```

0x11	0x11	*cc*	0	fs	fd	0x11
6	5	3	2	5	5	6

Move conditional floating-point single false

```
movf.s fd, fs, cc
```

0x11	0x10	*cc*	0	fs	fd	0x11
6	5	3	2	5	5	6

Move the floating-point double (single) from register fs to register fd if condition code flag *cc* is 0. If *cc* is omitted, condition code flag 0 is assumed.

Move conditional floating-point double true

```
movt.d fd, fs, cc
```

0x11	0x11	*cc*	1	fs	fd	0x11
6	5	3	2	5	5	6

Move conditional floating-point single true

```
movt.s fd, fs, cc
```

0x11	0x10	*cc*	1	fs	fd	0x11
6	5	3	2	5	5	6

Move the floating-point double (single) from register fs to register fd if condition code flag *cc* is 1. If *cc* is omitted, condition code flag 0 is assumed.

Move conditional floating-point double not zero

```
movn.d fd, fs, rt
```

0x11	0x11	rt	fs	fd	0x13
6	5	5	5	5	6

Move conditional floating-point single not zero

movn.s fd, fs, rt

0x11	0x10	rt	fs	fd	0x13
6	5	5	5	5	6

Move the floating-point double (single) from register fs to register fd if processor register rt is not 0.

Move conditional floating-point double zero

movz.d fd, fs, rt

0x11	0x11	rt	fs	fd	0x12
6	5	5	5	5	6

Move conditional floating-point single zero

movz.s fd, fs, rt

0x11	0x10	rt	fs	fd	0x12
6	5	5	5	5	6

Move the floating-point double (single) from register fs to register fd if processor register rt is 0.

Floating-point multiply double

mul.d fd, fs, ft

0x11	0x11	ft	fs	fd	2
6	5	5	5	5	6

Floating-point multiply single

mul.s fd, fs, ft

0x11	0x10	ft	fs	fd	2
6	5	5	5	5	6

Compute the product of the floating-point doubles (singles) in registers fs and ft and put it in register fd.

Negate double

neg.d fd, fs

0x11	0x11	0	fs	fd	7
6	5	5	5	5	6

Negate single

neg.s fd, fs

0x11	0x11	0	fs	fd	7
6	5	5	5	5	6

Negate the floating-point double (single) in register fs and put it in register fd.

Floating-point round to word

round.w.d fd, fs

0x11	0x11	0	fs	fd	0xc
6	5	5	5	5	6

round.w.s fd, fs

0x11	0x10	0	fs	fd	0xc
6	5	5	5	5	6

Round the floating-point double (single) value in register fs, convert to a 32-bit fixed-point value, and put the resulting word in register fd.

Square root double

sqrt.d fd, fs

0x11	0x11	0	fs	fd	4
6	5	5	5	5	6

Square root single

sqrt.s fd, fs

0x11	0x10	0	fs	fd	4
6	5	5	5	5	6

Compute the square root of the floating-point double (single) in register fs and put it in register fd.

Store floating-point double

s.d fdest, address   *pseudoinstruction*

Store floating-point single

s.s fdest, address   *pseudoinstruction*

Store the floating-point double (single) in register fdest at *address*.

Floating-point subtract double

sub.d fd, fs, ft

0x11	0x11	ft	fs	fd	1
6	5	5	5	5	6

Floating-point subtract single

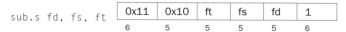

sub.s fd, fs, ft

0x11	0x10	ft	fs	fd	1
6	5	5	5	5	6

Compute the difference of the floating-point doubles (singles) in registers fs and ft and put it in register fd.

Floating-point truncate to word

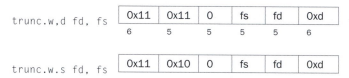

trunc.w,d fd, fs

0x11	0x11	0	fs	fd	0xd
6	5	5	5	5	6

trunc.w.s fd, fs

0x11	0x10	0	fs	fd	0xd

Truncate the floating-point double (single) value in register fs, convert to a 32-bit fixed-point value, and put the resulting word in register fd.

Exception and Interrupt Instructions

Exception return

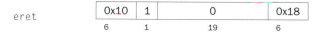

eret

0x10	1	0	0x18
6	1	19	6

Set the EXL bit in coprocessor 0's Status register to 0 and return to the instruction pointed to by coprocessor 0's EPC register.

System call

syscall

0	0	0xc
6	20	6

Register $v0 contains the number of the system call (see Figure A.9.1) provided by SPIM.

Break

break code

0	code	0xd
6	20	6

Cause exception *code*. Exception 1 is reserved for the debugger.

No operation

nop

0	0	0	0	0	0
6	5	5	5	5	6

Do nothing.

A.11   Concluding Remarks

Programming in assembly language requires a programmer to trade off helpful features of high-level languages—such as data structures, type checking, and control constructs—for complete control over the instructions that a computer executes. External constraints on some applications, such as response time or program size, require a programmer to pay close attention to every instruction. However, the cost of this level of attention is assembly language programs that are longer, more time-consuming to write, and more difficult to maintain than high-level language programs.

Moreover, three trends are reducing the need to write programs in assembly language. The first trend is toward the improvement of compilers. Modern compilers produce code that is typically comparable to the best handwritten code—and is sometimes better. The second trend is the introduction of new processors that are not only faster but, in the case of processors that execute multiple instructions simultaneously, also more difficult to program by hand. In addition, the rapid evolution of the modern computer favors high-level language programs that are not tied to a single architecture. Finally, we witness a trend toward increasingly complex applications—characterized by complex graphic interfaces and many more features than their predecessors. Large applications are written by teams of programmers and require the modularity and semantic checking features provided by high-level languages.

Further Reading

Aho, A., R. Sethi, and J. Ullman [1985]. *Compilers: Principles, Techniques, and Tools*, Addison-Wesley, Reading, MA.

Slightly dated and lacking in coverage of modern architectures, but still the standard reference on compilers.

Sweetman, D. [1999]. *See MIPS Run*, Morgan Kaufmann Publishers, San Francisco, CA.

A complete, detailed, and engaging introduction to the MIPS instruction set and assembly language programming on these machines.

Detailed documentation on the MIPS-32 architecture is available on the Web:

MIPS32™ Architecture for Programmers Volume I: Introduction to the MIPS32™ Architecture
(http://mips.com/content/Documentation/MIPSDocumentation/ProcessorArchitecture/
*ArchitectureProgrammingPublicationsforMIPS32/MD00082-2B-MIPS32INT-AFP-02.00.pdf/getDownloa*d)

MIPS32™ Architecture for Programmers Volume II: The MIPS32™ Instruction Set
(http://mips.com/content/Documentation/MIPSDocumentation/ProcessorArchitecture/
ArchitectureProgrammingPublicationsforMIPS32/MD00086-2B-MIPS32BIS-AFP-02.00.pdf/getDownload)

MIPS32™ Architecture for Programmers Volume III: The MIPS32™ Privileged Resource Architecture
(http://mips.com/content/Documentation/MIPSDocumentation/ProcessorArchitecture/
ArchitectureProgrammingPublicationsforMIPS32/MD00090-2B-MIPS32PRA-AFP-02.00.pdf/getDownload)

A.12 Exercises

A.1 [5] <§A.5> Section A.5 described how memory is partitioned on most MIPS systems. Propose another way of dividing memory that meets the same goals.

A.2 [20] <§A.6> Rewrite the code for fact to use fewer instructions.

A.3 [5] <§A.7> Is it ever safe for a user program to use registers $k0 or $k1?

A.4 [25] <§A.7> Section A.7 contains code for a very simple exception handler. One serious problem with this handler is that it disables interrupts for a long time. This means that interrupts from a fast I/O device may be lost. Write a better exception handler that is interruptable and enables interrupts as quickly as possible.

A.5 [15] <§A.7> The simple exception handler always jumps back to the instruction following the exception. This works fine unless the instruction that causes the exception is in the delay slot of a branch. In that case, the next instruction is the target of the branch. Write a better handler that uses the EPC register to determine which instruction should be executed after the exception.

A.6 [5] <§A.9> Using SPIM, write and test an adding machine program that repeatedly reads in integers and adds them into a running sum. The program should stop when it gets an input that is 0, printing out the sum at that point. Use the SPIM system calls described on pages A-43 through A-44.

A.7 [5] <§A.9> Using SPIM, write and test a program that reads in three integers and prints out the sum of the largest two of the three. Use the SPIM system calls described on pages A-43 through A-44. You can break ties arbitrarily.

A.8 [5] <§A.9> Using SPIM, write and test a program that reads in a positive integer using the SPIM system calls. If the integer is not positive, the program should terminate with the message "Invalid Entry"; otherwise the program should print out the names of the digits of the integers, delimited by exactly one space. For example, if the user entered "728," the output would be "Seven Two Eight."

A.9 [25] <§A.9> Write and test a MIPS assembly language program to compute and print the first 100 prime numbers. A number n is prime if no numbers except 1 and n divide it evenly. You should implement two routines:

- `test_prime (n)`   Return 1 if n is prime and 0 if n is not prime.

- `main ()`   Iterate over the integers, testing if each is prime. Print the first 100 numbers that are prime.

Test your programs by running them on SPIM.

A.10 [10] <§§A.6, A.9> Using SPIM, write and test a recursive program for solving the classic mathematical recreation, the Towers of Hanoi puzzle. (This will require the use of stack frames to support recursion.) The puzzle consists of three pegs (1, 2, and 3) and n disks (the number n can vary; typical values might be in the range from 1 to 8). Disk 1 is smaller than disk 2, which is in turn smaller than disk 3, and so forth, with disk n being the largest. Initially, all the disks are on peg 1, starting with disk n on the bottom, disk $n - 1$ on top of that, and so forth, up to disk 1 on the top. The goal is to move all the disks to peg 2. You may only move one disk at a time, that is, the top disk from any of the three pegs onto the top of either of the other two pegs. Moreover, there is a constraint: You must not place a larger disk on top of a smaller disk.

The C program below can be used to help write your assembly language program.

```c
/* move n smallest disks from start to finish using
extra */

void hanoi(int n, int start, int finish, int extra){
    if(n != 0){
            hanoi(n-1, start, extra, finish);
            print_string("Move disk");
            print_int(n);
            print_string("from peg");
            print_int(start);
            print_string("to peg");
            print_int(finish);
            print_string(".\n");
            hanoi(n-1, extra, finish, start);
    }
}
```

```
main(){
    int n;
    print_string("Enter number of disks>");
    n = read_int();
    hanoi(n, 1, 2, 3);
    return 0;
}
```

Index

CD information is listed by chapter and section number followed by page ranges (CD9.1:1-2). "In More Depth" references are listed by chapter number followed by page ranges (IMD4:5-6). Page references preceded by a single letter refer to appendices.

A